Coming *to* *Shore*

Coming *to* Shore

Northwest Coast Ethnology,
Traditions, and Visions

Edited by
Marie Mauzé,
Michael E. Harkin,
and Sergei Kan

UNIVERSITY OF NEBRASKA PRESS
LINCOLN AND LONDON

Publication of this book is made possible,
in part,
by the generosity of
the Claire Garber Goodman
Fund for Anthropological Research
at Dartmouth College,
the University of Wyoming Research Office
and College of Arts and Sciences,
and the Wenner-Gren Foundation.

Library of Congress Cataloging-in-Publication Data
Northwest Coast Ethnology Conference (2000 : Paris, France)
Coming to shore : Northwest Coast ethnology, traditions, and visions / edited by Marie Mauzé,
Michael E. Harkin, and Sergei Kan.
p. cm.
Papers presented at the Northwest Coast Ethnology Conference held in Paris, France in June 2000.
Includes bibliographical references and index.
ISBN 0-8032-3230-6 (cl. : alk. paper) — ISBN 0-8032-8296-6 (pbk. : alk. paper)
1. Indians of North America—Northwest Coast of North America—History—Congresses.
2. Indians of North America—Northwest Coast of North America—Social life and customs—
Congresses. 3. Ethnology—Northwest Coast of North America—Congresses. 4. Applied
anthropology—Northwest Coast of North America—Congresses. 5. Northwest Coast of
North America—Social life and customs—Congresses. I. Mauzé, Marie. II. Harkin,
Michael Eugene, 1958– III. Kan, Sergei. IV. Title.
E78.N78N69 2000
305.897—dc22   2004049849

CONTENTS

Texts and Narratives

History and Representations

Politics and Cultural Heritage

ACKNOWLEDGMENTS

The Northwest Coast Ethnology Conference held in Paris, France, in June 2000 benefited from the financial help of the Wenner-Gren Foundation, the Centre national de la recherche scientifique, the Canadian Cultural Centre, and the Laboratoire d'anthropologie sociale. Marie Mauzé wishes to express her appreciation to Gilles Duguay, minister in charge of cultural affairs at the Canadian Embassy, and Orietta Mugnier-Doucet, Chief of Academic Relations at the Canadian Embassy, who supported the colloquium in assigning special funds for native scholars. She would like to thank Nathan Wachtel, professor at the College de France and the then director of the Laboratoire d'anthropologie sociale for providing the facilities of the Amphithéâtre Guillaume Budé at the Collège de France. Her thanks go to Philippe Descola and Harvey Feit, who participated in the conference as discussants and to Laura Bliss Span, who kindly lent a copy of her film dedicated to Frederica de Laguna, *Reunion under Mount Saint Elias*. In addition, the two American co-editors, Michael Harkin and Sergei Kan, would like to express their deep gratitude to their French colleague Marie Mauzé and her husband, Michel Izard, for hosting an editorial réunion at their house in Casaneuve in the summer of 2001.

EDITORS' INTRODUCTION

Marie Mauzé, Michael E. Harkin, and Sergei Kan

This volume represents the culmination of a several-year collaboration among many of the most prominent researchers in the field of Northwest Coast ethnology, centered around a conference held at the College de France in Paris in June 2000. Why organize such a conference and publish a volume at this point in the history of anthropology? Why, in particular, emphasize the connections among French, Canadian, and American anthropologies of this region? As for the first question, it appears that the time is ripe for such a reassessment and overview. This represents the first collaborative collection on Northwest Coast ethnology since 1966 (McFeat 1966) and arguably the only one to incorporate a wide range of perspectives. Previous collections have explored specific cultural and linguistic groups (Arima et al. 1991; Hoover 2000; Seguin 1984). Festschriften for Wilson Duff (Abbot 1981), Viola Garfield (Miller and Eastman 1984), and Douglas Cole (Wickwire 2000) have explored closely related sets of themes, generally within the context of Canadian anthropology. In 1974 a special session of the annual meetings of the American Anthropological Association was devoted to continuity and change in Northwest Coast ceremonialism (Blackman 1977), and in May of 1976 Mary Lee Stearns organized a large conference at Simon Fraser University, with some of the same goals as our own Paris conference. Five years later John W. Adams (1981) produced an annotated bibliography. Finally, in 1990, after a considerable delay, the Northwest Coast volume of the *Handbook of North American Indians* came out (Suttles 1990).

The contrast with the present work is due to several factors. Conditions in the field and in the academy have changed enormously since 1966 and considerably since 1976. Our foci are no longer art, myth, ritual, kinship, and ecology, and the circumstances of our fieldwork and our collaboration with native colleagues, consultants, and communities is considerably less onesided. Northwest Coast studies, along with the rest of the human sciences, have incorporated postmodernist, feminist, indigenist, and other critiques, and as a result many scholars in this field have abandoned the certainty of perspectives such as cultural ecology, historical particularism, configurationism, Marxism, and structuralism, which characterized Northwest Coast ethnology in its "modern" phase. Moreover, the political climate of "the field" has been transformed by great historical events, such as the Alaska Native Claims Settlement Act of 1971, the Boldt decision of 1974, the Supreme Court of Canada's Delgamuukw decision in 1997, and the Nisga'a settlement of 1999. Increasingly, as several of the chapters point out, anthropologists, involved in close collaboration with native people, are working in a variety of capacities to further the aims of specific native communities. Research that was once designed primarily or exclusively for an academic audience is now read, and read carefully, by the native communities themselves, with an eye toward the way it treats issues such as intellectual property and the implications it may have for political and legal struggles. The old divisions between "pure" and "applied" research no longer hold, since almost any type of ethnographic or ethnohistorical information may wind up as evidence in a courtroom or ammunition in a political debate.

The location of the conference in Paris and the participation of several French scholars (some, such as Gérard Lenclud, François Hartog, and Maurice Godelier, presented papers at the conference that are not included in this volume) are notable, not only for the fact that one thinks of the Northwest Coast as a locus classicus of "Americanist" anthropology, but because it is viewed in some quarters as outside the swim of contemporary theoretical innovation and of little interest beyond the region. The Paris conference was organized by the three editors, with Marie Mauzé as the chief organizer. Her idea to host the conference was initially spurred by Claude Lévi-Strauss's 90th birthday (as it turns out, the year before the conference took place). In 1970 Pierre Maranda and Jean Pouillon had edited a festschrift in honor of Claude Lévi-Strauss's 60th birthday; the 2000 conference was in some ways inspired by that publication (Pouillon and Maranda 1970). Propitiously the conference coincided with the temporary reunification of the two Nisga'a stone masks at the new Louvre gallery, Pavillon des Sessions, reminding the participants of the important French role in collecting and appreciating, as major world art, Northwest Coast objects (Jonaitis 1981; Mauzé 1992a, 2000).

Claude Lévi-Strauss, as the honoree, was an important presence at the conference. His small memoir of the Northwest Coast published here is a valuable document in the intellectual history of our field. Lévi-Strauss's interest in the Northwest Coast dates back to the 1940s but was strongly reinforced during his 1973 and 1974 visits to British Columbia, which led directly to his monographs on Northwest Coast art, ritual, and social organization (Lévi-Strauss 1975, 1979, 1982). It is difficult to single out concepts from this rich material, but two represent especially well the points of contact between Lévi-Straussian and Boasian anthropology: the theory of inversion through diffusion and the concept of the house. The latter is, in some ways, a refinement of Boas's struggle with the cognatic descent group, which he described in his early work as a *clan* (much to the distress of Durkheim) and in his later work as a *numaym*, a term he borrowed from the Kwakwak'wakw (Kwakiutl) themselves. Lévi-Strauss's inversion theory, which holds that as plastic forms are transmitted between cultures, meanings change, and vice versa, is a structuralist twist to Boasian-Ratzelian theories of diffusion.

The French tradition stands in contrast to the two North American national traditions. The contributors to this volume represent both American and Canadian institutions and perspectives. These traditions have been intertwined for so long that it is no longer possible to separate them in any meaningful way, at least in the context of Northwest Coast studies. This is not to say that the Canadians have succumbed to American hegemony, but rather that the two have successfully cross-pollinated for several generations (see Darnell 2000, 2001:282–289). The uniqueness of the Paris setting was that, unlike all previous Northwest Coast conferences, neither side played "host" to the other's "guest," and as a consequence, the issues relating to differences and perceived differences were perhaps more openly addressed. In any case, it was clear that, as the field of Northwest Coast studies matures, it is enriched by Canadian, American, French, and other European scholars (several of whom presented papers at this conference) who are eager to collaborate and to share ideas.

One senior Northwest Coast scholar who had come out of the Boasian tradition but had also been strongly influenced by French (and other European) archaeologists and ethnologists of the 1930s is Frederica de Laguna. Although she was unable to attend the Paris conference, her autobiographical essay published here is an eloquent testimony to the various European influences on her development as a scholar and a unique blend of American and European intellectual traditions that her approach to fieldwork and her vision of anthropology represent, such as her firm commitment to the four-fields approach to Northwest Coast and North Pacific Rim studies, her Boasian and Sapirian commitment to getting at the native culture "from the native point of view," and her interest in history and ethnohistory.

One of the biggest changes that has occurred in Northwest Coast studies since the 1960s, and in large part drawing on the inspiration of de Laguna (1960, 1972), and that several of the essays in this volume reflect, is a move away from an ahistorical or synchronic representation of native societies toward an ethnology that is deeply concerned with historical changes and that utilizes published and unpublished written sources. Although ethnohistorical work by area specialists began in the middle of the 20th century (Codere 1950; Wike 1951), it is only in the last few decades that a substantial number of ethnologists began seriously mining the archives in order to reconstruct the general history of Indian-white relations on the coast (R. Fisher 1992) as well as more specific issues such as the maritime fur trade (J. Gibson 1992), missionization (Bolt 1988; Harkin 1993, 1996; Kan 1985, 1987, 1996, 1999; Usher 1974), suppression of the potlatch by the Canadian missionaries and authorities (Cole and Chaikin 1990), collection of native art and artifacts (Carpenter 1975; Cole 1985) and their display in museums (e.g., Jacknis 1985, 2002; Jonaitis 1988), native participation in the fishing industry (Boxberger 2000b), and other domains of the labor market (Knight 1978). The works dealing with indigenous institutions such as the potlatch (Kan 1989a, 1989b; Mauzé 1992a) and slavery (Donald 1997) have been written using a diachronic perspective. A number of scholars have also combined ethnographic and historical data to reconstruct the history of specific indigenous peoples and communities (Brink 1974; Boyd 1996; Mauzé 1986, 1989, 1992b). More general regional studies have also adopted an ethnohistorical bent (Boyd 1999; Newell 1993; Tennant 1990). Ethnographic studies of contemporary communities, as opposed to Boasian reconstructions based on memory ethnography, have also increased in number, despite the fact that some of these communities have decided to limit access by anthropologists (Bierwert 1999; Dombrowski 2001; McDonald 1989; B. Miller 2001; Stearns 1981). It appears that today native anthropologists are in a better position than in the past to research and write about some of the more sensitive topics related to the contemporary life of the coastal peoples (Dauenhauer and Dauenhauer 1994, 1995, 1998).

Northwest Coast anthropology has recently focused on the topic of representation of native peoples by non-natives — by tourists (Duncan 2000) and photographers (Darnell 2000; Wyatt 1989) — and by anthropologists, with a detailed account of Sapir's research on the coast (Darnell 1990) as well as an essay on McIlwraith's ethnographic work among and relationship with the Bella Coola (Nuxalks) (Harkin 2001). A few anthropologists have begun reflexively scrutinizing the circumstances of their own ethnographic research (Bierwert 1999; Kan 2001).

Recent work on the history of ethnographic research on the Northwest Coast includes serious attempts to fully document and evaluate the contribution of native ethnographers and thus finally to give them credit for their enormous contribution to the field. George Hunt is obviously the best known of these scholars, and thanks to the work of Judith Berman (1996, 2001, 2004) and Ira Jacknis (1991) we now have a much better understanding of the nature and the extent of Hunt's contribution to the corpus of ethnographic materials on the Kwakwaka'wakw. However, recent works have focused on other indigenous ethnographers such as Louis Shotridge (Dauenhauer and Dauenhauer 1994, 2003), Henry Tate (Maud 2000), and William Beynon (Anderson and Halpin 2000).

Finally, the most recent work by area ethnologists reflects an interest in the roles of artists (Cole 2000), environmentalists (Harkin 2000), museum curators (Ames 1992; Black 1999; Jonaitis 1991), and anthropologists in the politics of cultural representation. Attention to the role of the latter is a relatively new development that reflects the postmodernist concern with ethnography as textual strategy. While Boas's own ethnographic and ethnological work in the region has for obvious reasons been the focus of a number of recent books and articles (Berman 1996; Cole and Long 1999; Harkin 2001; Mathé and Miller 2001; Thom 2001), relatively new developments in local cultural and political life — the movement to repatriate traditional ceremonial artifacts from the "mainstream" museums and establishment of tribal museums to house these objects and develop new interpretations of indigenous history and culture "from the native point of view" — have taken center stage in recent Northwest Coast ethnology (Ames 1992; Jonaitis 1991;

Clifford 1997a; Erikson 2002; Hope and Thornton 2000; Masco 1995; Mauzé 1992a, 1999; B. Saunders 1997).

Regna Darnell argues convincingly for an organic relation between Lévi-Straussian structuralism and Boasian anthropology. This is consistent with Lévi-Strauss's own view of himself as something of a Boasian, formed in his New York years through his intensive study of Boas's works and his contact with Boas. A romantic reading might hold that his presence at the death of Boas at the Columbia University faculty club in 1942 entailed a sort of transfer of spiritual essence. Lévi-Strauss's Northwest Coast writings, especially his article on split representations (1963a) and his one Northwest Coast book (1982), pursue explicitly Boasian agendas. His similar love of the text and his holistic view of culture (quite possibly making him one of the few scholars, within or without Northwest Coast ethnology, to read carefully George Hunt's salmon recipes) place him very much within the Boasian framework. Indeed, *La voie des masques* goes back to Boas's intellectual origins in German diffusionism; this, in fact, goes against the grain of the standard reading of Boas, as interested only in discrete cultures, but recovers what was at the heart of his motivation for undertaking Northwest Coast studies in the first place. For instance, in his publication "Tsimshian Mythology" (1916b), Boas undertakes a massive comparison of mythological elements within various Northwest Coast cultures, similar in spirit to Lévi-Strauss's own comparative work.

This "perverse" reading, as Darnell calls it, is in fact very persuasive, perhaps too much so. Their common distaste for British structural functionalism and its colonialist application made them natural allies in the midcentury intellectual milieu. Lévi-Strauss's mentalism, although its roots were almost exclusively in Francophone sources, was compatible with the emphasis on symbolic culture within the Americanist tradition (see Darnell 2001). It is easy, given all this, to argue too strongly that Lévi-Strauss is an Americanist and indeed a Boasian. The roots of Lévi-Straussian anthropology in structural linguistics (De Saussure, Trubetzkoi, Jakobson) and even more in Annals sociology (Durkheim, Hertz), as well as in a more general French intellectual context defined by philosophers such as Rousseau and Descartes, place him in many ways worlds apart from Boasian particularism and empiricism.

In the final analysis, Lévi-Strauss is less an Americanist than a sympathetic outsider, one who strove to find points of contact between his own intellectual project and that of Boas. Surely his personal history is related to this. His fondness for his American hosts during his period of exile and the vibrancy of New York City during the war contributed to his friendly readings of Boas. It is indeed a testament to both the richness of Boasian ethnography and to the creative intelligence of Lévi-Strauss that such connections were made and provided such rich rewards.

Frederica de Laguna or "Freddy," as she has been affectionately called by her colleagues, offers us a fascinating account of the history of her scholarly career, which spans seven decades and includes ethnographic and archaeological research among the Athapaskans of Alaska's interior, the Chugach, the Eyak, and the coastal Tlingits (Birket-Smith and de Laguna 1938; de Laguna 1947, 1956, 1960, 1972, 1995; Emmons 1991). While rooted in the Boasian tradition she developed her unique and comprehensive approach to doing anthropology. Thus she was one of the first ethnologists on the Northwest Coast to conduct archaeological excavations and utilize historical documents in her work on reconstructing native cultural history. Like Boas himself, but unlike some of her colleagues, she has always viewed the coastal cultures in a larger regional perspective that in her case includes Pacific Yupiit and Athapaskans (de Laguna 1975b). A long-term colleague of A. Irving Hallowell, de Laguna also produced one of the earliest essays on Northwest Coast ethnopsychology (de Laguna 1954, 1965), which influenced the work of younger generations of scholars of this area including one of this volume's editors (Kan 1989c). While the story of Freddy's graduate work in anthropology and subsequent research in Greenland and North America has already been described (de Laguna 1977, 2000a; McClellan 1988, 1989), her early sojourn in Europe and interaction with and impressions of British and French scholars have not.

Marie-Françoise Guédon, a student and colleague of de Laguna's, has carried forth Freddy's program of empirical research in the northern borderlands of the Northwest Coast. Her own Francophone (Algeria and Québec) background provides a point of contact with de Laguna's European influences. Above all, the graduate training received from de Laguna, which emphasized a deep commitment to fieldwork and the communities in which field-work is done, has defined her own body of work. Guédon's commitment to long-term ethnographic research across the culture area boundaries has echoed Freddy's own. With her interest in the circumpolar shamanism and her research and writing about Athapaskans, Inuit, and Tsimshian, we see the continuity of de Laguna's legacy (Guédon 1974a, 1974b, 1984a, 1984b, in press).

Marie Mauzé explores the long history of the curious relationship between French anthropology and the Northwest Coast. One value of Mauzé's essay for North American readers is its discussion of lesser-known French ex-plorers and scholars. Beginning in the 18th century, explorers such as Lapé-rouse, Marchand, and de Roquefeuil visited the coast as part of scientific and commercial surveys of the region. If any of these names are known to North American readers, it is probably Lapérouse, but all made valuable ob-servations on the early contact period on the Northwest Coast. This tradi-tion continues into the 19th century but declines as the French move out of post-Louisiana North America and focus their attention on other regions, especially Egypt and Polynesia.

The record of French ethnography in the Northwest Coast is not long, although it too has produced some interesting and important results. Al-though few French anthropologists (Mauzé among them) carried out field-work in the region, this fieldwork has represented a significant presence in the French ethnographic imagination. It is clear that this distant gaze has not always produced understanding; Durkheim, in typical armchair fashion, ac-cuses Boas of not knowing what a clan is, because the concept of the *clan*, as a unilineal descent group, did not apply to the Kwakiutl. A decade later Georges Bataille produced a work of immense influence that achieved an effect remarkably similar to that of his American contemporary Ruth Bene-dict in terms of misunderstanding the potlatch. Or, if that is too harsh an assessment, both at least fixed in the mind of a broad public the notion that the potlatch was exclusively an agonistic and effete institution.

Of course, not all such *regards eloignés* were equally myopic. Georges Davy and Marcel Mauss achieved a certain understanding of the region, which has in turn influenced contemporary research in the region through the 1954 translation and later republication of *The Gift* (Mauss 1969). Claude

Lévi-Strauss, who, one is surprised to hear, never visited the region until the 1970s and never conducted extended research in situ, accomplished something truly remarkable in his profound understanding of the region's cultures. To cite but two famous examples—his introduction of the technical concept of the "house" into discussion of cognatic descent groups and his analysis of the Tsimshian Asdiwal myth—Lévi-Strauss has achieved something quite rare: the respect of specialists. Mauzé's discussion of Lévi-Strauss's long interest in Northwest Coast culture and his immersion in Boasian anthropology adds to the portrait of Lévi-Strauss as something of a Boasian himself, as Darnell (this volume) argues. After all, at a time when much of American anthropology was turning its back on the Boasian collection of massive amounts of quotidian data, such as recipes for preparing salmon, Lévi-Strauss, in a fashion at once generally Gallic and specifically Lévi-Straussian, views these as a key to understanding culture itself, with its implicit canons of gustatory and, by extension, categorical compatibility and incompatibility.

In the end, Mauzé argues, the Northwest Coast "haunting" of the French ethnographic imagination has been interesting but not sufficiently rigorous and sustained to be of great significance. Whether or not one agrees with this assessment, Mauzé has given us a valuable resource for considering this question further.

Lévi-Straussian structuralism is perhaps the last great overarching paradigm in anthropology. Outside of France it first attracted the attention of such British social anthropologists as R. Needham, E. Leach, M. Douglas, and C. Belshaw. Structuralism reached North America slightly later, in the late 1960s and early 1970s. However once Lévi-Strauss's method of analysis became known in the New World, it gained numerous followers in several major anthropology departments, including the University of Chicago, the University of Montreal, and the University of British Columbia. Pierre Maranda, a French-Canadian anthropologist interested in semiotics and one of the best scholars of structuralism, played a major role in introducing and promoting structural anthropology at the Department of Anthropology and Sociology at the University of British Columbia, where during his five-year tenure he organized well-attended courses and seminars that resulted in a number of important papers and dissertations; unfortunately they remained unpublished (S. Reid 1976; M. Reid 1981; Halpin 1973).

Closely related to Maranda's essay is the one by Marjorie Halpin on the various applications of Lévi-Straussian structuralist methodology to North-west Coast materials. Tragically, Marjorie passed away three months after our conference and did not have a chance to revise her piece for publication. However, because of its importance we are publishing her paper, which serves as a tribute to the memory of a distinguished specialist in our field. The essay reflects Halpin's somewhat narrow view of structuralism, which resulted in her discussion of the work of only a few scholars. They are the ones who in her opinion applied Lévi-Straussian models to his favorite topics of analysis: kinship and alliance, mythology, totemic classification, and art. Her vision is rather skewed toward Canadian scholarship and leaves out some important works by Americans who would not define themselves as strict Lévi-Straussians but who have been influenced strongly by the French anthropologist's ideas about Northwest Coast culture and social organization or who have applied his structuralist method. One could say that some of us working on the topic of the Northwest Coast, particularly those who studied at the University of Chicago, absorbed Lévi-Strauss's concepts (without necessarily citing him or agreeing with him on every specific issue) in the context of studying with Valerio Valeri, Marshall Sahlins, and Ray Fogelson (see Harkin's [1988] analysis of contact narratives and Kan's [1983, 1989b] analysis of Tlingit oratory, cosmology, and ethnopsychology).

Sometimes the American scholars' enthusiasm for Lévi-Strauss's structuralism resulted in rather careless reading and misunderstanding of his complex work. Lévi-Strauss himself, who has always been a careful reader and reviewer of North American works on the Northwest Coast, has pointed out specific errors and misinterpretations by these scholars. Thus, for example, he criticized Rosman and Rubel's (1971) incorrect structural analysis of the Tlingit, Haida, and Tsimshian marriage system (Lévi-Strauss 1986). He has also disagreed with Jay Miller's (1999a) application of the notion of the "house" to the Salish (Lévi-Strauss 1982, 2000). Finally, in his review of Jonaitis's (1986) work on Tlingit art the French scholar takes her to task for breaking her subject into two artificial categories, sacred and secular (albeit categories with a distinctly French pedigree), saying that a book on Tlingit art is still to be written (Lévi-Strauss 1987a).

Margaret Seguin Anderson's reanalysis of the story of Asdiwal uses Lévi-Strauss's (1967) famous essay as the starting point for an excursion into modes of understanding, ethnographic data, and the relationship between anthropologists and communities of Tsimshian-speaking people. In his analysis Lévi-Strauss sees Asdiwal as a disquisition on Tsimshianic social structure and marriage practices. Lévi-Strauss's view is that Asdiwal teaches by negative example what types of marriage are appropriate for upper-class Tsimshian, Nisga'a, and Gitksan people. In the end a cultural model of preferred matrilateral cross-cousin marriage is adduced. This practice mediates between the two opposing conditions of Tsimshian life: kinship group membership and residence. This problem is "solved" by the preferred marriage, which allows children to grow up with both their father and maternal uncle and provides for the concentration of material and nonmaterial property within the two intertwined lineages.

Lévi-Strauss's analysis has faced considerable opposition from North American anthropologists, most of whom have attempted their own analysis of the ethnographic material as a means of contesting it. Thus, John W. Adams (1974) has faulted him for suggesting that cross-cousin marriage was a viable possibility in Tsimshian society, much less a preferred practice. Such critiques were superficially plausible, given the fact that Adams and some of the other critics had conducted fieldwork among Tsimshian-speaking people, and that Lévi-Strauss had not, at that point, even visited the region. What Anderson finds, however, is that Lévi-Strauss was very careful in his use of available published material on this question. Moreover, as a well-situated insider, Anderson is able to test such hypotheses against contemporary elite Tsimshian opinion. It turns out that Lévi-Strauss was substantially correct in his analysis, at least on the matter of cross-cousin marriage.

This finding is, of itself, sufficiently important to justify an essay. However, Anderson goes beyond it to explore some of the epistemological issues involved in the construction of ethnographic knowledge. She quotes a contemporary Gitksan elder, Hanamuux, to the effect that knowledge is a layered affair, and that different levels are attainable by persons differently situated sociologically. This is a useful corrective to the crude positivism that even sophisticated scholars will embrace in the event of an argument. It also reminds us of the importance of context. For example, Alice Kasakoff's (1974) data on marriage were indeed based on real information but were skewed by a failure to consider class. Moreover, her data address a different issue entirely from Lévi-Strauss. While it may be a statistically insignificant practice, preferential cross-cousin marriage was nevertheless a cultural model that was realized under the proper circumstances. Although the vice president of the United States has succeeded to the presidency only a few times in 225 years, the fact that this rule exists is vital to legitimate government. Similarly, although it may have been relatively rare in the past (about this we are not really sure), matrilateral cross-cousin marriage was the keystone to an elaborate protocol of marriage and kinship pertaining to the upper stratum of Tsimshian society.

Judith Berman's essay is an important contribution to the literature on Northwest Coast contact narratives, drawing upon earlier works such as Harkin 1988 and Daunhauer and Daunhauer 1987. It is significant that this represents a departure from the Boasian emphasis on precontact narratives, to the exclusion of what Boas once called "idiotic stories" (quoted in Stocking 1968:204; but see Emmons 1911 for an early recording of a "first contact" narrative). Bringing such texts into the scholarly viewshed is an important methodological move, pregnant with both theoretical and practical implications. As for the latter, it is clear from essays in this volume by Bruce Miller and Dan Boxberger that historical narratives have an important and increasing role to play in the courtroom, as ongoing territorial and sovereignty claims draw on such texts.

Berman's sophisticated reading of the Shotridge narrative draws on both linguistic and ethnopoetical analysis. The quotative mode, which she calls Q, is a linguistic marker of pastness and contact with the sacred. As Berman convincingly argues, this is best viewed not within a linear construction of time and events, but something close to what Eliade (1959:21) called the *illud tempus*, the sacred era of transformation, which can reappear through the regular return of the sacred season, as well as through unexpected encounters with spirit powers in hunting and warfare and the historical encounters with Europeans (S. Reid 1976).

From an ethnopoetic standpoint, what this creates is tropes of opposition: particularly dramatic tension and irony, which inhabit the space between worldviews marked and unmarked by Q. Miguel Cervantes played on much the same structure of the conjuncture. Unlike in *Don Quixote,* irony is not the master trope of the Shotridge text, but it is present nonetheless. In the Shotridge narrative the "naïve reaction" of Tlingit warriors — people who, by definition, were in control of their territory, both physical and conceptual — is implicitly ironic, as is that of the Heiltsuk elders in the Heiltsuk narrative of first contact (Harkin 1988). It is significant that the shift in worldviews is occasioned by food in both texts, for both the obtaining and sharing of food had profound spiritual implications in the Northwest Coast lifeworld. Hunting represented a spiritual contract with the world of other-than-human-beings, and commensuality established a "ritual congregation," in Irving Goldman's (1975) phrase. This situation represents a sort of cosmological-historical irony, in the Boasian sense (see Hymes 1999; Krupat 1990). Berman's essay represents a healthy step away from that aspect of the Boasian tradition, in which the juxtaposition of native people and historical events was inherently problematic.

The Haida oral narratives collected by John R. Swanton at the very beginning of the 20th century are usually seen by anthropologists as being divided into four main genres: myth, lineage story, history, and song. In his rediscovery and retranslation of these texts published under the titles *A Story as Sharp as a Knife: The Classical Haida Mythtellers and Their World* (1999), *Ghandl of the Qayahl Llaanas: Nine Visits to the Mythworld* (2000), and *Being in Being* (2001), Robert Bringhurst, a prominent Canadian poet, presents this material primarily as literature rather than ethnology. He compares Haida literature to the European Classical traditions to emphasize its importance and the unique quality of authorship. His adoption of the methods of transcribing an oral text and of presenting it formally as poetry, especially his use of a stanza structure, is deeply indebted to the work of Dell Hymes (1981, 1990, 1996). This addresses a problem that goes back at least to Boas: how to represent an oral tradition in textual form. As Hymes points out in his seminal work in the 1970s and 1980s, such performances are rigorously structured, as much so as Classical and early modern English poetry, which was intended to be spoken aloud. Thus, Bringhurst's connection between Haida narrative and verse in the Western tradition is not as far-fetched as it may seem.

Both face the problem of presenting a large amount of material orally. Metric structuring supplemented thematic structuring, making the piece both easier to memorize and more memorable. Beginning in the 20th century, poetry was less often spoken and more often read, leading to the contemporary situation where most poetry is not, technically speaking, poetry at all. Thus, the dilemma faced by Bringhurst is to create a place for a formal literature that cannot be compared to contemporary forms. This problem is addressed by evoking the classics of our own tradition, going beyond text to other media (in this essay, 17th-century European painting) to shed light on the nature and dynamics of storytelling and the creative role of the storyteller (Bringhurst and Steltzer 1992). He also ascribes a philosophical meaning to these myths, which some anthropologists might find a bit too broad and general.

His unique understanding of and appreciation for the Haida oral traditions stem from both his own poetic work and many years of close collaboration with the great Haida artist Bill Reid (Bringhurst and Reid 1984; Reid and Bringhurst 2000). This collaboration was clearly fruitful. Such collaborative efforts are, as is evident from several of the essays in this volume, increasingly common. Despite this productive connection, it is worth pointing out that many contemporary Haidas object to Bringhurst's project. This, too, is increasingly characteristic of the Northwest Coast scene.

Another example of productive scholarly cooperation between native and non-native scholars is the recording, editing, and publishing of life histories of local indigenous people. Although this genre is fairly well established in Northwest Coast studies, the more recent projects tend to differ significantly from the earlier ones. As elsewhere in North American anthropology, Boasian scholars specializing on the Northwest Coast tended to use autobiographical narratives or life histories as sources of ethnographic, linguistic, and occasionally historical data and would usually guide the narrator with their questions (Krupat 1985; Brumble 1988). Once a life history had been recorded, it was often edited (sometimes heavily) before being published (e.g., Ford 1941; Spradley 1969; Blackman 1982). In recent years indigenous persons have finally been able to have a much greater say in how they would present their life's story, with the anthropologist's comments being reserved for the introduction and the notes (see Dauenhauer 1994). The best example of this new work is a collection of life histories of three First Nations Tlingit and Athapaskan women from British Columbia recorded and published by Julie Cruikshank (1990).

The essay by Martine Reid and Daisy Sewid-Smith represents this approach to producing indigenous people's life histories as well. ʔAx̌uw̓ (Mrs. Agnes Alfred), a monolingual Kwakwak'awakw (or more precisely Kwikwa-sutainux) elder and an accomplished storyteller from Alert Bay, was the grandmother of Daisy Sewid-Smith (1979, 1997), an educator, linguist, and historian fluent in Kwakwala. Martine Reid (1981), an anthropologist who conducted ethnographic research in Alert Bay in the late 1970s and early 1980s, has been collaborating with Daisy ever since. This, of course, means that there was a great deal of rapport and understanding between the narrator and her audience. As the two authors explain, ʔAx̌uw̓ chose to discuss only certain parts of her long life and presented it in a style that does not correspond to standard Western literary conventions. In their essay Reid and Sewid-Smith describe this style and provide an interesting perspective on their work with this remarkable native woman. Once ʔAx̌uw̓'s life history is published it will be a very important document for her community and the larger non-native audience. Anthropologists should also find it very interesting, especially since it would contrast with previously published Kwakwak'awakw autobiographies, including that of ʔAx̌uw̓'s son-in-law James Sewid (Spradley 1969).

Sergei Kan's essay, along with Harkin's, addresses tourism directly (although the papers on collections and museums certainly have some bearing on this topic). Arguably, tourism is one of the most important modalities of interaction between native people and outsiders, primarily well-to-do urban Americans and Canadians. The Northwest Coast has only recently acquired the status of tourist destination comparable to that of the American Southwest, but the roots of this development can be found in the Gilded Age. As Kan makes clear, this form of tourism was somewhat different from its successor. In addition to the (rather passive, by today's standard) appreciation of the sublime landscape (see Raban 1999), tourists enjoyed the *tableau vivant* of native life, which seemed to them to perfectly illustrate themes of cultural and moral evolution. Through a dialogic process involving both mimesis and othering, groups of native people were classed as more or less civilized, depending upon their external appearance and their willingness to participate in such ritual representations. The residents of the Presbyterian school presented visitors with the spectacle of progress in its most paradigmatic form, although still retaining some of what Bhabha (1994) identifies as the contradictions entailed in such projects. In particular, the assumed gap between moral advancement and racial inferiority is commented upon by observers, who are alternatively amazed at and skeptical of the ability of religion and education to overcome what were universally believed to be profound innate disadvantages.

From the standpoint of the Tlingits who participated in it, both opportunities and dangers were presented by the tourist trade. Most obviously, material gain derived from the sale of curios and posing for photographs allowed Tlingits to supplement their cash incomes. Given the importance of wealth in Northwest Coast culture, this benefit should not be underestimated. At the same time, the gaze of the tourists (sometimes assisted by binoculars) extending into the Tlingits' domestic space was an unwelcome intrusion. Between these two poles, a range of interactions took place that together constituted an economy of representation, in which both groups sought advantage.

Neither Tlingits nor tourists were monolithic. Some white tourists were more sophisticated and sympathetic, although most shared the fundamental racism and ethnocentrism of the age. Tlingits pursued different strategies, including withdrawal. Interestingly, neither side attempted to achieve the sort of "middle ground" arrived at in the Southwest, where the Hopi and other groups performed sacred dances in front of audiences composed in part of romantic and largely intellectual whites. Canons of secrecy were somewhat different in Hopi culture, but perhaps the more important difference is the dynamic of interaction itself. Neither were tourists inclined to look for the Noble Savage in the woods of southeastern Alaska, nor were Tlingits inclined to allow outsiders in to view, photograph, and comment upon their still-rich ceremonial life. Tourists were more likely to classify Tlingits with Asians (business acumen and physical appearance seemed to be diagnostic of "orientalness") than with the Indians of the Southwest or the Plains, the popular representatives of *homo americanus*.

Ira Jacknis's essay on the Northwest Coast Indian Hall at the American Museum of Natural History offers a historical perspective on the displays of native cultures and their impact on the ways in which scholars, artists, writers, and the general public perceived or represented Northwest Coast cultures in the 20th century. Deeply rooted in the development of anthropology, permanent museum exhibits reflect both the history of collecting and the status of ethnographic specimens arranged according to a comparative evolutionary typology or as illustration of specific cultures. Jacknis painstakingly describes both the major changes and some of the minor alterations that occurred from the time of Boas to the present. He is correct in his insistence that the "Boas Room" has had a special place in the museum and has gradually acquired mythological status at a time when such ethnographic displays became increasingly irrelevant to anthropological praxis.

In the 1940s the Indian Hall became more of an "aesthetic" object. This was the time when Claude Lévi-Strauss and his French surrealist friends discovered it. Jacknis discusses the various modes of appropriation of Northwest Coast art by the surrealists and the New York abstract expressionists manifested in private collecting of objects. While this process contributed to the development of a primitivist aesthetic, it also encouraged a genuine appreciation for the high quality of Northwest Coast art seen by Lévi-Strauss as "being comparable to those of Egypt, Persia and the Middle Ages" (1943). Unlike the artists and Lévi-Strauss, the novelists who visited the Northwest Coast Indian Hall interpreted the objects they saw in ways completely unrelated to the meanings attributed to them by Boas, Wissler, and other curators. For the former, this experience gave rise to a sense of a familiar place within the cultural geography of New York, forever frozen in time. Ironically, because it has failed to renovate its exhibit, the Northwest Coast Indian Hall contributes to this reification.

One of the major new developments in Northwest Coast ethnology has been an active involvement of native scholars in collecting and publishing new ethnographic data as well as rereading, reinterpreting, and republishing "classic" native texts collected by Boas and the Boasians using new and more accessible orthographies and new perspectives based on what Geertz calls "experience-near" perspectives (Dauenhauer and Dauenhauer 1987, 1990, 1994; Hilton et al. 1982). This important work was referred to by Margaret Seguin Anderson and Deanna Nyce at the Paris conference in a paper titled "Two Ways to Re-Voice in Aboriginal Histories" as "the repatriation of knowledge."

Of course, as we have already mentioned, native scholars (erstwhile "informants") have always played a major role in ethnographic research on the Northwest Coast. Imagine what our knowledge of the area's language, folklore, and ethnology would have been without the work of George Hunt, Henry Tate, William Beynon, Louis Shotridge, and a number of others (see Berman, this volume). However, in the past native scholars did not usually have a chance to set their own agenda for research but carried out projects that had been designed at least in part by their non-native employers and by scholarly patrons and collaborators (see Berman 1996).

Since the 1960s and especially in the last two decades the situation has changed dramatically. Although the number of native linguists, folklorists, and ethnologists working on the coast is unfortunately rather small, it is growing, and most importantly, the projects they undertake are usually of their own design. In carrying out field research, native scholars often have a strong advantage. Not only is their command of the native languages often better than that of their non-native counterparts, but as insiders they are more likely to have access to sensitive information and are in a better position to properly comprehend and contextualize the data they are collecting. In addition, native ethnologists are more likely to live in a native community and thus have a much better sense of the long-term sociocultural processes occurring in them.

One major example of first-rate research carried out by a native scholar is the work of Nora Marks Dauenhauer. Together with her husband, Richard Dauenhauer (a linguist and folklorist who has lived in southeastern Alaska, has been learning the Tlingit language for over 30 years, and has become very much a part of the Tlingit community), she has developed a new user-friendly Tlingit orthography and has been collecting, transcribing, and publishing important Tlingit texts ranging from ceremonial speeches to clan histories and from folktales to autobiographical narratives (see Dauenhauer and Dauenhauer 1987, 1990, 1994). These publications have not only been of great interest to scholars but have been widely read by the native community and have encouraged many young Tlingits to learn more about their cultural heritage. In addition, the Dauenhauers have published a series of important scholarly papers on the technical, emotional, and political issues related to the work they have been doing, including attitudes toward Tlingit literacy and language loss (1995, 1998, 1999).

Besides doing research, the Dauenhauers have been participating for decades in Tlingit ceremonies and working with or for several native political and cultural preservation organizations. This long-term exposure to the various aspects of native life has given them a unique opportunity to serve not only as native ethnographers but also as cultural critics. It is in the latter capacity that they speak in the essay published here. Although those of us who see culture as something that is constantly being reinvented (e.g., Harkin 1997b; Mauzé 1997) might take issue with some of the Dauenhauers' strong criticism of the recently invented Tlingit traditions (e.g., the so-called "Tlingit National Anthem"), we must take into account the unique intellectual and political position that colors their perspective. Regardless of whether we agree with their approach, we do learn a great deal from their essay about important sociocultural changes occurring in the Tlingit community. Moreover, in the current political climate, it is perhaps more appropriate for native scholars than outsiders to criticize recently invented practices that are being presented as "ancient traditions."

The issue of invented tradition is a recurring one in Northwest Coast ethnology, going back to Boas's and Hunt's take on the establishment of the "Eagle" class of potlatch chiefs. In his essay Aaron Glass summarizes contemporary anthropological approaches to tradition and innovation (see Harkin 1997b; Hobsbawm and Ranger 1983; Linnekin 1991; Mauzé 1997; Pouillon 1997) and discusses the different ways in which native peoples and anthropologists approach this complex and controversial issue. Drawing on his own field research, Glass then presents the diverse and often contradictory views of the Kwakwak'awakw (Nimpkish) of Alert Bay on the modern-day performance of the Hamat'sa (Cannibal) dance. A key element of the late-19th-century Kwakwak'awakw ceremonial, the Hamat'sa ritual has since become a reified expression of native cultural life. The information on the indigenous discourses that Glass presents shows that there are certain limits to how much innovation can be accepted by a community that considers such ritual dances as a privilege jealously guarded by noble families. The essay deals with two contemporary debates about the Hamat'sa dance: its performance in a tourist setting by native professional non-Kwakwak'awakw dancers, who had received the right to enact it as a show by a local chief, and a new practice of some Kwakwak'awakw women performing this dance, which had formerly been performed exclusively by men. Such manifestations bring to light tensions between a more traditional system of family ownership of ceremonial privileges and more global representations of Kwakwak'awakw identity.

The example of the incorporation of women in the Hamat'sa ritual is viewed by some members of the native community as an expression of cultural disintegration caused by the influence of the mainstream Canadian culture, which encourages women to claim "equal" rights. However, other Kwakwak'awakw see it as a means of keeping ceremonial privileges within a family in those cases where there is no male heir to bestow them upon. This controversy sheds light on the gender ideologies and relationships in Kwakwak'awakw society, an issue rarely dealt with in ethnographic literature.

Both cases exemplify negotiations about representations of native culture on a collective and individual level. As Glass astutely points out, "The fact that this specific issue revolves around the gender of the Hamat'sa may suggest that the larger issue of cultural representation and the politics of identity has become gendered as well." The conflicts are not easily described as between "traditional" and "progressive" factions but are part of an evolving discourse in which differently positioned persons contest cultural meanings and representations.

Bruce Miller discusses the important question of the role of anthropologists in the representation of cultural practices, especially as they relate to matters of politics and law. He suggests the invention of a tradition of consensus that does not serve contemporary communities especially well in their attempts to construct alternatives to the criminal justice system. This "patrimony" of intellectual property present in the ethnography of earlier generations of anthropologists, especially those working in the first half of the 20th century (who collaborated with consultants born before the imposition of Euro-American and Euro-Canadian hegemony and thus were presumed to have access to precontact cultures), is in many ways a skewed representation of the past and a poor model for the present. Two important issues arise here: ethnohistorical concerns and ethnographic representation.

From an ethnohistorical standpoint, Miller questions the assumptions of ethnographers and their audience who willingly accept the picture of 19th-century Salish society as both autonomous and relatively conflict free, in an atemporal ethnographic present. On the contrary, Miller argues that Salish groups were already encapsulated in white society and, moreover, were suffering through a period of intense conflict and dislocation. So the picture of Salish society presented by Wilson Duff, William Elmendorf, and Wayne Suttles is an artifact of a collaboration shot through with wishful thinking, false memory, and a well-intentioned desire to present a positive image of these societies to the outside world. Such a representational strategy involved both reification and invention, which is necessarily bound to create problems for contemporary Salish people, who are thus deprived of the truth about their own past.

This is a harsh assessment, and one with which few of Miller's colleagues would entirely agree. Representations, either ethnographic or ethnohistorical, are always characterized by principles of selection and formation. The narrative coherence required by traditional textual strategies always results in a certain degree of reification and imposed consensualism. This does not eliminate the value of such material, any more than an overarching view of the sweep of French history in the 18th and 19th centuries vitiates the work of Michelet (see Barthes 1987; H. White 1978:69). At the same time, as Miller suggests, much more information, especially about conflict, power relations, and coercive practices, exists in the field notes, archived in libraries and, increasingly, in native institutions as well. As Anderson, Glass, Boxberger, the Dauenhauers, and Erikson discuss in their chapters, this repatriation of knowledge is one of the major trends in contemporary Northwest Coast society. Only Glass and the Dauenhauers explicitly discuss the conflicts this causes within these communities, perhaps lending credence to Miller's argument that anthropologists prefer consensus and harmony. Indeed, in Boxberger's view, one of the most important roles for the contemporary anthropologist is to aid in the construction of politically viable portrayals of native societies. In the end, as all these essays remind us, the representational choices of anthropologists have pragmatic consequences.

Daniel Boxberger examines the role of the "expert witness" in contemporary resource, land claims, and sovereignty cases. These are of primary importance to native people and represent their best opportunity since the establishment of colonial rule to recover both land and a measure of autonomy.

Anthropologists have been heavily involved in these cases, a role that Boxberger critiques on several grounds, both ethical and methodological. Fundamentally, he argues that a body of knowledge may be transformed from "hearsay" into acceptable court testimony via an alchemy achieved by the intervention of credentialed scholars, who do little more than filter native intellectual property through a screen of objectivist rhetoric. This critique is generically related to, but not directly influenced by, the postmodern critique of the 1980s (Clifford and Marcus 1986). Rather, it is based on empirical analysis.

In the Delgamuukw case, anthropologists attempted and, in the first instance, failed to persuade the court of the legitimacy of the Gitksan and Wet'suwet'en claims to sovereignty over territory. In the McEachern decision, the judge was unswayed by anthropologists' claims to expertise that in a sense the court could recognize as something other than interested hearsay. Since that decision anthropologists have been more successful, having perhaps learned from their past errors as well as having found more sympathetic judges. Eventually, upon appeal, the Delgamuukw case was decided in favor of the plaintiffs, with the establishment by the Supreme Court of Canada of the principle of aboriginal title (Cassidy 1992; Culhane 1998; Mills 1994; Persky 2000).

Despite such successes, Boxberger finds fault with the system as it exists. Important issues of intellectual property and access to justice are involved. Why, for instance, is a judge much more likely to be persuaded by a usually white anthropologist than by a native elder who may have been the anthropologist's source of information? The legal system thus marginalizes certain modes of knowledge and discourse characteristic of native culture, while accepting those that originate in the institutions of Euro-Canadian and Euro-American culture. As Georges Davy (1922) argued long ago and Adams (1973) pointed out more recently, native institutions such as the potlatch have juridical status and have been used to adjudicate issues of property and sovereignty. At the same time, one might argue that in order for such aboriginal institutions to be appreciated by the powers that be, anthropologists must play an important role. Boxberger, who has been called on to be an expert witness, is in the end more equivocal about the role of anthropologists in this process.

The question of property rights connects this essay to those by the Dauenhauers, Miller, Erikson, and Glass. One issue that Boxberger highlights is the circulation of knowledge. In many cases native people have been caught in a double bind: in order to assert legitimate claims they must release sensitive information beyond the boundaries of the relevant in-group (see Harding 2000). Similarly, anthropologists who are expert witnesses (either for or against a particular group) frequently draw on archival or published information that is thereby thought to be "public domain" but that continues to be regarded as private property by the originating group (see Darnell 2001:330–332). Problems of this sort are bad for both anthropologists and native communities; this promises to remain a central issue in Northwest Coast ethnography well into the 21st century.

Since the latter part of the 19th century ethnographic museums have played not only the role of keepers of important collections of objects belonging to peoples thought to be on the verge of disappearance but above all the role of producers of knowledge on societies they represented in exhibits. The cultural authority of museums has been significantly challenged in the last three decades or so by native peoples who demand to control the representation of themselves by Western institutions (Ames 1986a, 1986b; Karp and Lavine 1991; MacClancy 1997). The next step occurred with the establishment of tribal community museums such as the Makah Cultural and Research Centre inaugurated in 1979. Drawing on the momentum generated by the Ozette excavation of the 1970s, a collaboration between museum staff and native people has been established. The Makah have become, through training programs, actors in the (re)construction of their culture.

Patricia Erikson's essay is a contribution to a Northwest Coast museum "autoethnography" or ethnographic (and museographic) self-representation through the exhibit of trinket baskets and various basketry trade items. The autoethnography is also shaped by oral traditions offering "individual, family, and tribal self-portraits." Testimonies convey a sense of time, continuity, and identity, excluding de facto such Western concepts as "cultural disintegration," "acculturation," or "cultural purity," and bring to the fore narratives on the complexity of native identity dynamics within the Euro-American colonial society. Autoethnography is a strategy to establish the authenticity and the legitimacy of the native voice, which, in the case of the exhibit *In Honor of Our Weavers*, essentializes a Makah culture envisioned through the female trade of basket weaving. This demonstrates the chasm between a contemporary anthropological view influenced by the postmodern deconstruction of the culture concept and a native appropriation of the modernist notion of culture as essential (see M. Sahlins 1993).

Ethnographic research on the various forms of indigenous knowledge including ethnogeography (or ethnotoponymy) has a long history in Northwest Coast ethnology. It began in the late 19th century with Boas's (1934) work on the Kwakiutl and Emmons's (1991) work on the Tlingits, continued in the 1920s (Waterman 1922), and intensified in the 1940s and 1950s (de Laguna 1960, 1972; Goldschmidt and Haas 1998). However, it is only in the last decades that ethnographers began a very systematic identification and mapping of native place-names, using the latest survey technology and working in close cooperation with native elders. This research, which has already had major implications for land claims (Goldschmidt and Hass 1998), is becoming increasingly urgent as the number of fluent speakers of native languages, well versed in the intricacies of the traditional geographic knowledge, continues to decline (Galois 1994; Sterritt et al. 1998).

In the essay appearing in this volume, Thomas Thornton, who has already made a major contribution to this field (Thornton 1995, 1997, 2000), addresses a more specific issue of the relationship between Tlingit ideas about place, personhood, and character. Thornton brings together the findings from his own previous work on the traditional ecological knowledge (TEK) of the Tlingits (cf. Hunn 1993) with Tlingit ethnopersonality concepts, first investigated systematically in the 1940s and 1950s by de Laguna (1954, 1972) and more recently by Kan (1989c) and Richard and Nora Dauenhauer (1990).

Drawing on a variety of sources, from the native ideas about the construction of the social order to mythology, Thornton convincingly demonstrates that place is an essential yet dynamic element of personhood and character among the Tlingits. As he puts it, "the idealized person in Tlingit society is one who not only knows the character of his or her ancestral lands but embodies and draws upon the character of the land in a variety of material and symbolic ways to develop, instill, and reflect individual and social group character."

With the imposition of colonial rule on the indigenous peoples of British Columbia, they have lost much of their control over the ancestral lands. Not only have many of their food-producing areas and sacred sites been occupied or disturbed by the newcomers, but even the names of many of the area landmarks have been changed. The local landscape has become a contested ground where the interests of the aboriginal persons and communities clash with those of the logging and mining companies, commercial and recreational hunters and fishers, ecologists, and tourists (from the thousands brought in annually by the cruise ships to the more recent eco-tourists).

This phenomenon should represent an important and interesting new research agenda for historians and ethnologists. However, so far very little work has been done on it by scholars specializing in Northwest Coast research, except those who have been hired by various state agencies to prepare the "multiple use" assessment studies (see, however, Catton 1997).

Michael Harkin's work on the topic is a major exception. He has concentrated on the various, often conflicting, representations and multiple discourses about them by 19th-century colonial geographers, more recent commercial developers, and the region's resources, environmentalists and tourists of various stripes, and, of course, native peoples themselves. While his recent paper "Sacred Place, Scarred Space" (Harkin 2000) examined these various forms of place-making and spatial discourse in several ethnographic or geographic contexts in British Columbia, his essay in the present volume focuses on the Clayoquot Sound and more specifically the "Walk the Wild Side Heritage Trail" developed in the 1990s by the local Nuu-chah-nulth people with assistance from environmental organizations.

Drawing creatively on the ideas of such French scholars as Michel de Certeau, Michel Foucault, and Henri Lefebvre as well as the Russian semiotician Mikhail Bakhtin, Harkin demonstrates that despite the Nuu-chah-nulth attempt to improve the local economy by promoting eco-tourism in their ancestral territory, their views and uses of the landscape continue to differ greatly from and clash with those of the eco-tourists. Harkin's findings are particularly important because the Nuu-chah-nulth people's predicament is not unique. As other indigenous peoples of the Northwest Coast and beyond struggle to balance survival as distinct ethnic, cultural, and political entities with economic viability within an increasingly globalized world, they would often be tempted to open their ancestral lands to various forms of development, including eco-tourism. As Harkin suggests, the outcome of these ventures would depend not only on the various economic and political factors but also on the nature of discourse generated by the native peoples and their non-native interlocutors.

Janine Bowechop's essay recounts the difficult yet rewarding experience the Makahs had in resuming the traditional whale hunt. Told from an insider's perspective, this piece is a valuable document in our attempt to understand the persistence of traditional practices among Northwest Coast societies, often amid widespread opposition. Several interesting points are raised. First, the degree to which cultural transmission with respect to whaling had been successful, despite the dramatic social and cultural changes occurring in the 20th century, is quite remarkable. On a superficial level, it is clear to outsiders that the Makahs do not live as their ancestors did but live in modern-style houses and avail themselves of the latest technologies. More profoundly, language knowledge is in decline, and esoteric knowledge concerning many specialized areas of activity is reduced with the passing of each elder. However, it is clear that much of this knowledge is indeed transmitted. Despite a hiatus of three generations, knowledge (both ritual and practical, to make a distinction that the Makahs would surely not make) has survived. The revival of the whale hunt, like the earlier revival of canoe making and regattas, is best viewed not as invention of tradition but an updating of it (see Harkin 1997b).

A second issue that arises is one that has been the subject of considerable debate recently, in both academic and political circles. That is, generally speaking, the way in which mainstream assumptions about both traditional and contemporary native lifeways has systematically distorted images of Indians, and the way in which these distortions have narrowed the options that contemporary communities have available to them. In particular, the image of "the ecological Indian," based on environmentalist ideology and counter-cultural propaganda, has led a gullible public to believe that all native groups lived in complete and bloodless harmony with nature, "praying to the winds, and maybe living off of vegetables and roots," as Bowechop ironically notes in her chapter (see Krech 1999). This cluster of images, while superficially positive, can quickly turn poisonous when Indians are perceived to be forsaking this clearly invented tradition. This is compounded by the uncritical assumption that people who live in frame houses and have televisions and automobiles cannot possibly be "real Indians." Such outsiders prefer their native people to be quaintly living in the past, without access to the many benefits of modern life. Such an attitude becomes particularly noteworthy in the matter of the technology used for hunting. Makahs were roundly criticized for using a high-powered hunting rifle, rather than a harpoon, to take the whale. The rifle fits in better than the harpoon — native technology though it is — with the overriding cultural concern with a swift and pain-less death for the whale. Indeed, from any reasonable ethical perspective, the rifle was the correct choice. Injured whales typically lashed out, sinking canoes and killing entire crews of Makah or Nuu-chah-nulth whalers even when the art of whaling was at its historical peak (in this case, one could well imagine a whale even taking out a Greenpeace boat). What purpose would have been served by thus endangering both crew and spectator with the death throes of the agonized whale? Indeed, such natural and necessary changes in hunting technology (such as the use of snowmobiles by Cree and other subarctic hunters) provide a convenient explanation for the opposi-tion of radical environmentalist groups to aboriginal peoples' continuing in traditional subsistence practices.

It would be interesting to know more about the political and cultural context of the decision to resume the hunt and the possibility for more hunts in the future. Was this one hunt so traumatic that the Makahs, who, like most native communities, prefer a peaceful life out of the spotlight of interna-tional media, have abandoned this revival? Will it be another 75 years before it is attempted again? Or, by contrast, has the hunt acted as a catalyst in a broader cultural revitalization among the Makahs?

The essays collected here represent, of course, a snapshot, a brief slice of time in the history of a region and a field of study. We cannot claim that they are any more than that, any more than manifestations of diverse theoretical, national, and generational perspectives that fit together in only a loose sort of way by virtue of some shared interests and commitments. However, this millennial moment is of particular interest, for the very fact that they came together at a particular time and place and spoke to one another. In the most obvious way, this represented a link between the early 20th century, with strong roots in the 19th, in the persons of Claude Lévi-Strauss and Frederica de Laguna, both of whom were influenced by Franz Boas, although in strik-ingly different ways, with the dawning of the 21st century, represented by those (e.g., Aaron Glass) who will spend their entire professional lives in the new century. Although human history, and especially intellectual history, is not obliged to follow the artificial divisions of the Gregorian calendar, it often does, although not always exactly on cue.

Most of us have felt the field of anthropology generally, and that of Northwest Coast ethnology in particular, to be in a liminal or perhaps "experimental" phase since the 1970s (see Clifford and Marcus 1986). Whether this represents merely the transition between phases of "normal science" or a more or less permanent extraparadigmatic state of affairs, it is characterized by an intense hybridity of discourse (see Kuhn 1970). This hybridity, characteristic of the field as a whole and of many, if not most, authors within it, limits our ability to make authoritative social science pronouncements and limits the sorts of "detachable conclusions" that can possibly derive from such works. However, rather than a situation of paralysis or confusion, such a set of circumstances has given rise to what we think and hope is the vitality of the hybrid.

Coming *to* *Shore*

Claude Lévi-Strauss. © Collège de France.

REFLECTIONS ON
NORTHWEST COAST ETHNOLOGY

Claude Lévi-Strauss

Delivered at the Collège de France on June 21, 2000

With these opening words I would like to thank the organizers for symbolically joining my name to the title of this conference. Nothing could move me more than this appreciation, from my distinguished colleagues, of my emotional and intellectual ties to the Pacific Northwest Coast. The peoples who have lived there for thousands of years, their social institutions, and their art have played an essential part in my theoretical thinking, just as they have affected me profoundly aesthetically.

Of all my ethnographic experiences, closest to my heart are the weeks I spent in British Colombia, on two separate occasions some 25 years ago. It would be presumptuous to say what I did there was fieldwork, even though I still have vivid memories of a night I spent in 1973 in a communal house in a Salish community near Vancouver to participate in a Guardian Spirit Dance, of another night in 1974 in Alert Bay, of my trip in a camper that same year throughout Vancouver Island from the Skeena Valley to the furthest stretches of Gitksan, and lastly of the Fraser Valley. These peregrinations were more in the spirit of a pilgrimage, however, a devoted homage to a major sanctuary of Native American civilization.

The Pacific Northwest is in this eminent position primarily because of its art, which, for all those who approach it, holds the same power of fascination. Better, perhaps, than any other, it captures the supernatural in a graphic and plastic representation and not, as in our own religious art, as merely an embellishment or amplification of natural phenomena. It is an art that puts us in the very presence of a *sui generis* — yet living — reality, the result of that rare blend of prodigious inventiveness and an extreme exactitude in execution. It could be likened to speaking a language governed by strict grammatical rules, and just as with language, abiding by the rules is exactly what allows for unlimited expression, while at the same time giving the boldest of imaginations an accent of truth.

I once saw a clear illustration of this exactitude in execution in rather amusing circumstances that I would like to share with you. Some 15 years ago the Musée de l'Homme organized an exhibition on the Americas. A short time before, Bill Reid accomplished the great feat of restoring the traditional techniques of building and decorating a large monoxylic canoe. This gave birth to the idea of inviting Reid and a group of Haida people to partici-pate in the show. They were to bring the canoe to Paris, which was to be the highpoint of the exhibition.

I will never forget that day, late in the afternoon, when the Haida crew literally landed at the Musée de l'Homme. The inauguration was supposed to be the following evening, but, as usual, nothing was ready, and the workers had left all their tools scattered about on the floor.

As a backdrop for the exhibition, the organizers had the idea of display-ing a life-size facade of a Haida house. The designated painter had settled on a very approximate depiction based on a photograph, intended even to be a little artistic. The Haidas were furious; grabbing buckets of paint, they splat-tered the facade in white and then, armed with the very rulers, set squares, and compasses the carpenters had left lying about, traced and painted the decor, not in any impressionistic style, but as it should be in reality. This skillful and exact execution, using professional instruments, made me feel that we were the ignorant ones, and our visitors the masters.

Reflecting upon — some 60 years ago — the displays at the Museum of Natural History in New York dedicated to the Northwest Coast, I thought to myself: this art deserves its place alongside the art of Ancient Egypt, the Orient, and Medieval Europe. Who would have thought that as I speak such works are entering the Louvre! This is just one of those consecrations this art — having the extra virtue of being a living art — is getting at last, after being relegated to the ranks of ethnographic specimen for so long.

I wonder, all the same, whether it is because of its profusion and bril-liance that we tend to underrate the neighboring societies whose aesthetic expressions are at a more modest level. This seems especially true of the small communities that inhabited — and many of which still inhabit — the Puget Sound area. I am not suggesting we have neglected them in our studies. The names of Gibbs, Eells, Wayne Suttles, Marian Smith, Elmendorf, and others are enough to prove the contrary. Yet, too concerned with locating the differences, the specialists of this region have never clearly ascertained what their social structures have in common with those of the peoples further up north. Reading a recent book by Jay Miller on the culture we refer to as Lushootseed, I found it gratifying that in order to characterize certain traits of the social organization, the author referred several times to aristocratic European houses.

Yet my proposition of making a place for the notion of house within an ethnographic typology, alongside that of phratry, gens, clan, lineage, and family, was what I had hoped — and still believe — would offer the key to resolving some of the enigmas we come up against when we try to understand the institutions of the Northwest. We were undoubtedly right to set out by identifying the social organizations of each people and showing accurately in what ways they differ from one another: the Kwakiutl, the Haidas, the Tsimshian, the Tlingits, and so on. But the analyses of our precursors, however indispensable, tended to lose sight — notwithstanding the economic, political, cultural, linguistic, and religious differences — of what a large ensemble of societies stretching from Alaska to Northern California (for in this regard the Yurok belong indisputably to this group) have in common, notably a form of social organization without equivalent anywhere else in America. For we can identify them only by comparing them to those institutions that our own societies and those of the Far East possessed centuries ago (and which in some cases survived a long time).

I began this brief interjection with some thoughts on the art of the Northwest Coast. That it is now recognized as one of the highest forms of art is indeed cause for celebration. Let us not, however, dissimulate the fact that despite all the studies that have already come out, this art remains shrouded in mystery. An external mystery to begin with. How are we to explain the formal analogies that we have intuitively perceived between this art and that of ancient China? The hypothesis of distant relationships seems less inconceivable now that we know that distinctive traits in the art of the Northwest Coast have been proven, on site, to belong to a period at least contemporary with the Shang and Zhou dynasties in China. But if we are not to settle with the too simplistic answers offered by diffusionism, the more plausible hypothesis whereby certain autonomous developments dispersed throughout the Pacific stem from a common core actually poses more problems than it resolves.

It is an internal mystery, too, as the peoples of the Northwest Coast have been so closely linked through war, the capture of slaves, commerce, and alliances that it is often difficult to assign a precise provenance to those productions we qualify as works of art. And when we do venture to do so, it is most often for negative reasons. Such and such an object, it seems, could *only* be Kwakiutl, another *only* Haida, and still another *only* Tsimshian, and so on. Yet we can barely say what exactly differentiates the arts of these societies, as historians of European art routinely do for 16th- or 17th-century French, Flemish, or Italian painting. Over the entire stretch of the Northwest Coast, we believe we can identify stylistic tendencies: "audacious" for the Kwakiutl, "hieratic" for the Haidas. But giving in to the temptation of contrasting a Tsimshian human sensibility with the Tlingits' dreamy poetry would be to forget that many of the works we attribute to the latter group were, in fact, what they commissioned from the former.

Scholars have diligently studied the Northwest Coast for more than a century, treating as much its art as its social organization, and yet they have by no means exhausted the task. This is what justifies this conference, and the communications and exchanges to follow will mark, I have no doubt, significant advancement in the field. To the very old man that I am, you give the joy of knowing that the studies to which I have dedicated part of my life are being continued. For several days they will be brilliantly illustrated in this house in which I have had the honor to teach for twenty-two years, a house I consider partly my own.

Translated from the French by Unity Woodman

THE LEGACY OF
NORTHWEST COAST RESEARCH

TEXT, SYMBOL, AND TRADITION IN NORTHWEST COAST ETHNOLOGY FROM FRANZ BOAS TO CLAUDE LÉVI-STRAUSS

Regna Darnell

The Americanist anthropology that I practice has evolved to its present stature and structure in great part as a result of the intersection of a culture area — the Northwest Coast — with the work of two seminal scholars — the German-turned-American Franz Boas and the Frenchman Claude Lévi-Strauss, who mined the broad ethnological fields of the Americas within a theoretical range not entirely incompatible with a characteristically Americanist historical particularism. To be sure, there is a degree of perversity in this reading. These two intellectual giants are hardly the only scholars to work on the Northwest Coast, as evidenced by the number of distinguished scholars contributing to this volume, both French and North American. Without question, there are dramatic and fundamental differences in the paradigms of historical particularism and structuralism. But there are also similarities, continuities amid the rhetorics of revolution and discontinuity (Darnell 1998). In this context, Claude Lévi-Strauss becomes a Boasian of sorts (Darnell 2001). These border crossings between the French and Americanist traditions come into focus on the Northwest Coast, which, I suggest, provides a veritable microcosm for the history of anthropology (Darnell 2000).

Americanist anthropology has been remarkably insular, a myopia reflected more in superficiality of historicist consciousness than in actuality. Recognition is long overdue that European colleagues (in the case of the Northwest Coast, particularly French and Russian colleagues) have contributed to the peculiar mélange of ethnological insight that constitutes our disciplinary heritage.

My own work as a historian of anthropology has focused on the Americanist tradition because it seems to me to have been submerged without intellectual justification in a wave of post–World War II enthusiasm for over-seas fieldwork (already practiced by Lévi-Strauss in Brazil a decade ear-lier) and British colonialist functionalism becoming degraded into implicitly ethnocentric interpretation, perhaps best exemplified by E. E. Evans-Pritch-ard's conclusion that the Azande were capable of rational thought but mis-taken in the tools with which they thought. These tools were presumably deployed properly only by post-Victorian gentlemen in the field. I exagger-ate, of course—in an attempt to highlight and reevaluate the Americanist position developed by Boas and his students during the first half of the past century.

The distinctive features of the Americanist tradition, as I have argued elsewhere (Darnell 2001; Darnell in Valentine and Darnell 1999), are mental-ist, products of the human mind. Despite contrasts of the inductive and de-ductive methods, giving a dissimilar surface appearance to ethnographically based arguments, I suggest that these distinctive features characterize the work of Claude Lévi-Strauss as well as that of Franz Boas and his students.

In sum: culture is a system, a structure if you prefer, of symbols con-tained in human minds situated in the context of particular social traditions. Language, thought, and reality are inseparable, their forms colored indelibly by categories learned through socialization. The database that provides ac-cess to these products of the human mind is encapsulated for study in texts, preferably volunteered in an interactional context and preferably in the na-tive language. Such texts reveal the "native point of view," "the culture as it appears to the Indian himself" (Berman 1996). The Americanist commit-ment to recording texts so that the accumulated knowledge preserved in oral traditions will not be lost to human history finds its downside, however, in an ethnocentric nostalgia for the formerly primitive that denies the contem-porary vibrancy of First Nations (as we call Native Americans in Canada) communities and traditions. My own anthropological predilections lead me to treasure what Helen Codere (ed. 1966) called Boas's "five-foot shelf of Kwakiutl ethnography" and to believe that this corpus has contemporary use-value in the communities that legitimately and inalienably own this ir-replaceable intellectual property. Whatever we might want to say about the intractability of anthropologists, First Nations traditions are far from static. From this it follows that First Nations communities and individuals are not objects to be studied. Rather, at least ideally, and varying across individuals, communities, and contexts, they are collaborators and consultants, embodying the possibility of respect coexisting with, perhaps even mutually reinforcing across, difference. My final suggestion for a fundamental characteristic of this Americanist tradition is that the fieldwork takes a long time. Northwest Coast ethnologists tend to devote a lifetime to a single nation or at least to the culture area. My own mentors, Frederica de Laguna when I was an undergraduate at Bryn Mawr and Dell Hymes when I was a graduate student at the University of Pennsylvania, both ensured that I would remain immersed in this tradition. Over my more than three decades in Canadian anthropology, the presence of the Northwest Coast has been inescapable in my anthropology.

If the history of anthropology is reflected in this culture area, then conversely, a personified Northwest Coast has in turn contributed to the history of anthropology by imposing its particular characteristics on visiting ethnologists. Richard Fardon (1990) assembled reports of the area-specific attitudes and practices of anthropologists working in culture areas around the globe, albeit Native North America is represented in his collection only by Eskimo hunters. Over a professional lifetime, scholars absorb many forms of habitual thought from the peoples with whom they work, and they come to share without conscious effort much that must be explained to colleagues who have worked elsewhere. (Sense of humor provides a telling example. My colleague Keith Basso, whose work on Western Apache jokes about white men has pioneered in this area, is himself a masterful raconteur. Nonetheless, we have always been able to finish one another's stories from the field; they arise from a similar set of cultural assumptions.)

If we are to understand this process of interaction between a field site and a particular anthropologist, or a succession of anthropologists, it behooves us to identify what is unusual about the Northwest Coast. Indeed, we must consider why the concept of the culture area still seems to work for ethnologists trying to delimit the purportedly "natural" scope and boundedness of their investigations. "Franz Boas worked there" is insufficient explanation for the significance of Northwest Coast examples in theoretical and comparative work across national anthropological traditions, especially the French (including Marcel Mauss as well as Claude Lévi-Strauss) and the Americanist (e.g., Ruth Benedict's use of Boas's Kwakiutl ethnography in *Patterns of Culture* [1934]).

For both Boas and Lévi-Strauss, the Northwest Coast provided a convenient laboratory for controlled comparisons, in contrast to the casual absence of context in classical evolutionary reasoning. The Northwest Coast environment was relatively constant, with rich maritime and riverine resources permitting cultural fluorescence and sufficient leisure for *Bildung* or individual creativity. Despite cultural and physical proximity, however, the various groups apparently remained distinct over long periods of time. Boas was introduced to the Northwest Coast through its art as exhibited in Europe. He notes he was enchanted by the "flight of imagination . . . compared to the severe sobriety of the eastern Eskimo" and mused over the "wealth of thought" that "lay hidden behind the grotesque masks and the elaborately decorated utensils of these tribes" (Cole 1999:97). Already, before his first visit to the Northwest Coast, Boas realized that traditional domains of culture (art, material culture, and myth) overlapped.

His choice of field site, albeit constrained by sponsorship of the British Association for the Advancement of Science and the Bureau of American Ethnology, enabled Boas to explore the complexity and interconnection of cultures reaching from southern Alaska to northern California. Culture was widely shared, although linguistic affiliations were wildly diverse. Joel Sherzer's areal typology of Native North American phonology and morphology (1976) viewed the Northwest Coast as typical of the continent's most developed type of linguistic area, characterized by intermarriage, trade, and multilingualism among relatively small and settled groups. Borrowing was the most obvious historical process.

In 1910, in reference to "Ethnological Problems in Canada," Boas clarified the need for areal-controlled comparisons, using the Cambridge Torres Strait Expedition and his own Jesup North Pacific Expedition as examples (1940a:332): "Brief reports on local conditions were well enough when even the rough outlines of our subject had not come into view. Since these have been laid bare, a different method is needed. Not even exhaustive descriptions of single tribes or sites fulfill the requirement of our time. We must concentrate our energies upon the systematic study of the great problems of each area."

Lévi-Strauss, in *A World on the Wane* (1961b:237) and *Tristes Tropiques* (1955b), conceptualized the culture area framework as yielding generalizations more significant than any study he might conceivably carry out of any single tribe: "I planned to spend a whole year in the bush, and had hesitated for a long time as to where, and for what reason, I was to go. In the end, with no notions that the result would be quite contrary to my intentions, and being anxious rather to understand the American continent as a whole than to deepen my knowledge of human nature by studying one particular case, I decided to examine the whole breadth of Brazil, both ethnographically and geographically."

Indeed, the emphasis on culture area functioned positively to distinguish American from British anthropology. British functionalism erred, in Lévi-Strauss's view (1975:145), in focusing on "isolated tribes, enclosed within themselves, each living on its own account a peculiar experience of an aesthetic, mythical, or ritual order"; populations coexisted "elbow to elbow" and deployed various "modalities according to which each explained and represented the universe to itself . . . elaborated in an unceasing and vigorous dialogue." The ethnography of each group provided a window to larger perspectives. Lévi-Strauss believes that his own commitment to concrete and detailed ethnographic data has been misunderstood (145). "Only those whose entire ethnological outlook is confined to the group they have studied personally are prone to overlook my almost maniacal deference for the facts."

We might reformulate the question of the importance of studying the Northwest Coast as: "Why did Boas move away from studying the Eskimos of Baffin Island to the people he called Kwakiutl (now Kwakwaka'wakw) and other cultures of the Northwest Coast?" Boas went to Baffinland, as it was then called, to decide for himself whether environment determined culture, as many of his geography professors in Germany had maintained. He returned firmly committed to the interaction of culture with an environment that played a constraining rather than a determinant role. He found that the Central Eskimos, despite the extreme character of their environment, possessed a highly elaborated "mental" or symbolic culture. Environment, therefore, held little further interest for Boas. He had moved irrevocably from geography to ethnology, the link among his successive professions being the effect of the observer on the phenomena observed (a position deriving from his doctoral work in psychophysics on the color of sea water). If "the mind of primitive man" was not set into its characteristic pattern by environment, then variability of cultures in history became, almost by default, the paradigmatic problem for anthropology. Such attention to the epistemological status of the observer applied both to the Eskimo hunter observing and taming nature or environment by culture and to the observing anthropologist. By this mentalist route, methodology moved to the center of Boasian theory.

In "The Aims of Anthropological Research," for example, Boas directly linked the inadequacy of economic determinism to the impossibility of any single historical explanation: "Undoubtedly the interrelation between economics and other aspects of culture is much more immediate than that between geographical environment and culture. . . . Every attempt to deduce cultural forms from a single cause is doomed to failure, for the various expressions of culture are closely interrelated and one cannot be altered without having an effect upon all the others. Culture is integrated. It is true that the degree of integration is not always the same" (1940:256).

Although Boas is frequently dismissed as a mere descriptivist, he in fact practiced a deconstructive method that has come into its own with structuralism and its intellectual descendants. Diffusion provided the core concept for Boas's redefinition of "history," another heritage from his German geographical training. By identifying separate foreign elements, the analyst could trace the process of their integration into particular cultures. The method foreshadows that of Lévi-Strauss, although the explanation of distributional features was diffusion in one case and a universal structure of the human mind in the other.

Interestingly, Lévi-Strauss has on occasion acknowledged that Boas "never thought structural analysis was incompatible with ethnohistorical investigations" (1975:162). In the first volume of *Structural Anthropology* (1963a:281), he noted:

> In the history of structuralist thought, Boas . . . made it clear that a category of facts can more easily yield to structural analysis when the social group in which it is manifested has not elaborated a conscious model to interpret or justify it. Some readers may be surprised to find Boas's name quoted in connection with structural theory, since he has often been described as one of the main obstacles in its path. But this writer has tried to demonstrate that Boas's shortcomings in matters of structural studies did not lie in his failure to understand their importance and significance, which he did, as a matter of fact, in the most prophetic

way. They rather resulted from the fact that he imposed on structural studies conditions of validity, some of which will remain forever part of their methodology, while some others are so exacting and impossible to meet that they would have withered scientific development in any field. A structural model may be conscious or unconscious without this difference affecting its nature.

Boas, "the great master of modern anthropology," produces an analysis of remarkable but "mainly theoretical" "elegance and simplicity" (260). "Our analysis thus converges with that of Boas, once we have explored its substructure" (262), which manifests both social and formal features.

George Stocking (1974) has argued that the Boasian theoretical paradigm was essentially complete by 1911. Boas's two-pronged critique of classical evolution tacked between psychology and history. On the psychological front *The Mind of Primitive Man* (1911b) denied that "primitive" "man" was different in kind from the anthropologists who studied him or her, while on the historical side his introduction to the *Handbook of American Indian Languages* (1911a) analytically distinguished race, language, and culture. In practice, however, Boas considered the psychological questions premature and called for detailed investigation of the histories of particular tribes. This research program required him to develop reliable methodologies for reconstructing the cultural histories of peoples without writing.

In "The Limitations of the Comparative Method of Anthropology" in 1896, Boas wrote: "A detailed study of customs in their relation to the total culture of the tribe practicing them, in connection with an investigation of their geographical distribution among neighboring tribes, affords us almost always a means of determining with considerable accuracy the *historical* causes that led to the formation of the customs in question and to the *psychological* processes that were at work in their development" (1940a:276, emphasis added). Throughout Boas's career, history and psychology remained sides of a single interpretive coin, sides that were to be examined in constant alternation (1940a:264): "Understanding of a foreign culture can be reached only by analysis and we are compelled to take up its various aspects successively. Furthermore, each element contains clear traces of changes that it has undergone in time. This may be due to inner forces [psychology] or to the influence of foreign cultures [history]. The full analysis must necessarily include the phases that led to its present form."

Boas and Lévi-Strauss were in agreement that the analysis they fore-grounded could not be carried out entirely from within a culture. In the introduction to the *Handbook of American Indian Languages,* Boas insisted that "the grammar has been treated as though an intelligent Indian was going to develop the forms of his own thoughts by an analysis of his own form of speech" (1911a:70). The psychological element of the Boasian paradigm, the "native point of view," however, resonated very differently for Lévi-Strauss, who was not much interested in Native interpretations of cultural forms because he assumed that people did not easily articulate their unconscious understandings of cultural phenomena.

Like Lévi-Strauss, Boas was fascinated by myth variants. He wrote to George Hunt (BPC: September 1, 1906) attempting to uncover the history of particular versions and to establish the "correct" version. He valued the individuality of such variable texts as a means to make the culture come alive as well as to reconstruct history through the working out of principles of rank "in the case of a number of particular men and women." These stories focused on rights to masks and dances and the stories that went with them (Boas to Hunt, BPCApril 4, 1913:).

In his Northwest Coast diaries (Rohner 1969:38), Boas emphasized the scientific value of collecting material culture objects for the American Museum of Natural History that were accompanied by the stories that made cultural sense of them. Comparably, a ceremony made no sense unless its meaning was explicated by a member of the culture. Boas noted on one such occasion: "George Hunt was not here, and so I did not know what was going on" (188). Boas, determined that his students would not restrict their topics to single domains of culture, stated: "I have instructed my students to collect certain things. . . . Consequently, the results of their journeys are the following: they get [museum] specimens; they get explanations of the specimens; they get connected texts that partly refer to the specimens and partly simply to abstract things concerning the people; and they get grammatical information" (Berman 1996:270). It is a short step to the domain plasticity of Lévi-Strauss's concept of structure, with his exemplars moving freely across visual, verbal, and semantic representations.

In his 1927 study *Primitive Art,* Boas continued to emphasize the "two principles" of psychology and history (1955:1): "the fundamental sameness of mental processes in all races and in all cultural forms of the present day" and "the consideration of every cultural phenomenon as the result of historical happenings."

Form was constant although its meanings were variable, "not only tribally but also individually," in art, mythology, and ceremonialism alike (Boas 1955:128). Meaning "was tacked on according to the peculiar mental disposition of the individual or the tribe" (129). The underlying mental processes, however, "do not take place in the full light of consciousness" (155):

> The single tribe cannot provide a reasonable perspective: There is probably not a single region in existence in which the art style may be understood entirely as an inner growth and not as an expression of the cultural life of a single tribe. Wherever a sufficient amount of material is available, we can trace the influence of neighboring tribes upon one another, often extending over vast distances. Dissemination of cultural traits that has made the social structures, the ceremonials, and the tales of tribes what they are today has also been a most important element in shaping the forms of their art. . . . Their strong individuality proves that their present distribution must be due to mutual influence among various North American cultures. We cannot determine where the pattern originated but it is quite certain that its present distribution is due to cultural contact. (176)

A long section of *Primitive Art* is devoted to the "North Pacific Coast of North America." The men's style of wood carving and painting is symbolic, distinct from the women's style of weaving, basketry, and embroidery. The general features of symbolic art include "an almost absolute disregard of the principles of perspective, emphasis on significant symbols, and an arrangement dictated by the form of the decorative field" (1955:183). The "exuberant" decorative designs have developed "only recently" (279); this symbolic style is now used by the Kwakiutl for house paintings and posts and for masks (288).

Lévi-Strauss's treatment of split representation draws heavily on Boas's formulation. His sample transcended the Northwest Coast as a culture area, including China, the Amur, the Neolithic, the Maori, the Eskimo, and the Amazon. That is, his own areal work in Brazil, compared with the Northwest Coast where Boas pioneered in the anthropology of art, posed a wider question about the causes of social hierarchy and their correlation with masks and split representations.

For Boas, however, masks were not a single phenomenon, although "a few typical forms of their use may easily be distinguished" (1940a:274–275). What Boas found interesting was "the intelligent understanding of a complex phenomenon" (305): "I aligned myself clearly with those who are motivated by the affective appeal of a phenomenon that impresses us as a unit, although its elements may be irreducible to a common cause." "The historical development of primitive cultures" had to be "inferred" from "very inadequate material," but Boas believed this could be done, at least in part, although "the uniqueness of cultural phenomena and their complexity" probably precluded laws "excepting those psychological, biologically determined characteristics which are common to all cultures and appear in a multitude of forms according to the particular culture in which they manifest themselves" (311). In 1936, the year he retired from Columbia, Boas acknowledged that the battle against premature evolutionary generalization had been won, but he insisted that similar logical errors continued with "the imposition of categories derived from our own culture upon foreign cultures" (311), by which he meant not the epistemology of observation but the apparent inevitability—belied by the subsequent revitalization of traditional cultures and languages—of "acculturation."

As early as 1895, in "The Growth of Indian Mythologies," Boas described "a dwindling down of an elaborate cycle of myths" (1940a:429) in a process leaving traces of historical movement of folklore elements. Mythologies as such were not "organic growths, but have gradually developed and obtained their present form by accretion of foreign material" which "must have been adopted ready-made" and modified "according to the genius of the people who borrowed it." Such historical inferences could not be expected to reflect "the native point of view." Rather, "explanations given by the Indians themselves were often secondary," relative to origins, and "complex."

The culture area framework allowed Boas to move toward theory or at least generalization (1940a:433–434):

> The analysis of one definite mythology of North America shows that in it are embodied elements from all over the continent, the greater number belonging to neighboring districts, while many others belong to distant areas, or, in other words, that dissemination of tales has taken place all over the continent. In most cases we can discover the channels through which the tale flowed, and we recognize that in each and every

mythology of North America we must expect to find numerous foreign elements. And this leads us to the conclusion that similarities of culture on our continent are always more likely to be due to diffusion than to independent development.

Boas went on to study what he called "the interesting psychological problems of acculturation," that is, "what conditions govern the selection of foreign material embodied in the culture of the people, and the mutual transformation of the old culture and the newly acquired material" (435).

In "The Decorative Art of the North American Indians" in 1903, Boas (1940a:557) suggested that borrowed motifs were assimilated "to some indigenous and familiar form" against the grain of the original "motives." He concluded that ceremonial objects were much more realistic than decorative objects for ordinary use. Art styles proved themselves much more widely distributed than explanatory styles, demonstrating the secondary and "late" character of such explanations; interpretation and style were not necessarily correlated although they influenced one another (562). Both artistic style and explanatory style were products of the particular group history. "The historical explanation of customs given by the native is generally a result of speculation, not by any means a true historical explanation" (563).

Boas's 1908 paper on "Decorative Designs of Alaskan Needle-Cases," based on museum exhibits, made the case against historical accuracy of Native interpretations even more strongly: "The only satisfactory explanation lies in the theory that the multifarious forms are due to the play of the imagination with a fixed conventional form, the origin of which remains entirely obscure" (1940a:588).

Boas understood the folk tale "primarily and fundamentally" as a form of primitive art. Already in 1914 (1940a:480), he considered style as a reflection of "constant play with old themes" having little to do with origins: "The explanatory element would then appear, not as an expression of native philosophy, but rather as an artistic finishing touch required for the tale wherever the art of story-telling demands it." Through such questions of psychological reality, Boas was led to the study of the individual in culture (482): "The contrast between a disorganized mass of folk-tales and the more systematic mythologies seems to lie, therefore, in the introduction of an element of *individual* creativeness." This helps to explain the contradictions in systems of myth, both within and across traditions: "These contradictory traditions are the result of individual thought in each community, and do not come into conflict, because the audience identifies itself with the reciting chief, and the truth of one poetic creation does not destroy the truth of the other one."

In 1916 (1940a:397) Boas set out his method for analyzing folktales and myths, the core of his textual research program. Wide distribution of elements, however, "rarely only" provided "internal evidence" of origin or borrowing. Nonetheless, particular forms of tales were characteristic of localized versions. The versions developed for psychological reasons (401–402): "The artistic impulses of a people are not always satisfied with the loose connection of stories, brought about by the individuality of the hero, or strengthened by the selection of anecdotes. We find a number of cases in which a psychological connection of the elements of the complex story is sought. . . . We must infer that the elements were independent and have been combined in various ways." Each region, through the "imagination of the natives," selects "preponderant themes, in the style of plots, and in their literary development"; "there is comparatively little material that seems to belong to any one region exclusively, so that it might be considered as of autochthonous origin" (403).

Ritual and social system "have been foisted upon the myths" so that variants "tend to establish harmony between mythology and social phenomena" (Boas 1940a:422). The historical vista emerging from the method he applied to the myths of the Thompson River Indians captured Boas's own imagination (424): "It would seem that mythological worlds have been built up, only to be shattered again, that new worlds were built from the fragments."

In 1916 Boas turned to "Representative Art of Primitive People." On the Northwest Coast "the principle of representation of an object by means of symbols is carried to extremes" (1940a:538), with little attention to realistic animal forms. Rather, "all characteristic parts" of the animal were shown conventionally. These symbols were then "squeezed" into a decorative field.

Lévi-Strauss brought his Boas-inspired immersion in Northwest Coast ethnology to bear on the question of mask cultures in *The Way of the Masks* (1982). Across this "vast region" peoples maintained close contacts through "migrations, wars, borrowings, commercial and matrimonial exchanges, of which archaeology, traditional legends and history supply the proofs" (1982:

129). The borrowings, such as between mainland and inland or Dene and coastal peoples, have a consistent symmetrical character.

Fascinated by Northwest Coast masks from his first exposure to them in interwar New York, Lévi-Strauss acknowledged "profound respect . . . undermined by a lingering uneasiness" because "their plastic justification escaped me" (1982:10). The problem could not be resolved within the domain of art. Myths and masks were less separate objects than semantic relations (12): "Looked upon from the semantic point of view, a myth acquires sense only after it is returned to its transformation set." Coherence involves transformation and contrast, a "restringing of the segments" (27); for example, the original mainland versions are built up logically and become less coherent as they move to the islands: "Any myth or sequence in a myth would remain incomprehensible if each myth were not opposable to other versions of the same myth or to apparently different myths, each sequence opposable to other sequences in the same or other myths, and especially those whose logical framework and concrete content . . . seem to contradict them" (56). Plastic, sociological, and semantic points of view are all needed to "articulate . . . scattered traits . . . into a system" (39). Works of art, like masks and myths, cannot contain their entire meaning. The mask domain combines myth, social or religious function, and plastic expression (57): "Hence, they will justifiably receive the same treatment." The "ideal mask" can be predicted ("described and reconstructed" on theoretical grounds) and then discovered "in reality" (59).

Both elements and wholes are integral to the structuralist position: "the relics of a common stock [provide] the elements of myths, rites, and plastic works forming this organized whole," "a cultural complex" of mask types whose "traces" are found in particular tribal instantiations (1982:189). What is finally delimited is a "semantic field" (223).

Data for such reconstructions, however, are difficult to obtain. Group styles are clearly distinguished, with the Kwakiutl taking a "hieratic, more lyrical and more violent" approach (1982:40). Ambiguous relations reverse at all three levels. For the Kwakiutl, "rich though they may appear when compared with others," these data are "far from exhaustive," and their distributions are not fully clear (68). The parts of such a system are transforms of one another (93): "Except for stylistic differences, all the plastic characteristics of the Swaihwe masks are found in the Xwexwe masks of the Kwakiutl, but the latter, being avaricious instead of generous, fill a function opposite to that of the former. By contrast, the Dzonokwa mask (which dispenses riches like the Swaihwe and, like it, transfers its wealth from the wife's family to the husband's) has plastic characteristics which, down to the smallest details, constitute a systematic inversion of the Swaihwe mask's characteristics." This method can be extended as far as parallels are found. Alliance and exchange protect against intracommunity marriage and provide security from foreign incursion. "The coppers and the masks constituted two parallel solutions to the same problems for two different but contiguous populations" (139).

Lévi-Strauss even concludes that historical reconstruction can provide greater time depth than local explanations postulate (1975:141): "I would prefer to suppose either that the existence and diffusion of the Swaihwe mask go back to a more ancient period than the various local traditions suggest, or that, in the form in which they have come down to us, the coppers and the masks perpetuate, each in its own way and in more or less parallel fashion, archaic themes." These forms "share the same spirit" and metaphor (143): "a mask does not exist in isolation; it supposes other real or potential masks always by its side, masks that might have been chosen in its stead and substituted for it. A mask is not primarily what it represents but what it transforms, that is to say, what it chooses *not* to represent" (144). (This is not the language of individual psychology but of culture as collectivity.) Thus, style is both original and a product of borrowing and the "conscious or unconscious wish to declare itself different" (144).

The method, adapted from Boas, acknowledges that the "short-run and localized history of a people without writing eludes us by definition"; nonetheless, structural analysis can sometimes "document the concrete conjectures from which a mythic transformation has sprung" (1982:152). The "mechanisms" through which masks spread "by inheritance, marriage, conquest, or borrowing remain visible" (162).

In sum, then, the theoretical positions of Franz Boas and Claude Lévi-Strauss concur on many points and intersect significantly in the history of anthropology. Both scholars define culture and myth within the symbolic domain and apply a comparative perspective from outside the culture studied to answer larger questions of history and group interaction, if not of origins. Both take for granted what was once called the psychic unity of mankind, although Lévi-Strauss is more likely than Boas to assume these universals in the products of the human mind to be accessible to anthropological investigation. Boas thought that such psychological questions might be answerable sometime in the future but placed priority upon historical questions.

There is, of course, a generation of substantial duration between these two scholars and their encounters with the Northwest Coast. Without Boas's groundwork documenting the distribution of myth themes and correlating masks, ceremonials, and stories, the comparative project of Lévi-Strauss could scarcely have been formulated. He adopted both the database and the historical comparative method of Boasian Northwest Coast scholarship and applied the method to revised theoretical purposes. The structures he compared throughout the Americas were not "historical" in precisely the Boasian sense, although their historical interactions provided evidence of universal mental processes. In this, Lévi-Strauss's approach is French, his thinking a product of an Enlightenment rationalism and universalism thoroughly alien to Boas's own Germanic emphasis on the unique Weltanschauung of particular cultures, including his own. That American anthropology has, for the most part, taken the Boasian direction should not preclude attention to the French side of the coin. If Lévi-Strauss was not precisely a Boasian, he did build directly upon Boasian guidelines in fundamental ways — producing a productive cross-fertilization for both national traditions.

BECOMING AN ANTHROPOLOGIST

My Debt to European and Other Scholars Who Influenced Me

Frederica de Laguna

Report to Paris

I met Dr. Marie Mauzé in Canada in 1991 at a symposium on shamanism organized by my former student and present colleague, Dr. Marie-Françoise Guédon, professor of anthropology at the University of Ottawa. We were guests in her large, rambling house in the province of Quebec, just across the river from Canada's capital. Here the informal hospitality, *en famille,* was conducive to nurturing friendships and the exchange of scholarly chitchat. I was fascinated by what I learned there about some of the recent developments in French anthropological-ethnological studies, for ill health and failing eyesight had gradually been cutting me off from the learned world.

I once spoke French with ease, if not always correctly, but the papers given in French at the Ottawa symposium showed me how much of that language I had forgotten. The French I knew was now incredibly old-fashioned, since I was ignorant of the completely new vocabularies and idioms spawned by the technological inventions and the social upheavals of the past 70 years.

So when Dr. Mauzé invited me to Paris to join the symposium on the Northwest Coast, I rejoiced in anticipation of this unique opportunity for relearning French, for "catching up" with recent scholarship, for meeting colleagues new and old, and perhaps for revisiting some of the scenes of my childhood and student days in France. Professor Claude Lévi-Strauss would be at the conference, and I could join other colleagues in paying him honor.

Alas, my health would not permit the journey. Since, I am told, Professor Lévi-Strauss has spoken of my fieldwork with approval, I am very grateful for this chance to write on what I should have liked to discuss in person and especially to acknowledge my debt to the French scholars who gave me their generous help when I was a student in France and who did so much to shape my career.

I also thank Dr. Sergei Kan, professor of anthropology at Dartmouth College and coeditor of this volume, as well as my literary executrix, Marie-Françoise Guédon, Mrs. Mary Campo, and my longtime friend Richard Davis, professor of anthropology at Bryn Mawr, for their help in finishing this chapter now that my eyesight has failed.

My Background: My Parents and Their People

My connections with France go back several generations. My father's father, Alexandro Francisco Lopez de Leo de Laguna, whom I never knew, was born in Eu, Haute Normandie, in 1831 or 1832. His parents were French citizens, although the father was, I believe, of Sephardic *converso* descent, and his mother's ancestors had been Italian. No record of my grandfather's birth or of his family has been found in the provincial archives, now in Amiens, but it has been suggested that they may have been hidden by friends during World War II to protect the remaining family members from the Nazis.

None of this, however, had any direct effect on me, for young Alexander, like so many European immigrants to America, cut all ties with his former home and became a United States citizen as soon as possible. His name appears in Philadelphia about 1850 as a "professor of languages," where he taught Spanish. He eventually married one of his pupils, Fredericke Bergner, the daughter of a woolen mill owner who had fled Saxony with his family and friends after the abortive revolution of 1848. He settled in Philadelphia and ran a brewery, since the owner was a compatriot to whom he had loaned money, and this was the only way he could regain the loan. Young Alexander took his bride to San Francisco in 1856, mistakenly thinking that the Anglos there would want to learn Spanish. Instead of teaching that language, he found himself undertaking a variety of activities: as proprietor of the "Laguna Saloon," founding a business school, and, lastly, running the Chelsey House, a family hotel in Oakland where Robert Louis Stevenson spent his last days.

Although both my parents became professors of philosophy, they were not members of an "intelligentsia" as Andrei V. Grinev stated (1999–2000), for there is no such class in this country. Individuals may become academics, but there is no guarantee that their children will follow a similar profession.

My father, Theodore, was the ninth and youngest child in his family, inheriting his father's facility with languages and his German grandfather's liberalism, especially with respect to women. My father revolted against his mother's strict Lutheran piety, which lingered in the household long after her death. Since she died when he was still young, he was brought up by his older sister Frederica (for whom I was named) but was largely neglected by his own father. He was self-directed in his education and, luckily for my mother and me, was a sincere feminist. He took his A.B. and M.A. at Berkeley and then escaped the dogmatic confines of his family by going to Cornell University for his Ph.D. There he encountered two charismatic teachers, who fortunately were diametrically opposed, so that neither was able to make him a disciple. His freedom was secured when, in 1901, he volunteered as one of the first group of American teachers, "the Thomasinos," to go to the Philippines after the Spanish-American War and the Filipino Insurrection. He did more learning than teaching, however. His experiences of three years in the jungles, capped by a trip to Japan, were essentially like those that initiate the field ethnologist-anthropologist into that liberating and exacting discipline and that confer citizenship in the universal brotherhood of humankind. It was this experience that my father wanted for me, when he recommended anthropology as a career and sent me to Columbia University in 1927 to study under Franz Boas.

My mother, Grace Mead Andrus, was, as her name suggests, a Connecticut Yankee of old New England stock. During the Civil War, her father, Wallace R. Andrus, then not yet 20, had served heroically in the 17th Connecticut Volunteers, before being captured by the Confederates. After 11 months of hardship in prison camps, he was exchanged and returned home in broken health. He married, had three children, and eventually became land agent for the Northern Pacific Railway when it was being built. He went west with his two sons, Howard and Lester, but as soon as enough track had been laid, his wife, Annis Mead, and their little daughter, Grace, followed him into Oregon Territory (later to become Washington State). Although my mother experienced a frontier childhood, her driving ambition was to come east to college, and her great achievement was to get the necessary funds despite the depression of the 1890s.

Both my parents, therefore, had made their own ways to secure their education and intellectual freedom. They met in the Sage School of Philosophy at Cornell University, where my father had a minor teaching job after his return from the Philippines, and where my mother received her Ph.D. in philosophy. They were married as soon as my father secured a suitable position. In 1907, a year after my birth, we went to Bryn Mawr College, where my father's liberalism won the approval of its strong feminist president, M. Cary Thomas, who soon had both of my parents teaching philosophy. After my father's untimely death at the age of 52, just before the start of the academic year in 1930, my mother buried him in the Vermont village where they had summered (I was in Alaska then, ignorant of my loss) and put aside her grief to take his place as chair of the Department of Philosophy. Somehow, on her single salary, she managed to help both my younger brother, Wallace, and me to complete our educations through the Ph.D.

This was my background. I do not know to what extent it was typical of other Americans. I was, however, lucky in having more international experiences in my childhood and youth than most young people of my generation.

Memories of the First World War

My education in French began early. Professor of psychology James Leuba and his wife, Berthe, both French Swiss from Lausanne, were among my parents' close friends at Bryn Mawr College, and Tante Berthe delighted in teaching Wallace and me French rhymes and jingles, including the charming songs of Jacques Dalcrose. This was even before we met French children. My parents' sabbatical years (1914–15, and 1921–22) were planned so that the summers could be spent in Switzerland, where James Leuba, an accomplished alpinist, could introduce us to his beloved mountains. The winters were to be in France, when my parents could attend international conferences in Paris, especially on philosophy and psychology. They read French, of course, and could speak and understand the spoken word well enough for these meetings.

I was eight years old and Wallace was about three and a half when we landed at Genoa in 1914 on the day that Archduke Ferdinand was assassinated at Sarajevo. We were in Switzerland when World War I broke out. A retired Russian general who had experienced the horrors of war urged us to go at once to Paris. We arrived there the day mobilization was declared. I have vivid memories of Paris during the first weeks of the war, of fleeing Paris on the last crowded boat train to the Channel just before the Battle of the Marne, and of passing the British Expeditionary Force headed for the Front. Few of those young men who waved to us so gallantly from their box cars (designated in French for 8 horses or 40 men) would survive the machine-gun fire that awaited them.

The American government would have brought us home from England, but my parents had invested too much in their European sabbatical to give it up. We spent the autumn at Cambridge and the spring at Oxford and returned to Paris in the early summer of 1915. By then, the fighting seemed immobilized in the trenches, and the Channel temporarily clear of submarines. I remember the elegant ladies and the handsome French officers in their red and gold *képis,* eating wild strawberries at outdoor cafes along the boulevards. Paris seemed very gay as I saw it on our way to Switzerland.

After spending the summer in the Alps, we made an exciting departure from Bordeaux, for a German sub had just sunk a ship outside the port. Because this particular submarine was no longer in the vicinity, the U.S. consul advised us to sail while we could. We were given an early dinner on board, all lights were extinguished, and our ship crept down the river to the open sea. We had to spend the night on deck in our lifebelts, the lifeboats already hanging over the side. The grownups spent an uneasy night while we children slept. When we woke in the gray dawn, I remember a destroyer (maybe two) escorting us westward until we were beyond the reach of any submarine.

When we returned home, we found few who shared our conviction that the European war was ours too, until the sinking of the *Lusitania* proved that it was. I also knew in September 1939, when the Nazis marched into Poland, that not only was this the beginning of a second terrible world war, but that it would inevitably engulf my own country. Because of these experiences, the Battles of the Marne and of Verdun became as much a part of my historical background as are the storming of Omaha Beach in Normandy and the Battle of the Bulge. If I could have gone to the symposium in Paris, I would have wanted to pay my respects to those buried on these fields of honor.

School in France

During my parents' sabbatical of 1921–22, I attended the Lycée de jeunes filles in Versailles for six months. I had, of course, studied French at school, but my father knew this was not enough, and he prepared me in his own fun way. He sat me down and began to read aloud and explain the first chapters of Alexandre Dumas's *Les trois mousquetaires* (two volumes). Although

I was fascinated and asked for more, he was always too busy to continue, so I simply plunged into the story, doing the best I could without dictionary or other help, learning more as I advanced. I evidently had read the two sequels, including the six volumes of *Le vicomte de Bragelonne,* by the time I was to enter the Lycée in the fall. I remember that when the mistress of the house (*pavillon*) in which I was to live mentioned, among the excursions to be taken by the students, one to Fontainebleau, I shocked her by bursting out, "Would we see the royal oak where Lavallière confessed her love for the King?"

French girls of my age did not know about such things, although a familiarity with Dumas's romances might be among the peculiar requirements of Bryn Mawr College entrance examinations. I could keep my books, provided they were kept locked away from the other pupils; they remained in my trunk, for I found plenty of other interests in my new life at boarding school.

In addition to the regular courses in French history, composition, mathematics, and so forth, I took the special class in *dictée* offered for foreigners. This last was delightful because of the humor of the passages selected and the beautiful reading voice of our teacher. This year gave me an excellent grounding in French. I became fluent in speaking it, although my spelling was always shaky, as it is in English. My closest friend at school was a mulatto girl from Martinique, perhaps because we were both so far from home and often a bit homesick.

In my math class I particularly appreciated the combination of plane geometry and algebra and wished later that I had studied the bit of trigonometry also included. But I had no time, for that year I also had to prepare for the entrance examinations for Bryn Mawr College. I had failed my first trial at Latin prose authors; I now had to face that, as well as Latin poetry and Latin composition. Since the French pronunciation of Latin confused me, my father gave me work in Latin outside of class, correcting the exercises I submitted to him each week. Later that spring he had me read Caesar without using a dictionary or attempting to translate, and when I could read five pages an hour with some degree of understanding, he said I would pass the exam. He advocated reading aloud *ten times* a passage that one understood, but I balked at that.

I was not sorry when my parents took me out of the Lycée at Easter so that we could all spend the spring at Grenoble, getting in shape for a summer in the Alps. I was by that time tired of the strict life in the Lycée, for its novelty no longer compensated for the curtailment of the freedom I would have enjoyed at home. I would have found it difficult to hear my own country criticized in the history class, which was scheduled to cover "United States Imperialism" in the last weeks of the term.

My Introduction to Anthropology

I entered Bryn Mawr College in 1923 and in 1927 received my B.A., together with the coveted European Fellowship, which I postponed for a year in order to start my study of anthropology at Columbia University.

I was disappointed the first semester, for anthropology was not yet asking the questions to which I wanted answers. That was to come later, as was the realization that what bored me was the emphasis on refuting the thesis of cultural evolution in Lewis Henry Morgan's *Ancient Society* (1877), with its stages of savagery, barbarism, and civilization. Instead, I wanted to hear about fieldwork and what anthropologists actually did. Some insights were provided by firsthand accounts by former students and by others, fresh returned from the field, who might speak at the weekly seminar. Otherwise, the seminar would be only a student's report on some book assigned by Franz Boas.

There were also other compensations. Ruth Benedict's class in folklore was fun, revealing among other things that the Omaha Indians had a real sense of humor. Their story "Great Turtle's War Party" mocked their own serious conduct of such a raid and the warrior's ceremonious counting of "coups" (war honors). Boas's own class in linguistics was not clearly organized, for we practiced phonetic transcriptions of Dakota from Ella Deloria and of Yoruba from a former royal drummer from Africa, now getting an M.B.A. at Columbia. The second semester of my first year passed quickly, and I was satisfied with my choice of study.

When I went to Europe in 1928–29, it was to gather material for my doctoral dissertation. The subject had been given to me by Franz Boas: Was there sufficient similarity between Upper Paleolithic and Eskimo art styles to support the argument that the modern Eskimos were the descendants of the Upper Paleolithic hunters of France who had followed the reindeer north at the end of the Pleistocene? Since I had nourished a childhood ambition to live among the Eskimos ever since my father had brought home books on Arctic exploration, I was content with this assignment. Boas, I noticed, was inclined to recall with nostalgia his youthful Arctic experiences whenever winter ice in the Hudson began to bump the ferry that he took to his New Jersey home. For me, the Arctic was the magic land of adventure.

It was not Boas's habit to tell his students how to accomplish the tasks he set for us. He preferred to let us struggle with the problem and devise our own methods of solution. He appreciated not only the depths of our ignorance but also our capacity for learning. So he left us — myself, at least — to find our own way into the world of anthropological scholarship.

A Graduate Student in France

I spent the summer of 1928 with the American School of Prehistoric Research, a group led by George Grant MacCurdy of Yale. Although we visited the most noted prehistoric sites in England, France, and Spain and excavated a Mousterian rock shelter in the Dordogne, even I could see that the instruction given us was rather superficial, except for introducing us to the famous sites and their discoverers or those now studying them.

We saw the finest examples of prehistoric cave painting at Altamira in Spain. We met the Abbé Breuil deep in the cavern of Trois Frères, where he was sketching the remarkable frieze of horses below the "sorcerer" on the rock walls of the cavern. We were led by one of the original discoverers, a son of Count Bégouen, into the depths of the adjacent cave, Tuc d'Audoubert, where the bare footprints of prehistoric adults and children were still fresh in the mud. There were also fresh hand marks where people had scraped up the mud from which they molded the figures of the bison family at the far end of the cave. The thrill of these experiences has never left me.

That fall in Paris I attended the Abbé Breuil's lectures on Paleolithic art. I could not take notes in French; I could only listen and marvel at the skill with which he covered the long blackboard with beautiful images. He personally taught me how to make pen-and-ink drawings of the specimens I was sketching in the collections of the Musée des antiquités nationale at St. Germain-en-Laye. These were used in my dissertation, along with some of the pictures of Mesolithic and Eskimo art I later made in Scandinavian museums. Though the pupil could never equal the master, what I gained of that priceless skill served me the rest of my life.

That winter in Paris I also attended lectures by Dr. Marcellin Boule at the Institut de paléontologie humaine and studied independently with him, but I had a closer association with Dr. Paul Rivet, curator of the Musée d'Ethnologie, in the old Trocadero building. This structure had the opera house at the front, but the museum was tucked into the labyrinthine rear end almost as a bizarre afterthought. Here Dr. Rivet cleared a place for me in his office where I could sketch specimens. He also taught me how to take bibliographic notes and citations fully and carefully, the notes accompanied by accurate page numbers and references, so that they could be used in any subsequent scholarly writings without the necessity of returning to the original documents. (It is best, however, to check them all in proof.) I have ever since been grateful for his teaching me these indispensable scholarly habits.

These were the days of the famous Glozelle frauds. Baked clay tablets with alphabetic or syllabic signs had been allegedly found at a Paleolithic site near Vichy, albeit one known to have been "salted" for the benefit of Louis XVIII and suspected to have been further "developed" by the farmer who owned the property. I was absorbed by the debate over the authenticity of the tablets, especially since they were alleged to be stained by the newspapers on which they had been dried before firing! A few antiquarians protested that it was unfair to subject such objects to "a post-mortem, like a corpse of the *Rue Mouffetard* in Paris." This struck home, since it was on that very street that a fellow student from Bryn Mawr and I were living at the time.

Many of these discussions took place in the unheated halls of the Musée des antiquités nationale in Saint-Germain-en-Laye or in Dr. Rivet's dusty office in the Trocadero. The prehistory museum was always cold, for the scanty allowance for fuel was only enough to heat the living quarters of the young curator and his wife, who did their best to warm my chilled hands with a cup of hot chocolate when I finished my sketching. When the Trocadero suffered from the all too frequent failures of electricity, Dr. Rivet and I would not know whether to sit out the period of darkness or to grope our way toward the exit. The telephone company refused to answer his calls because the museum was too poor to pay the usual bribe. So we were all poor and cold together, suffering these difficulties in comradely fashion.

In looking back on my experiences as a graduate student in France, I marvel at the way in which I, a veritable beginner in anthropology, was treated as a colleague and generously made welcome in discussions by these European scholars. I had grown up among the faculty friends of my parents, and so I was used to academic society and was not shy in such company. I could and did enter their discussions when appropriate, but the Bryn Mawr College professors did not treat me as an equal. Thus I was surprised by the reception I received in France and later in Scandinavia and appreciated the opportunities thus given me by senior scholars. I did not know if they found my manners unusual for a student; possibly I was a little too forward, or maybe pleasantly different. They were always gracious and helpful.

A Term with Bronislaw Malinowski

After Christmas I went to London to read at the British Museum, and at the "Lent Term" I matriculated at the London School of Economics and signed up for three courses, including one in ethics (about which I remember nothing) and one by C. G. Seligman on Africa, which up to that time had been a really "dark continent" for me. The latter course was especially important since the reading led me to discover patterning in whole cultures. This was most clearly shown in Henri A. Junod's *The Life of a South African Tribe* (1912–13) in which the same rituals were repeated at all the important stages of tribal life. This interest in cultural patterns was to remain dormant until the late 1930s when I encountered the treatment of cultural patterns by Ruth Benedict and Alfred Kroeber, discussed below.

The third and most important seminar I took at the London School of Economics was on "Magic, Science, and Religion," given by the great Bronislaw Malinowski, whose arrogance was in striking contrast to the attitudes of all the other European scholars I had met. He held a grudge against Franz Boas and set out to make my life miserable by exhibiting my shortcomings as an example of Boas's faulty teaching — unfair tactics, since Boas had me as a student for only one year. The first hour of the two-hour seminar was usually devoted to attacking the United States. This was, I believe, because he had failed to win the acclaim of the American anthropologists to whom he had expounded his new gospel of "functionalism" during a recent visit to the United States. Eventually I discovered that the entire material for the seminar was contained in his article "Magic, Science, and Religion" (1924; not the book of the same title he later published). I committed this article to memory, and when I answered his questions in his own words, this spoiled his fun. To give a whole seminar on an article already published was, I felt, cheating the students. Yet he craved the worshipful attentions of a circle of disciples.

I was defeated by the rigid British class system that effectively separated student from professor. I had already met Sir Arthur Keith the previous spring through Dr. MacCurdy, but when I wanted to see him again to ask his opinion about the alleged Eskimo affinities of Chancelade Man, Professor Malinowski gave me to understand that only an introduction from him would be proper. Yet he never made it. Instead, as if to punish me, he sent me to study physical anthropology with his archenemy, the extreme diffusionist W. J. (*Children of the Sun*) Perry. The latter scholar was kindness itself and even gave me his own copy of A. Irving Hallowell's doctoral dissertation, "Bear Ceremonialism in the Northern Hemisphere" (1926). Perry also directed my attention to Malinowski's "Magic, Science, and Religion" article.

Malinowski's treatment of me did not lessen my early admiration for his work as a descriptive ethnographer. At the time, however, I wondered why he could write about the Trobrianders' sense of beauty without mentioning their magnificent wood carvings. I think now that he may have been unable to perceive it as art. As the years passed I saw that his functionalism, like that of A. R. Radcliffe-Brown, was only a static formula, unable to accommodate the changes of a living culture. It also became evident that Malinowski had tried to re-create the once primitive picture of the Trobriands by simply removing the tin cans and other signs of contact with civilization, and he had woefully neglected the importance of women's ceremonial exchanges.

I was definitely not pleased when, years later, Malinowski greeted me as "my spiritual child!" This was in Copenhagen, in June 1938, at the First International Congress of Anthropological and Ethnological Sciences. I was an official delegate from the University of Pennsylvania Museum and read a paper titled "Eskimo Lamps and Pots" (de Laguna 1940a). Malinowski had evidently discovered my association with Drs. Therkel Mathiassen and Kaj Birket-Smith, our hosts at the congress, which now rendered me worthy of Malinowski's notice.

My Debt to the Danes: Arctic Greenland

In the spring of 1929 I embarked from England on a tour of museums in Denmark, Sweden, Norway, and Finland, where I found a warm welcome and kindness at all. At Oslo an artist was put at my disposal in sketching specimens; curators gave me copies of their publications. After I had been in Copenhagen only a week, Dr. Mathiassen asked me to accompany him to arctic Greenland as his assistant. I thought I could go for six weeks but of course stayed for the full six months. This archaeological expedition proved the turning point in my life (de Laguna 1977). I experienced the delights of fieldwork and living among native peoples. I was challenged by the high standards and devotion demanded of the professional anthropologist and determined to follow such a career. This proved to be a hard choice, but it was the right one for me.

In 1929 no American man could have taken me, an unmarried young woman, on such a field trip. My parents were certainly taken aback when I announced Mathiassen's invitation, and they needed to be reassured by Boas. But Danish women were more independent than we Americans were, and all the Danes I asked assured me that my going was perfectly proper since it was a *scientific* expedition. Mathiassen observed all the proprieties of his country background, unwilling even to address me by my first name, and I learned in Greenland how to secure privacy even when sharing the same cabin or tent. All this was to prove very useful in my field research in Alaska.

Independent Fieldwork in Alaska

My fieldwork in Alaska began sooner than expected, even before I had finished my course work at Columbia or had written my dissertation, because Dr. Kaj Birket-Smith wanted to excavate in Alaska's Prince William Sound in the summer of 1930, and I was to be his assistant. When he fell ill on the eve of sailing, I was able to persuade the University of Pennsylvania Museum to send me to look for sites that we might excavate later, when his health permitted. The museum imposed an additional assignment in Cook Inlet on what appeared to be an impossible mission. My father generously invested in this venture, making it possible for my brother, Wallace, to go with me, for my father saw clearly how important my success on that first trip would be for my subsequent career.

With luck and hard work, we found not only the sites in Prince William Sound to which Birket-Smith and I returned in 1933 but also other sites in Cook Inlet that justified my independent excavations in 1931 and 1932. These sites fortunately sampled the prehistoric sequence on Cook Inlet through at least three thousand years, including the Kachemak culture (or "Tradition"), which solved the question in which the museum had been particularly interested (de Laguna 1975a). During the years 1931–35 I could boast the lofty title of "assistant and field director" in the museum's American Section and received a modest salary in the winter and field expenses in the summer.

There were many rock paintings in this part of Alaska. I remembered my French friends and our mutual interest in such art, and I boldly submitted an article titled "Peintures rupestres eskimo" (de Laguna 1933) after enlisting my friend Melle Germaine Brée to correct my French. This same Melle Brée was to receive the *Croix de Guerre* for heroism during World War II.

Although Franz Boas approved of my fieldwork in Alaska, he was in no way directing it. I was carrying out my own ideas, though with the financial support of the University of Pennsylvania Museum and grants from the National Research Council in 1931 and 1932 and with guidance from Dr. J. Alden Mason, head of the museum's American Section.

As a Student of Franz Boas

I had, of course, reported fully to Boas on my work in Europe as soon as I returned to the United States, although this was not until January 1930. With his characteristic disregard for university regulations, Boas succeeded in giving me full academic course credit for my time in Europe and Greenland. He also secured for me a university fellowship, which generously provided for more than my support during my last year as a student (1930–31). In return, I was expected to show and explain to other students the anthropological collections of the American Museum of Natural History in New York City. In this way I not only became familiar with this rich material but also got to know personally many scientists on the museum's staff.

At the museum I encountered its marvelous collections from the Northwest Coast and was inevitably drawn to the art. I found it wonderfully satisfying, although I did not understand the structure of the elegant northern style (Tlingit, Haida, Tsimshian) in contrast to the heavy, almost brutal Kwakiutl treatment of the same themes, until I read Bill Holm's seminal paper on the northern "formlines" (1965), about which I wrote an enthusiastic review.

Meanwhile, I finished writing my dissertation, and Boas allowed a single oral examination not only to serve for defense of the thesis but also to satisfy other requirements, such as being able to read German and being familiar with diffusionist theories.

At that time though all requirements for the Ph.D. might have been met, I could not use the degree until a certain number of *printed* copies of my dissertation, including a vita, were deposited in the Columbia University Library. Professor Mary Swindler of Bryn Mawr College, then editor of the *American Journal of Archaeology,* published my dissertation, "A Comparison of Eskimo and Paleolithic Art," in 1932–33. I was naturally grateful to her, especially as she afterward remarked that if she had realized all the editing required, she would not have undertaken the job. Despite what some readers have reported, I was unable to conclude whether or not there were sufficient similarities to prove a connection between Paleolithic and Eskimo art styles.

The Danish-American Expedition to Alaska

The influence of Danish scholarship on me was increased in 1933 when Kaj Birket-Smith and I collaborated on a joint archaeological-ethnological expedition to Prince William Sound. He, unlike Mathiassen, came from a background that was urban, sophisticated, and scholarly. Yet he was fiercely patriotic, he was uncomplaining and patient when facing hardships or nagging inconveniences, and he was ready to use first names like everyone else in Alaska. He had read widely himself and complained to me that most American anthropologists were not acquainted with the classics in their discipline, a shortcoming which I henceforth tried to overcome.

In 1930 I learned from H. C. Cloes, the U.S. deputy marshal in Cordova, that there were members of four major linguistic groups (or tribes) in Cordova and vicinity: the Chugach of Prince William Sound, Atna Athabaskans from the Copper River, Tlingits from southeastern Alaska, and the Eyak. "Those Eyak are altogether a different breed of cats from the others," Mr. Cloes said. "Don't let anybody tell you different."

Did Mr. Cloes's vehement statement refer to the "official" opinion, expressed in the *Handbook of American Indians North of Mexico* (Anonymous 1910, vol. 2:862) that the Eyak were a small group of Chugach who had been so strongly influenced by the Tlingits as to be recognized as part of that nation? This opinion was based on information furnished by William H. Dall in the 1870s.

My curiosity was aroused, although I did not fully understand the implications of this emphatic statement. Few people outside this part of Alaska had ever heard of the Eyak, but Birket-Smith and the Russians, who zealously collected vocabularies from all the tribes encountered, were well aware that these natives formed a distinct group. While the English designation *Eyak* referred to the name of a former village, the Russians knew these people by names derived from the designation used by the Chugach, *Ugalentsi* (with Russian plural) and *Ugalachmiut* (the Eskimo form), with these two forms suggesting to later researchers that there were two tribes. Their self-designation was *Daxunhyu*.

In 1930 my brother and I, with Galushia Nelson, an Eyak man, as a guide, visited sites on the Copper River delta occupied by the Eyak when Nelson was a small boy. In 1933 Birket-Smith and I decided to spend the first three weeks of the expedition in an intensive study of the Eyak who were living at Old Town, Cordova. Our assistant, Norman ("Sandy") Reynolds, a graduate student in anthropology at the University of Washington, proved to have considerable linguistic ability. Like myself, he was familiar with the phonetic symbols used by the American Anthropological Association. He diligently collected Eyak names and words and as much grammatical information as he could. Birket-Smith knew only symbols for writing Eskimo, but by using the latest edition of the British *Notes and Queries for Travellers,* he led us to investigate every aspect of Eyak culture.

I sent this linguistic material to Boas, and he in turn passed it on to Edward Sapir of Yale. They were excited because this language seemed to be a new member of Sapir's Na-Dene stock, falling between Tlingit and Athabaskan. We wanted Sandy Reynolds to be given support in studying this language, but Boas and Sapir felt that such a study should be made only by a mature linguist who was already skilled in Athabaskan, but they could not decide who should be sent.

As the years passed and the numbers of Eyak dwindled, I became more and more anxious to have someone make a proper study of Eyak. Although a few linguists did nibble away at particular features of the language, it was not until this small group of Eyak speakers was on the verge of extinction that Michael Krauss made a thorough study of Eyak (1970a, 1970b). There is now only one Eyak speaker alive, Marie Smith, chief of the tribe.

Birket-Smith and I coauthored *The Eyak Indians of the Copper River Delta, Alaska* (Birket-Smith and de Laguna 1938) and shared our work and notes on the Chugach Eskimos of Prince William Sound, so that he wrote their ethnography (1953) while I dealt with their prehistory (1956). The archaeological specimens were divided between the University of Pennsylvania Museum and the Danish National Museum. It was during this expedition that I received my doctorate in absentia from Columbia University.

In 1934 the University of Pennsylvania Museum published the results of my Alaskan excavations, *The Archaeology of Cook Inlet, Alaska*, with a grant from the American Council of Learned Societies (1975). Although Bruno Oetteking of the Anthropology Department at Columbia contributed a section on the racial types represented in the skeletal material, I doubt that Boas ever read the manuscript; he was too busy for me to bother him with it. J. Alden Mason, however, said that the book lacked a conclusion and insisted that I write one. I reluctantly complied, although I felt (correctly) that I was not ready to commit myself.

I have maintained to this day an interest in the Arctic and especially in Greenland through my friendships with colleagues in Denmark. In addition to those already mentioned, the individual who probably influenced me the most during my early professional life, up to about 1948, was another arctic enthusiast, the late Henry B. Collins, archaeologist and one-time chairman of the Smithsonian's Bureau of American Ethnology. He and his wife Caroline made their home in Washington DC a center for everyone interested in the Arctic, and I was a favored visitor. Although he was painfully shy, refusing to speak in public, he shared his fund of knowledge in private. During his years of active fieldwork he made many brilliant contributions to arctic archaeology, winning the gold medal offered by the Danes for the best work on the origin of Eskimo culture (1937). We shared many interests in anthropology and in public affairs and were in constant contact with each other. I believe he knew more about my interests in anthropology than any other individual, and therefore his influence on me was always very strong.

The Yukon and the Great Depression

In 1935 the museum sent me to the interior of Alaska, in the hopes of discovering traces of the First Americans, or Paleo-Indians. Failing in that endeavor, our small party was nevertheless able to gather a considerable amount of information on the more recent sites in the Yukon Valley, as well as ethnographic data that was welcome because the region was then almost unknown to anthropologists.

The great interior of Alaska was a whole new dimension of the northern landscape, something I had not hitherto encountered. It demanded drastic adaptations of the anthropologist just as it did of the native inhabitants.

During the years of the Great Depression, I was entertaining two diverse interests: the historic development of the northern cultures and the experiences of actual individuals living in their particular cultures and how best to understand these in relationship to cultural patterning.

When I returned from the Yukon in the fall of 1935, my immediate job prospects were grim. Because of the Depression, the museum could no longer afford to send me into the field or give me a job. Although unemployed, I still had obligations to my data. Therefore, while supported only as a cataloguer by New Deal Programs (PWA and WPA), I finished my report on our archaeological activities in the Yukon Valley: *The Prehistory of Northern North America as Seen from the Yukon* (1947) — even though it had to wait until after World War II for publication. I eventually managed to use the ethnographic information in my survey titled "Matrilineal Kin Groups in Northwestern North America" (1975b) and in *Tales from the Dena* (1995) and *Travels among the Dena* (2000b).

The archaeological report as finally published turned out to be a mammoth distribution study, such as the Scandinavians and many Americans were making at that time. Though I came to distrust that method as a way of reconstructing cultural history, the exercise was good, since it introduced me to the prehistory and ethnography of a good part of the circumpolar world and adjacent areas (de Laguna, 1994). I studied the work of the Jesup Expedition in tracing circum-Pacific distributions, especially as I came to know personally some of the members of that expedition. At the same time I was breaking free of the Danish obsession with a two-level conception of Eskimo cultural history (Paleo-Eskimo/Neo-Eskimo or ice hunting/snowshoe hunting). The short papers that I published in 1936 show the confusion in my own thinking.

My interest in tracing trans-Pacific cultural similarities and in reconstructing cultural history survived the Depression and the interruption of World War II; in fact, it has never left me. For example, in 1949 I reviewed André Leroi-Gourhan's *Archéologie du Pacifique-Nord: Matériaux pour l'étude des relations entre les peuples d'Asie et d'Amérique* (1946). I was impressed by his scholarship, but if I was unduly critical of his emphasis on trade as the only mechanism of cultural diffusion between Siberia and North America, I am now inclined to believe that I then underestimated the importance of the aboriginal trade routes as avenues for diffusion.

The Southwest

In December 1935 I was offered the lucrative position as associate soil conservationist in a group headquartered in Albuquerque that would make surveys of Indian reservations in collaboration with the Bureau of Indian Affairs. We began on the Pima Reservation in southern Arizona, although our efforts were of dubious value since all the policy decisions had already been made before we started. But it was my introduction to a new world, one with which I maintained contact in the summers, even after I began to teach at Bryn Mawr College.

I received a National Research Council Fellowship to study the distribution of Eskimo archaeological types outside the known Eskimo area. This research was to begin in the fall of 1937, and I pursued it during the following winters in various Canadian and U.S. museums, including those in Seattle, where I joined my mother during her sabbatical year of 1937–38. The Eskimo research resulted in a paper written at the request of Douglas Beyers: "The Importance of the Eskimo in Northeastern Archaeology" (1946). However, its publication was delayed by the war, and it was out of date when it appeared. It made unjustifiable assumptions about the importance of the Thule Eskimo culture, and the suggested modest time depth involved was shot to pieces by radiocarbon dating, which began in 1950. The illustrations, which I drew myself, are the only valid survivors.

The prospect of the fellowship enabled me to resign from the Soil Conservation Service at the conclusion of the Pima Project in June 1936. Then I asked my mother to join me in Albuquerque and purchased a dealer's demonstrator car (nearly "demonstrated" to death), a tent, and complete camp outfit. With letters of introduction from kindly scholars at Santa Fe, we set out on a tour of the Southwest, visiting active excavations. I knew that if I ever secured a position teaching anthropology at Bryn Mawr College, or anywhere else, I would be expected to teach a course in American archaeology. There were then only two areas in North America where real archaeological sequences had been established: the Arctic, which I already knew firsthand, and the Southwest, which I still had to study. We visited all the important sites in New Mexico and Arizona, including the Paleo-Indian site near Clovis, New Mexico. Dr. Edgar B. Howard, of the University of Pennsylvania Museum, who was directing the excavations, welcomed me because I could testify to the fact that the clay layer over the mammoth bones and the associated flint tools was intact. It was a gloriously successful summer.

Through friendships we established that first summer in the Southwest, especially with Dr. and Mrs. Harold Colton, founders of the Museum of Northern Arizona in Flagstaff, my mother and I began to spend our summers there, and I took part in the weekly discussions of anthropology conducted by Dr. Colton for his associates and for visiting scholars at the museum. He had me report on Alfred Kroeber's *Cultural and Natural Areas of Native North America* (1939). It was one of the most difficult assignments I had ever faced, because I was used to defining culture areas by their substantive *contents* (traits), but Kroeber was dealing with intangibles such as intensity of culture. Later, I discovered his *Configurations of Culture Growth* (1944). When his new, completely revised edition of *Anthropology* appeared in 1948, he became a major influence on my thinking, even before he and Theodora Kroeber became my good friends.

The Northwest

In Seattle, where my mother and I spent the academic year of 1936–37, members of the University of Washington's Department of Anthropology gave me private instruction in linguistics and made it possible for us to witness a Salish "Power Dance" ceremony, one seldom seen by whites. We saw that the descendants of the Makah whalers still guided their dugouts with superb skill through the heavy surf, though their crafts were now powered with outboard motors. Our academic colleagues also guided us to many prehistoric sites on Vancouver Island and to native villages in northern Washington State.

In this way I was led into personal contact with members of many different western tribes from British Columbia to California. My introduction to these peoples was often with the guidance of the leading scholars who knew them best. Members of these various tribes were no longer anonymous, shadowy figures in ethnographies but real persons, actively living their cultures and distinguished from each other by individual as well as cultural traits. At the same time I was discovering the patterning in whole cultures. Ruth Benedict saw those patternings in psychological terms, as the ethos or personality of a culture. There was still no adequate psychology to supply the descriptive terms we needed. Edward Sapir, who never lost sight of the individual, suggested that anthropology needed the psychiatrist. But now at last I felt anthropology was beginning to ask the right questions and was becoming the science of humankind that I had sought for in vain when I first began my studies.

Bryn Mawr College

In 1935 I became a lecturer at Bryn Mawr College, but it was only to teach a single elective course in anthropology. However, I was able to wangle extra courses each year until by 1938 I was given a full-time position as assistant professor of anthropology. Although I taught in the undergraduate major in sociology, offered by the Graduate Department of Social Work, I was the first to introduce anthropology to Bryn Mawr. In the summer of 1941 I took six Bryn Mawr students on an excavation near Flagstaff, sponsored by the Museum of Northern Arizona and funded through the generosity of retiring president Marian Edwards Park, who used the funds raised in her honor to establish American archaeology at the college. This was the year my mother retired and our last trip west until 1945.

Lucien Lévy-Bruhl

It was just at the beginning of my teaching career that I became re-acquainted with French scholarship. While I am sure that Lucien Lévy-Bruhl had been around during my student days in Paris, I do not remember meeting him or even hearing about him then. Yet I believe it was in 1921–22 that my parents acquired his first publications, for they were certainly in our house in 1935 when, shortly after the author's death, I was asked by the editor of the *Philosophical Review* to write a critical appraisal of his work. I had access to four of his six major books, but since these formed a systematic development of the same fundamental thesis, I felt that I had at hand enough to justify an overall review of his work from 1910 to 1935. In my review, published as "Lévy-Bruhl's Contributions to the Study of Primitive Mentality" (1940b), I wrote: "We can roughly place Lévy-Bruhl . . . as . . . a member of the French sociological-anthropological school of Durkheim and Mauss, in this sense a successor of Comte, and on the other hand, the opponent of the British school represented by Tylor and Frazer" (552).

Lévy-Bruhl's thesis was that primitive mentality was culturally determined and should be explained only in its own terms, not those of logic or individual psychology. Therefore, Lévy-Bruhl rejected Tylor's theory of animism, which implied that primitive man was a naive philosopher, reasoning from wrong assumptions. Lévy-Bruhl, however, seemed to hold this same view that he attacked, for he argued that a good ethnographer who had entered into the native's way of thinking could explain it so well that the native's actions would seem to us reasonable, rather than absurd.

Lévy-Bruhl was among the anthropologists who still clung to the notion that all cultures had evolved, or were evolving, in the same direction, through the same stages. The mentality of peoples in each stage would be similar, since they were subjected to similar conditions. In the attempt to understand "pre-logical" mentality and activities, it was legitimate to jumble together any observations of similar thinking or behavior, provided they were of peoples at the same evolutionary stage. This was the "comparative method," which brought together and equated cultural traits from all parts of the world. This outmoded method was forced on theoretical scholars by a dearth of detailed, sound ethnographic reporting. While Lévy-Bruhl's insights were vindicated by his faulty methodology, his demand for better data helped us to see what was needed and how to obtain it. Although I had to reject his evolutionary bias, I found his views otherwise congenial, for he was "asking the right questions" and helping anthropology to become what I had hoped it would be.

Even now, chapter 12 of La mentalité primitive (1922) on the natives' reaction to modern medicine could be read with profit by all government officials who deal with American Indians. In the same book he advocated making acculturation studies, but it was only in 1937 that the American Anthropologist began to accept such studies for publication.

According to Lévy-Bruhl, the fundamental difference between civilized man and the savage was that the thought and behavior of the latter was dominated by "collective representations," and the notion of "participation." Collective representations rather vaguely defined complexes of several related fundamental ideas and the emotions and values with which they were associated. They were shared by all members of the society, and they were acquired largely in the emotional atmosphere of tribal ceremonies. "Participation" was not simply sharing the qualities or condition of some other entity or entities but implied an actual merging with them to such an extent that their identities as individuals were blurred or lost.

Although Lévy-Bruhl was concerned to exhibit the most fundamental and extreme differences between pre-logical thought and our scientific rationality, he erred in failing to recognize that primitive mentality is not really homogeneous; each culture in which it was formed and manifested was a unique, integrated, and functioning system. His problem was not to understand primitive mentality, but primitive mentalities. "Yet because he has attacked some of our unconscious assumptions he has enabled us to become more objectively critical of others. His pioneer formulation of the problem was a necessary preliminary to more adequate formulations, and his mistakes can be as illuminating as his durable contributions" (de Laguna 1940b:566).

Even when his explanations of "the mystic experience" or other various notions of causality seemed to miss the mark, I found them stimulating. I was especially excited when the particular examples he analyzed as an illustration resembled incidents with which I was familiar. Often these suggested to me more accurate interpretations that could be built on his. For example, in a number of cases he erred because he took the natives' statements literally, not metaphorically, or symbolically, or figuratively, as they should have been. One has to know the whole cultural background in order to understand what the natives are saying and meaning. Firsthand experience, better than travelers' reports, will prove that the intensity of emotions in the native community may range from great excitement (fearful or joyful) down to complete indifference, depending on circumstance. Again and again, I found that Lévy-Bruhl was asking questions of importance, and that only better fieldwork could supply the answers.

World War II

I would not really be established in my profession until after World War II. In September 1942 — after one year as assistant professor — I joined the U.S. Naval Reserve as a lieutenant junior grade and became one of the first teachers at the Naval Reserve Midshipmen's School for Women on the Smith College Campus at Northhampton, Massachusetts. I realized at the time that I would never again have such enthusiastic and strongly motivated students as these women midshipmen. Although I chafed for more active duty, I nevertheless think this was my best contribution to the war effort, especially in the teaching of communications (codes and ciphers).

In the spring of 1943 I was transferred to Naval Intelligence in Washington DC, where my duties were often vague and unimportant. I remained here for the rest of the war, eventually reaching the rank of lieutenant commander just after the Japanese surrendered.

Unfortunately, the navy men looked upon us as their fathers had looked upon the suffragettes only 22 years before, when they reluctantly gave women the right to vote. Their fragile male egos could not accept us as "sisters-in-arms," although this gracious phrase was used by one of our co-instructors at Northampton. Our position was anomalous. We were in the naval reserve but not full members of it; we were necessary but a nuisance. The original notion that there could be a dual command was, of course, nonsense and was rapidly abandoned. For those of us who wanted to be fully accepted, the uncertainties were frustrating and ignominious. I knew I should have had more training, if I were to give the best service of which I was capable, but I did not know how to get it.

What I learned in the navy probably applies to all large organizations, including business corporations. The real work is accomplished, not through adherence to the vertical ups and downs of the table of organization, but through the horizontal, sidewise interaction of an unofficial network of petty officers or secretaries. Unless there is something obviously unfair or dishonest, the boss should keep his nose out of this network and let his subordinates accomplish the job through an exchange of favors, in this way cutting through the masses of bureaucratic red tape that would clog up the works.

Postwar Plans

A Rockefeller Post-war Fellowship (secured for me without my knowledge) gave me a year (1945–46) in which to catch up with anthropology and to write before going back to teach at Bryn Mawr. My mother and I spent the fall in the peace and quiet of northern Arizona, while I drew up unrealizable plans for a study of the Ainu in Japan. George Atcheson, the husband of my first cousin, Mariquita de Laguna, was at that time an ambassador to Japan under General Douglas MacArthur, and I counted on his hospitality and protection. He told me, however, that only a member of Congress was permitted to enter that devastated country. For about two years I kept hoping that conditions would change. Then George was killed on a trip to the State Department in Washington when his plane went down in the middle of the Pacific. Mariquita did not long survive his loss, and I, brokenhearted at this double tragedy, abandoned the Ainu project.

I Find My True Vocation

I was now ready for a complete change in the direction of my research interests. I planned a combined archaeological, historical, and ethnographic study of Tlingit culture. I hoped to be able to trace the development of a recognizable Tlingit pattern from ancient to modern times.

In 1949, therefore, I began with a survey of Northern Tlingit communities to determine the most suitable one for such a study. Starting at Yakutat on the Gulf Coast of Alaska, I found the natives so welcoming and their cultural history so complex and interesting that I could hardly tear myself away after a six-week stay. In 1950, when I decided to try out this combined approach with a party of four at Angoon on Admiralty Island in southeastern Alaska, I began the happiest period of my career as an anthropologist.

I knew my future was secure when I was promoted to associate professor of anthropology. I enjoyed my teaching and in 1950 became chair of an independent Department of Sociology and Anthropology, although the combination of these disciplines, which attract such different personalities, was not my choice. We did not secure our "divorce" from sociology until 1967, when I was president of the American Anthropological Association. I had become a full professor in 1955.

I was happiest in my fieldwork. Thinking (mistakenly) that ethnography would be less physically demanding than archaeology, I turned over the latter to others, though keeping control of the project as a whole. I was now free to do what I found most satisfying: working with the native people while enjoying the companionship of my former student, now colleague, Dr. Catharine ("Kitty") McClellan. Because we went through some rough times and had to rely on each other, we developed a special relationship. The same was true with Marie-Françoise Guédon, now my literary executrix, when she went into the field with me in 1968. I still retain rich field notes and happy memories from those years.

After the year at Angoon we worked in Yakutat for three seasons and later spent four summers concentrating on an ethnographic study of the Athabaskans of the Copper River and their Upper Tanana neighbors. Kitty also conducted independent research in Yukon Territory, where she became the acknowledged authority, and Marie-Françoise later did several years of dissertation research among the Upper Tanana people, who made her their own. The mid-1950s and 1960s provided summers on the Copper River for perfecting our research methods in ethnography and other summers and sabbaticals for writing and publishing my major work on the Yakutat Tlingits (de Laguna 1972).

During this period A. Irving ("Pete") Hallowell, professor emeritus of anthropology at the University of Pennsylvania, who had been giving a seminar at Bryn Mawr College, became a major influence in my life. His wife, Maude Frame, had been my mother's graduate student in philosophy, sharing her special interest in psychology, and it was Maude who introduced him to my mother, knowing that they would have much in common. The Hallowells and de Lagunas soon became fast friends, dining at each other's houses several times a month and sharing lengthy intellectual discussions.

The influence of these conversations can be detected in some of the essays published by my mother in her book *On Existence and the Human World* (G. de Laguna 1966). She was careful in acknowledging the specific ideas or suggestions made by specific persons, but we had all talked them over so thoroughly that I could not recognize as mine some ideas she attributed to me. These were, however, her last writings, for she was already developing macular degeneration, that most cruel affliction for a scholar.

Hallowell's brilliant concept of "The Self and Its Behavioral Environment" became for me the key to understanding the culturally conditioned views of the world and the places in it of human beings and "other-than-human selves." It avoided the one-sided implications of the usual "ego and alter ego" approach.

In the spring of 1954, to celebrate Hallowell's 60th birthday, his many friends and fellow anthropologists decided to republish as volume 4 of the Publications of the Philadelphia Anthropological Society a collection of Hallowell's own widely scattered articles, the selection to be made by Hallowell himself. He titled the book *Culture and Experience* (1955). The president of the society was at that time J. Alden Mason, and the chairman of its Publications Committee was Loren C. Eiseley. I was a member of that committee and happened to be teaching a course in culture and personality, then a popular subject. The proposed volume would be snapped up as a text for such courses, I said, but no one would believe me. In consequence, the University of Pennsylvania Press, which registered the copyright on the book, insisted that we pay in advance all the costs of publication. The society was able to do this only because of the generosity of an anonymous donor and the Wenner-Gren Foundation for Anthropological Research. Although it was never put into writing, I recall that the press, in the highly unlikely event that the book made a profit, was to reimburse the society. Even though the first edition sold out, as I had predicted, and a second edition (with a less fancy binding) was issued, the society received nothing, nor were royalties paid to Hallowell.

When Hallowell died in 1974, at the end of a long and painful illness, I felt as if I had lost my own father. All his students loved him.

Claude Lévi-Strauss

Although I recently discovered that I was two years and one month older than Claude Lévi-Strauss, our careers as anthropologists differed, as would be expected, but they also paralleled each other's in a reversed sort of way, with both of us similarly delayed or interrupted by the Depression and World War II. Thus, in 1927, when I began graduate work in anthropology, Lévi-Strauss also began his studies of philosophy and law at the Université de Paris, lasting until 1931, while I ended my graduate course work in 1930. After teaching at a secondary school, he went to Brazil and from 1935 to 1937 was professor of sociology at the University of São Paolo. He also did fieldwork among the Indians. In 1934 I had just received my Ph.D., and even though I was still looking for a job, I had already begun independent fieldwork. Whether by accident or by temperament, fieldwork itself was probably never of primary importance to Lévi-Strauss. Rather, he seemed to have seized the opportunity to experience it mainly because he was already in Brazil. I followed his dusty steps in *Tristes Tropiques* (1955b) with great interest and sympathy, for in the end he and his savage encounter could not communicate with each other. I, on the other hand, relished the firsthand contact with the native peoples, among whom I always found some who already spoke English. Unemployment gave me the opportunity to write and publish, while Lévi-Strauss's most productive period came after he was professionally established. So, in addition to a historical novel for young people and two detective stories written to earn money, I published my Ph.D. dissertation (1932–33), wrote *The Archaeology of Cook Inlet, Alaska* in 1934 (1975), coauthored with Birket-Smith *The Eyak Indians of the Copper River Delta, Alaska* (1938), and wrote the report of my Yukon Valley trip.

During the war years, while I was in the U.S. Naval Reserve and for a time teaching future women officers, Lévi-Strauss was a visiting professor at the New School for Social Research in New York City (1941–44). Here he was associated with a group of structural linguists, among whom Roman Jakobson was the most influential. In New York City he also came face-to-face with my old friends, the wondrous Northwest Coast art objects in the American Museum of Natural History. Later Lévi-Strauss was one of the most important people in bringing this art to international attention. Whereas Lévi-Strauss profited professionally from these war years because they brought him new insights, for me it was as if the war years had been completely wasted, and I still had to complete three more years as assistant professor before I could be considered for promotion.

When hostilities ceased, books we had begun or even finished before the war now began to appear. These included my *Prehistory of Northern North America as Seen from the Yukon* (1947) and *Chugach Prehistory* (1956) and Lévi Strauss's *Les structures élémentaires de la parenté* (1949), *Tristes Tropiques* (1955b) on his field experiences in Brazil, and *Anthopologie stucturale* (1958a).

In 1950, when he became director of studies at the École pratique des hautes études, I became chair of the new department of sociology and anthropology at Bryn Mawr College. In 1959 he became chair of social anthropology at the College de France, a position of considerable prestige. The majority of his most important publications followed this appointment. *La pensée sauvage* and *Le totémisme aujourd'hui* both appeared in 1962. His influential *Mythologiques* was published in four volumes between 1964 and 1971. Fortunately for contemporary students there is no retirement from his position at the College de France, and he is still able to participate in conferences and to give advice to students. Teaching, administrative duties, and fieldwork in Alaska made me postpone most publications except for *Under*

Mount Saint Elias (1972). With the help of former students and colleagues I hope to be able to publish the ethnographic reports that I have never finished.

Although Lévi-Strauss's and my goals were dissimilar, we agreed that the anthropologist/ethnographer should patiently sort through the details of cultures to discover their underlying individual patterns. Unlike Lévi-Strauss I was not primarily concerned with the universal experiences of human life and universal thought patterns but was absorbed by the detailed and varied experiences of an individual life alien to me. Since 1933 I believed that the ethnographer should know enough about a culture to be able to use it as a setting for a novel, and I realized the insufficiency of the average ethnographic report when even a shoebox full of my notes taken from historic sources on the Eskimos was insufficient for a single scene in a children's story that I wished to write. In contrast to Lévi-Strauss's research into the hidden and inexplicit rules governing the "grammar" of cultures, I wanted to understand the specific opportunities and choices offered or forced upon particular individuals by the distinctive cultures in which they lived. Lévi-Strauss's analyses of culture are in terms of opposites such as the raw and the cooked, culture and nature. His rules for choosing the opposites are not apparent, and the system, according to his own admission, does not work for Eskimo mythology. It would also seem to be difficult to apply it to the world of the Athabaskans. It serves best in cultures that use the symbolism of their ceremonials not to achieve specific ends but rather to express their own inner nature.

On Anthropological Inquiry

Let me paraphrase my presidential address for the American Anthropological Association (de Laguna 1968:474). Anthropology is different from every other scholarly discipline or profession. It is a way of life. That is, no matter what branch of anthropology one pursues, it involves contact with aliens, living with aliens, adapting to their culture, getting to know them as individuals, and winning their confidence and cooperation. To do this involves transforming one's own self and fulfilling hitherto hidden potentialities. Those who remain in their laboratory or library, or even in the streets of our cities, perform their scholarly functions and play their professional roles without ever losing their civic status or their sociocultural identities.

But the field anthropologists are taken out of their ordinary life and out of themselves. In the constraints of the field they find new freedoms and new personalities. If only in their imagination, they have been forced to accept the aliens' values and concepts, and when the field anthropologists return, they must translate these into terms that their colleagues can understand. Thus they have gained dual citizenship.

When I write, I am compelled to use the term *anthropology* in the American sense of the word. It is not limited to biological studies, as in Europe, and it also includes more than ethnology, the study of living cultures. There is more here than a difference in terminology. Rather, *anthropology* for me designates that holistic discipline that would embrace studies relating to all aspects of human existence and activities. It offers a general program, as it were, in which all such special studies and interests can find a role. It is more than Sir Edward Tylor's (1946) capacious carrying frame that lightens the student's burden of learning by holding together the various aspects of the "science of Man and Civilization," making them more intelligible by showing how they are interrelated. This is an understanding not derived from the pursuit of belles lettres, or the classics, though it can appreciate them, nor does it spring from the dusty speculations of the armchair sociologist. Rather, according to Alfred Kroeber, anthropology is the child of natural science, a product of the great voyages of discovery that shattered forever the narrow medieval world, because men now came face to face with strange new lands and creatures and civilizations that the Bible could not explain.

Culture cannot be understood as something outside of the world of nature. Culture is both a human creation and something that creates symbol-using human beings. Without it, we could not survive. Rather, it is the human form of adaptation to the natural world. As anthropologists our privilege is to learn something about every aspect of the whole world of humans. And this for us means that we must explore the beginnings of that culture through two million or more years of human development and evolution. What other scholars can boast such a heritage?

> It is not given to us, or at least to most of us, to be a Boas or a Kroeber who can work at first hand in all branches of our discipline. But we can share their vision and stand on the mountain top, surveying all the vast world laid out below. We can have a hand in drawing the map, knowing that it will never be completed, and that we as individuals may never

travel more than a few leagues across it. Still we shall know where we are, and where the blank spaces lie, if we take our bearings on a common beacon, and speak [to] each other as we pass. Because we have not sought the safety of familiar, well-buoyed waters, but claim a wide universe for our domain, we shall always, I fondly hope, find ourselves sailing towards continents of spice and treasure. We will be asking questions of import, for which there are no certain answers. (de Laguna 1968:476)

The chart we are creating is two-dimensional, but the reality that we are trying to understand has many dimensions. This means there are vistas that we cannot see in advance, new aspects to explore that come into view only as we climb the hills. The importance of new discoveries is illustrated by the sudden broadening of our knowledge brought about by the discovery of DNA's structure, which had implications far beyond the field of biology and now permeates our entire culture. The program in anthropology should be capacious enough to provide a place where such unexpected insights may be seen in relationship to each other and to the whole. I envisage such a program as the plan for a vast, capacious cabinet with multiple cubbyholes and shelves. This cabinet has niches still unfilled but ready for what we shall discover in the future. There is a place for everything, and it is all ours! But when that cabinet fills to bursting, it will be a sign that this paradigm — as has been the case with all others before it — must change to accommodate new knowledge.

Note

Additional biographical information on Frederica de Laguna may be found in her own autobiographic narrative (de Laguna 1977, 1994) as well as in McClellan (1988, 1989) and Grinev (1999–2000). See also Guédon (this volume).

CROSSING BOUNDARIES
Homage to Frederica de Laguna

Marie-Françoise Guédon

The development of Northwest Coast studies is marked by underlying features, which may become visible when one is looking closely at individual careers, especially when those careers stand at important cross roads of our field of study. Frederica de Laguna presents us with one of these careers.

She occupies a special place in the anthropology of the North Pacific Coast, having produced substantial studies of the northern Northwest Coast for more than 60 years. She also commands several of the great junctions in our field. First, her work on Prince William Sound and among the Tlingits places her at the geographic and cultural hinge between the Amerindian Northwest Coast and the Aleutian-Eskimo North Pacific area. Second, she maintained throughout her life a definition of the work of the anthropologist as an integration of archaeological, linguistic, ethnographical, and even ethnohistorical data. Furthermore, what is less well known is that she developed herself as a scholar at the junction between American and European social sciences, with strong connections with both North American cultural anthropology and French and Danish scholarship. Finally, her life of research spans more than 60 years of fieldwork on the Pacific coast, from Boas and Birket-Smith through the Second World War to the present. In every case she rose to the challenge by constructing links between different geographical and cultural areas, different disciplines, and different approaches.

Culture Areas

When teaching in the classic setting of a North American university, one is quickly drawn by the textbooks into a reduced definition of *Northwest Coast* as something that starts with the Salish and ends with the Tlingits, excluding both the Plateau and anything north or west of the Tlingits. Barring the exception, such as volume 7 of the *Handbook of North American Indians*, edited by Wayne Suttles (1990), it is only in archaeological studies, or linguistics, or in the work of a few "generalists," such as Bill Holm, Wilson Duff, or Claude Lévi-Strauss, that our angle of vision increases and that peoples such as the Eyak, Aleuts (Unangan), Chugach (Alutiiq), or even Yupiit are brought back into the picture. Correspondingly, the northern North Pacific Coast specialists in Alaska do not as a rule foray into the southern regions, that is, south of the Tlingits.[1]

Much of de Laguna's work concerns the northern regions of the Northwest Coast. There, she went from Cook Inlet to the Eyak, then to the Chugach and the Dena'ina, and finally to the Tlingits and the Ahtna, studying and reconstructing a rich and diverse cultural environment, which she took as a whole regional complex, embedded in the still larger North Pacific Rim context (cf. Fitzhugh and Chaussonnet 1994). But she had come to the North Pacific Coast via Greenland. Greenland was not an accident. In 1929 it was a deliberate step. It demonstrated the breadth of her geographic and cultural orientations and remained in her work as a steady northern anchor (see de Laguna 1977). From this perspective the arctic regions, the Bering Strait, and the Pacific Coast are part of the same complex. This perspective resulted in a dual circumpolar and circum-Pacific reference, which Frederica de Laguna wove into her research, her teaching, and her links with her colleagues (de Laguna 1994). In the 1970s her graduate seminar on the northern cultures typically placed the Inuit first, not in the northernmost part of North America, but on the shores of the Arctic Ocean. The Dorset and pre-Thule immigrants were never far from her discussions of Prince William Sound, and the Bering Strait was presented as a gateway between the two continental masses of Eurasia and America, as well as between two oceans.

During the Northwest Coast Ethnology Conference Claude Lévi-Strauss (see Lévi-Strauss, this volume) asked participants to reinstate the southern part of the North Pacific Coast back into our field; Puget Sound and the Coast Salish area, he said, contribute important facts and represent a valuable component of our field of study. In many ways we hear the same kind of message coming from Frederica de Laguna, this time about the northern regions of the Pacific Coast. According to her, Prince William Sound, for instance, is a key area in the development of the Pacific Coastal cultures and must have been a well-populated and culturally complex center of activity for many millennia (including a possible link with early Dorset cultures). Correspondingly, one cannot understand the cultural developments on Vancouver Island without knowing something of the Chugach, Aleuts, and Yupiit, for instance.

A third dimension of this geographical bridging is left out in textbooks relying on cultural areas separating coastal manifestations from inland adaptations. Frederica de Laguna has traveled up the Yukon and the Tanana Rivers, and her recent research deals with the Athapaskan, or Dene, peoples and cultures of the Copper River valley. This interest in the interior and her consideration for inland connections are continuations of her contextual approach. Her important 1975 study of matrilineal kin groups in Northwest North America exemplifies the results of that approach. In her introduction to this study, she states that she is not trying to build a theory of clan development but simply to bring together all the information available. Yet this simple study effectively silences the idea that matrilinearity developed on the Northwest Coast and then diffused and spread inland (de Laguna 1975b).

Throughout her work, we are invited to recognize the enormous complexity and the contributions of series of cultures, past and present, which cannot be apprehended locally without reference to the past or to the neighboring communities, both on the coast and inland. Indeed, questions of connection have surfaced again and again in Northwest Coast ethnography. From Philip Drucker's survey of secret societies and winter rituals (1940) to the Crossroads of Continents exhibition (Fitzhugh and Crowell 1988), the diversity of Northwest Coast culture is played against a formidable background of exchanges and contrasts. What else can we expect from the studies of cultures, which define themselves against each other, as Claude Lévi-Strauss reminds us in *La voie des masques* (1975).

Interdisciplinary Boundaries

The relationship, or lack of relationship, between scholars of different disciplines is defined by research and teaching institutions. Archaeologists, linguists, historians, and ethnographers are supposed to meet but are rarely encouraged to work together. At least this has been the official picture of the Northwest Coast field until recently. In 1949 Frederica de Laguna wrote a complimentary review of André Leroi-Gourhan's 1946 *Archéologie du Pacifique-Nord*. She was writing from experience — she had been working in Cook Inlet and Prince William Sound since 1930 with additional trips along the Lower and Middle Yukon as well as to the Tlingits and the Eyak peoples. Her intellectual kinship with Leroi-Gourhan extended beyond this review. Like Leroi-Gourhan, and following a road almost parallel to that of Franz Boas, who had encouraged her in that direction, Frederica de Laguna included archaeology among her professional disciplines from the beginning of her career. In response to the doctoral research topic assigned to her by Boas, which asked for a foray into Paleolithic cultures and "Eskimo" cultures, past and present, she sought first a contact with Paleolithic European archaeology, meeting the leading French and Danish archaeologists of the first quarter of the 20th century; then she was introduced to archaeology in the Arctic with Therkel Mathiassen in Greenland (de Laguna 1977, 1994). It was in Greenland that she also first got exposed to ethnography. From then on, both subdisciplines remain linked, a linkage that she addressed more and more decisively. As she herself recently pointed out, "I can no longer conceive of ethnography as something separated from linguistics, archaeology and history." As her studies progressed, she included linguistics and ethnohistory as well as mythology in her methods and interests.

This methodological position has all kinds of consequences. An archaeological approach coupled with history, on the one hand, and ethnography, on the other, leads one sooner or later to perceive culture as a process rather than a thing. What de Laguna taught her students in the field was comprehensive anthropology complemented by detailed studies of geological, botanical, and faunal studies as well as historical and even administrative contexts, with attention being paid to both the present and the past.

The history of Northwest Coast studies shows that Frederica de Laguna is not alone in crossing the disciplinary boundaries. Her students and the students of her students followed her example and forged dual research careers or lasting partnerships with other disciplines. The work of George Mac-Donald and his crew among the Tsimshian is also an example of such a process. Bill Holm and his studies of Native Northwest Coast Indian art are embedded in "participant observation." Margaret Seguin Anderson incorporates linguistics into her ethnographic works, and in the end, we are all jacks-of-all-trades.

From Boas to Breuil and Lévi-Strauss: The French Connection

At first glance, to judge by the literature, Northwest Coast studies are a creation of American cultural anthropology. Most of the early studies during the first half of the 20th century were accomplished by Boas or Boas's students or colleagues (often with Boas's authorization) or scholars from the University of Washington, many of them Boasians themselves. Frederica de Laguna could be represented, at least technically, as one of Franz Boas's students, even though she frowns at such a label. Yet surprisingly it is because of Frederica de Laguna that one can make a case for a significant French participation in the development of our field. Her personal history is strongly marked by a French theme, as can be read in the autobiographical account published in this volume. It evolved from her childhood and her father's influence, depended on personal encounters with French archaeologists working in Europe, and fitted with the intellectual climate of her early career when most anthropologist were polyglots. This theme would be difficult to perceive without autobiographical data, since in de Laguna's case it has less to do with theories and much more with perspectives and methods. As de Laguna relates her encounters with French archaeologists and ethnologists, she describes the transmission of essential skills and specific methods (from drawing artifacts to taking notes to excavation methods). She was drawn to the expertise of French and Danish archaeological circles and acknowledged their search for precision and scientific rigor. Frederica de Laguna's students and the students of her students may not know that the organization of their field notes is indeed related to methods developed by French and Danish archaeologists before 1930, but the quality and reliability of the ethnographies influenced by de Laguna depends largely on such exchanges.

Because she could speak and read French, and because she was interested in European anthropology and French *ethnologie,* Frederica de Laguna read French ethnographies and theoretical works, noting such authors as Leroi-Gourhan, Lévy-Bruhl, and Lévi-Strauss, following their careers and integrating what she needed from their views into her own scholarly perspective (as well as her teaching). She did not so much borrow their ideas as use them to broaden her own horizon. After La Pérouse's trip, one could think that the French connection with the Northwest Coast was practically gone (but see Mauzé, this volume). Yet, the French intellectual world, though represented by a few individuals, continues to have an impact on the study of this culture area. It continues to be strengthened by the pioneers who, in their own individual ways, brought their own contributions, especially to the methodological perspectives and modes of analysis: Marius Barbeau and his wealth of ethnographic data, Leroi-Gourhan and his North Pacific perspective, and Claude Lévi-Strauss with his endorsement of the value of Northwest Coast art and his tantalizing use of structuralism. They are walking along the same path as Frederica de Laguna.

The Importance of a Long-Term Perspective

Many contemporary researchers know Frederica de Laguna mainly as the author of the monumental three-volume study on the Yakutat Tlingits (1972), complemented by her gathering, completing, and editing George Emmons's manuscript, *The Tlingit Indians,* which she published in 1991. These studies, while not her last, are also the culminating result of 40 years of fieldwork, teaching, research, and writing. Even today when anthropologists are working with low budgets and short-term fieldwork conditions, Frederica de Laguna stands out because she has managed to return to the communities and places she chose to study for more than three-quarters of a century, interacting with four or five generations of informants and learning about the local languages and mores (see de Laguna 2000a). Her ethnographic research context already framed by archaeological considerations is never frozen in time; it takes time — and change — as a fundamental dimension of culture. There is no ethnographic present.

The essence of her ethnographic work lies in her relationships with her informants. This is obvious in her fieldwork. It is equally valid in her writings. Coming back to the same communities field season after field season for several years has its obvious advantages deriving from experience and familiarity with places and people. For de Laguna, it meant more than being greeted by people who knew her. It also meant that she could reciprocate by greeting these people on their terms. Grace de Laguna, her mother, once reflected in one of her philosophy articles that the ethnographic work had a lot in common with acting on a stage. The stranger learns to understand a different culture by acting, by behaving in ways that copy or mirror the others. In Frederica's case, this participation in the community is not simply a tool toward accurate description; instead, one's research becomes a tool through which one can meet people. The more one can know, the more satisfying the encounter for all parties involved. An ethnographic description is an encounter and an act of respect.

A long-term framework also brings past and present together from the standpoint of an observer who has witnessed the changes she is to describe. As an archaeologist, Frederica de Laguna is very much aware of time and of cultural changes, not only in archaeological times but also in historical time; she never falls in the trap of considering cultures as unchanging entities captured in an abstract isolation.

For Frederica de Laguna, this ethnographic practice is built on definite theoretical choices that are no less real or less important for not having been spelled out in her monographs. Her most important choices have to do with the concept of culture. On the one hand, ethnography allows for the recognition of culture as a mental object, carried by thinking beings that live in and contribute to a culturally constituted behavioral environment. Culture becomes that which is carried, invented, and transmitted by individuals, a move that recalls Edward Sapir's decision toward the end of his career to favor biographical and even autobiographical accounts as a source of data, and culture "as lived" as the focus of anthropological research.[2] This implicit but firm theoretical position permeates all of Frederica de Laguna's ethnographical work. On the other hand, culture, as an object of research and writing, is that which is described by the ethnographer. Long before postmodernism de Laguna taught her students the necessity for ethnographers to be aware of their own intervention in shaping their account of cultures, whether they were archaeological data, museum collections, or written accounts. One of the metaphors she used to define culture, in the methodological sense of the term, as a kind of intellectual cabinet, was a teaching tool she used in her seminars to emphasize the fact that a culture, from an ethnographer's perspective, is a construct that depends as much on his or her experience and a priori categories as on the lives observed in the field. The more explicit the categories, the more externalized the categories of description and analysis, the more transparent the intervention of the ethnographer. In Catherine McClellan's words, even though Frederica never "'felt prepared to do theory' . . . she set out a consistent viewpoint revolving around questions of objectivity and subjectivity in her fieldwork, values, the individual culture, and the historic sweep of cultures" (McClellan 1988:42).

Another dimension of her ethnographic work is worth noting. While many of us, dealing as we do with rapidly changing cultures and landscapes, may be tempted to capture what is left of the past using the categories handed down by our predecessors, Frederica de Laguna views ethnography and culture in the future tense as a tool to prepare for knowledge to come. She sees anthropology as the "only discipline that offers a conceptual schema for the whole content of human experience" (McClellan 1988:42). This complementary view of culture, both as lived by individual informants and constructed by individual ethnographers, can be sustained only though rigorous methodology. But it brings to the fore a dimension of Northwest Coast studies that has not been recognized fully, though it may apply to all intellectual endeavors.

Frederica de Laguna's participation in the Northwest Coast field of studies is that of an idiosyncratic, well-defined, and truly original personality, fed by encounters and exchanges shaped in turn by the personality of each interlocutor, whether it be her parents, Franz Boas, the Abbé Breuil, Paul Rivet, Therkel Mathiassen, or Kaj Birket-Smith, whether chance encounter or planned meeting. Looking at the Northwest coast studies in the light of Frederica de Laguna's experience, one is struck by the large amount of work accomplished by such a small number of authors; one should notice as well the imprint of their individuality on their accounts. The few anthropologists whose works now rest as classic foundations for Northwest Coast peoples' cultural history, men and women, were each driven by passionate but unique yearning: Edward Sapir, Marius Barbeau, George Swanton, Franz Boas, George Hunt, Edward Curtis, Viola Garfield, T. F. McIlwraith, George Emmons, among others no less than Wilson Duff or Marjorie Halpin. The stronger the personality, the more influential the work.

Singular events and encounters marked the lives of these individuals no less than they mark Frederica de Laguna's accomplishments. From this angle the entire field seems to be built serendipitously on contributions offered by distinctive individuals who made specific choices as to what and how to study for reasons of their own.[3] Who went where and did what was partly influenced by leading personalities such as Franz Boas and by the museums that financed the anthropological expeditions. Yet the researchers were strong enough to shape the content of their ethnographic work and therefore part of the knowledge now available on Northwest Coast cultures, languages, and history as a whole. In that process some communities were forgotten, while others were elevated to the status of distinct or representative "culture." Certain notions such as "crest," "potlatch," or "chief" became cultural icons. Others were left unexamined for the following generation to rediscover, assuming they would still be there.

This individualism on the ethnographers' side and the role played by single events and circumstances in their lives and research work are matched in the indigenous communities. The emphasis found in Northwest Coast societies on the charismatic personalities of chiefs, shamans, artists, and travelers, including, of course, informants, has shaped social life, historical events, and political situations. Even in smaller communities, as among the Athapaskan peoples, individual personalities are very much in evidence, both in the shape of their communities and in the ethnographers' accounts. Though one can read larger social structure components and cultural combinations arching from one culture to the next, like the crest system in the north, the spirit dances in the south, the secret societies along the entire coast, or the spread of the Tsimshian Simhalait dances and costumes, each community is different and is proud to be so: each lineage is different and has its own version of the local myths; each island, each camp, has its own story. Moreover, when the ethnographer meets the communities, each informant has a different interpretation to offer to the academic world. George Hunt is one of the most obvious examples. On the one side the need for the Aboriginal people to present, at least from time to time, a united political front and on the other side the need for the researchers to generalize concepts and ethnological findings do not lessen the power of the general underlying idiosyncrasy that underlies both research and the cultures under study. Frederica de Laguna's legacy reminds us that understanding the singularities stemming from such idiosyncrasy may be what Northwest Coast studies are about; this is still what anthropology is all about.

Notes

1. As Judith Berman noted in her chapter (see Berman, this volume), one has to come to Paris for these boundaries to dissolve and for formally redrawing both the notion of cultural area and the boundaries of an eventual Northwest Coast area.
2. This notion of culture is also used by Cornelius Osgood in his Athabaskan ethnographies (see Osgood 1936a, 1936b, 1937).
3. Frederica de Laguna relates (this volume) how Boas had decided against letting a young though talented linguist work on the Eyak language at a time where it was still fluently spoken at the mouth of the Copper River.

WHEN THE NORTHWEST COAST
HAUNTS FRENCH ANTHROPOLOGY

A Discreet but Lasting Presence

Marie Mauzé

To speak of French anthropology and the Northwest Coast is first of all to point out the general lack of fieldwork research in North America by French scholars. This might be the result of French intellectuals' lack of interest since the end of the 18th century with questions and problems regarding the former French possessions of Canada and Louisiana. From the 1870s onward French Americanism primarily involved the study of Mesoamerican archaeology, mainly pursued by amateur scholars who belonged to the Société des Américanistes (founded in 1893) and contributed to its journal, the *Journal de la société des Américanistes* (originally published in 1895). The first international meeting of Americanists was held in Nancy in 1875. An international school of American archaeology and ethnology was created in Mexico City in 1910 under the auspices of France and Germany (Descola and Izard 1991:52) and the United States, thanks mainly to Franz Boas's efforts. Today, Americanism is well developed in other regions of Latin America such as the Andes and Amazon Lowlands (Descola and Taylor 1993). North American studies have always represented a poor relation in French anthropological research. When French anthropology became professionalized with the creation of the Institut d'ethnologie de l'université de Paris in 1925, students who were to undertake fieldwork chose the French colonies of Africa and New Caledonia.[1] As Lucien Lévy-Bruhl wrote in 1926, the institute was to "work for the progress of the ethnological science" while at the same time "putting the results of this science to the disposal of our native policy when needed" (Fournier 1995:62, my translation).[2]

It was only in the 1960s and 1970s that a few anthropologists undertook fieldwork among native societies in the United States and Canada.[3] Some, notably Bernard Saladin d'Anglure and Dominique Legros, finally chose to pursue careers in Quebec. Today "North Americanism" is represented by only a handful of professional researchers, each working in a different cultural area (Northeast, Plains, Southwest, Northwest Coast, and Arctic). There was an attempt at fieldwork earlier in the century when Henri Beuchat, a student of Marcel Mauss, was to study "the language, manners, customs and religious beliefs" of the Eskimos in the Canadian Arctic (Barbeau 1916:109–110; Jenness, 1991:9).[4] Beuchat, who had collaborated with Mauss in the publication of "Essai sur les variations saisonnières" (1906), was recommended by Marius Barbeau, one of the first members of Edward Sapir's team in Ottawa to set up the Canadian Artic Expedition of 1913–16.[5] The expedition was to be led by Gustav Stefansson (Darnell 1990:67; Fournier 1994:308). Beuchat and Barbeau had met in Paris while they both attended Mauss's lectures at the Ecole pratique.[6] Unfortunately, in January 1914 the boat on which Beuchat was traveling, the *Karluk,* sank. The young French ethnographer who could have become an expert on Eskimo culture died of cold and hunger on Wrangell Island off the coast of Alaska. In an "In Memoriam" piece Mauss wrote: "Beuchat ranked among the best of Americanists. . . . He was a remarkable linguist and observer. He knew many things and knew them well" (Mauss 1925b:20, my translation; see also Barbeau 1916). Beuchat's participation in the Canadian Artic Expedition could have been an incentive for younger generations to undertake fieldwork. His tragic death may have put an end to the development of French research in North America.

The French Discovery of the Northwest Coast: Early Observations

The Northwest Coast became known to the French public at the close of the 18th century and the beginning of the 19th through the publication of the journals of French explorers and traders reporting on various aspects of native life and trade relations. The accounts by Jean Galaup de Lapérouse (1785–88 [1985]), Etienne Marchand (1791) (see Gunther 1972; de Laguna 1972), and Camille de Roquefeuil (1816–19) provide descriptions of the Tlingits, Haidas, and Nootka. Lapérouse, who commanded the *Astrolabe* and the *Boussole,* was the first to reconnoiter Lituya Bay, which he named Port des Français. He briefly comments on the Tlingits' clothing, ornaments, and body decorations but is not very informative on native art and crafts. In contrast to Lapérouse's rather laconic observations on the Tlingits, those of

Captain Prosper Chanal and surgeon Claude Roblet, both members of the commercial expedition led by Etienne Marchand, are detailed, especially in the domain of the art of the Tlingits of Sitka Sound and the Haidas of the northern part of the Queen Charlotte Islands (Haida Gwaii). Chanal and Roblet furnish one of the earliest and best historical records on different types of Haida house structures. We are also indebted to them for the most detailed description of elaborately carved wooden poles and painted house panels. From a historical viewpoint their observations are important because they testify to the presence of large wooden posts erected before European arrival, a fact questioned by some anthropologists, notably Marius Barbeau (1930), who preferred to think that monumental sculptures had been a by-product of contact. They also show a rather remarkable understanding of design arrangements painted or carved in low relief on two-dimensional artifacts. Chanal and Roblet compared Tlingit designs to hieroglyphs. Both men assumed that the symbols they saw on paintings were part of a writing system. The combination of recurrent images and designs appeared to them as a written text having a hidden meaning they could not decipher. Paintings and sculptures were thought to be a means for the people to remember the gods they venerated.

Although there were several visits by French ships during the early years of the 19th century, the third official record is the account of the trader Camille de Roquefeuil (1823), who anchored his ship, *Le Bordelais,* in Nootka Sound in 1817. He returned for another visit in 1818. While Roquefeuil's journal is mainly based on published accounts, the main contribution made by Roquefeuil and the ship's surgeon, Yves-Thomas Vimont, who also wrote a journal, to the early ethnography of the Nootka is the description of the Mowachaht whaling shrine first discovered by Vimont in September 1817 (Mauzé 1991).[7] At Boas's recommendation the now famous shrine was collected by George Hunt in 1904 for the Museum of Natural History in New York (Jonaitis 1999). Roquefeuil's and Vimont's accounts are of the utmost importance as they provide the only firsthand description of a ritual site, still used by the Mowachaht, which was not the case when Hunt acquired it almost a century later.

For the late 19th century one should mention the name of the explorer Alphonse Pinart. A self-trained linguist and ethnologist, Pinart traveled between San Francisco and Norton Sound in 1871–72; he again visited British

Columbia (Victoria and Nanaimo) and Alaska in 1876 (Parmenter 1966). Pinart collected Koniag (Alutiiq) and Aleut artifacts invaluable today as well as some Northwest Coast pieces, among them the rare Nisga'a stone mask with open eyes. Since April 2000 the mask has been exhibited at Le Louvre in the new section devoted to non-Western art.[8] Pinart is rightly credited with having written some of the earliest ethnographic descriptions of the Aleuts and Koniag and collecting Northwest Coast linguistic material. However, it may well be true that the lists of Cowichan, Tlingit, and Nootka vocabularies were copied from other sources (Kinkade 1990:99).

The Northwest Coast and the *Année sociologique*

At the turn of the 20th century French anthropological conceptions of North American native societies principally relied on the data collected by American anthropologists, not French scholars. In this regard the French school of sociology founded by Emile Durkheim, whose ambition and scope were largely anthropological, played a great role as demonstrated by the *Année sociologique* (1896–1913; n.s. 1923–24, 1925). Reflecting the works of Durkheim and young students—usually of philosophy—such as Marcel Mauss, Camille Bouglé, Georges Davy, Robert Hertz, and Henri Hubert, the *Année* developed a methodological framework for social anthropology based on a deep-level comparison. They wished to understand social phenomena from other times and places as part of an attempt to lay the foundations for a rational sociology of the contemporary world (see Nandan 1980:16–17). As Mauss (1998:33) remarked, the aim of the *Année* was "to enable us and himself [Durkheim] to put forward our point of view on all sort of sociological topics. However in all our minds, it soon became something quite different from a vehicle for propagating a method or a platform for opposing the various schools of economists, historians of religions, theoricians of jurisprudence, and so on. Under Durkheim's direction, and I might add, to some extent under my own impulsion, we all agreed to try to organize in the journal not merely ideas but above all facts."[9]

The pieces in the *Année* dedicated to reviews and analyses of an impressive amount of materials from different disciplines were the result of a systematic collaborative enterprise (Lukes 1973:292) within which each member's task was to verify and criticize each other's use of facts. The *Année* could be compared to "a sort of handbook, continually updated, of one of the most recent and important science[s]" that comprised ethnology (Mauss 1998:30, 34). All domains of sociology were covered by original papers ("Mémoires originaux"), reviews ("Analyses"), and notes ("Notices"). Mauss was the chief reviewer of the section entitled "la sociologie religieuse" under which appear most of the reviews concerning publications on the North American Indians. This section is further divided into subsections such as "religions of primitive societies," "traditions and beliefs," and "religious *représentations*," which included "mythology" (Lukes 1973:291-292; Salomon 1960:249). While ethnographic texts on Native Americans reviewed in the *Année sociologique* were numerous, the place they occupy in the journal certainly does not compare with the publications on Australia, which provided Durkheim with the materials for his well-known essays titled "La prohibition de l'inceste et ses origines" (1896–97), "Sur le totémisme" (1900–1901), and "Sur l'organisation matrimoniale des sociétés australiennes" (1903-4). In any case, North America was almost the exclusive domain of Mauss, who analyzed in the first twelve volumes (1896–1913) the early North American field-workers' writings and those of Europeans involved with American research institutions.[10] He was above all impressed by the richness of the great amount of mythological data collected by Boas's collaborators on the Jesup North Pacific Expedition (1897–1902): "among the many Jesup Expedition publications we think the sociological domain in which the American ethnographers is best expressed is still mythology. Their contribution is of the utmost importance" (Mauss 1901-2:248, my translation).

Besides the Northwest Coast and the Artic extended to Siberia, the cultural areas concerned by his reviews were the Plains, California, and the Southwest.[11] From his own research Mauss produced two main essays: "Essai sur les variations saisonnières" (1906; *Seasonal Variations of the Eskimo*, 1979), in collaboration with Henri Beuchat, and "Essai sur le don" (1925, 1950; *The Gift*, 1967). But before turning to *The Gift*, it should be noted that Mauss wrote ten reviews on Northwest Coast topics.[12] These reviews of publications by James Teit, Franz Boas, John Swanton, and Charles Hill-Tout treat issues of social organization and mythology and their relation to totemism.

Social Organization and Totemism

At the end of the 19th century and in the first two decades of the 20th, totemism constituted a defining issue in the numerous ethnological debates between European and North American scholars. The *Année* (1898–1913) contributed significantly to the centrality of that issue in anthropological literature of the era. Durkheim made it a major concern, as shown by the list of books, treatises, and articles he reviewed in the *Année* (Pickering 1975:311–313). Like many scholars of his time (Frazer, Wundt, Jevons), he tackled the question within an intellectual and scientific context deeply influenced by evolutionism. Durkheim envisioned totemism as the most primitive form of religion, epitomized by Australian totemism. The Australian material provided him with data to flesh out his theory, grounded in the comparative method, which he outlined in his *Elementary Forms* (1915).[13] He used the American ethnographic literature as a supplementary way "'to illuminate and lend precision to the Australian facts': for though the American Indians' civilization was 'more advanced,' the 'essential lines of the social structure remain the same as those in Australia; it is always the organization on a clan basis'" (Lukes 1973:453; see also Durkheim's remarks in Pickering 1975:178).

In the *Année* totemism is generally discussed under such rubrics as "Elementary religious phenomena" and "Primitive religions." However, the place assigned to Northwest Coast totemism — mostly under Mauss's pen — is rather difficult to circumscribe as it is dealt with under various headings such as "Social organization," "Legends and tales," and "Religions of lower societies," and within the latter under "Religious systems with advanced totemism," as is the case for Swanton's publications on the Tlingits and the Haidas. It is likely that this rather imprecise framework reflects more of an attempt to describe the content of the monographs than to explicitly address the issue. It is nonetheless symptomatic that even though Mauss remarked that the wording "lower or primitive societies" was not quite right he still thought this was the best way to "account for the length and the greatness of all the evolutions" (Fournier 1994:497, my translation).

Both Durkheim and Mauss considered that totemism was a real social institution based on a clan organization (Durkheim 1915:222) with distinctive characteristics (exogamy, totemic taboos, the use of totemic emblems, beliefs in descent from the totem, etc.). These are the characteristics they tried to track down in Northwest Coast monographs on the Kwakiutl, Bella Coola, Haidas, Tlingits, and Interior and Coast Salish. While data on the social organization of the Haidas and the Tlingits were not questioned, the overall structure being characterized by exogamic phratries (later called

moieties) subdivided into clans, Durkheim and Mauss had difficulty understanding the complexities of the Kwakiutl and Bella Coola social organization. In his review of Boas's 1897 work *Social Organization and the Secret Societies of the Kwakiutl Indians* (1970), Durkheim, who agreed with the "totemic
clan theory" developed by McLennan and Morgan, accepted Boas's findings
of totemism among the Kwakiutl in the form of crests transmitted matri-
lineally; in addition he rightly remarked on the mixed system of descent
as privileges transmitted from the father-in-law to the son-in-law in trust
for the children yet to be born. While admitting the transitional status of
the Kwakiutl, Durkheim (and Mauss as well) dismissed Boas's hypothesis of
their shift from an originally patrilineal form of organization into the direction of matrilineal descent (Durkheim 1898–99:339). For Durkheim such a
case is "highly improbable" as it would appear as an example of a regressive
expression vis-à-vis the widely accepted scheme of the evolution of human
society. On the basis of facts described by Boas, Durkheim maintained that
maternal descent principles are too clearly expressed to be of recent origin
(337).

Durkheim questioned Boas's ability to analyze Kwakiutl facts in his letter to Mauss (November 1899): "I am reading Boas. He is far from having
new ideas. He absolutely does not know what a clan is. Hence a lot of confusion. Do not give in so easily to your readings" (Durkheim 1998:228, my
translation). In fact, Boas and Durkheim were following the same line of
thought but taking a different side of the argument. Boas believed he had
found evidence against the well-established theory of cultural evolution,
which posited movement from matrilineal to patrilineal descent, but not
vice versa. Later Boas (1920) changed his mind and described a system predominantly governed by patrilineal rules, which in reality functioned as a
cognatic system of affiliation (Lévi-Strauss 1982:168).

The French sociologist was probably unaware that Boas was trying to
grasp the seeming paradox of Kwakiutl society that we now know can be
understood only in terms of acquiring, transferring, and above all keeping
and accumulating privileges within what at the time Boas called the *clan*.
Such operations were subjected to strategic devices that did not follow strict
rules of descent and exogamy. In his analysis of Boas's 1898 publication *Mythology of the Bella Coola Indians*, Mauss questioned Boas's assertion of cases
of endogamy "to keep myths and rituals within clans except for certain chiefs

who marry outside to acquire more 'magic riches.' . . . If it were to be true," Mauss wrote, "it would be very interesting but the information given by Boas is hypothetical" (Mauss 1901–2:249). Finally, criticizing Boas's diffusionism, a method that Boas used within the context of the Northwest Coast to study the borrowing and adaptation of cultural elements by neighboring groups, Durkheim concluded vis-à-vis the nature of Kwakiutl secret societies that "in order to account for a total social fact, [Boas] more often contents himself with investigating where it could have been borrowed" (Durkheim 1898–99:340, my translation).

Both Durkheim and Mauss found that the features displayed by Northwest Coast totemism were sufficiently pronounced to be recognized as belonging to this social and religious complex. Some elements of totemism were present whereas others were expressed in a very weak way. This is the case for the Kwakiutl, among whom there is no totem as such. In fact, the totem that is a crest does not represent the ancestor. It is only a fetish (or a sacred object) that the mythical ancestor brought to the descendants of the clan. What is left from the ancient clan organization is exogamy (Durkheim 1898–99:337). The Thompson River Indians (belonging to the Plateau) have no totemic clans or rather have totems but no clans. Mauss concluded that some elements such as sexual taboos, descent in female line, and cases of individual totems described by Teit could be considered as surviving forms of totemism (Mauss 1898–99:278). The example of the Statlumh (Lillooet) described by Hill-Tout shows that totemism among them existed in a decaying form, which nonetheless was based on "extremely primitive forms" from which clan and [secret] societies cults originate (Mauss 1905–6:236). The case of the Haidas and the Tlingits described by Swanton (1905a, 1908) is puzzling as totems do not operate as a distinctive mark of clans since the same crest is shared by two phratries (moieties), and within a phratry the same crest is common to several clans. Following Swanton, Mauss considered the overlapping of crests as the result of a historical process characterized by the borrowing, exchanging, and lending of crests through marriage and potlatching. Therefore the inventory of Haida crests could not be considered as a means of identifying social groups but reflected their use for social and political purposes (see also Boas 1916a). Mauss explained the successive acquisitions and alienations of totems by the weakening of their religious character and their transformation into material property. He remarked that names derived from the totem remain the property of the clans and therefore kept their primitive character. In short, for Mauss, the Haidas and the Tlingits offer an example of a shattered totemic organization that broke down under various circumstances, while retaining some archaic forms that testify to what it was once (Mauss 1906–9:117). Durkheim, who considered the Northwest Coast societies to have a "more highly developed mentality" that those of Australia (1915:190), concluded: "It is true that these are societies (the Haida, Tlingit, Tsimshian) where it is no longer admitted that a man was born of an animal or a plant; but these ideas of an affinity between the animals of the totemic species and the members of the clan have survived there nonetheless, and expresses itself in myths which, though differing from the preceding, still retain that is essential" (192).

Having examined the social and religious data from these societies, Durkheim and Mauss came to consider them an intermediate category between properly totemic religions and tribal religions. Northwest Coast totemism persists but is "in a process of giving birth to new forms or religion." What is remarkable, according to Durkheim, is that "the clans themselves, whilst sometimes remaining recognizable, include religious subgroups which . . . are differently organized. These are the brotherhoods so often and wrongly called secret societies. We shall call those religions which are to be found particularly among the Indians of North America, *primitive religions evolved from totemism*" (Pickering 1975:100–101, 167).

No doubt the origin of totemism and the discussions pertaining to the "American theory" was of interest to Durkheim and Mauss. The theory is based on the idea that the clan totem grew out of the personal guardian spirits of individuals. For the Northwest Coast, Boas was the first one to point out an "analogy between totem legend and guardian spirit tale among the Kwakiutl" (Boas 1916a:319). Boas's theory was taken up by Hill-Tout, who generalized it to all the British Columbia native societies to make one single category of the individual spirit, the tutelary animal of a secret society, and the clan totem. Mauss, who had a good knowledge of Northwest Coast mythology and traditions (Mauss 1901–2:249), saw a necessary link between totemism and mythology but doubted that Hill-Tout's research on the existence of such a "complete totemism" would have escaped earlier observation (Mauss 1905–6:237). But Mauss was so puzzled by the transformations of clans into secret societies and the transition from individual totemism to collective totemism that he advised Barbeau to undertake for his B.Sc. thesis at Oxford (1910b) research on Northwest totemism, investigating the relations between "manitous (totems), crests, names and social units" (Nowry 1995:82).[14]

The Potlatch

The "Essai sur le don" (*The Gift*), which Mauss first published in 1925, is the result of research on archaic forms of contract and on the potlatch that Mauss had undertaken before World War I. His interest in the potlatch goes back to the time when he was working on his "Essai sur les variations saisonnières" (*Seasonal Variations,* 1979), which appeared in 1906. It is his reading of Swanton's works that really triggered his curiosity about "this strange institution" (*curieuse institution*) (Mauss 1906–9:115; Tarot 1999:599).[15] In 1905–6 he lectured on the topic at the Ecole Pratique des hautes études (Mauss 1969:58–60; Fournier 1994:308) and again took up the subject in 1910–12, drawing on the ethnographies of the Tlingits, the Haidas, and the Kwakiutl.

In 1913 Mauss extended his research to Melanesia with the review of C. G. Seligman's *The Melanesians of British New Guinea* (1976). After World War I he delivered several papers at the Institut d'anthropologie, among them "L'extension du potlatch en Mélanésie" and "L'obligation de rendre les présents." Malinowski's *Argonauts of the Western Pacific* (1922) introduced the kula system to Mauss, on which he lectured at the Ecole pratique in 1923–24 (Fournier 1993:332, 1995:63). In homage to his friend Charles Andler, he also published a short article entitled "Gift-gift" (1924) that analyzed how in a system of total prestations donors and receivers are bound on magic, religious, and jural levels.[16] The examination of facts in their entirety led Mauss to develop a general theory of the "Forms and Functions of Exchange in Archaïc Societies," which introduced the notion of "total social facts."

Mauss (1998:37–38) reflects on his research program in the following way:

> I have tried to explain the reciprocities and antagonisms that develop in a society by pointing to the way in which it distributes men, women, and generations among its internal divisions. I have thus identified systems of moral phenomena of considerable importance: . . . above all the phenomena labeled by the term potlatch, within which I prefer to

distinguish systems of social prestations and systems of agonistic prestations or the potlatch proper.

In connection with the latter, guided by Boas's admirable descriptions of the American Northwest [and?] by a suggestion from Durkheim, I was able to identify a whole system of phenomena that are extremely widespread in most archaic civilisations. . . . From the whole I drew out the idea of the gift as simultaneously religious, mythic, and contractual. . . . I also analysed the collective nature of archaic forms . . . and, above all, the notion of "total facts" which set in motion the whole collectivity, as an entity simultaneously economic, moral and religious, aesthetic and mythic.

In this essay Mauss showed that in primitive societies exchange more frequently consists of reciprocal gifts than of economic transactions. He stressed the reciprocal aspect of giving and receiving and the mutual obligations an exchange imposes upon the participants. He categorized the potlatch as a "total phenomenon" having social, religious, economic, magic, jural, and moral functions. The social dimension appears in the gathering of tribes, clans, and families that are involved as moral persons; the exchange of gifts serves to establish publicly the status of a group or family; not only material goods are exchanged but intangibles, rights, and persons.

While these points provide a good framework within which to analyze the potlatch, other aspects of Mauss's argumentation give a distorted view of the institution. Mauss based his theory on Northwest Coast ethnographic literature that he considered a "sound documentation,"[17] but he failed to provide legal, economic, and demographic data much needed for a thorough analysis of the potlatch (Mauss 1967:99n104). Certainly Mauss lacked detailed data that would have strengthened his analysis, but he understood the necessity of collecting incomplete information about "primitive" societies that were doomed to disappear soon (Mauss 1969:428–429). Conversely he ignored the social, demographic, and economic changes affecting the Northwest Coast societies at the end of the 19th century, which led to radical transformations of its basic principles (Codere 1950; Drucker and Heizer 1967; Mauzé 1986; Schulte-Tenckhoff 1986). On the basis of the available ethnographic information, he came to define the potlatch as a gift exchange marked by violence, rivalry, and antagonism (1967:32, 33) often expressed in the consumption and destruction or goods (35). One of the functions of the potlatch is to surpass a rival in generosity or to crush him under the burden of mutual obligations: "Political and individual status in associations or in clans, and rank of every kind," Mauss wrote, "are determined by the war of property, as well as by armed hostilities, by chance, inheritance, alliance or marriage. But everything is conceived as it were a war of wealth," (35) whence his interpretation of the potlatch as a system of agonistic prestations. Characterized by antagonistic confrontations disrupting the usual pattern of reciprocity in gift giving, the potlatch is conceived as the "monster child of the gift system" (41). Although built on misinterpretations of a Northwest Coast ethnography rife with ambiguities, this becomes *the* French definition of the potlatch.

Drawing on Boas (1899), Mauss wrongly interpreted the notion of credit in the potlatch: "by substituting for Boas's terms words like 'gifts made and returned' (which Boas does use eventually) one sees clearly the function of credit" (Mauss 1967:101n112). Mauss relied on Boas's article, which he considered one of the most illuminating texts ever written on the topic by the American anthropologist (100) and in which the potlatch is defined as an "interest-bearing investment." A version of this article appeared in part a year earlier in the *Province,* a local Victoria (BC) newspaper (March 6, 1897). Boas's article aimed at defending the native institution threatened by the implementation of the Potlatch Law and making some of its mechanisms understood by a large public (Mauzé 1986). By drawing a parallel between the potlatch and the Western investment system, Boas emphasized a late but widespread phenomenon (especially among the Kwakiutl) that exclusively concerned the accumulating of property by making high-interest loans. Mauss ignored Dawson (1888) and Curtis (1915), who clearly distinguished the lending of property from gift exchange (Mauzé 1986; Schulte-Tenckhoff 1986; Suttles and Jonaitis 1990). In any case Mauss understood the gift in archaic societies as "necessarily imply[ing] the notion of credit," two processes that were once different but were eventually pulled together in barter (Mauss 1967:35). He concluded that the potlatch was a transitional stage in evolution characterizing "societies which have passed the phase of 'total prestation' but have not yet reached the stage of pure individual contract, the money market" (45).

Mauss's Legacy and the Potlatch

In France Mauss's essay was well received (Fournier 1993:333, 1995:66).[18] Soon *The Gift,* enhanced by ideas expressed in earlier writings, came to be considered as Mauss's masterwork, which "introduced and imposed the notion of *total social fact*" (Lévi-Strauss 1987b:25). In Great Britain Malinowski read the "admirable article with the utmost interest," but Raymond Firth criticized Mauss's use of the native notion of *hau* set up as a universal principle (Fournier 1994:524).[19] In the United States Franz Boas (1926) wrote a letter to Mauss declaring it an "interesting investigation" (Fournier 1995:67), but to my knowledge Boas never made the essay known to his students.[20] It is remarkable that Mauss's essay, translated in 1954, has been ignored by the bibliographies of Northwest Coast scholars, although the potlatch has been the subject of much scholarly attention.[21] It may well be that the post-Boasian anthropologists have always grounded their research empirically, thus distrusting critical analysis. It may also be the case that Mauss's definition of the potlatch as "an exchange marked by antagonism and rivalry, destruction of property and an expected return of gifts at usurous rates of interest" (Irvin 1977:67) was thought inaccurate by field-workers. However, Mauss brought to the fore elements that provided a theoretical framework for future analysis of the potlatch within the context of Northwest Coast societies, a fact that Terry Irvin (1977) acknowledged in his assessment of Mauss's famous paper.

By contrast, Mauss's essay had a great influence in French anthropology. More than his reviews in the *Année sociologique*, *The Gift* made the Northwest Coast societies known to French scholars in the various fields of social sciences and is also considered as a seminal study on the potlatch.[22] Three major works were directly inspired by Mauss's research: *La foi jurée* (1922) by Georges Davy and "La notion de dépense" in 1933 and *La part maudite* in 1949 (1967; English translation in 1988) by Georges Bataille.

Mauss's research is said to have been partly appropriated by one of his students at the Ecole pratique, Georges Davy, who published his thesis three years before "Essai sur le don." Although Davy's work raised a lot of controversy, its scope is more limited than Mauss's analysis.[23] Davy considered the potlatch from a juridical perspective, leaving aside its religious, economic, and mythological dimensions, which make it in Mauss's terminology a "total phenomenon." From an evolutionary perspective, Davy brought to the fore the transition from a "totemic communism" characterized by collective prestations to the emergence of a "feudal and commercial individualism" represented by a wealth-based elite. From being collective the exchange of gifts became individualized; thenceforth the potlatch operated as a form of juridical contract giving rise to unequal status among clan members. Thus Davy interpreted the potlatch not as a collective institution bounding phratries and clans but as one of the main mechanisms whereby the individualization of power is made possible. He also remarked on the role of secret societies, which substitute for clans to provide wealthy chiefs the necessary religious power to guarantee their status (Davy 1922:250–251). For Davy the potlatch is "the means for the individual to claim his personal status and prestige" (350, my translation). In short, the contractual nature of gift giving serves to define the legal status of individual chiefs. Davy's thesis on juridical contract and political sovereignty in "potlatch societies" is distinct from the general theory of obligations stemming from the exchange of gifts (see Cefaï and Mahé 1998:216).

In France contemporary readings of Mauss's essay are mediated by Georges Bataille's interpretation. Bataille, the writer and essayist who founded the Collège de sociologie in 1937–39 with Michel Leiris and Roger Caillois (Hollier 1988), first became familiar with the potlatch (as well as Aztec human sacrifice) through his conversations with Alfred Métraux, when the latter reminisced about Mauss's seminars (Métraux 1963).[24] His encounter with ethnographic data, combined with his knowledge in various fields (poetry, religion, economy, politics), led him to develop his theory of general economy, distinct from that of the Western world in which production of goods and reinvestment of surplus is the general rule. In general, in archaic societies the production of goods is turned toward prodigality in gift giving and destruction and toward *consummation,* or nonproductive expenditure. The notion of "expenditure" is associated with that of the "accursed share" (*part maudite*), defined as what is given or wasted without being returned. The sun provides the best example of nonreciprocity: "The source and essence of our riches are given in the effulgence of the sun, who dispenses energy — riches — without a counterpart" (Richman 1982:17).

Bataille's theory is rather ambiguous, not to say paradoxical, when it comes to potlatch, which he regards as one of the historical forms of the universal phenomenon of expenditure (Schulte-Tenckhoff 1986:186). The notions of gift and expenditure, although distinct are in some cases interchangeable or overlapping. In contrast to *gift,* which connotes reciprocity, *expenditure* does not necessarily do so. For Bataille, gift giving, in extreme cases, equates with dilapidation and destruction of goods. To give, to lose, and to destroy are one and the same thing (Bataille 1967). In Northwest Coast ceremonies involving chiefs destroying great amounts of goods and precious objects such as coppers to crush their rivals and increase their prestige (32–33), Bataille found that expenditure becomes acquisitive, the economic loss turning into a social or symbolic gain. "Potlatch cannot be unilaterally interpreted as a consumption of riches," stated Bataille. "Only recently was I able to reduce this difficulty and give to the principles of a general economy a sufficiently ambiguous basis, which is that a dilapidation of energy is always the opposite of a thing, but can only be considered once it has entered an order of things, transformed into a thing" (Richman 1982:19). The "thing" acquired is power, honor, and prestige (Bataille 1967:112–124). Moreover, potlatch giving entails the establishment of a social hierarchy when the receiver cannot reciprocate. "In potlatch," according to Bataille, "the rich man distributes the products furnished to him by other men. He seeks to elevate himself above an equally rich rival, but the ultimate goal is to raise himself above these miserable creatures. Thus dépense [expenditure], though it may serve a social function, ends up as an antagonistic act of separation, in appearance anti-social. The rich man consumes the waste of the poor by creating for him a category of abjection which opens the way to slavery" (Richman 1982:61–62).

In his own wording, Bataille agrees with Mauss when the latter writes: "Even destruction of wealth does not correspond to the complete disinterestedness which one might expect. These great acts of generosity are not free from self-interest. . . . Between vassals and chiefs, between vassals and their henchmen, the hierarchy is established by means of these gifts. To give is to show one's superiority, to show that one is something more and higher, that one is *magister*" (Mauss 1967:72).

The potlatch has been raised to the status of an anthropological category by Mauss and Bataille. The main difficulty is that its elaboration as a concept was drawn on ethnographic data ignoring the historical dimension of Northwest Coast societies, resulting in a simplistic approach toward the complex native institution. After successive shifts in meaning, the potlatch came to be reduced, in French thought, to an institution of ostentatious rivalry (Mauzé 1987).

Finale

Claude Lévi-Strauss's interest in Northwest Coast ethnology paradoxically developed quite independently from Mauss's research on the potlatch. Although Lévi-Strauss, in his "Introduction to the Work of Marcel Mauss" prefacing Mauss's first major collection of writings, *Sociologie et anthropologie* (1950), places himself in Mauss's footsteps, he reconstructs the framework within which Mauss elaborated the notion of "total social fact" without reference to a Northwest Coast that Mauss had in his own way explored with the help of Boas. The intellectual encounter between the two giants of French anthropology occurred without reference to the Northwest Coast, despite its importance in the intellectual development of each.

Lévi-Strauss's interest in the Northwest Coast cannot be explained simply by his academic research. He has frequently avowed his "emotional" and "intellectual" ties to the Northwest Coast, by which he means a deeper sort of connection, a meeting of the minds, that occurred in the first instance in his encounter with Northwest Coast art (Lévi-Strauss, this volume). He took to the study of the arts and culture of these societies during his New York exile in the early 1940s, but he was already attracted to this outstanding civilization of the North Pacific Coast as exemplified through the acquisition of his first Northwest Coast piece—a Haida argilite pipe—at the Parisian antique dealer Level in 1936 (Lévi-Strauss, personal communication with author, December 1998). In New York he bought a fairly important collection of Northwest Coast artifacts (Carpenter 1975:9–10; Lévi-Strauss and Eribon 1991:31, 33; Mauzé 2000a:31–32; Jacknis, this volume). It was also in New York that Lévi-Strauss met Boas on several occasions (Lévi-Strauss 1984:8–9; Lévi-Strauss and Eribon 1991:36–37) and became familiar with the American anthropologist's writings and more largely with Northwest Coast ethnographic literature. Lévi-Strauss always refused to follow the steps of those who have been criticizing Boas's ethnography and "his aversion for theory" (e.g., L. White 1963). On several occasions he assessed the great American anthropologist's contribution to the field of anthropology (Lévi-Strauss 1991a:117; Lévi-Strauss and Eribon 1991:38). Lévi-Strauss detected in Boas's ethnology the constant reference to ethnographic facts treated in their diversity, which in his opinion underscores "the everywhere identical operation of universal laws of the human mind" (Lévi-Strauss 1991a:117). Henceforth, without saying so explicitly, Lévi-Strauss acknowledged Boas's work as prefiguring structuralism. Lévi-Strauss (Lévi-Strauss and Eribon 1991:39) is further indebted to Boas: "The Kwakiutl recipes gave me the key to certain mythological problems by revealing relationships of compatibility and incompatibility among foods, relationships that are not solely a question of taste." Boas's meticulousness in collecting seemingly trivial detail, which earned him the scorn of more "theoretical" Anglophone anthropologists, is utterly vindicated by a characteristically French juxtaposition of food and thought.

Northwest Coast ethnographic material played a paradigmatic role in Lévi-Strauss's research on mythology, art, and social organization. His ambitious program concerning the structural study of myths (1955a) was implemented for the first time in the analysis of a corpus of Tsimshian myths collected by Franz Boas. In *La geste d'Asdiwal* (1958c; *The Story of Asdiwal,* 1967) Lévi-Strauss brought to the fore different levels of meanings of the myth involving geographic context, techno-economic life, social organization, and worldview and analyzed the relationships between those levels while comparing different versions of the same myth (see also Lévi-Strauss 1985b:162; Seguin, this volume). The object of the experiment was to reveal the formal structures of myths. References to Northwest Coast mythic material are scattered in *Les mythologiques* (1964–71), notably in *L'Homme nu* (1971), in which Salish mythology offers a methodological interest to elicit transformation rules and structures.

The second example is Lévi-Strauss's deep interest in Northwest Coast art. In his famous article published in 1943, he evoked his emotion at discovering the Northwest Coast gallery at the National Museum of Natural History, which we imagine was also shared by his surrealist friends. Relying on Franz Boas and Leonard Adam, among other authors, Lévi-Strauss published in 1945 a comparative study on the split representation in Asia and America (1958b), a topic he lectured on the previous year at the New School for Social Research (Waldberg and Waldberg 1992:184–185, 203). Whereas Boas interpreted the split representation as the extension to flat surfaces of a technique appropriate to three-dimensional sculptures, Lévi-Strauss took this interpretation further and demonstrated that split representation has to do structurally with specific types of hierarchical societies in China and on the Northwest Coast.

Both mythology and art form the focus of *La voie des masques* (1975). Lévi-Strauss discussed the relationships between art (here, masks), social structure, and worldview. He insisted that "as is the case with myths, masks too, cannot be interpreted in and by themselves as separate objects" (Lévi-

Strauss 1982:12). He further noted "the social or religious functions assigned to the various types of masks, which we contrast in order to compare, have the same transformational relationship with each other as exists between the shaping, drawing, and coloring of the masks themselves when we look at them as material objects" (14). Lévi-Strauss demonstrated the above hypothesis in analyzing relations of opposition and correlation between the Salish Swaihwé and the Kwakiutl Xwexwe masks and Dzonoqwa masks on both plastic and semantic levels. These transformations are related to the old Boasian problems of diffusion and social organization.

Northwest Coast kinship systems do not come within elementary forms. In his research on complex structures of kinship, Lévi-Strauss introduced the notion of the "house," elaborated from Northwest Coast data. In the second edition of *La voie des masques* (1979), he reexamined the social organization of the Kwakiutl and applied the concept of the house, thus pointing out similarities between the *numaym* and medieval European houses, which he thought "would offer the key to resolving some of the enigmas we come up against when we try to understand the institutions of the Northwest" (Lévi-Strauss, this volume). He astutely defined the house as a moral person "holding an estate made up of both material and immaterial wealth, which perpetuates itself through the transmission of its name, its goods, and its titles down a real or imaginary line" (Lévi-Strauss 1982:174) in which descent and alliance are equally important and mutually substitutable as long as the house's estate is looked after.

Lévi-Strauss's influence on Northwest Coast research was probably at its climax in the 1970s, which saw the application of structuralist methodology in the domain of kinship, myth, ritual, and art (see Halpin, this volume). Although Lévi-Strauss is not quoted in Wilson Duff's *Images, Stone, B.C.* (1975), the author's quest for "inner meanings" of Northwest Coast images fed on "psychosexual theories of psychoanalyis" (Ames 1981:19) and also benefited from the structural system of oppositions as exemplified in Lévi-Strauss's works. Duff explicitly referred to Lévi-Strauss's method as demonstrated in *La voie des Masques* when he declared in his "Notes to myself": "I say images are structures. They are systems. They involved transformations. The transformations involve laws" (Duff 1996:212).

The most discussed text by Lévi-Strauss in Northwest Coast circles is probably *The Story of Asdiwal,* as shown by Margaret Seguin Anderson (this volume). Anderson recognizes that Lévi-Strauss's method is pertinent for the understanding of crucial issues pertaining to marriage and residence rules among the Tsimshian-speaking peoples and rightly criticizes certain field-workers' questioning Lévi-Strauss's mastery of the ethnographic literature. Conversely, she ironically remarks that the data they themselves relied on and the interpretations they gave were not without flaws.

As suggested by the title of this essay, the Northwest Coast has haunted French anthropology since the very beginning of the 20th century as shown by the works of Durkheim, Mauss, Davy, and Bataille. Another sign is provided by what could be considered as a mere editorial incident. In the *Dictionnaire de l'ethnologie et de l'anthropologie* (1991), one is struck by the fact that two of the biographies of anthropologists are linked in a remarkable way: Lévi-Strauss is both the "object" of an article by Jean Pouillon—one of the best analysts of French structuralism—and the author of the article devoted to Franz Boas. It is as if a continuity was established between the founding moment of the American cultural anthropology at the beginning of the 20th century and that of a French social anthropology, which, through Lévi-Strauss, inherited the Durkheimian and Maussian legacy, in turn, indebted to Northwest Coast ethnology. In giving a new status to the notion of *maison,* as the encounter between a Kwakiutl social organization trait and an old aristocratic European institution, Lévi-Strauss attested, in some way, to several decades of intellectual relationships between both American and French anthropologies.

Notes

Thanks are due to Michael Harkin and Sergei Kan for their support and constructive comments as well as for kindly correcting the "infelicities" in the text.
1. Mauss's idea to create a department of ethnology was thwarted by World War I. The idea was taken up again in 1924. The institute was run by Marcel Mauss, Paul Rivet (professor in anthropology at the Muséum national d'histoire naturelle and director of the Musée d'ethnographie du Trocadéro), and Lucien Lévy-Bruhl (professor in the history of modern philosophy at l'Université de Paris). Mauss's "Instructions" were published in the *Manuel d'ethnographie* (1947).
2. The goals of the institute were to co-ordinate the various teachings in ethnology in different institutions (Ecole pratique des hautes études, Muséum national d'histoire naturelle, Ecole nationale des langues orientales vivantes) as well as

to reunite the main anthropological knowledge in France so as to legitimate ethnology as a scientific and academic discipline (Jamin 1991).

3. In the 1930s Paul Coze was sent by Rivet to eastern Canada to gather a collection of objects; these were shown at the exhibit "Peaux-Rouges d'hier et d'aujourd'hui" (May 15–June 15, 1931). The same year a young woman, Ms. Dijour, undertook a linguistic field trip among the Thompson River Indians in British Columbia. She collected archeological and ethnographic artifacts and plant specimens that she donated to the museum in 1931 (*Bulletin du Musée d'ethnographie du Trocadéro* vol. 2:59, 61–63; vol. 3:28, 120–121). For more details on North American ethnographic artifacts in French collections see Mauzé 2000a. North American collections certainly cannot equal those gathered during the most famous expedition launched by the Musée du Trocadéro in Africa (Mission Dakar-Djibouti).

4. Barbeau also recommended Diamond Jenness, a former classmate of his at Oxford, as a member of the Canadian Artic Expedition.

5. For details on Beuchat's collaboration with Mauss see Fournier 1994:301–302.

6. Beuchat was first registered as a student of Marcel Mauss at the Ecole pratique des hautes études in 1901–2. Marius Barbeau, then a student at Oxford under R. R. Marett, attended Mauss's lectures during the years 1905–6, 1908–9, 1909–10 (Fournier 1994:299, 308).

7. Vimont left an unpublished journal (see Niaussat 1983).

8. Most of Pinart's collection is housed at the Musée de Boulogne-sur-mer (Rousselot 2001; Salabelle 2001), and some pieces remain in the collections of the Musée d'ethnographie du Trocadéro. Pinart acquired the mask from an antique dealer in Victoria in the summer of 1876 (Mauzé 2000c). It has been temporarily reunited (June 2000) with its twin mask from the Canadian Museum of Civilization, collected by I. W. Powell in Metlakatla in 1879.

9. This text was probably written in 1930 when Mauss was a candidate for election at the Collège de France (James and Allen 1998:29).

10. Durkheim reviewed two publications by Boas: *The Social Organization and the Secret Societies of the Kwakiutl* (1898–99) and *The Mind of the Primitive Man* (1909–12a).

11. The works discussed are those by Fewkes, Voth, Dorsey, Radin, Kroeber, Fletcher and La Flesche, Boas, Teit, Swanton, and Bogoraz. These were published in the following journals: *Reports of the British Association for the Advancement of Science,* the *Reports, Bulletins and Memoirs of the U.S. National Museum and the Bureau of American Ethnology, Reports of the Jesup North Expedition, American Anthropologist,* and *Popular Science Monthly.*

12. For a complete list of Mauss's reviews see Fournier 1994:770–795.

13. For a critique of Durkheim's theory on totemism see, for example, Lukes 1973: 455–465, 478–484. See earlier comments by Goldenweiser (1975) and Richard (1975). Conversely, see review of Goldenweiser's seminal essay on totemism (1910) by Durkheim (1909–12b:100–101). Durkheim underestimated Goldenweiser's attempt to move totemism away from an evolutionary perspective to inscribe it in what Shapiro calls a "proto-structural view of totemism" (1991: 600). However, Durkheim accepted Goldenweiser's definition of totemism as "the tendency of definite social units to become associated with objects and symbols of emotional value," or "Totemism is the specific socialization of emotional values." Goldenweiser wrote later that the emotional values "constitute the content of totemism" and the specific socialization, "the form" (1918:280). For a wider overview of Northwest Coast totemism in the anthropological literature see Mauzé 1998b.

14. Barbeau's thesis was prepared under R. Marett's supervision. In a letter written in French to Mauss dated June 23, 1910, Barbeau wrote: "Vous vous souvenez sans doute que c'est vous qui avez suggéré ce sujet" (1910a; You no doubt remember that it's you who suggested this topic).

15. The potlatch is scarcely mentioned in Mauss's reviews except for Swanton's publications on the Tlingits and the Haidas (1906–9) and Boas's "The Kwakiutl of Vancouver Island" (1909–12). In the latter review Mauss was especially interested in the juridical aspect of the rules governing the invitation of guests to feasts.

16. For reference to cited works see the collection of texts reunited by Victor Karady in Mauss 1969 (29–103). See also Fournier 1994; Lévi-Strauss 1987b; Tarot 1999.

17. Mauss noted: "Our survey is necessarily incomplete. We make an abstraction from a large number of tribes, principally the following: Nootka, Bella Coola, Salish tribes of the Southern coast" (Mauss 1967:99n103).

18. See Fournier 1994 for an analysis of the political context in which the essay was written and especially an examination of Mauss's socialist views, his interest in the cooperative movement, and other economic alternatives to a capitalist economy. See also Godelier 1996.

19. Some 70 years later Firth wrote: "In his Essai sur le don he had taken a Maori text as the pivot of his argument about reciprocity in the gift. But I felt he did not really understand the Maori, and in fact he glossed one word of the text quite wrongly. The Maori elder spoke of a gift having an immaterial essence which demanded a proper return. Mauss misread this as implying that part of the personality of the giver was involved" (James and Allen 1998:23).

20. Letter dated March 26, 1926. Boas wrote to Mauss: "My dear Dr. M. Mauss: I received this morning a copy of 'L'année sociologique' with your interesting in-

vestigation for which I wish to thank you most cordially. I hope we may have an opportunity to discuss the matter when you are here" (Archives M. Mauss, Collège de France).

21. Mauss, Davy, and Lenoir's research is taken into consideration by Goldman (1975:128–130). Recent exceptions are Kan 1989b and Harkin 1997a. I am not including myself (Mauzé 1986) because of my French intellectual background. An overview of the literature on the potlatch shows that Mauss's essay is rarely referenced in American anthropological research. Codere (1950) never acknowledged Mauss although she did remark that the potlatch equates a war of property. The exceptions are Alan Dundes (1979:395) and Suttles and Jonaitis (1990: 85). Irvin (1977) is right when he points out that Stuart Piddocke (1965), without quoting Mauss, develops a similar view to that of Mauss. Piddocke writes: "The potlatch had no one essential function, but several. . . . The potlatch was, in fact, the linch-pin of the entire system" (1965:258). *The Gift* has become a required reading in a number of leading American and Canadian graduate programs in anthropology since the 1970s (Kan, personal communication, August 2001).

22. Mauss's theory on exchange and the potlatch is being continually reassessed. The latest examples are Godelier (1996) and Testart (1998). Godelier pays homage to Mauss's work and re-evaluates the French sociologist's interpretations of classical forms of "total social fact," primarily the *hau,* the potlatch, and the kula. Godelier focuses on two categories of objects he claims to apply to a general configuration of exchange, that is, things than can be given or traded and things that cannot be given or traded, the most important of the latter being sacred objects, such as Coppers on the Northwest Coast. Testart questions the universality of reciprocity in gift giving. In his critique of Mauss's use of Northwest Coast data he examines the question of enslavement for debts (for which the information is rather scarce) and attempts to demonstrate that in the potlatch failing to return gifts entails a social sanction but not a legal one. Issues raised by Testart are somehow rather foreign to those usually tackled by field anthropologists.

23. Davy's dissertation relied on data gathered by Mauss. Unable to attend the defense, Mauss was critical on a few points. He thought the analysis superficial and the information insufficient. Davy's dissertation gave rise to a controversial debate initiated by Marcel Granet, who replaced Mauss on the examining committee, and Raymond Lenoir (1924), another student of Mauss's. See Besnard 1985; Fournier 1994:486–487. In *The Gift* Mauss acknowledges Davy's work only to mention that he himself analyses the potlatch from a wider perspective (Mauss

1967:36–37). Lenoir (1924) insisted on the religious connections between potlatch, warfare, and winter ceremonies (see Goldman 1975:128).

24. Métraux and Bataille used to walk up and down rue de Rennes, where Bataille
    lived. Bataille was thrilled at Métraux telling him about Kwakiutl chiefs destroy-
    ing great mounts of property to smash their rivals and increase their prestige
    (see Mauzé 1987).

STRUCTURALISM AT THE UNIVERSITY OF BRITISH COLUMBIA, 1969 ONWARD

Pierre Maranda

Context

Claude Lévi-Strauss's structuralism made a strong impact in European and American universities already in the early 1960s. At that time several of his papers published in English became required readings in Oxford and Cambridge as well as at Harvard and in departments of anthropology in other universities. Actually *Tristes Tropiques* (1955b), *Anthropologie structurale* (1958a), and *Le totémisme aujourd'hui* (1962b) were all published in English in 1963, followed by *La pensée sauvage* (1962a) in 1966. In 1963 Douglas Oliver at Harvard, in conjunction with Rodney Needham in Oxford, took the initiative to have *Les structures élémentaires de la parenté* (1949) translated into English (1969b). Paperback editions of those titles became available soon after the hardcovers and were widely read in American and other Anglophone universities.

Anthropology at the University of British Columbia

Structuralism was implemented in the Department of Anthropology and Sociology at the University of British Columbia in the fall of 1969. The head of the department, Cyril Belshaw, had recruited new faculty who had already contributed structural analyses: Brenda Beck, Michael Egan, myself, and, a year later, my late wife, Elli Köngäs Maranda. Upon our arrival the program committee set up undergraduate courses and graduate seminars in structural anthropology, in which, obviously, the works of Claude Lévi-Strauss figured prominently. Students flocked to learn about what they perceived as the best approach to dynamically "x-ray" live and thus moving social facts without pinning them down in the manner butterfly collectors stock their catches (to use Edmund Leach's metaphor to uphold structuralism).

Structuralist momentum built up: it generated M.A. theses, Ph.D. dissertations, informal extracurricular regular meetings where faculty and students together took up topics on which structuralism could contribute fresh views. American colleagues, mainly from the states of Oregon and Washington, traveled up the coast to participate in those meetings. Interactions with Amerindians also developed in that context, and Lévi-Strauss engaged in them when he came to British Columbia.

I had the privilege and joy of seeing Lévi-Strauss accept two invitations to the department in 1973 and in 1974. He gave a well-attended high-level seminar in the framework of which several colleagues and advanced students presented papers. The National Film Board of Canada had a team follow Lévi-Strauss for three weeks, the outcome of which was the film *Behind the Masks*. This documentary shows Lévi-Strauss doing such things as interviewing an Indian totem-pole carver and analyzing masks in the Victoria Museum. The main component of the film consists of his giving a very lively lecture to a specialized audience at the university. Actually, it offers a masterful presentation of the main axis of *La voie des masques* (1975). Unused footage—the leftover sequences after the editing process—should be available from the National Film Board if someone wished to use the film as complementary data on Lévi-Strauss in British Columbia. Another notorious event was a public lecture that Lévi-Strauss gave at the university. It attracted such a large crowd that it overflowed the big auditorium where it had been scheduled and had to be broadcast simultaneously in other halls on the campus to accommodate the unexpectedly high number of people who had come to hear him.

Several publications singled out UBC structuralism as a strong pole in social anthropology, such as papers delivered in international conferences as well as publications by faculty members, especially Brenda Beck and Michael Egan (see Beck 1972, 1978a, 1978b, 1982), by me (Maranda 1971, 1972a, 1972b; Maranda, ed., 1972, 1974, 1978), by my wife and me (Maranda and Maranda 1970, 1971, 1974a, 1974b; Maranda and Maranda, eds., 1971), and by graduate students such as Dominique Legros (1978), Carol McLaren (1978), David Moyer (1978), David Turner (1978), John Leroy, Robert Tonkinson, and Éric Schwimmer (1967, 1969a, 1969b, 1970, 1973, 1978). Other UBC advanced graduate students published structuralist chapters in a book I edited, *Soviet Structural Folkloristics* (1974): Wolfgang Jilek with Louise Jilek-Aall (1974), Susan Reid (1974), and Monique Layton (1974); this chapter was quoted by the newspaper *Le Monde*. And structural analysis expanded beyond anthropology, namely in political science with Laponce (1981).

When at UBC I edited, with my wife, *Structural Analysis of Oral Tradition* (1971), containing as its first chapter "The Deduction of the Crane" by Lévi-Strauss and contributions by such well-known scholars as Edmund Leach, Dell Hymes, Victor Turner, A. J. Greimas, and Roberto Da Matta. In the same year my wife and I coauthored *Structural Models in Folklore and Transformational Essays,* a book that was devoted to the investigation and applications of Lévi-Strauss's canonical formula for the analysis of myth and that was translated into German, Hungarian, and Russian. Actually, the formula stirred up much interest among the students and incited them to rethink the epistemology of modeling in anthropology. I should mention a recent spin-off of that book: *The Double Twist: From Ethnography to Morphodynamics* (Maranda, ed., 2001), which opens with a chapter by Lévi-Strauss ("Hourglass Figures"). The ten chapters of the book all focus on the canonical formula through an interdisciplinary convergence (social anthropology, of course, and classics, computer science, logic, mathematics, philosophy, and morphodynamics).

Salish Amerindians—some of whom Lévi-Strauss met both in the context of a Winter Dance and in individual encounters—were enthusiastic partners of structural studies. We worked together on the analysis of their myths in cooperation with the British Columbia Indian Languages Project headed by the linguist Randy Bouchard. One of the outcomes of that synergy consisted of a large computerized corpus of Salish and Okanagan myths, a view of which can be found in Maranda, Taylor, and Flynn (1984).

When my wife and I accepted offers from Université Laval and moved from Vancouver to my native Québec City in 1975, colleagues carried on structuralism at UBC and continued interacting with us and colleagues at Université Laval (Bernard Saladin d'Anglure, Bernard Arcand, Éric Schwimmer, who was professor of anthropology at the University of Toronto before joining us at Laval, and Yvan Simonis) and at the Université de Montréal (among them, Rémi Savard, Jean-Claude Müller, and Pierre Boudon). Joined by others, we produced a special issue of the Canadian journal *Anthropologica* (1978) in honor of Lévi-Strauss's 70th birthday, entitled *L'Appropriation sociale de la logique.*

And how about structuralism in 2001? Enthusiastic prepublication reviews of *The Double Twist* suggest that Lévi-Straussian anthropology moves ahead in a powerful way. Actually, I was repeatedly told by younger colleagues in international anthropological meetings over the last few years,

> "Structuralism is coming back! That's the only way out of the postmodernist aporia."

> "We are shaking off the obscurantism of postmodernism and are rediscovering Lévi-Strauss. Good for us!"

> "Structuralism is back, and strong. And Lévi-Strauss is where it's at."

LÉVI-STRAUSSIAN STRUCTURALISM
ON THE NORTHWEST COAST

Marjorie Myers Halpin

In this chapter I review the milestones in Claude Lévi-Strauss's application of structuralist methodology to the anthropology of the Northwest Coast and look at the work of others who have participated in the Lévi-Straussian tradition.[1] Finally, I consider why there have been so few.

A Brief Sketch of Lévi-Straussian Anthropology

One of the pleasures of doing this research and now presenting it in France was re-encountering the charming story Lévi-Strauss tells about the social ceremony he witnessed among strangers in cheap restaurants in the south of France. The patrons sit together at a long communal table, where each finds beside his plate a bottle of wine. Before the meal each man pours his wine into his neighbor's glass. Wine offered calls for wine returned, followed by conversation. Society appears where there was none before.

In *The Elementary Structures of Kinship* (1969a),[2] the first major work in structural anthropology and the founding work of alliance theory, Lévi-Strauss links social reciprocity to the prohibition of incest:

> Exchange . . . is from the first a total exchange, comprising food, manu-
> factured objects, and that most precious category of goods, women.
> Doubtless we are a long way from the strangers in the restaurant, and
> perhaps it will seem startling, to suggest that the reluctance of the south-
> ern French peasant to drink from his own flask of wine provides the
> model by which the prohibition of incest might be explained. Clearly
> the prohibition does not result from this reluctance. Nevertheless, we
> believe that both are phenomenon of the same type, that they are ele-
> ments of the same cultural complex, or more exactly the basic complex
> of culture. (Henaff 1998:48)

The exchange of women produces alliances, the cornerstone of culture, and brings with it all manner of other reciprocities, of gifts and counter-gifts, by which cultures are maintained. In other words, "the incest prohibition is . . . the basis of human society; in a sense it *is* the society" (Lévi-Strauss 1976:19).

Whatever form the incest prohibition takes in a specific culture, it has a unique nature due to two elements that remain the same: "(1) it is a universal prohibition; and (2) it is defined by a rule of reciprocity" (Henaff 1998:46–47). Lévi-Strauss's (1969a:123) solution to the problem of cross-cousin marriage — which he calls the "veritable *experimentum crucis* in the study of marriage prohibitions" — demonstrates how the two are connected. His answer to the question why cross-cousin marriage is favored and parallel-cousin marriage prohibited in a wide range of societies is the demonstration that the former is simply marriage by exchange or reciprocity.[3]

The basis of all structural analysis is a shift from terms to relationships between them. In alliance theory the simplest structure, the "atom of kinship," is the quadripartite system of relationships between brother and sister, husband and wife, father and son, and maternal uncle and nephew (Lévi-Strauss 1976:84). This in turn rests upon the incest taboo, which amounts to saying that a man must obtain a woman from another man who gives him a daughter or a sister. At the heart of both matrilineal and patrilineal systems stands the avunculate, the relationship between uncle and nephew. To the system of relationships he adds a system of attitudes that he describes as follows: "the system of basic attitudes comprises at least four terms: an attitude of affection, tenderness, and spontaneity; an attitude which results from the reciprocal exchange of prestations and counterprestations; and, in addition to these, two unilateral relationships, one which corresponds to the attitude of the creditor, the other to that of the debtor. In other words there are: mutuality (=), reciprocity (±), rights (+), and obligations (−)" (1963a:47). He also formulates a predictive structural law: "the relation between maternal uncle and nephew is to the relation between brother and sister as the relation between father and son is to the relation between husband and wife. Thus if we know one pair of relations, it is always possible to infer the other" (40). As Ino Rossi (1982:7) summarized this idea, "since this structural relationship remains always operative, no matter what the principle of descent is, it must be considered as a more fundamental explanatory principle than the principal of descent."

Following his work on marriage rules, Lévi-Strauss turned in 1950 to the study of New World mythologies to more clearly demonstrate that the universality he revealed in kinship analysis is that of the unconscious human mind itself. Unconscious, that is, as the operations of language are unconscious: "for it is linguistics and most particularly structural linguistics, which has since familiarized us with the idea that the fundamental phenomena of mental life, the phenomena that condition it and determine its most general forms, are located on the plane of unconscious thinking" (Lévi-Strauss 1987b:35). This unconscious, moreover, is not a content but a form.[4] "As the organ of a specific function, the unconscious merely imposes structural laws upon inarticulated elements which originate elsewhere—impulses, emotions, representations, and memories" (1963a:203).

As Lévi-Strauss puts it, "Starting from a binary opposition, which affords the simplest possible example of a system . . . construction [of a myth] proceeds by the aggregation, at each of the two poles, of new terms. Chosen because they stand in relations of opposition, correlation, or analogy to it. It does not, however, follow from this that the relations in question have to be homogeneous. Each 'local' logic exists in its own right" (1963b:161).

In *Totemism* (1963b) and *The Savage Mind* (1966b), which can be considered prologues to the *Mythologiques*, Lévi-Strauss examines such local logics, which he calls "the science of the concrete," as systems of classification based on sensible properties. He also defines the *bricoleur*, the mythic handyman who works with whatever detritus from earlier projects is at hand. According to him, "It might be said that the engineer questions the universe, while the 'bricoleur' addresses himself to a collection of oddments left over from human endeavors" (1966b:19).

The significant images of myth, the materials of the *bricoleur*, are elements that can be defined by two criteria: they have *had a use*, as words in a piece of discourse that mythical thought "detaches" in the same way as a *bricoleur*, in the course of repairing them, detaches the cogwheels of an old alarm clock; and *they can be used again*, either for the same purpose or for a different one if they are at all diverted from their previous functions (1966b:35). This logic works rather like a kaleidoscope, an instrument that also contains bits and pieces by means of which structural patterns are realized (36).

Due to the flexibility of what Lévi-Strauss calls the "species operator," so-called totemic classifications, classifications that "are not only thought but lived" (1963b:66), are especially widespread. In his view, "The differences between animals, which man can extract from nature and transfer to culture . . . are adopted as emblems by groups of men in order to do away with their own resemblances" (107). He calls them "medial classifiers."

In 1958 Lévi-Strauss published "La geste d'Asdiwal" (translated into English in 1967), undoubtedly the best-known and most controversial analysis of a myth ever published. The story of Asdiwal is not a fully developed structural analysis but a demonstration of (1) how various codes — geographic, economic, sociological, cosmological — are transformations of an underlying structure, and (2) how different versions of a myth from the Tsimshian-speaking people reflect economic differences between the peoples of the Nass and Skeena Valleys.

But Aswidal was just a taste of what was to come. Beginning his astounding four-volume *Mythologiques* in 1964 with the Bororo in South America, Lévi-Strauss traces mythic oppositions, constants, and transformations through more than 800 myths (almost twice that number if variants are taken into account).[5] His methodology is precise, his use of the existing ethnographic record meticulous. "I propose to give the name *armature*," he writes (1969b:199), "to a combination of properties that remain invariant in two or several myths; *code*[6] to the pattern of functions ascribed by each myth to these properties; and *message* to the subject matter of an individual myth." In volume 1 of the *Mythologiques* Lévi-Strauss demonstrates how in mythic transformations between a Bororo myth and a Sherente myth, "[as] we move from one to another, the armature remains constant, the code is changed, and the message is reversed" (199). Although one can do a structuralist analysis of myths from a single culture or culture area, the method demands crossing cultural boundaries to discover the transformations that more readily reveal mythic structures. "Since the purpose of myth is to provide a logical model capable of overcoming a contradiction (an impossible achievement if, as it happens, the contradiction is real), a theoretically infinite number of slates [variants] will be generated, each one slightly different from the others. Thus myth grows spiral-wise until the intellectual impulse which has produced it is exhausted" (Lévi-Strauss 1966b:226). "We need only assume that two opposite terms with no intermediary always tend to be replaced by two equivalent terms which admit of a third one as a mediator; then one of the polar terms and the mediator become replaced by a new triad, and so on" (221).

In other words, all myths are transformations of other myths, or as he puts it, "A group of myths must never be interpreted alone, but by reference . . . to other groups of myths" (1976:65). Tracing mythic transformations throughout the Americas, he arrives in volume 4 at the coastal Northwest Coast region from south of the Oregon River to beyond the Fraser River (the "Oregonian area"), six thousand miles away. Here he finds a "mythological microcosm which contains, in a condensed form, all of the major themes broached since the beginning of my inquiry." It is on the southern Northwest Coast that he "extracts the quintessential mythic formula" (1981a:564): the "one myth only," "the fundamental theme behind all these myths" — the problem of the origin of fire (589). In Lévi-Strauss's words, this rounds off his analysis of a vast system, the invariant elements of which can be represented in the form of a conflict between the earth and the sky for the possession of fire (598). He concludes by stating: "In the last resort, there is only one absolutely undecidable sequence. . . . When reduced to its essential features through a series of transformations, this sequence boils down to the expression of an opposition. . . . there is the sky and there is the earth; between the two there can be no conceivable parity; consequently, the presence on earth of that celestial phenomenon, fire, is a mystery; since celestial fire is now present here below on the domestic hearth, it must have been brought down from the sky by an expedition which went up from the earth to fetch it" (602).

In the 1970s Lévi-Strauss turned his attention to the plastic arts in *La voie des masques* (1975), translated into English as *The Way of the Masks* in 1982. Questioning the strange form and appendages of the Coast Salish Swaixwey mask, he writes: "I was unable to answer any of these questions until I realized that, as is the case with myths, masks, too, cannot be interpreted in and by themselves as separate objects" (1982:12). In his view they had to be returned to their transformational set to discover the echoes of the other forms that they transform. As he puts it, "My hypothesis, then, which extends to works of art (which, however, are more than works of art), a method validated in the study of myths (which are also works of art), will be proven right if, in the last analysis, we can perceive, between the origin myths for each type of mask, transformational relations homologous to those that, from a purely plastic point of view, prevail among the masks themselves" (14). On the structuralist assumption that the Swaixwey can be understood only when another mask can be found whose purpose is to contradict it, Lévi-Strauss finds its opposite in the Kwakwaka'wakw Dzonokwa mask and its mediating form in the Kwakwaka'wakw Kwekwe. In a breathtaking synthesis of Northwest Coast myths, art, social organization, and geography, he then weaves a dense fabric of transformational themes from throughout the region. The "canonical formula" for the relationship discovered first with the Swaixwey, Kwekwe, and Dzonokwa is as follows: "*When from one group to another, the plastic form is preserved, the semantic function is reversed* [Kwekwe]. *On the other hand, when the semantic function is retained, it is the plastic form that is inverted* [Dzonokwa]" (1982:93; my emphasis).

There's more, of course, a lot more. But I think that the texts reviewed and cited here are the major contributions of Claude Lévi-Strauss to the anthropology of the Northwest Coast.

Northwest Coast Anthropology in the Lévi-Straussian Tradition

Surprisingly few anthropologists have published structural analyses in the Lévi-Straussian tradition using Northwest Coast materials. In this section I present brief synopses of their analyses as well as those of several others whose claim to be using a structural methodology I reject. Their work is instructive of the way Lévi-Strauss's method is misunderstood and misused.

Marriage

The major work on Northwest Coast marriage to couch itself in structuralist terms was Abraham Rosman and Paula Rubel's *Feasting with Mine Enemy: Rank and Exchange among Northwest Coast Societies* (1971). Here they write: "Our method in developing these structural models has been to follow the procedures used by Lévi-Strauss in *The Elementary Structures of Kinship.*" The originality of their approach was to organize their study of six Northwest Coast societies around answers to the questions "Who does one potlatch to? Who is present?" (Answer: "one potlatches to one's affines.") The authors then attempt to account for variations in potlatches according to marriage preferences. They argue, contra Lévi-Strauss (1976:191–194), that both the Haidas and Tlingits prefer a patrilateral cross-cousin marriage, a pattern that he claims produces a weaker social integration than the matrilateral preference.[7]

This issue is logically resolved for the Tsimshian by John Dunn (1984). Dunn reexamines the accepted notion of four exogamous matrilineal groups (*phratries* or *clans* to anthropologists, *tribes* to Native speakers). Based on more recent fieldwork in Coast Tsimshian and Gitksan villages (Adams 1973; Dunn and Dunn 1972), he discovers an older pattern in which only two groups are present in any village, in a pattern corresponding to the inter-ethnic moieties of other North Coast cultures. The quadripartite structure of Metlakatla and Port Simpson were postcontact developments arising out of the amalgamations of people from older villages. However, Dunn discovered another quadripartite structure, one that is egocentric or relative rather than sociocentric or absolute. For the Coast Tsimshian this structure consists of one's own house, inside versus outside, and in terms of one's crest, of (1) one's own side of one's house, (2) the unrelated ("other") side of one's house, (3) one's own tribe of another house, and (4) the unrelated (Dunn 1984:41–42).

A key term in the kinship system, especially as it relates to property distributions following death, is *grandfather,* which connotes both "ancestor" and reciprocal of "cousin grandchild," or "cousin grandfather" (Dunn 1984:43). This also has significant implications for the old debate about marriage preference. In Dunn's words, "no matter how families may contrive marriage [matrilateral or patrilateral cross-cousin], the purpose of grandchild inheritance is incompatible with any attempt to retain property exclusively in any kin group. On the contrary, the purpose of grandchild inheritance is the redistribution of wealth throughout the quadripartite village division. This must be the case since any combination of cross-cousin or non-lateral marriage will result in the presence of inheritor grandchildren in each of the four village divisions" (52).

Myth

I found only two structural studies of Northwest Coast myths in a Lévi-Straussian manner by other anthropologists: Allan Jensen and Martine Reid.[8]

Allan Jensen's "A Structural Approach to the Tsimshian Raven Myths: Lévi-Strauss on the Beach" (1980) analyzes five Tsimshian Trickster myths collected by Franz Boas. Using the Lévi-Straussian method quite scrupulously, Jensen (62–63) finds both an "invariant" armature and "basic constant message" revealed through different codes—auditory, gustatory, tactile, visual, emotional—based on sensory experience. While he (163) discovers "many alterations of code and inversions of elementary detail . . . these changes simply augment one another. They do not alter a basic, constant message." This message is that "of the necessity of cultured beings, spirits or men, to observe social conventions."

In 1984 Martine Reid reported on her dissertation (1981), in which she analyzed in a Lévi-Straussian manner some 19 versions of the myth of the origin of the Hamatsa (Cannibal) ritual of Kwakwala speakers (Heiltsuk, Kwakwaka'wakw, Oweekeno, Haisla) through time—1897 to 1980. In the earlier versions her analysis follows Lévi-Straussian themes about the consequences of the irregular marriage of a young woman to the supernatural Cannibal and her return to her family bearing the dance privilege of his impersonation. However, after 1940, the myth loses the part that dealt with the girl and her marriage to the Cannibal. Also, whereas the 19th- and early-20th-century versions of the story dealt with an exclusively male privilege, the contemporary story legitimizes the privilege for women as well. That is, the changes shift the story from dealing with marriage to dealing with potlatch privileges.

Totemic Classification

In my 1973 doctoral dissertation (see Halpin 1984) I analyze Tsimshian totemism using Lévi-Straussian notions about classification developed in *The Savage Mind* (1966b). Basing my study on some 750 crest names and descriptions culled from museum documentation and the Marius Barbeau and William Beynon field notes, I find the category of the "totemic operator" especially useful. Plant and animal species are admirably suited as logical vehicles because of their "intermediate position as logically equidistant from the extreme forms of classification: categorical and singular" (Lévi-Strauss 1966b:149). Being thus a "medial classifier," the species concept can widen its referent upward in the direction of associated elements (e.g., sky/earth) and categories (high/low), or contract it downward in the direction of proper names. The totemic operator thus suggests logical movement or connection between the concrete and individual on the one hand and the abstract and categorical on the other. I was also able to add to the horizontal axis of totemism (the differences between species corresponding to the differences between social groups) characteristic of the Haida and Tlingit systems, a uniquely Tsimshian vertical axis that expresses differences in rank.

Masks

Lévi-Strauss's *The Way of the Masks* was followed by only two other structural examinations of Northwest Coast masks: David Penney's 1981 analysis of Nootka Wild Man and Rosman and Rubel's 1990 study of Kwakwaka'wakw masks.

Penney analyzes Nuu-chah-nulth (Nootka) "wild man" masks in ethnographic records and museum collections and finds considerable variability, including both plastic and semantic echoes in Kwakwaka'wakw masks. He writes that "each one of these masks seems to be defined, reciprocally, by what another is not" (1981:100). What is surprising is that within this set there are indications of the emergence of structural contrasts reminiscent of those Lévi-Strauss noted between the far more polarized concepts of Ts'onoqoa and Xwaexwae (107). Penney postulates that structural contrasts evolved gradually, becoming more pronounced over time: "The ethnographic record can be read as pointing to a historical and sociological process in which structural oppositions would become progressively sharper over time. In other words, the variants of the forest-spirit masquerade tradition grew apart through the development of more and more terms of contrast."

Rosman and Rubel (1990) compare and contrast Kwakwaka'wakw masks from the Baxus (secular) and Tsetsequa (sacred) seasons of the ceremonial year. In the Baxus season, dancers dramatize family histories in which ancestors are the descendants of supernatural animals. In the Tsetsequa, dancers enact the relationship between humans and secret society spirits. They find that "stylistic elements characteristic of each of the two sets can be paired. Thus, one stylistic element of a *baxus* piece may be paired with another stylistic element in the piece in the *tsetsequa* realm with which it corresponds" (1990:621). In brief, the Baxus animals are naturalistic, while the Tsetsequa are "fabulous." Although they write that "in our analysis, we shall adopt a structuralist perspective derived from the work of Lévi-Strauss" (620), their "analysis" consists merely of identifying Baxus and Tsetsequa pairs from Audrey Hawthorn's *Kwakiutl Art* (1979). This kind of empirical procedure bears no relationship to Lévi-Strauss's methodology that I can recognize.

Other Material Culture Studies

Two eminent anthropologists working with Northwest Coast materials, Wilson Duff (1975, 1981) and George MacDonald (1981), also claim "structuralist" status, although it must be said that their work is merely Lévi-Straussian in ideology since neither engage the detailed ethnographic materials necessary to the Lévi-Straussian method. In the first of his "structural" texts Duff (1975:12) refers to his own work as "anthropology with a great deal of artistic licence" and as "my most audacious imaginings" (13). In the same volume with Duff's (1981) second and posthumous structuralist text George MacDonald (1981:225) writes that "[Duff] was intrigued by the structuralist approach . . . in that it confirmed his own conclusions about the consummate logic inherent in various Northwest Coast cultural forms," and cites the following passage: "Myth, like art, seems to have as its hidden agenda the problem of coming to terms with the terrible dilemmas of the human condition. As Lévi-Strauss has taught us, the provisional answers lie in the logic implicit in the resolution of the myths" (Duff 1975:57).

Duff is not dealing here with the ethnographic "local" logics explored by the Lévi-Straussian method; his "terrible dilemmas of the human condition" are universal existential problems, "our" problems, notably sex and death. As he puts it, "Art seems to deal with that which is terrifying and that which is taboo, and it does it in the guise of dealing with that which is familiar and controllable. We penetrate its guises at our own peril, and most of the time, the best common sense is not to try. But the terrifying and the taboo — in a word, the sacred — will not be ignored, and it seems to be the mission of great artists to show us how to come to terms with them" (1975:56).

In his second structuralist text Duff (1981:210) expands his argument, using historic as well as the prehistoric artifacts of the first and employing a more precise vocabulary, including a Lévi-Straussian concept of *armature*, adapted to visual forms. In his words, "Armatures are the structural relationships between symbols. They are the ways of making visual equations. They are the predicates of statements in which symbols are the subjects. They are the inner structures of images" (210). Duff goes on to say that he wants to move beyond the accepted ideas of images in the Northwest Coast—art as either spirits or crests or "pure" design—to reveal deeper, hidden agendas at work. These principally concern sexual imagery, which is surprisingly absent from historic Northwest Coast artifacts. According to him, "sexual symbolism is so important in the arts of the world and elsewhere that I feel its virtual absence on the surface of Northwest Coast art permits us to suspect that we might find it in metaphorical forms below the surface" (214). Which he does. And once again, he asserts that this level of symbolism is both sacred and taboo: "For the art is also about being human; ultimately, about those aspects of being human which are the most sacred and therefore most repressed and tabooed" (210).

Lévi-Strauss met Duff several times and recalls giving him "logical" and "technical" answers to two questions about the meaning of masks, the latter in a letter in which he suggested that Duff look into Tsimshian mythology for representations about the meaning of stone. In Lévi-Strauss's words, "Wilson Duff never answered my letter. Once again, I had probably disappointed him by offering him an explanation that was too simple for the great mysteries his soul was seeking" (1981b:260).

In his "Cosmic Equations in Northwest Coast Indian Art," archaeologist George MacDonald (1981) mentions Lévi-Strauss by name some ten times, which certainly implies commonalities in their approaches to Northwest Coast cultures. This impression is dispelled when MacDonald refers to "the shared concepts of a shamanic cosmology that are becoming apparent throughout the New World . . . [and] which provides the basis for cultures to influence each other in covert, often secret, exchanges between ritual specialists" (220). MacDonald then reviews, without citing any literature, the "fundamental concepts of a shamanic cosmology" (221): "The shaman, as the key intermediary between man and the cosmos, is a microcosm which must be completely harmonized with the powers of the macrocosm to be effective" (227). He then applies this shamanic framework to the arts of the Northwest Coast. Although not universalist in the same way as Duff, MacDonald's undocumented notion of a shared shamanic cosmology stretching from Siberia through the Americas generates an analysis that is the antithesis of Lévi-Straussian structuralism.

Unfortunately both Duff and MacDonald may have fueled the suspicion of English and North American empiricists that structuralism is more mystical than methodological.

Conclusion

So, I discovered only five structural studies by anthropologists (other than Claude Lévi-Strauss) using materials from the Northwest Coast: Rosman and Rubel, Martine Reid, Jensen, Halpin, and Dunn. One reason, as Kronenfeld and Decker (1979:536) have also concluded, is that "structuralist anthropology proved to be too hard to do."

Our examination of the literature has convinced us that structural analysis has been little done in American and British anthropology. Most of what one sees are either works of Lévi-Strauss himself or discussions of his work. Lévi-Strauss himself has discussed the difficulties of his method. In "The Structural Study of Myth" (1955a and 1963a:215) he deals with the problem of coding all the variants of a myth, stating, "we have seen that the structural analysis of *one* variant of *myth one* belonging to *one* tribe (in some cases, even *one* village) already requires two dimensions. When we use several variants of the same myth from the same tribe or village, the frame of reference becomes three-dimensional, and as soon as we try to enlarge the comparison, the number of dimensions required increases until it appears quite impossible to handle them intuitively." And in an interview with Didier Eribon (1988:4), he said:

> I began work on mythology in 1950 and I finished Mythologiques in 1970. For twenty years, rising at dawn, drunk with myths, I really lived in another world . . . these myths appear first of all as puzzles. They tell stories without head or tail, full of absurd incidents. One has to "hatch" the myths for days, weeks, sometimes months, before suddenly a spark bursts out, and in some inexplicable detail in a myth, one recognizes a transformation of some inexplicable detail in another myth, so that by this expedient they can be brought together as a unity. Each detail in itself need mean nothing; it is in their differential relationships that their intelligibility is to be found.

Globally, Lévi-Strauss's influence on scholarship in the social sciences and arts has been profound and unparalleled. Locally on the Northwest Coast, anthropologists necessarily work within the political context of Native interpretations and explanations. This has implications for the kind of anthropology we do here that go beyond the decline of structuralism, which was itself wounded by the political events of May 1968 in Paris.[9] In his Massey Lectures on CBC Radio Lévi-Strauss (1995:41) compared an older anthropology using mythic materials with more recent books by Chiefs Walter Wright (1962) and Ken Harris (1974) based on the *adaawk* (family histories) of their respective Houses among the Canyon Tsimshian and Gitksan:

> What is misleading in the old anthropological accounts is that a kind of hodge-podge was made up of traditions and beliefs belonging to a great many different social groups. This makes us lose sight of a fundamental character of the material — that each type of story belongs to a given group, a given family, a given lineage, or to a given clan, and is trying to explain its fate, which can be a successful one or a disastrous one, or be intended to account for rights and privileges as they exist in the present, or be attempting to validate claims for rights that have since disappeared.

In the 1990s anthropologists were increasingly contracted by First Nations to write their histories. Although I do not have time here to elaborate on particular instances, it does lead me to a concern that when anthropologists work for Native groups, their claims to objectivity can be compromised by political loyalties and realities. Perhaps all that is needed in such cases is a statement of personal situatedness on the part of the anthropologists. Perhaps we should all celebrate the shift in power relations between Natives and anthropologists that this reflects. At the very least we need to recognize publicly what is happening.

Lévi-Strauss (1995:43), writing before anthropologists began writing history for and with Natives, considered the books by Chiefs Harris and Wright to be "continuation[s]" of mythology and, as such, both equally "true" or "valid" (41–42). What about the Native histories, or myths if you will, co-constructed by anthropologists?

Notes

Marjorie Halpin's manuscript has been edited by volume editors Michael Harkin, Sergei Kan, and Marie Mauzé.

1. I am considering only published works.
2. *The Elementary Structures* was Lévi-Strauss's doctoral dissertation and was writ-

ten during his exile in New York in the 1940s, but it was not translated into English until 1969.

3. Assume there are two patrilineal groups, x and y. If a man of x marries a woman of y, their children will be x, as will the man's brother's children, their parallel cousins. But if the man's sister, who is also x, marries a man from y, their children will be y as well, and cross-cousins to the first man's x children. A marriage between cross-cousins is, therefore, exogamous (marriage out of the group), while a marriage between parallel cousins is endogamous (marriage within the group), establishing no exchange or alliance.

4. This is very different from the Freudian unconscious: "The unconscious ceases to be the ultimate haven of individual peculiarities — the repository of a unique history which makes each of us an irreplaceable being. It is reducible to a function — the symbolic function, which no doubt is specifically human, and which is carried out according to the same laws among all men and actually corresponds to the aggregate of these laws" (Lévi-Strauss 1963b:202–203).

5. As Lévi-Strauss puts it, "We define the myth as consisting of all its versions" (Lévi-Strauss 1966b:213).

6. Sociological, economic, sensory, meteorological, astronomical, technological, etc.

7. Margaret Anderson recently reviewed issues raised by the original analysis of Asdiwal and subsequent criticisms, including challenges to Lévi-Strauss's conclusion that the Tsimshian preferred matrilateral cross-cousin marriage (see Anderson, this volume — Eds).

8. Dell Hymes used a couple of Lévi-Strauss concepts in 1982, although his analysis is more in the style of American cognitive structuralism than Lévi-Straussian structuralism. In the process of editing this chapter, the volume editors had asked Dell Hymes to provide additional comments on Halpin's statement. Here is what he wrote: "One criticism that can be made has to do with verbal detail. Hymes praises the work of Lévi-Strauss as indispensable, but sometimes open to alternative. On the one hand, only a double transformation, such as he employs, explains a myth told to Boas by the Kathlamet Chinook Charles Cultee. In Cultee's account, the Sun is a generous woman, who offers a chief who has come to her and her daughter continuing wealth. Yet he cannot resist a desire to have the shining thing she carries about the world each day. When he starts back to see his people again, he cannot be refused that thing, but is given an axe as well. In returning to his home, he destroys his own people, five villages in turn. Surely this account of destruction through hubris is a thinking through of the destruction of most of the people in the area through disease. There is no analogue in the narratives of the area known to us. But a double transforma-

tion, such as Lévi-Strauss has introduced, allows us to see a source in a myth in which a young man comes to Sun, who is male and evil (and overcomes him). Sometimes such permutations, however, can gloss over significant detail. Such is the case with the Wintu (California) myth of Loon Woman. Lévi-Strauss makes the story an essential part of showing the unity of myth throughout the New World but in doing so treats an incident involving hair as arbitrary (Lévi-Strauss 1981a:389). Another reading, from within the language and culture of the Wintu, finds it important to the form and outcome of the myth. (That involves the Wintu concern for bases of knowledge, expressed in part by evidential suffixes at turning points [see Hymes 2002:198–199]). Such details may be more apparent when a narrative is presented, not in paragraphs, but in lines and groups of lines. Oral narratives increasingly appear to be organized that way in many, perhaps all, languages. None of this detracts from Lévi-Strauss's original and fundamental contribution."

9. Catherine Backès-Clément's (1968) charge that "It is clear that structures don't take to the streets" is quoted in Françoise Dosse's (1997:116) history of structuralism.

ASDIWAL
Surveying the Ethnographic Ground

Margaret Seguin Anderson

Structuralism is no longer a hot-button topic among scholars, and this is an appropriate time to review several of the published studies in the light of contemporary understandings of the ethnographic context and the original languages. In this essay I look at Lévi-Strauss's analysis of the Asdiwal story and several critiques in the context of current studies of Tsimshian, Nisga'a, and Gitksan *adawx* and then explore the ethnographic validity of several of the published critiques.[1]

In his British Columbia court decision on the Delgamuukw case, Allan McEachern (1997) dismissively sniffed that there were so many exceptions to every stated precept that the Gitksan could not be said to have laws at all. He was, of course, wrong in this statement (and in my view, his comments reinforce racist stereotypes). It is true, however, that the anthropological literature on the Gitksan, and their closely related neighbors the Nisga'a and Tsimshian, is notably complex and sometimes controversial. Trying to sort out some of the issues in this literature is relevant to the contemporary political aspirations of these peoples, as well as to understanding the significance of Lévi-Strauss's structural analysis of the Asdiwal story.

Hanamuux (Joan Ryan, Gitsegukla) recently reminded me that it is important to understand that there are many levels of comprehension in Gitksan culture. Speaking of masked *halayt* dance performances, she said that small children see only the surface level and laugh or scream in terror according to the actions of the performers. As young people grow and experience more, they come to understand the performances and take part in the dramatizations, and their awareness deepens. Eventually the significance of the metaphors reveals itself according to the ability of each person to comprehend, and the spiritual force of each performance and its links to the spiritual power of the House become manifest. (Interview 1997). Operating at the deepest level of understanding are those whose abilities and insights are so profound that they can breathe fresh life into song, dance, regalia, and, of course, the *adawx* (oral histories) that bind these to the Houses. The *adawx* of the Houses of the Gitksan, Tsimshian, and Nisga'a are the accumulation of thousands of years of such genius. Since the time of Boas, anthropologists have sought to appreciate the meaning and aesthetic force of this corpus, but except for occasional flashes of insight, we are often still working at superficial levels — in fact, we don't even have all the basic information sorted out clearly.

Claude Lévi-Strauss's analysis of the Asdiwal text (1958c; 1967a) certainly had the force of a masterstroke of insight and brought the *adawx* of the Tsimshian-speaking peoples to the attention of the academy. It is of interest to assess the impact of his study as it enters its fifth decade in the literature.[2] For a retrospective symposium on the impact of the publication in English of Lévi-Strauss's *Story of Asdiwal* at the American Ethnology Society (AES) in 1998, I was encouraged to consider the question of ethnographic validity in Lévi-Strauss's work on Asdiwal and also in that of his commentators and critics (M. Anderson 1998). It has been quite an eye-opener to revisit the literature, and in the following discussion I point to continuing gaps in our understanding of several of the most vexing topics, especially in the areas of marriage and residence rules or preferences and the implications of these, which were the crux of Lévi-Strauss's analysis.

Marriage and Residence

Lévi-Strauss argued that the Asdiwal story was a mythic exploration of areas of cultural tension, reconciling people to the contradictions of their society by exploring and attenuating oppositions. The cultural contradictions or tensions he highlighted centered on the cluster of matrilineal kinship and group membership among the Tsimshianic groups:

> matrilineal exogamous crest group descent and inheritance;

> childhood residence in the father's House;

> a subsequent shift in residence to the House of the matrilateral uncle from whom a chiefly name and territory would be inherited (for elite male heirs to chiefly titles); and

> a stated preference for matrilateral cross-cousin marriage.

In this cluster Lévi-Strauss saw a contradiction between the pressures of kinship and residence patterns that was partially resolved through matrilateral cross-cousin marriage. He argued that in the myth this compromise was justified through the demonstration that alternatives in marriage choices and residence patterns had as many drawbacks as the status quo. For Lévi-Strauss, therefore, Asdiwal was a "what if" story. As he put it, "Such speculations, in the last analysis, do not seek to depict what is real, but to justify the shortcomings of reality, since the extreme positions are only imagined in order to show that they are untenable" (Lévi-Strauss 1964:121).

It is crucial to an understanding of the impact of Lévi-Strauss's work then to have a clear picture of the marriage and residence patterns of the Tsimshian, Nisga'a, and Gitksan. While a number of authors have discussed Lévi-Strauss's analysis of Asdiwal, there is still no real closure in the literature on these very fundamental issues, as is apparent from the following summary.

Lévi-Strauss's Ethnographic Information

Lévi-Strauss's *La geste d'Asdiwal* (1958c, 1961a; English translation, 1967a) cited the following primary sources on Tsimshian ethnography: Barbeau 1950; Beynon 1941; Boas 1895, 1902, 1911c, 1912, 1916b; Durlach 1928; Emmons 1910; Garfield 1939; Garfield et al. 1951; Goddard 1934; Sapir 1915; Swanton 1909a, 1952. Lévi-Strauss's presentation assumes that the Tsimshian (including the Nisga'a, Gitksan, and Coast Tsimshian) have a preference for marriage with the mother's brother's daughter: "In a society like that of the Tsimshian, there is no difficulty in seeing why this type of marriage could be thought ideal. Boys grew up in their fathers' homes, but sooner or later they had to go over to their maternal uncle when they inherited his titles, prerogatives, and hunting-grounds (Boas, 1916[b], p. 411, where he contradicts p. 402. We shall return to this contradiction later.). Marriage with the matrilateral cousin provided a solution to this conflict" (1967a:24–25). Marriage preferences and residence patterns are the ethnographic issues that are the heart of the matter for Lévi-Strauss and for the discussion that follows here.[3]

Lévi-Strauss managed to consult most of the primary sources that were in print when he was working, but he did not refer to several unpublished sources that have a bearing on the issues. Among these is Garfield's 1931 study of changes in marriage patterns among the Tsimshian; I include some detail here about her findings in that study, as these data are relevant to later authors' arguments. Garfield obtained information on "older customs" from Sidney Campbell, then 85, a highborn Tsimshian who was 10 or 12 years old when the missionary Duncan came to the Tsimshian in 1857, and who had been through several naming ceremonies. Her interviews with him confirmed the information Boas had extracted from myths. Two of her conclusions are particularly germane here.

> Descent is reckoned directly through the mother, but inheritance of property and social and political position is in the male line, though passing indirectly through females. It is not a man's son but his oldest sister's oldest son who normally succeeds him and inherits from him. Since a man and his mother's brother's daughter are of different clans, their marriage is proper according to clan regulations. It is the preferable marriage especially when the parents are of high rank or possess wealth which it is desirable to keep in the blood family. Children of sisters were always of the same clan; those of brothers might be, depending upon the clan affiliation of their wives. Since members of the same clan were forbidden to marry, children of sisters were taboo to each other. Because of the possibility of belonging to the same clan, the taboo includes the children of brothers also, with the result that no parallel cousins may marry. While the marriage of any cross cousins conformed with the early rules of exogamy, we find that one particular cross-cousin relationship was preferred; that between a man and his mother's brother's daughter. Cousin marriage is now frowned upon, but this is not so strong a taboo as the extra-clan rule. (Garfield 1931:4–5)

This summary is a succinct expression of the canonical preference for matrilateral cross-cousin marriage that interested Lévi-Strauss. Garfield also found a strong overlay of sentiment against the custom of cousin marriage: "Our own taboos against cousin marriage have been superimposed upon the clan taboos of the Tsimshian. All of the early reports agree with the traditions, which are that the normal type of marriage is that between a young man and his mother's brother's daughter. The following statements bear this out. [At this point Garfield quotes Boas (1916b:166, 185, 176, 441) regarding marriages to the mother's brother's daughter.] Now cousin marriage is also looked upon as unconventional by the natives though the families are so intermarried that remote blood relationship is difficult to avoid" (Garfield 1931:15). This superimposed view of cousin marriage as "unconventional" may be the basis for denials of such marriages in later researchers' data.

When Lévi-Strauss wrote he apparently had access to some, but not all, of the unpublished materials collected by William Beynon and Marius Barbeau. In particular, the large collection that Beynon sent to Franz Boas was then lost to scholars due to a cataloging error at Columbia University Library, where the materials had been deposited on Boas's death; this was rediscovered and made available two decades after Lévi-Strauss's publication on Asdiwal. It includes a wealth of material relevant to his analysis, including texts of *adawx* with themes resonating with Asdiwal, such as the "The Heat of Her Breasts: Sun's Daughter," which Dunn analyzed for the 1998 AES symposium. At this point it is possible to begin to assess Lévi-Strauss's analysis in the fuller context of these unpublished materials.[4]

In 1974 Alice Kasakoff published "Lévi Strauss's Idea of the Social Unconscious: The Problem of Elementary and Complex Structures in Gitksan Marriage Choice," one of the first critiques that was ethnographic in focus rather than methodological or comparative. Based on field interviews and a statistical analysis of 750 marriages in genealogies from 1850 to the 1970s, Kasakoff's conclusions about Gitksan marriage differ from the earlier sources on which Lévi-Strauss had based his discussion. "Far from being determined by an unconscious logic expressed in the elementary structures, marriage choice seems to be based on universal factors of age, residence, political status, group size, and economics, which are as much available to the consciousness of natives as any other set of factors in their lives" (Kasakoff 1974:165).

Several of Kasakoff's specific claims about Gitksan marriage patterns differ radically from other sources on marriage among the Tsimshian-speaking groups, which may indicate that the Gitksan are more divergent from the Tsimshian and Nisga'a than had been believed, or that there is some problem with Kasakoff's data. Kasakoff put forward the following claims:

> that marriage was prohibited with either first cross-cousin; hence the reported preference for matrilateral cross-cousin marriage is wrong or "purely mythical";

that more distant "cousin" marriage was practiced only as a specific strategic move when a chief had no heirs and was not a preferred strategy in any sense;

that there were some patterns of Houses linked by marriages, but in Kasakoff's analysis these appear to be artifacts of a more general trend for marriages within villages and for those whose own House is not local (i.e., a child of a woman married-in) to marry a person who has rights in the village in which they are residing.

Kasakoff also alludes to a structural pattern, not described by other ethnographers except Adams (who did his fieldwork with Kasakoff), in which each House had two "sides" that were not genealogically related — this is not explicated in Kasakoff's brief commentary on the Asdiwal story, and it is somewhat difficult to interpret what is being described.[5]

In assessing Kasakoff's data it is crucial to bear in mind that she did not consider social class at all in her analysis as she was unable to obtain reliable data on class for deceased people in the genealogies she collected. The patterns of marriage and succession on which Lévi-Strauss's analysis hinges are especially relevant to the heirs to chiefly titles, which makes Kasakoff's statistically grounded but classless generalizations immaterial. It should be noted that Kasakoff's field research among the Gitksan was during a highly politicized period, and she did apparently encounter some negative reactions to her inquiries; this may have had some effect on data collection in areas perceived as sensitive, such as cousin marriage. There is some evidence that the Nisga'a did not maintain exogamy by rank as strictly as the Tsimshian (Duff n.d.),[6] and it may be that the Gitksan shared this pattern. Nonetheless, the Nisga'a were firm in their assertions that the nephew who was in line to succeed a chief should marry his uncle's daughter.

John Adams (1974), in "Dialectics and Contingency in 'The Story of Asdiwal': An Ethnographic Note," concluded that Lévi-Strauss was wrong about the significance of Asdiwal's life: "So as we go through the myth, translating some of the references and adding what insight we can obtain from examining the typical patterns found throughout the entire Tsimshian corpus of myths, it becomes increasingly apparent that the narrative is not concerned with exemplifying a life-history which is a fantasized overcoming of the contradictions inherent in the categories which Tsimshians use to structure their social life, as Lévi-Strauss suggested. Instead, it becomes clear that the life of Asdiwal is a really possible life among the Tsimshians" (1974:177).

With respect to the issues of marriage and residence, Adams, along with Kasakoff, has introduced several positions that require clarification to ascertain whether they are accurate, and if so, whether they are unique to the Gitksan. Specifically, Adams claims that

> The most general rule [of Gitksan marriage] is that no two people who share rights to the same resources can marry each other (a rule which Asdiwal violated when he shared resources with his brothers-in-law). Everybody in this culture has rights to resources from both his (or her) mother's and his (or her) father's group, and though the latter are secondary, this rule effectively eliminates relatives on the father's side from marriage. Kin marriages are rare and when adequately documented may be seen to occur only when a person has been adopted into a different resource-owning group from the one he was born into or when biologically unrelated persons inherit the status of a kinsman. Hence there is no regular form of first-cousin marriage at all. (1974:171)

As noted in the preceding discussion of Kasakoff's work, the claim that there is no first-cousin marriage is contrary to all of the earlier ethnography with the Gitksan, Nisga'a, and Tsimshian, and there are well-documented first-cousin marriages attested among the Coast Tsimshian, though this is now generally thought to be "too close." More generally, marriages to spouses from the father's House are also easily attested among the Tsimshian, contrary to Adams's assertion. Adams further claims that the chiefly kin groups are very small due to an idiom of reincarnation that limits "true" members to descendents of grandmothers; this is not attested by other ethnographic sources and is inconsistent with data from Coast Tsimshian and Nisga'a communities, where the definition of House membership is not limited in this fashion. It is also inconsistent with *adawx* that frequently feature a theme of recognition of distant "true relations." Adams correctly notes that a man may have rights on his brother-in-law's territories, as he is "feeding" the owner's sister and her children (including possible heirs to the territory). However, he does not note that this is not a boundless right—use of resources beyond the level required for this purpose is not acceptable; so the fault of Asdiwal may not have been that he hunted on the territories belonging to his brothers-in-law, but that he killed far more than could have been needed to feed his wife and children, using his brothers-in-law's territories for self-aggrandizement — he killed off all the sea lions! If this is accurate, then Asdiwal did not lead a possible life among the Tsimshian, as Adams claims, but in fact violated a norm of Tsimshian society, as Lévi-Strauss suggested.

Adams also raises a concern regarding the proper translation of a passage that has proven problematic for several other authors, and this should be sorted out as far as is possible: "Finally the episode (recounted in a sequel [Boas 1916b:243]) of Waux's marriage to his mother's cousin, which Lévi-Strauss considers an ethnographic error on Boas's part (p. 24, n. 11) is frequent among Gitksan: it remakes a tie and is a form of marriage employed especially when, as in Waux's case, a child has no father living" (Adams 1974:172). The text of the note by Lévi-Strauss cited by Adams on this is significant.

> Boas's informant seems to have made a mistake which Boas has only partially corrected. In Boas (1916[b]) the text is as follows "Before his mother died she wanted her son to marry one of her own cousins, and he did what his mother wanted him to do" (p. 244). Thus it would be a cousin of the mother and not of the son. The corresponding native text is to be found in Durlach (1928, p. 124) of which herewith a transcription (in simplified signs): *na gauga(?) dem dzake na'ot da hasa'x a dem naksde lguolget a k!alda lgu-txaât* . . . The kinship term *txaâ* denotes the father's sister or the mother's brother's children — that is to say, all cross-cousins. *Lgu-* is a diminutive. The suffix -*t* is a third person possessive. In his summary of the story of Waux, Boas repeats the suspect phrase: "He marries one of his mother's cousins" (Boas 1916[b], p. 825). But in the commentary he corrects his interpretation by placing this example quite rightly with all those he quotes of marriages with a matrilateral cross-cousin. "The normal type of marriage, as described in the traditions, is that between a young man and his mother's brother's daughter. Thus . . . a mother requests her daughter to marry her cousin (244)" (Boas 1916[b], p. 440). Since p. 244 only mentions Waux's marriage, it is clear that this time Boas rectifies the kinship relations, but confuses the sex of the husband and wife. From this there arises a new contradiction, for this cousin would be the father's sister's daughter.

The real meaning seems to be: before dying, his mother wanted him to marry one of his own cousins. (Lévi-Strauss 1967a:44 n. 11)

Adams's position is that Lévi-Strauss is wrong, that the first translation is correct, and that the marriage in question was not between a man and his cross-cousin, but rather between a man and his mother's cross-cousin, which he states is a useful political strategy in certain circumstances.[7] There are still sufficient fluent speakers to test the two theories against their intuitions about the passage in question, and this should be done in a situation in which people can discuss the matter. I have informally queried several speakers about this passage, and so far it appears that either of the proposed translations might be accurate, with a leaning toward Lévi-Strauss's amended reading by which the marriage was with the son's own cross-cousin. Grammatically, the passage is ambiguous and in context could possibly mean that the son should marry a cross-cousin of the mother, but this is a more strained interpretation of the text since "her son" (literally "her child") is the closest possible antecedent to the gender-neutral third-person singular pronoun -t in *lgu-txaât* "his/her cousin." Charles Ackerman (1975) further confused the literature dealing with the interpretation of this passage with a reading that the intended marriage was with a patrilateral cross-cousin (see below).

There is a need to address other aspects of Adams's argument as well, but these are beyond the scope of this discussion:

Adams conflates the use of father's territories with the special case of adoption of a son by a father;

he appears to conflate several types of names, including *halayt* names and territory-linked House names (though these tend to be more intermingled among the Gitksan, where many of the names used by House chiefs have associated *halayt* performances, than they are among the Coast Tsimshian, where this is rare);

he incorrectly assumes that all Gitksan names are about overcoming negative traits (for types of names see Halpin 1973; Guédon 1984a);

he assumes that there are "levels" of hunters, with no ethnographic grounding (Adams 1974:176).

I must disagree with Adams's claim that Asdiwal's career was a recognizably Tsimshian one—although rules can be broken, Asdiwal performed none of the ritual processes by which violations can be legitimated in Gitksan, Tsimshian, and Nisga'a society—no cleansing feast "shut the mouths" of the people, and other people can "talk about" his mistakes with impunity (and indeed his very name puns on this).[8]

Lynn Thomas, Judy Kronenfeld, and David Kronenfeld (1976) published a close examination of the consistency of Lévi-Strauss's analysis with the sources he had used; this did not provide a definitive answer to the questions of Tsimshian, Nisga'a, and Gitksan marriage and residence. There are some difficulties in their grasp of the ethnography. For example, they indicate that perhaps Asdiwal's difficulties with one of his sets of brothers-in-law might be "hostility of inferior, ungrateful hungry Coast Tsimshian towards the great Gitksan hunter. Perhaps what is relevant here is that what would normally be a poor, backward Gitksan is getting the upper hand over normally wealthy Coastal Tsimshian" (Thomas et al. 1976:161).

This passage wrongly identifies Asdiwal as Gitksan. At the beginning of the text, however, Asdiwal's mother was traveling downstream to meet her own mother, who was herself traveling upriver from Canyon (Kitselas), and the text is explicit that this is the mother's own village. Hence, she and her daughter were Kitselas women, and the daughter's son, Asdiwal, is not a Gitksan; he is Tsimshian. Despite this error, and other problems in their control of the relevant ethnography, Thomas, Kronenfeld, and Kronenfeld offered a boldly phrased conclusion that may have caused some readers to conclude that, as their title intimates, Lévi-Strauss's analysis of Asdiwal had crumbled:

> While some of his assertions, isolated from context, are intuitively plausible or interesting, his analysis as a whole, embedded as it is in a complex, elaborate, and too frequently arbitrary system, does not, in any intuitive sense, illuminate or make explicit a set of relations we perceived to exist in the myth and felt to be connected. In the absence of such illumination and in the absence of a set of explicit procedures, we can only conclude that Lévi-Strauss creates a set of problems so ill-

defined as to be meaningless, and provides solutions to match, to paraphrase Adams (1974:171). [Thomas et al. 1976:170–171]

The issues of marriage preference and residence patterns become even
more convoluted in the work of Charles Ackerman and Brad Campbell.
These authors follow Lévi-Strauss's structuralist approach closely but argue that the preferred marriage is actually with the father's sister's daughter, not the mother's brother's daughter, and this changes the details of the
significance of the Asdiwal text. Unfortunately, the evidence they adduce
includes inaccuracies and mistranslations. For example, Ackerman thinks
that Asiwa (the hero's name in another version) might be glossed as 'without feet' and hence connect somehow to an issue with respect to territori-
ality. This is simply wrong. Ackerman relies on a list of morphemes from
Boas to concoct this analysis, but in fact the particle wa- "without" is always
word-initial and never word-final, so it could not be the final morpheme
in this name; the word-initial restriction on wa- was correctly indicated in
the Boas glossary Ackerman cites. Other pieces of Ackerman's and Campbell's evidence are also suspect. For example, they attempt to link semen
with bones, which seems to be a wayward or wishful import from the New
Guinea ethnography—they cite no evidence for the idea from Tsimshianic
languages or ideas about procreation (Ackerman 1982). Further, there is no
independent support for the notion that a man's own grandson should be
his reincarnate, and there is no reason to believe that a man would be symbolically "killed" if his children's marriages were not arranged in such a way
that his son's son is also his nephew's nephew (the result of repeated patrilateral cross-cousin marriages). As elegant as the kinship diagram might be
if the marriage preference were as Ackerman suggests, this is not sufficient
grounds for revisionism in the face of clear and unambiguous statements
by Nisga'a, Tsimshian, and Gitksan that the preferred marriage was with the
mother's brother's daughter. Both Ackerman's and Campbell's interpretations, intriguing as they are—and they are well worth reading as compelling
attempts at the application of the structuralist model—are simply not tied
to the factual ground of the languages and cultures of Tsimshian-speaking
groups.

To return to the main line of inquiry into the ethnographic grounds
for Lévi-Strauss's reading of Asdiwal, McNeary's excellent fieldwork-based
ethnography of the Nisga'a (1976) suggests that matriliny is an instrument

of alliance, ensuring bonds through children that are more enduring than affinal relations. His position is clear in the following passages: "If affinal ties are uncertain, how can enduring alliances be ensured? The answer, I believe, is that it is the children of the marriage who unite the Houses of their parents. After the birth of a number of children a chief could even return his wife to her relatives without any hint of insult. I would argue that it is through the institution of matrilineal descent that children form such an effective bond between houses" (McNeary 1976:5). McNeary also comments on rights to resource access:

> Ties of paternity are prominent in Tsimshian ideas about access to re-
> sources. Naturally, a man has full rights to the resources of his uncle's
> House, since he possesses one of the ancestral names of the House and
> usually resides there as an adult. He also has rights to the resources of
> his father's House, where he was raised and where he received his early
> instruction in subsistence techniques. These rights are active as long
> as his father is alive and may continue longer if he makes the proper
> contributions to his father's funeral. A man also has rights to the re-
> sources of a third House, that of his wife's brother. This is not phrased
> as a purely affinal relationship. Rather, he holds these rights because he
> uses the wealth obtained from his brother-in-law's lands to support his
> own children, who are the ultimate heirs to his brother-in-law's posi-
> tion. (McNeary 1976:6)

Finally, McNeary addresses the question of marriage preferences:

> I would like to return, briefly, to the problem of marriage. Boas (1916[b]:
> 440) and Garfield (1939:231–232) both recorded a preference for mar-
> riage with the mother's brother's daughter. Both sources also give in-
> stances of classificatory father's sister's daughter marriage, and my in-
> formants saw no objection to marrying back into the father's House, as
> long as the relationship was not too close genealogically. But the stated
> preference, for the nobility, is marriage with the mother's brother's
> daughter. This preference is phrased two ways. One way is to say that
> chiefs like to keep two names linked through marriage over the gen-
> erations. That is, if George marries Martha in one generation, so in the
> next generation the names George and Martha should be united in mar-
> riage. A moment's reflection will show that given matrilineal inheri-
> tance of names, this formula amounts to matrilateral cross-cousin mar-

riage. Clearly, such marriages perpetuate the relationships of affinity and paternity between Houses. The advantage of the system is said to be that it keeps the wealth, and knowledge of esoteric House histories, within a limited circle of the nobility. There does not seem to be any implication of an asymmetrical or ranked relationship such as Rosman and Rubel have postulated (Rosman and Rubel 1971:10–33). The other way of describing marriage preferences (and it amounts to the same thing) is to say that a chief wants his heir to marry his daughter. One of Boas' informants went so far as to say that a chief's nephew must marry the chief's daughter in order to inherit his uncle's title (Boas 1916:185). I think that Lévi-Strauss has correctly interpreted the function of this marriage preference: it helps to reconcile the difficulties inherent in a system of avunculocal residence (Lévi-Strauss 1967:24–27). [McNeary 1976:9–11]

If McNeary's views on the significance of children of a marriage as instruments of alliance is correct, it might be productive to add this perspective to our reading of Asdiwal.

Finally, Dunn (1984) brings fresh data from fieldwork in Kitkatla to bear on the issue of matrilateral cross-cousin marriage and finds a compelling rationale in the effect that such marriages have on patterns of relationship and inheritance. In brief, he locates the genius of Tsimshian matrilateral cross-cousin marriage in maximizing retention of wealth in the House, re-distributing goods evenly among the quadripartite structure of a traditional village, and enhancing prestige by making a chief an ancestor to all four sections of the village — a position of honor beyond price. Details of the Gitksan feasts recorded by William Beynon in 1945 in Gitsegukla provide independent corroboration for the quadripartite structure Dunn posits on the basis of kinship denotata/connotata — specifically, the gifts given by the various categories of those related to the House at feasts manifest the four categories he discusses:

House chiefs and heirs — the "inside-inside" of the House;

Out-married women and their children — the "inside outside";

Married-in women and their children — the "outside inside"; and

Guests who receive gifts but do not contribute, comprising the fourth "side" — the "outside outside."

Dunn offers important information to add to the layers of context through which we can productively read Asdiwal. Additionally, Dunn has produced a series of careful retranslations of *adawx* sent to Franz Boas by Tsimshian ethnographer William Beynon, applying ideas pioneered by Dell Hymes (1990). Dunn's exegesis of the poetic structures that shape these texts reveal stylistic features that may be connected to specific storytellers or to other aspects of the specific context of their telling. It is useful to note that these *adawx* were told in various forms for different audiences. At feasts it was typical to present a synopsis sufficient to demonstrate rightful possession of specific prerogatives, but not to recount the entire House history. On the other hand, during training of successors the entire *adawx* would be imparted and explicated in minute detail.

As a final comment I will point out one thing that seems apparent in the literature but that has been unremarked. There has been a considerable under-attention to the role of the Sigidm'naa'ax, "chiefwoman," specifically the wife of the House chief. If marriages are about political alliance, and if women, men, and children are the instruments of the formation of such alliances, the chiefwoman is a crucial agent of its success. Lévi-Strauss and others have pointed to the number of failed marriages in the texts and located significance in the institutions of marriage and residence. Yet these failures can also be read as commentaries against the examples of successful Houses, in which the chief and chiefwoman epitomize the ideal of Tsimshian moral order. In many villages people still revere particularly effective couples who were leaders of their communities in past generations, and who fulfilled all of the obligations of their positions and truly became ancestors of the entire village. Perceived shortcomings of contemporary community leaders are often measured against the virtues of these "mothers and fathers" of the community. Such examples are also strong counterpoints to Asdiwal's repeated failures as he attempted to establish himself.

Conclusions

It is ironic that the name of the hero in the text that has so captivated our discipline puns on "making a mistake," because we have certainly made a lot of mistakes in trying to understand it. Clearly, the anthropological literature dealing with the topic of the marriage and residence rules and preferences among Tsimshian-speaking peoples has remained unsettled to a remarkable degree for a very long time — in Hanamuux's terms, our level of understanding is still quite rudimentary. Despite this, however, it is clear that Lévi-Strauss's analysis identified issues of crucial import to the Tsimshian, Nisga'a, and Gitksan, and that the approach that he developed is a useful part of the toolkit we can bring to understanding the oral literature of these peoples. There are several other approaches to understanding stories that may help deepen our insights into the meaning of Asdiwal's story. As noted above, John Dunn has been working recently on careful poetic exegesis of several Tsimshian texts: these have been discussed with fluent speakers and refined to capture their understandings, a process sorely needed for Asdiwal. Keith Basso's insights on Western Apache "Stalking with Stories" point to the types of meanings conveyed by contextualized storytelling, including the significance of place-names, audience, and context; if more information can still be gathered about the actual context in which *adawx* are or were narrated, this approach could be useful in understanding the Tsimshianic corpus. There are doubtless others as well of which I am not yet aware. I certainly hope that whatever approach they bring to it, the next generation of students will continue to find the story of Asdiwal as compelling as we have.

After a review of the literature relevant to the Asdiwal text, it seems clear that Dell Hymes's comment (1965) on the appalling state of the "toolkit" for the study of aboriginal languages should be expanded to include a call for attention to the state of our knowledge on the significant ethnographic issues — if we can't come to a definitive consensus, we need to at least maintain a coherent sense of the state of our knowledge. We need a literature in which the basic questions are clarified rather than simply tossed into the air for dazzling displays of theoretical virtuosity. When an *adawx* is recounted in a feast among the Gitksan, Nisga'a, or Tsimshian, the role of the educated audience is crucial — their job is to keep the teller honest. With respect to our scholarship, this function is still "under construction."

The *adawx* of the Tsimshian, Gitksan, and Nisga'a retain contemporary relevance in communities, though now only the older generations understand them in their original languages.[9] *Adawx* are used in teaching university-level Tsimshian Sm'algyax language courses and have been adduced in discussions in the codification of the Ayukwhl Nisga'a (Laws of the Nisga'a) for their new post-treaty Nisga'a Lisims government. Within some communities names that had not been publicly assumed for decades are being brought out again, and matrilineal genealogies are being documented to support claims for succession — or to dispute them. The issues of marriage and residence that bedeviled poor Asdiwal continue to be flashpoints in conflicts, albeit in new forms and in new contexts. Recent disputes have revolved around

> the rights of succession of children of married-out women (in the context of patrilineal band membership laws under the Indian Act that still give "resident outsiders" substantial power and strong incentive to exclude matrilineal House members who grew up elsewhere; it is not unheard of for all the direct matrilineal descendants of a House to be nonresidents of the village where the House originated);

> the involvement in community governance of those whose orientation is to their birth community but who reside "off reserve";

> the residence and resource rights of people who are married in to communities (or whose mothers or grandmothers married in) and whose proper House membership is elsewhere;

> the proliferation of ḵ'aats (within-crest group) marriages, even among those who are assuming chiefly names, leading to embarrassment in the feast hall as spouses from the same crest origin are seen to sit together; and

> attempts by patrilineal descendants and "adoptees" to assert priority over matrilineal descendants in the line of succession within some Houses (an issue not confronted by Asdiwal).

At the same time, rights in land and resources are framed and fought over in the rhetoric of traditional cultural forms, even by those who may have violated fundamental tenets of the culture. It is clear that the immediate future will be turbulent in some communities, though it is generally believed that the strength of the traditions will win out in the end.

Finally, with respect to the original question of the ethnographic reality of Lévi-Strauss's analysis of Asdiwal, while it may be a sterile exercise to track down the intellectual roots of every misperception, it is important to confirm as far as possible the most accurate account of the ethnographic context. I conclude this discussion with a summary of the conscious norms and regular practices of the Tsimshian-speaking groups prior to missionization. It is my view that the overwhelming body of evidence from published and archival sources indicates that these were as follows:

Descent and Kinship Relations

The Tsimshian, Nisga'a, and Gitksan all have four matrilineal exogamous *pteex* (referred to in the literature as clans, phratries, or crest groups): Gispudwada/Gisgahast; Laxgibu; Ganhada/Laxseel; and Laxskiik. Kinship terminology distinguishes between parallel and cross-cousins. Extensive life-long public ritual significance attaches to the *kswaatk* ("father's side"), continuously reconfirming individual rights and obligations in the matrilineal House through an idiom of respect and obligation and contracting with the father's side for all ritual services and paying for these publicly. Ideally each person has relations of every category, and maximizing the web of relations is a factor in arranging marriages; this is evident at feasts through the life cycle and especially at death. Where two individuals stand in two relationships (e.g., father's side and affine), gifts at a feast may be contributed in one or both categories as a sign of respect.

Marriage

Marriages were arranged and approved by the House. There were strict rules of crest-group exogamy on the one hand and upper-class or high-rank endogamy on the other. The stated preference for matrilateral cross-cousin marriage was probably pertinent only to the elite chiefly class, specifically to those being prepared to assume chiefly responsibilities. There was no barrier to patrilateral cross-cousin marriage, but no preference was expressed for this pattern. As explicated by Dunn (1984), the cultural logic of matrilateral cross-cousin marriage is a strategic maximization of prestige as ancestor of all sections of a village, and retention of resources within a House, and this logic is manifested in the categories of gift givers and recipients at feasts. There are specific kinship terms for men married to sisters and for women married to brothers. "Sister-exchange" (or at least marriage of both men and women from one House to mates in another) was not uncommon, and there was no pattern of wife givers or wife takers with differential prestige. A woman's reproductive capacity did not transfer to her husband's

House at marriage, as she and her children were members of her own and her brother's House. Siblings might well be married to individuals from different crests and Houses and to spouses from different villages; conversely, the men and women married into a House would likely be drawn from more than one crest group, several Houses, and several villages. To have the maximum success, a House needed strong guidance and leadership from both the Chief (Sm'oogyet) and Chiefwoman/matriarch (Sigidm'naa'ax).

Residence

Idealized residence for the elite males on whom such texts as Asdiwal are focused was to live in the dwelling of their father from birth and to move to the dwelling of their mother's brother in late childhood. This made it possible to exercise the prerogatives of House membership on House territories. Eventually the heir succeeded to the House chief position of his uncle. An alternate pattern is mentioned repeatedly in *adawx:* the son of a very high-ranking woman married in from another village or nation might remain in the village of his father and found a new House after being given territory by his father, who might even relinquish precedence to his son's new House.[10] For an elite woman the norm was the mirror of the male's pattern, either marrying the cross-cousin who would succeed to her father's position and remaining in her father's or husband's dwelling after marriage, or marrying into and moving to a different village, establishing and consolidating relationships of economic and political significance. After her children matured, a woman might move to the House of her brother with her son, her brother's successor.

Succession

According to ideal formulations, a man is succeeded by his eldest sister's eldest son, though depending on age, ability, political support, and wealth, the actual successor may be a younger brother, a different nephew, or a more distant matrilineal relation. A woman takes the name of a woman from her matriline—her mother, maternal aunt, grandmother, or other relative. Where there is no eligible heir within the House, adoption of a distant matrilineal relation at a feast may be sanctioned by the House members, or a woman of the House may carry a man's name, in which case she is addressed as a man in feasts. Very rarely a House may sanction adoption of a daughter to provide future successors through her progeny; such adoptions require expensive distributions to "shut the mouths" of critics, and even so there are sometimes disparaging comments made for decades, especially if there is a rival claimant to rally around, or if the adopted successor is less than generous and judicious in demeanor. While adoptions are increasingly common in contemporary communities, none are attested in the *adawx*; a strategy that is attested in *adawx* is to elevate a son through gifts of territory, so that the son becomes founder of a new House, supplanting the father's House in rank (see the section on residence).

Inheritance

Individuals distribute property to their own House members prior to death; the personal property of a deceased person is burned at death. House members, members of other Houses in the same crest group, children of the House (those for whom the House is the "father's side"), and spouses of House members all contribute for the totem pole raising (now usually a gravestone moving) and memorial feast by the nephew/successor, and payments for services and gifts are given at these events to the guests not in the hosting group. Nonmaterial property (names, crests), territories, and objects bearing House crests, such as regalia, stay in the House as property of the nephew/successor or are passed down to other House members. Women inherit names and House privileges from their mothers and grandmothers.

It is notable to me that in each of these categories the best evidence supports the same ethnographic assumption that grounded Lévi-Strauss's analysis of the story of Asdiwal.

Notes

1. Asdiwal puns on the phrase for "make a mistake." *Asdi* "aside"; *waal* "do"; *asdiwaal* "make a mistake." This is a productive construction type, parallel to, e.g., *asdihaw,* "misspeak." This is true in all three Tsimshianic languages, spoken by the Coast and Southern Tsimshian, Nisga'a, and Gitksan. These three groups have all been referred to as Tsimshian in the anthropological literature, but it is now preferred to use their own designations to refer to them and to use the term Tsimshianic or Tsimshian-speaking peoples to refer to them as a whole.
2. Lévi-Strauss first published his analysis of Asdiwal in 1958 (1958c); the English translation became available in 1967 (1967a).
3. When Lévi-Strauss's study was first published in English, there were a num-

ber of commentaries and critiques published with it, but none of these dealt with sorting out the issues of Tsimshian-speaking peoples' actual marriage and residence patterns definitively, so they will not be addressed in this context.

4. Another resource not available when Lévi-Strauss was writing is Wilson Duff's *Tsimshian File* — several thousand pages of notes made by Wilson Duff on the Barbeau and Beynon materials in the Salle Barbeau at what is now the Canadian Museum of Civilization in Gatineau, Québec. Duff prepared the *Tsimshian File* as the foundation for a study of the social organization and ceremonial life of the Tsimshian, Nisga'a, and Gitksan, which was never completed. The present author has recently completed a virtual version of Duff's *Tsimshian File* as a research tool on CD.

5. Kasakoff does not seem to be referring to a sometimes misunderstood but frequently encountered category of kin termed *wilnat'ał* (relatives who share the same origin, written as *wilnadahl* in Gitksan and Nisga'a). Since House members share a single origin, this rules out the *wilnadahl*. It also doesn't seem to denote married-in resident spouses and children of the House. As Kasakoff describes the "sides," she seems to be referring to two distinct lines of House members; such a category has not yet been confirmed by other studies, though Dunn (1984) discusses another sense of "sides" of a House.

6. "Our [Nisga'a] arrangements differ from the Tsimshian. The Nass River [people] don't use leka'get; only in the Tsimshian language. No word here to mean the same. Cannot see the reason why difference in organization from Port Simpson. Port Simpson royal chiefs can marry only among their class, not among leka'get. Different with nisge. They can marry with anyone (not own crest)" (Duff n.d.).

7. As one of the press reviewers commented, whether the marriage was to a mother's brother's daughter or to a mother's mother's brother's daughter, it would still place the heir to a chiefly title on his own House's territories, with his uncle or his uncle's uncle. Hence, the difference to Lévi-Strauss's analysis is insignificant.

8. See note 2 above regarding terminology.

9. All three of the Tsimshianic languages are endangered, and the fourth, Sküüxs, is virtually extinct. Each of the nations has active programs for language revitalization.

10. Walter Wright's published *adawx, Men of Medeek* (1962), includes an example of this pattern. See also versions of the epic of Neqt in Dunn n.d. and Duff n.d. See M. Anderson n.d. for an inventory of the latter.

TEXTS AND NARRATIVES

"SOME MYSTERIOUS MEANS OF FORTUNE"

A Look at North Pacific Coast Oral History

Judith Berman

Introduction

Since Franz Boas's time a considerable body of oral history narratives has been collected from the indigenous peoples of the North Pacific Coast. Some of the major published and unpublished sources are the Kwakwaka'wakw materials of Boas and George Hunt; Coast Tsimshian oral history recorded by William Beynon for both Marius Barbeau and Boas (Cove and MacDonald eds. 1987; BBN, BCU); Haida oral history scattered through Swanton's publications (1905b, 1909a); and the extensive Tlingit materials collected by Swanton (1909b), Louis Shotridge (1919, 1920, 1922, 1928, 1929, UEN), Ronald Olson (1967, ROP), and Frederica de Laguna (1960, 1972). The sources contain narratives in native-language text and original English as well as reduced to English summary or paraphrase.

Despite these riches, attention has focused to a far greater extent on myth, song, and poetry — what is more typically considered verbal art. Boas argued for recording myths and folktales on the grounds that such stories "probably contain all that is interesting to the narrators" (1935:v). If nothing else, the sheer quantity of North Pacific Coast oral histories tells us these narratives, too, contain a great deal that was interesting to their narrators.

This essay considers the oral histories both as a form of history and as a form of traditional literature, drawing primarily on materials written down between 1900 and 1940. Although the examples are taken largely from two coastal groups — the Tlingits and the Kwakwaka'wakw — it is anticipated that the major outlines of the discussion apply more widely along the coast. The degree of interest in history is an areal phenomenon, and as is further touched on below, it is surely linked to other social and economic characteristics of this cultural province (McFeat 1966:vii–ix; also Kroeber 1923).

Oral History as History

The term *oral history* raises the question of how these narratives are "history." The question can be considered both from the viewpoint of Western cultures and from the viewpoint of the indigenous peoples who narrated the stories (see also Marsden 2001). Let us examine each of these in turn.

Although there are always a number of questions regarding the interpretation of North Pacific Coast oral histories, the narratives often contain a great deal of what would, from the Western standpoint, be considered accurate historical information. The Natives of the region traditionally maintained a deep historical consciousness of almost astonishing detail. For instance, George Hunt and Ronald Olson collected Kwakwaka'wakw and Tlingit genealogies, respectively, containing over 15 generations (Boas 1921: 836–884; BPC: Hunt to Boas, January 10, 1899, July 14, 1916; ROP). The deepest known genealogies are the Kwakwaka'wakw lines of chiefly succession that Hunt recorded in the *laǧaɬəm* or "cry songs," which reach up to 25 generations into the past.[1] If we estimate 25 years between generations, this is a time depth of over 600 years. Although these narratives merge into mythological time at their farthest end, when the very first ancestor of a descent group removes his or her animal mask to assume human form, their historicity, in a Western sense, should not be discounted.

One measure of historical accuracy is agreement of detail from community to community. As Olson commented with respect to the Tlingit genealogies, "So detailed was all this genealogical information that J. B. [Cora Benson] was able to give me accurate information on many hundreds of persons, not only from her own clan and tribe [the Chilkat G̲aanax̲.teidí] but also from tribes as distant as the Stikine. The genealogical charts I constructed reached through twelve generations and meshed perfectly with data I obtained from other informants" (1967:vi).

An example illustrating this point is a famous marriage between S'eiltín, a high-ranking G̲aanax̲.ádi clanswoman of the Taant'ak̲wáan division at the extreme southern end of Tlingit country, and Taax̲sha (or Taax̲shaa), a young Kaagwaantaan chief from Icy Strait in the north. This marriage figures in oral history narratives collected in the early decades of the 20th century from the Taant'ak̲wáan and at Sitka, and mention of the wedding is even made at Yakutat, almost 200 miles north of Icy Strait at the extreme opposite end of Tlingit territory (Olson 1967:84; Shotridge 1929; see also Swanton 1909b:401, de Laguna 1972:1226).[2] The approximate date of the union can be estimated from Taant'a̲kwáan genealogical and oral historical materials supplied in the 1930s to Ronald Olson by George McKay, a descendant of the couple and a member of S'eiltín's G̲aana̲x.ádi clan (ROP). McKay was also, incidentally, a cousin of George Hunt, the part-Tlingit coworker of Franz Boas who shared both McKay's clan affiliation and his descent from S'eiltín.[3]

The marriage of S'eiltín and Taa̲xsha appears four generations above George McKay and five above George Hunt; these men were born in 1867 and 1854, respectively (Paul 1971:14; BPC: April 7, 1916, January 6, 1919). At 25 years between generations, S'eiltín and Taa̲xsha would have been born around 100–150 years before McKay and Hunt. If they married at about age 20, the famous union took place around 1750–90.[4]

There are significant differences in the stories about the wedding of S'eiltín and Taa̲xsha. There is also, however, agreement on important details, including the names and the clan and tribal affiliations of the principals. Both versions, also, recall that Taa̲xsha dressed up for his arrival at the Taant'a̲kwáan village in the Kaagwaantaan Petrel Hat. And both mention the dense fog that greeted the northerners on their arrival, although they attribute it to different causes. According to Louis Shotridge's Sitka version, the fog came from grease burned by the bride's party in the attempt to impress the north erners "that they were visiting the land of plenty" (1929:146). McKay implied that donning the Petrel Hat itself caused the fog. His version resonates with the Tlingit myth in which Petrel traps the boastful Raven by putting on his Fog Hat (k̲ugáas' s'úuxw). Lost in the fog, Raven is forced to admit that there are powers older and greater than he (UEN: "Emblems: Gànù.k s'á.x""; Swanton 1909b:10–11). The Petrel Hat said to have been worn by Taa̲xsha is presently at the University of Pennsylvania Museum. Shotridge states that it was said to have been made "long before the Tlingit discovery of iron" (AHL: "G̲ànùk s'á·x""), and it is indisputably a very old piece.[5]

We also find points of contact between oral histories of entirely different groups. For example, in the early 20th century the Kwakwa̲ka'wakw at Fort Rupert recalled the mid-19th-century slave-raiding forays of a Coast Tsimshian adventurer they called ʔamɛxs. This was undoubtedly Haymaas, a dangerous warrior remembered as something of a renegade even among his own people (KM V:5418–20; BPC: Hunt to Boas, December 14, 1921; Cove and MacDonald eds. 1987:135–138, 139–146, 150–156).

Similarly, both the Tsimshians and Tlingits preserved accounts of a conflict between the Taant'akwáan Tlingits (called Gidaganiits by the Tsimshians) and the Kitkatla Tsimshians (Olson 1967:88–89; Cove and MacDonald 1987:36–37) as well as one between the Stikine Tlingits and the Ginaxangiik Tsimshians (Olson 1967:80–82; Cove and MacDonald 1987:135–138, 147–149, 187–190; note also Marsden 2001). In these oral histories of Tlingit-Tsimshian conflict, each version emphasizes the prowess of its side's warriors and the damage inflicted upon the opposite side to such an extent that, other than the identification of the participants, the narratives share virtually no details in common. There are also, however, Tsimshian narratives that describe incidents in a later war between two Tlingit clans, the Stikine Naanyaa.aayí and the Sitka Kaagwaantaan, in which Ginaxangiik men were said by the Tsimshians to be witnesses and advisers. These Tsimshian versions do contain points of correspondence with both the Naanyaa.aayí and Kaagwaantaan accounts of that war. Incidents that all versions share in common include the death of the nephew and heir of Sheiks, the Naanyaa.aayí chief, and a terrible massacre at a peace-making ceremony (Cove and MacDonald 1987:147–149, 187–190; Olson 1967:71; Emmons 1991:329; de Laguna 1972:279–284).

Further indication of genuine historical content in North Pacific Coast oral histories lies in the congruence between archaeological sites and specific locations mentioned in the narratives. MacDonald, for example, has examined relationships between oral tradition and certain archaeological features in the Tsimshian and Gitksan areas, most notably between the group of narrative texts MacDonald titles "the epic of Nekt" and the Kitwanga Fort site (G. MacDonald 1984, 1989; note also de Laguna 1960:140–143; Boas 1966: 42–43).

Perhaps the most convincing measures of historical accuracy are the matches that can be discovered between indigenous accounts and early European historical records. The Russian historian Tikhmenev, for example, writing in the 1860s, noted the Kaagwaantaan-Naanyaa.aayí massacre; the date he supplies is 1852 (1978:353; see also LSC: Shotridge to MacHugh, September 28, 1927; AHL: "Genealogy—notes [Sheiks succession]"). A genealogy given by Cora Benson of Klukwan (ROP) contains a series of individuals cited in European documents (Figure 1). The earliest of these is Yeilxáak, head of the Klukwan (Chilkat) G̲aanax̲.teidí clan. Yeilxáak is almost certainly the powerful Chilkat chief "Ilkhak" who met the Russian explorers Ismailov and Bocharov in 1788 at Yakutat, where he had come on a trading visit (Shelikhov 1991:93–103; Olson 1967:8; see also de Laguna 1972:135; Dauenhauer and Dauenhauer 1987:436–439). Benson's genealogy, incidentally, extends nine generations, or over 200 years, above Yeilxáak.

At Yakutat a few years later, in 1791, Alejandro Malaspina's Spanish expedition encountered a powerful local leader whom they referred to as "Juné." While "Juné" apparently is not represented on Benson's genealogy, a Yakutat chief with the L'uknax̲.ádi name of X̲'unéi does figure in Tlingit oral histories of a long and bloody war between the L'uknax̲.ádi clan of Yakutat and Yeilxáak's G̲aanax̲.teidí clan of Klukwan. In this war Yeilxáak was killed (Swanton 1909:160–165; de Laguna 1972:139–145; Shotridge 1919:45–46, AHL: "Gànkà· yé·ł").[6]

In 1802 fur traders putting in at present-day Wrangell on the ship *Atahualpa* reported meeting "Cockshoo," who was said to be chief of the Stikine group of the Tlingits (Krause 1956:217). There are two Stikine men on Benson's genealogy named K'ux̲shóo, at least one of whom headed the very powerful Naanyaa.aayí clan. One K'ux̲shóo was Yeilxáak's father; the other, Yeilxáak's sister's husband (see also Olson 1967:81).

One of Yeilxáak's sister's sons, Shkeedlak̲áa, accompanied an 1834 Russian expedition ascending the Chilkat River from Klukwan. Shkeedlak̲áa was a noted artist and the head in his time of the Klukwan G̲aanax̲.teidí (Emmons 1916:24; Emmons 1991:62). In 1852 Shkeedlak̲áa's son Laatx̲ítshx̲ (better known in European accounts as Shartridge) led an overland raiding party that destroyed the Hudson's Bay Company post of Fort Selkirk and restored the Tlingit fur-trading monopoly in that region (Emmons 1916:10; Emmons 1991:15). Laatx̲ítshx̲ died at an advanced age in 1887 (1991:278). Missionaries and scientists in Klukwan in 1881–2 met his son Yeilgoox̲ú (George Shotridge), at that time a young man about 25 years old (Willard 1995:196, Krause 1956:93,99). Laatx̲ítshx̲'s grandson was Louis Shotridge, the Native ethnographer already referred to.

The existence of such deep historical interest, shared among many if not all of the indigenous peoples of the coast, raises questions about its source and its exact nature. It is undoubtedly linked to North Pacific Coast

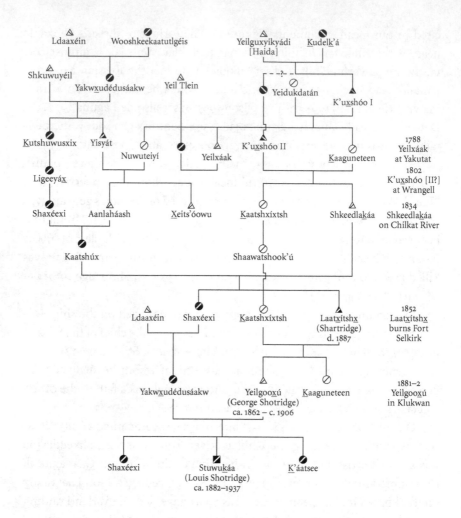

1. Part of Cora Benson's genealogy: (ROP), showing elements of the Klukwan Kaagwaantaan and Gaanax.teidí chiefly lineages, with dates of some figures appearing in European historical documents.

social organization, especially to traditional concepts about rank and the continuity of the group. The basic unit is traditionally an internally ranked corporate descent group. This descent group, which consisted of a chiefly descent line, lower-ranking nobles, and commoners, takes the form of a matrilineal clan over large parts of the region. Traditionally the chiefly descent lines within the clan not only possessed significantly greater social and political status but were considered to partake of a more powerful, more pure, and even more spiritual nature (Boas 1966:43–44; Kan 1989; Berman 1991:72–75). They were the group's "real" members (Boas 1940b:357). The head of the chiefly descent line was the most pure and the most powerful of all. Among the 19th-century Kwakwaka'wakw he was literally the "head" (ʔuǧəmiʔ) of the group and also the "top of the head" (ʔuxλɛ), the part of the body where the soul resides, while commoners were the group's "body" (ʔuǧidiʔ) (Berman 1991:72–75, 79–83). Or, in another metaphor—as Hunt wrote—the chief "is a body of a wɛlkw or great cedar tree, and the branches of this tree is the tribe [descent group] . . . Hanging onto the chief['s] body" (BPC: Hunt to Boas, April 11, 1918).

The social body is laid out in time as well as space: the chiefly ancestor is giqagiwiʔ, "chief at the forehead" (Boas 1921:841; Berman 1991:84–95). Anchoring the chief-as-tree are the chief's ancestors, called ʔəwaṅəwiʔ, the "root" of the tree (Boas 1921:836; BPC: Hunt to Boas, February 4, 1918). (In Tlingit usage, ancestors are also likened to roots of a tree; Dauenhauer and Dauenhauer 1990:395).

There was a very strong feeling about the importance of chiefly ancestors. Olson reported that "It was said of the really high-caste people, especially those of Chilkat, that they would lie awake at night for long hours thinking on the great names and great deeds of those 'through whom they had come'" (Olson 1967:vi).

Along with this feeling comes a pervasive sense of being situated between ancestors and descendants, between past and future. Worthwhile existence occurs within lineage continuity. This notion is expressed in the Tlingit word shuká, which can mean both ancestors and descendants, both past history and the future yet to come (Dauenhauer and Dauenhauer 1990:19). Or, as George Hunt said in an 1894 potlatch speech (this is Franz Boas's English paraphrase), "This is not my way of doing. Chief Nɛqáp!ɛnkɛm and Áwad taught me this way and I followed them. My name is L!aqwagila, on account of the copper which I had from my grandfather [i.e., great uncle?]. My name is Q!omogwe on account of the ermine and abalone shells which I have from my grandfather. I do not give this festival that you may call *me* a chief. I give it in honor of these two [his children] who are dancing here" (Boas 1966:190–191; emphasis added).

Although the present is situated between past and future, the past is morally and ontologically privileged: the proper relationship between Kwakwa̱ka'wakw chiefs and nobles and their ancestors was expressed in such Kwak'wala terms as *hayigiʔ*, "to imitate, to follow, to use someone else's existence as a model for one's own," and *duǧigiʔ*, "to look back and imitate deeds of one's ancestors" (Berman 1991:86–87; note similar Tlingit sentiments in Dauenhauer and Dauenhauer 1990:95–96, 253).

In this worldview both what we might call "myth" and "history" are part of a single system of knowledge about the past, a system shaped and unified by the persistence of chiefly descent lines that are anchored in the past and extend into the future. George Hunt gives us an ethnogeneric classification made by the 19th-century Kwakwa̱ka'wakw (Berman 2001; 1991:117–124). Although this system is specific to that culture and time, its general outlines probably apply more broadly.

Hunt divided Kwakwa̱ka'wakw narratives into four genres, two belonging to the age of myth and two to the *ba̱x̌əs* or "ordinary, secular" age that followed. From his viewpoint these four categories of Kwakwa̱ka'wakw narrative did not differ in their factual accuracy — all were true narratives.

Stories about the primordial beings Hunt called *nux̌nim̓is*, a term he translated as "myth People" or "History People" (KM 3:4624). The History People "were Birds and anamals yet they can talk to Each other and understand Each other" (KM 6:4969). Generally speaking, the *nux̌nim̓is* stories refer to the origin of important features of the present-day world that are shared by many social groups, features such as the origin of salmon, the tides, summer and winter seasons, and cycles of storm and fair weather. The final story of this era is the myth of Mink and the Wolves, which recounts the origin of the first winter dance. In order to perform the ceremonial, the History People took off their animal shapes. At the end of the dance, some of them dressed once more in their animal masks, while others remained in human form (Boas and Hunt 1905:489; Boas 1930:57–92; also Boas 1966:258;

Berman 2000). This was the beginning of the separation between the human and spirit realms.

After the *nux̌nim̓is* comes the second genre of myth-age stories, called *nuyəm*. These are myths concerning the first generations after the first winter dance. In these stories the first human beings and their children and grandchildren grow to adulthood, found descent groups, and venture into deep forest or out to sea. There they encounter denizens of the spirit world and acquire from them various forms of spiritual treasure or "good fortune" (*λuǧiʔ*): names, songs, crests, dances, and other gifts (KM 6:4969, 2:4624). The *nuyəm* stories belong to the descent groups whose origins they narrate.

The efforts of various transformers to render the world safe and bountiful for human beings cumulatively brought an end to the second half of the myth age and ushered in the *bax̌əs* or "ordinary, secular" era. The first genre of the secular age Hunt called *q̓ayuɬ,* or "tale[s] about the forefathers" (KM 3:4624). Hunt included the recitation of genealogies as *q̓ayuɬ* (BPC: Hunt to Boas, January 10, 1899). Last there is the genre that Hunt called *q̓ayoɬa,* the personal experiences of living people (KM 3:4624).

It is possible for a single narrative to move through all four genres, covering the entire time span of the world. Hunt, for example, recorded one *laǧaləm* or mourning song that contained "the whole History of [a chief's] family ... [beginning] from the Whale before it turn into a man" and ending with a chief who had just died (BPC: Hunt to Boas, July 4, 1916; Boas 1921:836–885).

While Hunt placed the four genres on a kind of evolutionary timeline, the relations between the myth age and the historical era are more complex. In some contexts, such as the mourning song just mentioned, the four genres do indeed seem to be conceived of as set during successive eras of the cosmos, as lying on a unidirectional arrow of time. But in other contexts the mythic and "secular" time periods appear to be more like states of being — or, as Boas expressed it, "qualities." These "qualities" not only succeed each other in cosmogony, but, since that first winter dance performed by human ancestors, they also alternate cyclically, between the winter ceremonial season and the *bax̌əs* or secular portion of the year (Boas 1966:172; Berman 2000). During the secular season the spirits dwell deep in the wilderness of forest, sky, and sea. They visit human realms only in the form of animals and usually to offer themselves as game. During the winter dance season, however, certain spirits travel to human communities. The spirits bring with them all their primordial power and danger and renew the myth age for a season within the secular, historical world. A Kwak'wala term used to describe the change from secular to winter dance "seasons" is *lix?id*, "to turn over or revolve" (e.g., Boas and Hunt 1905:470).

Mythic and secular "qualities" succeed each other; they alternate over the course of a year. Myth and history also coexist generally in North Pacific Coast ethnoliterary space. We have both "historical" and "mythic" versions of some events; such pairs of stories provide evidence for how historical knowledge both persisted in its own right and was assimilated into the formal patterns of myth and ceremony. There are, for example, both historical and mythic versions of the acquisition of the Wolf crest, a form of spiritual wealth, by the Tlingit Kaagwaantaan clan. In the mythic version, a Kaagwaantaan man out camping encounters a wolf, whom he helps. The wolf later appears to him in a dream and tells him "something to make him lucky"; the Kaagwaantaan thereafter use the Wolf crest (Swanton 1909b:233). In the historical version, the Kaagwaantaan seized a set of Wolf-crest house posts from the Teikweidí clan during a raid (Swanton 1909b: 338–346; Olson 1967:42; UEN, "Mythology: Wù·ckìná-yàs-yá," "Emblems: The Tè·qʷè·dí Nation").

Or again, Boas and Hunt provide two versions of the acquisition of the Kwakwaka'wakw *nułmał* or Fool Dancer from what Hunt called "Back of the woods living tribe," the At'łasamk. In the mythic version, the At'łasamk are a population of spirits (Boas 1897:468); in the historical version, they are the population of human beings otherwise known as the Xuyalas, a division of the Kwakwaka'wakw who were nearly exterminated in a war and who subsequently fled into the forest for self-protection (KM 5:5601–5602).

This kind of coexistence between myth and history also appears in the two versions of the story of Taaxsha and the Petrel Hat: in one, Taaxsha, like Petrel himself in myth time, creates fog by putting on the hat; in the second the fog is caused more prosaically by burning grease.

There is at least one further type of relationship between myth and history: both the mythic and secular "qualities" are potentially accessible at any moment along the arrow of time; one is merely dominant, and the other is muted at any given time (Boas 1966:172). Under the right circumstances the muted "quality" can become dominant for a period. What changes is the relationship of the two "qualities" to each other and to the present.

One insight into the modalities of their synchronous relationship is provided by the discourse use of the Kwak'wala "quotative" suffix -ła, which we can refer to as Q (Berman 1991:357–369). Hunt connected the use of Q to what he called the "old story"; when narrating an "old story," he remarked, Kwakwaka'wakw storytellers of his day began each sentence with a form containing Q. In anything not an "old story" they omitted Q (BPC: Hunt to Boas, September 18, 1917). At first glance it might appear that by "old" Hunt meant "set in the myth age," and that the use of Q coincides with the linear, progressive model of 19th-century Kwakwaka'wakw cosmogony. As it happens, texts belonging to the two myth genres are heavily marked with Q, with an occurrence in nearly every sentence, while in the two genres of historical narrative Q is quite rare. Moreover, in the deep genealogical narratives the further in the past an event takes place, the more likely the clause is to be marked by Q.

But when we look at the circumstances in which Q is absent in mythic texts (which should mark the "recent" parts), or present in historical ones (which should mark the "old" parts), it is clear that what Hunt intends by the English term *old* is not quite this straightforward.[7]

For example, in one myth we find Q lacking in all clauses that describe the establishment of present-day, secular-era names, customs, prerogatives, and institutions. This might be expected; these are the parts of the myth that refer to the present day. We also find Q missing from a second group of clauses where human beings are depicted as separate, inferior beneficiaries or witnesses of spirit power (Boas 1943:189–209). What these two types of "recent" Q-less circumstance have in common is the *opposition* and *distance* between past and present, spirit and human, mythic and secular.

In contrast, in a historical narrative of a war expedition Q is absent except for a few clauses in which the warriors, in the moment of battle, "become excited" (x̌asa) in their winter dance personae (Boas 1921:1263–1279). "Our season will change from bāxus [bax̌əs, 'secular'] to ts'əts'aəqa [čičeqa, 'winter dance'] as soon as we cut off the head of a man" (Boas 1897:429; see also 664). Such "old," Q-marked moments in historical narrative are like the cyclically recurring winter dance season, when the mythic "quality" comes to the fore, and the distance between the present and the myth-age past disappears. The difference is that, here, the mythic moments are not tied to the yearly cycle.

With respect to Q, then, "old" and "recent" do *not* correspond to a linear model of time. In Hunt's use of the term, "old" (Q-marked) means a superimposition or conflation between present and mythic past, human and spirit, the secular and the winter dance season. "Recent," Q-less parts of stories, on the other hand, lack conflation—but not relationship—between present and past, human and spirit. What replaces conflation is ranking and opposition. The spirit has marvelous power; the human is ordinary, secular, and powerless. The spirit or ancestor, or moment in the past, was the origin; the present is descended from that origin.

In the two mythic genres almost the entire narration is "old"; it is as if the very act of myth telling is a form of superimposition of the myth age on the present day, with "recent" parts coming only at special moments. In the two historical genres it is the "old" parts that come only at special moments. The distance between past and present expressed in genealogical narratives is perhaps why all of them seem to be classified as *q̓ayuɬ* even when partially set in the myth age. The historical narrations focus almost exclusively on the human, secular side of the "recent" ranked, distant human/spirit opposition, with the spirit side being invisible and muted. What the use of Q shows us, however, is that even the most secular-seeming historical narratives take place in a framework of relatedness to the spirit world, to the mythic "quality," and to the deep, mythic past.

Oral History as Oral Literature

This discussion has thus far looked at how oral history is "history"; what features make it possible to term it "literature"? First, although a much smaller proportion of histories were recorded in the original words of their narrators, and little analysis has been directed to the subject, it does appear that the ethnopoetic forms of oral history narratives differ only slightly from those of mythic narratives within in the same ethnoliterary tradition. Form and style in Tlingit mythic and historic narratives, for example, appear to be quite similar (Dauenhauer and Dauenhauer 1987; see especially 15–20). And the Kwakwa̱ka̱'wakw histories published by Boas are narrated in exactly the same sort of "measured verse" found in Kwakwa̱ka̱'wakw mythic narratives (Berman 1982; 1994; 1991:389–432; 2004). ("Measured verse," as Dell Hymes [1981] and others have shown, is a form of poetry where the poetic units—lines, verses, stanzas, and so on—are "rhetorical" structures built out of patterns of narrative action. These structures are marked by particles and changes in setting, topic, and focus, rather than by features like meter and rhyme. The types of patterns, the pattern-numbers that inform the rhetorical structures—whether they fall into 2-, 3-, 4-, 5-part or other types of patterns—and the ways in which the structures are marked are specific to each ethnopoetic tradition.)

Second, the subject matter of historical narratives is by Western standards at least as "literary" as that of myths, if not more so. Myths tell of world creation and transformation; the historical narratives examine human situations, particularly human morality and appropriate behavior— what could be called *virtue.* This notion of virtue is linked to the ideas mentioned above about "imitation" of ancestors and of being situated between past and future. The histories look backward for examples that current and future generations should live by or avoid. "The clan and lineage were the important things," and the stories cluster around chiefly clan or descent-group ancestors (Olson 1967:vi). The story of the high-caste couple S'eiltín and Taax̱sha, for example, was repeated at Sitka weddings as an ideal for newlyweds, especially newly married women, to strive toward.

The subject matter of historical narratives is very diverse, ranging through weddings, diplomacy, trade, war and peace, shamanic dreams and rivalries, the creation of famous art objects, and much more. Historical narrative can be humorous as well as dramatic, as in the story of the Tlingit commoner K̲ase who won a monumental eating contest intended to kill him (UEN: "Warfare: Wú.cx-dàgà").

A brief example illustrating the character of these stories comes to us from Dan Katzeek of Klukwan through Ronald Olson. Olson states that he wrote down the story "verbatim" (1967:vi), but the published version is clearly a paraphrase.

One of the main characters in the story is Katzeek's paternal grandfather, Kichgaaw Éesh of the Klukwan Dak̲l'aweidí clan. The story begins when a man of the G̲aanax̱.teidí clan kills Kichgaaw Éesh's sister and her child. In retaliation Kichgaaw Éesh shoots and kills the murderer.

> Now two Dak̲l'aweidí were dead but only one G̲aanax̱.teidí. The G̲aana-x̱.teidí chief, Saayíduwús', called his clan together and asked for a volunteer [to even the score]. . . . But no one volunteered so Saayíduwús'

said, "I'll go myself." He put on his ceremonial robe, and when he came out of the house he was shot by Kaxanáa [a Daḵl'aweidí] . . .

After this the new chief of the Ḡaanax̱.teidí, Yeilx̱áak (the brother of Saayíduwús') and Gaxayí of the Daḵl'aweidí [the brother of Kaxanáa], arranged a peace which has lasted to this day (Olson 1967:72–73).[8]

Both the narrator and his grandfather Kichgaaw Éesh belonged to the Daḵl'aweidí, the injured clan. The hero of the brief story is nevertheless Saayíduwús', the Ḡaanax̱.teidí chief. The story emphasizes the powerful moral obligations of chiefs. After the first pair of killings, to even the score and thus forestall further bloodshed, a member of the murderer's clan had to die, someone of equal rank to the victims (Olson 1967:70–71). Saayíduwús' had no personal involvement in the crime, but when no one volunteered, he offered his own life in order to prevent a war. The fact that this story of courageous sacrifice is narrated by a member of the offended clan shines an even brighter light on the chief's nobility of spirit.

Very different in character is a narrative from George Hunt that belongs to Hunt's fourth genre, q̓ayoła, "stories of events witnessed by living persons" (from Boas 1921:713–718). Unlike the story above, its focus is aberrant rather than exemplary behavior — the weakness of virtue.

The story begins when Hunt asks a twin woman how she came by a scar on her chest. (Hunt wrote this story in Kwak'wala; the following is my English rendering.)

> Yayax̌əyiga . . . just laughed. She said to me, "Don't you know? I'm a Salmon changeling, and my lover is my fellow twin. . . . What you're asking about was made by a spear . . . when I was a sockeye salmon. The spear . . . broke off. I went home to Mɛʔisila [guardian of salmon]. . . . Then I asked my lover Maməntayiʔ, who was an oolachan, to leave our tribe with me, because they were talking about [our being lovers]. . . . So we entered the body of our pretended [i.e., their human] mother. . . ."
>
> [Now] Maməntayiʔ . . . says that he is returning home, and that his soul has already gone . . . [with] the souls of the Salmon that died in the rivers after spawning . . . to the seaward edge of our world. Maməntayiʔ never has any strength [any more]; he sleeps all the time, he has no happiness.
>
> I asked Yayax̌əyiga why [his] heart was bad [Ẏagəm noqaẏas]. . . . She just laughed. She said, "His heart is bad because I am married to Max̌məwis."

Hunt then asks her many questions about the nature of the soul and the towns at the far edge of the world where souls go to after death. For a while Yayax̌əyiga answers willingly, but then she breaks off.

> She said, "I won't answer any more questions. . . . I've made the Salmon angry . . . because I have talked about it; they're going to take me [home]. . . . She was really crying . . .
> Her brother Mamənłayiʔ, whom Yayax̌əyiga referred to as her lover, was always sleeping. He was depressed [x̌əlsi noqaẏas, literally, "his heart was withered"]. His father . . . went up to the roof of the house. He called Mamənłayiʔ to come up and help him. Mamənłayiʔ immediately went up. . . . He had just reached . . . his father . . . when his foot slipped. He fell through the roof of the house. He was killed. Yayax̌əyiga just said that his soul had returned home long ago. . . .
> Yayax̌əyiga said to her mother . . . "You and your husband are very bad, for you do not know how to treat us properly. I am returning home, and I will take the souls of my older sisters." . . . Only three days later . . . she died . . . Her three older sisters died [before the winter was over]. Their parents soon followed them. That is all there is to say about this.

The larger moral framework of this story has to do with beliefs about salmon and the supernatural powers of twins, who were believed to be salmon incarnated among humans. Hunt does not fully commit himself to these beliefs, but he narrates the story as if it suggests their truth. The chain of cause and effect is complex, with different causes for the various deaths. When Yayax̌əyiga chastises her mother, she uses the Kwak'wala term ʔaʔikila, "to treat well." Hunt uses this term elsewhere to refer to the proper treatment of spirit powers, including the careful observation of taboos (e.g., Boas and Hunt 1905:303–304). Yayax̌əyiga, in other words, accuses her parents of not having taken appropriate care of their spirit children. She is apparently blaming them for her brother's death, although she does not mention any specific fault on their part, and in fact Hunt seems to be saying that her accusation is entirely false. After all, it was Yayax̌əyiga who broke a taboo when she talked too much to Hunt about matters of the spirit realm; she predicted that this would result in her death. The overall structure of the story suggests that Hunt saw her death as the consequence of *her* error.

Side-by-side with this framework, however, is another framework of cause and effect that is psychologically more fraught. Here, the core of the matter is the incestuous, unhappy love of the twins for each other. The twins' belief that they are salmon is not just a neutral cognitive judgment. Yayax̌əyiga experiences her salmon-ness as profound alienation. She and her brother are only visitors to their "pretend" family, as she refers to them, and to humankind in general. But she was also unhappy in her true home, the land of the salmon, where the twins' incestuous love was just as abnormal. In this light the mutual longing of brother and sister, wrong in both salmon and human communities, is the ultimate cause of the other deaths in Yayax̌əyiga's family. The brother's accident resulted from carelessness, perhaps suicidal, that was brought on by severe depression. If the parents are to blame for that death, as Yayax̌əyiga's accusation suggests, it can only be because they tried to prevent the incestuous union by marrying the daughter to another man. While Yayax̌əyiga's death may have come as a punishment for her talking too much, there is also the suggestion that grief was a contributory cause, and she used her own supernatural power to punish the rest of her family.

Oral History and the Contact Experience

There is much recorded oral history from the north Pacific coast concerning events of the 18th and 19th centuries. Interestingly, however, although the contact experience begins in the 1770s, with Cook and the Spanish expeditions, and indirect influence begins even earlier, following the first Russian landfall in southeast Alaska in 1741, white people rarely figure in these narratives. When their presence is indicated, it is usually in the form of an oblique reference, such as a mention of firearms, or of a journey to trading centers such as Fort Simpson or Victoria. From this it would appear that despite being the focus of a considerable amount of economic activity, and the cause of increasing disruption, whites were generally irrelevant to the sense of history and the moral framework that informed these stories and their narrators' lives.

There is, however, a class of exceptions where, in one sense or another, the subject of the historical narrative is itself contact. Like other historical narratives, the contact narratives often have morality or appropriate behavior as their subject and are thematically structured by the presence or absence of virtue. In these narratives, however, there is an additional thematic axis—ignorance versus knowledge of what appropriate behavior might be.

Because the contact narratives are very often a commentary on situations in which the main characters did not know the appropriate action to take, and in some cases did not understand their state of ignorance, these stories are fundamentally ironic in a way that other historical narratives are not.

One example from George Hunt relates an incident that occurred a few years before his birth. The incident, which began when hunters from the T'łat'łasikwala division of the Kwakwaka'wakw killed three Hudson's Bay Company deserters and escalated into a pitched gun battle between two divisions of the Kwakwaka'wakw and the British Navy, has been the subject of debate among historians of the North Pacific Coast (Bancroft 1887:274–275; Gough 1984:32–49; R. Fisher 1977:51–52). I have compared Hunt's version with those of white historians in more detail elsewhere (Berman 2001:184–186); here I would like to consider it as an example of contact narratives.

Hunt's story, given in English only, focuses on the character, virtuous or otherwise, of individual Indians; on ambivalence and conflict within the Native community; and particularly on the consequences of the Indians' unfamiliarity with the ways of the white men. At one point, when the British man-of-war arrived at the village of P'atłams, this last issue becomes explicit and is the subject of argument among the Native actors in the narrative. In response to the British demand that the Native murderers be handed over, one old T'łat'łasikwala chief said, with some disgust, "If I had Power over these two Bad men. I would send them off to the . . . man-of-war. and let them Do as they like with them" (IICU 14:3939). But if the two murderers were unpopular, they were still important members of the community. They argued that they had only done their duty: "the Rules given to us By our forefather is to kill the first foreigner or stranger we meet" in the territory controlled by their division.

This argument was accepted by most of the villagers. Hunt writes, "lots of the men . . . cryed out we will fight against the white men. sooner than let them take *tslāgE·yos* and *yEmgwās* away. and turn our great warriors into slaves. and we know well that threat to Burn Down our Houses . . . has no meaning" (14:3839).

The young chief Yaquλas pondered the best course of action. "What can I say my tribes People . . . it is true we Dont know the ways of the white People. about the murder and the only thing I say [is] for you all to take good care in case they carry out thier threat" (14:3840).

The British did indeed carry out their threat. The outcome of this narrative is the death of Yaquʌas—the character who best exemplifies virtue in the story—and the destruction of two entire villages, leaving their residents homeless and impoverished at the onset of winter. Unlike the chief's self-sacrifice in Dan Katseek's narrative, which prevented a war, Yaquʌas's death was pointless, and his exemplary acts were ultimately without effect.

Although virtue is not as ineffective in every contact narrative, the pervasiveness of irony in these stories suggests that they in some way stand in opposition to the worldview expressed in the mythic and ordinary historical narratives. This is particularly evident in narratives about the *first* encounter with whites (e.g., Harkin 1997a:45–65; Cove and MacDonald 1987:158–159; Emmons 1911:294–298; UEN: "Public School Lectures: First White Man"; Dauenhauer and Dauenhauer 1987:292–309). The remainder of this chapter focuses on first-encounter narratives, particularly an unpublished story written down in the 1920s by Louis Shotridge (UEN: "History: When Ta·nt'aqʷán Met the White Man").

"When Taant'aḵwáan Met the White Man"

Shotridge's story is a fragment. He penned at the bottom of the manuscript that it was to be "continued," but the rest was either destroyed or never written. It was intended either for Shotridge's unpublished monograph on Tlingit culture and history or for the *Museum Journal,* where his other articles appeared. Although Shotridge conducted his fieldwork in Tlingit and certainly received the story from his sources in that language, this is his retelling for a white audience. Shotridge does not name his source, but he collected at least some of his Taant'aḵwáan (Tongass Tlingit) narratives from Chief Johnson (*Ḵuxteech*), the elderly head of the Gaanax̱.ádi Gijook House (UEN: "Warfare: Encounter of the Haida and Tlingit").[9]

In the Hymesian verse analysis of the text that is presented here, I am preserving Shotridge's somewhat nonstandard punctuation and usage exactly, though I have corrected two misspellings and attempted to render Shotridge's transcription of the Tlingit names in the Story-Naish orthography in widespread use today. The arabic numbers to the left of the text mark Shotridge's original paragraphs. Shifts in topic and focus suggest these are genuine rhetorical verses, and I have treated them as such. The basic rhetorical unit in this text appears to resemble the basic unit of measured verse in Kwakwaka'wakw oral tradition, a unit that in Kwak'wala is often marked by particles or discourse auxiliaries, and that I have called a *stich* (Berman 1991:389–432; 1994; 2004). Here I have chosen to treat as stichs each of Shotridge's English sentences (identified through grammar rather than punctuation). Each stich begins at the left-hand margin; each clause or, in some cases, parallel phrase is set off on a separate line of type. Indentations of clauses within stichs reflect judgments about the rhetorical structure of the text.

When Taant'akwáan Met the White Man (fragment)
by Louis Shotridge

[A. The hunt]
(1)   It was on their hunt for sea otter,
                that Xax'áan of the Teikweidí,
                        with Atch'éiyi, his brother-in-law,
                one day paddled far out into the ocean from their camp
                                                on the southern shore of Yéix,
                        the island which is now known as Duke Island.
        Being their first good day after a severe weather
                the two good hunters were eager
                        to bag all the game
                                that they could catch.

(2)   Yéix had already lowered its base into the ocean
                and the shadows on it had turned into one solid mass of
                                                smoky color,
                        but on that day all the animals of the sea seemed
                                to have sensed their presence,
                and the course they took appeared
                        as if it had been washed clear of game.
        All during [since] the break of day
                they had speared and hauled aboard but two animals.

[B. Discovery]
(3)   After a hard paddling,
                the canoe was adrift in silence.

In their disappointment the two hunters could not think of
                                    anything worth while to talk about.
In his relaxed position at the bow
        X̱ax'áan was resting his eyes by looking at the
                                            bottom of the canoe.
It seems
        that he could not even recall his dream of the passed
                                            night,
        "What was it that he had in mind to tell his friend?"
The hunter was still trying to think of what to say
        when his steersman spoke:
"I never knew that such island was in this position,
        "or have I been deceived by my eye-sight?"
After looking around
        X̱ax'áan followed the stare of his steersman. —
There over the horizon appeared an object,
        it does not look like an island,
        it can never be one,
                because such had never been heard
                or known of in the position,
                        and the hunter was well acquainted in the
                                            neighborhood,
        thus he spoke:

(4)   "No, it is not an island . . .
        "It may be
                "that a living sea monster has sensed our presence,
                        "an octopus perhaps,
                        "such monsters are often deceiving."

[C. The approach of the monster]
(5)   The canoe was in such a position
                that even if the men made an effort
                        to escape such sea monster as the octopus
                        [it] would be of no avail,
                so the only thing for them to do was to lay still

and watch their chance.
    As the great object approached landward
        it began to take another form,
          it was more like a great sea bird of some unknown species,
        moving slowly over the rolling sea
          with its great wings spread out into the light
                  southeastern breeze.

(6)   It may be
        the hunter's canoe was detected through a spyglass perhaps,
          for the "monster bird" of a sudden made a turn from
                its direct course inland
        to where it lay adrift.
    When the hunters realized
        that the great monster had detected them
          their feeling of course was not like that of a man at
                  peace.

[D. X̱ax'áan's fortitude]
(7)   "Much depends upon thine courage my friend,
      "and thou can wish
        "for no other to die with than thine beloved brother-
                  in-law."

(8)   Atch'éiyi use to tell
        that his companion said these words to him in a very
               calm manner,
      and that it made him
        feel like a little boy
          who had been encouraged to perform
            that which was dangerous to him.

[E. The mystery]
(9)   The two men sat up
        and prepared themselves
          to be swallowed,

as the monster approached,
but in spite of his excited feeling
X̱ax'áan seem
to sensed the presence of a rational being within
the presence of the strange monster.
It was strange to feel—
hope perhaps—
the great monster was coming upon them
not to destroy them
but to bestow upon them some mysterious
means of fortune.
In truth such thing had been told of in some myths.

(10) As the great object came at close range
the feeling of the hunters gradually changed,—
until the feeling of wonder entered into them
they never knew
that they had been afraid,
and for the moment each man did not know
how to wear away the sign of shame.
The great "monster" was but a floating town,
but what kind of beings dwelled therein was yet to be
learned.—
"Might these be the gods of the universe,
"or are they the ghosts of brave sea-faring men
"who had passed on to the great beyond through the
great ocean,
"[who] came to pass over once more the waters which
they had loved to navigate."
Come what may of this meeting
X̱ax'áan was there then to find out.

[F. The meeting]
(11) At last the great floating town came near
and its great sails was swung to leeward,
and on a high level upon it climbed men

who shouted to the hunters in some unknown

        tongue.

(12)   "Da<u>k</u>w aa tu<u>k</u>uháani sákwshí yé<u>k</u>uwanóok,[10]

      "What manner of denizens be on a mission?"

      Was a reply shouted back by <u>X</u>ax'áan.

   It was here

      that the Tei<u>k</u>weidí warrior put to test his

          character of fortitude,

    and all the way through his encounter with the strange

          people of unknown nature

     he never showed a sign of cowering of feeling.

(13)   Presently an odd looking canoe was lowered down the cliff-

          like side of the town,

   and this,

      manned by men carrying what later turned out to be

          firearms,

     rowed up to the hunter's canoe,

   and after many signs and much motioning

     the two hunters were taken aboard the floating town.

   Their canoe also was hoisted aboard.

There are a number of interesting points in the text. While Shotridge's English can often seem repetitious, florid, and even opaque, once the prose is written in verse form, its inner structure begins to appear. The prevalence of couplets and parallelisms surely reflects traditional Tlingit rhetorical forms (see Dauenhauer and Dauenhauer 1987:15–20). Couplets, in fact, comprise seven of the thirteen verses, while one other verse has four stichs and another has eight. (Of the remaining four verses, three have one stich, and one, verse 9, has three stichs.)

Not only are verses often couplets, but they often contain parallel internal structures. For example, both of the stichs in verse 1 tell us that two men are going sea hunting. The first stich gives biographic and geographic detail, the who and where; the second stich adds the circumstances—that it was the first good weather in some time. Verse 2 has considerably more internal structure. The first stich has two parts: first, a description that tells us that it is now evening and, second, a comment that they had encountered little game. Each of these parts is doubled. The first two lines of the verse describe the appearance of Yéix in two different ways; the second four twice describe the absence of game. The second stich of this verse repeats the structure of the first, but more concisely. Its first line repeats the time interval; its second, the fact that the hunters had obtained hardly any game.

The overall rhetorical structure of the text suggests higher-level units that we can call stanzas. These are pairs of verses—in one case a triplet of verses—linked by common subject matter. I have given each of the six stanzas a descriptive title.

The following six-part analysis suggests itself:

> Stanza A: The hunt
>> verse 1 (2 stichs)
>> verse 2 (2 stichs)
> Stanza B: Discovery
>> verse 3 (8 stichs)
>> verse 4 (2 stichs)
> Stanza C: The approach of the monster
>> verse 5 (2 stichs)
>> verse 6 (2 stichs)
> Stanza D: X̱ax'áan's fortitude
>> verse 7 (1 stich)
>> verse 8 (1 stich)
> Stanza E: The mystery
>> verse 9 (3 stichs)
>> verse 10 (4 stichs)
> Stanza F: The meeting
>> verse 11 (1 stich)
>> verse 12 (2 stichs)
>> verse 13 (2 stichs)

A good deal more could be said about the rhetorical structure of this text. In terms of the present discussion, the point of greatest interest is the pattern of irregularity in verse form. The four verses that are made up of an odd number of stichs, verses 7, 8, 9, and 11, cluster at the moment of greatest intensity in the story. Three of the four "irregular" verses—7, 8, and 11—have only one stich. These are the verses in which X̱ax'áan encourages his young companion to face his death with fortitude and in which the strange visitors call out to the hunters.

The third odd-numbered verse, which describes the initially mythic appearance of the ship, has three stichs. This is verse 9. Both its unique form and its content suggest it is the crux of the story.

Threaded through the narrative is a series of interpretations in which the two men try to comprehend the strange object bearing down on them. On very first sighting, in verse 3, the steersman thinks the ship is an island. But the two hunters quickly realize the thing is in a place where no island could be, and moreover, it is moving. In verses 4, 5, and 6 they decide it is a sea monster, perhaps a gigantic octopus; then, as it comes closer, it begins to resemble a "monster bird."

In verse 9, the two hunters prepare to meet a supernatural being that will either destroy them or grant them spiritual treasures. Up through this verse, the story closely follows the North Pacific Coast mythic pattern already referred to, in which the hero encounters a supernatural being who grants gifts that will become the spiritual wealth of the hero and his or her lineage—what Shotridge calls "some mysterious means of fortune."

There is evidence from other sources that the encounter with whites was, in fact, initially framed in terms of the mythic pattern. A Haida first-encounter narrative, collected by Swanton, reports the perceived supernatural powers of the strangers, which resemble the exploits of mythic shamans: "When one of the white men shot with a gun, some of the natives said he did so by striking it on the side; another, that he blew through it; and a third, that a little bird sat on top and made it go off . . . A single bullet was procured by the people of this town; and the rumor went around that, if it were thrown at an opposing force, all would be killed. Other towns were consequently in terror, and the fortunate possessors kept it carefully wrapped up in skins" (Swanton 1905:105–106).

At the Taant'ak̲wáan village of Kaduk̲guká, the G̲aanax̱.ádi clan erected a crest pole in 1883 to commemorate the first encounter with white men a century earlier. The carvings on it included a Raven at the bottom and, at the top above a long shaft, a bearded white man.[11] This pole in effect framed the first white men as similar to Raven, Bear, and the other beings on the crest poles from whom spiritual wealth had been obtained. In this instance it may be relevant that, as mentioned, the Taant'a<u>k</u>wáan were heavily invested in the sea otter trade, a source of enormous material wealth, from its inception in the 1780s.

An encounter incident from European historical sources resonates with a group of myths in which the hero travels across the ocean to a mystical land of wealth, often the home of the salmon or the Copper Maker, and brings back treasures to his village.[12] In the 1780s, a Nuu-chah-nulth man from Nootka Sound named Comekela, the brother of the chief Maquinna, journeyed on the white man's ships to Canton, China, where he lived for several years. He was given return passage in 1788 by Captain John Meares, who hoped to use him to gain trading advantages. Meares described Comekela's return to his village:

> His scarlet (regimental) coat was decorated with . . . quantities of brass buttons and copper additions of one kind or another. . . . At least half a sheet of copper formed his breast-plate; from his ears copper ornaments were suspended, and he contrived to hang from his hair, which was dressed en queue, . . . many handles of copper saucepans [which he had obtained from the cook]. . . . A general shout and cry from the village assured him of the universal joy which was to be felt on his return.
>
> The whole body of inhabitants moved toward the beach, and . . . welcomed him on shore. . . . After the first ceremonies of welcome were over the whole company proceeded to the king's house, into which persons of rank were alone permitted to enter, and where a magnificent feast of whale blubber and oil was prepared (Quimby 1948:250–251).

There are additional first-encounter narratives that explicitly state that the Native actors perceived whites as supernatural beings. Even where this was not true, the many new and marvelous objects brought by whites might well have seemed to be a form of spiritual wealth. In general, while the acquisition of European goods has often been treated by anthropologists as a loss of traditional culture, there is plenty of evidence from the North Pacific Coast that interest in new, unusual, and beautiful objects was deeply rooted in tradition and was linked to the chiefly prerogatives of display. Possession of rare objects was an emblem of wealth in a practical sense, as chiefs traded over great distances and spent great riches to obtain such objects. An unpublished historical narrative from Shotridge tells how the aristocratic trader K'uxshóo brought the first Chilkat blanket from Kitlatla to Klukwan, a distance of over 450 miles as the crow flies. To acquire the blanket in the first place, K'uxshóo had been compelled to give a box of rare berries from Klukwan, a delicacy much valued and otherwise unobtainable in the south (UEN, "Textile: Notes on the origin of the . . . Chilkat blanket").

In the early postcontact years, with its expanded range of new and rare objects, K'uxshóo brought to Klukwan another Tsimshian "masterpiece," an extremely expensive headdress depicting a fish hawk that was ornamented with tin from the first tin cup and copper from the first copper plate acquired by its makers.

> When the . . . Head-piece was brought to Klukwan, the whole popu-
> lation of the great Tlingit town turned out to view the exhibition of
> it. . . . . "It was indeed a formal occasion. . . . The great hall [of the
> Kaagwaantaan Killer Whale House] was packed to its full capacity
> with people. . . . The metal ornamentation shone like the rays of mid-
> summer sun . . . the light played over the polished parts, which made
> the thing looked as if it were alive, and moved by men's admiration.
> 'Indeed it is a wonderful piece.' It was such praise that a man of wealth
> had always sought" (AHL: "Gidju·k [Fish Hawk]").

And in the Tlingit village of Angoon nobles in the Deisheetaan clan used a Tahitian breastplate as part of their regalia until early in the 20th century (Katz 1986). About this object, Shotridge wrote, "Being the only one of its kind the strange piece, for a time, was an object of high esteem with its owners, because it had been the work of unknown hands, 'And it could be well compared with those objects improvised by the great Raven, as described by legend'" (LSC: Shotridge to G. B. Gordon, July 22, 1925). The possessors of this rarest of objects, in other words, likened it to works Raven had created in myth times, even though the people it had been acquired from were not themselves considered to be mythic.

In all the first-encounter narratives the nature of the strange visitors is at first unknown — it is potentially or incipiently mythic. It is the very shift in viewpoint, as the potentially mythic turns into something else, that forms the thematic core of Shotridge's Taant'akwáan encounter story. Up through the pivotal verse 9, Shotridge tells us what could be a myth, and he even pauses in the crucial moment, just as the mythic encounter is about to occur, to add the third, "extra" stich of this verse: "In truth such thing had been told of in some myths." In the very next verse, however, the potential "mysterious means of fortune" transforms into something entirely different.

From this point on, most first-encounter narratives focus on the naive reaction of the Natives to the unprecedented situation. The narrator tells how his or her ancestors thought rice to be maggots, pilot bread to be fungus, and molasses to be water from the village of the land-otter men, or the black liquid from human decomposition. The newcomers, as a Heiltsuk narrative comments, had to "feed them just like you feed kids" (Harkin 1997a:49). "The fight with a reflection: 'Not until we became more accustomed to the white man's way of thinking did we come to realize how comical we had appeared in presence of the stranger. And our aged persons, usually with a suppressed smile recited some of these drolleries in which some of us appeared to act the part of a buffoon[']" (UEN, "History: And the pig lay in state"; see also Olson 1967:88; UEN, "Public School Lectures, History"; Cove and MacDonald 1987:158–159).

These stories, however, are not just about acquisition of knowledge of the white men and their ways. They are about a fundamental shift in world-view, the entry into an ironic world in which the old virtues of the forefathers and ancestors are not sufficient. The Tlingit warrior in one contact narrative who tries to fight the double he spies in a mirror is faultlessly brave, but that does not stop him from looking humorous or absurd to his more sophisticated descendants (UEN, "History: And the pig lay in state"). In Harkin's words (1997:62), the encounter stories portray the arrival of "a new historicity."

These stories are indeed like myths, but their importance is not just the degree to which they follow the mythic pattern. It is, crucially, also the ways in which they deviate from it. These stories are something like anti-myths. Just as true myths are the charter for traditional life, these can be seen as forming the charter for the transformation of that traditional worldview.

When these stories were retold 100 or 150 years after the first encounter, narrators and listeners were well aware of all that had happened since. The context of their lives provided numerous reversals in relation to the mythic pattern. The encounter, in the long term, had weakened rather than strengthened the power of chiefs. It did not lead to wealth pouring out of the spirit realm; it brought devastating diseases, impoverishment, loss of autonomy, and ultimately loss of the land itself.

Moreover, encounter stories can be seen not just as anti-myths but also as anti-histories. Where traditional historical narratives hold up an example for current and future generations to emulate or avoid, in this class of historical narrative even the most virtuous ancestors can be ridiculed.

There is even some evidence that the arrival of the flawed and ironic postcontact world is presented as a further development tacked onto the traditional cosmogony: as a kind of second transformation that altered the landscape of the aboriginal historical era in a manner comparable to the way the myth-age transformers changed the myth world. For example, in those encounter stories where the first sailing vessel is thought to be Raven's boat (e.g., Dauenhauer and Dauenhauer 1987:298–309), the narrators may be drawing an implicit parallel between Raven's actions in myth times that were beneficent to human beings — such as releasing water, light, or salmon into the world — and the different transformations that whites will bring.

It is tempting to view first-encounter stories as if they are direct evidence of that historical moment of shifting perspective, a record of the transformation of the pristine indigenous worldview into a colonized, ironic one. It is certainly possible to search in them for Western-style historical content (note, for example, Emmons 1911). The first-encounter narratives that we have, however, were not collected at the time of the encounter. They were largely recorded during the 20th century, at the same time as the major collections of north Pacific myths and "traditional" historical narratives, and often from the same people. The encounter stories are — and this is a critical point — *commentary* made 100 or more years later. All three types of narrative, in other words, were being offered synchronously by 20th-century storytellers as different ways of seeing the past and, it is assumed, of understanding their present and future.

We can suppose that, as commentary on contemporary life, all three types of narrative (myth, "traditional" history, encounter story) address *contemporary* Native relationships both to traditional cultural values and to the dominant society. The diversity of narrative types might then stand for coexisting "ways of thinking and feeling" (Boas 1935:v) about past and present. Time progression and the stages of cosmogony might then function in part as a metaphor for the degree of tension and dissonance.

This line of argument brings us back to the discussion about the variety of relationships between myth and history in the Boas-Hunt Kwakwa̱ka̱'wakw materials. The mythic and secular "qualities" are presented not merely as successive stages of the cosmos; they are also cyclical conditions recurring yearly; they can coexist as two different ways of understanding the origins of important institutions; and the mythic quality can, in fact, under the right circumstances, be brought to the fore at any narrative moment (and moment of experience?) occurring in secular time. We can speculate that to the storytellers who gave us all three types of narrative, the ironic, anti-mythic "quality" of encounter narratives intertwines in narrative and in real life with the other two "qualities" in a similarly complex way. First one, then another, dominates.

Certainly indigenous storytellers could "turn over" — as Hunt's Kwa-k'wala refers to the change between qualities — the dominant ironic quality of contact stories and use them for the traditional purposes of history, to construct a positive reinterpretation of traditional virtues. In the Heiltsuk narrative published by Harkin, the Heiltsuk move from paralysis and fear during the encounter to a new mastery of their world through acquiring and displaying the new forms of power — a passage, in fact, that repeats the mythic model. In his Taant'a̱kwáan narrative, Shotridge focuses on the value of the traditional virtues in and of themselves: X̱ax'áan's "character of forti-tude," which allows him to maintain his courage and composure in the face of every bizarre occurrence.

Another Tlingit first-encounter story from Shotridge, this one from Klawak, illustrates this point more explicitly (UEN, "Public School Lec-tures"). As in other first-encounter narratives, the Tlingits initially perceive the first white man's ship to be a monster. The story describes a number of actions they undertake out of ignorance, including the fact that they only dare look at the ship through holes in a devil's-club root. But what Shot-ridge emphasizes is that they do not run away. Instead, a brave man goes out to investigate because, as Shotridge writes, "were the strange monster a distructive kind the hunting grounds for his people would be no longer safe."

Like the ordinary historical narratives in which virtue is an important theme, this story, which Shotridge composed as a lecture for Philadelphia schoolchildren, holds up the behavior of its main character as exemplary. Shotridge wrote,

> When I imagined myself . . . walking out from the forest with no defense or means of escape,- what was the use of carrying the bow and arrows, such weapon was like a baby s toy at that moment; coming out to be devoured by a monster which had never been heard of in the country, the blood began to rush to my head; there I sat before the narretor, an example of a modern coward. You know, the fellows who can do what this man did are not many now. . . .
>
> It is not what these peoples did, when they first met, that I have in mind now, but the unselfish part which Tánah took. You Imagine the great danger, had this ship turned out to be in reality a dangerous living being. So it was ever in a real man's mind: "Some one must sacrifice in order to insure safety for all."

Shotridge's virtue of sacrifice for the greater good recalls Dan Katseek's traditional historical narrative in which the Klukwan chief offers his life to forestall a war. And like those narratives, Shotridge's story also looks forward — it is offered to a group of young children as an example to be admired, even imitated. In this instance, though, Shotridge is working yet a further change on the self-portrayal of Natives in these narratives. He, a Native, is holding up the naive but courageous Native character to *white* children as an example of a "real man."

Conclusion

This essay explores several aspects of the extensive oral history materials from the North Pacific Coast. It examines these materials both for evidence of Western-style historical accuracy and in terms of some of the indigenous notions of history that inform them. These historical narratives are also examined as a form of oral literature comparable to North Pacific Coast myths.

The essay also looks at a particular class of historical narratives: stories of contact — in particular, first contact — with whites. This class stands in opposition to the "traditional" mythic and historical narratives in several ways. They depict an ironic, almost "post-historical" world in which mythic expectations are subverted, and traditional virtues are often shown to be insufficient. Storytellers could also, however, use first-contact incidents as a means to reinforce the work of myth and to exemplify traditional virtues.

This is a rather superficial tour of a very large territory. It represents only a first step toward better understanding of this marvelous, complex, and moving body of narrative, where deeper exploration promises rich rewards.

Notes

An earlier version of this essay, titled " 'Some Mysterious Means of Fortune': Literary Patterns in North Pacific Coast Oral History," was given at the conference titled *Perspectives on Native American Oral Literature,* held March 5–8, 1998, at the First Nations House of Learning and Green College, University of British Columbia, Vancouver. I would like to thank Michael Harkin and Sergei Kan for their helpful comments on this earlier draft; Nora Dauenhauer and Christopher Roth for their aid with, respectively, some of the Tlingit and Coast Tsimshian spellings; and Igor Kopytoff for his insights into the personal experience of cultural transformation, which spurred me to a better understanding of contact narratives.

1. Kwak'wala words are written in one of three orthographies. Common terms for social groups (e.g., Kwakwaka'wakw) appear in the orthography of the U'mista Cultural Centre of Alert Bay, BC. Other Kwak'wala words are written in an orthography that follows that of Lincoln and Rath (1980), with, however, retention of nonphonemic schwa (ə) for ease of reading. In quotations from Boas or Hunt, words appear as originally transcribed. Tlingit, except in cited titles of Shotridge manuscripts, has been transcribed in the widely used Story-Naish orthography.

2. Swanton gives the groom's name as Gunahéen. This may be another name used by Taaxsha, or it may indicate another marriage in a later generation. The fact that names repeat from generation to generation frequently makes interpretation of these materials problematic.

3. McKay's genealogy, as set down by Olson, is in parts quite difficult to interpret. As it stands, however, both men are shown as descendants of S'eiltín's oldest son. McKay was also descended through the youngest son as well, appearing six generations below S'eiltín through this link.

4. McKay's genealogy extends seven generations further into the past to a Gaana-x.ádi clan ancestress named Joon, a female shaman, whose history McKay also related to Olson (1967:115; see also Swanton 1905b:248–249). According to McKay's genealogy, Joon might have lived around 1560–1600.

5. About the Petrel Hat, art historian Steve Brown states, "Its small size and the style of workmanship and flat design all point to something at least early- or readily even pre-eighteenth century" (personal correspondence, July 5, 2002).

6. Nora Dauenhauer kindly supplied the spelling and clan affiliation of the name X̲'unéi (personal correspondence, July 18, 2002). Three other men on Benson's genealogy are mentioned in connection with this war: Shkuwuyéil, apparently Yeilxáak's predecessor as head of the Klukwan G̲aanax̲.teidí; Ldaaxéin (or Ldaaxéen), Shkuwuyéil's father-in-law and a high-ranking member of the opposing L'uknax̲.ádi clan; and Yeil Tlein, Yeilxáak's own father-in-law, also a L'uknax̲.ádi. Shotridge's information (AHL: "Gànkà yé·lì") suggests that Yeil Tlein is X̲'unéi, the chief encountered by the Spanish at Yakutat in 1791, but Swanton's account (1909b:160–165) has these two as different men.

7. These statements apply to myths narrated using the most heavily marked discourse style.

8. Where knowledge permits I have corrected Olson's often-faulty transcriptions of Tlingit names. There are several additional problems with Olson's published version: for instance, the murdered woman is said to be Katzeek's paternal grandmother, obviously an error as she is Dak̲l'aweidí, and his paternal grandmother would belong to the opposite moiety. White military authorities as well as the missionaries living in Klukwan give more elaborate accounts of these events, which took place in 1881, and there are, as always, a number of questions in reconciling the different stories (Willard 1995:38–41; Emmons 1991:50–51).

9. Internal evidence suggests that this story might have been told by someone who had heard it from the steersman Atch'éiyi, though this does raise questions about the date of the encounter. The Taant'ak̲wáan were early participants in the sea otter trade, and by 1793 "Clement City," as it was called, later the site of the Tongass winter village Kaduk̲guká, was already well-known to European and American fur traders (Paul 1971:13; Gibson 1992:110, 207). The encounter must therefore have occurred before 1790. The steersman seems the younger and less experienced of the hunters, but even so Atch'éiyi would have been elderly by the mid-19th century, in his 70s or 80s. It is not inconceivable that Chief Johnson, who was himself quite elderly in the 1920s, overlapped with Atch'éiyi, but there may also have been intermediary narrators passing on the story. Moreover, there are several other versions of the Taant'ak̲wáan first encounter (Paul 1971; Olson 1967:87–88) with different participants, suggesting several first-contact or early contact experiences.

10. I am grateful to Nora Dauenhauer for her aid in retranscribing this line; she offers yóo k̲uwanóok for Shotridge's yé-qùwà-nú.k.

11. In Tlingit it was known as the Proud Raven pole, but as a photograph of Abra-

ham Lincoln served as the model for the white man, it is more generally known as the Lincoln pole (Paul 1971:6, 10; Olson 1967:87).

12. This type of story is well represented among the Boas-Hunt materials from the neighboring Kwakwaka'wakw and is also found among Salishan groups; to what degree it can also be claimed for the Nuu-chah-nulth is uncertain (see Bierwert 1996:232–233 for discussion of versions from Puget Sound and vicinity).

THE AUDIBLE LIGHT IN THE EYES

In Honor of Claude Lévi-Strauss

Robert Bringhurst

I

The whole of France, according to Camus, is a place where human time and nature's time have mingled past division. And according to a calendar that mingles nature's time with man-made time like a glass of wine or a vase of flowers, today is summer solstice in the year 2000: a good day to be in Paris.

One hundred years ago this month, in a land where the peaceful mingling of time had been violently upset, a young man by the name of John Reed Swanton was beginning his career, defending his doctoral thesis at Harvard. It was a study of the grammar of two closely related languages: Kathlamet and Shoalwater Chinook, whose last fluent speaker had been dead since 1897. Linguistics was not taught at Harvard in those days — Roman Jakobson was only four years old — but after taking two degrees at Harvard, Swanton had begun linguistic work with Franz Boas in New York. A student doing this today would be expected to transfer to Columbia, where Boas was on staff. A century ago, *alma mater* had a meaning it has lost. Swanton had become a Harvard man, and on the strength of Boas's recommendation, Harvard gave him his doctorate as well.

Three months later — Tuesday, September 25, 1900 — Swanton stepped ashore in the Haida country, off the coast of British Columbia. In his pocket was a five-page letter of instructions that Boas had written the previous June. Before him was a world where smallpox and missionary pressure had exercised their powerful effects. The skeletons of ancient Haida structures were still standing in the ghost towns, but in the two inhabited villages, all the traditional houses, and nearly all the monumental sculpture, had already been destroyed. Yet as soon as Swanton asked to hear a story in Haida, the world he was seeking reappeared. Just beneath the surface, a rich tradition of Haida oral literature lay secretly alive.

Swanton's Haida teachers saw at once how his talents could be used. They told him what they wanted written down; and what they didn't want written, they did not tell. Swanton cheerfully accepted that arrangement, ignoring Boas's instructions. He took dictation and language lessons six days a week for nearly a year and spent another two years editing the texts he had transcribed. These texts include the following:

1. a myth-cycle of epic length (close to eight hours long in oral form; in printed form about 5,500 lines) dictated in October 1900 by the poet Skaay of the Qquuna Qiighawaay;
2. the longest and by far the most complex version of the Raven Cycle ever recorded on the Northwest Coast, about 1,500 lines, again dictated by the poet Skaay;
3. a village history of great literary stature and of epic length — at least six hours in oral form; in printed form about 4,000 lines — dictated in December 1900 by Kilxhawgins of Ttanuu;
4. about 80 independent narratives, averaging 20 to 40 minutes but ranging in length up to two hours each, dictated for the most part by three oral poets named Ghandl, Haayas, and Kingagwaaw;
5. several thousand lines of autobiography dictated by an old warrior and trader by the name of Sghaagya; and
6. much else belonging to the four main genres of Haida oral literature, which are *qqaygaang* (myth), *qqayaagaang* (lineage story), *gyaahlghalang* (history), and *sghalaang* (song).

In short, what Swanton heard, and single-handedly transcribed, was a literature of classical dimensions and complexity and power. At the end of his first month of transcribing, Swanton likened the work he was hearing to Homeric epic, and indeed the resemblance is deep although the surface similarities are few.[1]

When they were made, Swanton's Haida texts formed the largest body of literature transcribed in any native language north of Mexico and by far the largest literary corpus from the Northwest Coast. This has not remained the case. Boas and his colleague Q'ixitasu' (George Hunt), working separately and together from 1886 until 1931, wrote about three times as much in Kwakwala as Swanton did in Haida in the course of that one year, and thanks to the work of other devoted scribes, working steadily for decades, there is now much more to read in Navajo, Inuktitut, and Cree than there is in Haida.

The eight-hour cycle that I mentioned, dictated by the Haida poet Skaay of the Qquuna Qiighawaay, nevertheless remains the longest and most complex single work of oral literature ever recorded on the Northwest Coast. And embedded in Sghaagya's autobiography is a set-piece poem composed and performed as part of a peace-making venture some 50 years before Swanton wrote it down. It dates, in other words, from roughly 1850. As such, that little poem appears to be the oldest single piece of literature we have from the Northwest Coast. It may, by a slim margin, be the oldest extant actual text in any Native Canadian language. More to the point, the major authors in Swanton's collection — Skaay, Ghandl, Haayas, Kingagwaaw, and Kilxhawgins — have survived as major authors, patiently waiting for the rest of us to recognize how good they really are.

Back in Washington and New York, neither Boas nor anyone else appeared at first to see the value of this work. The most important of Swanton's manuscripts sat unpublished in Boas's office for more than 30 years and has been sitting unpublished since his death in a Philadelphia library. The rediscovery, retranslation, and publication of these texts as literature rather than anthropological data or folklore therefore stands as a new phase — not an entirely peaceful phase at the moment — in the generally bleak and ugly history of interaction between Europeans and Native Americans on the Northwest Coast.

The appreciation of Native American oral literature as literature is not, however, a new idea. Native American audiences have been appreciating the skill and wisdom of their mythtellers for centuries, no matter how slow outsiders have been to catch up. And not all the outsiders were so slow. The literary qualities of Native American literature were a central concern to Jeremiah Curtin, who was born two decades earlier than Boas, and the example Curtin set was important to Edward Sapir. But Curtin spent little time on the Northwest Coast and did his most serious work on Seneca. In a more technical sense, the study of native literatures as literature starts late in the 1950s. That is when Dell Hymes began his lifelong study of literary form in Native American oral literature. This has proven an extremely fruitful line of enquiry. Like the work of Vladimir Propp, Roman Jakobson, and Claude

Lévi-Strauss, it also proves the essential seamlessness of literary studies and linguistics — a seamlessness that far too many linguists, and far too many literary critics, still deny.

Swanton is important in this respect not just because he took a lot of texts that are literarily superb, but because a sense of literature, of poetry, of literary value, is something he and his Haida teachers shared.

I would like us all to stop referring to these texts as Swanton's texts, after the man who wrote them down. I think we ought to call them, like other works of literature, after the names of their actual authors. But Swanton's contribution was essential. He did far more than take dictation. He *asked* for stories to be told; he paid the tellers to tell them, and he paid, in every case, for a capable and fluent Haida listener, so that he as the transcriber was always in a tertiary position. He also almost always *let the storyteller choose* the size and scope and content of the work. The effects of this procedure are easy to see. During his year in the Haida country Swanton functioned not just as a linguist and ethnographer but also as a major patron of the literary arts. No better use was ever made of the Bureau of American Ethnology's congressional appropriation or the American Museum of Natural History's budget for ethnographic research.

Along with John Swanton, the significant transcribers of classical North American oral literature include Leonard Bloomfield, Franz Boas, Ruth Bunzel, Roland Dixon, Fang-kuei Li, Pliny Goddard, Berard Haile, John Hewitt, Melville Jacobs, William Jones, Michael Krauss, Ekkehart Malotki, Douglas Parks, Paul Radin, Edward Sapir, Cornelius Uhlenbeck, and Gene Weltfish: all familiar names to specialists but to the literary public quite unknown. Yet they are just as important to the sustenance and propagation of culture as Carnegie or Morgan or Guggenheim or Barnes.

Four of the great transcribers published significant theoretical work and so acquired considerable renown in scholarly circles. These four are Boas, Bloomfield, Radin, and Sapir. But the people who told them the stories — even the best and most prolific of those who told them the stories — and who deserve the fame the most, have attained it least of all. I am thinking of myth-tellers such as Kainaikwan in Blackfoot; Q'eltí in Chinook and Kathlamet; François Mandeville in Chipewyan; Kâ-kîsikâw-pîhtokêw and Sâkêwêw in Cree; Anna Nelson Harry in Eyak; Skaay, Ghandl, and Kingagwaaw in Haida; Hetsmiixhwn in Hanis and Miluk; Sam Brown and Mrs. Molasses in Hupa; Bill Ray in Kato; Kootye in Kawaiko; Pahlnapí in Kutenai; Hánc'ibyjim in Maidu; Chiishch'ilíts'ósí and Charlie Mitchell in Navajo; Saayaacchapis and Qiixxa in Nootka; Kaagigeepinäsi and Midaasuganj in Ojibwa; Ctaahaaritkari' in Pawnee; Gwìsgwashaán in Takelma; and Tumaka and Leo Zuñi in Zuni. In any honest and nonpartisan study of North American literature, these and other indigenous authors would be given a prominent place—no less so than authors whose language is English or Spanish or French. Yet the names of these Native American mythtellers and poets are just beginning to appear, furtively, in a few encyclopedias of literature and bibliographical catalogues.[2]

Enlightened North Americans who advocate equality for persons of all races and all creeds are often far less liberal, or far less self-aware, in their attitudes toward language. Literature is very often taught, in the Americas, in much the way that pizza, wine, and cheddar cheese are sold: as something foreign at its root, now also made—bigger if not better—in the good old U.S.A. Poets and mythtellers—even the greatest among them—working in the languages indigenous to Canada, the United States, and all the nations to the south, have in general been regarded as perfectly irrelevant to the culture and identity of the countries in which they were born.

Yet there are all those texts to read: all that proof that literature belongs to the Americas as fully as salmon, corn, and squash.

The patron saint of all this text collecting is, of course, Franz Boas. Like many saints, he proves to be a highly complex character with secular as well as sacred interests. I would like to spend a moment considering the impact made upon his work by two men less well known. One of these was French. The other was one of the greatest Native American oral poets ever recorded.

The first substantial anthology of Native North American texts was made by Émile Petitot, a native of Dijon, and published in 1888 in Alençon. The main texts are in Chipewyan, Dogrib, Slavey, and Gwichin, with a tiny supplement in Cree, and all with parallel French translation. The book was subsidized by a well-to-do philologist, the Comte de Charencey, who was dissatisfied with Petitot's first treatment of these stories: a bowdlerized and prettified translation published in Paris in 1886 as part of a library of popular literature. That bowdlerized edition is still in print.

Boas rarely mentions these two books, but I think they had considerable impact on his thinking. Directly after the first and more popular version of

Petitot's anthology was published, Boas started working on a popular collection of his own: *Indianische Sagen von der Nord-Pacifischen Küste Amerikas*. Most of the work for this anthology was completed by the fall of 1889, and all of it by summer 1890, though the full text was not issued until 1895. In the meantime, two important events had occurred. First was the publication of the more rigorous version of Petitot's anthology, with full aboriginal texts and much more literal translations. The second was Boas's meeting, in the summer of 1890, with a 58-year-old oral poet named Q'eltí. The jubilant letters Boas wrote his wife and parents to commemorate that meeting show that Boas sensed, early on, what later and more careful study would confirm.[3] In years of pestering Native Americans for stories, Q'eltí was the first great mythteller, the first real poet, the first substantial *man of oral letters* that Boas had ever met.

Culture is not genetic; it has to be learned, where biological identity does not. And it has to be learned from those who possess it. Like the Haida poet Skaay, Q'eltí was not only a poet; he was a library: a living means for the reproduction of his own civilization.

Boas had done serious transcription work before, with the two Tsimshian mythtellers and singers he called Old Matthias and Mrs. Morison, but he recognized Q'eltí as an artist of a different order. Accordingly, Boas abandoned most of his travel plans and spent three seasons with Q'eltí, in 1890, 1891, and 1894. These were some of the most fruitful years of Boas's life. Through his transcription, Q'eltí became the author of two books: *Chinook Texts* (Boas 1894) and *Kathlamet Texts* (Boas 1901). These are the first indigenous texts of genuine substance published by Boas himself and the first substantial collections, in any language, of work by an individual Native North American author.

Another result was less direct. In 1896, under Boas's direction, John Swanton had started doctoral work on Lakhota. Then, brooding on the brilliance of the stories told him by Q'eltí, and on the imminent extinction of his languages, Boas overruled his student's decision. Swanton never met Q'eltí, but Q'eltí's great literary gifts are among the reasons Boas pressured Swanton to set aside his study of Lakhota and work on Chinook and Kathlamet instead. Swanton learned his sense of Native American literary form and literary value from Q'eltí. He spoke very little about this sense of form and value, but his actions leave no doubt that he possessed it. That was the sense he put to work when he arrived in Haida Gwaay, where he sat with fanatical patience at the feet of the best mythtellers he met. It was the sense he put to work again a few years later, defending his transcriptions against everyone's attempts, including Boas's, to cut them down to preconceived dimensions.

The way to prove what I have said about these texts would be to offer some examples, but listening to myths takes time, and listening for style in a foreign tongue or through the veil of translation takes a lot of time. In printed form this time turns into space. A thousand pages, I have discovered, is barely sufficient to lay out the evidence.[4] What I would like to do instead, in the time and space we have, is attempt a short demonstration of certain familiar features of mythtelling. These are features often found in the masterworks of Native American literature, but I will show them to you here in a different form, relying on mythtellers who work in a different medium and belong to a different tradition.

II

Figure 1 is an instance of mythtelling. The medium is oil on canvas instead of spoken words, and the mythteller — Diego de Silva y Velázquez — is a figure known by name to millions of admirers of European art. In almost every other respect this work can be directly and closely compared with accomplished instances of mythtelling transcribed in North America by linguists such as John Swanton. The painting was made in Seville about 1618. It is known now as *The Kitchen Maid and the Supper at Emmaus,* and it hangs in the National Gallery of Ireland.

Most of the things in the painting are actually *not* part of the myth. They are part of the mythteller's mental and physical world. But because they are here in the company of the myth, the myth affects them. That is a feature typical not only of Velázquez's early paintings but also of narrative poems told in Haida by Skaay and Ghandl, Kingagwaaw and Haayas. Myth illuminates the quotidian and vice versa.

The myth in this case is the story of the dead Christ rising from the grave, walking toward Emmaus, meeting some old friends along the way, and joining them for dinner, where belatedly he is recognized. The myth per se is stated only in the upper left corner of the canvas (Figure 2). Yet the light cast by the myth inundates everything around it: everything within the frame of the painting and everyone outside that frame who comes up to the painting

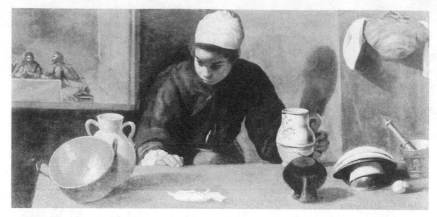

1. Diego Rodríguez de Silva y Velázquez. *The Kitchen Maid and the Supper at Emmaus.* c. 1618. Oil on canvas, 55 × 118 cm. National Gallery of Ireland, Dublin.

2. Detail of Figure 1: the myth scene.

3. Diego Rodríguez de Silva y Velázquez. *Christ in the House of Martha and Mary.*
c. 1618. Oil on canvas, 60 × 103 cm. National Gallery, London.

4. Detail of Figure 1: the dishes.

and allows it to keep saying what it says. This is another feature typical of many of the finest Haida stories Swanton heard. The myth illuminates the life and times of those *outside* the frame as well as those within it.

For this to happen, it is necessary to enter the world of the story, but not to violate the frame. For the myth to do its work, the hearer or the reader or the viewer of the myth must learn the language of ideas in which the myth performs its function—but that is not to say that one must join any ethnic community or religion. Velázquez's painting can and does work its magic on non-Christians, the plays of Sophocles can and do work magic on non-Greeks, and the narrative poems of Skaay and Ghandl can have plenty of meaning for non-Haidas.

Figure 3 is another painting made by the same painter, in the same place, at nearly the same time: *Christ in the House of Martha and Mary,* now in the National Gallery in London. The surface structure—to borrow Chomsky's term—is much the same in these two paintings, though symmetrically inverted. There is a background scene confined to one far corner and a foreground scene located in a kitchen. But I am not sure that in this case there is any fundamental separation between the realms, as there is in the previous painting. The women in this kitchen may be myth creatures just as fully as those in the farther room.

Like works of Haida oral literature, these paintings disobey one of the central tenets of modernism, that form and content ought to be the same. Form is something more (or something less) than an extension of content in mythology just as it is in human language. Forms exist in their own right, like cups and bowls and sentence structures. Forms exist as independently as chairs, in which anyone may sit unless restrained by social rules.

Incidentally, there is food in this painting. There are fishes, boiled eggs, a broken bulb of garlic, a capsicum pepper. In the *Supper at Emmaus,* there is no food at all apart from garlic—but that is a painting in which the central character no longer needs to eat; and where food is no longer required, purification may well be needed instead. The central character in the *Supper at Emmaus* is painted with a few quick strokes and tucked away in a back corner, but his story fills the frame. This kind of atmospheric effect and symbolic detail is typical, once again, of well-told works of Haida oral literature.

One of the former owners of the *Supper at Emmaus*—we do not know who it was—had the myth painted out. The alteration was forgotten and re-mained undetected until 1933, when the painting was cleaned. So for much of its life, this piece of mythtelling lay in obscurity, misunderstood. In that respect again, it resembles some of the finest works of Native American oral literature. There is some authority, though, for the alteration. Mythtellers—young ones especially—are very often interested in other things than myth. Figure 5 is a mythless version of the painting (now in Chicago) apparently made by Velázquez himself.

It seems to me that its mythic dimension is crucial to the *Supper at Emmaus,* but there is also plenty to be learned from the quotidian details. Notice if you will the basket and its towel, the upright pitcher, the mortar and pestle, the inverted stack of dishes (Figure 4). In Velázquez's original paint-ing those dishes are lit by the myth—but they didn't come from the myth. They came from the mythteller's circumstance. They came, in all probability, from Velázquez's mother's kitchen.

Another work by the same painter, also dated 1618, is known as the *Old Woman Cooking Eggs* (Figure 6). It is in Edinburgh now, in the National Gal-lery of Scotland, though it was painted in Seville, where Velázquez was born and where he lived until 1621. There is the same basket, the same towel. There is the mortar and pestle. There is the pitcher. The story, however, is gone, replaced by another in which eggs have a very different connotation. Myths are stories, and stories, like music, like painting, like language itself, are full of repetitions. Forms, phrases, images, and rhythms are repeated, forming patterns whose content is subject to change.

Figure 7 is yet another painting made in the same years: *Two Young Men at Table,* now in the Wellington Museum, London. There is the same inverted stack of dishes, and the same mortar and pestle, here also upside down. This kind of imagistic echo, this recycling of luminous detail, is frequent in poetry worldwide, and Haida narrative poetry is no exception.

Stories can be inverted just as easily as kitchen utensils and bowls. In Velázquez's version of the *Supper at Emmaus,* the kitchen maid is in the fore-ground, Christ and his disciples in the back. But when Rembrandt painted the same scene in Leiden about 1628, he reversed them (Figure 8). Here the myth is right up front. The serving maid is in the background, opening her oven. This painting is in Paris, where it hangs in the Musée Jacquemart-André. The paraphernalia in this painting isn't reused, so far as I recall, in

5. Diego Rodríguez de Silva y Velázquez. *Kitchen Scene.* c. 1620. Oil on canvas, 56 × 104 cm. Robert Waller Memorial Fund, 1935.380. The Art Institute of Chicago.

6. Diego Rodríguez de Silva y Velázquez. *Old Woman Cooking Eggs.* c. 1618. Oil on canvas, 99 × 117 cm. National Gallery of Scotland, Edinburgh.

7. Diego Rodríguez de Silva y Velázquez. *Two Young Men at Table.* c. 1619. Oil on canvas, 65 × 104 cm. Wellington Museum, London.

8. Rembrandt van Rijn. *Pilgrims at Emmaus.* c. 1628. Oil on paper over panel, 39 × 42 cm. Musée Jacquemart-André, Paris.

other works by Rembrandt, but there are qualities of light and color here that belong to him alone. Art historians and amateurs alike perceive them as the Dutch mythteller's signature. In Haida literature as well, we find inversions of this kind and equally personal touches.

Such inversions are explored in some detail in one of the most imaginative works of 20th-century scholarship, Lévi-Strauss's *Mythologiques*. But it is important, I think, to remember that they occur in the domain of the individual just as much as in the domain of the cultural type. We encounter such inversions when comparing the works of individual Haida mythtellers or of individual European painters, just as we do when comparing themes and forms across great spatial and temporal distances.

III

Close attention to individual artists and their works is a well-established practice in European studies, and the museum collections are built with that approach in mind. Native American art has rarely been collected, catalogued, or stored in the same way. But when we look at Native American art more closely and pay it the same attention and respect to that we routinely pay to works from Europe, we always find that Native American artists are individuals, too. I will try to demonstrate this fact in a token way through a single pair of illustrations.

Figure 9 is a stone dish carved in low relief by the Haida artist Daxhiigang (1839–1920). It was made, I believe, around 1880 and is now in the Field Museum of Natural History, Chicago. The material is argillite, a soft black stone much used by Haida carvers in the nineteenth century, but not for works that were intended to remain within the community. The theme is a much-loved episode in the story of the Raven. Skaay put this episode in the final movement of his poem *Xhuuya Qaagaangas* (*Raven Travelling*) when he dictated it to Swanton in October 1900. In that performance, it goes like this:

> Gyaanhaw sta lla qaaydang, wansuuga.
> Ll qqagighans gutxhanhaw
> jaasing lla xadangxidang, wansuuga.
> Gyaanhaw jaaghang qquhlgha jaasing lla qqaawdas.
> Gyaanhaw sta lla tluuqaaydang, wansuuga.   5

9. Daxhiigang (Charlie Edenshaw). *The Raven and His Bracket Fungus Steersman.*
c. 1880. Argillite plate, 35 cm diameter. Field Museum of Natural History,
Chicago. © The Field Museum, # A102063.

Taana qan·kkugya lla ttsaa'anhlingas
gyaan qqadang lla isdas.
Kittaw ising lla isdas.

Gyaanhaw ll qaadla qqayghudyas gutgwiixhan guttagahliyasi.
Gyaanhaw llaghan aaxhana ghyalgaay dluu   10
ll aadagaghihls.
Gyaanhaw lla dangat styaalang, wansuuga.

Gyaan ttlaayttlaay ising lla ttsaa'anhlingas
gyaan lla dangat ising lla gittaxidas.
Llaghan aaxhana ghyalgaay dluu   15
lla ising haaying xitxidaginggwangas.
Gyaanhaw giina wadluuxhan ghaduu lla ghitsgyas.

Gyaan gyalgas naangha lla qqalingas
gyaan ttaangghaa lla tsaadlnadas.

10. Daxhiigang (Charlie Edenshaw). *The Raven and His Bracket Fungus Steersman.*
c. 1892. Argillite plate, 32 cm diameter. National Museum of Ireland, Dublin.
(Top and side views.)

Gyaan, "agang aa qqadangaadang ttaas   20
gaystlgangan hla," han lla lla suudas.

Gyaan lla dangat lla tluuqaaydasi.
Llaghan aaxhanaghilaay dluu
haying qajing lla qqaynaangas.

Gyaanhaw nang yuuwan at nang xajuu lla kitxhaghadlgas   25
gyaan dangat lla stiihlsi.
Gyaanhaw ll isghaawas
gyaan jaaghang ghan lla ghaghuyins
gyaan gii nang lla ttl guusgidas.

Gyaan jaasing gi ising nang lla istas.   30
Gyaan Siiwas sghayhlas.
Gyaan han lla suudas,
"Haw skkyaan dang gyaagha qagana aldasghasga."

Then he left the place, they say.
And as he was leaving,
he picked up his sister, they say.
He left his sister with his wife.
Then, they say, he set off by canoe. 5

He asked the Junco to serve as his steersman
and took him aboard.
He also took a spear.

The things he had come for were sprawled on the reef
over top of each other.
As soon as they drew alongside, 10
the Junco went mad.
He brought the Junco back, they say.

Then he asked the Steller's Jay to be his steersman,
and they headed out together.
As soon as they drew alongside, 15
the Jay started shaking and flapping his wings.
Whoever tried to do it failed.

Then he painted a face on a bracket fungus
and seated it in the stern.
"Look alive there, and backpaddle 20
as soon as we come alongside," he said.

Then he headed out with him.
When they drew alongside,
the fungus nodded his head.

The one we speak of speared a large one and a small one, 25
and he brought the two of them home.
He went ashore there
and called his wife to come
and put one of them on her.

Then he put the other on Siiwas, his sister. 30
She started to cry,

and he said to her,
"Yours will be safe, my darling."
(Skaay 2001:335–336)

Skaay never says point-blank what the Raven and his bracket fungus steersman are hunting. His Haida audience knew as well as he that the quarry was a crucial part of feminine anatomy, without which the Raven's wife and sister were clearly incomplete. Skaay was not the least bit bashful in such matters, nor was he hiding his light under a missionary bushel—but he did possess an ancient virtue: hunterly reserve. To name the quarry plainly in the poem might have been as pointless as to carve the quarry's image naturalistically in the midst of a formline sculpture.

The old Haida villages were filled with public painting and sculpture. House poles, memorial and mortuary poles, masks, rattles, frontlets, storage boxes, serving bowls, canoes, and other objects were dense repositories of images. The Raven and his Bracket Fungus Steersman is a subject not found on any of these works, but it was a favorite theme of Daxhiigang's, and he carved it in argillite at least three times. The Field Museum's plate is the earliest extant example. Another, which remained for many years in private hands, is now in the Seattle Art Museum. The last version known, made about 1892, is in the National Museum of Ireland (Figure 10). These three plates were made for export, yet each is intelligible only from within Haida intellectual culture, for that is where Daxhiigang's graphic language has its roots and where the story itself was (and still is) told.

There is a real sense, then, in which these works are international. They were made in and for a world with a cultural outside and a cultural inside—but one in which the outside and the inside did not exclude each other. Beyond that, of course, they tell us something about the individual artist who made them. They tell us how Daxhiigang's sense of form and his sense of the Raven's character changed over the space of a decade or so, and how his sense of spatial organization had remained the same.

If we had several transcriptions of Skaay's poem *Raven Travelling*, made over the space of a decade or more, we could compare them in the same way. We do not have that luxury in his case, nor in the case of any other Haida author. But during the single month of October 1900, as he dictated some 7,000 lines of Haida narrative poetry to Swanton, Skaay returned many times to certain themes. We can watch him reuse certain phrases and ideas, in much the way that the young Diego Velázquez reused a stack of dishes. We can also watch him vary the arrangement of components, changing the pace from one occasion to the next, and focusing on certain aspects here, other aspects there.

IV

Every skilled performance of a myth, it seems to me, whether the medium is oil paint or words or something else, can speak at least three languages at once. It can speak to us about the human species, and about the local culture, and about the individual telling the myth. The fact that myths are timeless stories, capable of traveling the globe, does not in any way prevent them from exploring local conditions or from expressing individual emotions. The mythtellers Swanton met in Haida Gwaay a century ago used shared and inherited stories to speak not only of timeless concerns but also of deeply personal matters, including the deaths of their wives and the loss of their villages.

Along with these three kinds of information, I think there is usually a fourth, which is there because myths are not just stories; they are narrative hypotheses, personified theorems that address the very nature of the world. Myths are not like landscape paintings, which are merely *about nature* or nature's position vis-à-vis the human domain. Myths are about the nature of nature. They are, for all their marvelous concreteness, also wonderfully abstract. They routinely do what art does and what science does as well. They are, I wish to say, a means of art and a means of science, too: a means not just of recording impressions but of investigating and organizing principles of form and content that extend beyond our species.

This brings us, if you will, to another *inversion*, another transformation in which content is divided but maintained while its form undergoes a drastic change.

In mythtelling cultures, theorems that address the nature of the world are expressed in personified form. A grammatical statement made with personified elements is what we call a *story*. Where the languages of myth are displaced by those of mathematics, the inverse assumption is made. Even where everyone knows better, both the constants and the variables are treated as if they were dead. A grammatical statement made with depersonified, depersonalized elements is known by and large as an equation. We find them in music, abstract painting, and academic prose as well as in mathematics. These are the inverted forms of myths, in principle no better and in principle no worse. Tradition matters in both cases. But in both cases, who is doing the telling, and how, matters every bit as much.

Nearly 40 years ago, in the overture to the first volume of *Mythologiques,* Lévi-Strauss expressed the essence of his undertaking in a simple, lucid sentence: *Nous ne pretendons . . . pas montrer comment les hommes pensent dans les mythes mais comment les mythes se pensent dans les hommes, et à leur insu* (We don't pretend to show how people think in myths, but how myths think themselves in people, and without their even knowing this occurs; my translation). That sentence has lingered in my brain since the day long ago when I first read it. I think that it expresses Franz Boas's aim, too, though Boas himself was never quite sufficiently articulate to put it in those terms.

In my own studies of Native American literature I have turned more and more in the other direction, to dwell on the contributions of individuals. This, it seems to me, is what Swanton also wanted at the start of his career, though again, he never said it plainly. It is something that Edward Sapir and Leonard Bloomfield also valued highly, and Sapir is the one who stated it most clearly.

But these are not in the end alternatives. There are no individual artists without a tradition, and there are no artistic traditions that don't depend for their existence on the work of individuals. *The ways myths think themselves in people* are intimately linked, *à leur insu,* with *the ways people think themselves in myths,* and the study of each enriches the study of the other.

Notes

1. Swanton's statement on this subject—contained in a letter to Charles Newcombe—is published in Bringhurst 1999:175.
2. W. H. New's *Encyclopedia of Literature in Canada* (University of Toronto Press, 2002), which pays considerable respect to aboriginal literatures, is the best example I have seen of this new attitude.
3. These letters are published in Rohner 1969:121–122.
4. Bringhurst 1999; Ghandl 2000; Skaay 2001.

Martine J. Reid and Daisy Sewid-Smith

In recent years autobiography as a genre has come under a good deal of scrutiny. Is an autobiography a fiction of the self? A story of a story? "A novel that dares not speak its name" (attributed to Roland Barthes without any further citation in Heilbrun 1988:28)? North American First Nations autobiographical material especially has been the subject of much discussion in anthropological literature. Even treated as "a culturally specific narrative genre" (Cruikshank 1990:x), autobiographies still raise many issues, as we shall see in this essay, which explores new perspectives on the writing down (textualization) of a nonliterate First Nations individual's verbal art. This essay is a preamble to the forthcoming publication *Paddling to Where I Stand: Agnes Alfred, Qwiqwasut'inuxw Noblewoman,* edited by Martine Reid and translated by Daisy Sewid-Smith (in press).[1]

Autobiography

There are several ways to record a person's life. The subject may tell it and write it, in what she or he chooses to call a self-written first-person narrative, or an autobiography. A biographer may write the person's life from direct or indirect sources in what is called a biography. Preliterate North American First Nations individuals have narrated their lives (or episodes of their lives) to intermediaries, such as ethnographers, ethnologists, historians, and doctors, and these life history narratives form another category of writings, known as "as-told-to autobiographies." Georg Misch (1951) and Karl Weintraub (1978) have described their histories of Western autobiography "as the history of the rise of the idea of the individual in the West" (Brumble 1988:4). Although the history of Western autobiography spans some 4,500 years, starting with the ancient Greeks, this genre as we know it in its most popular form is relatively recent and began to be common only after the 18th century.[2] Since then it has become so well entrenched, so structured by convention, that Western readers now consider it to be a "natural" genre not requiring explanation. The familiar model comes from written autobiography, a first-person narrative that purports to describe the narrator's life or episodes in that life customarily with some chronological reflections about individual growth and development.

In *Le pacte autobiographique* Phillippe Lejeune defines autobiography as a "retrospective account that an actual person makes in prose of his own existence, stressing his individual life and particularly the history of his/her personality" (1975:14). The subject of this essay, ʔAx̌uw̓, was not explicit about the history of her personality in her narratives. Nevertheless, her telling of her life and social roles offers an unparalleled insight into her personality and the way she saw herself.

Life histories provide a method of assessing the individual in society: the relationship between a sense of self and a community. The use of First Nations life histories as ethnographic documents can be traced back to Franz Boas, the putative founder of North American modern scientific anthropology, whose intensive relationship with the Kʷakʷakəwakʷ and emphasis upon the collection of Native texts and personal interpretations of those led him to regard descriptions cast in the imagery of the people themselves as the "true" and "authentic" rendering of culture (Blackman 1981:65; Goldman 1975:xi). Scholars who followed Boas intellectually similarly valued the usefulness of the life-history document. One example among many is Paul Radin's 1926 publication *Crashing Thunder: The Autobiography of an American Indian,* (1983), perhaps one of the most popular narrated Indian autobiographies presented by an anthropologist.[3]

The methods and theories of the personal narrative have been applied and debated in anthropology for some time. North American literature, especially, is vast on the subject for which this is only a brief review. Some anthropologists recorded life stories either to "salvage" elements of "disappearing races" (reviewed by Krupat 1985; Brumble 1988) or to add a "human" dimension to anthropological science by presenting the individual "informant's" perspectives on his or her "worldview" or "culture" (Langness 1965:8). By the middle of the century the debates in anthropology centered primarily on the verification of the life story or on the validity of an individual's perspective vis-à-vis the ethnographer's "objective" observations from a range of other sources (Kluckhohn 1945; Langness 1965). Arnold Krupat in his work *For Those Who Came After* (1985) points out the necessity for collaborators in any cross-cultural project to see themselves as individuals present in a given place and time if they are going to begin to understand the nature and consequence of their work. At the boundary of the discipline First Nations women involved in personal narrative groups "have found that personal narratives provide insights into culture and society not afforded by conventional anthropological methods" (Howard-Bobiwash, 1999:117–118).[4] Such diverse methods underscore how personal narrative has been used to fit some theories while other researchers focused narrowly on its factual contribution.

On the one hand the past 20 years have seen an upsurge of autobiographical material, while on the other hand "anthropology's claim to provide authoritative interpretations of culture is being challenged from both inside and outside the discipline" (Cruikshank 1990:1).[5] Audiences for ethnological writings are changing and have become multiple as members of the described cultures are becoming increasingly critical readers of ethnography. Debates about how to represent cultural experience may be partly responsible for recent scholarly attention on these orally narrated life stories, but possibly there are other reasons for the recent proliferation of literary autobiographical documents. For example, some "ethnic biographers have produced brilliant explorations aimed at rediscovering the sources of language, and thereby also the nature of modern reality" (M. Fisher 1986:199). Also, renewed anthropological interest in life histories coincides with increasing attention to analysis of symbolism, meaning, and text. Much of the contemporary philosophical mood (in literary criticism and anthropology, as well as philosophy) is to inquire into what is hidden in language, what is conveyed by signs, what is pointed out, what is repressed, implied, or mediated.[6] What initially seem to be individualistic autobiographical accounts are often considered to be revelations of traditions and recollections of disseminated identities (M. Fisher 1986).

Fisher again in his essay "Ethnicity and the Post-Modern Arts of Memory" (1986:197) discusses this phenomenon of contemporary reinvention, or re-creation of ethnic identity through remembering, as perhaps a reaction to globalization and the fear of becoming leveled into identical "hominids." Furthermore, if First Nations (especially those who are literate) are going to be portrayed in the literature, they want these renderings written by themselves, not by others who may not understand things as the persons themselves understand them. The debate about autobiography as fiction is not new. The debate comes down to this: who writes what, about whom, and how?

Why is autobiography a fiction? Many factors are at play. In the case of a literary person, autobiography is a fiction by the writer of the story she or he has to tell, a construction of the self. No autobiography can be a "true" representation of the self in any absolute sense. But self-written autobiography is at least the subject's own fiction. With the as-told-to autobiographies of nonliterate First Nations persons, on the other hand, it is the recorder-editor who decides what is to be the final shape of his or her subject's "autobiography." Hence the roles of the editors must be disclosed. As-told-to autobiographies should be considered "bicultural documents, texts in which the assumptions of Indian autobiographers *and* Anglo editors are at work" (Brumble 1988:11).

Various authors have noted the natural human tendency for an autobiographer to select those experiences and events from his or her life that conform to or substantiate a fictional or mythic view of the self. We agree on this point of selection when we see that ʔAx̌uw̓ has on several occasions consciously deleted—by not telling—some relevant information. On the other hand if ʔAx̌uw̓ has, consciously or not, deleted some elements of her narratives, it perhaps has something to do with the belief that knowledge is power, and that she must never reveal all of what she knows (such as sacred notions or taboos, which can be harmful if revealed). That would be consistent with her view of what her life story is or should have been. There are some silences that are inherent to a particular life in a particular culture. ʔAx̌uw̓'s tellings as well as her silences, if they are interpreted, will have to be interpreted accordingly. This brings up a question of ethics. Do we reveal, if we happen to know from other sources, what the narrator, for whatever reasons, chose not to tell? Do we respect these forms of silence?

Writing Down As-told-to Autobiographies

Writing down another culture is not without flaws as the recorder-editor records, transcribes, and translates what the First Nations subject gives orally. Sally McClusky in her critique of *Black Elk Speaks* by John Neihardt (1932), titled "Black Elk Speaks, and So Does John Neihardt" (1972), is the first North American literary scholar to draw attention to the problem of editor-narrator relationships. Brumble (1988), Sarris (1993), and many other life history critics have concurred.

We are all aware of this problematical method. Ethnologists have approached informants to relate life history, asking questions along the way to guide them and to ensure adequate details. Ethnologists then edit these great bundles of material (now usually in translation) into something like chronological order, selecting content and making other changes necessary to transform a collection of transcripts of individual oral performances into a single, more or less continuous narrative, often editing out repetitions that are important stylistic and rhetorical features. The new imposed chronology distorts the narrator's sense of time. As Brumble pointed out, the whole process is a construction of the Western mind with Western habits of mind (1988:66).

According to Brumble, the published version of an autobiography without the hand of a non-Native editor is very rare. Of the 600 published American Indian texts that are autobiographical, more than 83 percent were narrated. Of these, 43 percent were collected and edited by anthropologists, and the other 40 percent were collected and edited by non-Natives from other disciplines.

Whether narrated or written, autobiography is not someone's life but an account or story of his or her life. ʔAx̌uw̓'s narrated life story is an account of an account, a story of a story. ʔAx̌uw̓'s story is, as it were, doubly edited: first during the encounter between herself (as narrator) and us (as recorder-editors) and second during the literary reencounter of the translation and editing process (see Sarris 1993:85). In the encounter between ʔAx̌uw̓ and us it is important to remember that for whatever personal or cultural reasons, she may have edited and shaped her oral narrative in certain ways. A selection may have taken place in her memory.

All autobiography is shaped by narrative convention, and the history of American Indian autobiography parallels the history of Western literary tradition in many ways (Brumble 1988:4–5). Among those researchers who followed Boas to the Northwest Coast and who valued the utility of the life history documents are Sapir, whose studies focused on a Nootka man (1921), Jenness on a Katzie man (1955), and Marius Barbeau on Haida carvers (1957). Four Northwest Coast life history documents span four successive generations of Southern Kʷakʷakəwakʷ cultural history and are particularly valuable for their documentation of continuity and change in that culture. In 1940 the Kʷakʷakəwakʷ informant Chief Charlie Nowell dictated his life to Clellan Ford (1941), and following him, in 1969 Kʷakʷakəwakʷ chief James Sewid, the father of translator Daisy Sewid-Smith, related his personal history with the editorial assistance of anthropologist James Spradley. Finally, Kʷakʷakəwakʷ chief Harry Assu of Cape Mudge collaborated on his life story with anthropologist Joy Inglis in 1989. In 1981 Chief James Wallas told Kʷakʷakəwakʷ legends to Pamela Whitaker, which include a very short portrait of this elder man. With the exception of the life history of Haida elder Florence Davidson by Margaret Blackman (1982) and the recent works by Julie Cruikshank on life histories of First Nations women from the Yukon (1990, 1998) (all interviews conducted in English), and by Dauenhauer and Dauenhauer (1994), most other documents of the lives of Northwest Coast Natives are about male individuals. As Augé has written, "anthropology is produced and received by men of a particular epoch and society, in a determinate intellectual political conjuncture" (1982:6).

As Margaret Blackman noted some 20 years ago, there has been a familiar pattern of shortcoming in ethnographic accounts: male ethnographers who were interested in life histories focused upon the roles and activities of Native men while similar data on women were incidental and incomplete, limited to discussions of the crises of a normal life cycle: birth, puberty, marriage, and death (1982:65). Although there is a growing body of anthropological literature that has attempted to correct the prevalent male viewpoint so pervasive in the discipline, this bias, so frequently lamented in the anthropological literature on women, is typical of the Northwest Coast ethnological material.[7] Anthropological literature on Native North Americans included a few examples of women's biographical accounts (Lurie 1961; Marriott 1948; Washburne 1940), but through the early 1970s, at the time we began our research, very few Native women had written their own autobiographies (Campbell 1973; Willis 1973). Northwest Coast ethnology, which is relatively rich in accounts on men's lives, is still lacking in similar materials on women.[8]

Aware of this lacuna in the anthropological literature and the pressing need for biographical material on women, and also for more personal than academic reasons, Daisy and I began work with her grandmother, Mrs.

Agnes Alfred, known as ʔAx̌uw̓, a nonliterate elderly Qʷiqʷasutinux̌ʷ woman of Alert Bay who was in her 80s when we started in 1978. ʔAx̌uw̓ died in 1992 at the approximate age of 103.

What were our objectives and methods? Our primary immediate objective was ʔAx̌uw̓'s primary objective, that is, to fulfill her will to record everything she was willing to tell for the written record. She urgently felt the need to pass on her knowledge to the younger generation, especially those of her family. ʔAx̌uw̓ was acutely aware that the younger generations of Kʷakʷakəwakʷ people needed her knowledge as well as other elders' help to ensure the continuity of cultural identity and traditions.

We wanted to capture her verbal art in her native tongue, Kʷak̓ʷala, and to ensure accuracy of the transcripts by having them translated by someone versed and fluent in her language and culture. That person is her granddaughter Daisy [Mayanił: Precious One], the daughter of Chief Jimmy Sewid and Flora Alfred, ʔAx̌uw̓'s second offspring. With the growing interest of younger Kʷakʷakəwakʷ people in reclaiming their native language, we plan to transcribe phonetically the unedited original recordings for further study. (All original materials, tapes, and transcriptions were deposited at the archives of the Museum of Anthropology at the University of British Columbia, and copies were made for ʔAx̌uw̓'s family).

We wanted to hear from ʔAx̌uw̓ what it was like to live the life of a Qʷiqʷasutinux̌ʷ woman at the turn of the 20th century. We wanted to render the portrait of this five-times great-grandmother, who happened to be one of the last great storytellers of the Kʷakʷakəwakʷ people, as she would like to be remembered, that is, in terms of her knowledge and life experiences, by the workings of her memory, and by mounting a memorial in words. Thus our work is an homage to ʔAx̌uw̓ and to all the talented Kʷakʷakəwakʷ storytellers, for whom remembering meant not just drawing on rote memory but engaging in an awesome creative activity. *Paddling to Where I Stand* represents our endeavor to capture, as accurately as possible, both ʔAx̌uw̓'s sparkling verbal waves and her equally intense moments of deep creative silence.

Our intention was not to write another interpretation of Kʷakʷakawakʷ culture. Our clear objective was to privilege ʔAx̌uw̓'s voice throughout the text. Our less immediate objective was to examine ʔAx̌uw̓'s sense of self, her identity. We know from previous studies in this field that preliterate autobiographies put before us conceptions of the self that were often foreign to modern, individualistic societies. At a later date we want to piece together a sense of who ʔАx̌uw̓ was, the substance of her self, from the stories of her knowledge and experiences, as well as her narrative style.

In *Paddling to Where I Stand*, ʔАx̌uw̓'s narratives mean much more than "the course of a lifetime," hence our choice of "Memoirs," her rememberings [to remember: m̓əlq̌ʷəlla; memory: m̓əlǧʷəĺ]. Her narratives allow us to see the remarkable complexity of Kʷak̓ʷakəwakʷ life from the point of view of a Qʷiq̌ʷasutinux̌ʷ woman and an accomplished storyteller told through myth [n̓uyəm], chants, tribal and personal history, and episodes of some other people's lives. More specifically the myths [n̓uyəm] include several versions of the Baxbaǩʷalanux̌ʷsiweỷ (Man-Eating Spirit) paradigm and several other myths, some of which could be considered as educational narratives routinely told to young boys and girls.⁹ Historical accounts or news of particular events [c̓ek̓alləm] include, for example, the last deadly raid by the Bella Coola on the Qʷiq̌ʷasutinux̌ʷ that took place around 1840 at Ǧʷayasdəms on Gilford Island for which, ʔАx̌uw̓ confessed—by breaking decades of silence—her great-aunt was responsible. The consequences of the raid for the Mamaliliqəlla, Ǧʷawaʔenux̌w, D̓awadaʔenux̌w, and Qʷiq̌ʷasutinux̌ʷ continue to this day.

ʔАx̌uw̓ related lengthy genealogies, making sure we understood the complex kinship relationships of the people she talked about. She recounted personal and tribal collective life experiences, such as her arrest with her husband Moses for illegally participating in the infamous 1920 Village Island potlatch. She shared her knowledge of culturally specific traits surrounding the complexity of the potlatch. Although ʔАx̌uw̓ spoke some Chinook,¹⁰ she never used the word *potlatch* in her narratives but used instead *p̓əssa* (to invest within your own tribal group), *ỷaq̌ʷa* (to give at rites of passage for witnessing), and *max̌ʷa* (to invest among several tribal groups). She also told of the practice of witchcraft, its effects and remedies.

Marriages took a prominent place in ʔАx̌uw̓'s narrative, with their complex formalities involving dowries and the usage of Coppers. Several types of marriages were described, such as the prearranged one performed for her future husband, Moses, when, as a child, he was married to a dead girl from the West Coast of Vancouver Island. She related several episodes of other lives, such as that of her aunt who was taken as captive by the Bella Coola and later escaped. ʔAx̌uw̓'s own life was revealed in her telling of important events, such as how she was married before having menstruated and how she had thirteen children. Her intimate knowledge of the land and place-names of the Q̌ʷiqʷasutinux̌ʷ — with their fishing sites and digging and hunting grounds — her daily activities, and her personal fears, joy, and emotion were revealed.

Why ʔAx̌uw̓ Was the Subject of Our Collaboration

ʔAx̌uw̓ was a respected, nonliterate, octogenarian woman of reliable memory who had witnessed undreamed of changes in the condition of her people while retaining her position as a noble [noxsola] Kʷakʷakəwakʷ matriarch.[11] Being nobility gave her access to a certain education and knowledge shared only between her equals. ʔAx̌uw̓ had virtually no Western education and did not speak English. Although she could understand a few words in the idiom, she was one of the few individuals still fluent in Kʷak̓ʷala, in both its classical and everyday form, and was recognized by her peers as a talented storyteller and orator with a long and accurate memory.

We do not know precisely when ʔAx̌uw̓ was born as there were no birth certificates for any First Nations children born in the late 1800s (i.e., before the arrival of a federal agency for the administration of Native affairs). She identified herself as a Q̌ʷiqʷasutinux̌ʷ woman. ʔAx̌uw̓'s father, Ǧuɫəlas, was a Mam̓aliliqəlla (both his parents were from Mim̓kʷɔmlis, Village Island); her mother, Puλas, was part Nəmǧis (from Yəllis, or Alert Bay) and part Q̌ʷiqʷasutinux̌ʷ (on her mother's side; from Ǧʷayasdəms, Gilford Island). She married Moses Alfred, Koddiy̓, a Kʷaguɫ from Fort Rupert, giving her the fourth component of her identity, as she put it. ʔAx̌uw̓ called herself a Q̌ʷiqʷasutinux̌ʷ, and not a Mam̓aliliqəlla, therefore stressing her matri-lineage.

ʔAx̌uw̓ did not call herself a Kʷaguɫ either. Most of what we know about the Kʷakʷakəwakʷ comes from Boas and his disciples. His contribution to Kʷakʷakəwakʷ ethnography and ethnology is enormous, but he was also responsible for making a huge, somewhat confusing, generalization.[12] The people whom he visited on the northern tip and western corner of Vancouver Island and the adjacent mainland, plus the many islands situated in between, belonged to 28 well-defined local groups that he referred to as "tribes." They all spoke a common language: Kʷak̓ʷala. As a nation, they

ʔAx̌uw̓, or Agnes Alfred. ʔAx̌uw̓ was small and slightly stooped, with white hair that she often braided, but she commanded attention through her deep voice. Photograph by David Neel. *Our Chiefs and Elders: Words and Photographs of Natives Leaders* (1992:27).

called themselves then, as now, the Kʷakʷakəwakʷ, that is, the Kʷak̓ʷala-speaking people. Because Boas worked mostly with the people of Fort Rupert, home of the Kʷaguł proper and with informant-interpreter George Hunt,[13] the whole nation became known as the Kwakiutl ("ancient smoke that brought people together"), after the most commonly used Anglophone spelling. But many of Boas's publications on the ethnology and ethnography of the Kʷakʷakəwakʷ people pertained not only to the Kʷaguł of Fort

Rupert but to the Nəmǧis of Alert Bay, the Ḷawiċis of Turnour Island, the Qʷiqʷasutinux̌ʷ of Gilford Island, the Nak̓ʷaxdax̌w̓ of Blunden Harbour, and so on. This explains why ʔAx̌uw̓ called herself a Qʷiqʷasutinux̌ʷ and not a Kʷaguł. Whenever ʔAx̌uw̓ spoke about the Kʷaguł people as a tribe, she was referring specifically to the Fort Rupert people. In her memoirs, unless otherwise stated, we follow ʔAx̌uw̓'s use of the term *Kʷaguł*.

We thought that it would be rather refreshing to hear about the Kʷakʷa-kəwakʷ people from someone not closely related to the Hunt family. Although ʔAx̌uw̓ was in some ways related to the Hunts, she made clear her tribal affiliation and her personal identity. Furthermore, she had not been "trained" as a professional informant and therefore was not anticipating nor expecting random questions from us.

The most important reason for selecting ʔAx̌uw̓ was her willingness to speak out, her own motivation. Although ʔAx̌uw̓ did not know how to read, she grew to know the power of the written word. She had been made aware of George Hunt's writings done in collaboration with Boas; she had seen the translation of Christian hymns into Kʷak̓ʷala, and she had contributed information to some of her granddaughter Daisy's publications.

In her eagerness to pass on her life experiences and knowledge to her descendants, ʔAx̌uw̓'s memory was future oriented. We thought ʔAx̌uw̓'s life story could be used in some strategies for cultural continuity among the Kʷ̓akʷakəwakʷ people. At closer examination we found several other secondary motivations besides her willingness to pass on her knowledge to the younger generation. She, consciously or not, took the opportunity to clear up community rumors and set the record straight about certain facts and their consequences. She conveyed her grief or view of what happened to others, and she demonstrated to others, mainly commoners [x̌amalla], how knowledgeable she was about her cultural and personal history.

Paddling to Where I Stand addresses readers who are interested in seeing the world through ʔAx̌uw̓'s eyes, who are willing to read with imagination her life experience told in her ways. We see her memoirs as the chance to come to know her and her culture from within. *Paddling to Where I Stand* is ʔAx̌uw̓'s book. She titled it after one of her favorite names, Six̌ʷasuw̓. This potlatch name, meaning "Many People Are Paddling toward Me," implies that many guests attended many potlatches that were given by the family members who passed the name on to her. And she added, "today when I am old, people are still coming towards me, but this time they are seeking my knowledge about my people."

Our questions to her were few. Some questions remained unanswered. We wanted her memoirs to be her own, with as little interference and suggestion as possible. ʔAx̌uw̓ told only what she wanted to tell. Sometimes reflective, she often commented on specific points, making sure that we understood. Whether discussing genealogy, marriage, or potlatch "rules," her intention was to inform, to reveal, to educate. Her silences were respected. Her sense of humor, her laughter, and her wit were recorded.

Since ʔAx̌uw̓'s granddaughter, Daisy, was the translator, we greatly reduced the risk of producing a fictional character such as we described earlier. Daisy grew up immersed in her culture and speaks her mother tongue; she has witnessed and "lived" oral performances and has done extensive experimentation in oral rendition. She recorded several elderly relatives in the past, which led her to write and publish several articles as well as the well-known *Prosecution or Persecution* (Sewid-Smith 1979), which deals with the anti-potlatch law and its consequences on the Kʷakʷakəwakʷ people. As a First Nations instructor for School District 72 in Campbell River, British Columbia, for the past 20 years, Daisy has been working on grammar books in order to aid the teaching of Kʷak̓ʷala (1998).

As for me (Reid), the ethnographic qualifications I originally brought to our collaboration combined some training in anthropology received at Paris University and the University of British Columbia, followed by several long sojourns since 1976 among Kʷakʷakəwakʷ people, some rudiments of Kʷak̓ʷala and international phonetics, and considerable enthusiasm for recording oral tradition, which I did with ʔAx̌uw̓ and other elderly Kʷak̓ʷala speakers prior to meeting Daisy.[14] As our friendship grew deeper, the three of us decided to collaborate on ʔAx̌uw̓'s memoirs.

Paddling to Where I Stand is neither a classic ethnography nor a literary autobiography, as documented by Gretchen Bataille and Kathleen Sands in *American Women: Telling Their Lives* (1984). It is not organized according to Western literary conventions, which usually entail ordering material in a linear past-present-future chronological sequence. ʔAx̌uw̓ did not present her stories in a linear chronological sequence. Her stories moved in and out of different time frames and often implicated Daisy, other family members, or me.

The chronology of sorts in *Paddling to Where I Stand* unfolds according to how ʔAx̌uw̓ saw herself and her life. ʔAx̌uw̓ lived to be over 100 years old. This means that preceding her own memory, which spanned four or five generations, and the memory of her immediate ancestors, which spanned another few generations, was myth time. Then animals—beasts and monsters—and humans all spoke a common tongue, lived in great houses, and were honored as the forebears of the Kʷakʷakəwakʷ nation, lending their iconic images to the crests of the great human families. As ʔAx̌uw̓ grew from childhood to womanhood as the wife of a Kʷaguł nobleman, myth time slipped even further into the background, but the bond that secured her to her past and formed a pattern for her present was never broken. Until the end, from her home in the small fishing village of Alert Bay, her connection to her mythic past and to her people remained strong.

When ʔAx̌uw̓ spoke we were faced with an awesome compression of time. She was born one generation before the last slaves disappeared and two generations before storytellers relied on the written word. She very clearly made a distinction between the times of myth [n̓uy̓əm] in chapter 1, the times she had heard about but not experienced [ćeḱalləm], with actual facts relating to events or people that have been discussed and passed down in chapter 2, and the times she had lived and known personally in chapter 3. This sequence became the basic chronology of her memoirs, but her stories often wove the three time periods together in a nonlinear way.

Because this was to be ʔAx̌uw̓'s book, we did not interrupt her voice in the body of the text. Our comments are restricted to the introductions in each chapter that explain to non- Kʷakʷala readers obscure or untranslatable concepts and establish the context for what is to follow.

Style and Translation

Translation is far from being an absolute and accurate process. Rubel and Rosman address the problem of translating words, ideas, and meanings from one culture to another in a recent publication entitled *Translating Cultures: Perspectives on Translation and Anthropology* (2003:1–22). If perfect translation is impossible and is at best relative and disputable, our duty remained to be as faithful as possible to ʔAx̌uw̓'s original words and intended meaning.

ʔAx̌uw̓ spoke with at least two voices (chanting could be considered a third voice). In her formal voice she followed the tradition of pure oral literature, the classic style of oral myths, legends, and historical accounts. We have tried our best to retain as much of ʔAx̌uw̓'s formal voice as is possible in the context of translations. By this, and in agreement with Richard Bauman, we are referring to a context "in which the words spoken are to be interpreted as the equivalent of the words originally spoken [in Kʷakʷ̓ala]" (Bauman 1984:10). We have retained the format and presentation of the text that Westerners normally associate with autobiographical accounts—that is, we follow normal paragraph style rather than a continuous narrative. ʔAx̌uw̓'s classic style of speech, as opposed to the style of everyday speech, was marked by certain stylistic features such as repetitions, which have a wide range of functions, ranging from aesthetic and structural to expressing emotion (Hendricks 1993:78–79). For this reason we have not edited out repetitions, even though some readers may find them tedious. As Nora Marks and Richard Dauenhauer (1987:15–16) have pointed out with regard to Tlingit oral literature, good oral composition involves the constant use of repetition. This is because repetition emphasizes main ideas, lends the story a musical rhythm and balance, or simply gives listeners a break so that they need not receive too much new information all at once. ʔAx̌uw̓ also used repetitions to aid her in oral composition, to give her time to think, and to enable her to formulate what was to come next. She often repeated the name of a place or person or certain anecdote, to underscore a theme or idea. Some names were repeated over and over again to achieve a certain effect or response from us, or simply because it was integral in some way to the story as she understood it and remembered it for herself.

ʔAx̌uw̓'s informal style was similar to that of daily speech. In this voice she told us where she was born, where she grew up, and what she did during her childhood and adulthood (chapter 3). At times the more formal style overlapped: one of the few questions we asked was if an individual could be reincarnated in a lineage [ṅumay̓əm] different from her or his own. After a long reflective pause, she said she did not think so and immediately started telling a myth to prove her point. ʔAx̌uw̓ would often respond to questions with a myth or sometimes with a chant.

The most salient aspect of ʔAx̌uw̓'s tellings was that her stories were not dead and buried somewhere in what we call the past. The stories were alive for her in her immediate present. We have tried to preserve much of the flavor of ʔAx̌uw̓'s storytelling as it moved back and forth from tribal history to myth and to personal reminiscences, so that the written text became the story of our hearing her stories. We wanted our readers to experience something like our own experience of listening to ʔAx̌uw̓ telling stories.

Conclusion

In light of the constitutive features of narrated North American Indian autobiography and of critical work surrounding the genre, we hope that our approach will result in a portrait of ʔAx̌uw̓ that mirrors her life as she saw it. Of course, we should ask ourselves: To what extent have we created a fictional character as many others have done? If we have, we hope the fiction is as close to ʔAx̌uw̓'s reality as we could possibly make it.

We hope this work will contribute to preserving and transforming Kʷakʷakəwak culture, and that ʔAx̌uw̓'s memoirs attest to the endurance of First Nations storytelling as it is transformed into a new literary form that in turn enlarges the sense of life's possibilities.

Notes

We are most grateful to all family members related to ʔAx̌uw̓ for their precious collaboration; Marie Mauzé, Michael Harkin, and Sergei A. Kan for organizing the Northwest Coast Ethnology Conference; Dell Hymes for his editorial suggestions; and our friends Edith Daly-Iglauer and Rodney A. Badger for their editorial help and continuous moral support.
1. There are several ways of spelling Kʷakʷala, depending on which phonemic system we choose. Here we are using the system developed by the language program at the Carihi Secondary School in Campbell River BC.
2. See Karl Weintraub (1978) on life episodes of the Greeks and Georg Misch (1951) on the records of Egyptian pharaohs' deeds (cited in Brumble 1988:4). *The Confessions* of Jean Jacques Rousseau is a good early model of the genre.
3. John Neihardt's 1932 publication *Black Elk Speaks* (1972) is equally well known.
4. For a feminist approach to women's life see *Feminist Fields: Ethnographic Insights* (Bridgman et al. 1999).
5. See also Clifford and Marcus, *Writing Culture* (1986).
6. For a philosophical approach to autobiography, see Wollheim, *The Thread of Life* (1984).
7. See, for example, Buckley and Gottlieb (1988); Strathern (1972, 1988).
8. According to Rohner (1966:198), Julia Averkieva is said to have collected some life history material from Kʷakʷakəwakʷ women in the 1930s while recording

genealogies. Her published work, however, is mainly on slavery and string figures among these people.

9. For an analysis of the Baxbakʷalanuxʷsiweẏ myths and subsequent studies, see Martine J. Reid (1981, 1984) and Martine de Widerspach-Thor [Reid] (1981).

10. The trade language, Chinook jargon, not the "Chinook" spoken by Charles Cultee and others at the mouth of the Columbia River on its northern side and recorded in Chinook texts by Boas (1894) and grammatically described in the first volume of the *Handbook of American Indian Languages* (1911a).

11. *Noxsola* is a generic term that refers to the entire class of chiefs and the nobility. See Boas (1921:1416).

12. See also Judith Berman for a reevaluation of some of Boas's translations (1992: 125–162).

13. George Hunt was born from a Tlingit mother and a Scottish father and was raised among the Kʷaguł in Fort Rupert.

14. See Martine de Widerspach-Thor, *Kwakiutl Marine Mythology* (1978).

HISTORY AND REPRESENTATIONS

"IT'S ONLY HALF A MILE FROM SAVAGERY TO CIVILIZATION"

American Tourists and Southeastern Alaska Natives in the Late 19th Century

---

Sergei Kan

In the last decades of the 19th century, with the establishment of a regular railroad service between the two coasts and the complete "pacification" of the Plains Indian tribes, touring the western part of the United States became a popular activity among upper-middle-class Americans (see Pomeroy 1957; Hyde 1990). "Sublime" landscapes and "picturesque" Indians were the region's major attractions, with the desert Southwest quickly becoming the most popular destination. Tourists flocked to witness what railroad company brochures promised: majestic scenery, poignant ancient ruins, exotic native rituals, and authentic crafts. The visitors watched and photographed Hopi Snake Dances and purchased beautiful Pueblo pottery and returned home refreshed with by their encounter with a fascinating and peaceful "vanishing race" (Dilworth 1996). Once regular steamship service between several West Coast ports and southeastern Alaska had been established, a smaller but steadily increasing number of well-to-do Americans began touring the Inside Passage as well. If in 1884 there were only 1,650 visitors to the area, by the end of the summer of 1890 some 5,000 travelers had toured southeastern Alaska (Hinckley 1965:71). As in the Southwest, a combination of beautiful scenery and exotic natives were the two main magnets that drew curious visitors to the recently acquired United States territory.

While the reasons for a strong and persistent American fascination with the indigenous peoples of the Southwest and the mythic images of the region's Indians constructed by and for the tourists have been explored in a number of studies (e.g., Wade 1985; Weigle 1990; Dilworth 1996; Howard and Pardue 1996), little has been written about the early Alaskan tourism.[1] The main exceptions are a brief but important pioneering article by a historian on the Inside Passage tourism (Hinckley 1965) and a study by an art historian of the work of two major area photographers (Winter and Pond), which was stimulated by and, to a large extent, served the turn-of-the-century tourist market (Wyatt 1989). Given the importance of the early southeastern Alaska tourism in the process of constructing a distinct image of the area's native peoples (most importantly Tlingits but also Haidas and Coast Tsimshians) and stimulating a proliferation of the manufacturing of marketable arts and crafts by them, this lack of scholarly interest in the subject is surprising.

The goal of the present essay is to fill this gap by focusing on the images of the Tlingits constructed by those visitors to Alaska's Panhandle who wrote travel books and thus played a major role in shaping those representations. My argument is that, although these images had been influenced by such earlier ones as those of the "noble/picturesque" and the "primitive savage" as well as the "vanishing Indian," they differed significantly from those of the Plains or the Southwestern indigenous peoples. In fact, in the popular and semipopular literature of this era, the coastal natives were often described as being very different from and even totally unrelated to those of the rest of the western United States. These differences had to do not only with the area natives' distinct physical characteristics and way of life but also their unique socioeconomic and political status. In fact, the tourist writers' insistence on the coastal peoples' uniqueness had itself been inspired to a significant extent by these visitors' encounters with the Protestant missionaries and government officials (who in the early days of U.S. rule were often the same persons) who had preceded them by less than a decade but had played a key role in "civilizing" the local natives (see Hinckley 1972, 1982; Kan 1999:174–244). Reading the missionaries' writing and conversing with them on this subject as well seeing the results of their efforts convinced many of the turn-of-the-century visitors that the Tlingits, the Haidas, and the Coast Tsimshians were superior to the Sioux or the Hopis and could save themselves from extinction by becoming civilized and productive "lower class" citizens of the new territory. Paradoxically, however, the coastal Indians' "progressive" potential and impressive commercial skills made them less "exotic" and "picturesque" and thus less interesting to many of the tourists. Consequently, by the 1910s the majority of the visitors to the Inside Passage were paying a lot more attention to the area's glaciers and native-made artifacts than to its native inhabitants.

One popular tourist site was of particular importance for those wishing to witness the Americanization of the local natives. It was the town of Sitka, the capital of Russian America and of the Territory of Alaska (until 1900), which boasted not only a large Indian village but a thriving Presbyterian boarding school for native children and a separate American-style cottage settlement inhabited by that school's graduates. Given the town's relatively small size, it took a tourist less than half an hour to walk from one of its native settlements to the other and witness what one author described as native progress from "savagery to civilization" (Collis 1890:123–124). Hence one could argue that Sitka was "read" by its visitors as a "text" or a "morality play" (cf. Brown 1987:19–21) about the past, present, and future life of its indigenous inhabitants. Another reason for Sitka being the focus of this essay is the fact that much of my own ethnographic and ethnohistorical research for the last 20 years has concentrated on its Tlingit community; hence I am in a good position to compare the images of the local native life constructed by the early tourists with the reality of that life (Kan 2001).[2]

Tlingit Culture and Society in the 1880s–1890s

By the time the first groups of tourists began to arrive in southeastern Alaska, its aboriginal inhabitants had already experienced two decades of American rule marked by the military and civil authorities' as well as the missionaries' efforts to civilize them.[3] While the Tlingits resisted the American authorities' heavy-handed interference in their lives and the American settlers' encroachment on their hunting and fishing territories, they did not flee from contact with the people they called "Waashdaan Ḵwáan" ("Washington People") but, on the contrary, tried to benefit from the new sources of wealth that the interaction with them offered. Thus by the end of the 19th century many natives were already fishing for the canneries and working in them; they also worked in the lumber and mining industries, packed freight on the docks of Sitka and Juneau, and manufactured artifacts for sale to the tourists.

Having always been interested in acquiring exotic foreign goods to serve as markers of status within their own community, the Tlingits were quick to develop a taste for American household furnishings and clothing. Partly because of this desire to imitate the powerful newcomers and partly due to the American pressure, Tlingit villages began to change their appearance, especially in places like Sitka, where the native people were under a constant critical gaze of the local white residents. Thus large American-style houses gradually replaced the traditional winter longhouses, and boardwalks began to be built in front of them. Moreover, determined to partake of the newcomers' spiritual power and knowledge (especially reading and writing) and envious of the success of their southern neighbors, the Tsimshians, in doing so, the Tlingits throughout southeastern Alaska in the late 1870s began asking American missionaries to establish churches and schools in their own communities. By the 1890s the majority of the Tlingits (especially in Sitka) had at least nominally become Christian, with many youngsters attending day schools and boarding schools (Kan 1999:201–211).

Contrary to the Presbyterian missionaries' expectations, however, this movement toward "civilization" did not mean a dramatic abandonment of the traditional ideology and social relations. On the contrary, with the exception of a relatively small cohort of devout Presbyterians, many of whom were the graduates of the boarding schools in Wrangell and Sitka, the majority of the Tlingits remained committed to such key manifestations of their precolonial sociocultural order as moiety exogamy, matrilineal descent, collective ownership of land, houses, and ceremonial property by matrilineal groups, and the elaborate and lavish feasts or "potlatches" hosted by them. Much of that persisting traditional life had to be concealed from the Presbyterian missionaries and their secular allies. In fact, as I have argued before, a sudden turn to Russian Orthodoxy by many of the natives of Sitka and of several other Tlingit communities, which took place in the mid-1880s, had a lot to do with their displeasure with the methods used by the American reformers in their struggle against the so-called old customs. While determined to take advantage of the material and spiritual benefits Christianity seemed to offer them, these Tlingit people chose a mission that demanded fewer social and ideological changes from them, whose rituals appealed to the more traditional natives, and whose staff was much smaller and much less powerful than that of the Presbyterians (Kan 1999:245–278).

Of course, this picture is accurate only in general terms — considerable differences remained between the more conservative Tlingit villages (especially Angoon/Killisnoo, Hoonah, and Klukwan) and the larger, somewhat more urbanized communities where the Tlingits had to live side by side with the "Creoles" (descendants of the Russified Native Alaskans and persons of mixed Russian and native parentage) and the Euro-Americans. Since the steamer rarely stopped in the more traditional native communities and since the majority of the tourists visited the Inside Passage in the summer when almost no potlatches and other ceremonies took place and when many Tlingits were engaged in traditional subsistence activities and cannery work away from their permanent villages, the impressions of native life acquired by the visitors were rather skewed.

A Gilded Age Tour of the Inside Passage

Although some American visitors toured southeastern Alaska in the late 1870s and early 1880s, tourist traffic in the region began in earnest in 1884, when the Pacific Coast Steamship Company initiated summer excursions through the Inside Passage, and persisted until World War I. The cruise's itinerary remained pretty much the same during this entire period. The voyage usually originated at an American port, such as San Francisco, Portland, Tacoma, Seattle, or Port Townsend, Washington. After stopping at Victoria and a couple of smaller British Columbia ports, such as Nanaimo and Metlakatla, the ship finally entered Alaska waters, always making stops at Wrangell, Sitka, and Juneau. In addition, it often made brief visits to such small Alaskan communities as the Haida village of Kasaan, the recently established Tsimshian settlement of New Metlakatla, and the Tlingit village of Killisnoo (Hinckley 1965:69; Pacific Coast Steamship Company 1887–1894; Scidmore 1885; Collis 1890). After docking at Sitka, the ship either went back south or continued north to the Tlingit village of Yakutat in order to view Mt. St. Elias. Sometimes the trip was also extended north from Juneau up the scenic Lynn Canal to a mixed white-native town of Haines. A visit to the spectacular Glacier Bay (north of the Tlingit village of Hoonah) was the highlight of the entire journey, at least as far as the scenery was concerned.

The entire trip lasted no more than two weeks and was often even shorter. This allowed for only relatively brief stops at each port, with the one in Sitka, which lasted 24 hours, being the longest. The brevity of these stops did not allow for any in-depth exploration of the communities being visited, and this was pointed out in several publications about southeastern Alaska and its native inhabitants authored by those Americans who had spent long periods of time living there. Thus, for example, a book written by Frances Knapp and Rheta Childe, entitled *The Thlinkets of Southeastern Alaska,* contrasted its own detailed portrayal of native life with those offered by tourists, with the latter being described as "somewhat superficial" (1896:11–12).[4] In the words of Knapp and Childe, "The tourist sees only the larger villages where the people are directly under government and missionary influence. To study native life it its original simplicity, one must be a resident of Alaska, with opportunities for visiting the out-of-the way villages off the steamer route altogether" (14).

Although it is difficult to estimate how many of the visitors to the Inside Passage actually read this particular book or another detailed amateur ethnography of the Tlingits written by a Presbyterian missionary (Jones 1914), it is likely that the majority of them were more familiar with such popular tourist-oriented publications as George Wardman's *A Trip to Alaska* (1884), Charles Hallock's *Our New Alaska: The Seward Purchase Vindicated* (1886), Abby Woodman's *Picturesque Alaska* (1889), Matilda Lukens's *The Inland Passage: A Journal of a Trip to Alaska* (1889), Septima Collis's *A Woman's Trip to Alaska* (1890), and a more detailed and scholarly *Alaska: Its Southern Coast and Sitka Archipelago* by Eliza Scidmore (1885), a noted geographer, photographer, and author who was the first woman to serve on the Board of Managers of the National Geographic Society (Griffin 2000:16).

Like the authors of many other late-19th-century tourist-oriented books describing journeys to the American West, these authors were clearly inspired by patriotic sentiments and thus tried to convince their readers to forsake the usual trips to Paris, Rome, or the Swiss Alps and visit America's own recently acquired lands (see, e.g., Collis 1890:1; cf. Pomeroy 1957, Hyde 1990).[5] Often explicit comparisons were made between Europe's famous sites and those of southeastern Alaska, with the latter being depicted as more "grand" than the former.[6]

Those tourists whose primary goal was to partake of coastal Alaska's scenery, praised so enthusiastically by none other than America's famous outdoorsman and conservationist John Muir (1993, 1988), were rarely disappointed. Among the region's most frequently admired natural sites was the majestic Glacier Bay as well as several other glaciers and snow-covered mountains. In fact, short informational brochures produced by the Pacific Coast Steamship Company devoted a lot more attention to the region's scenery than its native inhabitants and emphasized the health benefits of a sea voyage to Alaska. Here is my favorite passage on this subject:

Having arrived home you will find your eyes clear and speaking, your appetite keen, your step more elastic, your general health immensely improved, and, in case you were not up to a proper and healthy standard when you started out, your *avoirdupois* increased anywhere from five to thirty pounds. You will be delighted at having made the journey. You will have lots of stories to tell of your experience, which will make you the lion of social gathering and envy of those who stayed at home or went to the springs. This is the invariable experience of those who take this trip to Alaska. (Pacific Coast Steamship Company 1894:19)

However, for those visitors who were more interested in the native inhabitants of southeastern Alaska than in its natural wonders, the tour of the Inside Passage was probably a bit of a disappointment.

Looking for the Picturesque and Noble Indians

Whereas the abandoned native villages, especially those of the Haidas and the Southern Tlingits that had totem poles still standing, presented a rather romantic and "picturesque" view, the native sections in Wrangell, Sitka, and Juneau had few visible features of "authentic" Indian settlements. Here is how Collis (1890:77) described Ft. Wrangell: "Ft. Wrangell is perhaps today as uninviting a spot as any in the world, save for the few curiosities in the way of Indian graves and totem poles, and the very excellent work done by the missionaries in the Indian schools." With totem poles being considered the local natives' most unique artistic creations, a number of authors lamented the fact of their decline and inevitable disappearance. As Scidmore put it, "The disappearance of the totem poles would rob these villages of their greatest interest for the tourists, and the ethnologist who would solve the mysteries and read the pictures finally aright, should hasten to this rich and neglected field" (1885:54). The same author complained that in Sitka, "there are no totem poles, or carved gravehouses to add interest to the village" (175). I wonder how many of these visitors realized that the central and northern Tlingit villages never had any poles except for the short and simple mortuary and memorial ones.

Sitka natives, with their freshly painted houses and Western clothing were a particular disappointment to those tourists who sought glimpses of the "Noble Savage." Thus Scidmore complained that the Sitka Indians "are too much given to ready-made clothes and civilized ways to be really picturesque" (1985; cf. Field 1897:8).

The only exception to this were the Tlingit women who continued to wear blankets on top of their store-bought dresses. As the steamship company's brochure informed the visitor, "You will be amused to the squaws, on the arrival of the steamer . . . sitting around the sills of the wharves, dressed in their best raiment" (Pacific Coast Steamship Company 1894:18). Another blow to the romantic expectations of the tourists was the fact that the Indians were not always neatly dressed (at least according to Euro-American standards) and tended to paint their faces black to protect themselves from the sun and mosquitoes. As one visitor to Sitka observed, "we wander up Lincoln Street . . . and behold many of the natives who, though unkempt and repulsive, present a certain artistic fitness for their surroundings" (C. Taylor 1901:269; cf. Collis 1890:97).[7] Only a more open-minded observer, willing to view a native person wearing European clothing as an interesting sight, succeeded in catching a glimpse of the "picturesque Indian." Here is Scidmore's description of a scene observed at the Kasaan fishery: "A group of Indians gathered on shore, their gay blankets, dresses, and cotton kerchiefs adding a fine touch of color to the scene, and the men in the fishery, in their high rubber boots and aprons, flannel shirts and big hats were heroic adjuncts to the picturesque and out-of-the-way scene" (1885:31–32). An even more romantic account of a native scene was offered by Abby Woodman, who sailed by an Indian fishing camp on the shore of Kupreanof Island:

> Several Indian men were sitting upon some stones in the edge of the forest, as if they had just come out from the wigwam, which stood behind them under the shadows of the fir trees. Drawn upon the shore in front of them, were several bark and log canoes, and about them lay scattered their various camp furnishings, piles of skins, etc. Red blankets and shirts were hanging over a pole near by, and strung upon another pole were a dozen or more split salmon, drying in the sun and air. It was a real storybook scene, and came well up to our childhood imaginings of Indians in the wild woods. (1889:179).

Another disappointment awaiting those visitors who had expected to encounter simple and naive "children of Nature" in the Inside Passage was the fact that the local natives turned out to be shrewd and aggressive traders who demanded high prices for their artifacts, knew very well how to bargain, and even insisted on being paid for having their pictures taken. As Collis (1890:97–98) observed, the prices asked by the Tlingit women for their baskets, spoons, bracelets, rings, miniature totem poles, and so forth "were exorbitant in the extreme, and they [the sellers] seemed to have a trades-union understanding among themselves that, having once fixed a price, they would adhere to it to the last." Scidmore (1885:90) echoed this author's sentiment, pointing out that "there was no savage modesty or simplicity about the prices asked."

Of course, from the visitors' point of view, purchasing the region's distinct native-made objects was a major part of the journey, just as it was for the tourists riding the Santa Fe railroad through the Southwest. In its rather crude and straightforward way, the Pacific Coast Steamship Company brochures made that point very clear when they reprinted a passage from the *Juneau Free Press* describing the Tlingits as "the artistic savages of the world" whose "marvels of savage work" would serve as perfect "romantic remembrances of a yet more romantic journey back to civilization" (1887:12).

Although some visitors admired the great business skills of the Tlingit women, who dominated the sale of artifacts to tourists, others were bothered by them, referring to them as having "the shrewdness and business instincts of a Jew and a Yankee rolled into one" (Finck 1891:241). Nonetheless, like most tourists everywhere, the visitors to southeastern Alaska felt compelled to bring home at least a few Indian-made "curios." Most of them did not know much about the local material culture and artistic styles and thus were most likely satisfied with their purchases. Only a more sophisticated visitor, like Scidmore, complained that few of the artifacts sold by Indians were "truly authentic." Thus she was bothered by the proliferation of objects manufactured specifically for the tourist trade, mentioning, for example, that one prominent Wrangell silversmith "has given up carving the emblematic beasts of native heraldry or heavy barbaric wristlets, and now only makes the most slender bangles, adapted from the models in an illustrated jeweler's catalogue that some Philistine has sent him. Worse yet, he copies the civilized spread eagle from the half-dollar, and, one can only shake his head sadly to see Stikine art so corrupted and debased. For all this, the lame man cannot make bracelets fast enough to supply the market, and at three dollars a pair for the narrower ones he pockets great profits during the steamer days" (1885:49–50).

The fact that the tourists were clearly impressed with the local natives' superior commercial skills was underscored by the fact that the only Tlingit resident of Sitka mentioned by a number of the guidebook authors by name was the so-called Princess Tom, who served as an intermediary between the native manufacturers of various crafts and the Euro-American visitors. Thanks to her energetic purchasing of artifacts from several local native communities and what one observer described as her great "energy and shrewdness," this woman had become quite wealthy. Although her title was a pure Euro-American invention (harking back to the popular American myth of the "Indian princess") and her enormous wealth was probably an exaggeration, Princess Tom did capture the imagination of numerous visitors to Sitka who stopped by her house to purchase "curios" and take her picture (for the latter, see Knapp and Childe 1896:106–107).[8]

In their search for the picturesque, most visitors to Sitka and other native communities did not hesitate to enter native homes without being invited. In fact, there was a great deal of voyeurism in the tourists' behavior. While these visits were ostensibly conducted in the pursuit of additional "curios," they also gave the tourists a chance to observe the daily life of the "savages." Thus, Scidmore, a more sophisticated observer than most others, admitted that the visitors violated the Indians' privacy, but she remained rather unperturbed by that. In her words, "In all the houses the Indians went right on with their breakfasts and domestic duties regardless of our presence; and the white visitors made themselves at home, scrutinized and turned over everything they saw with an effrontery that would be resented, if indulged in kind by the Indians" (1885:60). At another location a group of tourists, unable to visit a native settlement, went as far as observing minute details of daily life through a telescope (Woodman 1889:145).

The general impression that these visits to the native villages and homes made on the Gilded Age tourists was a negative one. There were some exceptions, particularly when it came to Sitka's "Indian Village," which in the 1880s had undergone a thorough cleaning under pressure from the local navy officers maintaining law and order in the area.[9] Thus Scidmore (1885: 175) characterized the village in the following way: "Entering thought the old stockade gate, the Indian *rancherie* presents itself, as a double row of square houses fronting on the beach. Each house is numbered and white-washed, and the ground surrounding it graveled and drained. The same neatness marks the whole long stretch of the village: the reason for this are the heavy fines and threat of imprisonment imposed by the captain of the man-of-war on the Indians who maintain their houses. Indians are made to keep their village quiet and clean." Most of the visitors, however, were far from impressed with the villages that, with their canoes and drying fish racks, looked a lot different from a typical American one, and especially with what they saw inside the native homes. Thus Collis (1890:103) gave the future tourists who might venture into the Sitka Indian village the follow-ing advice: "Walk slowly, tread carefully, talk loudly so as to give notice of your coming, or send of your party ahead to give notice, for you are about to experience a most revolting, almost sickening sight, and their nor-mal condition in costume being bad enough, you don't care about being met by any surprises which may prove embarrassing." The same author as-serted that she had visited "some of the huts in which these [Tlingit] families . . . reside, and there can be nothing worse in the slums of London than what I saw here" (81). Aware of a negative reaction many of the tourists might have toward visiting the native homes, the Pacific Steamship Com-pany even recommended that they purchase "Indian curios" not from their manufacturers but from the American-owned stores in Sitka and Juneau (Pacific Coast Steamship Company 1894:18). Thus the coastal Alaskan Indi-ans turned out to be neither particularly noble nor particularly picturesque but rather crafty and unclean.

"They Are Wholly Unlike the Typical American Indian"

Although the degree of anti-native prejudice exhibited by each visitor-author varied a lot, most of them agreed that the coastal Alaskan natives were radically different from and generally superior to the rest of the indige-nous peoples of the United States. This impression was based on both the natives' physical characteristics and their lifestyle.

The promotional brochures issued by the steamship company empha-sized that "the native people of the Territory are not Indians in the common acceptance of the term; they are wholly unlike the typical North American Indian in personal appearance, habits, and customs. Their features are of the Mongolian race;[10] and, as compared with the Red Man of the States and Ter-ritories, they are naturally bright, intelligent people; they are industrious, shrewd, keen traders, and among them can be found some good mechan-ics, and many skillful carvers in wood, ivory, and gold and silver" (Pacific Coast Steamship Company 1893:71). With the Plains Indian wars still fresh in the minds of many of the Americans, their accounts often emphasized the friendly attitude of the coastal Indians toward the whites, which was sometimes contrasted with their past bellicosity. As Hallock (1886:86) put it, "As a whole the Indians of Alaska . . . as far as we know, are normally peaceable, tractable, intelligent, clever, eager to learn, useful, and industrious to a degree unknown elsewhere among the aborigines of America." The fact that, unlike the Plains Indians, the coastal ones could still pursue much of their traditional subsistence activities seemed to escape our observers, who thought about the differences between ethnic groups and "races" in biological rather than cultural terms.

Native Alaskans—Tlingits, Yup'iks, and Athapaskans alike—were frequently compared to the "Orientals," especially the Chinese and the Japanese (e.g., Hallock 1886:92). Japan was particularly popular as a country to which the origin of the coastal Alaskan native could be traced (e.g., Wiley and Wiley 1893:158). By placing the Tlingits and their neighbors on the same evolutionary ladder as the Japanese, American visitors were emphasizing their superiority to the rest of the indigenous inhabitants of the United States but also distancing them, as far as their intelligence and degree of "civilization" went, from the country's "white race."

In fact, racial prejudice, marked by an anti-Asian bias, was quite pronounced even in the writing of those visitors who insisted on the coastal natives' superiority to the rest of America's Indians. Even Scidmore, a well-educated and well-read observer who praised the Tlingits for their ability to work hard, trade, and produce beautiful arts and crafts, could not avoid heavy anti-native prejudice: "These Thlinket Indians of the coast have broad heavy faces, small eyes, and anything but quickness or intelligence in their expression. They are slow and deliberate in speech, lingering on and emphasizing each aspirate and gutteral, and any theories as to a fish diet promoting the activity of the brain are dispersed after watching these salmon-fed natives for a few weeks. Many of their customs are such a travesty and burlesque of our civilized ways as to show that the same principles and motives underlie all human action" (1885:57–58). Even such writers as Knapp and Childe (1896:194–195), who claimed a much better understanding of Tlingit life, based on a long-term residence in southeastern Alaska, and who did give the coastal natives credit for their desire to learn the "white man's ways," exhibited a strong biologically derived, racist, and evolutionist anti-native prejudice, typical for this era. Their evaluation of the Tlingits' potential for becoming civilized is so blatantly racist that it is worth quoting in its entirety:

> It is a commonly admitted fact that development and the power of assimilating knowledge ceases much earlier in the lower races than in the highly civilized. In youth, the barbarian, even the savage, is generally quite as quick-witted and intelligent as a European child of the same age. Philanthropists observe this, and leap to the conclusion that all that "the heathen" needs is a chance of enlightenment. As a matter of fact, in a very few years, at adolescence in the lowest races, the brain becomes dulled, inactive, and retrogression both of body and mind is rapid; just as the ape, which approaches the human type in its first years, recedes and becomes more brutal, mentally and physically, when full grown. This is true, in a much less marked degree, of civilized man. Precocity is not to be confounded with intelligence; and even of true intelligence we must not expect too much. Information, knowledge itself, is but the seed-grain of wisdom. The actual structure of the brain must change before a hitherto unrecognized truth can become so much part of it as to have an influence upon the character and the general view. Education, in the highest sense of the word, is simply growth; and for that we have always to wait.

Occasionally an outright negative depiction of coastal natives as savages without any redeeming qualities, harking back to all the old anti-Indian stereotypes, found its way into the tourist literature. Thus a British guidebook author characterized the natives as "low on the scale of humanity as North American Indians generally are: that is ignorant, ungrateful, treacherous, cruel savages" (Pierrepont 1884:157–158). Nonetheless, most of the late-19th-century writers who commented on the level of intelligence and the degree of evolutionary development of the coastal Alaskan natives, placed them above those of the rest of North America.

From Savagery to Civilization

In the last quarter of the 19th century the notion that the aboriginal inhabitants of America's recently established Alaska Territory were radically different from and superior to the rest of the country's natives was being actively promoted in the writing of such leading "Alaska boosters" as the founder of the Alaska Presbyterian mission and the General Agent for Alaska Education, Sheldon Jackson, a Presbyterian missionary-turned-businessman and politician, John Brady, and most of Alaska's other governors. In fact, Jackson and Brady insisted that the Tlingits and other indigenous peoples of the territory had to be called "Alaska Natives" rather than "Indians" (Hinckley 1962, 1966, 1972, 1982). These missionaries, businessmen, and politicians were hoping that, given the beneficial effects of civilization and Christianity, these "Natives" would eventually turn into Alaska's hard-working "lower classes."[11] For these "agents of civilization," the best proof of their argument was the coastal natives' eagerness to learn and imitate the ways of the "superior" newcomers, participate actively in the labor market, send their children to school, and go to church.

In order to emphasize how far the Tlingits and their coastal neighbors had already progressed along the road to civilization, these authors liked to contrast the "evils of prejudice and old-fashioned customs," which they claimed only the oldest and the most conservative natives still adhered to, with the modern-day native behavior and lifestyle.[12] The missionaries' most-favorite example of the former were such customs as female infanticide, polygamy, intertribal warfare, slavery, shamanism, and violent persecution of witchcraft. Needless to say, they tended to sensationalize the pre- and early-contact native customs in order to drive their point home. Sheldon Jackson, whose 1880 *Alaska and the Missions of the North Pacific Coast* was a standard reference book on the subject, was particularly prone to this sort of exaggeration and misrepresentation. Many of the writers of the period's tourist guidebooks repeated his assertions without bothering to verify them (e.g., Woodman 1889:149).

However, for most of those who commented on native life in southeastern Alaska, there was hope. All they had to do was to look at the well-dressed, well-behaved, English-speaking students of the missionary boarding schools and the life they led after graduating from these institutions.

Sitka, with the largest school of this kind and its settlement of Presbyterian Tlingits, provided a powerful visual example of the merits of the missionaries' argument. A visit to the Sitka Industrial School (as the Presbyterian boarding school was called) and the nearby neat Victorian-style "Cottages" inhabited by the school's graduates, who had intermarried regardless of the law of moiety exogamy, was part of every tourist's itinerary (e.g., *The Alaskan*, 7 May 1890:2). Thus a visitor to Sitka could literally make a journey from "savagery" (i.e., the old Indian Village) to "civilization" (the Industrial School and the "Cottages") in less than half an hour.

Septima Collis articulated this idea most eloquently when she wrote the following:

> To me Sitka was the vestige of a departed empire; the home of a decaying race of aborigines; a depot for the sale of Russo-Indian relics and curios; a pretty little town timidly hiding away in among the mountains; and for that I had come to see it and had been amply repaid. But the "Mission" I had never thought of. . . . Be that as it may, hereafter no man, nor woman either, shall outdo me in words of praise and thanks for the glorious Godlike work which is being performed by the good people who are rescuing the lives, the bodies, and the souls of these poor creatures from the physical and moral deaths they are dying. (1890:119)

> I went first into one of the classrooms of the males, where I saw perhaps twenty dark-skinned Siwash[13] Indian boys, whose Mongolian faces and almond-shaped eyes had assumed an expression of intelligence, so different from the stupid, blear-eyed appearance of the same age and race who I had seen in the rancherie, that it was difficult to realize that they could possibly be twigs of the same tree. (121)

> It is said somewhere that it is only a single step from civilization to barbarism,—perhaps so. If all wrongdoing is barbaric, the saying is not only trite but true, for a false civilization often begets the very worst of crimes. But I and those ladies and gentlemen who accompanied me through the rancherie and the schools at Sitka can vouch for the fact that it is only half a mile from savage, uncivilized ignorance, superstition, filth, and immorality to education, deportment, thrift, domestic felicity, and all human happiness. Thank God I have seen "le revers de la medaille." To have gone back to my comfortable home in New York and to the embraces of my bright, healthy, intelligent children, feeling that these poor little wretches at Sitka were to remain outcasts during the brief time that disease and degradation should permit them to exist on earth, would have been a great sorrow. Thanks to the Presbyterian Board of Home Missions . . . the reverse is a great joy. (123–124)

Thus, for Collis and most other tourists who came to southeastern Alaska looking for the "picturesque noble savages," the search ended on the southern edge of Sitka among the English-speaking Protestant Tlingits.[14] In fact, during the fist decade of the 20th century the Sitka Indian Village was already losing much of its exotic appeal, while the missionary school, with its well-dressed and well-behaved native children, and the neighboring "Cottages" continued to attract the tourists. Thus a 1910 guidebook does not even mention the Indian Village as a site worth visiting (Higginson 1910:193). Similarly, an 1897 "Tourist Guide to Sitka," published in the local newspaper, mentions it only as a place where one of the graduates of the Sitka Industrial School, Rudolph Walton, a prominent silversmith, had set up his store (*Alaskan*, 5 June 1897:1). Thus by the early 1900s the old "Indian Village" had become thoroughly domesticated, and its inhabitants could now be dealt with on a commercial basis without the fear of being assaulted by "uncivilized" smells and sights.

Conclusion

To conclude this essay, I would like to take another look at the similarities and differences in the tourists' impressions of the native people of the American Southwest and the Alaska Panhandle. While in both cases the tourists were lured by the beauty of the scenery and the exotic nature of the local Indians, the latter factor played a much bigger role in the Southwest, where native ceremonies, especially the sensational Hopi Snake Dance, could still be observed. In Alaska no major "authentic" rituals that could attract a tourist audience took place in the summer, while attempts to organize native dances for the entertainment of the tourists were very rare.[15] This suggests that despite their interest in benefiting financially from the tourist trade, the majority of the Tlingits and other coastal natives were unwilling to allow the outsiders to witness any aspects of their ceremonial life. It is possible that having been criticized harshly by the missionaries for clinging to the "old customs," they were reluctant to admit to the outsiders that these customs were not a thing of the past. Judged by the success of one performance of "authentic Indian dances," organized by a White Juneau entrepreneur in cooperation with a local Tlingit headman (Collis 1890:168–174), native singing and dancing could have generated a great deal of interest among the tourists and made southeastern Alaska more attractive to those seeking "the exotic and picturesque Indians."

In the absence of such entertainment the most "picturesque" sites of southeastern Alaska were the abandoned villages, particularly in its southern portion where totem poles and remnants of large winter houses could still be seen. While the abandoned prehistoric ruins of the Southwest could to some extent be compared to these coastal villages, there were still plenty of romantically looking inhabited pueblos in the Southwest, whereas the only "exotic" looking structure a tourist could still occasionally see in Sitka was a decaying wooden gravehouse behind the Indian Village depicting its owners' animal crest.

Another major difference between the images of the Southwestern and coastal Alaskan natives that developed within the tourist enterprise had to do with the fact that the Southwestern Pueblo Indians were depicted primarily as makers of arts and crafts, whereas the coastal Alaska natives tended to be seen as fishermen first and as woodcarvers, basket weavers, and jewelers second. Moreover, farming, the primary subsistence activity of the Pueblos, was viewed by the tourists as more benign and "civilized" than the fishing and hunting in which the Tlingits and their coastal neighbors continued to engage (cf. Dilworth 1996).

Furthermore, despite their generally friendly attitude toward whites, southeastern Alaska natives continued to be portrayed as former warriors who, as fishermen and especially hunters, had retained their traditional physical and emotional toughness.[16] In contrast to them the Southwestern farmers were usually portrayed as peaceful.[17]

Finally, unlike the Southwest, southeastern Alaska never became a region that drew romantic Euro-American artists and writers. Except for its scenery, it had little to offer to the likes of Adolph Bandelier, D. H. Lawrence, or Charles Lummis. The coastal climate was much less benign than that of the desert, and the Panhandle Indians were much less romantic than the Pueblos. Even such enthusiasts of Alaska as John Muir tended to extol the unique beauty and attractiveness of its scenery and not of its indigenous inhabitants. Similarly, resident photographers (such as Merrill of Sitka and Winter and Pond of Juneau) were much less inclined to romanticize native life than their counterparts in the Southwest (Dilworth 1996; Gmelch 1995; Wyatt 1989). In the end even the "quaint, picturesque and historic" Sitka was a far cry from Santa Fe (Wilson 1997). At the same time, the coastal Alaska natives did not seem to fit the "vanishing Indian" stereotype as easily as the Southwestern Indians. Unlike the latter, who continued to cling to their ancient ceremonies and were not particularly eager to send their children to school, the Tlingits, the Haidas, and the New Metlakatla Tsimshians seemed to be undergoing rapid Americanization. Echoing the argument put forth by Presbyterian missionaries and Alaska civil authorities, most of the writers of tourist books praised the coastal natives' progress and predicted a brighter future for them than for the rest of the "Red race." Even such a maverick as Muir, who had spent a much longer period of time in southeastern Alaska than an average tourist and had a somewhat critical view of the activities of the missionaries, ended up echoing Sheldon Jackson's and John Brady's views on the future of the region's natives. Here is an eloquent passage from one of Muir's "Letters from Alaska," written in 1879–80. It begins on a sad note of lamenting the demographic and cultural decline of the Tlingits and the negative effects of the evil influence of the Euro-American "civilization" on them, but it ends on a hopeful note:

> These noble ruins [of an abandoned village] seem to foreshadow too surely the fate of the Stickene tribe. Contact with the whites has already reduced it more than one-half. It now numbers less than 800 persons, and the deaths at present greatly exceed the births. Will they perish utterly from the face of the earth? A few years will tell. Under the present conditions their only hope seems to lie in good missionaries and teachers, who will stand between them and the degrading vices of civilization and bestow what good they can. Thus a remnant may possibly be saved to gather fresh strength to grow up into the high place that they seem fully capable of attaining. (1993:40)

In the years preceding the Great Depression, when tourism in the American West declined significantly, the Alaska Panhandle's native inhabitants were no longer a major tourist attraction, while the Pueblos continued to draw numerous visitors, collectors, artists, photographers, and writers to the Southwest (Dilworth 1996). Only decades later, with the establishment of a regular airplane connection between southeastern Alaska and the "lower 48," followed by an explosion of the cruise ship tourism and the native arts and crafts renaissance of the 1960s–1970s, American and foreign visitors once again descended on the region in large numbers (Dunning 2000). This time the local native people began to have a greater say in how they were presented to the tourists and portrayed in the tourist literature. Unlike the late-19th-century visitors, the modern-day tourists could now observe native singers and dancers, dressed in their crest-bearing regalia and using traditional drums and dance paddles. However, only in the last decade did several Tlingit communities in the area begin to establish their own tourist ventures aimed at improving the native economy and presenting the native culture and history from the native point of view (Kan 1998, 1999:519–527; see also Dauenhauer and Dauenhauer, this volume). But that is another story.

Notes

1. The only monograph on tourism in another region of North America that addresses the images of the local native people constructed by the Euro-Canadian visitors is Patricia Jasen's fine work titled *Wild Things: Nature, Culture, and Tourism in Ontario, 1790–1914* (1995).
2. For my major publication on the history and culture of the Sitka Tlingit see a monograph (Kan 1999) as well as a recent essay detailing the circumstances of my research in that community, which began in 1979 and continues to this day (Kan 2001).
3. This summary is based on my own research (Kan 1999:174–292) as well as the work of Hinckley (1972, 1982, 1996) and Richard and Nora Dauenhauer (1994: 30–103).
4. Although I was unable to identify who Rheta Childe was, I do know that Frances Knapp was the daughter of Lyman E. Knapp, Alaska's governor in 1889–93.
5. The fact that many of these books were written by women and several, especially Collis's popular *A Woman's Trip to Alaska* (1890), for women is a special topic that merits further study.
6. Here is Charles Hallock making this point: "I doubt if there is a more enchanted site in the world than Sitka. It has been compared to Naples; but Naples, though serenely sweet, is not so massive, not near so grand. In the varied combination of its picturesque environment Sitka is both placid and stupendous, benign and majestic, alluring and severe. It entices while it warns" (1886:181).
7. The steamship company brochure was less charitable in its description of the native women's habit of painting their faces black, saying that "[this] added to their natural ugliness makes them look like the old Nick himself" (Pacific Coast Steamship Company 1894:18).
8. In all fairness it should be pointed out that the local Euro-American residents were well aware of the fact that noble origin and wealth of this woman was blown out of proportion by the naive visitors (e.g., Knapp and Childe 1896:106–107).
9. Most of the visitors, including the more sympathetic ones, referred to the Sitka Indian village as the "Ranch(e)" or "Rancherie," pejorative terms used by the

local whites, which were most likely brought by them from California in the first decade following the purchase of Alaska by the United States.

10. Alaska governor Alfred P. Swineford was even more emphatic, stating that the Tlingits "have not a drop of Indian blood in their veins" (1898:94).

11. "Lower classes" is the term used by Swineford: "there is not a more independent, prosperous, and contented 'lower class' in any country on earth than the native population of southeastern Alaska" (1898:99).

12. In fact, the Protestant missionaries tended to be much less racist in their evaluation of the Alaska natives' potential for becoming civilized than the secular writers quoted in this essay (cf. Coleman 1980).

13. *Siwash* was a standard term for coastal natives, derived by the local whites from the Chinook Jargon, which in turn had acquired it from the French *sauvage*. According to Thompson and Kinkade (1990:51), by the mid-19th-century this regional English term "had become derogatory and offensive to Indians."

14. A number of visitors also commented favorably on the neatly dressed and well-behaved Tlingit parishioners attending services at Sitka's Russian Orthodox cathedral (e.g., Collis 1890:110–114), but the Presbyterian natives always received the highest praise.

15. I found only one reference to a Tlingit headman organizing a "war dance" for the entertainment of the tourists (Sessions 1890:116).

16. Thus a number of the tourist guidebooks on the Inside Passage mentioned the retaliatory bombardment of the Tlingit villages by the U.S. Navy—Kake in 1869 and especially Angoon in 1882, which had occurred just a few years prior to the establishment of tourism in the region.

17. This image of the Pueblos was perpetuated not only by the tourist literature but by much of the anthropological writing about them (see, for example, Parsons 1991; cf. Dilworth 1996).

"A MAGIC PLACE"

The Northwest Coast Indian Hall at the
American Museum of Natural History

Ira Jacknis

There is in New York a magic place where all the dreams of childhood hold a
rendezvous, where century old trees sing or speak, where indefinable objects
lie in wait for the visitor with an anxious stare; where animals of superhuman
gentleness press their uplifted little paws, clasped in prayer for the privilege of
constructing for the chosen one the palace of the beaver, of guiding him into
the realm of the seals, or of teaching him, with a mystic kiss, the language of
the frog and kingfisher. This region, to which disused but singularly effective
museographic methods grant the supplementary prestige of the clair-obscur
of caves and of the crumbling heaps of lost treasure, can be visited daily from
ten to five o'clock at the American Museum of Natural History, New York. It
is the vast gallery on the ground floor devoted to the Indians of the Northwest
Coast.

Claude Lévi-Strauss,
"The Art of the Northwest Coast
at the American Museum of Natural History"

When Claude Lévi-Strauss arrived in New York City in the spring of 1941,
one of the first things he did was visit the Northwest Coast Indian Hall at the
American Museum of Natural History. Two years later, in the pages of the
Gazette des Beaux-Arts, he extravagantly praised the gallery for the high aesthetic quality of the Native art that it contained. The French anthropologist
had come at a special moment in the hall's now century-plus history. Although renowned as the repository for the collections and displays of Franz
Boas, the appearance of the hall had already changed radically from Boas's
time as a curator at the museum, 1895–1905. The hall that Lévi-Strauss saw,
however, has changed little in the succeeding decades. This essay, a case
study in anthropological displays, offers a history of the hall—its construc-

tion and its influence on scholars, artists, and the general public. With the world's largest collection from the region, the displays of the American Museum of Natural History have played a critical role in forming our image of Northwest Coast Indian cultures.[1]

The Hall before Boas (1880–1895)

The American Museum of Natural History began its anthropology department in 1873, four years after its founding by naturalist Albert S. Bickmore. By 1877, when it moved to its current site on Manhattan's Upper West Side, it had ethnological specimens on display. The debts and poor attendance that plagued the institution during the 1870s soon became a memory under the effective presidency of Morris K. Jesup (1881–1908), a retired railroad banker. At the same time, Jesup vastly increased the collections and encouraged the conduct and publication of systematic scientific research.

Because of the interest of trustee Heber Bishop, the museum began to acquire ethnological specimens from the Northwest Coast (Jonaitis 1988:71–113). Bishop, who visited the region in 1880, offered a contract to Dr. Israel Wood Powell, the superintendent of Indian Affairs for British Columbia. Gathered between 1880 and 1885, his collection was especially rich in Haida material. The most spectacular object was a 64-foot Haida canoe — the largest Northwest Coast canoe in any museum — which arrived in 1883. Although the Powell-Bishop collections were important, they were greatly eclipsed by the horde of mostly Tlingit artifacts purchased from naval lieutenant and amateur ethnologist George Thornton Emmons — 4,000-plus objects in 1888–93, and a second 2,500-piece collection, which arrived in 1894.

At the museum's opening, the ethnology collections occupied part of a mezzanine gallery, overlooking the second-floor hall. The large Haida canoe was suspended from the ceiling, floating in the well above the bird gallery (Figure 1). As museum display has always been strongly influenced by commercial design, it is not surprising that the exhibits looked like the innovative department stores of the time (Leach 1993): many similar objects, generally arranged by type and crowded on shelves in finely made glass and mahogany cases. Despite having some spectacular pieces, the anthropology collections lacked a curator; they were supervised, instead, by Director Bickmore. Consequently, their display was not especially noteworthy. Given the relatively small scope of the collection, all the ethnology holdings were ex-

1. View of Haida canoe, suspended above Bird Hall, American Museum of Natural History, New York, c. 1883. Courtesy AMNH Library, neg. no. 483.

hibited together. Because they were grouped by collector, they tended to be in regional clumps. In 1887 the Powell collection was removed in order to show 1,284 pieces from the collection loaned by Lt. Emmons, who came to New York to supervise its installation (Jonaitis 1988:106, 108). The canoe and other items from the Northwest Coast elicited most appreciative comments in the pages of the *New York Times,* which spoke of the canoe's "graceful outline," the "tasteful decoration" of an argillite plate, and a raven rattle, "colored in the highest style of barbaric art."[2]

The Hall of Franz Boas (1895–1905)

The anthropology collections were first put on a professional footing in 1894, with the appointment of Frederic W. Putnam as curator and chairman of the department. Simultaneously professor of anthropology at Harvard and director of its Peabody Museum, Putnam immediately set out to hire Franz Boas (1858–1942) as assistant curator. Following his first field trip to the Northwest Coast in 1886 and his immigration to America the following year,

Boas had taught at Clark University before joining Putnam in 1892 in the preparation of the anthropological displays at the World's Columbian Exposition, held in Chicago in 1893.

Boas's entrée to the American Museum was a commission to collect materials for a life group. Related to biological habitat dioramas (Wonders 1993), these life groups consisted of costumed mannequins acting out a scene from Native life. Boas favored life groups because they showed the functional context of museum specimens. Very innovative at the time, they were popularized by the Smithsonian, especially at the Chicago fair. Boas's diorama was to be the first for anthropology in the American Museum. He spent the fall of 1894 in Fort Rupert, Vancouver Island, gathering objects for two Kwakwaka'wakw displays: one for the Smithsonian's National Museum, depicting the return of the hamatsa initiate, and one for New York, illustrating the uses of cedar. For this Boas commissioned a set of artifacts made of cedar bark and then had a woman demonstrate the use of these crafts so that the scene could be photographed as a model for the museum's preparators (Jacknis 1984:14, 33–36; 1985:97–103).

After supervising the installation of his display in the fall of 1895, Boas was able to parlay this into a permanent position (Jacknis 1985). In the decade that he spent at the museum Boas's greatest achievement was the direction of the Jesup North Pacific Expedition (1897–1902), which among its other results produced a great deal of highly exhibitable material. Boas and his Kwakwaka'wakw assistant George Hunt were able to balance the museum's Tlingit, Tsimshian, and Haida holdings with large collections of Nuxalk, Kwakwaka'wakw, and Nuu-chah-nulth specimens.[3]

In a time of great expansion for the anthropology department, all of its exhibits were moved to galleries in a new wing. Those for the Northwest Coast, placed on the ground floor of the original museum building, were opened to the public on November 30, 1896, in the same room that has ever since been devoted to the Northwest Coast Indians. Along with material from that region, the Ethnology Hall held Eskimo, northern Mexican, and Melanesian artifacts. Already on display were a model of a Kwakwaka'wakw village, the life group depicting cedar crafts, and plaster busts of physical types. When the new West Wing was completed in 1900, the other ethnological specimens were moved out, leaving the entire hall for the Northwest Coast. Though Boas was trying to arrange a more or less permanent display,

each year more material came in, and it was placed on exhibit as it was catalogued and researched. Items too large for the hall—tall totem poles, grave
and house posts, petroglyph casts—were placed in the adjoining Western
Vestibule, but still there was a constant shortage of exhibit space. In 1901
the previous artifact arrangement by collector was replaced by a fully tribal
order. Boas thus began by integrating the rich Powell and Emmons collections with the new acquisitions he and his team had collected on the Jesup
Expedition. Although the Annual Report for 1902 stated that the North Hall
was "completed in its main features," work on the hall continued for several
years.

Like all the ethnology halls in the American Museum, the unity and
rationale of this gallery was geographical, a direct implementation of Boas's
argument in his 1887 debate with Smithsonian anthropologists Otis T. Mason
and John W. Powell (Jacknis 1985:77–83). As he had suggested, artifacts
could be arranged in two series: "First, a general or synoptic collection of
specimens obtained from the entire area, designed to illustrate the culture
of the people as a whole; Second, several independent collections, each illustrating the peculiarities of the culture of a single tribe" (Hovey 1904:41).
These first synoptic cases followed a plan popular in ethnographic monographs of the period, running from matter to spirit: natural products and
materials, industries and tools, house furnishings, dress and ornament, trade
and barter, hunting and fishing, travel and transportation, armor and weap-
ons, musical instruments, decorative art, and clan organization.

The tribal series followed, starting with the northernmost Tlingit and
proceeding south in order through the Tsimshian, Haida, Nuxalk, Kwakwa̱-
ka'wakw, Nuu-chah-nulth, and Coast Salish. At the end was a group of cases
for the interior Plateau tribes. Though neighboring, they have a culture distinct from that of the Coastal tribes, and Boas was juxtaposing these two
areas in the hall to drive home his point about the effects of local geography
and history. The material within each tribal set basically followed the order
of the synoptic series, with local omissions and additions as they occurred.
Historical concerns were evident in the cases of archaeological remains and
in labels stating, for example, that Bella Coola "culture is considerably affected by that of the inland tribes, with whom they have always traded" (Boas
1900:8).

Visually the hall was typical for its period, while firmly revealing the

2. Northwest Coast Indian Hall, American Museum of Natural History, New York, c. 1902. Courtesy AMNH Library, neg. no. 12633.

concerns of its arranger. A large rectangular space, the room was divided into two longitudinal series of alcoves formed by alternating polygonal and flat cases (Figure 2). The bulk of the collections were contained in these ethnology cases, but the synoptic series occupied only the first four alcoves on the east side. The tribal series snaked down the rest of the east side and looped back up the west side. Running down the center were two parallel rows of waist-high table cases for the archaeology. Although the room was no longer open to a floor below, as the mezzanine had been, Boas again suspended the Haida canoe from the ceiling, along with oversize nets and several smaller canoes. Totemic sculptures and large boxes were piled around columns on the tops of cases.

The focal point was a large case containing the life group (Figure 3). In a guide to the hall Boas described its action:

> The importance of the yellow and red cedar is illustrated in the group case in the center of the hall. A woman is seen making a cedar-bark mat, rocking her infant, which is bedded in cedar-bark, the cradle being

3. Life group exhibit, *Uses of Cedar*, Northwest Coast Indian Hall, American Museum of Natural History, New York, c. 1904. Courtesy AMNH Library, neg. no. 351.

moved by means of a cedar-bark rope attached to her toe. Another woman is shredding cedar-bark, to be used for making aprons. A man is taking red-hot stones out of the fire with tongs made of cedar-wood, and is about to place the stones in a cedar box. The Indians have no kettles or pots, but cook in boxes, heating the water by means of red-hot stones. A second man is engaged in painting a box. A young woman is drying fish over the fire. (1900:3–4)

As an archaeologist who spent little time at the museum, Putnam left ethnological matters to Boas, who acceded to the chairmanship in 1903 with Putnam's retirement. Although Boas was able to arrange the Northwest Coast Hall largely as he wished, his insistence on the priority of research and publication over exhibition was not received sympathetically by the museum administration, and by 1905 he felt he had to resign (Jacknis 1985:105–108).

The Hall of Clark Wissler (1905–1942)

Boas's position was assumed by his former student Clark Wissler (1870–1947), who had joined the museum staff in 1902. As Boas had been curator during the "Jesup era," so his successor fits neatly into the "Osborn era." Henry Fairfield Osborn, however, was not nearly as supportive of anthropology as Jesup had been. A nephew of J. P. Morgan, Osborn had been curator of vertebrate paleontology since 1891, but with Jesup's death in 1908 he also became president. As a scientist, president, and wealthy patron, he wielded enormous power until his retirement in 1933. Osborn naturally emphasized displays from his own discipline, but he maintained a strong antipathy toward anthropology. As he once remarked, "Between ourselves, much anthropology is merely opinion, or the gossip of the natives. It is many years away from being a science. Mr. Jesup and the Museum spent far too much money on anthropology."[4] For their part, the anthropologists (including Boas, Wissler, Lowie, and Mead) returned the sentiment, opposing his racism and eugenic beliefs, as well as his personal and administrative style (Rainger 1991:178).

While loyal to his former professor, Clark Wissler attempted to respond to Osborn's requests. As a former schoolteacher, he was more committed than Boas to making the exhibits appealing to the general public. For instance, in 1907 he separated out the "study series" from those specimens on display in public corridors. In an effort to simplify the Northwest Coast Hall, Wissler and assistant curator Harlan I. Smith removed Boas's initial synoptic series and arranged all the material geographically, "so that the visitor in passing from south to north through the hall encounters the tribes as if he were actually traveling from south to north in the country" (American Museum, Annual Report, 1909:38). In 1908 they removed the low center cases of archaeological specimens, replacing them with the giant Haida canoe that had been suspended from the ceiling. Boas's cedar life group was broken up and moved to side and back cases. More importantly, all of the former curator's large polygonal cases were replaced with smaller and lower ones.

In 1910 an even more dramatic effort was made to simulate the Northwest Coast habitat. First about 20 mannequins were placed inside the canoe, representing a chief and his retainers on their way to a potlatch (Dickerson 1910; Figure 4).[5] Based on life casts, the figures were formed out of plaster by

4. Northwest Coast Indian Hall, American Museum of Natural History, New York, October 1910. Courtesy AMNH Library, neg. no. 33003.

sculptor Sigurd Neandross (Neandross 1910). At about the same time painter Will S. Taylor was commissioned to create a series of 16 murals—executed between 1910 and 1926—depicting typical scenes from tribal life (W. Taylor 1910).[6] To prepare for this work Taylor visited British Columbia with Smith in the summer of 1909 to collect artifacts and sketch the scenery (Fassett 1911). Over the next few years more side cases were removed, as were artifacts from the remaining cases, producing a much less cluttered effect. Totem poles were placed around the columns, giving "the final ethnic touch to the whole exhibit" (American Museum, Annual Report, 1917:91; Figure 5).

The exact responsibility for the renovation remains obscure, but it was the result of a complex collaboration among several players. It was probably not a coincidence that the life group was introduced shortly after Osborn became president. Osborn, who had long been interested in art, firmly believed in the educational efficacy of large and spectacular exhibits, especially

5. Northwest Coast Indian Hall, American Museum of Natural History, New York, 1919. Courtesy AMNH Library, neg. no. 37672.

large mounted dinosaurs and stunningly realistic habitat groups (Rainger 1991:160). Director Hermon C. Bumpus, who also advocated large dioramas, was formally given credit for the "conception" of the canoe group (Dickerson 1910:227; cf. Wissler 1943:121–123).[7] Wissler, however, seems to have been inactive during the construction of the canoe group, due to a "severe breakdown in his health" that he suffered in early 1909 (Freed and Freed 1983:806). Instead, scientific direction of the project was given to Harlan Smith, who had worked with Boas at the Chicago exposition and on the Jesup Expedition. Apparently it was the central administration — Bumpus or Osborn — who chose George T. Emmons to supervise the production and installation of the canoe group. Emmons, of course, was well known to American Museum staff from his earlier collections, but Boas had formed an intense dislike for the collector (Cole 1985:149; Jonaitis 1988:112–113).[8] It is unlikely that Wissler or Smith would have turned to him.

Perhaps because of the strong administration role, Clark Wissler disliked the resulting canoe life group. After Bumpus had left the museum, Wissler wrote to museum secretary George Sherwood that "the really courageous thing to do is to admit that the group has failed; dismantle it, swing the boat up to the ceiling as it used to be, take the group of figures in the stern for a dancing group to be placed in a case in the middle of the hall, or, as an alternative, construct a model canoe two thirds the size for which the water line shall be near the floor."[9] Wissler may have also agreed with Boas, who, although basically supportive of human dioramas, found that large, dramatic life groups distracted visitors from the basic point of cultural representation (Jacknis 1985:97–103). In any event Wissler's critique was ignored.

The Northwest Coast Hall continued to undergo refinements until about 1930. Details were changed in the canoe group, the adjacent Eskimo exhibits were removed in 1916, and ceiling lamps were painted with designs of Tlingit baskets. In the summer of 1922 associate curator Pliny Goddard collected more totem poles, which when added to the hall completely covered the columns. "The totem poles and other objects in the hall have been adjusted so as to give the mural panels an artistic setting. These very important secondary features of the North Pacific Indian exhibit add greatly to the habitat function of the installation" (American Museum, Annual Report, 1918:87). During these years, when the great Akeley Hall of African Mammals was taking shape, full-scale habitat groups were very much on the minds of the museum administration. An environmental setting was reinforced at some point, probably in the late 1920s, when all the windows in the hall were blocked up, greatly reducing the ambient lighting. Whether intentional or not, this had the effect of further simulating the shadowy coastal forest suggested by the totem poles.[10]

To some extent the pace of changes to the hall reflected the relative rate of collecting. Acquisitions were substantial in the decades between the accession of the Powell-Bishop collection in 1881 and the last receipts of the Jesup Expedition in 1904. Boas, who was deeply committed to research on the Northwest Coast, revised his display repeatedly as new specimens arrived. After he left, no curator had a personal interest in the region, and collecting declined. As at the rival Field Museum and Smithsonian, the American Museum had already accumulated massive collections. Contemporary Indians, apparently bereft of much of their traditional material culture, were no longer considered picturesque. The principal exceptions were the few totem poles, acquired more for aesthetic than scientific reasons, that suggested a forest. After these initial cosmetic transformations, the exhibit remained static.

The Hall after Wissler (1942–2002)

The Great Depression—followed by World War II—hit American museums particularly hard. The private philanthropists who had formerly funded them now had less to give, and the foundations that took their place were not interested in museums. According to F. Trubee Davison, president of the museum between 1933 and 1951, "Because of the Depression, our salaries were reduced, some of our positions were abolished, our great exploration program was suspended, and ten of our exhibition halls were closed, for part of the time, in rotation. The City reduced its allotment to us, and the trustees could no longer be counted on to make up the annual deficit" (Hellman 1969:213; J. Kennedy 1968:226–232). Exacerbating the deficit were the many new buildings and halls that the museum continued to open: the grandiose Theodore Roosevelt memorial wing in 1936 and habitat halls for South Asiatic mammals, African mammals, and North American mammals (opened in 1930, 1936, 1942, respectively).

The problem of what to do with the museum's many expensive exhibits was the topic of much discussion during these years. Desiring a "permanent" exhibit, Osborn looked forward to the day when the anthropology department could devise "an ideal arrangement [of objects] that would stand the test of criticism for all time" and would never have to be tampered with. In an effort to be accommodating, Clark Wissler explained the Boasian logic of museum arrangement: "It is because of the universal feeling that association of ideas and their diffusion is the chief factor in the origin and distribution of cultures, that museum plans are projected on a geographical basis with confidence that such plans need never be materially revised to meet future requirements."[11]

Franz Boas, however, would have been the first to point out that these displays would need to be modified to reflect changes in our knowledge, which is always relative (Jacknis 1985:107). In fact, in 1937 he wrote to the museum's president, Roy Chapman Andrews: "The habitat halls enabled the

6. Northwest Coast Indian Hall, American Museum of Natural History, New York, March 1943 (cf. Lévi-Strauss 1943, fig. 1). Courtesy AMNH Library, neg. no. 318931.

Museum to be very successful for a while. They also armored the Museum, like a dinosaur, against change. It is odd that Professor Osborn, who was a paleontologist, did not recognize that the huge expenditure of capital tied the Museum almost irrevocably, for many years, to the exposition of one particular aspect of science and made it almost impossible for it to respond to changing scientific interests."[12]

Well before Wissler's retirement in 1942 the Northwest Coast Hall had settled into its current state as an "aesthetic" object (Figure 6). Some alterations and minor revisions were made to the hall between 1946 and 1948, but it was not until 1960, with a new director and a new curator, that any substantial changes were made. Although marine biologist Albert E. Parr, director between 1942 and 1959, marked a radical contrast from the Jesup and Osborn years—when the president called the shots and directors were weak—his interests lay primarily in ecology. Just as he was arriving, the museum had sponsored two reviews of its programs (Hellman 1969:161, 183), and although both were severely critical of the exhibition program, with the exception of the new Hall of Human Biology (opened in 1961), the anthropology department was ignored.[13]

A sign — or perhaps the cause — of this neglect was the lack of a curator of North American ethnology between Wissler's retirement and the hiring of his successor, Stanley A. Freed, in 1960. With a great deal of energy Freed started out systematically renovating the North American halls. Appropriately, he began in 1960–61 with the most important of these, the Northwest Coast Hall. However, the hall received only a cosmetic renewal. Instead, Freed put his efforts into a more thorough treatment of the Eskimo gallery (opened in 1964), directly off the Northwest Coast Hall, before a complete transformation of the two connected halls for the Indians of the Eastern Woodlands and Plains (1966, 1967, respectively; see Freed 1966). The museum spent the following two decades renovating virtually all its other anthropology halls (with the exception of that for the Indians of the Southwest — including California — which was demolished).[14]

When Freed arrived he found that the Northwest Coast Hall was already being renovated in preparation for the museum's centennial celebrations in 1969. According to the Annual Report, "Our aim is to improve the appearance of exhibition areas that are scientifically and structurally sound, but that, with the passage of time, have become dingy and, in some cases, outmoded in form of presentation" (American Museum, Annual Report, 1959–60:56). The work was being directed, on a volunteer basis, by Bella Weitzner, who had joined the museum in 1908 as Clark Wissler's secretary and since 1956 had served as curator emeritus of ethnology.[15]

With the help of her sister, Weitzner made numerous changes throughout the hall. Some of the cases were reconfigured — their back panels replaced and painted in new colors, and crumbled cork spread on the bottoms — and some new wall cases were constructed; some objects were removed, and others were rearranged within the cases. The Taylor murals were cleaned, new lighting was installed, and the graphics were partially redesigned (using raised-letter titles). Stanley Freed's major responsibility was rewriting some of the labels; he also identified some of the totem poles that had lost their catalogue numbers. As part of this renovation, in 1960 came the most substantial change to the hall since 1930: the large Haida canoe was relocated to the lobby just outside the hall. This removal of the hall's popular

7. Northwest Coast Indian Hall, American Museum of Natural History, New York, 1962. Courtesy AMNH Library, neg. no. 328715.

landmark encouraged the use of the gallery as a corridor to the auditorium (especially after the construction of its giant IMAX movie screen in 1982). Most of the renovation took place during the first two years, and although it was quite substantial, the general content and effect of the hall was left intact (Figure 7).[16]

Things remained quiet on the first floor until art historian and museum vice-president Aldona Jonaitis began reviewing the Northwest Coast collections in the late 1980s. In 1989–91 the 17 mannequins in the Haida canoe were completely refurbished (Coffee 1991). Although Jonaitis's 1991 exhibition, *Chiefly Feasts: The Enduring Kwakiutl Potlatch,* was a major rethinking of the museum's relationship to Northwest Coast peoples, as a temporary exhibit it had little impact on the permanent hall. One of the commissions for the show, a totem pole carved in 1992 by Kwakwaka'wakw Richard Hunt, was subsequently installed in the hall (before being moved to the nearby Discovery Room in 2001).

In the last decade or so, the hall has also been modified for pragmatic reasons. An entrance placed in the east wall for a temporary gallery necessitated the removal of some cases, and plastic panels were placed around the bases of the totem poles to prevent damage from the prying fingers of eager school children. One factor contributing to the hall's stasis in these years was the protracted merger negotiations between the American Museum and George G. Heye's Museum of the American Indian, with the prospect of combined exhibits (Force 1999:118–336). The talks, which began in 1982, finally broke off in 1985, with Heye's museum becoming part of the Smithsonian in 1989. With the retirement of Stanley Freed in June 1999 and the appointment of Peter M. Whiteley at the beginning of 2001, the hall began its life under a new curator.

The Northwest Coast Hall as Cultural Influence

As the American Museum's anthropological displays became increasingly irrelevant to anthropology, they took on a vitalizing influence among artists and the general public. The museum's spectacular habitat dioramas of the 1930s made it one of the city's leading attractions. By mid-decade the museum was reportedly the second most important tourist site for visiting dignitaries, after the Empire State Building (Gallenkamp 2001:294–295). In 1941, when Lévi-Strauss arrived, a total of 1,163,318 people visited the museum (American Museum, Annual Report, 1941:35), and attendance figures continued to grow through the war years. By 1944 the institution was so much a part of the city's popular culture that a scene of the Broadway musical *On the Town* took place in the museum, where one of the main characters worked as an anthropologist. The Haida canoe, a notable feature, was a popular meeting place for museum visitors. It was so beloved that "sometimes parents would lift their children up and set them inside the canoe" (Coffee 1991:32). Some of these children grew up to become scholars—for example, the comparative mythologist Joseph Campbell, who dated the inception of his life's work to a visit to the hall in 1910 (Cousineau 1990:xxv, 1).

Artistic Reflections

According to one city guide book, the museum's Northwest Coast totem poles and masks were "works of the highest aesthetic quality, which excite the admiration of modern artists" (Federal Writers' Project 1982:364). Indeed, the museum and its Northwest Coast Hall had been attracting artists since the first decade of the century (Levin 1984; Rushing 1995:41–96). Max Weber, associated with the photographer and gallery owner Alfred Stieglitz, had studied tribal artifacts in European museums while part of the community of Parisian artists. Upon returning to New York in 1909, Weber frequented the Pueblo and Northwest Coast collections at the Museum of Natural History. Attracted to the flatness and strong decorative sense of Indian art, he synthesized his interest in Native American art with influences from a wide range of African, pre-Columbian, Asian, and modernist art (Rushing 1995:44).

By coincidence, Lévi-Strauss arrived in New York just as an influential exhibition of American Indian art was opening at the Museum of Modern Art (Rushing 1992). It was curated by Frederic Douglas, curator of American Indian art at the Denver Art Museum, and René d'Harnoncourt, general manager of the Department of Interior's Indian Arts and Crafts Board and later director of the Museum of Modern Art. Many objects from the American Museum of Natural History—such as a Haida portrait mask, a Tlingit war helmet, and a Nuu-chah-nulth painted screen—were lent to the show, which highlighted the aesthetic qualities of the objects. In his large Northwest Coast section, d'Harnoncourt, a master of museum display, used an ambient darkness cut by spotlights, simulating firelight in a plank house set in a forest of totem poles. Although he was influenced by Coastal environments, which he had visited in 1938, undoubtedly d'Harnoncourt was also responding to the American Museum's dark hall, which he certainly knew. In turn, d'Harnoncourt's dramatic style became an archetype, if not a cliché, in later displays devoted to the region (Jacknis 2002:123–126, 243).

Many of the artists that Lévi-Strauss came to know in New York were excited by Northwest Coast Indian artifacts. This émigré community of French surrealists included Max Ernst, Kurt Seligmann, André Breton, Yves Tanguy, Roberto Matta, Georges Duthuit, Robert Lebel, and Enrico Donati. The surrealists had been attracted to artifacts from the region since the beginning of their movement in the early 1920s (Cowling 1978; Maurer 1984; Mauzé 1994). These artists found in Northwest Coast artifacts an art that was true less to surface appearance and more to imperatives of the subconscious, a subconscious that was collective and universal. Among the first to value this art on the level of humankind's greatest achievements, they spread their enthusiasm in exhibitions and publications.

Collections from the Northwest Coast were not plentiful in France, but these artists visited other European museums and consulted illustrated publications.[17] Several built their own collections from the few Northwest Coast artifacts on the market. Once in New York, they were excited to discover new sources. In a good-natured competition, they carefully selected their gems from the curio and "junk" shops on Third Avenue, racing each other up to George Heye's Museum of the American Indian, where he casually offered to sell them items from his collection. A collector of "exotic curios" since his youth, Lévi-Strauss acquired a number of Northwest Coast pieces from these sources (Lévi-Strauss and Eribon 1991:33; Mauzé 1990:52).[18]

Despite his anthropological status, Lévi-Strauss soon adopted surrealist aesthetics. "Contact with the surrealists enriched and honed my aesthetic tastes. Many objects I would have rejected as unworthy appeared in a different light thanks to Breton and his friends" (Lévi-Strauss and Eribon 1991:35). For all its ethnological references, his 1943 essay is a thorough piece of poetic art criticism. As he wrote: "This dithyrambic gift of synthesis, the almost monstrous faculty to perceive as similar what all other men have conceived as different undoubtedly constitutes the exceptional feature of the art of British Columbia" (1943:180). Lévi-Strauss and the surrealists shared an interest in myths and the irrational: "The surrealists taught me not to fear the abrupt and unexpected comparisons that Max Ernst liked to use in his collages" (Lévi-Strauss and Eribon 1991:35). The French ethnologist invoked this combinatorial freedom of the *bricoleur* in his books on mythology and the "savage mind."

The American abstract expressionists—stimulated by the surrealists—were also inspired by Native American and other forms of "primitive art" (Varnedoe 1984; Rushing 1995:121–190). Among those who responded to Northwest Coast art during the 1940s and early 1950s were Barnett Newman, Adolph Gottlieb, Richard Pousette-Dart, and Jackson Pollock. Also attracted to the region's art were the New York painters of "Indian Space" or "semiology": Will Barnet, Robert Barrell, Peter Busa, and Steve Wheeler (A. Gibson 1983). While the displays of the American Museum were most often frequented, these artists also visited the Museum of the American Indian and the Brooklyn Museum of Art (Weiss 1983:82). Most read and acquired scholarly volumes on the subject; Newman owned copies of Boas's *Primitive Art* and his 1921 monograph on Kwakwa̱ka̱'wakw material culture.

Like the surrealists, many (e.g., Gottlieb, Pousette-Dart, Newman) owned Northwest Coast art.

Of all these artists, Barnett Newman was the most intimately involved in Northwest Coast art. An active theorist and curator, he arranged an exhibit titled *Northwest Coast Indian Painting* at the avant-garde Betty Parsons Gallery in 1946. Although 4 of the 28 objects came from Max Ernst's own collection, most of the others were lent by the American Museum of Natural History, where they were exhibited not as art but as ethnology. Significantly, in this show Newman chose to focus on painting, not the more familiar sculpture. Its attraction for him lay in its all-over composition, bidimensionality, and abstracted realism. As he argued, these peoples "depicted their mythological gods and totemic monsters in abstract symbols, using organic shapes, without regard to the contours of appearance" (1946). Newman directly linked Native work to that of "our modern American abstract artists," who by working with a "pure plastic language" were "creating a living myth for us in our own time."

Comparing this art favorably to that of ancient Greece and Picasso, Lévi-Strauss wrote prophetically: "Certainly the time is not far distant when the collections of the Northwest Coast will move from anthropological museums to take their place in art museums among the arts of Egypt, Persia and the Middle Ages" (1943:175). Not only were these objects not in a specifically anthropological museum, but they were in one devoted to natural history, along with animals, plants, and minerals. Their disciplinary categorization was thus subject to transvaluation. As historian James Clifford has argued, these episodes of "primitivism" were expressions of the fluidity between artistic and ethnological circles: "While the object systems of art and anthropology are institutionalized and powerful, they are not immutable. The categories of the beautiful, the cultural, and the authentic have changed and are changing" (1988:229, cf. Rubin 1984). Not only did these artists reappropriate the Northwest Coast collections as art, but they were undoubtedly led to this position by the carefully crafted installation art of the American Museum of Natural History.

Literary Reflections

Unlike the painters, who looked to the Northwest Coast Hall as a locus of exotic and primordial reality, the novelists who meditated on the gallery conceived of it as a place of personal memory and desire. Perhaps the most striking of these literary reflections may be found in J. D. Salinger's *The Catcher in the Rye* (1951). At one point his protagonist, Holden Caulfield, visits the museum:

> I loved that damn museum. I remember you had to go through the Indian Room to get to the auditorium. It was a long, long room, and you were only supposed to whisper. . . . Then you'd pass by this long, long Indian war canoe, about as long as three goddam Cadillacs in a row, with about twenty Indians in it, some of them paddling, some of them just standing around looking tough, and they all had war paint all over their faces. There was one very spooky guy in the back of the canoe, with a mask on. He was the witch doctor. He gave me the creeps, but I liked him anyway. Another thing, if you touched one of the paddles or anything while you were passing, one of the guards would say to you, "Don't touch anything, children," but he always said it in a nice voice, not like a goddam cop or anything. They you'd pass by this big glass case, with Indians inside it rubbing sticks together to make a fire, and a squaw weaving a blanket. The squaw that was weaving the blanket was sort of bending over, and you could see her bosom and all. We all used to sneak a good look at it, even the girls, because they were only little kids and they didn't have any more bosom than *we* did. Then, just before you went inside the auditorium, right near the doors, you passed this Eskimo. He was sitting over a hole in this icy lake, and he was fishing through it. He had about two fish right next to the hole, that he'd already caught. Boy, that museum was full of glass cases. . . .
>
> The best thing, though, in that museum was that everything always stayed right where it was. Nobody'd move. You could go there a hundred thousand times, and that Eskimo would still be just finished catching those two fish, the birds would still be on their way south, and the deers would still be drinking out of that water hole, with their pretty antlers and their pretty skinny legs, and that squaw with the naked bosom would still be weaving that same blanket. Nobody'd be different. The only thing that would be different would be *you*. Not that you'd be so much older or anything. It wouldn't be that exactly. You'd just be *dif*ferent, that's all. . . . Certain things they should stay the way they are. You ought to be able to stick them in one of those big glass cases and just leave them alone. I know that's impossible, but it's too bad anyway (1951:120–22).

Salinger, who was born in New York City in 1919, would have known the hall primarily in the 1920s and 1930s, when it had achieved substantially its final form. In a comment to *Story* magazine in 1944, Salinger noted: "I . . . am more inclined to get my New York out of the American Indian Room of the Museum of Natural History, where I used to drop my marbles all over the place" (cited in Ducharme 1998:71).[19]

Although John Cheever does not comment on the hall at Salinger's length, in his 1969 novel *Bullet Park* one of his principal characters visits the museum in search of a young woman with whom he has just fallen in love: "It was a place I had visited once or twice a year for as long as I could remember and while there had been changes there had been fewer—far fewer—than there had been outside the walls. In fifteen years the Alaskan war canoe had traveled perhaps twenty-five yards, leaving a gallery of totem poles for a vestibule. Eskimo women in glass cases were performing the same humble tasks they had been performing when I was a child, clutching Gretchen Oxencroft's hand" (1969:211). Although written after the move of the war canoe in 1962, Cheever's passage is reminiscent of Salinger's musing, even to the comment on the unchanging Eskimo diorama. One wonders if Cheever was alluding, consciously or not, to Salinger.[20]

Perhaps coincidentally, both of these literary reflections of the Northwest Coast Hall emphasize the exhibits as stasis, as a place of refuge (Wonders 1993:222). As one first encountered in childhood, it was also a place of lost innocence ("The only thing that would be different would be *you*"). For both J. D. Salinger and John Cheever, the Museum of Natural History was a meeting place. It was an unchanging landmark, as well as a venue of enchantment, a fictional vision of perfect natural worlds. For Holden Caulfield, as well as many New Yorkers, "the best thing" about that hall was that "everything always stayed right where it was." Unlike Boas's desire for constant change, some visitors find pleasure in the moribund hall: "Certain things they should stay the way they are. You ought to be able to stick them in one of those big glass cases and just leave them alone."

The Northwest Coast Hall as Cultural Artifact

In fact, it is not quite true that everything in the Northwest Coast Hall has "always stayed right where it was." Because its appearance is so obviously antiquated, people commonly attribute the hall to its originator, Franz Boas.

Clifford refers to it as "the Boas Room" (1988:229), and Lévi-Strauss remarks of it, "Victim, like so many others, of the aberration of curators, the collection at the American Museum of Natural History has lost a good many of the attractions that Franz Boas' method of presentation had managed so well to conserve" (1982:9).[21] Although Boas must be credited with the hall's basic conception, as we have seen there is practically nothing about its appearance, as opposed to its contents, that can be found in Boas's version, with the notable exception of the ceiling and floor. The cases, old-fashioned as they are, as well as their arrangement, are due to Wissler and other museum staff of his period. Commentators reach back to an even older period because the hall has remained the same for so long—about seven, if not nine, decades.[22]

During Boas's time the Northwest Coast Hall was central to the debates of American anthropology. In the face of received wisdom of a comparative evolutionary typology, Boas used his own Northwest Coast Hall to implement his model of an ideal anthropology display, one based on functional contexts of cultural domains, set in a scheme of local geographical distribution. After Boas's departure, the changes to the hall were cosmetic, in the sense that they applied only to appearances and made no fundamental contribution to anthropology. In fact, after about 1930 the changes were hardly even cosmetic. The Victorian density of the 19th century, carried over by Boas, was radically simplified under Wissler. With minor alterations the hall was fundamentally untouched by the display innovations of the Bauhaus. Instead, these more abstract and conceptual styles were applied to the display of Northwest Coast artifacts, including those from the American Museum, by René d'Harnoncourt (Staniszewski 1998). As the hall remained static in the wake of constantly developing anthropological theory, it became more and more irrelevant to the discipline. In this it was like almost all other anthropology exhibits until at least the revival of museum anthropology in the mid-1960s. That museum displays are not inherently a-theoretical or outmoded may be seen in later attempts to incorporate change and culture contact (for example, at the British Columbia Provincial Museum of the 1970s, described below).

The American Museum, like most long-established museums, has been confronted with complex issues of preservation. Although curators are dedicated to preserving the artifacts (some of which have been on continuous display for over a century, in the case of the Northwest Coast Hall), many also find themselves maintaining old displays, which have been manufactured by the museum. The real truth of the so-called Boas Room is that it is not the product of any one person but a collaborative creation of over a century of museum personnel. As such, it resembles the dense layering and incorporation of a painterly pentimento or a literary palimpsest.

The Northwest Coast Indian Hall is only an extreme example of a "permanent exhibition." As Collier and Tschopik suggest, museum displays change little due to their initial high costs and their lengthy gestation time resulting from shortages of staff and money. Yet, as they argue, "one of the main causes of their apparent conservatism in this respect is that museums have vested interests — financial, intellectual, and occasionally, sentimental as well — in their collections and exhibits" (1954:774). Perhaps because they represent such an investment of labor, or perhaps because they are genuinely loved, life groups have been especially popular for curatorial recycling. Although Boas's Kwakwaka'wakw hamatsa display is now gone from the Smithsonian, many of its companions were retained during the last renovation in the 1950s (Ewers 1955). The American Museum still displays the figures from his cedar crafts group, and in its 1982 renovation the Field Museum kept its 1901 version of the hamatsa.

The maintenance of the hall through so many years was probably due more to neglect than intention. Yet, as patriarch Noah Cross remarks in the movie *Chinatown*, "Politicians, ugly buildings, and whores all get respectable if they last long enough." Such charm now seems to call for preservation.[23] As the museum recently reviewed the renovation of its exhibits, there was a consensus that "There is something noble and worth saving about these antiques, something that will show this and succeeding generations of museum visitors what a turn-of-the-century museum looked like" (Gardner 1985:76). From a more theoretical perspective Clifford has argued:

> It is important to resist the tendency of collections to be self-sufficient, to suppress their own historical, economic, and political processes of production. . . . Ideally the history of its own collection and display should be a visible aspect of any exhibition. It had been rumored that the Boas Room of Northwest Coast artifacts in the American Museum of Natural History was to be refurbished, its style of display modernized. Apparently (or so one hopes) the plan has been abandoned, for

> this atmospheric, dated hall exhibits not merely a superb collection but a moment in the history of collecting. (1988:229)

Paradoxically, preserving at least some aspects of the hall would return the Northwest Coast Hall, if not its putative subject, to history.

The American Museum and Northwest Coast Anthropology since 1965

Just as the hall reached its last incarnation in the early 1960s, the field of Northwest Coast Indian art, and its anthropological study, were about to undergo an explosive development. The mid-1960s witnessed the revival of museum anthropology in general, as well as the creation and study of Northwest Coast art. As the premiere collection from the region, the American Museum's holdings were critical to scholars such as Bill Holm (1965), Allen Wardwell (1996), and Peter Macnair (Macnair et al. 1998). In addition to these more formal and contextual studies, this collection and others were subjected to the postcolonial and reflexive critique of anthropology (Cole 1985; Clifford 1988). The collection also became part of the dialogic encounter with its originating communities in the *Chiefly Feasts* exhibit, carried out with extensive Native consultation and curation.

Museum displays have been important sources of inspiration for contemporary Northwest Coast artists, as they were for earlier artists in New York. Most of these artists, however, have learned from more local museums in Victoria and Vancouver, as did Haida Robert Davidson, when they did not learn from older masters, as did Kwakwaka'wakw Henry and Tony Hunt from Mungo Martin. More recently, a number have made trips to New York to study the collections more thoroughly; for example, Nisga'a artist Norman Tait, who visited the museum in 1985 to study the Haida canoe, among other things.[24] With the exception of the replicas that Aldona Jonaitis commissioned for *Chiefly Feasts,* the collections of the American Museum and other East Coast institutions have been mediated more by publications than actual inspection.[25]

The influential exhibition *Arts of the Raven,* staged in 1967 at the Vancouver Art Gallery, was emblematic of the shift in the scholarly study of Northwest Coast Indian art closer to its home. Curated by Bill Holm (of Seattle's Burke Museum), Wilson Duff (of Vancouver's University of British Columbia and formerly of the British Columbia Provincial Museum, in Victoria), and Haida artist Bill Reid, the exhibit used the American Museum as a source of display material. In the following decade major new permanent Northwest Coast galleries opened at the University of British Columbia in 1976 and the Provincial Museum in 1977. Although the Field Museum opened a new hall of *Maritime Peoples of the Arctic and Northwest Coast* in 1982, the Smithsonian, like the American Museum, left its American Indian displays unchanged.[26] This shift in the center of scholarship was indicated by Lévi-Strauss's own choice of the University of British Columbia as a base for his return to Northwest Coast studies in the early 1970s.

As the American Museum effectively ceased to collect Northwest Coast artifacts and then failed to renovate its exhibit, the culture of these peoples became reified in a timeless "ethnographic present" (cf. Fitzhugh 1997). While it may have had the world's finest collection from the region, it was not without its weaknesses and biases. To give only one example, there is no mention in the hall of the tremendous intercultural exchange that characterized the societies from which the artifacts were collected. And it goes without saying that the past century of cultural development on the Coast is omitted. As influential as it has been, no longer can this hall be said to fairly represent Northwest Coast cultures.

Envoi: Claude Lévi-Strauss, Franz Boas, and the Northwest Coast Hall

During the six years that Claude Lévi-Strauss spent in New York, first as a professor at the New School for Social Research and then as the French cultural attaché, he increased his familiarity with the work of Franz Boas and his students. "I was always interested in the Indians of the Northwest Coast," he recalled (Lévi-Strauss and Eribon 1991:38). As Boas "had written a great deal about them," he soon paid a visit to the master, and by chance he happened to be present when Boas died at the Columbia Faculty Club in 1942 (35–38). There is much in the Frenchman's thought that is reminiscent of Boas and Americanist anthropology in general (Darnell 1995, 2001:282–289) and of Boas's writings on Northwest Coast art in particular (Jonaitis 1988:240–241; Jonaitis, ed. 1995:320–325). In the analysis of art and myth, both Boas and Lévi-Strauss were interested in the comparative, cross-cultural analysis of discrete traits.

In Lévi-Strauss's work an important stimulus was the American Museum of Natural History and its Northwest Coast Hall, which so impressed him that four decades later he reprinted a portion of his 1943 essay as the introduction to his book on masks of the region (1982:3–8; cf. 1985a:264–265). Lévi-Strauss was not oblivious to the hall's antiquated nature. Like the New York Public Library, where he spent so many hours in research, "It had a great attraction for me. It was a little antiquated, as is often the case with old New York institutions, but full of charm" (Lévi-Strauss and Eribon 1991:43). In his essay he made a virtue of the Northwest Coast Hall's "disused but singularly effective museographic methods," which he felt granted "the supplementary prestige of the *clair-obscur* of caves and of the crumbling heaps of lost treasure" (1943:175).[27] Thus, like Salinger's Holden Caulfield and so many others since, Lévi-Strauss glimpsed a world of exotic beauty in a display that Franz Boas had begun over a century ago. Whatever its future, the Northwest Coast Hall has had a powerful past.

Notes

Acknowledgements: The American Museum's Northwest Coast Hall, which I have known and loved since my childhood, inspired my career in anthropology. Consequently, the research for this essay has spanned many years. Although it is difficult to cite my many obligations, I would like to single out Belinda Kaye, former Anthropology Department archivist at the museum, and Douglas Cole, who greatly encouraged my research into the history of Northwest Coast collecting. I am also grateful to Stanley Freed and Laila Williamson for correcting several errors and offering supplementary information, to Marie Mauzé for sharing with me her research on Claude Lévi-Strauss and Northwest Coast art, and to Peter Macnair and Jay Stewart for sharing their research on the history of the hall.

1. Although the story of the hall's construction process has been previously considered, much remains to be said about its status since the 1930s and its effect on its various audiences. Among the most significant scholarship on the American Museum's Northwest Coast collection and its display are Wardwell 1978 (cf. B. Holm 1979), Jonaitis 1988; Jonaitis, ed. 1991, 1999; cf. also Cole 1985; Jacknis 1985, 2002. While this essay goes into far greater detail on the American Museum hall than Jacknis 2002, that study should be consulted for contextual detail. Because of limited space, this essay does not offer a complete analysis of the content of the hall as a representation of Northwest Coast Indian cultures, nor the relationship of the Northwest Coast Hall to other anthropology exhibits at the American Museum.

2. "The Museum Curiosities: Rare and Valuable Additions to the Collection," *New York Times,* April 1, 1883, cited in Jonaitis 1988:82.

3. In this essay I employ the current spellings for the Kwakwa̱ka'wakw, Nuu-chah-nulth, and Nuxalk peoples, whom Boas and Wissler referred to as the Kwakiutl, Nootka, and Bella Coola, respectively.

4. Henry Fairfield Osborn to William Berryman Scott, May 22, 1908, cited in J. Kennedy 1968:163. Several of the trustees, such as Leonard C. Sanford and Cleveland H. Dodge, joined the president in these feelings (Hellman 1969:185; Wissler 1943:200).

5. About 40 mannequins were originally planned (Dickerson 1910:227–229), but only half seem to have been completed. About a dozen are visible in contemporary photographs (e.g., Jonaitis 1988:216), and 17 figures were present in 1989, when the group was restored (Coffee 1991:31).

6. Taylor's murals, a medium revived by the "American Renaissance" art movement of the late 19th century, were suggested by the background paintings of habitat dioramas. The most extensive murals in the museum were those executed by Charles R. Knight for Osborn's halls of dinosaurs and other ancient life, starting in the 1890s. In 1909 Frederick W. Stokes painted the first anthropology murals for the adjacent Eskimo Hall. Before enlarged photographs were possible, murals were a space-effective method of representing a scene, especially one that could not be effectively photographed (Wissler 1943:219–223).

7. The idea for the canoe group may actually have originated with Osborn. The president, who was known for his almost complete control of the museum, was then feuding with Bumpus. After accusing the president of mismanagement, Bumpus was forced out of his position in 1910 (Rainger 1991:65, 313–314).

8. Emmons, who grew up in Princeton NJ and later settled there, may have had a personal relationship with president Osborn, who was a student and professor at the university in the 1870s and 1880s. The two men also shared feelings of anti-Semitism.

9. Clark Wissler to George H. Sherwood, September 20, 1913, cited in Jonaitis 1988:220.

10. Unfortunately, I have been unable to determine when the hall's windows were blocked up; it seems to have gone unmentioned in the annual reports. Dated photographs from 1919 reveal windows (Jonaitis 1988:222); by 1943, they had been filled in (cf. Jonaitis 1988:227, which is dated as March 1943 in museum photo archives; see also Jonaitis 1988:236). Annual reports from 1942 (p. 21) and 1944 (p. 25) refer to plans for blocking out the windows in the adjacent 77th Street building so that the illumination could be controlled.

11. Henry Fairfield Osborn to Clark Wissler, July 19, 1910, and Wissler to Osborn, July 30, 1910, cited in Jonaitis 1988:218.

12. Franz Boas to Roy Chapman Andrews, November 19, 1937, cited in J. Kennedy 1968:204.

13. During the years 1942 to 1970, the chair of the anthropology department was physical anthropologist Harry L. Shapiro. A revised Hall of Mexican and Central American Archaeology opened in 1944. Between that and the opening of the Human Biology Hall in 1961, there was also an exhibit titled *Men of the Montaña,* devoted to the peoples of the eastern Peruvian rain forests. The kind of innovative exhibit advocated by director Parr, it employed recorded sounds, mannequins in the open, and dramatic lighting (American Museum, Annual Report, 1952–53:33). Although meant to be "temporary," it was on view between 1951 and 1973.

14. Halls for the peoples of Africa (1968), Mexico and Central America (1970), the Pacific (1971; moved and revised in 1984), Asia (1980), South America (1989), and a totally new Hall of Human Biology and Evolution (1993). The anthropology department also participated in a collaborative display titled *Mollusks and Mankind* (1975).

15. Despite her curatorial title, Bella Weitzner (1891–1988) had no formal training in anthropology; instead she learned on the job. She spent much of her tenure as editor of the department's scientific publications.

16. My review of the 1960s renovation is based on museum annual reports, comments from Stanley Freed (personal communication, September 2002), as well as an earlier Freed discussion (April 2002), kindly shared with me by interviewers Jay Stewart and Peter L. Macnair.

17. The surrealists differed in their use of anthropological research. According to Lévi-Strauss, André Breton "distrusted it, he didn't like having scholarly matters get between him and the object. Max Ernst collected objects but also wanted to know everything about them" (Lévi-Strauss and Eribon 1991:34).

18. For financial reasons, in 1951 Lévi-Strauss was forced to sell at auction his predominately Northwest Coast collection. Many of the pieces were subsequently donated to the Musée de l'Homme and the ethnology museum of Leiden, among others (Mauzé 2000a, b, c, d).

19. Like most New Yorkers, Salinger and his protagonist speak simply of the Museum of Natural History and refer to the Northwest Coast Hall as the American Indian Room.

20. The Eskimo gallery, just off the Northwest Coast hall, was the first exhibit renovated by Stanley Freed. Although two or three of the nine mannequins were recycled from the original installation of late 1906, the rest were new. "The faces of the old mannequins were life masks of real people. The newer mannequins

all had the same faces, a standardized Eskimo face." The hall was dismantled in 1999 (Stanley Freed, personal communication, 2002).

21. Although Lévi-Strauss may indeed be referring to Boas's own installation, most likely he was thinking of the hall as he had first seen it in 1941.

22. Although the Northwest Coast Hall gives the appearance of stasis, in fact it has changed slowly but constantly through the decades. Some of these subtle changes can be seen in a comparison of photographs from 1943 (Figure 6) and 1962 (Figure 7). Because the angles are not the same it is difficult to get a full sense of the changes, but one can see many different or moved cases in the latter picture. And the differences between 1919 (Figure 5) and 1943 are particularly striking, such as the columns, the cases, many of the objects displayed, and, of course, the windows. The problem is that most of these changes have been relatively small-scale and spread out beyond an individual's lifetime, thus giving the impression of constancy. Moreover, like an accumulation of dust or noise, these minor but numerous changes have, for the most part, been neither intentional nor systematic.

23. This is becoming a common museum problem. Among anthropology museums perhaps the most famous "classic" exhibit hall is Oxford's Pitt Rivers Museum, virtually unchanged from its installation circa 1890. When the American Museum recently renovated its paleontology halls, it installed radically modern displays but uncovered and restored the original architecture (Dingus 1996:45). Honolulu's Bernice P. Bishop Museum has also decided to restore its grand Hawaiian room, completed in 1903.

24. An ironic and amusing scene is recounted by Jonaitis (1988:250). Tait requested permission to get into the canoe in order to make more detailed studies. As he was standing there early one morning before the museum opened, two janitors walked by. "Look," said one, "there's a real Indian in with those statue Indians in the big boat!"

25. Haida artist Bill Reid fell in love with a painted Haida box from its illustration in Boas's *Primitive Art* (1955:276) and not directly from seeing it in the American Museum, where it was not on display. It was the first thing he borrowed for the *Arts of the Raven* show at the Vancouver Art Gallery in 1967 (1981).

26. The Provincial Museum was renamed the Royal British Columbia Museum in 1987. For a more extensive consideration of these exhibitions, see Jacknis 2002: 221–242.

27. This is the passage as taken from the original English publication. The French reads: "Ce lieu, auquel des méthodes muséographiques désuètes, mais singulièrement efficaces, confèrent les prestiges supplémentaires du clair-obscur des cavernes et du croulant entassement des trésors perdus" (Lévi-Strauss 1975:

7–8). As Stanley Freed and Laila Williamson pointed out to me, the original English is not quite accurate. A better rendering can be found in the translated reprint contained in Lévi-Strauss's book on Northwest Coast masks: "This place, on which outmoded but singularly effective museographic methods have conferred the additional allurements of the chiaroscuro of caves and the tottering heap of lost treasures" (1982:3).

POLITICS AND CULTURAL HERITAGE

EVOLVING CONCEPTS OF TLINGIT
IDENTITY AND CLAN

Richard and Nora Marks Dauenhauer

It is generally asserted and accepted that the clan is the basic social unit within Tlingit society. This certainly was true for traditional Tlingit culture of the 19th century and remains true for an ever-diminishing number of elders in contemporary Tlingit culture at the start of the 21st century, but we question the extent to which the statement applies and still holds true for the majority of the Tlingit population today. Does the clan truly function as the basic unit of Tlingit personal identity and sociopolitical discourse today? We suggest that while many symbols and emblems remain the same or similar, their perception, function, and patterns of use have changed, and that we are witnessing a fundamental reorientation in the thinking and social organization of most Tlingit people. We have been gathering examples of the present topic for years, because the elusive phenomenon of change in Tlingit social structure, specially the clan system, continues to affect our other projects. We are trying to learn how to step back and look at this frame in which all of our other work operates. While our previous publications (especially Dauenhauer and Dauenhauer 1990, 1994, 1995, 1998, 1999, 2003) address closely related and tangential aspects, this is our first essay to deal directly with the concept of changing clan identity.[1]

We do not wish to be negative regarding change and innovation. We do not want to judge what is "authentic." Rather, we want to observe and analyze as dispassionately as possible a process in which we are emotionally involved personally and professionally, and by which we are often bewildered. As we describe elsewhere (Dauenhauer and Dauenhauer 1995) our cultural mentors were of the generation of traditionally raised elders born between 1880 and 1910, now mostly departed. Our work of more than a quarter of a century has been informed and shaped by their desires and cultural dynamics, and we often find ourselves confused by the emerging—and conflicting—changes in patterns of cultural discourse and demands from younger generations. The examples indicate a fundamental change in concepts of personal identity and sociopolitical organization to ways that are now more congruent with Euro-American patterns than were the Tlingit patterns of previous generations. Because this phenomenon and our culture-specific, Tlingit examples are not unique, we consider some general concepts first, after providing some general background.

Background

Cultural Background

For a more complete background of Tlingit culture, see our various publications (Dauenhauer and Dauenhauer 1987, 1990, 1994) and other works cited therein. Space limitations demand that we restrict our comments here to those essential to our thesis of evolving concepts of identity and clan. Tlingit society is organized in two moieties (an anthropological term meaning "half"). The names of the moieties are Raven and Eagle, sometimes also referred to as Crow and Wolf. The moieties themselves have no political organization, leadership (other than some ceremonial titles), or power but exist only for the purpose of exogamy. In precontact time, and well into the 20th century for conservative families, one was required to marry into a clan of the opposite moiety. A person is born into his or her mother's clan but maintains a complicated ceremonial relationship with the father's clan.

The basic sociopolitical unit was the clan. Each moiety consists of several clans, some of which are historically connected. Clans owned houses and property, had leaders, conducted trade, and made war and peace. The term *moiety*, or "half," is appropriate, because clans operate (or at least traditionally operated) in reciprocal relationships and patterns of exchange of goods, services, and marriage partners with clans of the opposite moiety. Marriage partners came from the opposite moiety; love songs and oratory were composed and are still performed across moiety lines. Ceremonial exchange is at the heart of traditional spirituality and folklife. The most important aspect of this is in the funeral cycle, in which clans of the opposite moiety of the deceased offer assistance, and are repaid through potlatch, when the clan of the deceased hosts guests of the opposite moiety and gives them food and gifts. During the ceremonies, the guests respond to lamentations and oratory of the hosts with supportive songs and speeches of condolence.

Clans also own symbolic property, called *at.óow* in Tlingit (see Dauenhauer and Dauenhauer 1987, 1990, 1994), including emblems, songs, dances, stories, names, and spirits.[2] Thus it is significant in traditional Tlingit pre-Christian religion (shamanism of a circumpolar type) that the entire ethnic population did not have equal access to all the spirits of the group, but that each clan had its own, revealed to its shamans, and passed down as part of the clan inheritance. This is our conclusion based on years of field experience. Thus any traditional ceremonial event depends on the reciprocal exchange between clans of opposite moieties; both halves are needed to complete the whole. Guests at a potlatch console the grieving hosts by balancing the songs, dances, speeches, ceremonial regalia, and spirit powers of the hosts with those of their own clan. In this sense most of the serious Tlingit clan songs are not secular but are part of a sacred repertoire performed in a specific context. In contrast, love songs, while also clan owned and restricted in performance, lend themselves more easily to secular performance. Likewise hats, blankets, and other regalia are connected with the system of spirits and clan ownership, and their use is also restricted. Evolving concepts and patterns in contemporary Tlingit religion are discussed in R. Dauenhauer (2000) so are not included as examples here.

A few introductory words about inheritance are also necessary. As noted above, Tlingit society was traditionally matrilineal, meaning that one follows the mother's line. It is significant that a man's children are not of his own clan and moiety, but of the opposite moiety. Therefore, traditionally a person did not inherit from his or her father, because he was not of the same clan as his children. Inheritance followed from maternal uncle to nephew. Thus a person inherited from his or her mother's brother, and a man would pass clan property and position not to his sons but to his sister's sons. Both men and women can and did inherit property. Women typically inherit from female relatives, who would be of the same clan (and moiety). In Tlingit the terms for *niece* and *nephew* do not distinguish gender as they do in English but, rather, distinguish membership in the same or opposite moiety, regardless of gender. This, of course, runs contrary to Western law and custom, which is patrilineal. As might be imagined, this conflict of law has been a major issue in Tlingit communities for over a century.

Historical Background

For a general survey of Tlingit sociopolitical history see the introduction to our volume of Tlingit life stories (Dauenhauer and Dauenhauer 1994). Tollefson (1978) also provides a good overview of legal history culminating in the Alaska Native Claims Settlement Act of 1971 (ANCSA) and the formation of regional corporations, but this addresses the growth of corporations more than the reduction of clan roles and does not discuss any shifts in worldview away from clans as a focus of personal identity. Traditional autonomy was at the clan level. Whereas in the Russian period (1741–1867, especially 1794–1867) the Tlingits were able to be selective in their relationship with newcomers without surrendering local autonomy, with the American period (particularly between 1867 and 1912) they lost control of local political autonomy, property rights, subsistence economy, and access to natural and economic resources, communal living, civil rights, and the right to educate their children. The Alaska Native Brotherhood (ANB) was founded in 1912 and initiated legal efforts to regain what had been lost, eventually winning victories in voting rights, integration of schools and public places, and ultimately the land claims settlement. These legal, cultural, and social achievements were also accompanied by a shift in social organization. The nuclear family and single-family dwelling gradually replaced the community household (i.e., a clan house) as the unit of production. We also begin to see erosion of the clan and clan house as the basic ceremonial unit.

Our thesis of the weakening of the clan system or a shifting away from clan orientation does not originate with us. Tollefson (1977) describes a pattern of clan-hosted potlatches shifting to moiety-hosted events about the time of the founding of the Alaska Native Brotherhood in 1912, although Kan (1999 and personal communication in various years) suggests that this might be too early, and the history is more complex. Tollefson attributes the broadening sphere of potlatch to decreased population and loss of access to resources, and he notes that the shift to moiety-based events allows more people to participate and increases the wealth. Writing in 1946, Walter Goldschmidt and Theodore Haas observed the process well underway. They observed the trend toward patrilineal inheritance and general adoption of Euro-American customs, so that while Native law remained a force in daily life, the adoption of American customs "creates some confusion in the tenure system and social patterns—the sort of confusion that is generally attendant upon the adoption of a foreign civilization by a native culture." They continue, noting

> While the clan membership of an individual is important to him and to his community, and while he feels a strong tie to these relations, there has been, in the past 80 years, some weakening of this tie. In general, this loss of importance of the clan itself has been in favor of strengthening the importance of the village or tribe. This fact is not to be considered in any way surprising, for some of the sanctions that supported the old social system have given way before the adoption of many American customs, such as the increasing individualization of households in place of the large communal houses. (Goldschmidt and Haas 1998:17)

These observations remain applicable 50 years later and are perhaps even more acutely evident in the post-ANCSA era (described below).

Writing a generation before Goldschmidt and Haas, Tlingit ethnographer Louis Shotridge advocated a community-based solution to many questions of the day. While insistent on clan ownership and social structure as critical information for the contextualization of objects in museum display, Shotridge recognized the weakening of the clans. In 1923 he suggested the concept of a Tlingit nation. He noted that the decline in Tlingit population also decreased the impact of clans and clan history in the modern world. With the decreasing effectiveness of any single given clan, he suggested that a collective effort of all divisions within Tlingit society will be required to achieve sociopolitical ends (Milburn 1997:282).

This was certainly the thrust of the Alaska Native Brotherhood movement of the early 20th century (Dauenhauer and Dauenhauer 1994, 1995, 1997). The most recent and decisive step was the passage of ANCSA in 1971, which extinguished aboriginal claims and title and established a system of regional corporations with shareholders to administer a land and cash settlement in payment for lands taken during the Euro-American settlement of Alaska. All Native people of Alaska with the proper blood quantum and alive on December 18, 1971, were eligible to apply to an appropriate regional corporation and become a shareholder. Persons born after that date are not eligible for membership but may inherit stock. Now, some 30 years later, a substantial portion of each indigenous ethnic population is largely disenfranchised, and Tlingit shareholders are currently divided about 50–

50 whether to extend membership to them. The corporation to which the majority of Tlingits belong is called Sealaska Corporation, an acronym for Southeast Alaska. Like the other ANCSA regional corporations, it was created on the Western corporate model, with no parallel or precedent in traditional culture or clan structure. Shareholders now elect board members who elect a board president and hire a corporate CEO, so that for the first time in Tlingit history there is a single leader for all the Tlingit people (in contrast to traditional house and clan leadership). ANCSA also created a new class of leadership, drawing not from the traditional clan leaders, but from a younger, English-speaking generation (often speaking no Tlingit at all) with business or political experience.

Theoretical Background: Three Management Models

Perhaps the most succinct presentation and departure point for the present essay is Tollefson's "Tlingit Acculturation: An Institutional Perspective" (1984), in which he uses a conflict-management model to measure a century of changes in Tlingit political behavior. He selects three historical intervals as focus: 1880 (traditional clan household), 1930 (ANB), and 1980 (corporate). For each period he studies goals, rules of exposure (governing access and flow of information), spokespeople (leadership), and organizations for action, bargaining, and implementation. The traditional clan household of 1880 had as its basic goals subsistence living, well-being, and social respect. Membership was by birth through genealogy and kinship, leadership was through rank and seniority, and rule was essentially by consensus.

The ANB model of the 1930s had civil rights as a goal; membership was voluntary, open equally to all, and realized by paying of dues. Rule was in English by parliamentary procedures, officers were elected, debate was open, and majority rule prevailed. The 1980 corporate model has earning money and paying dividends as its goal. The paradox is that the ANCSA corporations are expected to be profit-making enterprises but also to serve the community needs of stockholders. Rules are essentially defined by corporate law, legal contracts, and policy manuals of operation. The board of directors is elected by proxy votes, and the board then elects its officers and hires corporate managers. The role of shareholders is limited, and many decisions are made in secret behind closed doors. Grass roots candidates have little chance of election to the board whereas management's candidates have access to corporate funds for campaign expenses (1984:239–241).

Tollefson argues that these changes occurred in Tlingit political process as people responded to new political demands, and that they deliberately made these changes in order to better cope with requirements for survival (1984:242–243). This is true, as is his assertion that all three models are in use and operation (244). However, the situation has changed in the 15 years since the Tollefson essay, and we believe that our examples from this period will show that, while the traditional system or model remains in operation for many people, more emblems and processes traditionally associated with the clan structure are now gravitating to the ANB and especially corporate structures. At any rate, it seems to us that the three models are not equally weighted, and that as more elders pass away, less understanding of the traditional clan system remains among the general Tlingit population. Tollefson observed that the roles are compartmentalized, with a certain amount of cultural ambiguity evident as people vacillate between asserting their ethnic identity and maintaining "a unidirectional orientation in the acculturation process" (244). He sees "a new synthesis or reaffirmation of traditional cultural values, as formerly various levels of assimilated Tlingit donned their dancing blankets and participated with drums and singers to express their ethnic soul" (245). This is perhaps a bit romantically stated, but we don't disagree. He continues, suggesting that "It is possible that these new political forms with their supporting cultural structures stretched the Tlingit ethnic identity to such a level of cultural dissonance that it forced the people to search for a revised and renewed ethnic identity and cultural integration. As the ANB leaders led the way for civil rights and for cultural preservation, so too are many of the directors of corporations also taking the lead to preserve relevant portions of that Tlingit culture" (246). He cites Sealaska Corporation's donating $100,000 to Sealaska Heritage Foundation in support of Celebration '82 (to be described below). He concludes, "A reaffirmation of traditional culture is surviving along with the Grand Camp [ANB] and the corporation. Each new level of Tlingit political organization filled a strategic cultural niche in their ethnic survival" (246). We agree that ethnic identity remains important, but we suggest that its emblems, models and manifestations are becoming increasingly corporate and not clan.

Some Concepts

Change

Cultures change. All cultures are changing all the time, some more noticeably than others. One might even argue that culture is a process and set of relationships, and that the only constant is change. Culture is not monolithic, but its meaning or meanings are negotiated among the persons who form it. Cultures are always in flux, not frozen, but adapting to fit changing needs (Dauenhauer and Dauenhauer 1995). Elements of traditional culture can be fossilized and look real, but be dead. Conversely, traditional cultural functions may continue through innovative forms that do not appear traditional (Dauenhauer and Dauenhauer 1998:73–76). As Marjorie Halpin suggests (Halpin, this volume), if the plastic form is retained, the semantic form is reversed; if the semantic form is retained, the plastic form is reversed.

There seem to be two extremes in popular notions of culture: either denial of change or "golden age" theories of an idealized past contrasting with the degenerate present in which the defense of tradition becomes a sacred duty. The concept of traditional Native culture as unchanging is widespread and even somewhat cliché. One often hears the politically correct claim that "Tlingit language and culture have not changed for thousands of years." Recently an ethnographic object of known historical manufacture was claimed to be "thousands of years old." (See also Mauzé 1997:5.)

The irony here is that some very self-conscious innovations are often justified in the name of tradition or quickly labeled "traditional." One hears people say that "In our traditional culture we do such and such," whereas in fact the cultural element may be very new. The implication seems to be that deliberate innovation, however useful or valuable or necessary, is not legitimate but must be veiled in terms of tradition, as if people are embarrassed over innovation and feel the need to defend or disguise it as tradition. As noted elsewhere, none of this is unique to the Tlingits. See Mauzé (1997) for accounts from other cultures and for theoretical discussion of the concepts they illustrate. Harkin (1997b) is especially relevant to Tlingit issues.

Deliberate and self-conscious change and innovation can provide a refreshing contrast. One example is the assertiveness of women in new ways. At a recent event in Juneau, a group of young Tlingit women drummed in Plains Indian style, sitting in chairs around a common suspended drum. Although clearly not a traditional style of Tlingit drumming, this seems to us an exciting, honest, refreshing, and positive change, perhaps because it is not falsely couched in a rhetoric of unchanging, ancient tradition but instead openly embraces innovation, in this case not of something entirely new but of a revitalized form of drumming as what Harkin calls a "latent symbol" (1997b, discussed below). Another example is that of the Naa Kahidi Theater, an internationally acclaimed performing group active from the mid-1980s to the 1990s that presented traditional stories but in contemporary ways that combine traditional Northwest Coast storytelling with European dramatic conventions.

Tlingit oratory offers a powerful example of how change can happen in ways that are unnoticed until two contrasting benchmarks become available as points of reference. Delivered only 12 years apart, the sets of speeches from Hoonah in 1968 and Sitka in 1980 show this (Dauenhauer and Dauenhauer 1990). In the 1980 speeches the elders felt the need to make explicit (perhaps because the context was an elders conference in which their roles were as teachers) what was implicit and understood by all in the speeches of 1968 (which were delivered in the ritual context of potlatch). The elders of 1980 were aware that children had mastered the texts of Tlingit songs but did not understand the social and spiritual contexts. The management and oratory examples are both indications that the former traditional clan system is no longer operating in the same way in social and political discourse.

Reinvention

Part of change is reinvention. Cultures continually reinvent themselves, consciously or unconsciously, as they change and adapt. This is a natural process and seems to occur in all cultures. One fascinating treatment of this is N. Scott Momaday's *The Names: A Memoir* (1976). Momaday describes how the entire Kiowa culture reinvented itself after moving from the mountains to the plains and encountering the horse. What was a recent, historical innovation soon became "traditional" and perceived as eternal, inalienable, and unchanging. Another challenging study is Jaroslav Pelikan's *Jesus through the Centuries: His Place in the History of Culture* (1985). Pelikan traces the development of Christian dogma and perceptions of Christ in the context of intellectual and cultural history and shows how each age adapts to make sense of what is theoretically changeless: "Jesus Christ, the same yesterday and today and forever" (Heb. 13:8). He examines the fundamental assumptions that believers within each given epoch unconsciously presuppose. Similarly, Everett Fox in the commentary and notes to his new translation of *The Five Books of Moses* (1995:312, 322) offers examples of the shaping of Hebrew scripture and religious life, as symbols are reframed depending on the sociopolitical needs of a given historical period. Harkin (1997b) explores the "tradition of invention" in Northwest Coast cultures culturally and geographically close to the Tlingits. In principle the models and methods of inquiry that these writers offer can be applied to the intellectual and material history of any given culture. They can help us understand the problem of how to accept innovation and change. It would seem that some patterns of change are unconscious, while other changes are more perceptible and self-conscious and are packaged accordingly as "revolutionary" or "ancient tradition." (See also Handler and Linnekin 1984 and Mauzé 1997.)

Birth vs. Choice

A basic concept in understanding Tlingit social structure is the distinction that sociologists and anthropologists make between a gemeinschaft society (in which one's membership is determined by birth or circumstance) and a gesellschaft society (in which one's membership is elective). The traditional Tlingit clan system is a classic gemeinschaft community, in contrast to a generalized Euro-American gesellschaft pattern characterized by a history of immigration and high levels of geographic and social mobility, so that the average citizen identifies with most social groups by choice. The contrast is between obligatory and elective membership. For most contemporary Euro-Americans, how Irish or Hungarian to be is usually a matter of choice. It may not be the same for a resident of Belfast or Budapest.

Our main point in the context of this essay is that Tlingit society is also experiencing change, and membership is increasingly more elective. This is what sociolinguist David Margolin describes as the shift from "traditional ethnicity" to "civic ethnicity" (Dauenhauer and Dauenhauer 1998:76–78). In "traditional ethnicity" of 200 years ago, an individual had no option but to operate within traditional Tlingit linguistic and social structure. As contact and social interaction with Russians and then Anglo-Americans increased, the options for identity increased, so that perhaps the majority of Tlingit individuals today have the freedom to identify with Tlingit culture or not. The "politics of identity" come into play as one makes these choices.

Whereas the traditional social structure was organized around the clan, a great number of Tlingit individuals today do not have a clear idea of what their clan is. Only 10 percent of the ethnic Tlingit population speak the Tlingit language, so that many individuals do not know the name of their clan in Tlingit but typically use English "nicknames" that are translations not of the clan name but of the most popular crest or totemic animal. We are not suggesting that the English names necessarily indicate a lesser sense of connection to or pride in one's clan identity (any more than to suggest that participating in a Catholic Mass in English is less valid than one in Latin); but in cases where the indigenous clan names are no longer known, this must certainly indicate a loss of historical understanding, and the fact remains that many people are not aware of their clan by any name. (This is often through no fault of their own, and many people in this situation are struggling to research their clan affiliation and personal names.) Tlingit clan names usually end in –eidí, -.ádi, or –taan, meaning "people of," thus encoding in their very names information about places of origin and migration. The popular nicknames such as Brown Bear, Killerwhale, Coho, or Sockeye do not convey this. Beginning with the clan names themselves, some aspects of the clan and clan system may seem increasingly alien as the culture moves away from it, and some elements of it may seem a threat to personal choice and control.

One often hears reference to Tlingit culture moving "from local clan to regional corporation" or "from the clan house to the boardroom," as if there were no underlying change in "the culture" as it "moves." In some cases such claims may have political purposes such as to legitimize new patterns of leadership by minimizing or downplaying fundamental differences in structure and constituency. The assumption seems to be that the traditional Tlingit worldview remains traditional, unchanged and unchanging, but merely expressed or framed in new technology. We argue the opposite: there is a fundamental shift in point of view and worldview, congruent with the shift in social structure and personal identity. Part of the transition to Western kinship and social models affects the interpretation and use of cultural items, including oral literature and traditional art.

Badges of Ethnicity: Identity Markers

As identity becomes more elective and personal, so also the selection of emblems of identity becomes more elective and personally charismatic. Choosing to identify with the traditional clan of birth now becomes one option, exercised at certain times, but no longer the single operating principle. A person's participation in potlatching, regardless of ability to speak the language, sing, or dance, may also serve as a marker of ethnic identity. For several years the Alaska Native Brotherhood has required members to introduce themselves in Tlingit. The most popular identity markers in the last two decades are singing and dancing and sewing of blankets for dancing. Other markers are food, weaving, and carving. Canoe carving and racing are becoming very popular. Language study is on the increase but will probably never match the popularity of singing and dancing because language is more abstract, more difficult to master, and offers far less immediate gratification. There is also an increase in the public use of language and literacy as display rather than for communication. This is seen in names of organizations, dance groups, schools, blankets and other objects, and personal names. These phatic or display examples are often in deliberately idiosyncratic spellings that ironically use Tlingit writing as an emblem of ethnicity, but that also make a statement of resistance to standardized spelling for indigenous language literacy.

Sealaska Heritage Foundation in Juneau has recently put considerable effort into marketing tangible items of ethnic identity. One example is a Pendleton wool blanket featuring a generic Northwest Coast design, executed in Plateau colors. The current best-selling item at Sealaska Heritage Foundation is the Tlingit Barbie Doll (complete with Tlingit phrases on the box, in nonstandard spelling).

As various elements of culture become recontextualized as identity markers, the question arises of symbolic value vs. "authenticity" and "purity." As one of our colleagues enjoys commenting, "If you want purity, go to a dog show." This process and phenomenon of redefining ethnic identity and selecting identity markers is not unique to the Tlingits but has parallels among the indigenous people of Siberia and the Far East in the former Soviet Union (Golovko 1997; Vakhtin 1997). (For more on the issue of authenticity in other Northwest Coast cultures, see Harkin 1997b.)

Some Examples of Changing Patterns

Celebration

For over 20 years Sealaska Heritage Foundation has sponsored a biannual gathering of Tlingit, Haida, and Tsimshian dance groups. It has grown into a major cultural event, with over a thousand dancers gathering in Juneau for three days of performances in even-numbered years. The first Celebration was held in 1982; the most recent in June 2004. Even by the end of the 1980s, after fewer than ten years of existence, the event was perceived and described by some as "traditional." Certainly the songs and dances are traditional and "authentic." But the performance context is different. Celebration is a secular folk festival. It is performance and entertainment oriented, with dancers on a stage and the audience not expected to participate. Some dance groups are clan based, and others are community based, including members of various clans. In contrast, in traditional performance, members of one clan would sing and dance as hosts in a ceremonial context, and a clan of the opposite moiety would reciprocate as guests. All this changes with "secular" performance, with "potlatch songs outside the potlatch" (Kan 1990; Dauenhauer and Dauenhauer 1990, 1994). Many people seem unaware of the difference between performance contexts. We have heard it suggested that Tlingits re-invented dancing to appeal to tourists. There may be isolated cases of this, but we see it in general as "going public." Dances were rarely performed outside of ceremonial contexts until the 1960s and 1970s.

We distinguish two aspects of Celebration. The more obvious focus is on the three intense days of performance, including parades and youth events. But often overlooked is the anticipated performance opportunity as motivation to learn and practice during the two years between Celebrations, so as to perform well. The hidden aspect fosters the more traditional pattern of local elders teaching the songs and dances to the young, and each Celebration features an increasing number of children's dance groups. This can also strengthen a community's ability to use the songs in traditional settings such as potlatch, but the "reentry" into ceremonial contexts may require explicit training by elders, so that the singers do not confuse performance on stage before an audience with performance in a ceremonial setting with cultural expectations of reciprocity. To use another example, a secular choir may technically master renditions of liturgical music but not be able to perform in the context of liturgy and worship.

In our opinion there is nothing wrong with Celebration; it is just not "traditional," although it is widely perceived as such. But this gives rise to the question: how long does it take for an innovation to become "traditional," like Paul Bunyan, the popular American Coca-Cola image of Santa Claus, or "Rudolph the Red-Nosed Reindeer"?

The Tlingit "National Anthem"

A striking example of the popular adoption of a non-Tlingit concept may be seen in the new "National Anthem." Shortly before his death, the late clan leader of the Lukaax̱.ádi, Austin Hammond, gave permission to people of all clans to sing one of his clan's songs ("Ch'a aadei yei unatee-gaa," composed by Joe Wright) as a political rallying song in the ongoing effort to protect the land. Austin did this at the 1989 ANB convention, and the anthem was used for the first time at Celebration 1990, with minor adaptation of words by Paul Jackson. At the Sealaska elders conference in Ketchikan, October 1990, Austin again spoke of his vision of people united from south to north, from one end of Tlingit Country to the other in defense of their land. For years clan members had popularly called the song their "land claims song" because of the central images in the text, "Lest my grandfathers' land grow desolate beneath us, you will always hear my voice on it."

The idea caught on, and people soon began calling the song the "National Anthem." Imitating Western protocols for national anthems, some community leaders began to insist that people stand when it is sung. This practice seems to have been well received, but many older members of the Lukaax̱.ádi clan resent being asked to stand for their own clan song. It is safe to say that most people today no longer perceive the song as a clan song they were given permission and encouragement to sing, but as a "national anthem." The song's identity has moved from the clan context to a "national" context. As the popularity of the "anthem" increases, so are new layers of legend slowly forming around the life of the composer and the circumstances under which the song was originally composed.

The Tlingit "National Anthem" even has a Web site now, created by a Native American support group in New York City. This is the ultimate in decontextualization and shows the extent to which not only Tlingit people but others of Native American ancestry can identify with the concept of a national anthem, whereas the concept of clan ownership of songs within a given tribal group is more alien, obscure, and troublesome. As with all Web sites and networking, there may be questions of quality control over what is published there. Enthusiasm can easily displace accuracy, but this is part of electronic folklore.

At some point in the process of change and reinvention there is a gradual redefinition of the self and the culture in terms of something new and other. Some elements of identity are adopted in the name of tradition, although they are traditionally alien to it. The item itself may be new and consciously adapted, like the new Kiowa horse or the new Tlingit "National Anthem," but the cultural patterns that the new element creates or in which the new element operates may not be as conscious. It is probably not as much self-conscious imitation of another culture but an adaptation because the new pattern makes more sense, and in the case of the anthem this suggests that the shift from clan to individual or community identification is nearly complete.

The danger is that imitation and emulation of cultural items from the dominant culture may be at the expense of the patterns of the indigenous culture. On the other hand, the widespread appeal of such dominant culture models suggests that they make sense where the traditional patterns no longer do. The indigenous tradition becomes increasingly alien, requiring more study and effort and threatening to the extent that it is not understood. On the one hand, the changes may be dangerous to the extent that people are not aware of them; but on the other hand, changes are exciting because they prove that the culture is alive and not fossilized.

The symbolic appeal of the Tlingit "National Anthem" is no doubt linked to a larger pattern of political rhetoric and symbols of nationhood current among Native American and Canadian First Nations people as issues of sovereignty are being defined both legally and emotionally. Harkin (1997b:98) reminds us that such reframing of symbols is always political. The shift illustrates our point that the interaction is no longer among members of autonomous clans within a larger, loosely defined "national" group, but of a Tlingit "Nation" redefining itself as a whole and as an autonomous national entity dealing with external local, state, provincial, and federal governments and agencies. It is beyond the limits of space to discuss this more fully, but there is also a political history of similar evolution at the local level through the organization of "federally recognized tribes" made up of more than one clan and moiety.

New Songs

A related example is the composition of a new song. Because Tlingit songs are clan owned and sacred as opposed to secular, arguments frequently arose in the context of Celebration over which songs everybody could sing during the grand entrance and exit by the massed dance groups, an impressive event involving about 1,000 singers and drummers. To resolve the recurring conflicts over rights, ownership, and appropriateness of singing traditional spirit songs in secular settings, one young Tlingit man, Harold Jacobs, in 1993 composed a new song as a gift to Sealaska Heritage Foundation, specifically for Celebration, and it was first used in 1994. Its text is based on words from a speech by departed elder George Davis: "We will open again this container of wisdom" (Dauenhauer and Dauenhauer 1990:315). We find this exciting, because the composition of new songs for new cultural situations prevents the song tradition from becoming fossilized by being limited to the singing of existing songs, with no new songs entering the repertoire. This example also illustrates a challenge facing other new cultural settings such as bilingual and language immersion programs. Teachers have been criticized for translating "school culture" songs into Tlingit, rather than using indigenous music, but in the absence of traditional secular music they have no clear alternative. This is also true for cultures such as Navajo (W. Holm 1993). It is our understanding that this is not true for popular program models such as Maori and Hawaiian, which seem to have strong secular music traditions that carry over more easily into classroom settings. We applaud the composition of the new song as an indication of the continuing vitality of Tlingit song tradition, even though it functions in a new and different social setting. A challenge created by changing times was met creatively and positively. The entrance song seems to be enthusiastically accepted, whereas some previous contemporary compositions were criticized for not being "traditional." (We should note here the bentwood box as another example of a "latent symbol" reactivated.)

Healing Totems, Drums, and Blankets: Symbols Recontextualized

One of the most striking patterns to emerge in recent years is the creation of organizational- or community-commissioned art objects such as blankets, drums, and totem poles. In the case of totem poles, part of the pattern includes community-sponsored potlatches in conjunction with the pole raisings. Traditional symbols are being recontextualized. We see this operating on two levels. One level is more superficial, public, political, and decorative. This is best illustrated in the numerous carvings commissioned by

ANCSA corporations, such as Goldbelt, Inc. of Juneau. In these works the form continues in traditional style, but the context is radically changed. (This parallels the performance of song and dance, wherein the forms remain traditional, although with gradual changes in musical style and pronunciation of words, but the context of performance is different.) As part of its business ventures in tourism, Goldbelt commissioned carvings for several venues, such as its hotel and its tramway to the top of Mt. Roberts overlooking Juneau, and for places visited by rafting and kayaking trips. Other village corporations have done the same. The designs are traditional and culturally appropriate, but the contexts and functions are decorative and symbolic. The traditional Tlingit context of a clan commission for ceremonial use following patterns of reciprocity and exchange (as described in Dauenhauer and Dauenhauer 1990) has now been adapted to a contemporary Native corporate and community context entirely congruent with Euro-American patterns of organizationally commissioned art in public places.

The second level we observe is deeper, more emotional, and more spiritual. Here again, traditional symbols are being recontextualized, but independently of the traditional clan context. The clan is no longer an organizing concept. Although the forms, and here even the functions, are traditional, the new contexts are more congruent with Euro-American cultural values and patterns, relating primarily to the individual on the one hand and to the community on the other. Harkin (1997b:97–98) calls these "latent symbols" or "symbols waiting to happen." These latent symbols are already present within the culture but are usually obsolete and need to be reframed. An English example is the royal coach, which was symbolically reframed in the 19th and 20th centuries as it became obsolete for practical transportation.

Two recent Tlingit examples are the "Healing Blanket" and the "Healing Drum" commissioned by Southeast Alaska Regional Health Corporation (SEARHC, pronounced "search"). The "Healing Blanket" was commissioned for use especially in drug and alcohol treatment and for dealing with grief in general. It met with mixed reception. Some people expressed violent opposition to it, denouncing it as deliberate neo-ritual or reinvention. Some conservative Christians have rejected it as pagan or neo-shamanic. Other people say, "Maybe so, but it works." Clearly the blanket works for people in ways that the traditional regalia should work but no longer do for a number of reasons. One reason may be the many cultural restrictions that limit the use of traditional regalia. For many young people, the "pure" Tlingit clan system is too encumbered with protocol regulating the use of "real" regalia to be personal and charismatic enough, on the one hand, or to be community-inclusive enough on the other. Another reason may be the lack of understanding on the part of younger generations of the traditional system and how it works.

Our personal feeling is that if such things as the Healing Blanket give meaning and healing to people in grief, if they lead to sobriety and reduce suicide and violence, then we are in favor of it. But our main point here is to note that such new pieces work precisely because they are no longer operating in the traditional system of clan ownership, reciprocity, and ritual ceremonial display. Ironically, as such a piece of regalia becomes more public and generic in terms of access and use, it also becomes more private in dynamics of use; as it operates more at the community level, the catharsis becomes more private and individualized. Traditional clan regalia serve the same purpose but are displayed in action in public ceremonial contexts and in more stylized and prescribed ways.

SEARHC also commissioned a "Healing Drum" for all people to use and recently sponsored an "All Tribal Memorial Ceremony" called "Feeding the Spirit," inviting all people to come and "honor our relatives who have passed on, in our traditional way, and through this bring strength and healing to ourselves." Such events are perceived and described as "traditional," but the pattern should now be familiar to readers: what was traditionally a clan-hosted process involving and requiring reciprocity with clans of the opposite moiety is now evolving to a community level, with an organizational sponsor and requiring no reciprocity. The concept of the whole is redefined. The symbols and emblems and even the actions may be the same or similar, but the social structure within which it is operating is Western and new. The new, community-based emblems, songs, and ceremonies make sense to people and are popular because they are congruent with the new Euro-American social structure in which they actually live and operate, which for most people is no longer traditionally Tlingit, even though people may retain clan and moiety membership through birth.

Another recent (1996) example is the "Healing Heart Totem" from the village of Craig, Alaska. Tsimshian carver Stan Marsden lost his son to a cocaine overdose and decided to use his grief to bring people together by carving a totem pole. The project slowly grew to involve his family, then the community, Native (Tlingit, Haida, and Tsimshian) and non-Native, in the carving and raising of the pole. The carver used the project to keep kids drug free, and he dedicated the pole not only to his son but to all the people who have died from drug and alcohol abuse in Alaska. The word TOTEM is also used as an acronym and acrostic:

toge	T	her
hon	O	ring
tradi	T	ions
and drug fre	E	
com	M	unities.

The irony here again is that this is not a "tradition." While carving is clearly a Northwest Coast tradition, the context here is new because the problem is new. The combination is a new adaptation to address new social and spiritual problems. Creativity and change are a healthy part of any living tradition. The cultural irony here is that the traditional form is now reemerging as part of a new, Western-based system and context that is personally and community based rather than clan based. The significant feature of all of these objects (totems, blankets, drums) is that they are explicitly created to function in traditional ways of comforting and community bonding, yet outside the traditional clan system. The widespread phenomenon suggests that neither traditional Tlingit spirituality in the form of a clan-based spirit world nor traditional Christianity is "working" for many people in the Tlingit community.

A major crisis in the Native community is how to deal with drugs and alcohol and related patterns of dysfunction, including violence to self, family, and community. Many people feel helpless and overwhelmed by this impact and are looking for new methods to deal with the new problems. The new generic healing objects offer a creative solution to the problem that is functionally traditional but structurally innovative. Tlingit regalia have always been used for spiritual healing, but in the patterns of clan reciprocity in ceremonial contexts (Dauenhauer and Dauenhauer 1990). One appeal of Christianity at the end of the 19th century (whatever other sociopolitical considerations influenced one's personal decision to become Orthodox or Presbyterian) must have been that of a personal, positive, ever-loving God, in contrast to the ambivalence of the traditional spirits, which could turn against the individual, if not handled properly. Also, Christian spirituality was common, universal, and individually accessible to all, in contrast to Tlingit spirits, which were (and are) clan owned, and depended on reciprocity across moieties to operate properly. The evolution and popularity of the new healing objects indicate that many young people find neither the traditional clan system nor traditional Christianity effective or supportive.

What seems to be evolving on the spiritual level is a blend of generic worldviews: generic pan-Christianity and generic Native American, with imported features from both sources. Some appear suspiciously "new age." The tribal-specific emblems remain vehicles of expression and symbolism, but the system within which they traditionally operated is now changed. The traditional emblems remain powerful as symbols, but only when functioning within the new context, because the traditional contexts are no longer understood, accessible, or meaningful for a number of reasons. For the self-esteem, strength, and power to combat the ravages of drug, alcohol, and grief in a unified way, a new system of unity is evolving, no longer based on clan ownership and reciprocity, but on community ownership and joint use. It would seem that what is now happening on the spiritual level parallels what happened on the political level as described above for the early years of the ANB.

Similar patterns are reported from Siberia regarding the mental and physical health of Native people in the post-Soviet era (Abruitina 1997). For the dysfunctional individual, family, or community, these new "healing" objects and activities are a kind of spiritual first aid applied at "ground zero." The first priority is to stabilize and then attempt more complex and permanent healing. Across Alaska various official Native organizations, often ANCSA related, are speaking in support of the return to traditional values as a strategy for coping with modern problems. Often they publish explicitly codified official lists of these "traditional values," which have been formally adopted by boards of elders as part of the effort to heal dysfunctional persons, families, and communities. In light of our thesis of changing patterns in Tlingit, it would be interesting to study how congruent the innovations in other Native groups are with the traditional social structures.

Canoes

Canoes are another "latent symbol." The Northwest Coast "Canoe Nations" movement has spread to Southeast Alaska and has generated renewed interest in canoe building, paddling, and racing, partly as cultural activities contributing to sobriety and pride. Harkin describes how "an obsolete mode of transportation is drawn out of the realm of praxis, where it scarcely continues to exist, is ritually framed, and becomes a symbol of a new sociopolitical order. . . . Ritual is a key element in activating such symbols" (1997b:108). Harkin discusses the irony or paradox in a term such as "new tradition." "The success of the canoe festival as an 'invented' ceremony belies the notion that new traditions are bound to be perceived as inauthentic and false. . . . A canoe became not an obsolete mode of transport but a symbol of, on the one hand, historic culture, and, on the other, the revitalization of contemporary culture. As such, it is a 'new tradition' in a real and ironic sense" (108). In the summer of 1999 there was a ceremony in Sitka for the launching of a new canoe. Each paddle was identified with a clan or community. Thus, all people were symbolically united in making the canoe move.

The Father's Clan: Conflicting Patterns of Inheritance

As noted above, the conflict between traditional Tlingit law, based on matrilineal inheritance, and Western law, based on patrilineal inheritance, has been ongoing for over a century. In Tlingit tradition, because a man's children followed the mother's line and were therefore not of his moiety and clan, inheritance followed within his clan, from maternal uncle to nephew and not from father to son. The steward of a clan house was not the owner of its clan regalia and property, but rather the custodian. Conflicts have arisen during the last 100 years over inheritance, with modernist children claiming to inherit from the father's clan. The situation may have been intensified by passage of the Native American Graves Protection and Repatriation Act (NAGPRA), through which Native cultural objects are being returned by museums to communities. As the objects are returned and recontextualized, arguments have arisen in some communities over ownership, often with descendants claiming to inherit from the father's side. In one community the ownership of a clan house was contested both in civil court and in Tlingit tribal court. In this case the deceased clan leader had formed a clan trust and designated trustees to administer the clan property after his death. This is a culturally innovative way of handling a traditional situation. Realizing that clans had no status in Western law, the late clan leader attempted to articulate the concept of clan in Western legal terms by forming a trust. However, the children, who are not of the same clan as the father, disputed this, claiming, among other things, that a clan house is not simply for a single clan but for the entire moiety, and that children can inherit their father's clan property. Both of these claims are without precedent in traditional Tlingit law and exemplify the disintegration of the traditional social structure and clan system and the resulting confusion. On the other hand, NAGPRA repatriation requests, which are proliferating, could work positively to contribute to an increase in clan identity and solidarity, providing that people understand the clan system in general and the specific genealogical details in particular, as well as the history of the object in question.

The Father's Clan: Children of the Father's Clan

As we have suggested above, the most insidious changes can be those that are not noticed, so that people mistakenly believe that they are doing as they have always done, whereas they are really doing something quite different. Of such changes, perhaps the most significant is the change in understanding of the ceremonial role of the father and the father's clan. In addition to the disputes over inheritance, the clearest evidence is in changing patterns of ceremonial reciprocity as shown through response to songs traditionally directed across moiety lines.

As described above, one traditionally married into the opposite moiety, and descent was matrilineal. Therefore, a person was always the same clan and moiety as his or her mother and not the same moiety or clan as his or her father. Whereas one's clan identity is ceremonially clear by personal name and the regalia worn, the father's clan is more abstract. The father's clan is recognized ceremonially through the important term and concept "Child of the Father's Clan"; in Tlingit: *[clan] yádi*, plural *[clan] yátx'i*. These terms are inserted after the clan name as part of one's genealogy and identity. For example, *Kaagwaantaan yádi* means "Child of Kaagwaantaan," and *Kaagwaantaan yátx'i* means "Children of Kaagwaantaan." The term refers not to persons who are of the Kaagwaantaan (Eagle moiety) clan itself, but to persons who are (following the rules of matrilineal descent) of the opposite (Raven) moiety and whose fathers were of the Kaagwaantaan clan.

This term is almost always the second line of a traditional "love" song performed across moiety lines, directed by the singer of one moiety to members (biological children or clan children) of the opposite moiety. Thus a singer of the Eagle moiety Kaagwaantaan clan might address his or her song to the "Children of Kaagwaantaan," who are members of clans of the opposite (Raven) moiety, inviting them to stand up and dance, to recognize and honor their fathers and their fathers' clan.

The crucial point here is that the children of Kaagwaantaan are themselves *not* Eagle or Kaagwaantaan, but of various clans of the Raven moiety, following the matrilineage of their mothers. The above example is of Eagles singing to Ravens, but the pattern works both ways. A singer of the Kiks.ádi clan of the Raven moiety might sing to "Children of Kiks.ádi," inviting these Eagle moiety persons whose fathers were Kiks.ádi to stand and recognize their fathers' clan. Thirty years ago this did not need to be explained. We have noted in the last ten years an increasing confusion over the meaning of this concept, and that more and more people stand when their own clan is called, not their fathers' clan. We attribute this in part to lack of understanding of the Tlingit language and the term, but more seriously due to loss of the entire concept of the father's clan as the opposite moiety, and that one is a child of the opposite moiety. The understanding seems to be shifting to Euro-American patrilineal thinking. For example, at a recent event in Juneau, the leader of a technically brilliant dance group explicitly, but incorrectly, instructed the audience to stand "when your clan is called," saying "if you're Kaagwaantaan stand up when you hear Kaagwaantaan yátx'i." He should have instructed the audience to stand for their father's clan. Sadly, many people stood up to recognize their own clans, and not their fathers' of the opposite moiety. Some people may have stood so as not to embarrass the song leader, but we suspect rather that the entire concept of reciprocity with the father's clan across moiety lines was lost on them.

This is admittedly a difficult concept to grasp, but it lies at the heart of the traditional clan system, and to the extent that it is no longer understood, it further demonstrates the replacement of the traditional matrilineal clan system based on reciprocity by a patrilineal, individualized, and community-based system of Euro-American origin, as the traditional Tlingit terms and concepts and patterns of interaction become increasingly alien and incomprehensible. From a traditional point of view, it is sad to see a new generation of singers learning the text of songs with this important phrase but not understanding the context and meaning. This will be a major and ongoing challenge for teachers of Tlingit language, culture, and dance.

Contemporary Potlatches

Restrictions of space prevent us from discussing numerous examples from contemporary potlatches. We cannot deal adequately with the complexities, which are deserving of a separate essay. See Harkin (1997b) for discussion of similar issues in Northwest Coast cultures to the south of the Tlingits. We can, however, highlight some of the structural problems that arise. The host-guest relationship and reciprocity of clans of the opposite moiety are central to a traditional potlatch. In the new, community-based ceremonies, these roles and boundaries are sometimes obscured, with a resulting confusion over protocol. In one extreme case, the interaction did not cross moiety lines but was only within the hosting clan; money and food were retained by the hosts and not distributed to the opposite moiety. This violates the fundamental concept of Tlingit funereal reciprocity and exchange: only by giving comfort to the living of the opposite moiety can symbolic comfort pass over to the clan departed in the spirit world and in the process give spiritual healing and removal of grief to the hosts. On the positive side, there seems to be a renewed interest in potlatching, and many families and communities have creatively and successfully adapted traditional forms to fit contemporary needs and social reality (such as same-moiety marriages).

Conclusion

In any culture "time will tell" regarding the acceptance of change. Some innovations are embraced, others are rejected as shocking; some changes are made without self-conscious awareness, and others are accepted after time. How Tlingit people think, talk, and act about things has changed in the last century and continues to evolve. (See Dauenhauer and Dauenhauer 1995, 1998, and 1999 for more on community reactions to issues of language maintenance, literacy, and publication, all part of this pattern, but beyond the scope of this essay.) Clan-centered identity has diminished, accompanied by resocialization according to Western structures and concepts that are more individual and community based. While the models are increasingly Western, they are often labeled or perceived as traditional. Certainly the rhetoric of political correctness is couched in traditional terms. Zeese Papanikolas (1995:3), in the context of discussing the American novel and Native American oral literature, offers the insight that cultures aspire to "an aesthetic of wholeness" when they are breaking up. This seems to describe the popularity of the new Tlingit "National Anthem," which, while inspiring wholeness is at the same time a monument to the breakdown of the traditional clan system. Although the anthem is a new symbol representing a new social structure, most symbols are traditional (totems, drums, blankets, the new Celebration entry song), but their meaning and function have changed, as have the group dynamics and traditional patterns of use and exchange. The emblems and concepts of the clan-based system are being replaced, reshaped, and reinvented on a broader, "national" base, with new concepts of individuality, community, membership, and interaction.

Whatever the emblems and evolving structures are, the concept of clan plays little or no role in their function and is no longer the actual basic organizational unit of Tlingit society (although it continues ceremonially and genealogically for many people, especially in the context of potlatch). Former clan identity continues to dissolve in two opposite but complementary directions: the individual and the community. Whereas in the past, clan membership was of a classic gemeinschaft type into which a person was born, the contemporary community structures are based on classic gesellschaft patterns of membership by individual choice. Clan identity remains important in kinship and genealogy for those who still cultivate such things, but clans no longer operate as the sociopolitical and ceremonial units they formerly were. One might imagine as a theoretical model that traditionally the "national whole," which existed only potentially, was realized situationally through reciprocal interaction of clans of the two halves, with a minimum interaction of at least one clan each of the opposite moieties. The converse seems to be the case in contemporary society. The whole is constant, but its membership in traditional terms is unclear, and clans play little or no role in forming or operating within it. In this model the clans no longer operate in reciprocal patterns across moiety lines, with each half uniting ceremonially and politically to create a "national" whole. The last vestige of the traditional model is the potlatch, which for many people continues to endure as a meaningful social and spiritual process and which is, in fact, gaining strength in many communities. Although it remains compartmentalized, we should reemphasize that traditional potlatching is still practiced and has the potential of helping to maintain the strength and identity of matrilineal groups. But in legal terms, modern Tlingit society consists of individual shareholders of regional and village corporations. And since the cutoff date of December 18, 1971, an entire generation of "new Natives" has been born. These individuals, often called "after-borns," are not shareholders and are disenfranchised. We see all of this as creating new patterns of sociopolitical discourse.

Whatever the outcomes, we believe that understanding and appreciation of traditional Tlingit social structure and patterns of social interaction (whether they continue to be practiced or not) will rely increasingly on explicit instruction, teaching, and explanation, rather than on implicit or intuitive transmission through models of conventional behavior, as those changing behaviors continue to move toward Euro-American structures and patterns. Confusion will no doubt continue, but it can be reduced by clarification of assumptions as "the Culture" comes to be understood not as monolithic and unchanging, but as in the process of being negotiated and shaped by its members.

Notes

1. Some of the ideas and ethnographic examples that appear in this essay were previously used in an earlier and different treatment published as "Tlingit Clans and Shifting Patterns of Socio-Political Discourse" in the volume *Discourses in Search of Members: Festschrift in Honor of Ron Scollon* (Dauenhauer and Dauenhauer 2002).

2. In this essay, as in our other works, we use the phonemically accurate standard coast Tlingit popular orthography originally designed by Constance Naish and Gillian Story. In the word *at.óow*, "a" is the "short a" as in *America;* "oo" is a long "u," as in *toot;* the acute accent indicates high tone; the period indicates a glottal stop; and "w" is as in English. Contrasting examples are: *at.óow* ("symbolic clan property"), *atóow* ("she or he is reading it"), *atóo* ("inside of it"). For a table of the popular orthography and equivalents in phonetic transcription see Emmons (1991:xiv).

THE INTENTION OF TRADITION
Contemporary Contexts and Contests of the Hamat'sa Dance

Aaron Glass

Every year in Alert Bay, a Kwakwaka'wakw community on the central coast of British Columbia, the T'łisalagi'lakw elementary school holds a cultural celebration in which children perform dances and songs learned as part of the standard curriculum. As is now customary for most potlatches or important local activities, a T-shirt is produced to commemorate the event. On the 1993 shirt, along with a design created for the occasion, are the words "Alert Bay, Village of Culture."

Invoking Tradition

Performances of this sort are commonplace in Native communities today, and such mobilization of "culture" is playing an increasingly important role in the maintenance of indigenous identities. In the age of land claims, treaties, and repatriation, a legal language of strictly bounded tradition is required of First Nations to demonstrate what is held to be the validity of their claims. Likewise, a discourse of tradition and cultural authenticity is used by indigenous people to market themselves in an expanding and vital tourist economy. At both local and global sites Native people engage in a complex dialogue with anthropology, rejecting its colonial legacy while appropriating the language and concept of culture, as well as specific ethnographic texts, in order to represent themselves.

While many anthropologists have spent the last 20 years interrogating the concept of culture, Native people often deploy a reified and essentialized self-image, for both themselves and others. Roy Wagner (1981:62–64) suggests that ethnography's methods of objectification tend to "invent" the people studied and to create "cultures" as discrete products that can be displayed, bought, and sold as needed. Furthermore, Dominguez (1992) describes how the anthropological concept of culture has become the defining feature of 20th-century ethnic, social, and political rhetorics of unique identity. Performances for outsiders are one major venue in which communities consolidate and display emblematic — and consumable — aspects of their cultural heritage, events that often require considerable local negotiation as to the specific content and public interpretations offered.

First Nations are also increasingly — if ambivalently — using specific ethnographic texts to help in the revitalization of their art (see King 1997:88) and ceremony (see Harkin 1997b:105). Ethnography tends to codify and "entextualize" what were fluid practices, thereby turning process into product (Bauman and Briggs 1990:72; Dauenhauer and Dauenhauer 1995:97). Anthropological texts — especially among the Kwakwaka'wakw, who inherit one of the largest bodies of ethnographic material in the world — have a feedback effect in communities: once "traditions" are codified in books, they are more likely to be "revived" by subsequent generations. This brings up the question of the origin of those traditions. Jeanne Cannizzo (1983) suggests that the classic ethnographic portrait of "The Kwakiutl" may in fact be biased toward the family, lineage, and village of Boas's chief informant and collaborator, George Hunt. Thus the entextualization of culture may be one of the routes whereby specific privileges or performances become transformed over time into national emblems.

The last 20 years have seen a growing debate in the social sciences over how to approach tradition both theoretically and ethnographically (see Boyer 1997:23–24). Normative or merely historical, used unconsciously or strategically, traditions are usually thought of as those aspects of social life most resistant to change and thus strong signifiers of authentic links to the past. By the 1960s social scientists began to view tradition as a more dynamic, processual phenomenon, open to strategic (re)interpretation within larger social dialectics, and most certainly not the conceptual antithesis of modernity (Barth 1966; Eisenstadt 1973; Shils 1981).

Empirically minded and often Marxist scholars tend to expose specific practices as "invented" at some historic moment to suggest how the manipulation of culture serves an ideological or political agenda (e.g., Hobsbawm and Ranger 1983; Clifton 1990). This trend is anchored in objectivist or positivist assumptions about history where cultural authenticity can be evaluated scientifically, and it tends to dismiss the "emic" value of Native discourse as mere political rhetoric. In contrast, more constructivist or interpretivist scholars tend to view all culture as a perpetual invention and argue that the question of the authenticity of specific practices is thus a red herring (Linnekin 1991). In this view, tradition emerges — as does culture — from the dialectical interplay of representations and their negotiated meanings, individual manipulations and social norms, the past and the present (Handler and Linnekin 1984: 273–276). The authenticity of traditions becomes an issue of their "usefulness" (Mauzé 1997; Tuleja 1997) to current cultural projects, their affectiveness and effectiveness (Harkin 1997b:98) in fostering in people a sense of historically anchored identity and political agency. This constructivist view frequently comes under attack by Native peoples and their advocates as it is perceived to directly undermine the claims of identity and title that First Nations are struggling to define for themselves in a presumably postcolonial world (see F. Hanson 1997; Linnekin 1992).

How then are we to discuss tradition(s) while avoiding both strict empirical judgment (academics accusing First Nations of falsifying specific practices as invented) and attacks by Native advocates (First Nations accusing academics of falsifying their entire culture as invented)? One way is to listen carefully to the ways in which people actually speak about tradition in evaluating their own current cultural transformations. People invoke concepts of tradition and culture to define, validate, and legitimize contemporary practices regardless of their actual historical pedigree. Tradition is in this sense a selective and "implied" history (Mauzé 1997:5), a "retroprojection" or "reverse filiation" of the present into the past — according to local and negotiated criteria of authenticity — as a means of justifying and explaining mobilizations of culture (Pouillon 1980:39; 1997:17). Ethnographically codified concepts and practices aid in the local selection of cultural elements chosen to play a central role in the representation of identity and heritage. The irony is that deployment of traditional culture as a powerful *concept* in service of such "intentional identities" (Tuleja 1997:138) demands the fluid nature of the actual *practices* subject to negotiation.

Innovation is thus not the practical opposite of tradition but its conceptual limit, the creative factor that grants tradition its rhetorical value as an appeal to (the illusion of) past stability and authenticity, as the legitimator of innovation (see Kan 1990:358). Both tradition and innovation have strong conceptual value as signifiers, and both are appealed to in different moments of contemporary cultural discourse. By insisting that tradition and innovation are part of the same social processes and products, we avoid making truth claims for current projects based on presumed historical accuracy, focusing instead on the ways in which people invoke concepts of tradition to negotiate, validate, contest, and control contemporary cultural transformations.

The following case studies explore some ways in which Kwakwaka'wakw implicate concepts of tradition and culture in response to current transformations of the Hamat'sa performance, described in the communities as well as in anthropological literature as their most important dance.[1] I focus on two recent debates as limiting cases as to how far one can innovate with the Hamat'sa before causing deep local resentments and forcing complex negotiations of contested claim to privilege and representational rights. The first issue is its performance (for money) by non-Kwakwaka'wakw dancers in a theatrical setting; the second surrounds the bestowing of the Hamat'sa (and the right to its performance) on women. Both issues are hotly contested in communities today, both intersect with individual and tribal scales of identity, and both have deep implications for the control of cultural representation, locally and globally.

The Hamat'sa in fact has a long history of centrality in issues of personal, social, and cultural identity, display, and representation.[2] The dance ceremonially enacts the removal, possession, taming, and resocializing of an initiate into the Hamat'sa Society (basically, the group of previous initiates with the hereditary or bestowed rights to the prerogative). Although acquired by the Kwakwaka'wakw in the early 1800s—sought after and incorporated through intermarriage or warfare with Owikeeno and Heiltsuk neighbors to the north—the Hamat'sa was almost immediately elevated within the secret society system of the Winter Ceremonial, and by the 1880s it was being spoken of as the highest-ranked, most sacred, and most important prerogative.[3]

The Hamat'sa is usually referred to as "The Cannibal Dance," due in part to consistent ethnographic translation of it as such.[4] The dance has certain cannibalistic imagery relating to its mythological origin stories, local interpretations, and (past) elaborate staging, but the extent to which human flesh was ever ingested remains obscure.[5] The violent imagery (whether real or staged) of the Hamat'sa contributed to the Canadian federal government prohibiting the potlatch in the 1884 Indian Act (Cole and Chaikin 1990). As missionization became more entrenched and effective due to residential school attendance, the values of the Hamat'sa were held up as representative of everything evil and uncivilized in Native life: dirty, wild, possessed, cannibalistic. In the 1950s and 1960s, when dancing was revived for local fund-raisers, tourist performances, and potlatches, the Hamat'sa was often presented as the "Wildman." Today most people describe the Hamat'sa (and present it publicly) as the Cannibal Dance.

Part of the Hamat'sa's 20th-century trajectory is its transformation from the most selective, secretive, and sacred prerogative of individual (chiefly) families to the most publicly visible, museified, and emblematic image of "The Kwakiutl" in general. One dancer called it "the marquee dance of the whole society." Although the Hamat'sa is now taught in many band-run schools to all children, Native and non-Native, a language of rank and restriction still surrounds it; only those with the hereditary privilege to claim it get initiated into the "secret" society.[6] One issue is the general secularization of a ritual once presumably central to individual spiritual practice (see S. Reid 1979). Related is the palpable tension between local contests (for individual status as well as over specific family and village rivalries) and more global representations of the dance as belonging to the Kwakwaka'wakw Nation (a reified and locally problematic scale of identity often employed in political and tourist productions).[7] Thomas calls specific attention to the role that anthropological objectifications play in the selection of emblematic customs and the dialogues of particularization and totalization that result between local and global scales of identity: "In particular, objectified practices and social totalities can be seen to be manifest in each other. . . . The community that is imagined is not simply conceived of in its empirical complexity; its distinctiveness is understood, rather, through particular resonant practices and characteristics. In a dialectical process, the group and the particular practices are redefined as they come to connote each other" (1992:214–215). It is important to note, however, that the rivalries within communities over control of cultural representation are emphatically not between "traditionalists" and "progressives" (cf. Kan 1989a). Culture emerges in the dialectic of stability and change, and everybody invokes concepts of both tradition and innovation at different moments of discourse. The more the Hamat'sa is continually—and intentionally—recontextualized and reinvented, the more important and emblematic it is becoming as a tradition.

Performing Tradition

It is precisely control over this transformation that lies at the heart of local controversy over the performance of the Hamat'sa by non-Kwakwaka'wakw in a touristic setting. Comparing performances (traditional or "heritage") to museum objects, Kirshenblatt-Gimblett (1998) suggests a political economy of display in which both are removed from their originating sources and recontextualized and reinterpreted elsewhere. She suggests that local rituals are performed in the context of their origin and ceremonial function, while the "hallmark of heritage productions—perhaps their defining feature—is precisely the foreignness of the 'tradition' to its context of presentation" (157). She further argues that "songs, dances, and ritual practices are also ethnographically excised and presented as self-contained units, though not in quite the same way as material artifacts. You can detach artifacts from their makers, but not performances from their performers" (62). Yet the following case study examines the dynamics occurring when the performers of the Hamat'sa are not in fact Kwakwaka'wakw; they may be inextricably tied to the stage movements, but it is their distance from the original owners, interpreters, and "makers" of the dance that elicits contestation over their right to perform it in the first place.

Rights to the Hamat'sa were—and still are spoken of as—secretive, selective, and restricted to a limited number of chiefly families. But there is also historical precedent for performance *for* outsiders as well as transference of the dance privilege *to* outsiders, be they non-Kwakwaka'wakw Natives or whites (see B. Holm 1977; Ostrowitz 1999). It was common for people to marry outside of Kwakwaka'wakw communities, with the Hamat'sa being included in marriage exchange. Along with its centrality in potlatch and Winter Ceremonial displays, the Hamat'sa was also performed for the general public as early as the 1880s, both locally (for passing cruise ships, for visiting dignitaries, and for Franz Boas's and Edward Curtis's cameras), and globally (at American world's fairs and in Europe) (see Cole 1985:129–131, 202). In addition, during the 1950s, some Natives gave Hamat'sa privileges to white scholars and friends, perhaps as part of the political outreach to a larger Euro-Canadian society. In all of these performative contexts—ethnographic, diplomatic, and touristic—there was an important shift away from local potlatch discourse that foregrounds individual (or lin-

eage) rights, ownership, and display to the presentation of dances as examples of Kwakwa̱ka'wakw culture. Such situations demand complex local
negotiation as to performative ethics and details, and many old debates continue today as some feel it is inappropriate to show ritual dances without
actually initiating anybody or giving away gifts to validate the display.

Such debates have crested since 1993, when a hereditary chief from Alert
Bay gave the American Indian Dance Theater (AIDT) — a pan-tribal, professional dance group from the United States — the rights to perform one of his
family's Hamat'sa dances as part of a new Northwest Coast segment of their
touring show.[8] The company is made up of many Native Americans, each
performing across strict tribal affiliation. The transferring of rights to the
Hamat'sa entailed being taught the dance movements and songs involved,
explanation of its meaning, and the loan of masks to use in its performance.
It also consisted of a more-or-less formal ceremony of transference that took
place at the U'mista Cultural Centre with the AIDT, the chief, and two elders,
and that was videotaped.

Opinion over the right of the chief to give the Hamat'sa away is hotly
contested.[9] For many cultural conservatives who take issue with any touristic performance, this was a double insult: it was done for entertainment
and money, *and* by non-Kwakwa̱ka'wakw. For them, the transformation of a
ceremonial practice into a "show" profanes the dance and endangers the cultural integrity of the Kwakwa̱ka'wakw. One woman suggested that "you got
to give money away, its too sacred to play around with," and when describing such shows for tourists, she quickly corrected herself when mentioning
"our sacred costumes — regalia, not costumes." Her son, a talented Hamat'sa
dancer and artist who used to perform for tourists in the 1960s, objected to
"giving it to a bunch of people who don't care, [for whom] it's just a show.
It's not a show, it never was a show, it's an ownership, property." One chief
distinguishes his movements in potlatches from those of the AIDT: "I'm not
a performer. When I perform, mean it. But when they perform, they do it
for the public. I can't do that. Because that's not the way I was brought up."
For the first half of the 20th century, when assimilation to Canadian society
was more highly regarded by those presenting dances to outsiders, it was
announced that performances were harmless diversions, mere playing. But
now, given the seriousness of traditional cultural representations in the era

of multiculturalism and land claims, people insist that "You can't go playing with the culture" (a common phrase for breaches in protocol).

Many people are specifically outraged because the performers have no hereditary rights to the Hamat'sa, because "some people care about these things *belonging* to families, you know. We don't fool around there." Without having been formally initiated in a potlatch context, and without receiving family-owned names, no transfer of the Hamat'sa can be traditionally validated. One person emphasized that the Hamat'sa privilege and the names bestowed with it "have to come from somewhere . . . you can't invent a name for a Hamat'sa, you can't make it up. It's got to go way back in history." Ultimately, this comes down to a matter of identity, though the scale of identification is variable. One woman characterized the AIDT as not only non-Kwakwa̲ka̲'wakw and American, but non-Native. One artist reports that according to the way it was done "in the old days . . . if you own a Hamat'sa, and you don't have a son, its not proper to give it to just anybody, you have to give it to a *blood relation*."[10] Even though the AIDT had the consent of the chief and U'mista Cultural Society's Board of Directors, they certainly didn't satisfy hereditary requirements. By stating that the rights to perform the Hamat'sa have to come from a chief in one's family, people are arguing for a historical pedigree, a genealogical tradition to validate the claim to ownership.

There is certainly recognition that not all privileges are acquired through genealogical channels, that they can (and always were) transferred in various other social exchanges.[11] For example, one man recounted the story of how the Hamat'sa was originally brought into Kwakwa̲ka̲'wakw territory through marriage and war, and then he challenged the AIDT's claim to it because they didn't earn it "when my ancestors went out and *fought someone for it.* When some poor woman had to go marry some stranger from up north to get it." Another individual, after acknowledging that "gifts" of the Hamat'sa and other ceremonial prerogatives are passed in marriage dowries (a traditional means of couching exchange in social rather than economic terms), then insists that "you can't just buy it."

More than anything, though, people complained that an individual has no right to give the Hamat'sa away. One dancer stated: "I don't think we have the right to do that. No one, *no one person*. . . . We have to answer to our nation, *all the time*." This shifts focus onto the fact that the exchange of performative displays is a social process, and one that tests the alienability of culture at the source (Kirshenblatt-Gimblett 1998:8, 165). The display of cultural heritage through touristic, theatrical, or museological productions alienates both the practices and the right of original owners to determine interpretive and performative content. Critics of this chief's decision point to their conviction that a single individual cannot determine how their entire culture is going to be represented in foreign contexts. One woman said the Hamat'sa is "not open to contemporary interpretation. Because it is cultural property. [That chief] did not have the right to give it. It is shared amongst high ranking Kwakwaka'wakw society. It is not like jazz or tap." For such critics these five factors — the *alienation* of the Hamat'sa from local ownership or control based on the (perceived) decision of a *single person* and its subsequent *theatrical* performance by *non-Kwakwaka'wakw* for *profit* — challenge the traditional importance and sacredness attached to the dance and the right to claim and display it.

Defenders of the act suggest just the opposite using the same language of tradition, arguing that a chief has always had the right to distribute his personal property as he sees fit, be it through potlatching, marriage, or trade. When people complained to U'mista's Board of Directors, the chief insisted that neither the Cultural Centre nor the Band Council much less the entire community was making this transfer, but that he was granting the rights to use his family's songs with the approval of the Centre and his elders. Others, speaking in general of the rights to arrange or transfer dance performances (or defending their own relatives' acts of doing so), suggest that the choice of display is always the chief's.[12]

Drawing on the traditional role of formal exchange, one person argued that giving the privilege away is acceptable "if it's paid for [and] witnessed by our people." As the chief had arranged to have the AIDT pay royalties from their performances to U'mista, one could say that it had been paid for. In terms of witnessing, his son described the "proper ceremony" that was held and documented on video, providing a lasting public record of the transaction. Furthermore, the chief had the power of traditional authority with him, because "there were a couple of our elders here that said he could do it, and he followed the instructions of his elders and, you know, who better to go to, I mean they're the final stamp of approval." This individual also justified the transfer in the language of temporary rights, that "its being loaned to them," and that ultimately, both the masks provided and the rights to perform would be "put back to where it belongs."[13]

For some, the fact that the AIDT are "professional" performers releases them from the ceremonial requirements of initiation and payment to witnesses. As the granting chief himself states: "no one was initiated, that's the misunderstanding that a lot of people have. We didn't initiate these guys, they were just more like actors. They didn't get any names . . . so the meaning of the dances to them and to their audience wouldn't have the same meaning to us." And they were, after all—in the words of a young man who had assisted in teaching the group songs—"other Natives." In other words, it is precisely their identity as disinterested (if admiring and respectful) outsiders (but not too far outside) that grants the troupe the freedom to present the Hamat'sa in a nonritual context; only true actors could perform the dance in a theater. The performance is thus justified in the name of educating the public about a uniquely Kwakwaka'wakw culture in a program otherwise dominated by the Plains and Southwest. "They were just trying to teach people . . . teaching people about us. . . . More people know more about the Cree than they do about our tribe." In fact, the chief in question identifies his main critics as a small faction of people who refuse any recording or photographing of songs or dances, who do not share his conviction that such ethnographic records are valuable educational and political resources. Numerous people voiced the opinion that as long as performers respect and honor the traditions, it is acceptable—and perhaps even beneficial—that they be enacted by and for outsiders. That is, as one young dancer said, "as long as they don't try and make up culture and make up who we are and make us look bad."

It appears that the AIDT issue became an occasion for families to enact specific rivalries and contests for interpretation as well as control of cultural capital. Although not a unique debate, the issue of whether the Hamat'sa belongs to individuals or to the Kwakwaka'wakw Nation addresses the problem of intellectual property and the scale of group identity more broadly. On the Northwest Coast, where dances and their specific variations are owned by particular individuals and families, the use of such practices as emblematic of First Nations as a whole becomes especially problematic. What is being negotiated here is the (traditional) rights of individuals to alienate their property and the (emergent) rights of members of the Kwakwaka'wakw Nation to determine how their culture is going to be globally represented.

Yet some of the contradictions and ambiguity in the language of justification or criticism is found within individual discourse as well as between individuals. For example, one chief from Ft. Rupert, when asked about the origins of the Hamat'sa in Kwakwaka'wakw territory, proclaimed, "it has always been amongst us. Yep, since time began, it has always been there." He also described numerous potlatch practices of recent origin with no apparent judgment. The same man at one point said it is ultimately up to the chief to decide how to handle his rights, yet 30 seconds later he added, "I think it's wrong to give a guy permission to do the Hamat'sa." These points are contradictory only to the extent that tradition is held to be based on objective and authenticated historical truth. This example suggests that individuals appeal selectively to tradition to understand, explain, and manage contemporary practices and meanings.

Engendering Tradition

In the course of interviews exploring the contemporary representational contexts and meanings of the Hamat'sa, at least a dozen women were mentioned who claim or perform the Hamat'sa privilege today, although most people said there are very few, and any given person only named a couple. There are various explanations for why and how these women came to claim it, and there is variation in its performative display.[14] Many scholars focus on cultural productions, performances, and representations as discursive formations or signifying practices whereby indigenous women are strategically negotiating their past and present, intentionality and ideology, individual and national identities (Lilley 1989; Emberley 1993; Ortner 1996). The political contexts in which these dialogues occur are multiple: local contestations for rights and appropriateness, more global constructions of identity at the village and national levels, places where unique Kwakwaka'wakw values intersect with those of Western modernity and feminism, and the superimposition of gender and other forms of differentiating discourse. Opinion in the communities is fiercely divided as to the details of both chief's and women's rights and responsibilities, although not along gender lines (many women were the most vocal critics) or along age lines (both young and old people debate the relative merits). Again, both critics and supporters invoke and debate traditional precedents to both condemn and legitimate the practice.

The historical evidence is often vague and contradictory. Boas (1966:52) mentions that women were not to receive hereditary status in the Winter Ceremonial, yet he also describes and illustrates a Koskimo woman being initiated as a Hamat'sa by her chiefly brother (1897:591–595). Along with most subsequent ethnographers, Goldman (1975:89) states definitively that "The hamatsa is always male." One chief suggested to me that it was population decline that required women to be given privileges that would have otherwise gone to men. By the late 19th century, new avenues to wealth and unprecedented intervillage amalgamation gave rise to more elaborate rivalry in the ranking system, and families scrambled to assert claims to ancestral names and privileges, often through marriage exchange. With this increase in the economic value of women may have come a transformation in the gendering of ceremonial life.[15] By the 1930s increasing accommodation to Western social values (through religious conversion, residential schooling, and participation in the market economy) may have promoted flexibility for women to reposition themselves. Since the 1950s and 1960s, many women have been employed as dance instructors and have participated in tourist performances under more flexible restrictions. As the Hamat'sa has always been critically entangled in hegemonic processes (being the privilege of elite males), it is no surprise that concepts of tradition are invoked to debate the relative merits of its innovation (see Kobrinsky 1975; Wolf 1999).

The harshest opponents deny the existence of anything like a female Hamat'sa and describe the current practice as further evidence of cultural disintegration: "If they want their own identity, then why don't they go and find their own identity, . . . but leave our Hamat'sas alone. Leave us alone. Because when they come and start doing that, we are just becoming Canadians, we are becoming North Americans, we are becoming Europeans. Very confused. We've already got our laws set down for us, so there will be no more confusion. And I am seeing it be broken apart. The circle is broken." This individual concluded the interview by emphasizing that his intention is not to be prejudiced, but "to make sure our culture is saved." Another, after acknowledging some early precedents and that some of the contemporary female Hamat'sas are his relatives, declared: "But you know, our ancestors had a really strict law, and for sure, it was a man's role, and that, you know, if we're going to start practicing our culture we need to get back to as close as what we can."

Numerous people tell stories of a female Hamat'sa from Kingcome Inlet early in the 20th century, and many claim that she was the only one they ever heard of. Apparently a chief there had no sons or nephews and decided to give his Hamat'sa to his infant daughter.[16] Even if people acknowledge that women were often given rights to hold in trust for a younger male, as some suggest for this case, they insist that she would never *perform* the dance. One man described this individual as "a little kid learning how to walk. . . . That's not a Hamat'sa. It wasn't even anything like a Hamat'sa." He also suggested that women were kept from dancing in Hamsaml̵ masks because it put them in a sexually compromising position vis-à-vis male audience members and participants. In any case, there is a sense that it is performance of the Hamat'sa that legitimizes claim to the rights, and if a woman merely holds the name, she is not an authentic Hamat'sa. Even if such women did exist, "their role wasn't as prestigious as the man's full-fledged Hamat'sa, I could almost guarantee that." Hence, another man identified it as "a special dance, not a real Hamat'sa dance."

A few people suggest that the women who now claim to be Hamat'sas were given the privilege because they asked for it directly or manipulated their families, not because they were in hereditary position to receive it (a suggestion the women themselves deny). Numerous people voiced the opinion that chiefs have no *traditional* right to bestow the Hamat'sa on their daughters simply because they love them deeply: "I think with the changing times, some people love and cherish their children so much that even a young lady might be initiated now, and with the changing times, I guess, that's acceptable now."

One of the most outstanding features of the criticism of female Hamat'sas is the marking of such women as deviants, as outsiders, as "others" of one sort or another. One man identified it as "just a matter of the Western world coming into our world. Its a matter of Caucasian thinking people who are all urbanites." He also suggested that the two worlds are irreconcilable: "One moment, they are totally women's liberation, next moment they're as traditional as can be." Another likewise invoked the influence of feminism, suggesting that women are supposed to be "servants for the Hamat'sa, they serve us our food. I mean, nowadays, they'll say 'Yeah, right. Sexism' and that kind of stuff." One man hinted and another claimed outright that all the women Hamat'sas are lesbians. In any case, there is the sense that contemporary female Hamat'sas mark the local infusion of modernity, Westernization, and feminism, resulting in changes to or "inventions" of tradition. These are all ways of semiotically marking these women as inauthentic participants in their traditional culture and articulating gender with other categories of difference.

Given the various practices recorded in both oral histories and anthropological texts, and the variety of current women's claims to the Hamat'sa, criticism of the practice draws selectively on the past (as well as the present) while arguing a strong case for tradition and the importance of its return. For some opposed to the practice, it indicates a dangerous acceptance of innovation, especially given current efforts to revitalize cultural integrity, economic stability, and political potency. "First we have to establish and live the way that was set down for us first, and then maybe we can make some changes after it becomes fluent." Another man explains that he would never pass his Hamat'sa onto his daughters despite the fact that he has no sons: "I'm a big believer in tradition myself. I think that if we start changing too many of the rules, we won't have any rule to follow." As if directly quoting from chiefs a century ago (see Boas 1897:592), one man argued that there were no traditional women Hamat'sas "*according to legend!* According to legend. Now if they got another legend to go with the woman Hamat'sa, then bring it on." There are those in the communities willing to take up his challenge.

At least two of the women who dance with other Hamat'sas claim specific family privileges that assert that the cannibalistic dancer be a woman, and some relatives can trace the legitimizing legends back in time (which often means to texts recorded by Boas and Hunt). Some claim these are not true Hamat'sas, and that the presence of validating legends sets them apart from the other women, but the fact that they dance with other Hamat'sas negates this distinction in most people's eyes. Others mention precedents "in the early days" at various villages. In fact, it is interesting to note that some people point to the case of the early-20th-century women from Kingcome as a traditional precedent for the contemporary practice, suggesting the historical boundary of "tradition" is itself fluid and open to negotiation.

There is some consensus that if a chief had no male heirs, he could "put" a Hamat'sa on his daughter in order to keep it in the family. This speaks to the right of chiefs to decide the fate of their privileges, and people point to such practices to validate the giving of Hamat'sas to women today, regardless of individual justification. For many people, the most important criteria in selecting candidates to receive the Hamat'sa are personal devotion, worth, and understanding. Two of the recently initiated women were selected by their families, despite the presence of possible male recipients, because of their deep interest and participation in the meaning of the dance; for both of them, being a Hamat'sa is about facing one's fears, confronting life's (and the community's) hostilities, and gaining self-understanding. One suggests that in the old days little children were never initiated because families waited to see which sibling would be worthy of inheriting and carrying the privilege. She said today people might initiate kids because they're cute when dancing, but you would never see a child dancing in "traditional ceremonies." One man favored returning to the importance of deep understanding and worthiness and mentioned a chief who is interested in getting "all the Hamat'sa together, and present[ing] what the role of that society is, and what they should be doing, and maybe that they need to be purified and practice those sort of traditional things." It is interesting to note that this chief gave his daughter a Hamat'sa. In shifting criteria for initiation away from primogeniture or rigidly gendered heredity, there is a reevaluation of tradition at the same time as people argue for the importance of cultural literacy over genealogy.

For such people, tradition is not meant to be a rigid adherence to the past, a past they hold to be selectively represented by certain individuals or families eager to consolidate representational authority. At least two or three of the women who have received the dance are lesbian, and their desire to take on the persona of the Hamat'sa may relate precisely to their perception of it as a traditional male prerogative, and one with which they may be fashioning their own gender identity at the intersection of traditional Kwakwaka'wakw cultural values and a Western feminist sensibility. An older woman invokes modern political changes to explain and justify contemporary female Hamat'sas: "Human rights say females are equal now (laughs). Did you hear that on the news? It's on females who should get paid equally as males for their jobs, [if] they got the same kind of job that get paid equally, and this will be retroactive to 1985. So this is applied to Hamat'sa (laughs)."

When one young woman desires to bring back initiatory isolation in the woods as part of reviving the personal meaning, symbolism, and ritualistic understanding of the Hamat'sa, she says some of the younger dancers "want to change a lot of things and make it more traditional."

So we can't simply assume that tradition is being used to validate conservative tendencies. While in some cases it bolsters claims to a reified and authenticated culture, it is also used to signify outmoded and no-longer-appropriate restrictions on behavior. The debates over gender are complex, and opinions divide along at least two axes, as they did in the case of the American Indian Dance Theater. One issue is whether such transfers were done in the past, and whether the chief has *individual rights* to pass on privileges to whomever he sees fit. As before, there is contradiction within individual discourse, as one man — totally opposed to women holding the Hamat'sa — demands that "it goes by who that chief thinks deserves it." The second issue is whether or not non-Kwakwa̱ka'wakw or women *should* be performing the Hamat'sa at all. Some who see traditional precedents also think it is wrong; others recognize such practices as innovative but have no problem with them. One vocal opponent of the practice, a talented Hamat'sa dancer himself, also helped prepare his female relatives for their own initiation. This highlights the fact that when directly questioned, people may invoke ideologically driven answers, normative "traditions" that are more fluid in everyday practice.

It also underscores the different meanings of the term *rights* mentioned above. One issue is that of ownership, the other that of acceptability or properness. Heath (1994:90) discusses this distinction in terms of "appropriation" and "appropriateness" and suggests that negotiations of cultural protocol and traditional performative rights — especially those linked to gendered roles and practices — become the sites for contests of ownership and control. The rights (of ownership) of individuals to alienate their cultural property and the rights (or worthiness) of others to perform it are negotiated for both local and national scales of identity. It is vital to distinguish between these two levels of dialogue. One is internal to Kwakwa̱ka'wakw communities and consists largely of negotiations over rights and responsibilities surrounding the representation of traditional culture. The late 20th century marks a shift in collective identification, and one reason for the extensive local conflict is precisely the degree to which previously disparate communities are now participating in collective expressions; various traditions are intersecting, and people are arguing over whose should be privileged. On the other hand, the Kwakwaka'wakw are recovering from the legacy of colonialism, and local contest for representational authority may be indicative of larger political claims for control over self-determination, resource management, and cultural property.

The fact that this specific issue revolves around the gender of the Hamat'sa may suggest that the larger issue of cultural representation and the politics of identity has become gendered as well. As Alexander (1994) and Fiske (1996) have argued, the gendered meanings superimposed on sexual identities provide the semiotic mechanism by which sexual symbolization of difference is projected onto political discourse. If hegemonic representations are often gendered, so too are resistance efforts. And if the Hamat'sa is one such formation, it becomes clear why local control has ramifications for global control. The performance of the Hamat'sa by women threatens some with images of cultural dissolution, images all the more dangerous in the climate of treaties and land claims. Lilley (1989:92) describes the importance of a strong rhetoric of cultural integrity and consensus to legitimize Australian treaty processes: "the kind of traditional past that they could marshal in defense of their collective interests was simply too diverse to encode their specific claim." Given the diversity of individual, family, and village variation in specific privilege and performative tradition, the slippage indicated by local contests over the past take on additional weight when the Kwakwaka'wakw Nation presents its generalized culture, or even more localized Nations argue their specific land claims.[17]

Kwakwaka'wakw women may be struggling to define their own identity against what they perceive to be the hegemony of tradition, yet Kwakwaka'wakw politicians are invoking tradition to fight the hegemony of colonialism. Just as the Hamat'sa played a central role in 19th-century local contests for rank and privilege as well as in the national rhetoric of potlatch prohibition and assimilation, so too is it deeply entangled in contemporary politics of identity and representation, locally, nationally, and internationally.

Conclusion: A Complex Cannibal

> Reference to tradition is a metaphor for identity. This means it encompasses and illustrates a past, a present and a future. It is not only the

memory of the past frozen in time that reemerges; it is also a reference necessary for elaborating a version of the contemporary world, which is the "space" where traditional and modern social life occur side by side. Tradition is primarily a political instrument for regulating both internal and external relations. (Mauzé 1997:12)

Twenty years ago anthropologists such as Wagner (1981) and Pouillon (1980) claimed that societies deploy reified notions of tradition in order to define themselves against others through invocation of a unique, authenticated past. More recently Appadurai (1996:12, 13) suggests that the "most valuable feature of the concept of culture is the concept of difference, a contrastive rather than a substantive property. . . . I suggest that we regard as cultural only those differences that either express, or set the groundwork for, the mobilization of group identity." He argues that culture serves a diacritical function similar to tradition, aiding in the construction and representation of identity in a shrinking global village. Within societies undergoing internal change, where historical or colonial pressures weaken normative structures, *differentiating* controls (limiting individual invention by consolidating authority) are often revitalized through conspicuous *conventionalization* (establishment of collective traditions) (Wagner 1981:59; Hobsbawm and Ranger 1983:4–5). In other words we are more likely to observe an official rhetoric of "national tradition" — defining and authenticating the boundaries of unique cultural units through appeals to historical continuity — in precisely those moments in which control over the practices used to define those traditions may be locally unstable and contested. I am suggesting that such a process is occurring amongst the Kwakwaka'wakw as they attempt to reconsolidate control over individual rank and privilege at the local level while establishing a unique cultural identity globally based on the presentation of emblematic forms.

The Hamat'sa has, in fact, always been central to representations of group identity at various levels, and it should come as no surprise that such a "key emblem" (Thomas 1992:219) shifted in signification over time. For example, the Hamat'sa (as locally elaborated) came to distinguish Kwakwaka'wakw from their neighbors; it was a chiefly rather than common privilege; it marks the transition from profane to sacred dances and from childhood to adulthood; it dramatizes savagery and its control by civilization (in both local cultural *and* colonial discourse). The cannibalistic imagery has always helped grant it significant drama and semiotic strength as a marker of both internal and external social distinctions, as well as larger political and cosmological boundaries.

Locally, the Hamat'sa concludes with the taming of the initiate, with his or her return to a "cultured" state as distinguished from the "savage" states of childhood and possession. As the Hamat'sa becomes transformed from an individual rite of passage to a national emblem, so too does this renewal imagery get applied to cultural history more broadly. In fact, some Kwakwaka'wakw today interpret the Hamat'sa as an image of the evolution of both the species (from animal to human) and the society itself (from savagery to civilization). One man articulates this view by stating "Kwag'iulth people already knew about evolution," and he goes on to describe the motions of the dancer through the sequence of songs as he stands progressively more erect, likening it to the transition from wild ape to noble man. He concludes, "to me, that's way before this Darwin guy."

He then equated the red color of the cedar bark (which is protective against the cannibal spirit and worn by both the initiate and the audience) with the blood of Christ in Church ritual, suggesting that this similar symbolic affinity for blood keeps one civilized, so that "you're not going to turn around and bite the person next to you because all of a sudden you're possessed." Later, after speaking of his personal maturation process, he mentioned that "it took us a century to become controlled, to calm down."

The fact that "traditional" cannibalism is once again emphasized in public interpretation of masks and dances may signify the exoticness of an authenticated indigenous past, the success of modernization, and the cultural uniqueness of the Kwakwaka'wakw. In terms of providing an oppositional identity, one man suggested:

> I think that we went through a rough time, and a lot of people accept it without even knowing the Western bullshit. . . . [Many people] have no sense of nationality, no sense of honor, no sense of anything. So, I think we're really lost as a—I'm not talking about the Hamat'sas, all the Hamat'sas are proud of who they are, all the Hamat'sas are insulted that they don't get fed first. Truly, you can put that down there, they are insulted by that. Hamat'sas know their rights in our society. And they're not getting it. . . . I'm looking at it from a different perspective than you as a European or as a Caucasian or a North American would look at it.

Another explained: "We have a different creator, not the God of the white-man. See, we were cannibals. Not recently, but back then." Thus a practice negatively evaluated against colonial standards of morality, yet codified and to some degree naturalized by ethnographic representations, now becomes a tradition positively valued as a distinguishing cultural trait. As Kirshenblatt-Gimblett (1998:161) puts it: "By narrowing the domain of what could be considered normative, critics of traditional ceremonies and customs simultaneously expanded the field of the nonnormative. What one was too ashamed to do, one could study, collect, and display. . . . The process of negating cultural practices reverses itself once it has succeeded in archaizing the 'errors'; indeed through a process of archaizing, which is a mode of cultural production, the repudiated is transvalued as heritage."

The importance of staging the Hamat'sa as a cannibalistic performance may have actually increased under colonization as people reacted to, and resisted, the imposition of Christian values. Thomas (1992:219) describes a similar occurrence of cannibalistic "performances" in the Pacific, where "islanders seem to have registered foreign perceptions of what was horrifying and to have paraded the horrifying practices in a taunting manner." What Thomas calls the "inversion of tradition", Tuleja (1997:9) calls "parodic parry": negative stereotypes are appropriated and reversed as a means of resistance. Since cannibalism represented that which was most removed from civilization, perhaps the Kwakwaka'wakw flaunted it in the face of missionaries, tourists, and government administrators in an attempt to remain just that: distinct from Victorian society.

Evidence of the continuing importance of the Hamat'sa is found also in a discourse of sacredness. Many suggest that it is too sacred to show to outsiders or tourists as mere entertainment. People report a recent change in attitude toward Hamsamł, the dramatic bird masks used in performance of the Hamat'sa; a few years ago these masks were performed for tourists in Alert Bay, but now generally they are not. People say the elders were unhappy that the masks were shown, as they are held to constitute the most important part of the ceremony. One young singer reports that "It is the most sacred of our dances, and our elders and everybody now are feeling that it shouldn't be brought out . . . for just public performances. Just within cultural, for cultural reasons and, you know, ceremonial events." This attitude does not extend as far as wanting all masks to come off display in museums, but it may mark the first stage in a resacralization process that could end in such requests (as did Coast Salish attitudes toward their Sxwó:yxwey masks; for a similar process among the Tlingit, see Kan 1990:363). It may be that as the Hamat'sa becomes more decontextualized and removed from local representational control, the more it may be intentionally removed from display contexts altogether and re-restricted to ritual.

Given the ways in which the Hamat'sa constitutes individual identities and is emblematic of national identities, it is no surprise that those held to have no rights to perform the dance are invalidated and marked as other in many ways. They are accused of "playing with the culture," of being "urbanites," or "culturally illiterate," or "Westernized", or "lesbian" or "C-31s"; in short, they are accused of being non-authentic Kwakwaka'wakw.[18] In appealing to tradition to evaluate the authenticity of contemporary identities, people are selectively remembering the cultural past in order to intentionally re-member present group boundaries.

The dialectic of innovation and tradition is complicated by shifts in the scale of identity and the context of representation, and these case studies illustrate the slippage when cultural forms circulate across certain boundaries. Locally, Kwakwaka'wakw are contesting specific prerogatives by appealing to or challenging the authenticity of claims; here we find a language of restricted access, rank, and sacredness applied to a dance taught to all kids in elementary school. On the more global stage, people are vying for the right to control generalized displays of a national culture through appeals to the traditional rights of individual chiefs; here we witness a language of aesthetics, drama, and emblematicity attached to a so-called secret society. Yet these contradictions in discourse do not indicate cultural instability or decay of tradition. They are part of the basic process whereby the past is put in service of the present.

Complicate this dynamic with the political climate of treaty negotiations, and we find academic, legal, and aboriginal discourses of tradition intersecting. Emblematic performances and specialized knowledge are offered as evidence of persisting cultural traditions and political unity. Yet when these practices are in flux locally, it undermines national claims. What is being negotiated in Kwakwaka'wakw communities is the rights and responsibilities of people with certain "inalienable possessions" to give and keep them appropriately (see Weiner 1992). The recent controversies around the Hamat'sa highlight the articulation of legal and aboriginal conceptions of intellectual and cultural property, control over which is crucial to the maintenance of both local and global identities. If cultural invention is held to be anathema to the maintenance of political sovereignty, then it is no wonder that tradition is invoked as the conceptual legitimator and delimiter of such change.

How does the postmodernist deconstruction of culture (as both structure and praxis) allow for the political language necessary in such cases? Anthropology has spent the last century helping to dismantle the notion of racial determinism, arguably in the best interests of Native people. But it has also reified the concept of culture, one that everywhere is internalized as the naturalized marker of difference (Dominguez 1992:38). Ethnography aids in the codification and reification of individual cultures, and its classic texts have been appropriated in order to build contemporary indigenous identities and political claims. Now deconstructivist, academic theories of culture threaten to undermine aboriginal performance of culture. I think we need to be very sensitive to the ways in which our current analytical attention to cultural innovation articulates with local Native discourses of tradition, in all their complexity.

Notes

This essay is adapted from my master's thesis in anthropology, University of British Columbia, 1999. I would like to especially thank the many Kwakwa̱ka'wakw people with whom I spoke, the Na̱mgis First Nation for granting my request to conduct research in Alert Bay, and the friendly and gracious staff of the U'mista Cultural Centre; G̱ilakas'la. In addition, this project greatly benefited from my conversations with Bruce Miller and Ruth Phillips as well as Jo-Anne Fiske, Dara Culhane, Julie Cruikshank, Bill Holm, Phil Nuytten, Marjorie Halpin, Jay Powell, Andy Everson, Nancy Wachowich, Aldona Jonaitis, Charlotte-Townsend Gault, and Margaret Stott. Thanks also to Marie Mauzé for inviting me to participate in the Paris conference.

1. The topics and material for this study emerged from interviews conducted in 1998 and 1999 with over 20 Kwakwa̱ka'wakw residing on reserves and in urban centers, supplemented by my own experiences with Kwakwa̱ka'wakw communities dating back to 1993. Participants represent a broad cross-section of the community and include both young and old, male and female, those with and without Hamat'sa privileges, those central and peripheral to public relations,

education, and performance activities. For the purpose of this essay, and due to the politically sensitive nature of the debates, respondents' quotations are left anonymous; all emphases in direct quotations are original.

2. I am currently engaged in doctoral research in anthropology at New York University on this history, which includes discussion of the acquisition and development of the Hamat'sa by the Kwakwa̱ka̱'wakw in the 19th century, the legacy of ethnographic accounts and representations of cannibalism, photographic and filmic depictions, performance at world's fairs and other touristic settings, museum and art gallery collection and display of masks, the appropriation of the dance by non-Kwakwa̱ka̱'wakw, and further contemporary dynamics.

3. Boas (1897:664; 1966:258) reports 1835 as the approximate date of acquisition of the Hamat'sa by Fort Rupert Kwag'iulth in a raid on the Heiltsuk. While this event is not in question *for the Kwag'iulth,* other Kwakwa̱ka̱'wakw villages have their own origin stories, reinforcing the view that Boas's "Kwakiutl" privileges Fort Rupert.

4. For example, in his earliest (1895) descriptions of Baxwbakwalanuxwsiwe', the possessing spirit of the Hamat'sa, Boas translates the name as "The first one to devour human flesh at the river mouth." In his 1897 work he changes that to "The first one to eat man at the mouth of the river, i.e. north," and describes the Hamat'sa as "a cannibal" (394). By 1905 he begins using the translation that would then remain consistent in future texts, "The cannibal at the north end of the world." Likewise, in 1897, although referring to cannibalistic imagery, Boas refers to the dancer as "the Hamat'sa." By 1910 he renders the word *Hamat'sa* as "Cannibal" in the English translations, and in the most used ethnographic treatment of the Kwakwa̱ka̱'wakw (1966), "Cannibal spirit," "Cannibal dancer," and "Cannibal society" are used throughout.

5. Continuing the recent trend of popular interest in cannibalism, McDowell (1997) attempts to uncover the historical factuality of reports of anthropophagy on the Northwest Coast. Instead, he makes a muddle of the historical, ethnographic, and interpretive literature. For more reliable assessments see Archer 1980; Wike 1984.

6. This has caused disruption at recent potlatches, as children with the technical knowledge but not the social right to perform the dance jump onto the floor with the other Hamat'sa dancers. In some cases they were pulled back or quickly accompanied by an older relative with a recognized claim; it is also encouraged that the families of such children make a public distribution of money or *digit'a,* to make amends for the breach of protocol.

7. The Kwak'wala-speaking people never had a pan-village political identity and,

locally at least, still do not. The largest (more or less) stable social units were a few amalgamated villages and alliances.

8. The AIDT had approached the U'mista Cultural Centre in Alert Bay, requesting the rights to perform the Hamat'sa as part of a video series they were involved in producing.

9. People refer to such acts as "giving the dance away," yet it may be more accurate to say that the privilege is kept and given at the same time, as performances on the Northwest Coast may be seen as "inalienable possessions" (Weiner 1992).

10. This illustrates the rhetoric of ethnonationalism in which heritage displays privilege "descent" over "consent" in determining group membership and rights to representation (Sollors 1982).

11. There are many cases where the Hamat'sa has been given to people from other families, or where the genealogical link is more tenuous, in order to foster specific relationships or validate individual status.

12. People will always challenge the claims and acts of chiefs in the potlatch context and outside of it. Part of the role of potlatching is to provide a public venue in which to hash out these negotiations. Perhaps part of the difficulty people have with this specific issue is that the transfer was done outside of the bighouse.

13. To my knowledge these conditions have not been met fully by the AIDT.

14. Two women are said to have inherited specific family privileges that entail female dancers; one because she was an only child; at least two because they asked their chiefly fathers for it; most because either there were no male children or those men in position to inherit it refused or were somehow not perceived to be worthy. Some acquired the privilege initially through formal, performative initiation whereas others received names alone; some women dance with other tame Hamat'sas at the conclusion of all new initiations during potlatches; some will perform only when their family hosts a potlatch, and they are required to display unique privileges; some never dance it, by choice or by family restriction; some occasionally dance it for tourists or in other cultural performances.

15. Over the course of the last century, other dances have undergone gender reversal, or at least a loosening of strict gender-specific requirements. People point out that women are doing many dances, (including the Tuxw'id, Madam, 'Ma'mak̲'a, and Xisiwe') that used to belong to men, and that men perform some dances previously held by women (including the Wa'a'a, or Pax̲lax̲, and in the case of one family, the Ladies Professional Dance).

16. The chief seems to have been Dick Webber, also known as K'odi Dick. One person identified the woman as Daisy Webber and one as Mrs. Sam Webber, but most people call her Anitsa (a relatively common Kwak'wala name). Mungo Martin recorded a song belonging to her with Ida Halpern in 1951 (notes in

U'mista Cultural Centre archives, card #12, "Woman Hamatsa Song"). He said
it was a well-honored, very old song (mentioning "27 years ago"), and that "she,
too, had to stay up in the woods." This is hard to reconcile with accounts of her
as a little child at the time.

17. There is occasionally the bizarre occurrence whereby someone will identify
themselves as, say, a member of the Namgis Nation, which is part of the Kwakwaka'wakw Nation, which is, of course, part of the nation of Canada.

18. Bill C-31, introduced to Canadian law in 1985, reversed previous policy that had
denied tribal status to indigenous women who married non-Native men, as well
as to their children. With the passing of the bill, many people returned to reserves to claim Native recognition and the benefits that accompany it, as well
as to integrate themselves in some cases into local politics and ceremonial life.

REREADING THE ETHNOGRAPHIC RECORD

The Problem of Justice in the Coast Salish World

Bruce G. Miller

The ethnographic record of the Northwest Coast lives on in many forms at present. Publications and field notes of our anthropological predecessors who worked with indigenous communities are now both part of the patrimony of the community members and the legacy of anthropology. And lest we think otherwise, these materials are regularly read and used by Northwest Coast people and are perhaps less likely to be pilloried in specific terms than our currently produced texts. This patrimony is employed in the (re)construction of indigenous ways of life and in internal debates about where communities should head. It is for these reasons that we might reexamine several issues and address questions that did not receive much anthropological attention in earlier generations. Valuable earlier materials can be reread in light of new problems and new understandings to make them more useful in addressing the contemporary world.

My work specifically addresses one corner of the Northwest Coast, the Coast Salish world, and one particular problem, namely, how people envisioned the establishment and maintenance of peaceful social relations in a hostile world. My argument is that these questions were addressed conservatively, if at all, by anthropologists of the early and middle 20th century, and this conservatism is now read into the record by indigenous community members themselves intent on making conservative representations of their own prior, historical justice practices for their own reasons. Discussions of law and justice in the ethnographic literature are ordinarily brief, descriptive, and normative accounts of communities that by then were long removed from the period of self-regulation, and many of whose practices of adjudicating differences between individuals and families had either gone underground or had disappeared. In some Coast Salish communities, particularly those in British Columbia, there is a kind of salvage ethnography underway for the purposes of treaty negotiation and for the establishment of new community institutions, such as diversionary justice practice, just as anthropologists vacate the topics of tradition and culture and focus on colonial processes and accommodation and resistance within aboriginal communities.[1] I am not proposing that a reinvigorated, redirected ethnography or a careful search of field notes will produce the truth of justice practices of a prior period and thereby provide clear models for communities to emulate in their efforts to restore self-governance. This would be a mistake on many grounds. However, I do suggest that ethnographic efforts can point to themes that can be explored in the debates within communities about where they should head.[2]

Perhaps the most thoughtful and interesting effort at using ethnographic materials to address contemporary justice was carried out in 1989–90 by the Northwest Intertribal Court System, a service provider for a consortium of tribal courts. Academics, lawyers, and elders worked together, and I provide this as an example of the contemporary discussion about justice within Coast Salish communities and the interplay with ethnographic materials. The NICS project "aimed to provide a background to the tribes and their tribal court systems and problematize how disputes were handled traditionally and how these processes and behaviors changed over time" (NICS 1991a:2). The NICS study is unable to reconcile its picture of conformity to cultural norms with the failure to conform or to resolve disputes, as indicated by the presence of ongoing blood feuding. The approach underplays the persistent theme of competition and struggle over resources and status within and between Coast Salish communities and individuals. Despite the conservatism of the ethnographic materials for the area, struggles do show up in descriptions of intercommunity gambling, in thinly disguised mock violence between antagonistic guests at potlatches, in episodic seizure of slaves and marriage partners, in village fissions, in the spiritual murder of those not yet strong with their spirit powers, in "evil doctoring" (the use of spiritual gifts for malevolent purposes), and in accusations of the slave status of someone's ancestors.

The authors of the NICS report are not unaware of conflict, but they acknowledge and address the undercurrents of violence and competition with a functionalist twist, observing that "Gambling and other challenge contests and games may also have served to alleviate tensions between families and communities" (NICS 1991b:45). But this, too, reflects the intellectual predispositions of the period in which much of the ethnographic writing occurred. For instance, Marion Smith, an ethnographer who wrote in 1940 that gambling was a substitute for fighting among south Puget Salish, is cited to support the view. The NICS report notes that the prestige of potlatch hosts was lost if serious trouble broke out between guests, although the literature suggests that, nonetheless, this happened and continues to happen today. The report quotes Smith's description of a *xadsitl*—"crowding against you"— that occurred as guests arrived at a potlatch. "The leader or warrior sang his power song and others joined in. According to Smith, each singer was calling on his power to protect against hostile shamans and to provide protection for the women and children. This was seen as offensive rather than defensive behavior." Further,

> In such situations men lined up along the landing place to receive the newcomers. These men were generally of one guest-group and the host and his followers and the other guests who might have already gathered did not participate, they watched, ready to interfere if occasion demanded. The waiting line held a pole parallel to the beach to be used in a tug-of-war with the landing group. In attempting to push each other across the goal line the contestants not only grasped the pole but tried to loosen each other's grip, cutting their opponents' hands with knives, pulling hair, etc. This contest sometimes became so serious that persons were badly wounded or killed. In any case, the losers 'felt bad and they gave presents to wipe out the stain.' (Smith 1940:108–109, quoted in NICS 1991b:44–45).

The NICS summary report concludes, however, that previously society was primarily cooperative. One passage reveals the documents' focus on consensus and cooperative coexistence: "The way in which the pre-treaty Salish societies were organized minimized open disputing and emphasized a cooperative coexistence that was essential to the survival of the family and village. With a strong community consensus about standards of behavior, various forms of indirect social control, rather than regulations and sanctions, pressured people to control their behavior." Other passages connected family discipline and training with group cooperation: "The family was the most important social group. When conflict arose within a family, every effort was made to resolve the issue within the family. Dispute resolution was learned from birth. Proper attitude and behavior were taught—primarily by elders—by example, lecture, storytelling and recounting of family history. Story telling, history and advice that was passed from generation to generation within the families ensured the continuity of tradition and identity." Further, "Children were trained from an early age in the qualities that led to continuity and flexibility within the communities. They learned to respect their elders and teachers, to refrain from boastfulness, and to value qualities of self-discipline, self-control, generosity, peaceful attitude and hospitality. Their training prepared them for their role in a society that was structured to minimize open expression of dispute" (NICS 1991a:4–5).

In these passages the significant phrase is the fear of *open* displays of hostility or dispute, which was avoided to a degree by the use of coded, oblique language in public oratory. These passages do not treat the issue of expressions of covert hostility, such as spiritual harm done through shamanic practice or even secretive efforts to harm others. Sally Snyder (1964), for example, notes the occasional effort to disguise aggressive actions, which could then, potentially, be found out by spiritual measures such as the use of the *skedelich* spirit boards.

The report's discussion makes a particular reading of the ethnographic literature concerning hierarchy in which persistent inequality is referred to, but not disagreement over rank. Winter ceremonials are mentioned as the time for putting aside difficulties in order to "pay tribute to their relationship with their spirit power" (NICS 1991b:19). However, contests between antagonistic spirit dancers are not mentioned, nor the dangers that coexist for humans in their personal and collective relationships with nonhuman beings.

Shamans are described within the benign context of "social control," a term that dismisses the sources and objects of domination. Their use of power is described as generally socially approved and operating within a "practical" ethical system that releases a shaman from blame if his "power went out of control," although, it is noted, if he caused too many deaths, he might be killed himself (NICS 1991b:23). This killing of shamans is reported widely among Coast Salish communities. This section also notes the likelihood that "violent bullies" who wronged their own family or village would "die soon" (23), although community stories reveal instances in which this did not happen and bullies continued to dominate communities that remained frightened of their physical and spiritual powers. An example of this is the story of the "Agassiz boy," noted in Duff (1952:42) and still told in various forms today. In this story a boy killed his sister's child and subsequently attacked travelers, killing for pleasure. His relatives at Agassiz disbanded their village and moved to the south side of the river about 1840 (as summarized in J. Miller 1999a:157).

The emphasis in the ethnographic literature and in elders' discourses on "quiet" leadership and on leading by example distracts attention away from the issues of how domination works and how subordination is experienced, issues that have received critical attention in social theory (Foucault 1979). The NICS report notes, for example: "Leaders had qualities that lent them authority and caused others to call on them for help. Stern provides examples of how people chosen to represent a family, to end feuds and personal quarrels, or to mediate a quarrel between spouses, were good speakers. . . . A leader never referred to himself as wealthy or important but in fact might belittle himself. From childhood, there was the teaching that it was improper to boast" (B. Stern 1969:72–73).

In this case the absence of boasting and the public use of coded language to ostensibly belittle oneself are confused with the absence of the exercise of power. A better case can be made that the mastery of oratory allows one to claim the right to exercise authority, and ultimately the power to impose one's own viewpoint, through culturally appropriate appeals to modesty. These claims to modesty are not to be taken as literal statements of the leader's self-assessment (nor did the speaker's audience make this mistake), but, rather, are themselves the tools of leadership and power (Duff 1952:80 implies something like this without developing it). Presentation of the self as humble left others to take precautions because "things were and never are what they seemed to be" (J. Miller 1999:146). Indeed, the report's reference to charisma disguises and naturalizes the play of power by implying that the exercise of charisma (noted on p. 34) is unambiguous and uncontested. Collins's commentary on the Upper Skagit "quiet leader" is cited to underscore this point: "A sia'p [upper class] showed that he deserved his title by behaving in a special way. He was not aggressive or disagreeably forceful. He was slow to take offense and display anger and often acted as a peacemaker within the family" (Collins 1950:334, cited in NICS 1991b:35).

A passage that cites Collins to convey the point that "people took time to consider the matter before deciding" (NICS 1991b:36) instead reveals something quite different. Collins, writing about councils called to "settle differences," indirectly points to the contradiction between an ideology of egalitarianism and the authoritarianism implicit in the pervasive hierarchy: "Anyone could speak for as long as he or she wished. *In actual practice only certain persons were likely to speak* since there was a tradition of formal oratory in which not all persons were skilled. These were more likely to be men than women" (Collins 1974:112–113, cited in NICS 1991b:36, emphasis mine).

In addition, leaders are described as emerging unscathed from the social field around the axes of birth, charisma, wealth, and ability (NICS 1991b:34), but not the politics of leadership and the undercurrents of dispute and contention that surround leaders, sometimes through their whole life or longer. Collins (1974) reported, and contemporary community members recount, for example, that one Upper Skagit leader was murdered because of differences of opinion even though he had dominated community life.

Finally, because distinctions of rank and class are naturalized in the document, the problem of social mobility, and the irritants this presents, are not considered. Ethnographic materials suggest that social mobility was limited and that a change in status to the upper class was not ordinarily available in one's own lifetime (Suttles 1987). The concentration of ethnographic material that shows the persistence of concern for social status suggests that issues of social hierarchy must have been significant and limits to social mobility must have been deeply felt and the source of conflict. More generally, then, the issue of stratification is treated as unproblematic and from the perspective of cultural continuity rather than that of conflict, domination, and subordination. While the NICS report indicates that there must have been conflict that was addressed by leaders and in councils, it does not purport to show the sorts of conflict or the *causes and sources of conflict.* The report thereby fails to reveal the ways in which those who exercised power and authority were implicated and the ways subordinated community members responded.

At present there appears to be political advantage in contrasting indigenous ideas of justice with those of the mainstream system, a stance that both reflects the problems of individual indigenous people facing the mainstream legal system in disproportionate numbers and supports the argument for separate, indigenized or indigenous institutions of governance and justice. Ultimately, I argue, this collusion between anthropological ancestors and predecessors and contemporary indigenous people is to no one's advantage, although there is a strong temptation to believe there is. Although this is central to my argument, I treat this in much more detail elsewhere (B. Miller 2001) and can only suggest the nature of this problem here. In brief, much of the discourse about justice, particularly among the Coast Salish of Canada as opposed to within the United States, features simplified language that obscures the nuance, the real strength, of earlier practice. The period of colonialism and the present-day period of renaissance of governance have produced a process of truncation and diminution of prior cultural practice; communities have long since produced paper-thin versions of their own practices for consumption by the outside world. Historian Alexandra Harmon (1998) notes that this process began by the middle of the 19th century among the Puget Salish, and it is certainly the case today.

Such discourses are based on a normative, consensus notion of culture that writes out conflict and is devoid of agency. Further, these discourses are at odds with present-day community diversity and the fact that justice practices must address difficulty and dissensus. Conflict is localized as internal or personal within healing and counseling discourses, rather than as systemic or social. Indigenous justice is often deduced as the opposite of Western justice in a process of binary logic that distorts in both directions. Elders are unproblematically treated as the source of resolution, a circumstance that overlooks how elders themselves are and were situated in family and community hierarchy and the practice of domination. A current problem around the creation of justice initiatives within the Coast Salish world is that prior culture is sometimes treated as Edenic, a response that assigns the topic of justice to the replication of culture. In this discourse people did the right thing because they were well trained and because to do otherwise brought shame on the family. Justice, then, is more about the avoidance of problems and of conflict, and less about what was done when things went seriously wrong.

Within anthropology, the few efforts to reconstruct the legal or justice concepts and practices suffer, as is true of the larger field of the anthropology of law concerning indigenous peoples, from the problems of accounts that idealize earlier culture or in which the processes whereby conflicts were treated were cleaned up in memory. Cases are thought to give principles, itself a conceptual problem. But the greater problem is that ethnographers just did not choose to explore this issue in detail in their publications. This is less true of field notes, however, and these give a much greater sense of the sorts of conflicts that existed in earlier periods, of the difficulties people had in resolving them, and of the means that were available to the reestablishment of peace under conditions of breach. It's clear from a look at the notes of early- and mid-20th-century ethnographers who worked in Coast Salish communities, such as Elmendorf, Snyder, Duff, and Barnett, that problems often were not resolved, that blood feuding was common, and that people gave very serious attention to how to both avoid and resolve problems. Recently Sonny McHalsie, Stó:lō Nation cultural adviser, presented a paper about the history of Stó:lō culture in a conference session entitled "A Community Forged in Conflict," an unusual recognition of these issues. My thoughts concerning Coast Salish justice concepts and practices are that they required great care for the nuance of society—of class, location, privilege, insult, knowledge. They were not crude processes that can be easily codified or described. They were personalized and case-dependent.

To start in on my own project, I must reframe my own statement of problem to encompass a more radical understanding of social practice and talk not merely of the maintenance of social relations and the restoration of peace, but of the processes of domination and the play of power in the pursuit of justice. Second, I wish to note that much of the Coast Salish ethnographic material was recorded in the period when indigenous communities no longer had a meaningful capacity of self-regulation. People were no longer free to move as individuals or as groups in times of difficulty, for example, nor were they able to escape the reach of colonial authority when major disputes arose. External authority had long usurped these powers, and many of the collaborators had only a dim picture of life before the regimentation of reserves and reservations, police and military, and of the chaotic circumstances of the violent period after contact when groups were dislodged and reserves were established. While prior forms of justice practice were not gone completely, they were attenuated and overlaid by new practices and concepts.

This last point raises an issue I cannot address in detail here, but one I wish to note. The experiences of the various indigenous peoples who voiced their views to ethnographers over the decades cannot be held to be equivalent. The Allen brothers who worked with Elmendorf, for example, were born in the middle of the 19th century, and their views reflect what they witnessed in the epidemic violence of that period of rapid displacement and what they were told by those born early in the century or in the 18th century. Those Stó:lō working with Duff in the 1940s grew up in a different area and experienced a very different world, that of long-established reserves. I now turn to my own rereading of the ethnographic literature to point to issues that can be considered in emergent Coast Salish practice of justice. In particular, I take note of the issues of power and social hierarchy and the concept of the self.

Theories of Power, the Self, Hierarchy, and Coast Salish Justice

Despite having noted these reservations about making claims about aboriginal law in the Coast Salish region, I venture some characterizations. An adequate theory of aboriginal justice depends on an articulation of the ideas of the self, of the social individual, of place, and of local theories of power. In the early–reservation period, and to some extent today, Coast Salish cultural ideas of the self have emphasized humans' subordination to, and dependence on, more powerful, nonhuman forces. These forces, some of which are anthropomorphized beings and others not, are potentially beneficial and dangerous and sometimes form relationships with humans who may be "favored by power" (Jenness 1955; Kew 1990). But the nature of human relations with nonhumans is never fully revealed to others, and the source and extent of their power are thereby unknown (Amoss 1977). The human being is made up of several components, these being the body; the soul, which only some can see, which continues after death, and which can be lost; the breath/vitality/life, which is not a condition, which can be disassociated from the body, thereby creating a state of illness, and which can be returned; and the shadow/reflection, which also can be lost or stolen. Although everyone has all four components, they are not well integrated in the young, the feeble, the ill, and others who are consequently vulnerable to spiritual dangers.

There is another part of the self that not all acquire: *Sil'ye,* the guardian spirit power. This power is gained in various ways, coming to some unbidden and to others through the rigorous process of fasting, training, and purification necessary to become acceptable prior to undergoing a quest for the spirit power. Once a relationship is established, a human becomes a different kind of human being. This relationship is invoked in the complex known as Spirit Dancing, or *Syowen,* a term that refers to the visible aspects of the nonhuman world given to humans. The initiate into Spirit Dancing draws closer to the nonhuman sphere and, eventually, gains new powers and abilities once the relationship becomes properly managed. The private relationship with the spirit power becomes dangerous if spoken of, and if the spirit is offended, and upset in the relationship can cause the death of the human partner. A healthy person, then, knows who they are (their self) and maintains a proper spirit relationship.

Coast Salish concepts of power follow from these conceptions of the self as a spiritual, psychological state, and of the individual located within society. Power is not seen as a property of an abstract entity, such as society, which might act on individuals or groups, or of social institutions, such as the family, but rather as a manifestation of largely unspoken human-nonhuman relations. Some individuals, however, were and are known publicly to occupy particular social roles as a consequence of their recognizable spirit powers. These include, among others, warriors, shamans, carvers, and public speakers. Although these ideas describe concepts widely shared in earlier generations, they still influence present-day conceptions and are still directly taught in the Winter Dance houses that are the centers of Spirit Dancing throughout Coast Salish territory.

The locus of power in individuals or nonhuman beings, rather than institutions or national entities, complicates the idea of domination by a social group. In addition, the authority of an individual was not thought to be easily generalizable; efficacy depended on circumstance, and someone skilled in one area of life was not necessarily an overall leader (Harmon 1998:22). Virtually all appropriate adults had access to spiritual power of some sort; these powers included the ability to acquire wealth, gamble successfully, cure, hold one's breath underwater to repair fishing weirs, eat prodigious amounts without manifesting, and seduce women, among others. Those without spiritual helpers were thought to be insignificant and weak. But because spirits might associate with anyone, even those without "advice" (including proper spiritual training), prudent people avoided giving offence to anyone. Amoss wrote that "Coast Salish Indians are . . . genuinely afraid of offending those whom they believe have strong spirit powers, because the spirits may take umbrage at the insult offered their human partners and re-taliate without the conscious participation of the injured person" (1977:134). One interpreter concluded that power "was not so much a means to domi-nate others as insurance against domination" (Harmon 1998:23). Bierwert commented on Coast Salish concepts of power and the lack of intersubjec-tive agreement that continues to characterize life and that imposes limits on the exercise of power: "Coast Salish social structures have been com-paratively decentered, a phenomenon attributable to the history of colonial oppression, but also reflecting laterally distributed power. . . . To use post-modern terms, the culture is destabilized and decentered; to use more classic terms, power is diffuse, laws and characterizations are applied ad hominem, and judgements are ad hoc" (1999:5–6).

But one must not assume that there was no operation of domination among the Coast Salish. Indeed, efforts to avoid domination suggest the presence of efforts to dominate. Over a long period, longer than the histori-cal frame of reference here, one could read Coast Salish society as oscillating between periods characterized by efforts to centralize and dominate and re-actions against this. Thom (1995), for example, connected the rise and fall of the practice of building elaborate burial mounds to a period of consoli-dation of regional authority by the political elite and subsequent successful resistance to this consolidation. McHalsie (1999) has argued that both a class system and social conflict are deeply rooted within Stó:lō history, and oral histories provide a glimpse of powerful leaders capable of controlling and regulating others.

The social field was not level in the historic period, and the local play of power by dominant members of society must also be taken into account in considering prior justice. In the Coast Salish world, domination did not ordinarily take the form of physical intimidation or direct attack. Rather, it was manifested through indirection, subtle intimidation, and efforts to con-trol public discourses about appropriate behavior. Duff (1952:80) observed, concerning what he called the "Upper Stalo," that birth into high-ranked family "constituted a tremendous advantage." Such a birth brought control of wealth, the possibility of important ancestral names being bestowed, and the opportunity to train for positions of respect. In addition, Duff wrote, Stó:lō beliefs were that children inherited the characteristics of parents and that the families of great people were thought to be superior and worthy of deference. He notes that despite the expected humility and mock denial of status by the elite, "there was never any doubt in anyone's mind that high-rank people were superior individuals. All children were thoroughly taught who were their social equals, and who were their inferiors" (1952:80). Barnett (n.d., field notes, 1935–36, folder 1–7) gives the sense of this by indicating that the practice of the payment of blankets in the event of a murder was not extended to "low people," who were said to be just good for "clam digging and drying fish."

It is worth noting that this domination, as elsewhere, regularly was quietly contested by subordinated people in such forms as storytelling and in the constant monitoring of elite people to see if they could maintain their propriety. For example, elite nonhuman beings (stand-ins for the local human elite) are revealed as pretentious and without the knowledge and bearing they claim in the oral traditions such as the story of Crow's marriage. Crow's claims to upper-class standing are belied by her reliance on slaves to make her marriage arrangements and on her crude voice (see Bierwert 1996; for a fuller development of this theme see Holden 1976).

For the Coast Salish, then, power was not ordinarily consolidated in social institutions that served to protect and reproduce the advantage of the elite, nor were there social boundaries insulating the elite from continual interaction with the non-elite. Power was regularly contested, and the capacity of others could be underestimated only at one's own peril. While power was thought to be an attribute of individuals with strong spirit helpers, access to power was not simply or easily passed intergenerationally. Power had both spiritual and material dimensions, and power differentials reflected raw demographic variables, primarily the size of one's family network, in addition to control over important resources such as salmon procurement stations and the personal abilities of leaders (Kew 1976). But important differences existed between individuals and families at any given moment, as indicated by the elites' abilities to influence community affairs and to impose their viewpoint in defining and redefining community goals and values. Differences in power were displayed publicly as well, in the layout of longhouses (the location of family quarters indicating status), in the conduct of potlatches, in control over important resources, and in deference shown at public gatherings.

Ancestors of the members of the current communities created justice practices that accounted for these views of the self, the social individual, and of the nature of human power. They employed a range of sanctions to control behavior and restore communities in the event of a breach. These sanctions included restitution, ostracism, social pressures, and even violent recrimination and are well documented in ethnographic literature. Public ceremonies were, and continue to be, carried out in the process of the public debate and resolution of conflicts. In addition, as the NICS report emphasized, the region has been characterized by a cultural emphasis on the avoidance of conflict through proper training in the absence of coercive authority in order to avoid disruption of economic activities. Ethnographic materials suggest that local kin groups bore responsibility for the behavior of members, and that damage to the personnel or property of another family constituted grounds for compensation. Meetings were held between senior members of the families to work out the terms of compensation, but if these were unsuccessful, rivalries or blood feuds could develop. The offender also had to undergo seclusion in the woods in order to fast and bathe to obtain purity and become acceptable to society. Although the ethnographic materials emphasize compensation in the event of a killing (accidental or otherwise), this may in some measure reflect the transformed, dangerous, more violent environment in the middle and late 19th century, and these processes also applied to other difficulties between families.

Although there are significant risks in making comparisons to Western legal concepts, there is some advantage in considering the issues of guilt and intention from the vantage point of social hierarchy. Perhaps the closest ethnographic examination of the intersections of justice and social hierarchy is found in the work of Sally Snyder (1964, n.d.), who combined her ethnographic work in the 1940s and early 1950s with an analysis of folkloric reflections on community values and practices. Snyder's Puget Sound materials derived from her work with elders from Swinomish, Samish, Lower Skagit, Upper Skagit, and other communities. In 1953 a Swinomish elder told Snyder a story about his own father concerning an episode that brought relations between members of two groups (Swinomish and Stillaguamish) to a dangerous point.

> When HbE's father was a small boy he was once walking home along the beach at dusk. He was half lost, and came to a Stillaguamish camp in front of which he had to pass. Nightguards had already been posted

there, and the child skulked along the shoreline in hopes that they would not see him. But they did, and his suspicious activity led them to think that he was trying to steal a canoe. They held him at their camp overnight. The next morning a man there recognized the boy and warned the others that they had made a grave mistake, that he was the son of important people and that they [the boy's people] would soon find out why he was detained — as a captive for slave-trade. The Stilla-guamish hurriedly released the boy and were ready to face a charge against them. Soon the boy's family arrived at their camp bringing a canoeload of valuables to the Stillaguamish and obsequious apologies for having a youngster foolish enough to lose his way at night. That was, of course, an insinuation of the Stillaguamish's guilt — one which could have been played up as an abduction and not a natural error. But all of this was supererogatory for the already anxious Stillaguamish who accepted the Skagits' offerings and then gave their visitors in return far more than they had received. (S. Snyder 1964:433–434)

This story reveals both the critical role of class and status in Coast Salish society and the pragmatic side of justice. Upper-class people in this tell-ing overawe lower-ranked people and dominate their thoughts and actions without restoring to force. Here the critical issue was not the boy's guilt or his intentions (apparently no one, either his family or his captors, made any attempt to determine if he had or had not tried to steal a canoe), but rather, power relations. But there is a second issue, namely the costs to elite people anxious to maintain their position in society. Snyder's field notes provide more detail about this episode, and the importance of this story is the in-terpretation given it by the elder while speaking to Snyder. He said that his grandfather's motives were that he "wanted to keep their record clean; to wipe out the accusation, rather than the crime or the supposed crime" (n.d.). Elmendorf (1993:192) provides a similar example of a Skokomish man who paid the father of a wronged slave in order to avoid trouble with the Klallam.

Snyder's field notes, recorded in 1953 with a knowledgeable Swimonish elder, provides insight into the related issue of intentionality: "If a [murder] is accidental a slayer will sacrifice some of his things as a sort of apology to that family of the deceased and then there will be no ill-feelings towards them. If you have intentionally committed a murder and still 'apologize' to seem innocent of intention, someone would know you had ill-feeling towards that person, he would still revenge." Another Swinomish elder told

Snyder in 1953: "Accidents had to be covered by payment, whether accidental or intentional. Intentional murders turn into long grudges between families, and a feeling to get even." Yet another Swinomish elder told Snyder that "with theft, if you didn't know who stole, you let it go, because you couldn't prove anything." The elder noted that if the murderer was not known, the wronged party would hire a person to find out. This was done spiritually, according to the way the *skedelich* (animated spirit boards) was interpreted. "This is just between the family and the hired party." This implies that the evidence of guilt produced spiritually did not create the grounds for demanding compensation or asserting guilt.

Snyder's work gives a picture of the occasional employment of secrecy, both in the commission of wrongdoing and in response. One elder gave an example of a murder within a family that was revenged by someone outside of the family "without the other parties knowing it." The same elder noted that intermarried families having a quarrel (blood feud) would "usually hire an Indian doctor to get rid of the guilty party, or hire a woman to poison, get him without shooting." The implication is that shooting would be more public and cause further difficulties. This elder also told Snyder that "One can shoot another who has gotten off his own territory and no one will know." A present-day Stó:lō elder pointed out that "I've heard stories too, where one or two people have had something happen to them while they're in the wrong people's territory but they won't be able to prove so they won't be able to do anything about it really because they can't prove why that person was harmed or injured or killed. But that thing is there, that maybe you could say, 'well that person was hunting in the wrong territory, see what happened?' But no one could say or find out how that person died" (B. Miller, notes).

Barnett, working with Squamish elders in the 1930s, noted that the practice of a face-saving potlatch ("wash blood") was only held if a fight was witnessed or if the damage was apparent. If the fight was not witnessed, the father of the combatant would "pay maybe $10," and the injured party would "give maybe $5," at which point, the combatants would "shake hands, just like married" (Barnett, n.d., field notes, 1935–36, folder 1–5). Similarly, he noted that if a man sickened and died there would be no "wash blood" unless the death was accidental or violent and was witnessed.

Ethnographic materials provide some insights into what might be known as rules of evidence and the use of precedent, to again make analogy to Western legal categories. Although the terms are foreign, the ideas are not. Coast Salish people, in common with others, faced the issue of what might be said about a given dispute or case of wrongdoing, by whom, and what weight might be assigned to a particular person's views of the matter. Present-day Puget Sound elders point out that people were free to make their views known. Yet, if some people didn't want to talk publicly they could hire a public speaker to talk for them. Stories of family and village history, genealogy, and legends could be presented to provide guidelines for resolving current disputes (NICS 1991b). However, these histories were not referred to for rules of precedent. A problem was not resolved in the same manner as a previous problem because of the implicit understanding that no two circumstances are precisely alike.

These details concerning the relative lack of emphasis on guilt, intention, and precedent can be connected to Coast Salish ideas of power, illness, and the control of will, particularly the notion that individuals can harm others through their failure to control their thoughts. Individuals must therefore guard against their injurious projections onto others (Swinomish 1991). This harm can be unintentional or intentional and yet produce similar results. In some cases a spirit helper of an individual has been said to act on the emotions of its human partner to harm enemies. These ideas explain the limited cultural emphasis on guilt and intention as guiding principles of justice since one is thought not to be at fault for such harm, although it is an indicator of a poor upbringing and a failure to consolidate one's relationship with a spirit helper. Because spiritual power might be exercised inadvertently in some instances, justice practices typically focus on repairing relations between families rather than punishing the individual. Stories reveal, however, that individuals might be restrained from raising further harm or even murdered by family members if it is apparent they cannot or will not stop. None of the discussions of justice appear to suggest any formal sense of precedent, then, because of the spiritual distinctiveness of each situation and because of the ambiguity of oral materials and the ability of tellers to apply them in a variety of ways.

Conclusion

Members of contemporary Coast Salish communities, in common with other indigenous peoples, have found value in examining older ethnographic materials that may contain insights into prior justice practices. But few of the anthropologists who worked in these communities in the first half of the 20th century gave much attention to the problems of community justice in their analysis and published materials. Further, what they did write was derived from a salvage paradigm and aimed at considering conflict within the constraints of a normative, rule-bound society. In many cases richer detail resides in field notes. These materials are useful in suggesting thematic elements of prior practice that can be, and are, usefully employed in the debates within communities about the directions they wish to take regarding self-government and justice.

On the other hand, the conservatively biased ethnographic interpretations have been employed by community members anxious to distance the practices of their community from those of the dominant society and to depict their own cultures as rule-bound, predominantly driven by spiritual values, and, ultimately, conformist. But because justice and law are not simply spiritual in nature, but rather are political as well, they concern defining crime and providing or denying access to legal processes. Disguising the workings of power and authority, I have argued, undermines the capacity of the new indigenous justice systems to achieve legitimization in the eyes of community members and to provide a real forum for the identification and resolution of problems. Much of the current discourse about justice is built on faulty notions, or at least public claims, of an earlier, Edenic society that cannot be emulated and that are ultimately unnecessary and self-defeating. I have further argued that the present-day discourses obscure much of what might be of value from earlier Coast Salish concepts and practices of justice.

These concepts are not forgotten by community members, however, and remain a significant resource for emergent formal systems in addition to anthropologists' field notes. In fact, in August of 1999 a Stó:lō transformer rock near the Fraser River was inadvertently destroyed by the Canadian Pacific Railroad, and commentary by Sonny McHalsie and elders published in the *Vancouver Sun* emphasized the role of the rock in community justice through its importance as a reminder to "do good."

Notes

1. Diversionary justice refers here to justice initiatives undertaken by indigenous communities in partnership with the mainstream society. These initiatives work

in a variety of ways; in sentencing circles, for example, elders, family members, and other members of a community advise court officials regarding sentencing. In all these initiatives, however, jurisdiction remains with the provincial/state or federal court.

2. Contemporary Coast Salish communities located on Vancouver Island, adjacent portions of mainland British Columbia, the lower Fraser River valley, southwestern Washington State, Puget Sound, coastal Washington, and northwestern Oregon are engaged in an array of new justice initiatives. These practices are all built on the concept of tradition and in the idiom of kinship, but they are radically different in nature. Over the last several years I have directed my attention to three among the several Coast Salish justice programs: the tribal court system of the Upper Skagit and other tribes of western Washington State, the justice initiatives of the Stó:lō Nation of the lower mainland of British Columbia, and the now discontinued South Island Justice Project of the bands of Vancouver Island. All have relied, to some measure, on anthropological materials in addition to the words of present-day elders and other community members in their construction. They have all struggled with the problem of contextualizing conflict and the enduring issue of the relationships between the individual, the constituent families, the tribe (or band), and the governance institutions that oversee regional interests.

WHITHER THE EXPERT WITNESS
Anthropology in the Post-Delgamuukw Courtroom

Daniel L. Boxberger

The Supreme Court decision in *Delgamuukw v. British Columbia* (3 SCR 1010 [1997]) established the validity of oral history as evidence in cases concerning issues of aboriginal rights. This marks a reversal of court procedures as have developed in Native rights cases in both the United States and Canada. In this essay I approach *Delgamuukw* as a turning point in the role of anthropological expert witness testimony. In keeping with the theme of this volume on assessments and perspectives, I see this decision as part of a process—a process of change in the nature of expert witness testimony, the nature of anthropological interpretation, and the nature of the flow of knowledge.

Over the past half century anthropologists, especially ethnohistorians, have assumed the role of expert witness in cases concerning Native land and resource rights. In fact, some anthropologists have become professional expert witnesses, devoting much of their careers to research and preparation of reports on behalf of tribes, law firms, and government agencies. Having served in the capacity of expert witness in two dozen proceedings in tribal, state, federal, and provincial courts, and having prepared testimony on behalf of tribes, individuals, law firms, and state and federal agencies, I have logged considerable experience in the role of expert witness. While not trained in law, as a participant in the legal process I have become familiar with court proceedings and especially how expert witness testimony is regarded in both U.S. and Canadian court systems. In addition I have had occasion to see how the role of expert witness is regarded by Native peoples and by fellow anthropologists. What follows is an analysis of expert witness testimony on the Northwest Coast, beginning with the first Native rights cases in the late 1800s through the Indian claims of the 1950s to 1970s and then anticipating how recent developments in the nature of expert witness testimony may be affected by the new sentiment concerning oral histories, both within the courtroom and in Native communities. Coupled with this analysis is a discussion of oral tradition as evidence and as property, within Native communities, the field of anthropology, and in courts of law.

For the last 25 years my research has focused on the political and economic aspects of Native American resource use and control (see, especially, Boxberger 1980, 1988a, 1988b, 1993, 1994, 1998, 2000a, 2000b). Throughout this time my view has changed little in respect to the political and economic factors involved in Native American adaptations to colonialism. The school of thought that envisions Native American societies as internal colonies resulting in dependent segments of the dominant society has, I think, powerful explanatory use. Although this approach has undergone considerable criticism in recent years (see, e.g., Wilkins 1993), it nevertheless has demonstrated a lasting contribution to the understanding of Native American underdevelopment (see, especially, Jorgensen 1972, 1978, 1990; Aberle 1983; R. White 1983). Where this approach has generally failed, however, is in the attempt to understand ideological components of cultural adaptation. The dependency approach relies on an analysis of external forces to understand the political economy and has been generally incapable of or uninterested in evaluating the internal modes of explanation, understanding, and transmission based within the continuing traditions of Native communities. As Roseberry (1996:77) has pointed out, we must look at hegemonic relationships as more than material and political; these relationships are embedded in power relations that operate within a process of domination and struggle. Within Northwest Coast Native communities a few key issues have been the central focus of this relationship of power and struggle. These issues have focused on land, resources, and self-determination. Since much of the discussion of natural resource use and control takes place within the arena of the court system this seems a reasonable place to begin this analysis.

In accordance with the approach I have followed until now, I view the use of oral tradition by expert witnesses as a form of intellectual hegemony. It is a process of usurpation of knowledge necessitated by the exigencies of land and resource claims and facilitated by the assumption of the role of *expert* by anthropologists. Certainly anthropologists bring certain analytical skills and theoretical and methodological expertise to their work; however, the type of information the courts need to make a decision is almost always based on descriptive data. One of the greatest contributions anthropology has made in this endeavor has been in the adoption of historical methods to supplement traditional anthropological methods. In fact, the field of ethnohistory emerged in response to the needs of Native claims. Although documentary evidence has played an important role in the submission of evidence and is the type of evidence that courts prefer, it is invariably supplemented by traditional ethnographic data collected either by other anthropologists or by the expert witnesses themselves. Paradoxically the field of ethnohistory has undergone a transformation in recent years with a shift away from overreliance on documentary evidence. The approaches that offer an analysis of both written and oral tradition argue that the symbolic elements embedded in both are engaged in a social process (Cruikshank 1992:21). The privileged status of documents as "factual evidence" as opposed to oral traditions as "mythology" has come under intense scrutiny. In the court system, however, it has long been standard practice to filter evidence obtained from Native testimony through *experts*. It is this type of intellectual property that has been filtered through the anthropologist as expert to give it validity, and the Western court system has empowered the anthropologist in this action. In this context tribal histories (read *knowledge*) might be viewed as a commodity, and like political and economic domination where Native peoples have lost control of land and resources, bit by bit Native peoples have been excluded from an active voice in presenting their own history and controlling the use of their traditional knowledge. On the Northwest Coast recent interpretive work (see, e.g., Bierwert 1999; Harkin 1997a; Kan 1989b, 1999; J. Miller 1997, 1999a) has entered into analyses that engage Native narratives in a dialogic process of interpretation of postcontact history. Tapping into Native ways of *knowing,* these approaches have reassessed the history of the colonial experience on the Northwest Coast, casting Native peoples as active participants instead of helpless bystanders in creating their own histories. Drawing on indigenous texts as well as the documentary record, this trend is an attempt to critically analyze the symbolic and ideological meanings embedded in Native interpretations of history. Given the precedent in *Delgamuukw,* suddenly these scholarly exercises take on new import as ways of translating knowledge into the context of positivist law where evidence is viewed as objective reality, and most commonly objective reality based on the evidentiary existence of documented history. How is indigenous knowledge, which is by nature oral, and as oral tradition subject to change and reinterpretation, to be evaluated? Whose standards will be used to validate oral tradition? The expert witness? The elders in the community? Tribal government? The individual, the family, the clan? The judge or jury?

It has become commonplace in North America to regard knowledge of sacred sites, the use of flora, and religious practices as intellectual property worthy of protection. Why is this same protection not extended to stories, histories, clan traditions, and other forms of intellectual property? This begs two questions. How did this come about? And how will it be affected by the changing trends in the nature of research and, in particular, research conducted for legal evidence?

Oral Traditions and Oral History

> Notwithstanding the challenges created by the use of oral histories as proof of historical facts, the laws of evidence must be adapted in order that this type of evidence can be accommodated and placed on an equal footing with the types of historical evidence that courts are familiar with, which largely consists of documentary evidence. (*Delgamuukw v. British Columbia* [1997])

This memorable conclusion has summed up an issue that has been going on outside of the court system for some time now. That oral history should be regarded as "real" history is old news to Native peoples and ethnohistorians. It has, however, been a transition a long time in coming. In an oft-quoted 1917 article Lowie chastised his colleagues for considering oral tradition as historical fact. Subsequent intellectual "giants" in the discipline such as Malinowski, Radcliffe-Brown, and Lévi-Strauss saw oral traditions as useful for understanding the psychology of other peoples, not as reliable portrayals of past events. In the early years of ethnohistory, documentary evidence was privileged over memory ethnography (Krech 1991:347). These general perceptions have held true until fairly recently when reassessments of oral traditions for the historical meaning imbedded in them have become a major focus of ethnohistorians (Steinhart 1989; Cohen 1989; Cruikshank 1990, 1998). For the purposes of this essay I use Vansina's distinction between oral history and oral tradition, not because I necessarily agree with this distinction, but because I think it has utility for understanding how oral testimony has been regarded in courts of law and by governmental agencies making administrative decisions that impact Native communities. "The sources of oral historians are reminiscences, hearsay, or eyewitness accounts about events and situations which are contemporary, that is, which occurred during the lifetime of the informants. This differs from oral traditions in that oral traditions are no longer contemporary. They have passed from mouth to mouth, for a period beyond the lifetime of the informants" (Vansina 1985:12–13).

While the discipline of ethnohistory no longer dismisses oral histories, in a more practical sense the disregard for oral history still plays a major role in Native claims. Take, for example, the United States Bureau of Acknowledgment and Research (BAR) statement on oral history.

> Oral history is the spoken record of a group, from the mouths of its members, its non-Indian neighbors, local officials and others.
>
> You may use oral history as direct evidence for the modern period. For example, interviews with your tribe's leaders about their tribal activities during the last ten years, may be very useful evidence for showing that your tribe exists as a political entity today.
>
> You may also use oral history when people are talking about their own lifetimes. If someone came and interviewed members of your group in the 1920's or 1900's, you may use those interviews for direct evidence about those times.
>
> When people talk about what they have heard—what their grandparents told them, for example—this evidence is not as strong as personal, first-hand accounts of actual experiences. But you can use such stories about long past events as guideposts to finding written documentation. (U.S. Department of the Interior n.d.)

Similarly, the provincial court ruling that preceded *Delgamuukw*, commonly known as the McEachern decision, characterized oral history as less useful then written documents. "When I come to consider events long past, I am driven to conclude, on all the evidence, that much of the plaintiffs' historical evidence is not literally true. . . . The history of the association of these people with the territory is a crucial part of their case and its proof is replete with difficulties. The plaintiffs undertook to prove amongst other things, the state, 200 years ago, of two separate people who had different, wholly unwritten languages and cultures, who kept no records" (*Delgamuukw v. British Columbia* [1991], 79 D.L.R. (4th) 185 [B.C.S.C.]). Likewise the government's statement titled "What Is Oral History?" concerning specific and comprehensive claims in Canada considers oral history as a limited form of information, even in the wake of *Delgamuukw* (Canada, Indian Claims Commission 1999). Since these guidelines have real importance for tribes seeking recognition, settling land claims, and adjudicating aboriginal rights, the estimation of the value of oral histories requires serious consideration. The reality is that the written record, even if incorrect, carries more weight than oral traditions. Thus we see the situation where an oral tradition written down in the past is valid history, but that same oral tradition alive in the community today is dismissed as biased.

In 1987 the Lummi Tribe of Washington State entered into a legal proceeding to establish jurisdiction over waters abutting reservation lands (*United States v. State of Washington*, 384 F.Supp. 312, Subproceeding 86-7 [1987]). The area in question included shellfish grounds and a rich fishing area that has traditionally provided a mainstay of the Lummi salmon fishery. The State of Washington refused to recognize Lummi jurisdiction because the area in question constituted "navigable waters," and the Organic Act establishing Washington State relinquished control over navigable waters to state government. The Lummi based their claim on oral traditions that relate a visit by territorial governor Isaac I. Stevens, who was the chief negotiator for the United States government during the Point Elliott treaty negotiations of which the Lummi were signatories. According to Lummi accounts Stevens met with Lummi leaders prior to the treaty negotiations of January 1855 to discuss the creation of the reservation. Standing on a large rock on the east bank of the mouth of the Nooksack River, Stevens held out his arms pointing toward Cherry Point to the northwest and Lummi Island to the southwest. Because the southwest line constituted a boundary from Treaty Rock to the southern point of the reservation, the Lummis have always argued the waters in question were included in Stevens's promise. This is a contention that has been repeated by various actions of Lummi leadership since the 1850s. For example, in 1916 Lummis seized a non-Indian vessel fishing within the claimed waters, creating a major incident for state fisheries management (Boxberger 2000:92–93). And, of course, the 1987 case was brought about because of continued conflict with the state of Washington.

This oral tradition was submitted to the court by a Lummi elder but dismissed as hearsay. When the court was presented with transcripts from a 1919 case involving a dispute over reservation tidelands (*United States v. Romaine,*

255 F. 253 [9th Cir. 1919]) where the same tradition was related and a 1940s version of the tradition from a local history (Jeffcott 1949:33), these were accepted as evidence despite the fact that the written accounts were of oral traditions written one and two generations removed from an "eyewitness" account. As this example painfully points out, the practical application of academic arguments concerning oral and documentary evidence are weak principles in a courtroom setting.

To suggest that oral traditions constitute unchanging accounts of past events would, of course, be untenable. To suggest, however, that oral traditions have no relevance to understanding past events is also untenable. Likewise, to suggest that written accounts are consistently accurate depictions of past events is also untenable. Oral traditions are criticized because of the nature of change, that is, the assumption being that oral traditions are reinterpreted by the teller to meet contemporary needs. What this ignores is the understanding that written documents are also subject to reinterpretation based on contemporary needs.

Recent discussions of oral traditions have focused on the adaptive nature of tradition. Knowledge, as traditional knowledge, is continuously reformulated in ways that help to make sense of contemporary social and political issues (Mauzé 1997). Traditional knowledge is expressed in a context of political agendas, and for the last century on the entire Northwest Coast this context has centered on land claims, resource rights, and political autonomy. Native peoples express their knowledge in the context of a subordinate population that understands, confronts, accommodates themselves, and resists their domination within the process of domination (Roseberry 1996). As such, traditional knowledge is power. It was power in the past, but now the power of knowledge is often acted out in a legal setting. The control of knowledge constitutes the control of power. Knowledge forms the basis whereby legal decisions are made, and control of and access to land and resources are affirmed or denied. Knowledge, of course, is not just limited to the legal arena. In fact, this is the area in which it has received the least attention. There has been much discussion of the transference of knowledge from Native communities, from Vine Deloria's *Custer Died for Your Sins* (1969) to Russell Means's *Where White Men Fear to Tread* (1995). Anthropologists have been the subject of much criticism for their role in Native communities and the transference of knowledge. Undoubtedly the control of traditional knowledge, however so defined, will constitute the major issue concerning research in Native Northwest Coast communities in the immediate future.

This discrepancy is not lost on Northwest Coast Native groups. In a number of communities there are programs engaged in "repatriating" knowledge. The collection of archival data, ethnographers' field notes, audio recordings, transcripts of courtroom testimony, photographs, and published data to stock tribal archives has incorporated written forms of knowledge into the traditional knowledge base of Native communities. Often the written knowledge is treated similarly to traditional oral knowledge, such as closely guarding certain types of written information and the censuring of information that might be considered sensitive.

It might be useful to distinguish between different types of knowledge in Northwest Coast Native communities. First, there is what we might call *public knowledge*—that is, knowledge freely shared and openly discussed within the community and with outsiders. Second, there is *privileged knowledge*, which is primarily shared within a certain group, be it a kin group, such as the clan or family, or a religious group, like a secret society. Third, there is *private knowledge*, which is rarely shared with anyone, even the most intimate. Commonly this involves religious experience, such as a guardian spirit encounter. Although in the past elements of all three types of knowledge were freely shared with ethnographers, this has changed dramatically in the last 25 years as Native groups have more closely guarded privileged and private knowledge, and to a certain extent, public knowledge as well. The release of knowledge in the past was commonly justified because it was in danger of being lost if not recorded. Or in the case of the legal system, traditional knowledge was necessarily given to provide evidence for Native claims, which might be seen as similar to the process Tennant (1990:68ff) calls the "politics of survival." Recently, as many tribes and bands have begun a process of "repatriating" knowledge taken from their communities, these new materials are collected with the intent of using them in legal battles, recognizing the validity assigned to knowledge in the written form. Written knowledge has also achieved some of the same status as orally transmitted knowledge in the sense of becoming property. Even materials that are in the public domain are sometimes jealously guarded by Native groups or members of the contributor's family. The Lummi Tribe, for example, is attempting to censure portions of materials collected in the past that are considered inappropriate for public use. Some of these materials contain highly sensitive material, such as spirit songs, that were perhaps recorded without understanding that they would be widely available. Spirit songs, which reincarnate, have been sung by one person but now belong to a descendent, or the person being recorded may have sung another person's song. These materials, collected in the 1950s and 1960s, or in some cases even earlier, contain interviews with elders now gone. As was common in the day, the materials were collected without obtaining informed consent nor with any directions regarding their disposal. As a result they are considered public domain by the repositories that hold them over the protests of descendents and the Lummi Tribe (Rasmus 2001).

Collected materials are sometimes characterized in ways that downplay their significance when they are alienated from the community. We have all heard the contemporary assertion that the elders simply lied to anthropologists. Ethnographers are presented as dupes who accept as fact anything told to them. Or, conversely, anthropologists are viewed as predators who swoop down on the community, gather information, publish it, get rich, and then are never seen again.

Rather than answering the questions posed earlier in this essay, this context poses new questions. Who owns knowledge? If a consultant works with an ethnographer, and the ethnographer has permission from the band or tribal council, does this constitute the transfer of ownership of that property (knowledge)? What if the consultant dies, and the descendents have a different point of view? What if band administration changes, and as a result the understanding of the agreement changes? Given the multitude of possibilities, how is knowledge to be transmitted, used, and controlled?

The Expert Witness and the Use of Knowledge

> All that life offers any man from which to start his thinking or his striving is a fact . . . and your business as thinkers is . . . to show the rational connection between your fact and the frame of the universe. If your subject is law, the roads are plain to anthropology, the study of man. (Justice Oliver Wendell Holmes, 1886)

The anthropologist has found a niche in the courtroom. The expert testimony provided by anthropologists is vast, including forensic analysis of human remains, the nature of religious communities, racial segregation, and the "cultural defense" in criminal cases. According to Mertz (1994:1), "Professional anthropologists have special value to courtroom litigators because as a group, their expertise and methods are broad enough to enable them to perform a wide range of research while maintaining a valid scientific methodology." Certainly the most common presence of anthropologists as expert witnesses has been in cases involving Native Americans. In the cases involving Native Americans in which anthropologists have supplied expert witness testimony, including issues of religious freedom, the consequences of forced culture change, and the nature of sociopolitical groupings, cases involving land claims and rights to resources have predominated.

There has been much written in the last 50 years concerning the nature of anthropological testimony in Native American cases (see, e.g., Steward 1955; Manners 1956; Rosen 1977; Stewart 1979; B. Miller 1992; Monet and Skanu'u 1993; Harmon 1990–91; Rosenthal 1990; Dyck and Waldram 1993; Mills 1994; Culhane 1998). In general the tenor of the discussions has been that the "good" anthropologists work for the Indians and the "bad" anthropologists work for the other side, whoever that might be. Many have pointed to the adversarial system of courts of law as pitting anthropologists against one another and as playing the role of advocate for their client (Rosen 1977:569; Beals 1985:151; Culhane 1998:71–72). There have been several attempts to propose a process to present data outside the adversarial system. In the 1950s Julian Steward pleaded for a system that would involve pretrial hearings with researchers presenting the evidence to the court in a fact-finding exercise (Manners 1956:75). In the 1970s Rosen argued for an approach that would allow for the presentation of evidence without the limitations of the question and answer format of examination and cross-examination. Beals (1985:152) suggested that the anthropologist be appointed "friend of the court" and present the evidence without regard to the help or harm it might bring to any party in the case.

Despite these attempts at reform the system is not likely to change. Anthropological testimony accelerated dramatically during the period of the Indian Claims Commissions (in the United States from 1946 to 1978; in Canada a claims policy was established in 1973, the Indian Claims Commission in 1991) and is only going to increase with the continuation of resource and recognition claims in the United States and specific and comprehensive land claims in Canada, all of which are only now beginning to reach a peak. If there is indeed a shift to reliance on oral traditions, will it give an advantage to Native groups in the court's adversarial method of examining the evidence?

The Good, the Bad, and the Confused

The nature of anthropological testimony has always been complex and controversial. There are those who condemn out of hand any anthropologist who "testifies against the Indians." I would argue, however, that the matter is not a simple black and white issue; these sorts of things seldom are. Presumably expert witness testimony is presented in order for the court to make an informed decision in a matter of law. Despite the image of justice as blind, decisions are made based on a variety of factors including prevailing social attitudes, idiosyncrasies of judges, persuasive attorneys, and the advocacy or adversarial attitude of the expert witness. Presumably expert witnesses are objective in their presentation of data, but as we all know, complete objectivity is not possible.

In real life expert witness testimony often benefits the oppositions' opinion, not all cases deserve to be won, and who is the "bad" anthropologist and who is the "good" anthropologist when two tribes are suing one another?

In *United States v. State of Washington* (384 F.Supp. 312 [1994], Subproceeding 89-3), the "shellfish case," there were 162 expert witnesses involved, of whom 155 were employed by the tribes. Nevertheless, in the final pleadings the tribal attorneys cited the testimony of one of the defendant's expert witnesses more than all the tribal expert witnesses combined. Although the data was presented in an adversarial situation, it nevertheless benefited the case of the plaintiffs. Clearly expert witnesses need to be true to their interpretations. Assuming the role of advocate can result in the disregard of their testimony or impeachment. Two recent discussions of the shellfish case (J. Miller 1999b; Hunn 1999) miss an important point. Decisions made in Indian cases are usually matters of law. Ethnography may serve to inform these decisions, so some historical or ethnographic data is better than none. If expert witnesses are true to the record and true to their interpretations, then it should not matter who requested the information. It is rather arrogant to assume that the anthropologists are the determining factor in cases of law. The anthropologists in the Gitksan-Witsuwit'en case discovered how their testimony could be summarily dismissed because of their advocacy position (B. Miller 1992). One might also ask, is it working "for the Indians" when the anthropologist accepts huge sums of money as consultant fees when the community is poverty-stricken?

When disputes over resources and land become intertribal, whose interests does the expert witness serve? Is being a "good" anthropologist negated when testimony is presented on behalf of a tribe in a case that may be detrimental to another tribe? We have seen this in the western Washington fishery, and we are going to see it in British Columbia over fisheries allocations and overlapping land claims.

I do not intend to be an apologist for cases in which I and others have been involved. My point is simple: the issue is complex, and millions of dollars are being spent to protect aboriginal rights when those monies are desperately needed elsewhere in the Native communities.

Anthropological testimony has not always been necessary in Indian claims cases. In the latter part of the 19th century and until the mid-20th century evidence was generally presented by members of Native communities, government employees, such as agents and surveyors, and eyewitnesses to treaty and other proceedings involving Native and non-Native negotiations. Pointing to a few representative cases from the three political entities on the Northwest Coast will illustrate this transition.

In the United States anthropological testimony for Native claims cases accelerated in the 1950s, the impetus being the Indian Claims Commission Act of 1946. Previous claims cases relied on Native testimony. One of the earliest cases involving aboriginal rights in Washington State was *Alaska Packers Association v. United States* (c.c. Wash. 79f 152 [1897]), a case concerning rights of access to traditional fishing locations at Point Roberts. Testimony of elders who had been present at the 1855 treaty negotiations was called to recount what promises had been made. The testimony of Old Polen was especially informative, as he recounted specific discussion of promises to allow the continued use of traditional fishing locations. This case was followed by a series of cases in the early 1900s also relying on eyewitness accounts. Perhaps the greatest use of oral history was presented in the case *Dwamish et al. v. United States* (79 Ct. Cl. 530 [1934]), which depended upon Native testimony collected in the 1920s.

In southeast Alaska cases emerged in response to the different status of Alaska Natives in the United States system of federal Indian policy. Fishing rights, land claims, and citizenship were issues that Tlingits, Haidas, and Tsimshians fought in the court system. In 1918 fishing rights in the waters surrounding Metlakatla (*Alaska Pacific Fisheries v. United States*, 248 U.S. 78, 39 S.Ct. 40 [1918]) and the famous voting rights case of 1922 both relied on Native testimony. The voting rights case involved Charlie Jones, then the incumbent Chief Shakes of Wrangell, who was denied the right to vote at the polls. The case was decided largely on testimony of elders who testified to the understanding of the status of Alaska Natives at the transference from Russia and in the creation of territorial government.

The famous 1944 hearings on aboriginal rights held in Hydaburg, Klawock, and Kake were transitory. The testimony of Tlingits and Haidas fill some seven volumes of evidence, mostly concerned with fishing practices and clan control of resource locations. Although anthropologist Viola Garfield had been retained by attorneys for the salmon industry, her testimony was not presented.

Subsequent to the 1944 hearings anthropologist Walter Goldschmidt was commissioned to collect evidence concerning aboriginal rights to land and resources. The 1946 report (see Goldschmidt and Haas 1998) formed the basis of anthropological testimony before the Indian Claims Commission in the 1950s. Subsequent cases, such as *Tee-Hit-Ton Indians v. United States* (348 U.S. 272, 75 S.Ct. 313 [1955]) relied upon anthropological testimony, following the trend of shifting from a reliance on Native testimony.

The battle for control of land and resources in British Columbia has a history as old as the province itself. Almost as soon as British Columbia entered confederation the Native groups sought clarification of their rights. In 1887 north coast leaders presented testimony in Victoria concerning a desire to clarify land and resource rights. Political pressure brought to bear by British Columbia Indian leaders resulted in the formation of the Royal Commission on Indian Affairs for the Province of British Columbia, commonly known as the McKenna-McBride Commission. From 1913 to 1916 this commission traveled the province collecting testimony from Native peoples. Thousands of pages of oral history are contained in the commission transcripts. (For a content analysis see D. Saunders et al. 1999).

A direct result of this activism was the passage of a prohibition on claims-related activity. Section 141, a 1927 amendment to the Indian Act, contained provisions making it illegal to receive payments for legal council

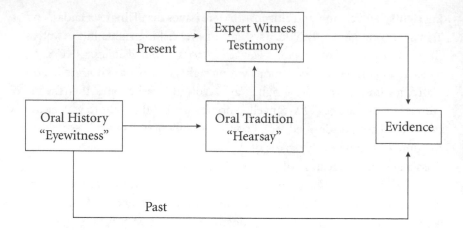

in pursuit of land claims. Although Section 141 was repealed in 1951 there were no court claims in British Columbia until 1963, when a case was presented that involved rights to resources in areas of Vancouver Island ceded by treaty to the Hudson's Bay Company (*Regina v. White and Bob [1964] 50 D.L.R. [2d] 613*). Heard by the Supreme Court of British Columbia in 1969, the courts depended upon the expert witness testimony of anthropologist Wilson Duff (Duff 1969). Subsequent to this case land and resource claims became commonplace in British Columbia and ultimately gave rise to the decision in *Delgamuukw*. All of the cases following *White and Bob* utilized anthropologists as expert witnesses.

What these cases illustrate for the general experience of Northwest Coast Natives is a shift of the control of knowledge of traditional life from Native leaders and elders to academic experts. This is reflected in the interpretation of evidentiary rules as a shift from eyewitness to hearsay testimony. This can be viewed as a hegemonic process that re-creates knowledge as commodity.

Knowledge as Property, Knowledge as Commodity

In Northwest Coast societies knowledge is a form of property. Oral traditions, songs, ceremonies, gossip, and genealogy are just some of the forms of private and privileged knowledge.

Anthropologists have always been conscious of the privileged nature of forms of knowledge in Northwest Coast societies, but this awareness has not precluded the open use of stories, songs, and family histories that were and are subject to rights of ownership and privacy within the Native communities. Instead, systems of access and ownership that regulate privileged knowledge are detailed along with other "traditional" institutions and ignore the prohibition outside the Native world (Rasmus 2001).

Identifying what constitutes privileged and private knowledge is a difficult and often contradictory task. What is explicitly identified as secret or private in one context is publicly shared in another. Ultimately that decision rests with the community, but even there opinions vary. Context becomes central to understanding processes of access, control, and ownership as they relate to privileged knowledge in Native communities. Much recent literature on the Northwest Coast stresses the importance of locating traditions, narratives, and histories within the context of their occurrence (Kan 1989b; Harkin 1997a), recognizing that issues of transmission, or reinterpretation, of knowledge are complicated through the separation of knowledge from the social, economic, and political milieu. Context also refers to the fact that cultures and cultural conceptions and expressions change over time. What was once considered public knowledge may no longer be.

Litigation requires the presentation of knowledge that results in benefits gained through clarification of aboriginal rights to land and resources. The exigencies of the assertion of rights often requires the transference of privileged knowledge into the public domain. Communities cannot afford to restrict certain forms of privileged knowledge, yet at the same time they regret having to do so. Some of the costs of this process are now being assessed by Native communities, as is the question, who is best suited to present this knowledge in a court of law?

Many forms of knowledge remain in the private domain, such as spirit songs, genealogies, origin traditions, family histories, and spiritual knowledge, although elements of these filter into the public realm. In the past, knowledge that was not meant for outside consumption was often shared, usually with the understanding of the privileged nature of this knowledge in the Native community. For example, audio recordings of spirit songs, which reincarnate, are found in numerous public collections. Contemporary owners of these songs would rather they not be heard.

This discussion is not meant to be an indictment of all work done with and for Native peoples. Rather, I think it is an attempt to understand control of knowledge as process. The trend remains to continue to disseminate knowledge within a system of knowing whereby the living aspects of the community become separated, peripheral, and lost within the "objective" nature of Western positivist analysis. The legal system not only encourages but relies on this separation, and the expert witness has been an active participant in the process.

Historical studies have analyzed the role played by the legal system in effecting transfers of land and resources to colonizing governments and settlers, in legitimizing the political sovereignty of colonial nations, in the extraction of natural resources, and in marginalizing Native peoples. A fundamental question that we must ask is, do we, as "expert witnesses," participate in this hegemonic process by adding intellectual resources to the list of effective transfers? And will *Delgamuukw* serve not to ensure a Native voice in the legal process but only to add one more dimension, as experts will now be called upon to validate that knowledge?

There is no easy answer to these questions. Not all Native communities feel the same way about these issues. Native communities, while universally embroiled in similar legal conflicts, follow their own paths to seek solutions. Often this includes the use of expert witnesses.

The anthropology of the past has been criticized for its role in the colonial process. Nevertheless this process continues under the guise of the expert witness. In the past Native peoples were seen as essential witnesses in presenting their own histories. A transition has occurred, however, where Native peoples are seen as incapable of presenting their own histories, as recently evident in the McEachern decision where Native peoples were described as a primitive people living a life that was "nasty, brutish and short" and incapable of comprehending how history really happened.

It should not be surprising that Native peoples are distrustful of researchers' motives nor that they are angry at having outsiders present their knowledge as trustworthy evidence. It should not be surprising that Native peoples are distrustful of researchers who purport to speak in the "Native voice." Although we might substitute terms such as indigenous knowledge, Native voice, dialogics, or oral tradition, we are still engaged in a hegemonic process over control of knowledge. Rather then giving Native people a voice in effecting the outcome of legal decisions, *Delgamuukw* will present one more avenue whereby the hegemonic process continues to extend over the production and reproduction of knowledge as commodity.

"DEFINING OURSELVES THROUGH BASKETS"

Museum Autoethnography and the Makah Cultural and Research Center

Patricia Pierce Erikson

Since the concept of the Northwest Coast as a culture area was invented, museums have been central to the anthropological study of Native American peoples. They have sponsored ethnographic field research and collected material culture; their resulting publications and exhibitions have profoundly shaped the representations of Pacific Northwest Coast peoples today. As a cultural anthropologist and anthropology-of-museums scholar who has worked extensively, but not exclusively, in the Northwest Coast, I pondered how my research with the Makah Cultural and Research Center (MCRC) might enhance a retrospective volume.

I decided to offer a snapshot of the present, an ethnographic portrait of one tribal museum and cultural center, to raise a set of broad questions: Why are museums and cultural centers an important aspect of Native American communities today in the Northwest Coast and elsewhere? How does the development of these institutions inform our understanding of Native American communities relative to American and Canadian societies in general and to the anthropological enterprise in particular? I share here some brief insights from a larger museum ethnography project to argue that the proliferation of institutions such as MCRC signals a sea change in Pacific Northwest Coast studies. In short, I would like to call attention to a process, the rise of museum autoethnography among Native American peoples. My review of an MCRC basketry exhibit — a Makah-curated exhibit narrating the place of basketry in Makah life — intends to provoke scholars to consider the benefits of collaborative research projects based out of these institutions.

Like other cultural anthropologists, my work takes me into many homes and in contact with the life histories of many individuals in a community. Because of my interest in museums and material culture, my work repeatedly leads me to the life histories of objects as well. Since I began working with the

Makah people in 1994, baskets have insinuated themselves into my research. In the course of my interviews in household after household, Makah families pulled solid-twine baskets of cedar bark, bear grass, and *či·bup* down from shelves or out of cabinets and tenderly removed their covers.[1]

I watched people pull from these baskets deeply browned newspaper clippings, olivella shell necklaces, and crisply folded slips of paper with tiny writing that detailed who made the basket, when, and for whom. These baskets often had been given as gifts to mark an important passage in life such as a wedding, a graduation, or a naming. Sometimes a weaver specifically made the basket for the occasion; other times she invited the honored one to choose a basket from her own collection. Each time someone lifted a basket lid in my presence, the opening released a story the basket had to tell. Through the exhibit that I describe here, these personal narratives found a new venue: the MCRC galleries.

In the winter of 2001 I relented. Building on my museum ethnography project (Erikson 2002) and my experience with Miwok and Pomo basket weavers while I was a doctoral student, I began to focus my research on basketry. I traveled to Neah Bay to study a basketry collection that Bruce and Linda Colasurdo had generously loaned to MCRC for a period that allowed Makah elders to analyze the baskets. While driving through town with Janine Bowechop, MCRC director, I asked her why she felt the baskets were meaningful to the Makah community. She answered, "Other than whaling, we have defined ourselves through baskets for generations." Whaling has been a significant aspect of historic Makah identity. With the reintroduction of the whale-hunting ceremony, the national and international media have positioned contemporary Makah identity as a high-profile subject in international environmental affairs (Erikson 1999). Bowechop's statement about the importance of baskets provoked me to go back to the MCRC galleries to listen to and learn from its curatorial voice. I chose Bowechop's statement as the title for this essay to highlight not only the importance of baskets to contemporary Makah identity but the "defining ourselves" process that is facilitated by a relatively new type of tribal institution — the tribal museum and cultural center.

The Makah Indian Tribe opened the Makah Cultural and Research Center in 1979, in part to exhibit artifacts unearthed from the precontact strata of a village named u·se·ʔil on Cape Alava (rendered "Ozette" by 19th-century English speakers). A joint Makah Tribe–Washington State University excavation began in 1970 and generated a compelling story of precontact longhouses, a catastrophic mudslide that buried them, and the extraordinary archaeological collaboration between anthropologists and Native Americans that followed (Cutler 1994; Daugherty 1971; Daugherty and Kirk 1976; Erikson 2002; Kirk 1980). The permanent galleries of MCRC interpret and represent precontact Ozette village life, based upon archaeological evidence and Makah oral tradition. The Ozette discoveries rippled through not only the community of Northwest Coast archaeologists, but the community of Makah basket weavers as well.

It was the occupation layer dating to 500 years before present that was astounding in its scope and degree of preservation. By 1981, after ten years of excavation, 55,000 artifacts had been removed from several longhouses; this included 179 categories of objects of which an inordinate percentage were excellently preserved organic materials (Mauger 1991:32). Artifacts ranged from an elaborate whale-fin effigy inlaid with hundreds of sea-mammal teeth to carved longhouse partitions to more than 3,000 woven objects (Daugherty 1995). One of these woven artifacts was a cedar bark basket, an intact tool kit belonging to a weaver. It contained a marvelously complete collection of awls, a spindle whorl, and some combs and blades. During the 1970s and 1980s these Ozette materials reinvigorated interest in carving and basketry among young Makah adults in Neah Bay. Once again cedar dugout canoes were made on the Makah Reservation and used for traveling and eventually whale hunting (Erikson 1999, 2002:166–169, 179–181). Continuing the 19th- and early-20th-century practice of selling carvings and weavings to tourists, Makah artisans stocked gift shops run by families and by the museum with baskets, carved masks, bowls, and clubs, cedar bark skirts, and much more (Erikson 2002:99–108).

When visitors walk through MCRC's permanent galleries, not only do they view precontact baskets from Ozette, but they may handle reproductions of Ozette baskets that were woven by young Makah weavers. To celebrate its 20th anniversary, MCRC turned to basketry and opened a temporary exhibit entitled *In Honor of Our Weavers* (hereafter *IHOW*) that presented the artwork and oral narratives of Makah basket weavers. Since 1999 the *IHOW* exhibit used baskets to tell some 20,000 visitors per year the story of the radical transformation since the precontact lifeways at Ozette.

Readers will derive more from my discussion of the rise of autoethnography through community museums in the Northwest Coast if I place the Makah example in a national context. In a comparative framework, it is easier to see how MCRC is one example of a widespread process: increasing Native American agency in historiography and ethnographic (self-)representation.

MCRC and the Native American Museum Movement

It is important to recognize that Native American tribal museums and cultural centers of the Pacific Northwest Coast represent one portion of a much more extensive movement throughout the United States, Canada, other nations in the Western Hemisphere, and beyond. Twenty-five years after the Ozette excavation began, I was drawn to MCRC by my fascination with how populations marginalized in states around the globe were appropriating the museum format. My early research mapped the "Native American museum movement" or the intensifying and shifting relationship between Native American communities and museology, beginning in the mid-20th century (Erikson 1996, 2002). I found that this movement spawned hybrid institutions that resembled a museum or art gallery yet diverged from them in significant ways. I have used the somewhat clunky term *museum and cultural center* to discuss this hybridity. Comparable to Native American cultural centers are the Chinatown History Museum, the Greenwood Cultural Center, and El Museo del Barrio — examples of self-representing institutions in Asian American, African American, and Latin American populations, respectively (Wei Tchen 1992).

Efforts to establish tribal community museums date back as early as 1828, when the Cherokee people tried to establish one; the implementation of the Indian Removal Act blunted their efforts (Abrams 1990; J. Hanson 1980). Native American individuals also opened museums in the first quarter of the 20th century; some of these have distinguished themselves with their continuous operation (Standing Bear, personal communication, 1994; Nicks 1996; Fawcett 2000). The majority of the institutions have been established in the twentieth century, however.

The relationship between museums and Native Americans began to change radically in the 1960s in the context of pan-Indian political activism. Specific critiques of anthropology and academia (Biddle 1977; V. Deloria 1969; Doxtator 1985; Forbes 1966; J. Hanson 1980; Horse Capture 1994; Medicine 1971; Biolsi and Zimmerman 1997) resonated with broader critiques of popular appropriations and distortions of Indianness (P. Deloria 1998; Green 1988; Jocks 1996). Establishing independent tribal institutions has been a stated goal since the occupation of Alcatraz Island (Forbes 1966; Fuller and Fabricius 1992). A number of federal agencies responded to the rise of Native American political consciousness by diversifying the funds available to cultural preservation projects (Fuller and Fabricius 1994; Parker 1991; Warren 1991).

The cadre of Native American scholars, artists, and activists that emerged from this era has, among other things, founded a variety of educational and cultural programs and institutions. While non-Native educational institutions have had a checkered historical relationship with tribal communities, these "mechanisms of control" are being "redirected" to rebalance power relationships, redefine popular stereotypes, and perpetuate living cultures (e.g., McBeth 1983; Garrod and Larimore 1997). Strategies for community empowerment have included founding tribal colleges or Native American Studies programs and departments in non-Native institutions. Tribal museums and cultural centers are another significant type of institution to emerge from this historical context (Begay 1991; Boss 1993; Clifford 1992; Cranmer Webster 1991; Erikson 1999, 2002; Fuller 1992; Hartman 1983; Knecht 1994; Pratt 1992).

For years the Smithsonian Institution's Center for Museum Studies (formerly the Office of Museum Programs) has kept track of tribal museums and cultural centers by compiling and publishing a tribal museum directory. By 1998 more than 100 Native American museums and cultural centers had been identified in the United States; only 40 were known to exist in 1981 (Cooper 1998; Fuller and Fabricius 1994). I have relied upon the Smithsonian Institution's definition of a tribal museum and cultural center: "a tribal museum is a museum owned and operated by a tribe . . . included are museums/centers operated in urban sites by conglomerate groups of Native Peoples; museums/centers managed by American Indian tribal entities; museums operated by American Indian individuals; and, finally, museums financed by non-tribal monies but located within tribal communities and hiring or partnering with residents of the community or otherwise viewed as presently serving as a 'tribal museum.' . . . The directory includes cultural centers which have exhibits, are open at posted times and which allow visitors to view those exhibits" (Cooper 1998). With the help of a student assistant, I updated the Pacific Northwest Coast portion of this Smithsonian directory.[2] As of the spring of 2001 there were at least 18 Native American cultural centers in the Pacific Northwest Coast culture area (see Figure 1 and Appendix). Although the earliest was founded in 1938, they were predominantly established during the 1970s and 1980s. Still more are developing, while others struggle to keep their doors open. Collectively, the tribal museums and cultural centers of the Pacific Northwest Coast constitute approximately 13 percent of the U.S. and Canadian distribution.

Native American museums and cultural centers take forms as diverse as the historical experiences of their hosting communities. Fuller and Fabricius (1994) have suggested that there are four types, the first being tribally operated institutions on reservation land. The Makah Cultural and Research Center is an example of this first type. The second category is composed of pan-Indian-operated cultural centers, often located in urban areas. Daybreak Star in Seattle is one of the most famous of these. The third category is Native American–controlled (but not owned) cultural organizations, such as the Southeast Alaska Indian Cultural Center located in a National Park Service building in Sitka. Museums owned by a family or individual constitute the fourth type, such as the one owned by Gladys Tantaquidgeon (although located in the Northeast [Fawcett 2000]).

The scale of Native American cultural centers varies widely, as does their financial stability. Not all cultural centers have enjoyed the consistent operating budgets of MCRC, let alone a continuity among staff members that can be counted in decades. Some harsh financial realities of running a nonprofit institution in the late 20th century have replaced the optimism, a hallmark of the 1970s, that cultural tourism would generate self-supporting institutions (Anonymous 1993; J. Hanson 1980). It would be a gross generalization, however, to say that all Native American museums and cultural centers operate on shoe strings. The newly founded Mashantucket Pequot Museum in Connecticut could be considered "the Smithsonian" of tribal museums if the National Museum of the American Indian (NMAI) didn't already play that role.[3] In spite of the diversity among Native American museums and cultural centers, they all must position themselves relative to the long history of the development of Western museums.

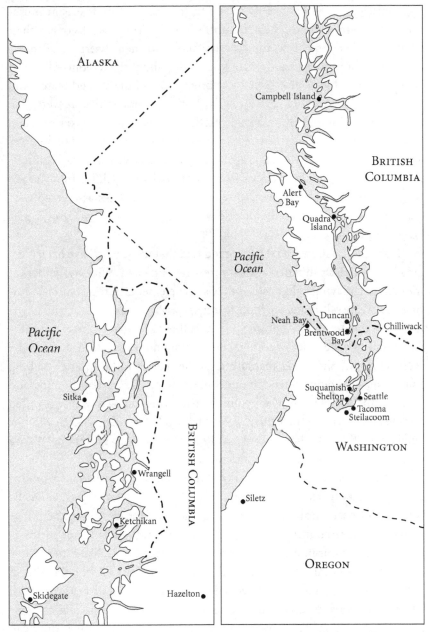

1. Locations of the tribal museums and cultural centers in the Pacific Northwest Coast.

Much has been written about the historic role of mainstream museums in Western societies: their concentration of priceless works of art, their amassing collections of meaningful artifacts, and their assertion of themselves as authoritative producers of knowledge about the (colonized) world (Hooper-Greenhill 1989; Clifford 1997b:188–219). In the United States, and the Western Hemisphere more broadly, Native American people were vital to these collecting and ethnological practices (Hinsley 1992, 1993; Krech and Hail 1999). Historically, mainstream museums have conceived of themselves as the center of knowledge making; in this vision Native American communities are left as the periphery or frontier of discovery (Clifford 1997b:192–193). This pattern is analogous to representation practices associated with colonization and nation building elsewhere (e.g., Haraway 1989:26–58; Anderson 1991).

Mary Louise Pratt (1992) has argued that that those who have been marginalized and discriminated against rarely remain passive like bystanders at the edge of a playing field. Instead they select elements of the dominant culture and create self-made portraits to engage with, accommodate, and negotiate with the dominant culture.[4] She calls these self-made portraits "autoethnography"; the space of colonial encounter and negotiation she calls the "contact zone." She writes that although the centers of knowledge making (museums, for example) tend to understand themselves as representing and determining the periphery, they blind themselves to the way the so-called periphery constructs the center. Along with others (such as Ruth Phillips and James Clifford), I have found that Pratt's transculturation model travels well to material culture studies and museum ethnographies.

Indigenous autoethnography is not new; it has taken various forms, including literary texts, artworks, and oral performances. Of interest to Pacific Northwest Coast scholars is that the translation of indigenous autoethnography into museum institutions potentially enriches not only our methodologies but also our interpretive frameworks. For example, like other Native American communities embedded in a Euro-American society, the Makah people historically have had to engage, accommodate, and negotiate with a *linear* model of cultural change, one that measures Native American cultural disintegration. This Western model has interpreted Native American communities and their art forms as either rapidly disintegrating or continuing to exist in a somewhat pristine form because of geographic and cultural isolation. Makah baskets — known as trinket baskets or trade baskets — are excellent examples of hybrid arts that embody processes of transculturation. What the curatorial voice of the *IHOW* exhibit communicated to me was that neither the model of cultural disintegration nor the model of isolated cultural purity captures the complexity of Makah historical experience. This is not news to cultural theorists, but ethnographers, museum curators, and movie producers still struggle to articulate the complexity of historic and contemporary Native American identity amid the received, dominant image of what a Native American is and looks like.

Baskets, like other tourist arts, represent forms whose so-called hybridities historically have been ignored in favor of analyses of the salvage ethnographic enterprise that determines what is purely Native. More than once in my research in museum collections I have heard a curator or museum educator refer to trade baskets as junk. One could interpret Makah trade baskets as marking the assimilation of the Makah people or as a degradation of their traditional art forms because of incorporation into the cash economy. However, since the 1970s anthropologists, art historians, and others have acknowledged the dynamism of Native American arts. This has nudged Native American studies further away from the era of acculturation theory (see Graburn 1999 for this summary; for examples see Jacknis 2002; Duncan 2000; Cohodas 1986; Lee 1991; Berlo 1990). New art historians have criticized classification systems that render some objects as curiosities, relics, trinkets, souvenirs, or tourist art, as opposed to fine art or traditional cultural artifact (e.g., Phillips 1998).

Of course, in their role as informants Native American individuals have always attempted to influence the content and interpretation of anthropological study. With the development of tribal museums and cultural centers, however, Native American peoples have greater resources for creating more authoritative autoethnography and mediating more directly between their community and the general public. At MCRC, the *In Honor of Our Weavers* exhibit uses baskets to create individual, family, and tribal self-portraits.

In Honor of Our Weavers: Weaving Identity and Stories of Weaving Baskets

MCRC's temporary exhibit titled *In Honor of Our Weavers* exemplifies autoethnography in the genre of museum exhibition. Before walking readers through this exhibit, I should explain that my Neah Bay fieldwork has biased my review and interpretation of this exhibit. When I moved to Neah Bay in 1994, I arrived intent upon writing a history of the MCRC, a history that would illuminate the contemporary role of museums in Native American social movements (Erikson 1996). With the benefit of hindsight, I realize that Makah people were, from the beginning, calling my attention to their family heirloom baskets and telling me stories about women weaving.

As with generations of anthropologists before me, the life histories that individuals shared with me in interviews repeatedly disrupted the narrative that I wanted to write. Master basket weaver Margaret Irving, in particular, was determined that I listen to her testimony about the place of basket weaving in Makah life. She once said to me: "I want to hand down what was taught to me. Basketweaving is part of our history. It's our tradition. It should be taught so you don't forget where you come from and who you belong to . . . I feel it's something we survived on way back. It should be kept alive. We still sell baskets to survive" (Irving 1995). Her older sister, Ruth, also emphasized to me the connection between baskets and a Makah sense of who they were and who they are: "Even though we don't have to have them [the baskets] to get groceries now, you wouldn't want to lose that history" (R. Claplanhoo 1995). Testimonies of basket weaving are strewn throughout the field notes that I began collecting in 1994. Unlike the thousands of tourists who would see the IHOW exhibit, I was already steeped in the extensive oral tradition in Neah Bay surrounding basketry before I first entered the gallery. My curiosity remained piqued, however. How had MCRC translated Makah oral tradition and material culture history into an exhibit? What did the interpretive framework of the exhibit reveal about MCRC's role in the hosting community and in the larger, encompassing society?

Since MCRC opened in 1979, its temporary gallery has hosted exhibits that focus on topics such as the photodocumentary record of the Makah people (Marr 1987) and on individuals such as Young Doctor, whose house posts, model canoes, and other carvings are prized by museums nationwide (MCRC 1989). Feeling that stories of weaving baskets deserved to find a broader and more public audience, MCRC director Janine Bowechop decided in 1999 to design an exhibit that focused on an aspect of Makah women's work and artistry. Several staff members collaboratively researched and curated the show, including Janine Bowechop, Melissa Peterson, and Theresa Parker. The staff selected baskets from MCRC's ethnographic collection; many had been donated by Euro-American families who had lived on the reservation as pastors, social scientists, and businessmen during the late 19th and early 20th centuries. Makah weavers had, in some cases, given rather than sold the baskets to them. Additionally, MCRC approached Makah families and successfully sought loans from the personal collections they treasured.

Community museums generated by the Native American museum movement have provided a forum for indigenous perspectives on basketry, a relatively undertreated aspect of Northwest Coast life. Compounding the general undervaluation of women's work was the academic devaluation of material culture that was produced for the market and hence reflects dramatic cultural change (Phillips 1998:17–18). Trade baskets were an important means to negotiate what Phillips calls the "texts of Indianness current in Euro-North American society" (14). In the wake of the encounter between Native American and Western systems of aesthetics and object valuation, these baskets historically have been left defined by what James Clifford has called the art-artifact paradigm (Clifford 1988). The intertwining of various intellectual movements has helped reverse this trend and has validated the importance of certain material culture categories, such as trade baskets. Feminist anthropologists and social historians of the 1980s and 1990s have also validated the historic importance of basketry. The *Masterworks of Washington: Contemporary American Indian Basketmaking* exhibit of the Washington State Capital Museum (Olympia, 1995–96) and the *Entwined with Life* exhibit at the Burke Museum of Natural History and Culture (Seattle, 2000–2001) are notable examples in the Northwest Coast of the increased attention to the basketry tradition. Increasingly, women's work is considered a viable subject for analysis and exhibition (McMullen and Handsman 1987; McBride 1990; Sarris 1994).

For Margaret Irving, baskets were far more than a beautiful art form. They were, somehow, the stuff that one's life, history, and identity were made of. Makah virtues saturated baskets and made them a source of pride; as Mrs. Irving and other weavers explained to me, making baskets helped avoid the dreaded "idle times"; basketry skills required commitment and practice; lastly, baskets symbolized the ability to work as a family "to get by." For Mrs.

Irving, basket making was one of the many ways that Makah lives had been interwoven.

Since I am using the *IHOW* exhibit to illustrate the nature and importance of autoethnography at MCRC, I structure my argument according to the four spatial elements of the exhibit: the introduction, the two cases comprising the main basketry display, the autobiographical sketches, and the basketry-as-fine-art display.

When visitors to the *IHOW* exhibit first enter the temporary gallery or "sun room," they may choose to begin by reading the introductory panel, which offers a segue from the permanent Ozette gallery. I share just a portion of this panel here:

> The time period represented by the Ozette artifacts you have just seen is in many ways not far removed from us. Basket weaving techniques from Ozette are still practiced here today, partly as a result of firsthand teaching through many generations, and partly as a result of the cultural renewal brought about by the excavation of these amazing pieces. . . . Baskets have played a role for us traditionally, as seen in the Ozette material, but also economically and socially. In this exhibit, we will take you from the rich heritage of our past, so beautifully exhibited in the Ozette basket materials, to the weaving which continues here today. The elders highlighted in this exhibit were weaving long before the Ozette excavation began. And the younger generation has been inspired not only by our living elders, but by the ones who left so much behind. We invite you to join us in honoring those who have continued our traditional weaving and created new and innovative forms and uses for this ancient art.

The introductory panel introduces four main themes: a Makah sense of time, the complexity of Makah identity, the notion of Makah culture as dynamic, and the desire to commemorate. The idea of the "vanishing American" established precontact indigenous peoples as pure and authentic, leaving historic and contemporary Native Americans with the uncomfortable labels of "mostly assimilated" or "hardly traditional." The relegation of Native American people to a "timeless" ethnographic past has been discussed widely in the literature and need not be repeated here.

Beginning with the introductory panel, the *IHOW* exhibit communicates a sense of time where the precontact past is neither disconnected nor distant from the present. At the same time, the *IHOW* exhibit neither diminishes nor denies cultural change to establish cultural authenticity. Instead, it embraces the complexity of Makah identity. The curatorial statement in the introductory panel attributes the state of contemporary Makah basket weaving both to "firsthand teaching" across generations (which is a traditional form of knowledge transfer) and to the cultural renewal brought about by the Ozette excavation (which involved extensive collaboration with non-Native archaeologists). Change and adaptability, or the complexity of the processes by which Makah identity survives, is a large part of what is being honored and celebrated in this exhibition.

After the introductory panel the exhibit presents two rectangular exhibit cases approximately ten by four feet and eight feet in height. Collectively the two cases, lined with black velvet, display 45 baskets on cedar pedestals of varying height. These baskets represent numerous weavers over more than a century of weaving, beginning in the late 19th century. Visitors are perhaps initially struck, as I was, by the tremendous variety of forms represented in the exhibit. Makah women wove not only trinket baskets or *pikuʔu* and *wa·bit* baskets (a basket taken to potlatches and community dinners for carrying home leftover food and dishes), but also rattles, anthropomorphic figures, handbags, shopping bags, matchbox holders, and much more. Visitors further discover the ingenuity of encasing shells and bottles with intricate twining (Figure 2).

In the third section of the exhibit a series of photo portraits and interview panels contextualizes the basket collection and focuses visitors' attention on the social and biographical dimensions of baskets. *IHOW* represents eight contemporary weavers — Ruth Allabush Claplanhoo, Mary Bowechop Greene, Isabelle Allabush Ides, Leah Smith Parker, Norma Pendleton, Vida Ward Thomas, Irene Hunter Ward, and Helma Swan Ward. These women, and members of their extended families, are among the artisans who created the baskets on display. The oral testimonies of these women — recorded by MCRC staff and transcribed for the interview panels — document up to a seven-generation chain of basket weavers reaching well into the 19th century. I quote from just one of the eight interview panels to illustrate how Makah oral tradition renders these baskets meaningful where each twining of bark or grass parallels the weaving of the social fabric. The Mary Greene

2. Ink bottle covered with wrapped twining and adorned with carving of an eagle. On loan to the Makah Cultural and Research Center for the *In Honor of Our Weavers* exhibit. Photo by Eric Long and Keely Parker. Courtesy of MCRC.

interview panel emphasizes trade baskets as one of the means for Makah women to participate in local, regional, and national economies: "When I was married, and the log industry was seasonal because of the weather, then my husband would go on unemployment. He made $15.00 a week. And so I would make baskets for bread and milk, bread and milk you know. And that's all I did, because 15 dollars went a long ways them days, and all I needed to do was make baskets for bread one day, and then milk the next, that's all." Other interviews testified that that for multiple generations the sale of trinket baskets supported household income and supplemented wage labor opportunities that were frequently seasonal.

The exhibit script reinforced what Makah oral tradition and federal records had taught me. By the late 19th century Makah people were participating in commercial sealing and whaling expeditions and later in commercial logging, fish canning, and hop-picking industries. As forest and marine resources became stripped by the late 19th and early 20th centuries, other sources of income were increasingly vital to economic survival. Women adapted their weaving skills to make trade baskets. For the most part, the sale of baskets were "thirdhand" exchanges of items that served as souvenirs of an encounter with a pan–Northwest Coastal culture (Duncan 2000:13–22; Phillips 1998:12). During the early decades of the 20th century baskets were generally priced at one dollar or less and as many as 3,000 to 6,000 baskets may have been made annually in the early years of the 20th century. Memories of this era are perhaps distilled by an exclamation quoted in the exhibit: "The whole town lived on baskets!" These are the conditions that produced the type of baskets in the IHOW exhibit.

The fourth section of the IHOW exhibit reveals a curatorial approach distinctive from the prior sections. In this section MCRC appropriated a more "fine art" approach. The staff selected three baskets whose workmanship was considered exceptional, isolated each in an individual exhibit case, and mounted them so that they appeared to float in the case unencumbered by any didactic materials. Contrary to the prior exhibit sections, these three baskets are allowed to stand outside their social and historic context, even though many Makah viewers would know the rich stories associated with them.

One particular basket in this section of the exhibit sensitized me to how viewers' responses to this display would vary widely. Loaned by the Claplanhoo family of Neah Bay, this basket was installed in an exhibit case inset into the corridor wall. Mirrors backing the case reflected the whale, bird, and canoe motifs on the back half of the basket. A label simply identified the weaver as Ruth Claplanhoo and the date as circa 1935. Just days before, Mrs. Claplanhoo and her son had, separately, shared with me the story associated with this basket distinguished by the initials "A.C." woven into it. Later, standing in the museum looking at the basket, I thought of the story Mrs. Claplanhoo had told me:

> By the way, did you see my basket up there [at the museum]? I made that for my late husband. It has his initial on the bottom. It's not a fine work. That was the first time [I put initials on it]. I had no idea my husband valued the basket[s]. We worked up the tower looking for fire for 9 years. Them years were the hard times, hard times. I got $45 per month and Art got $45 per month. We were glad to have that. Art said, "of all the baskets that you made, you never made one for me." Well, I thought to myself I never knew he wanted the basket. While we were out for the woods to look out for smoke, I used to take my basket material and go up the [fire]tower and make the basket, look around for smoke. That's when I made that basket for him. (R. Claplanhoo 2001)

Although this story is widely known in the Claplanhoo family and freely shared in the community, the exhibit leaves this story untold, allowing the fine weaving to appeal aesthetically to viewers.

This basket demonstrates an important point about the nature of auto-ethnography in tribal museums and cultural centers. Makah oral historians, curators, and others devise research goals after synthesizing and prioritizing various family, tribal, and professional value systems. They are then in a position to generate the potential for a unique research methodology and ethnographic self-portrait. Autoethnography should not be confused here with a static representation, however. The most ephemeral aspect of autoethnography in tribal museums and cultural centers is perhaps its most dynamic component: the impromptu oral performances in the gallery that occur when Makah staff, board members, volunteers, and consultants readily give tours to tourists, local and visiting school groups, and dignitaries. Tribal members unaffiliated with MCRC also use the galleries as mnemonic aids for stimulating narrative events and creating oral literature anew pertaining to one's family.

To use Ruth Claplanhoo's basket to elaborate the point, when the staff displayed it as fine art, they created the opportunity for a less familiar way of gazing at trade baskets. Showcasing the aesthetics of the fine weaving left the life history of this particular basket offstage. Members of the Claplanhoo family (and others who know the basket's story) may (and do) choose to augment the basket's presentation as fine art by narrating the associated family oral history. Previous sections of the exhibit had contextualized baskets using oral historical and ethnographic approaches. By juxtaposing these different modes, Makah staff have employed diverse representational and narrative strategies to construct the complex — and nonstereotypical — cultural portrait that they wish to present.

Centers of Collaboration: A Turning Point in Northwest Coast Studies

I was recently surprised to hear a prominent sociologist say that anthropology was suffering from so much ethical angst that it had retreated from field work into the archives, especially in North America. What about the anthropologists who *are* in the field, some of whom are Native American themselves, and are forging new types of working relationships? Whatever the effect of postmodern, post-structuralist, and postcolonial critiques on the rate at which anthropologists are working with Native American communities, the need for substantive dialogue on the future of the anthropological enterprise appears considerable. One of the most pernicious obstacles to improving upon the classic model of field work is the differential in power relations between the anthropologist, ensconced in the academy, and those studied, who (at least prior to the civil rights movement and the "studying up" initiative) were perceived as temporally, geographically, and socially distant from academia.

Critical theory has forced anthropology into a general critique of "representational texts," including ethnographic manuscripts and museum exhibits. The main assertion was that these representations were not simply "records of fact" but rather subjective literary works whose perspective had a history. Museum theorists have argued that while literary criticism has enhanced our understanding of museum subjectivity, there are many ways in which museums are *unlike* texts (Macdonald and Fyfe 1996). Despite these differences, museum autoethnography can be compared to literary and cinematic projects that assert "oppositional" or "returning" gazes to disrupt dominant ways of seeing (see discussion in Foster 1997). It is perhaps more accurate, however, to acknowledge that tribal museums and cultural centers are creating autoethnographies or representations of themselves with engaging with, struggling against, and accommodating dominant cultural systems (Erikson 2002: 143–214).

It is no longer enough to say that museums are "agencies of social control" that reinforce dominant ways of seeing, remembering, and feeling. The dramatic proliferation and relative democratization of museums globally necessitates a more nuanced analysis of museums. Historically, museum ethnology endeavored to salvage "the other" from the "zone of discovery" and reconstruct the other in museum galleries to educate the public (Stocking 1985; Orosz 1990). Although the correlation between museums and dominant social sectors remains strong, theorizing of museums must account for the diverse cultural logics that have appropriated the museum model (Macdonald and Fyfe 1996). As a cultural anthropologist who embraced the participant observation method and yet validated Native American critiques of anthropology, I was impressed with how tribal museums and cultural centers disrupted the anthropologist-Native dichotomy and offered an alternative.

Native American critics in large numbers have bashed anthropology as a rarefied academic enterprise since Vine Deloria's *Custer Died for Your Sins* (1969). Many scholars—Native American and non-Native—have argued that Deloria's critique stereotyped the practice of anthropology in Native American communities, jettisoning the nuance of the relationship. Christopher Jocks, a Mohawk scholar of religion, has offered a brilliant alternative to the Deloria-style critique: a persuasive argument that scholars should closely consider Native American critiques of anthropology for their hermeneutic value. His article "Spirituality for Sale" offers a five-point model delineating how scholars can forge productive working relationships with Native American communities. One point is as follows: "Scholars need to provide clear and comprehensive accounts of their relationships with the Indian communities they study. Moreover, the issue of motivation—*why* they are involved in this work—ought to be considered an integral part of its justification. Mere curiosity, or filling in lacunae in 'the research record,' should not be thought of as adequate reasons to probe into peoples' lives" (1996:426). Jocks clarifies for me why the rise of museum autoethnography marks a sea change in Pacific Northwest Coast studies. Who decides what are the "adequate reasons" for ethnographic study? This is where museum and cultural centers often insert themselves into the process of defining research projects.

Many, if not most, Native American tribes in the United States require that scholars formally approach the tribal council or other governing body for prior approval for their research. On the Makah Indian Reservation the Board of Trustees of the Makah Cultural and Research Center reviews requests to conduct research in the community. In my experience, the museum and cultural center had the authority (conferred by the tribal council and sustained through the approval of elders) to insist that anthropology make its research truly relevant and respectful to the community. MCRC staff trained me in their protocols for conducting oral history interviews in the community. Members of the tribal council and MCRC alike made clear to me that my critical audience was not simply a dissertation committee or a book editor; they insisted that they were colleagues, equal actors in Makah historiography who would insist that my work was done properly by their standards (Erikson 2002:51–67).

The Ozette excavation initiated long-term collaborative working relationships between the Makah Tribe and Washington State University, the University of Washington, the Royal British Columbia Museum, and the Thomas Burke Memorial Museum that were ahead of their time. Although this research approach is considered productive and ethical today, collaboration of this sort was still unique at that time (Spector 1993; Rice 1997).[5] The new kind of collaboration spawned by Ozette reverberated through anthropology and museology. Through training programs at the Burke Museum and at the Smithsonian Institution, Makah people shifted their position relative to museology from "outsiders" to "insiders" at the crucial time of the Ozette excavation and the planning stages of the Makah Cultural and Research Center (Erikson 2002:143–214). Consequently Makah individuals collaborated with other, non-Makah professionals to shape the subjectivity of MCRC—who it was for, what it communicated, how it did its business. The resulting, alternative notion of Native American community as constituency and audience had broad appeal.

Makah staff members brought their perspectives to a variety of museum training programs whose purpose has been (and remains) not only to provide technical training but to encourage reflection on the mission of cultural centers. Many of these workshops and educational materials are based out of the Smithsonian Institution and taught by Native American faculty (Erikson 1996; Fuller and Fabricius 1992; Mauger and Bowechop 1995; Sadongei 1991). I expect that the increasing number of Native American individuals working as museum professionals, some of them in their own communities, will tangibly affect the nature of future research in Pacific Northwest Coast studies. Certainly collaboration between ethnographers and Northwest Coast Native peoples that generates valuable ethnographic materials is nothing new; George Hunt's collaboration with Franz Boas is one of the older and most famous of these (Cole 1985; Jonaitis 1991; Jonaitis and Inglis 1992). However, the degree of agency and control involved in tribal museums and cultural centers contrasts starkly with a 19th-century model of collaboration.

A frequent query to my testimony is whether or not Native American museum autoethnography interferes with academic freedom. I choose to reframe the question. If we acknowledge the hermeneutical dimension of Native American critiques of academia, we can begin to hone a cross-cultural methodology (Jocks 1996:428). Collaborative research need not be the albatross to academic freedom; rather, it can challenge us to etch finer-grained, more accurate, and more reflexive ethnographies that respect the way notions of intellectual property rights vary cross-culturally. Native American museums and cultural centers offer Pacific Northwest Coast scholars potential community partners in cross-cultural research design and methodology. The hope is to forge new categories, new interpretive frameworks, and new theories that are relevant to the lives of contemporary people.

Appendix: Northwest Coast Tribal Museums and Cultural Centers

Alaska

Southeast Alaska Indian Cultural Center, Inc.
106 Metlakatla St.
Sitka AK 99835
Founded: 1969
This is run by the Alaska Native Brotherhood and has been a nonprofit cultural center with a small museum-quality collection since 1993.

Totem Heritage Center
429 Dock Street
Ketchikan AK 99901
Location: 601 Deermount St.
Founded: 1976

Tribal House of the Bear
P.O. Box 868
Wrangell, AK 99929
Location: Foot of Shakes St. on Shakes Island
This is a replica of Chief Shakes Tribal House dating from 1834
and includes artifacts.
Founded: 1938
This is also run by the Alaskan Native Brotherhood.

British Columbia

Coqualeetza Education Training Centre
7201 Vedder Rd. Bldg. #1
Chilliwack BC V2R 4G5
Location: 1 1/2 hours east of Vancouver on Hwy 1.
Founded: 1973

Quw'utsun' Cultural and Conference Centre
200 Cowichan Way
Duncan BC V9L 4T8
Founded: 1990

Heiltsuk Cultural Education Centre
P.O. Box 880
Waglisla BC V0T 1Z0
Location: Campbell Island
Founded: 1978

'Ksan Historical Village and Museum
P.O. Box 326
Hazelton BC V0J 1Y0
Location: 235 River Rd.
Founded: 1958

Haida Gwaii Museum at Quay 'Ilnagaay
P.O. Box 1373
Skidegate BC V0T 1S1

Kwagiulth Museum and Cultural Centre
34 Weway Rd., Cape Mudge Village
Quadra Island BC V0P 1N0
Location: short ferry ride out of Campbell River
Founded: 1979

Saanich Native Heritage Society
P.O. Box 28
Brentwood Bay BC V8M 1R3
Founded: 1985

U'mista Cultural Society
P.O. Box 253
Alert Bay BC V0N 1A0
Founded: 1980

Oregon

Siletz Tribal Cultural Center
201 S.E. Swan Ave.
Siletz OR 97380

Washington

Makah Cultural and Research Center
P.O. Box 160
Neah Bay WA 98357
Founded: 1979

Puyallup Tribal Museum
2002 E. 28th St.
Tacoma WA 98404
Founded: 1981

Sacred Circle Gallery of American Indian Art
Daybreak Star Arts Center
P.O. Box 99100, Discovery Park

Seattle WA 98740
Founded: 1977

Skokomish Tribal Center and Museum
N. 80 Tribal Center Rd.
Shelton WA 98584
Location: 10 miles north of Shelton
Founded: 1989

Steilacoom Cultural Center
P. O. Box 88419
Steilacoom WA 98388
Location: 1515 Lafayette St.
Founded: May 1989

Suquamish Museum
P.O. Box 498
Suquamish WA 98392
Location: 15838 Sandy Hook NE on the Port Madison Indian
Reservation, Poulsbo WA
Founded: 1983

Notes

1. Pronounced "chi-bup," *č*i·*bup* is also known as swamp or blade grass.
2. I am indebted to L. Burke Murphy, my student research assistant at Smith College, for her invaluable assistance in conducting this survey.
3. NMAI is the newest of the Smithsonian Institution's museums and is under construction on the Capitol Mall. The extent of Native American staff and Native American governing oversight and philanthropic support make it a transitional entity between what we might consider classic models of tribal and national museums.
4. Pratt credits Cuban sociologist Fernando Ortiz as the architect of the transculturation model in the 1940s (Pratt 1992:228).
5. Rice (1997:218) names the Ozette excavation and a burial relocation program on the Snake River as exceptional cases in the 1970s where contact with Native Americans was an integral part of project planning and studies; he goes so far as to say that "Apart from these exceptions, things only began to change with the legislative requirement for tribal consultation."

THE GEOGRAPHY OF TLINGIT CHARACTER

Thomas F. Thornton

Studies of place and personhood represent old and venerable domains of inquiry in both the humanities and the social sciences, and recently each has undergone somewhat of a renaissance. The philosopher Aristotle in his *Physics* observed, "The power of place will be remarkable," and characterized it as "the first of all things," an indispensable aspect of every substance, and a "vessel" or container that frames and holds things—perceptions, memories, feelings, and so on. Aristotle's theory of the primordiality of place has been expanded by phenomenologists, such as Heidegger (1962, 1977), Casey (1993, 1997) and Abram (1996), who have explored perceptual aspects of sensing place. Similarly, humanistic geographers (e.g., Tuan 1974, 1977; Relph 1976; Agnew and Duncan 1989), noting the shortcomings of purely quantitative and positivist analyses of specific environments, have charted a more experientialist approach to the study of place. In sociology this new interest in place prompted E. V. Walter (1988:215) to launch an ambitious new subfield called *topistics,* which he defines as "A holistic mode of inquiry designed to make the identity, character, and experience of place intelligible." Postmodern studies have underscored the importance of recognizing multiplicities of location and place in cultural analyses and the important connections between space, power, and knowledge in human societies (cf. Rodman 1992; Gregory 1994; Gupta and Ferguson 1997; Escobar 2001).

At the same time, ethnogeographically inclined anthropologists (e.g., Basso 1984, 1988, 1996; Cruikshank 1981, 1990; Feld and Basso 1996; Hunn 1994, 1996) have rekindled a theoretical interest, largely dormant since the Boasian era, in place making and place naming and their cognitive and social dimensions (see Thornton 1997a), as well as in landscape (e.g., Hirsch and O'Hanlon 1995). In Northwest Coast ethnology, perhaps more so than other culture areas, the interest in place has persisted in large measure due to the influence of students of Boas, such as de Laguna (1960, 1972), who continued work on the Northwest Coast with an attentive eye toward the human meanings of landscape, and more recent researchers who have taken up issues of place and identity (e.g., Thornton 1997b, 2000; Harkin 2000).

The study of personhood and character has followed a similar trajectory in anthropological research. After peaking with the heyday of the cultural and personality school in the 1930s to 1950s, which drew heavily on Northwest Coast ethnology (e.g., Benedict 1934), interest in the study of personhood has recently been revived under the new ethnopsychology (e.g., Kan 1989c) and ethnography on identity. A key linking figure between the two movements is Hallowell (1955), who recognized that personhood is a cultural construction with significant variation across societies but showed that this diversity is undergirded by certain universal concepts, such as the idea of "the self."

Similarly, anthropological studies of character proliferated as part of the culture and personality movement (e.g., Olson 1956), especially during the World War II era, when numerous national character studies were produced. But these have since fallen out of favor due to the nature of their assumptions, methods, and essentializing tendencies. Today, the study of character receives scant attention within anthropology or the broader social sciences, although a recent book by psychologist James Hillman (1999), *The Force of Character, and the Lasting Life,* sheds important new light on the unique and developmental qualities of character. Hillman argues that character is more than a set of traits to be identified or instilled; rather, it is a process of self-realization embodying a unique constellation of characteristics or traits that become more clearly inscribed (to use a term etymologically linked to character) on the individual and thus perceptible as lasting and defining images, only with age and experience. Thus character requires "additional years" and the important physiological and psychological changes that come with aging, in order to be fulfilled.

Hillman's emphasis on the individuality of character offers an important corrective to more totalizing national character studies that tended to portray character as a reflection of dominant personality traits, which, in turn, were molded in cookie cutter–like fashion by certain cultural institutions or enculturation practices. Hillman (1999:197) argues, "Unlike 'personality,' character is impersonal. Rocks, paintings, houses, even kinds of bacteria and logical propositions demonstrate character. The discourse of personality is human psychology; of character, imaginative description." To the extent that this conceptualization of character extends beyond persons to aspects of the natural and built environment, it is well suited to the study of indigenous peoples for whom character is typically viewed not merely as a manifestation of humanity but also as a force of nature.

In this essay I explore the relationships between place, personhood, and character among the Tlingits of Southeast Alaska with whom I have worked since 1989. In examining these relationships I emphasize the links that Tlingits themselves make between these domains. This involves attending to both the key cultural institutions that help to define personhood and "channel character," to use Olson's phrase, and the idiosyncratic assemblage of traits and qualities, stressed by Hillman, that forms around every individual as he or she develops and self-consciously engages in a particular set of life experiences. Based upon my research on sense of place, subsistence practices, and other dimensions of social life among the Tlingits, I argue that place is an essential yet dynamic element of personhood and character among this northern Northwest Coast group. The idealized person in Tlingit society is one who not only knows the character of his or her ancestral lands but embodies and draws upon the character of the land in a variety of material and symbolic ways to develop, instill, and reflect individual and social group character. To facilitate this analysis, I explore character at three levels: first as an expression of social identity; second as a collective process, and third as a landscape incorporating elements of geography.

Character as Social Identity: The Role of *At.óow* in Tlingit Personhood and Character

Shagóon ("heritage and destiny") and *at.óow* ("owned things") are key dimensions of personhood and character for the matrilineal Tlingits. These concepts have been discussed in detail by others (de Laguna 1972; Dauenhauer and Dauenhauer 1987, 1990; Kan 1989b), so here I highlight only their relationships to place, personhood, and character, elucidating first the role of *at.óow* and in the next section *shagóon*. Both terms are subsidiary to the more general concept of *shuká* ("ancestor," or "that which lies before us"), which Dauenhauer and Dauenhauer (1990:19) define as " 'ahead' or 'before' . . . those born ahead of us who are now behind us, as well as those unborn who wait ahead of us." Thus, the concept is temporally ambiguous and "faces two directions," referring both to the past—that which came before—and to the future—that which lies ahead.

At.óow consist of material and symbolic property claimed by the matrilineal clan or house group (a sublineage of the clan) as part of their shuká. Such property includes geographic sites, such as salmon streams, halibut banks, shellfish beds, fort sites, and prominent mountains, as well as symbolic capital, such as ceremonial regalia, stories, songs, spirits, and names. As with shuká, there is a collective and individual element to at.óow. Clan and house group members may share much at.óow (territory, songs, and stories, for example), but within the same lifetime two individuals never claim precisely the same at.óow (their names, for example, are different). As such, the sum total of a person's at.óow serves to mark that individual as a distinct member of the community, and constitutes a pillar of personal identity. In explaining the foundation role that these possessions play in identity and being, both past and future, one elder simply declared, "Our at.óow are our life" (Emma Marks in Dauenhauer and Dauenhauer 1994:v).

The life-sustaining role of material resources, such as productive salmon streams, is readily apparent, but the importance of the symbolic property in defining one's existence requires a deeper understanding of the production, meanings, and roles of at.óow in defining the individual and social group's existence in the world. At.óow are important precisely because they reference and encapsulate key elements of Tlingit social group history. "Through *purchase* by an ancestor, a 'thing' becomes *owned* by his or her descendants. The purchase and subsequent ownership may come through money, trade, or peacemaking, as collateral on an unpaid debt, or through personal action, usually involving the loss of life. The at.óow . . . recall the actions of ancestors whose deeds purchased them, and the at.óow are therefore precious to the Tlingit people" (Dauenhauer and Dauenhauer 1994:15). Events, beings, objects, and places typically become at.óow when they are crystallized as encapsulating images—usually in artistic designs—and consecrated through ceremonial use and formal dedication within the context of the ḵu.éex' (potlatch or party). Only after these representations or simulacrum become publicly invested with meaning and value through ritual is the prerogative of ownership recognized and the status of at.óow achieved. Additionally, in the sacred context of ritual, at.óow become more than mere images or representations: through mediation in expressive ritual forms such as oratory, song, and dance *at.óow* have the power to evoke and make present the spirits of those things they resemble and encapsulate.

Stories about special places in the Tlingit lifeworld constitute a special type of *at.óow*. In discussing the sacredness of particular legends of the trickster-demiurge Raven that are localized in the landscape (Chilkoot) claimed by his clan, the Lukaax̱.ádi, elder Austin Hammond (Daanawáaḵ, see Kawaky 1981) emphasizes how these *at.óow* connect place to being in a life-sustaining nexus:

> It was at Chilkoot [a place in northern Southeast Alaska, near Haines] that they [my grandfathers] taught me things about our Tlingit ways. My grandfathers said, "The time will come when these things we're going to tell will need to be heard again."
>
> I tell you for years and years we found in the river our livelihood and our food, the strength of our families. . . . And all along these shores were special places where the salmon come. And each place has its own name.
>
> It was Raven who showed us how to get our food. Raven knew what was good for us, and taught the Tlingit how to live. Raven exists in our legends and in our lives. Sometimes Raven is powerful and wise, and at other times Raven seems foolish. But always the stories of Raven hold special meaning for us. It was Raven who hung by his beak suspended from the clouds at the time of the Great Flood. It was Raven who taught our people to catch salmon.
>
> These are the stories my grandfathers passed on to me. These are the things I'm trying to teach my grandchildren. It is these stories which help guide our people as we live with the land. . . .
>
> For Raven taught us, if we live with the land, not against it, the land will take care of us. The land, the river, they hear us!

Thus *at.óow* are important for the earthly wisdom they embody and the character that they draw forth. As Hillman (1999:11) notes, the Greek word *mythos* is perhaps best translated not as "legend" but rather as "plot." "The plots that entangle our souls and draw forth our characters are the great myths," he observes. "Myths show the imaginative structures inside our messes, and our human characters can locate themselves against the background of the characters of myth." Places, the settings of myth, give resonance to these plots and make them tangible to future generations who follow their ancestors' footsteps, or *shuká*. Therefore, it is not only that the land and the river "hear" Tlingits, but also that Tlingits (ideally), through *at.óow* and other frames, "hear" the lands and waters speak their wisdom and use this guidance to construct behavioral models and meanings (Cruikshank 1998; Cruikshank et al. 1990) that help them realize their *shuká* as both heritage and destiny.

Beyond plot and narrative, *at.óow* represent this dialogic between person and place in a variety of ways, including mapping the landscape of the world and of history onto the landscape of the body as constitutive elements of personhood. This is done most poignantly through naming and the donning of regalia that clothe the body in clan crests and ornaments, which, in turn, clearly emplace the wearer geographically and socially. According to de Laguna (1972:758), Tlingit personhood may be conceptualized as possessing three aspects: "the body, a virtually sexless, immortal spirit or soul which is reincarnated in a series of bodies . . . and the name or names which indicate and also establish personal identity." Both personal and clan or house group names and titles are passed on from generation to generation and may be of geographic origin (see de Laguna 1972:789; Thornton 1997a, 1997b, 2000) or allude to particular landscapes. Such names fuse place and personhood in clear and inextricable ways. Similarly, as *at.óow* and *shagóon*, names evoke elements of character. As de Laguna (1972:790) observes, "It is through his name, and the meaning of his name, that a Tlingit knows himself. His name or names identifies the spirit or spirits, formerly animating a long line of forebears, that have come to live again in him, shaping his body or lending character to his personality."

I would argue that bodily *at.óow*, such as ceremonial headgear, Chilkat blankets, and other regalia, as well as ornamentation such as tattooing, face painting, and the like, effectively constitute a fourth dimension of Tlingit personhood. Through the embodiment of *at.óow* designs, these adornments literally extend and project the person as a social being. They also reveal another dynamic within the social structure beyond the clan and lineage, namely social rank. According to Kan (1989b:77–102), the ideal person in Tlingit is the leader (*hít s'aatí*, "master of the house") or "aristocrat" (*aan ḵáawu*, "person of the village," or *aanyádi*, "child of the village"), who is symbolized as being heavy, stationary, and dry like a rock, as opposed to

wispy, fleeting, and wet like a leaf. Accordingly, the ideal person is conceptualized as situated and emplaced, like a feature of the land itself, but also
as "heavy" in adornments and possessions, or *at.óow*.

In fact, the Chilkat and button-style blankets and other regalia that
adorn Tlingit leaders are literally heavy, but more importantly, they represent "weighty" and anchoring components of the collective being, including
stellar features of the landscape, such as rivers and mountains, which figure
prominently in the clan's *shuká*. These places are sacred sites for the clan
that displays them and are considered possessions (*at.óow*) through a transaction or "purchase" event, often in which a clan member was "exchanged"
(typically involuntarily) for the land. In the film *Haa Shagóon*, Lukaax̱.ádi
leader Austin Hammond (Kawaky 1981) wears the precious Sockeye Point
Robe (X̱'aakw X'aayí Naaxein; see Figure 1) and explains the event it sym-
bolizes and the purpose of its display:

> Woven into the blanket that I wear is an important legend. Two young
> boys were racing in their canoe when it capsized. As one boy pulled
> himself out of the water, up from the lake's depth appeared a giant sock-
> eye salmon, taking hold of the remaining boy to disappear beneath the
> waters. And after several days people from both clans gathered there to
> mourn his loss. It was decided to call the place Sockeye Point [X̱'aakw
> X'aayí]—the name repeated four times to carry the weight of the law
> and the emblem woven into a blanket. And to those who come asking,
> "Where is your history?" I answer, "We wear our history." Tradition-
> ally, we have not been writers of books. We did not have surveys or
> titles. But we wove into our blankets our brother the sockeye. On our
> clothing is the ownership and history of our land.

By this and other means, *at.óow* serves to merge place and identity in ways
that reinforce social group and geographic affiliations as well as Tlingit notions of personhood, social rank, and resource tenure. As Austin Hammond's example demonstrates, *at.óow* also inscribe character and serve as
touchstones for character building. In the case of Sockeye Point, the place
is the carrier of an important life-sustaining lesson about the dependence
of the Lukaax̱.ádi upon the salmon. The sacrifice of one of the clan's members to the sockeye allows his descendants to continue to harvest salmon in a
delicate moral and ecological balance suggestive of mutual respect between
equals.

1. Austin Hammond displays the Sockeye Point Robe (X̱'aakw X'aayí Naaxein), a sacred object (*at.óow*) of his clan, at a 1981 ceremony near Chilkoot Lake in Haines, Alaska. Among other things the robe encapsulates important clan history and signifies title to the lands and waters around Chilkoot Lake, where freshwater (spawned-out) sockeye salmon (x̱'aakw) are harvested. (Photo by R. Dauenhauer)

Character as a Collective Process:
Shagóon and the Practice of Social Being

Shagóon, like *shuká,* is often translated as heritage (or origin) and destiny, but *shagóon* specifically refers to the immediate forces of ancestry that affect clan members' being in the world. The late Austin Hammond, Daanawáak (Kawaky 1981), defined *haa* (our) *shagóon* this way: "It is what we are now, what we have been since the beginning, and everything that our children must become. *Haa Shagóon* — that is the way it is with us." As both heritage and destiny, *shagóon* constitutes an inalienable and indissoluble component and order of identity, and it is spoken of both at the collective (*haa*) and individual (*ax*) levels, with matrilineal clan and house group being the central social units and repositories of *shagóon.* The most literal gloss of *shagóon* is "head bridge" (Jeff Leer, personal communication, 1999), most likely an anatomical reference to the atlas bone that connects the head to the spine and body. The link between the common use of the term to refer to heritage and destiny, on the one hand, and the more literal anatomical reference, on the other, resides in the metaphoric connections between the individual and the larger social body and physical landscape.

The term *shagóon* also embodies places that were created or endowed with significance through ancestral activities. In this sense it is akin to the Australian aboriginal concept of the Dreaming. Like the Dreaming, *shagóon* recognizes the landscape as the ground of being, a potent congelation of past activities, and to the extent that the land embodies the wisdom of the ages and powerful ancestral spirits, a compelling force in contemporary life. Accordingly, it is through the landscape and one's knowledge of its historical and sacred places that the underlying order of the cosmos—and by extension one's *shagóon* or place within it—is revealed. As for Strehlow's (1947:31) Northern Aranda, the country is for the Tlingit individual a "living, age-old family tree" that continues to evolve and resonate through his or her own being and dwelling on the land. This is because geographical, biological, and sociological processes of individuation are intimately linked, especially in myth. Place-names serve as signifiers of these intertwined processes. Thus, Austin Hammond aspires to continue to fish for sockeye in the same locale where his ancestral relative was taken by the giant salmon and to dwell in the same landscape that his ancestor Raven helped to create through various deeds that are commemorated in toponyms such as Yéil Áx' Sh Wulgeigi Yé ("Place Where Raven Swung," a cut between two peaks) and Yeil Daa.áax̲u ("Raven's Bundle," a constellation of rocks in Chilkoot River) (Southeast Native Subsistence Commission 1995–2002). Lévi-Strauss (1966b) aptly describes the homology between the sociological and cosmological orders when he refers to space as "a society of named places."

The ordering implicit in *shagóon* is itself a dynamic construct that must be reinforced and reconfigured through the process of ritual. The memorial potlatch, which traditionally marked the (approximately one-year) anniversary of the death of a prominent individual (an *aanyádi,* or aristocrat) and the distribution of the clan *at.óow* to successors, was the most important public venue for configuring *shagóon.* It was here that notions about the ideal person as a thoroughly emplaced, knowledgeable, heavy, *at.óow*-laden, pure, and rock-like "high-class" person were celebrated, reconfirmed, and naturalized as part of the ethnogeographic order.

Drawing on Bourdieu's (1977) theory of practice, Kan (1989b:290) emphasizes that those aristocratic matrikin who were the custodians and controllers of their matrilineal relatives' *at.óow* and *shagóon* strategically used the hallowed structure of ritual to legitimize their dominant role in society. "Because they controlled much of *shagóon,* the *aanyátx'i* appeared to be the ancestors' mouthpieces. . . . Thus, their coercion of their lower-ranking matrikin was exercised not through brute force but mainly through 'symbolic violence,' i.e., oratory and other forms of ritual/symbolic action. . . . The hierarchical nature of this society was linked to and reinforced by the formalized language and ritual, so prominent in Tlingit life." By couching strategic political acts in the culturally reified and empathetic formats of ritual language and action, such as oratory, song, dance, cooperative feasts, and gift giving, members of the dominant strata could not only confirm their status and influence but raise and expand it (see also Boelscher 1989).

Yet, as Kan himself suggests (1989b:272), this framework takes us only so far, and "it would be a mistake . . . to see the potlatch rhetoric of love and respect for the dead and the living participants as only a mask hiding the brute facts of power, inequality, and competition." Indeed the ritual format can just as easily be seen as an institutional check on the worst forms of domination and self-aggrandizement and other sociopolitical and even emotional excesses. Olson (1956:686) emphasized that in ceremonies, as elsewhere, "Character was channeled to harmonize with the most important social group, the clan, and for most individuals the participation which they experienced was rewarding and satisfying." Indeed the potlatch and other ceremonies offered ample room for individuals not only to channel and reinforce social character and *shagóon* for collective and personal ends but also to extend and shape it in important new and positive ways that were consonant with clan and individual interests, and often transcended them. One important means of doing this was to create what I term *linking landscapes.*

A linking landscape is a terrain of the imagination, based on a geographic landscape, that is designed to bring people together. The best of Tlingit oratory and ritual action is filled with linking landscapes brought forth to promote solidarity, sharing, remembering, compassion, peace, healing, and other social, political, intellectual, material, and emotional ends. Linking landscapes are geographies of character. Let us consider one example, a speech by T'akdeintaan clan mother (Naa Tláa) Jessie Dalton, which has been carefully translated and analyzed by Nora and Richard Dauenhauer (1990:243–257, 385–397). The oration was delivered at an October 1968 memorial party for Jim Marks, a member of the Chookaneidí clan of the Eagle moiety and a child of the Lukaax.ádi clan of the Raven moiety, who died in October 1967. Jessie Dalton was chosen to make the central speech in the "removal of grief" portion of the ceremony in part because of her social position as an elder and clan mother (head of the T'akdeintaan women, collectively known as the K'eik'w Shaa or "Seagull [Kittiwake] Ladies") with ties to both hosts and guests, but also because of her outstanding individual character as a compassionate person and skilled orator. As Dauenhauer and Dauenhauer (1990:81) explain:

> An orator such as Jessie Dalton is selected to speak because of his or her sensitivity, and the orator is compared in Tlingit to someone who brings a very long pole into a house. In handling words, as in handling a pole, a speaker must be careful not to strike or hit anyone's face, or to break anything by accident. Referring to oratory during an interview, her own words were, "It is difficult to speak to someone who is respected. It is very difficult." Delivered carelessly, words can be dangerous and detrimental. But when delivered carefully, oratory can be a soothing medicine, a healing power and balm to one who is in pain. It can give spiritual strength. In Tlingit one says, *kaa toowú kei altseench*, "people gain spiritual strength from it," or *toowú latseen kaa jeex atee*, "it gives strength to the spirit." The effect of words in a good speech is described as *yándei kdusyaa yáx yatee du yoo x'atángi*, "his words were like cloth being gently spread out on a flat surface."

Alternatively, a well-delivered oration may also be seen as a "supportive wedge" or bridge linking two things — the past and the future (*shagóon*), the living and the dead, the grievers and the consolers, the hosts and the guests, and so on. In this respect Tlingits often characterize successful oratory as "imitating their ancestors," as a realization of their *shagóon*.

Jessie Dalton's speech builds on *at.óow* worn by her clan relatives, some of which have been referenced by earlier speakers. A button blanket, K'eik'w X'óow (Black-legged Kittiwake Blanket; see Figure 2), commemorating an ancestral T'akdeintaan site located by a prominent rock outcropping and

2. K̲’eik̲’w X’óow ("Kittiwake Blanket") refers to a sacred geographic site of the T’ak̲deintaan clan known as G̲aanax̲áa and is the central *at.óow* and key feature in the linking landscape employed by Jessie Dalton in her speech for the removal of grief at a 1968 memorial potlatch. (Photo by R. Dauenhauer)

kittiwake rookery named G̲aanax̲áa (on the outer coast of Glacier Bay National Park), becomes the central encapsulating image in the linking landscape that she lays out to clothe her hosts and aid in the removal of their grief. After invoking the central and supporting *at.óow* and the ancestral spirits they represent, Jessie Dalton transports her listeners to the landscape at G̲aanax̲áa for the purpose of healing:

> K̲’eik̲’w X’óow[1]
> Yes . . .
> A person who is feeling like you
> Would be brought by canoe,
> yes,
> to your father’s point,
> G̲aanax̲áa.
> That is when
> the name would be called out, it is said,

of the person who is feeling grief.
Yes.
(Dalton, in Dauenhauer and Dauenhauer
1990:245–247)

She completes the setting with references to other *at.óow,* similarly tied to T'akdeintaan land and *shagóon* and which also "show their faces" at Gaana-xáa, before consummating the image of the healing landscape by recalling the consoling acts of her ancestors, the kittiwakes — referenced here as "your father's sisters" to embrace the hosts of the opposite moiety (whose grateful responses are included in the excerpt) — at this sacred site.

> these terns [kittiwakes]
> Your father's sisters would fly out over the person
> who is feeling grief
> > (Willie Marks) *Áawé.*
> Then
> they would let down fall
> like snow
> over the person who is feeling grief.
> > (George Dalton) *Your brother's children are listening to you.*
> > (Harry Marvin) *Thank you.*
> That's when their down
> isn't felt.
> That's when
> I feel it's as if your father's sisters are flying
> back to their nests
> with your grief.
> > (Harry Marvin) *Thank you indeed.*
> *(Dauenhauer and Dauenhauer 1990:250–251)*

Thus, in the climax of Jessie Dalton's oratorical linking landscape for the removal of grief, the sacred k'eik'w literally cushion and absorb her host relatives' sadness and tears with their downy feathers and carry away the relatives' grief back to their nests at Gaanaxáa. She follows this with an extensive genealogical catalog of the bereaved hosts, whom she identifies, like the kittiwakes, by name and the appropriate kin term, before ending with a reference to another *at.óow* representing a mountain pass (Géelak'w) near Gaanaxáa from which the ancestors also "reveal their faces." In completing the genealogical catalog of relatives, as with the inventory of *at.óow* and sacred geography, Jessie Dalton effectively transcends or bridges the divisions of social groups just as she transcended the divisions of time, space, and body in transporting her audience to the spiritual landscape of her ancestors at G̲aanax̲áa. At the same time she reinforces the homologous linkages between the sociological landscape of those present at the memorial and the spiritual, temporal, and geographical healing landscape that she has just fashioned through her skillful oratory and mediation of *at.óow*. G̲aanax̲áa and other linking landscapes, then, serves as "chronotopes" (Bakhtin 1981:44–45; see also Basso 1984 and Thornton 1997b), or "points in the geography of a community where time and space intersect and fuse. Time takes on flesh and becomes visible for human contemplation; likewise, space becomes charged and responsive to the movements of time and history and the enduring *character* of a people. . . . Chronotopes thus stand as monuments to the community itself, as symbols of it, as forces operating to shape its members' images of themselves" (emphasis added).

The real beauty of this kind of oratory is that it both requires and engenders character. We learn what it means to be human, to be Tlingit, to be T'ak̲deintaan, as well as to be grief stricken, to possess *at.óow* and to be possessed by *shagóon*. With hardly a reference to "I," we also learn what it means to be Jessie Dalton, a clan mother and orator with particular relationships and responsibilities, who must rise to the occasion and weave a healing landscape into being with her own traditional knowledge and the materials (words, people, *at.óow*, *shagóon*, etc.) at hand. Furthermore, we see that she must commence the speech from her own location—her own place in Tlingit geography and social structure—but also transcend those structures in meaningful ways through words and images that inspire and move the assembly to new horizons of insight and terrains of being.

Critiquing the death of character in 20th-century Western consciousness and abstract thought, Hillman (1999:169) asks, rhetorically, "What would happen were character to return philosophically? Speaking would radically change, because it would tell about ourselves and the world as we appear. Characteristics need descriptions, faces are particular, phenomena present images. Language can respond by speaking more descriptively, imagistically." This is precisely what the linking landscapes of Tlingit oratory, as geographies of character, seek to accomplish.

Reading the Character of the Landscape

In linking the personal, social, and geographic elements of identity, Tlingits hold that character is not merely a manifestation of human nature but is itself a force of nature. The geographic basis of social group — clan, house, and _kwáan_ (from the verb "to dwell" and referring to the region one inhabits) — identity naturalizes the geography of character, but individual Tlingits, such as Jessie Dalton, also build their character on the basis of particular knowledge of and relationships with the lands and waters and other inhabitants of Southeast Alaska. This involves mastering important domains of traditional ecological knowledge (or TEK), such as place-names and their cultural meanings, but also learning to live in one's country through a broad range of activities, especially those projects that have come to be known as _subsistence._

The importance of TEK and subsistence food gathering activities to the maintenance of culture and of character can hardly be overemphasized. Sitka elder Herman Kitka (1998:48) put it this way: "Teaching subsistence occurred where our customary and traditional subsistence food supply was collected. This education was what made each Tlingit a good citizen in each community. The young people learn to respect the land they live on. They also learn to take only what each family needs to make it through the year. We need to keep teaching the children our subsistence lifestyle, culture, and religion. Without this education, our Tlingit cultures will be lost forever." As with ceremony, much could be written on the topics of TEK and subsistence (see Thornton 1998), but here I want to emphasize how ethnogeographic knowledge, especially the information that is embedded in place-names, was critical to both projects as well as to the process of character development.

Working with Tlingit tribes over the past decade to document approximately 3,000 Native toponyms, I have come to appreciate the breadth and depth of Tlingit ethnotoponymy (see Thornton 1995, 1997a, 1999, 2000; SENSC 1995–2001). The vast majority of major terrestrial and hydrographic features of Southeast Alaska were named by the Tlingits and other inhabitants of the region, and as elders often point out, "each name has a story behind it." An individual Tlingit's character is not only a product of knowing the stories behind these names, but also lies in his or her ability to read and adapt to the character of the landscape through TEK and the experience of living on the land. I label this capacity *place intelligence*, extending Gardner's (1993) theory of multiple intelligences (see also P. Stern 1999). Indeed, a fundamental characteristic of TEK is that it is *emplaced* knowledge — local knowledge that is developed in situ and is conditioned and sustained in vivo by the exigencies of subsistence life (Hunn 1993).

Geographic names exemplify these characteristics, and like TEK itself, indigenous toponymies can be viewed as culturally constituted systems of knowledge built up through the process of dwelling in particular landscapes. The empirical grounding of TEK in the named landscape, as we saw with the kittiwakes of G̲aanax̲áa, contributes to its force. Named places serve as icons and indexes of TEK, symbolizing and evoking historical knowledge, wisdom, and sentiments and making them "tangible and permanent" (Malinowski 1922:330) through the enduring features of the physical landscape. As Kake elder Fred Friday explained the relationship between Tlingit toponyms and ecological knowledge to land claims investigators in 1946, "The Native people know all the points and rocks and every little area by name. If I told you all the names of all the places that I know it would fill many pages. These areas were used so much that we were familiar with every little place" (Goldschmidt and Haas 1998:177). For him, the landscape of the physical world coordinates with the landscape of the mind in order to produce, organize, maintain, and recall TEK. There exists between these two landscapes, as Basso (1996) has shown, an interanimation. This is why Fred Friday suggests that the recounting of all the areas that he knows by name "would fill many pages." He is emphasizing not only the number of *names* he knows, but also what he *knows* about a number of names. In stressing these connections, Fred Friday, like Jessie Dalton, is suggesting something about his own character as an emplaced person in *Lingit aaní* ("Tlingit country").

Reading the natural landscape is not unlike reading the sociological landscape. One must be able to distinguish the character of individual places (like persons) and also to group them into meaningful wholes (like clans, etc.) as the context warrants. The cognitive patterns inherent in naming reveal these twin processes. For example, names distinguish important landmarks through precise topographic description (e.g., Geeshk'ishuwanyee or "Place below the base of the end of the edge of the kelp," a halibut fishing bank) but also group them under common generic terms (e.g., *héen* or creek, *geeyí* or bay). In his classic study of Kwakiutl place-names Boas

(1934:10) reported that once he came to understand their linguistic structure, he could often guess the names of landforms based upon their topographic appearance, "unless it so happens that specific interests attached to the place interfere with descriptive nomenclature" (i.e., they refer to historic events or other nonphysical or latent features of the landscape).

Another Northwest Coast ethnogeographer, Thomas Waterman (1922), observed that these naming principles bred a certain repetition or redundancy, wherein similar sites in different areas would inspire the same name. Even so, the logic of repetition involves more than unreflectively applying old names to new sites that resemble the originals. Like naming offspring after ancestors, naming places after similar predecessors involves a certain contemplation and comprehension of their character. Perhaps for the same reason, the geographies of mythic stories are often relocalized when groups move to a new setting. There is an important mitigating factor, too: distance. In general, features with the same name cannot be too close together. Thus we do not find two creeks named Gathéeni ("Sockeye Creek") in the same area. The logic of this rule would seem to be one of avoiding confusion in identification of key sites in practical navigation and in memory. Significantly, this pattern applies to the social world as well, where it is important that persons possessing the same name (especially honorific names and titles) not be too close together in social space (e.g., within the same localized house group) and time (e.g., the same generation), lest there be confusion.

There is another process that I term *ensemblage*, which also was reductively characterized as mere redundancy by early ethnographers.[2] A geographic ensemblage is a grouping and relating of separate landscape features into a meaningful whole, through naming. Ensemblages create regions out of otherwise disparate points. Typically one key landmark becomes the central organizing feature for a whole constellation of named sites within a circumscribed area. For example, there is a small island called Kéin at the entrance to the narrows above the village of Kake in central Southeast Alaska. Kéin (an unanalyzable term) is the central organizing feature for a geographic ensemblage that also includes Kéin Séet ("Kéin Strait/Pass," east of Kéin) and Kéin Yatx'i ("Children of *Kéin*," a set of islands southwest of Kéin). Although small and seemingly insignificant in itself, Kéin is a very important landmark for orienting travelers approaching and leaving Kake to the northeast. Its significance as a signpost is cross-cultural, as under-scored by the fact that the island, known as Turnabout Island in English, now houses a federal navigational marker for boats. But in the English toponymy there is no ensemblage—the subsidiary features of the island are not even named. Larger toponymic ensemblages in Tlingit may contain as many as 10 or 12 names related to a central feature.

The Kéin grouping is one of two ensemblages at the entrance to Keku Strait. The other one—the Teik ensemblage—orients the traveler approach-ing or leaving Kake to the northwest. Like Kéin, Teik is a small island, but in this case its derivative names refer to features on the island itself and are anatomical in nature—Teik Lunáak referring to the "nose" or point of the island and Teik Tukyee to its "anus" or outlet. Such anatomical references are common in geographical nomenclature and reflect another cross-cultural cognitive pattern: use of the body—the primary environment that we in-habit—as a metaphor or image schema for conceptualizing landscape (see Thornton 1995; Lakoff 1987). The metaphor of kinship offers another schema for relating places. Especially common is the "child of" metaphor, which de-fines a small feature proximal to its larger "parent"; Kéin Yatx'i ("Children of *Kéin*") is an example of this paradigm. Such ensemblages and schemata both reveal and shape Tlingit sensuous perceptions of the landscape, ren-dering the character of their country in human terms. Not far from Kéin is a place called Kéex' Luwoolk'í, or "Ring at the Base of the Nose [Rock] of Kake." Kake Tlingit dancers used to adorn themselves with large nose rings to emulate the shape of this rock, which had been a landmark to them during their migration north and still serves as a marker today (Clarence Jackson, personal communication, 1997). As with the Sockeye and Kittiwake blan-kets, which similarly map the character of the land onto the body, this too is a form of ensemblage. But the central feature of the geographic ensem-blage is not a place but persons, who place elements of the geography on their bodies in order to mutually inscribe their character on the land and the land on their character.

The character of the country is also defined by those nonhuman beings that inhabit it, including the kittiwake, whose eggs Tlingits sometimes con-sume, and hundreds of other species of plants and animals, many of which are utilized for subsistence needs. Boas correctly observed that "cultural in-terests" in landscapes, particularly those concerning food procurement, are reflected often in naming. G̲athéeni ("Sockeye Salmon Creek") is an example of a metonymic place name, meaning that the species characterizes the place by its presence there, usually in abundance. However, as the halibut bank example illustrates, these interests are not always obvious from the toponym itself. Often they can only be grasped by knowing the "story behind the name," or through interpretation of the name in its cultural-ecological context.

The case of sockeye salmon (*Oncorhynchus nerka*) is especially interesting from a cultural-ecological perspective. Sockeye streams, sparsely distributed in comparison to streams possessing other salmon, are named for this species nearly twice as often as all other streams are named for all other species combined, and three times as often as streams containing dog salmon and pink salmon (the most common types) are named for those species. A sockeye stream supporting other Pacific salmon (and all those in Southeast do, usually at least two other species) is rarely, if ever, named for those other species. This clearly reflects the "distinctions that make a difference" principle, but that alone does not explain the emphasis, for if that were the case, more of the also rare king salmon streams would be named "King Salmon Stream." The toponymic emphasis on sockeye also reflects the Tlingit interest in sockeye, which are valued for their high fat content, taste, predictable runs, and extended harvestability (they can be taken in freshwater streams and lakes even after spawning). So important are sockeye that we find overdifferentiation in the Tlingit classification as compared to Western science: Tlingit has a separate lexeme for populations of small sockeyes in the Sitka area, which are known as *dagák'* and their natal bay as Dagák' G̲eeyí or "Little Sockeye Bay."

Such anomalous and esoteric ecofacts are scrupulously recorded in the ethnotoponymy, and they are relished as TEK by knowledgeable Tlingits because they reveal unique aspects of the idiosyncratic character of their country, and therefore of themselves. Thus, Sitka Tlingits recognize the little sockeye or *dagák'* as a special salmon with its own unique personality, taste, habitat, and special harvesting and processing requirements. Their unique personality is celebrated in a phrase employed in ceremonial oratory: *Tleil dagák' Ahawateeni yík,* meaning "Don't leave insulted like those little sockeyes." The phrase itself is a humble way of saying to guests from the opposite moiety, "I hope I have not offended you," or "I hope I have treated you with respect so that you will return." Its meaning is rooted in an ecological fact. According to elder Herman Kitka (personal communication, 1996), "those little sockeye get offended if you don't leave them a hole in your [fish] weir; they won't come back if it [the stream] is all blocked off." Thus, this bit of TEK becomes immortalized in a place-name, serves as a metaphor of social relations, and instills a moral-ecological principle regarding escapement and conservation of salmon in a particular fishery. In its ecological context, it speaks volumes about the particular character of Sitka Tlingit country; in its social use it speaks volumes about the character of Tlingit ceremonial hosts.

Conclusion

In one of several important essays on Western Apache place-naming, Keith Basso (1984:48) notes that "American Indians, like groups of people everywhere, maintain a complex array of symbolic relationships with their physical surroundings, and that those relationships, which may have little to do with the serious business of making a living, play a fundamental role in shaping other forms of social activity." I have argued that geography—particularly knowledge of places and the stories behind them—forms an important basis for the development of Tlingit character and identity. Like Aristotle and the Apache, Tlingits recognize the primacy and revelatory logic of places and their vessel-like qualities as containers of wisdom. Thus, geographic knowledge goes hand in hand with ecological (TEK), social (at.óow, shagóon, shuká), and ritual (protocol, oratory, dance, etc.) knowledge to support Tlingits being in the world.

Hillman's emphasis on the unique and developmental qualities of character in the individual helps free us from some of the limitations of the culture and personality school's emphasis on enculturation and childrearing practices in the study of character and personality. At the same time, we can progress little in our understanding Tlingit character without recognizing that Tlingits had their own means of inscribing character onto individuals from an early age. Among the most important of these frameworks that survive today are the cultural institutions of shuká, at.óow, and shagóon.

To understand fully how place resonates with character, we must consider not only how places are apprehended and conceptualized, but also how they are transacted among people. As those in the phenomenological tradition point out, this means going beyond language and "speaking with [place] names" to include other modes of relating to landscape, such as visual art, contemplation, and subsistence, which similarly reveal the logic of place (Harkin 2000). If place names are truly signposts and vessels, then we must consider both the means by which people encounter and remember places and the ends they seek in doing so. For Tlingits, as with Basso's (1996) Western Apaches, "wisdom sits in places," but the apprehension of this wisdom requires an existing reservoir of traditional knowledge and the perceptual skills—what Merleau-Ponty (following Levy-Bruhl; see Abram 1996:44–59) calls *participatory perception* that comes through practical engagement, or what Heidegger (1977) calls *dwelling* with lands and people. Basso (1996:132) emphasizes the importance of what the Apaches term *smoothness of mind* in holding and applying the wisdom of place knowledge in appropriate ways. Tlingits, too, have a healthy appreciation for the respectful acquisition, maintenance, and pragmatic use of place intelligence. As the ethnographic examples above illustrate, it is in practice, through the strategic deployment of appropriate geographic knowledge, skills, and wisdom, that place intelligence is revealed and evaluated as an attribute of character. Austin Hammond's explication of the "Sockeye Point Blanket," Jessie Dalton's oratorical linking landscape for the removal of grief, and Herman Kitka's telling of the story behind the little sockeyes of Dagák' Geeyí are but a few superb examples of this integrity of place, wisdom, and character. For just as wisdom sits in places, so does character arise from places.

Notes

A seed version of this essay was presented at the 1999 American Anthropological Association Meeting in Chicago as part of a panel entitled "Place Names through Time." I am grateful to the participants of the panel for their comments on the paper, especially Eugene Hunn. My research has been supported by a grant from the National Park Service, which funded the Southeast Native Subsistence Commission's Native Place Names Project, and also by separate small grants from the Jacobs Fund and the Philips Fund. Harold Martin oversaw the SENSC project and taught me a great deal about place and character in the course of carrying out the research, as did the many Tlingit elders who participated in the project. Preparation of the manuscript was facilitated by a 1998–99 fellowship from the National Endowment for the Humanities and benefited from thoughtful reviews by Dell Hymes, an anonymous reader, and editors Michael Harkin, Sergei Kan, and Marie Mauzé. My insights into place and being among the Tlingits have also been enriched by conversations with Keith Basso, Julie Cruikshank, Richard Dalton, Nora and Richard Dauenhauer, Lydia and Jimmie George, Walter Goldschmidt, Ken Grant, Andy Hope, Fred Hope, Herb Hope, Joe Hotch, Mark Jacobs, Miriam Kahn, Matthew Kookesh, Ethel Makinen, John Marks, the late Amy Marvin, Pat Mills, the late Richard Newton, Robert Schroeder, the late Richard Sheakley, the late Mary Willis, Gary Witherspoon, Rosita Worl, and especially my wife, Patricia Thornton, and my Tlingit brother and teacher, Herman Kitka Sr.

1. I use the Tlingit phrase here, which the Dauenhauers translate generally as "Tern Robe," as do many Tlingits. Recent ethno-ornithological investigations (see Hunn et al. 2002), however, reveal _k'eik'w_ more precisely as black-legged kittiwakes (_Rissa tridactyla_), a relative of the tern, which roost at Gaanaxáa and are typically depicted with black legs in Tlingit _at.óow_.

2. I am grateful to Dell Hymes for suggesting the term _ensemblage_ in place of my original term _ensembling_.

THIRTEEN WAYS OF LOOKING
AT A LANDSCAPE

Michael E. Harkin

My title is drawn, of course, from Wallace Stevens's poem "Thirteen Ways of Looking at a Blackbird." This spare, imagist poem, reminiscent of Haiku, is theoretically interesting because it plays with and to a certain degree deconstructs the semiotic relation between human and nature. Observer and observed, signifier and signified, subject and object, are cut loose from their normal moorings in Western discourse. Nature and nature poet trade places. The plurality of perspectives offered by both poet and blackbird is reminiscent of anthropology's "Rashomon effect" (Heider 1988). With regard to landscape, both points are important. In order to take account of the phenomenology of place, we must resist the common view of place as mere object. Place takes on subjective qualities, of which humans may themselves become objects. Moreover, around any landscape a plurality, even an avian cacophony, of views arise. This is especially the case with respect to landscapes on contested ground.

Clayoquot Sound on the west coast of Vancouver Island, British Columbia, is the general area I am considering. Numerous perspectives have shaped the construction of Clayoquot Sound as place. I can only mention in passing the historically important ones of colonialism and the romantic picturesque, which I have discussed elsewhere (Harkin 2000). The colonial viewpoint is most eloquently expressed by Gilbert Malcolm Sproat, an English surveyor, government agent, and businessman, who was the first amateur ethnologist in the area. In 1868 he published *Scenes and Studies of Savage Life* about the Nuu-chah-nulth (Nootka) people of the area (Sproat 1987). His observations about place were informed by a fascinating hybrid of the military, navigational, logistic, and geological, which are entirely expected, with the aesthetic and picturesque, which are not. However, this combination was not unusual at the time. As the writer Jonathan Raban has recently (1999,

2001) argued, Romantic notions of "the sublime" were integral to the view taken by the English of British Columbia, beginning with the younger generation of officers on Captain George Vancouver's ship. Indeed, this celebration, even apparent worship of landscape, was evident in artists of the Northwest, such as Albert Bierstadt and Thomas Moran, and was also remarked upon by more direct agents of colonialism, beginning with Lewis and Clark (Allen 1972).[1] W. J. T. Mitchell goes so far as to say that landscape is the "'dreamwork' of imperialism" (Mitchell 2003:10).

The role of the aboriginal inhabitant of these landscapes is deeply ambiguous. The inhabitants of the Yosemite Valley were cleared out, by the typically brutal means practiced in 19th-century California, before Muir and Bierstadt saw the place. All indications of previous human occupation were "edited out" of the picture (Schama 1995:7–8; Bordo 2003:308–309). The effect was an apotheosis of landscape, in which certain elements are framed and fetishized. This reaches a climax in the photography of Carleton Watkins and, later, Ansel Adams, who, through various technical means, created the illusion of direct, unmediated access to the specific landscape features released from their ground (Snyder 2003:182–183).

However, for many observers, interest in aboriginal peoples as part of an organic landscape was pronounced; it was, after all, part of the package of Romanticism. Poets such as Wordsworth and painters such as Constable were interested in the people who dwelled in landscape, as well as in the landscapes themselves. Such Romantic taste in landscape reflects both nostalgia for agrarian modes of life as well as a belief that the ordering principles of social life, which placed such persons in positions of poverty and marginality, were essentially just (Bermingham 2003:98). Ruskin set forth the principles for this style of art, which was highly influential in both Europe and America (see Ruskin 1873). North American artists of the 19th and early 20th centuries, especially George Catlin, Paul Kane, and Emily Carr, placed Northwest Coast native people and their artifacts within the frame of the sublime landscape.

Emily Carr, who began her painting of Indian themes in Clayoquot Sound after meeting a local Ucluelet chief in 1898, epitomized the aestheticized view of native people and place. Interestingly, her meeting with the chief was wordless, as he spoke no English. She, however, believed that she understood perfectly what he thought: a nice metonym of the prevalent view of native people as mute, passive, and ultimately disappearing people who were classed with the natural world and could be represented as such (Cole 2000). Carr's intense fascination with the disappearing traces of the aboriginal past, especially totem poles, took her to "spooky places" haunted by the ghosts of dead and dying societies (Shadbolt 1979:28, 66). Indeed, there was a great deal of death and decline in this period, although the demographic nadir for most groups was 30 or more years in the past from the time of her most active painting of Indian subjects. There was even more an imagined decline, a product not of real historical forces but of the Claudian fascination with decay and traces of ancient peoples. In Carr, who is interestingly different from earlier British Columbia artists and writers, nature is an active force, even an agent, albeit one of entropy.

The imagined progress of entropy is traced in the trajectory of Carr's career. At the suggestion of fellow Northwest Coast landscape artist Mark Tobey, Carr eliminated all traces of aboriginal occupation. In the 1930s her paintings become "animistic" treatments of the forest itself, recalling her totem poles but no longer depicting them (Raban 2001:49). Had the Indians simply disappeared as she had indeed foretold, or was her art merely following an aesthetic of abstraction, such as that practiced by Tobey and other American landscape painters, such as Georgia O'Keeffe? Indeed, her development seems to draw on both sources. In a theoretical sense, one to which we will return, Carr was involved, along with fellow Canadians Marius Barbeau and the Group of Seven painters, in a project of "deterritorialization" and "reterritorialization" of the Canadian landscape, in Deleuze and Guattari's (1987) language (see Appadurai 1996; Slaney 2000). In the words of Frances Slaney, Carr's forest landscapes were representations "of a sense of place that included and revered indigenous inhabitants even while assimilating them into nature" (Slaney 2000:104). Marius Barbeau, the Quebecois ethnographer who was active in nationalist art and encouraged Canadian painters to paint specific, if archetypal, landscapes that carried a specifically Canadian sense of place, believed that Euro-Canadian artists had the right and the duty to carry on where aboriginal art left off. As native cultures, in his view, declined and lost their creative genius, white artists were obligated to adapt their place-making practices, re-animating landscapes in the service of a nationalist reterritorialization (Slaney 2000:93).

Marius Barbeau and many of his contemporaries believed that the problem of national identity was paramount. Canada, lacking a dramatic unifying national myth, such as that of the United States, and faced with the problem of almost insurmountable distances separating west and east, not to mention the French and English "two solitudes," was not an easily imagined community, in Benedict Anderson's (1983) phrase. Barbeau and his colleagues applied the technologies of landscape painting, ethnography, and folklore to the problem, rendering certain types of Canadian landscape: A. Y. Jackson or Tom Thompson's Canadian Shield-northern Great Lakes scenes, Barbeau's rural Quebec farmsteads, or Carr's dense rainforests, iconic: instantly recognizable symbols, even to those who had never seen them, of distinctly Canadian places.[2]

Discourse about place is thus generally both political and aesthetic. This remains the case today, in the United States and Canada, even as the terms of discourse have changed, and the discourses themselves have multiplied. Familiar discourses operate today almost as a shorthand for thinking about place — environmentalist vs. economic development, sacred spaces vs. open access to public lands — evident in the work of writers such as Gary Snyder and Wendell Barry (see Cronon 1995). Such paired opposites inject themselves easily into political debates about oil drilling, recreational uses of federal lands, and aboriginal claims on and uses of land. Such discourses conceal as much as they reveal, however. By looking at a specific case of place and the multiple discourses about it — resource management, environmentalism, tourism (of which eco-tourism and ethno-tourism are important components), and what I would call, for lack of a better term, traditional Nuu-chah-nulth place making — I hope to get at some of the complexities as well as the fundamental issues of deterritorialization and reterritorialization. I look at the related cases of Clayoquot Sound and the Walk the Wild Side Heritage Trail on Flores Island, British Columbia, as they developed during the 1990s.

Place and Space

The conception of space and location has become the object of considerable anthropological speculation over the past decade. As with the earlier examination of time concepts, this literature is useful in producing both phenomenological and critical accounts of what had been taken to be a "given," a universal, with little inherent anthropological interest (Basso 1996; Feld and

Basso 1996; Foucault 1980:63–77; Gupta and Ferguson 1992a; Kahn 2000). As Henri Lefebvre (1991) has phrased the matter, the problematization of space suffers from the Cartesian legacy of being viewed as *res extensa* in opposition to *res cogitans*. Lefebvre seeks to bridge this opposition by the creation of a "third space," which combines both the physical and spatial dimensions normally assigned to space and the mental and ideological ones normally assigned to culture. Lefebvre's approach has been adopted by Miriam Kahn (2000), whose recent article examines the construction of "third space" in Tahiti.

Similar to Tahiti, aboriginal landscapes in British Columbia are subject to an intersection of aesthetic, touristic, naturalistic, colonizing, and other discourses, which have combined to create spatial hybrids. In a previous article I (Harkin 2000) have examined deployments of place making and spatial discourse in several ethnographic contexts in British Columbia. Here I focus on Clayoquot Sound, and specifically on the trail project in Ahousaht called "Walk the Wild Side." It represents an intersection of several key landscape discourses.

The notion of "third space" is valuable in reckoning with the plurality of discourses that construct Clayoquot Sound as a place. Political and representational practices intersect and conflict in a contested third space. Similar to Kahn's Tahiti, discourses of tourism, environmentalism, and aesthetics are opposed to those of resource exploitation and national interest (in Tahiti played out over the issue of nuclear testing, in Clayoquot over the almost equally controversial issue of clear-cutting), while at the same time these discourses may themselves be contradictory in other contexts. However, although the notion of third space may give an adequate account of the play of discourse, it holds to an impoverished phenomenology. To begin with, Lefebvre and Kahn assume the existence of a "first space" that is purely physical and primordially outside human consciousness. This is the legacy of Descartes, and like any attempt to turn Descartes on his head, it ends up repeating the initial problems. Space as pure abstraction is the product of a radical reduction from the lifeworld that we know experientially. Why must we assume that a "first space" exists at all, except as the artifact of specific human discourses: cartography, geography, and geometry? Indeed, such ways of perceiving landscape had to be invented. It was not until the 18th century that what James C. Scott calls "cadastral mapping," the systematic, objective representation of space as resource, came into being, and this was clearly the handmaiden of the state (Scott 1998:38–45). The very use of the term *space* rather than *place* betrays its Cartesian ancestry.

Alternatively, Pierre Bourdieu (1991) views space as a socially determined and wholly arbitrary construct. Thus, place and all its culturally generated representations derive from an originary act of drawing a boundary. This arbitrary boundary drawing, which Bourdieu describes as a sacred act, is in fact a myth derived from the specific histories of European states. Although usefully preserving the "secondness" of representational space, it ignores the intrinsic qualities of landscape itself. Applying a Durkheimian structuralism, Bourdieu is hostile to the idea that meaning may be anything other than arbitrary or may reside outside the social and political structure. Even in Europe, with its famously shifting borders, those borders are not exactly arbitrary but usually follow ecological boundaries. The borders of England, the borders between the Holy Roman Empire and Burgundy, and other borders are clearly motivated rather than arbitrary (but see P. Sahlins 1989).[3] Moreover, inhabitants perceive landscape, often endowing it with agency, apart from any macropolitical acts, ritual or otherwise.

In the phenomenological tradition the inhabitants' view of landscape is primary; one speaks of "place" (Casey 1996). Unlike "space," place has intentional qualities, not mere extension. Place is a dwelled-in locus of human activity and intentionality and is imbued with subjectivity, including the ability to act. Thus, in Nuu-chah-nulth narratives about places in Clayoquot Sound, places become actors in a way reminiscent of Homeric narrative (Harkin 1998). Although the subject of discourse, including traditional narrative, place transcends discourse and is fundamentally a mode of being in the world.

Places acquire temporal meanings through the accretion of events that become associated with them. In this sense, the opposition between temporal and spatial perspectives is an artificial one on the local level. Like Australian aborigines who view landscape elements as transformations of ancestors, or as bearing traces of those transformations, Nuu-chah-nulth people use places to remember events. Places thus have a mnemonic function, similar to the spatial models of memory used in Europe in the Middle Ages. More than that, place is inherently a spatiotemporal agent, with an ongoing potential to effect transformations. Nuu-chah-nulth narrative, like that of other Northwest Coast cultures, is full of examples of persons undergoing profound transformations after an encounter with a place: change of species, change from poverty to wealth, change from life to death or vice versa. Caves, lakes, beaches, deep forest, and other liminal zones are especially possessed of this potentiality. Such a landscape is, before anything else, *inhabited*. It is saturated with habits of mind and body, with traces of ancestors and their actions. Place consciousness is homologous with historical consciousness, with a mere shift in modality; together, as Basso (1996:7) says, they are "a way of constructing social traditions and, in the process, personal and social identities."

Certain types of conceptualized landscape elements, which I have called "topemes," exist within cultural traditions such as the Nuu-chah-nulth (Harkin 2000). Thus, caves are likely to be places of great danger and also possibility for obtaining power (Harkin 1998). Beaches are places where political and military events occur. Beaches represent a liminal space between land and sea and thus a location of considerable strategic, economic, and supernatural importance. Caves were seen as portals to the underworld and thus the liminal space in which dangerous powers could be encountered.

Such topemes are, to some degree, semiotically motivated. Beaches, for instance, serve this political-military function because enemies, allies, and strangers come from over water and land on beaches. What is more, battles and contests took place on beaches, which were the only cleared-out space available for such encounters. Not only did such space provide adequate room to maneuver, but it allowed for a public viewing of events. Caves, on the other hand, are a natural interface between surface world and underworld, and for cultures possessing a vertical cosmology, these are likely to be places of power and danger. Thus, there are certain family resemblances among the motif of the cave in different traditions. Homeric narrative appears close to Nuu-chah-nulth, in this and other respects.[4] Odysseus is prevented from returning to Ithaca in several instances by the active intervention of places, including man-eating caves.[5] In an early story in the history of chiefly lineages of the Ahousaht, four brothers are trapped in a cave near Hesquiat Lake, which the eldest brother used as a ritual place. However, because the younger brothers are greedy and wish to take the eldest's whaling magic, the cave encloses them within, causing them to be devoured by giant rats.

If landscape acts, it also is affected by human events. In a story concerning the Tla-o-qui-aht chiefly line, an early chief is confronted by an overwhelming force of Ditidaht warriors. To this group he reveals his powerful stone club, his "death-bringer" (*mok'want*), which causes the warriors to fall down dead. The death-bringer was originally taken from spirit wolves, who gave humans the Wolf Dance (*tluqwana*), of which the death-bringer is an integral part (Curtis 1916:94–98; Drucker 1951:386–443). The dead warriors become transformed into landscape elements, humanlike stones that are to be found today on the banks of Clayoquot Lake. This transformation into landscape elements is, of course, reminiscent of Australian views of landscape (Morphy 1995; Munn 1973; Myers 1986). As with Australian landscape, discrete elements are created by ancestral acts. What is more, these places continue to play a role in human affairs by virtue of their power, as points through which the ancestors continue to operate in the world.

This view of history is anything but linear. Time is not unidirectional, but recursive. It is through places such as the rocks by Hesquiat Lake that ancestral powers are concentrated to the point that they affect the present. Such places are "perturbations in the space-time continuum where creative energy is transformed into matter" according to Robert Layton (1995:229), who is talking about Australian aboriginal places. Indeed, numerous examples of this phenomenon can be found in Clayoquot Sound. On Meares Island, a mountain on the northwest corner is the petrified form of a canoe that came aground at the time of the Great Flood. Such places are points of power, which may continue to act in the world, especially in situations where persons act in a ritual manner.[6]

In a more general sense, Nuu-chah-nulth sense of time and historical possibility may be said to be shaped by the landscape. As Schama (1995) forcefully demonstrates for Western history, dwelling in certain landscapes entails a consciousness of recurrent historical possibilities. Certain places, such as northern Poland, are, to be sure, located on historical fault lines that tend to erupt repeatedly. These eruptions emit overlays of historical sediment, which can later be read by the careful observer. More than an inscription of human events upon a natural surface, however, there is a sense that the landscape itself participates in these historical possibilities. Specific landforms and ecotopes, such as mountains, forests, and rivers, have meanings deeply rooted (we can scarcely avoid botanical metaphors) in Indo-

European language and culture (Friedrich 1970). Things are much the same in Clayoquot Sound. Topemes recur throughout history, with similar functions (Mauzé 1998a).

Trails

The forest trail is perhaps the best example of the interpenetration of landscape and human intentionalities. A trail, on the one hand, is "natural," since it follows physically the path of least resistance through dense temperate rain forest. This path follows higher, drier land through muskeg, perhaps along rock outcroppings or other areas that inhibit the collection of water and unstable soil that occurs most places. At the same time frequent use of the path makes it even more useful, by packing down soil and inhibiting the growth of flora, which in turn invites yet more human and animal traffic. In addition, specific actions may be taken, such as the felling of a tree, that alter the landscape in more sudden ways. However, rather than viewing this as an irrevocable break between a natural and an artificial environment, it is more accurately the intensification of a dialogic encounter between humans and forest. Trails, becoming increasingly efficient with use, deliver people into the heart of the forest to extract resources and to encounter nonhuman beings and sources of supernatural power. As the trail is increasingly characterized by human intentionality, humans who travel the trail become increasingly shaped by the nonhuman forest.

This paradox of the trail makes it a highly generative metaphor. In English and other European languages trails become metaphors and metonyms for history itself, which is thought to have a definite directionality. Literal trails, such as the Overland and Oregon Trails in the U.S. West, are metonyms of great demographic movements. Metaphoric trails, such as the development of flight or the computer, are opened up by "trail blazers," who constrain future movements. By contrast, trails in Nuu-chah-nulth culture are viewed differently. Traditionally they were a type of private knowledge that might be widely known, but that was shared within limited social circles. Trails led to economic resources and, perhaps more importantly, to loci of power well beyond the circumscribed social space of the village.

Other meanings of trails and trail blazing are relevant here. In the West and Northwest, the tradition of naturalism and conservation begin with the ancestral trailblazer, John Muir. Muir, known for exploring the Sierras of

California—probably the first white person to do so without economic incentive—traveled the West Coast as far north as Alaska, always seeking access to sublime nature. Aboriginal people were not especially important for Muir, except in cases where they could act as guides and bearers. Humans generally were framed out of the picture, which was focused on pure nature, especially those extraordinary features—Cathedral Rock in Yosemite, for example—that served as shrines of wilderness. It has frequently been noted that such attitudes constitute a secular religion, one predicated on natural, rather than artificial, sacred spaces. As such, it is an outgrowth of the Protestant search for signs of God in the immediacy of everyday life, rather than through the mediation of an ecclesiastical structure. Muir, raised as a Scottish Calvinist, was simply taking things a step further, dispensing with the church itself as unnecessary to, and indeed inhibiting, a communion with a divinity that was at once immanent and transcendent.

Muir is what Foucault (1998) calls a founder of discourse (although Foucault himself would probably have disagreed). That discourse has evolved and ramified over the last century, leading to social movements as diverse as deep ecology and eco-tourism. Both are represented in Clayoquot Sound, and both were important in defeating the 1993 proposal to clear-cut a large portion of the Sound. Environmentalists of all stripes, allied with aboriginal people and people whose livelihood was threatened unified in their opposition to the proposal, and many bravely went to jail for their opposition (MacIsaac and Champagne 1994; Dark 1998). However, in the years since, this coalition has become increasingly fragile, as substantial fault lines have been revealed between the discourses. And yet at the same time it would be a mistake to overstate these fault lines, as there remains considerable tolerance and goodwill among those who were united in opposition to clear-cut logging. Moreover, there is a certain hybridity of discourse at the moment, where elements from resource management, environmental, tourism, and aboriginal sovereignty discourses merge. This is, indeed, precisely what a "third space" model, although deficient in other respects, would predict. As Kahn (2000) describes with respect to Tahiti, there is a process of discursive creolization occurring to match the biological creolization of the population. One of her consultants, a creole professional photographer whose living is dependent upon eroticized and exoticized representations of his homeland, is in a position similar to that of many of the residents of Clayoquot Sound. Aboriginal people are fully integrated into the tourist infra-structure, as owners as well as workers. This imbrication of economic and political structures results in hybrid discourses about landscape. The most significant of these is eco-tourism (I retain the hyphen to emphasize its hy-phenated and contradictory nature).

My Canada Includes Clayoquot Sound

The current tourist boom arose in the wake of plans to clear-cut most of the forest in the Clayoquot Sound drainage in 1993 (see Dark 1998). Eco-tourists, along with environmental activists, were instrumental in defeating that ini-tial proposal. Of course, the tourists' presence itself threatens the landscape in a different way. Paradoxically, tourists are aware of this and do what they can to avoid the places already so corrupted. This leads to a cycle of penetra-tion and colonization of ever-new territories, in a parodic replay of colonial history (Harkin 1995). By the mid-1990s the tourist gaze had moved from the mainland (i.e., of Vancouver Island) and its coastal waters to outer islands and especially to native communities.

The eco-tourist discourse emphasizes the sanctity of certain semioti-cally framed natural areas. Paradoxically, the eco-tourist follows in the phys-ical footsteps of Muir, although participating in a commercialization of na-ture that Muir would have abhorred. Eco-tourism, along with its cousin, ethno-tourism, draws on a diverse background, which includes tourism as its prior and largest component. (How else could one justify the consump-tion and waste required to transport an "eco-tourist" from the metropole to the "unspoiled" wilderness, or the unavoidable damage done to the place by the tourist's very presence?) However, the notion of sacred place is the crux of the entire discourse. In this, eco-tourism and ethno-tourism are united; the difference is simply over what (or who) sanctifies a sacred place (tem-perate rain forest or aboriginal peoples).

There is no necessary contradiction between these two positions, at least in the mind of the contemporary eco- and ethno-tourist (who may very well be the same person). In fact, the presence of the aboriginal signifies to the eco-tourist a link with romantic ideas of the past, of authentic traditional cultures existing in harmony with the landscape: what Krech (1999) calls the myth of the "ecological Indian." This gaze is "sympathetic," as long as the aboriginal conforms to expectations. However, the use of the environment as resource — central to all aboriginal senses of place — is seen as a threat and an affront to the landscape designated "sacred" by the eco-tourist (see Scientific Panel 1995).

The bumper sticker quoted at the top of this section — seen frequently in the 1990s attached to a wide range of vehicles all over Canada — provides an interesting perspective on the issue. This slogan was a wordplay on an earlier political slogan, "My Canada includes Quebec," that betrays its explicitly nationalist character. Indeed, the two together would have delighted Marius Barbeau, who would have seen it as a vindication of his project of reterritorialization. The same uneasy relation to the aboriginal presence in that landscape is evident. Certainly claims of aboriginal sovereignty, and with them the right to use natural resources as First Nations see fit, coexist uneasily at best with an environmentalism predicated upon a nationalized sense of place.

The issue of economic "exploitation" of resources has led to bitter disputes between First Nations and environmentalists and eco-tourists in Clayoquot Sound (Dark 1998:202–223). Most recently, in May 2000, local Indians blockaded the only road to town on the day Prime Minister Jean Chretien arrived to announce the official designation of Clayoquot Sound as a UNESCO biosphere reserve. They were concerned that the designation would lead to the further alienation of traditional lands, which, in their view, should be returned through negotiation (Tla-o-qui-aht First Nation 2000). A potent undercurrent is the question of development. The biosphere designation would seem to prevent future development, although in reality it does not. However, any prior restrictions on land use violate the First Nations' sense of sovereignty. With astronomical on-reserve unemployment rates and low educational attainment, First Nations are desperate for economic development that will offer employment and financial security. Reasonably, leaders are aware as well that the settlement of land claims will lead to a new era of relations between First Nations and provincial and federal governments, one that is likely to see a decrease in transfer payments.

These very actions, and the unwillingness to exclude certain types of resource extraction from discussion, has led to an alienation between First Nations and their erstwhile allies, the environmentalists. According to what Dark calls the "sovereigntist" position, environmentalists believe that elements of aboriginal culture have been corrupted by capitalism, and that those elements, which are opposed by hereditary leaders, have come to the fore in negotiations with the government. This reading ignores a host of contradictions. A version of the aboriginal position was expressed well by Hesquiaht chief Simon Lucas: "Environmentalists talk about creating land or marine sanctuaries. We disagree on this: we don't believe in dissociating ourselves from any life. We must have learned our lesson by now that any time government declares an area as a *park* that it only opens up other areas for total exploitation" (Kosek 1993:20). When environmentalists speak of "sacred" landscapes, they necessarily make the Durkheimian distinction with the profane. Most landscape is thus profane, while the special places hold the interest and protected status. Although aboriginal activists employ the term *sacred* to refer to landscape, this does not accurately reflect the complex process of place making. Aboriginal sense of place in Clayoquot Sound entails the cultural modification of natural resources, in both traditional and nontraditional ways, in order to support the population. In a postmodern twist, this economic development of resources today includes strategies for attracting eco-tourists. Ironically, this type of development must conceal its very conditions of possibility, since "development" of any sort is anathema to the potential eco-tourist.

It is in the First Nation village of Ahousaht, about 20 miles north of Tofino and accessible only by water taxi, that one aspect of this process of tourist colonization of the landscape has played itself out. It is one of many islands in the area that are open to tourists; like several others, it has dedicated hiking trails for visitors to explore the temperate rain forest, of which the area has some of the finest surviving examples. This trail was constructed in the mid-1990s by the Ahousaht First Nation government along with the Western Canadian Wilderness Committee, whose prominent supporters include the environmental lawyer and activist Robert F. Kennedy Jr. (Dark 1998:179; Kennedy 1997). The Ahousaht trail is featured prominently in tourist literature for Tofino and environs and has spawned its own publication (Coull 1996:50; Sam 1997).

This hiking trail provides an interesting point of contact between tourist and native perception and discourse of landscape. For eco-tourists it is another of many such trails that promise access to (paradoxically) unaltered natural landscape. For the traditional Ahousaht, on the other hand, this place making is a means of constructing history. The trail is a trail into the past. Along the route are places commemorated in oral tradition, where events are inscribed upon the landscape. Stanley Sam, my Ahousaht consultant and the main consultant on the construction of the trail, narrated many of the events that occurred there (see Harkin 1998). It provides a spatial template for understanding this history and, more significantly, what Sam calls the "discipline" of traditional Ahousaht ritual and place-making practices (Sam 1997). Indeed, Sam initially balked at the idea of providing information in the sterile conditions of my hotel room, wishing instead to view the places in question by water and land. I attempted to accommodate him but was unable to hire a boat during the height of the tourist season. It was not until a year later that I was able to see the places for myself.

Garbage and Granola

My experience of the trail, when I finally got to hike it, was not what I had expected but was revealing in its own way. I was disappointed by the paucity of signage on the trail, since I knew many of the areas were those Mr. Sam had referred to. A statement in the literature to the effect that sacred landscape knowledge was to be kept from the view of outsiders was only a partial explanation, since areas that were marked included shamanic training places and the site of supernatural encounters. Clearly, decisions were political. No chiefly whaling shrines were marked, which was to be expected. However, relatively secular places such as battlegrounds were unevenly marked. Not having been present at the planning sessions, I cannot say exactly why many were excluded, except that they were probably objectionable to certain family groups in the community, or that they exhibited sensitive themes in Ahousaht political history, such as the limit conditions of chiefly authority (see Harkin 1998).

Directional signage was also rare, making the trail suitable only for advanced hikers. Unfortunately, the trail had not been well maintained in its five-year history, and many washouts of boardwalk trail had not been repaired, nor had signs been placed to indicate detours. At the same time, trash had been allowed to accumulate, especially in the section near the village. This illustrates in the clearest fashion the contradictions inherent in the project, which will possibly spell its demise. The essence of place making is dwelling in and knowing place. Dwelling in includes disposing of trash and has for thousands of years. Middens of village sites in coastal British Colum-

bia are often many meters deep. While it offends the aesthetic and environmental sensibilities of the hikers, it is integral to the human habitation of
this environment. Knowing place excludes the very idea of signage. I recall
as a child traveling through the U.S. southeast with an uncle who was an avid
amateur historian of the Civil War. We would trek to unmarked fields, and
after a conversation with a local landowner, we would explore precise spots
where critical events of the war occurred. At most, a single roadside marker
would indicate the general area of the battle. Likewise, for the knowledgeable
Ahousaht, signs along the trail were not only unnecessary but marring.

Although these practices arise from an authentically and pervasively aboriginal sense of place — I have never traveled to an Indian reserve or reservation that did not possess too much trash and too little signage from an
outsider's perspective — unfortunately, they may doom the project. On my
most recent visit, the Ahousaht Walk the Wild Side office had permanently
closed, and the Tofino-based tour office that handled bookings was barely
able to accommodate me, the first person wishing to hike the trail in several
months. They had booked, however, many people for the hot springs and
whale-watching tours, despite the foul spring weather.

The likely failure of yet another aboriginal tourist business is not in itself
surprising. The relative remoteness of the village, the lack of amenities, the
difficulty and potential danger of the trail all make this a difficult proposition
under the best of circumstances. And yet it signifies something broader: the
erosion of a temporary alliance between environmentalists and eco-tourists,
on the one hand, and First Nations people, on the other. The trail, launched
with much fanfare in 1996, is on the verge of returning to the forest at the
same time that Tla-o-qui-aht and other local groups blockade a road to
protest not logging but the declaration of the region as a biosphere reserve
(and some related land issues). As Shepard Krech (1999) has correctly noted,
the ecological Indian is a construction of Euro-American culture, albeit one
that some aboriginal groups have themselves bought into, at least for the
purposes of public relations.

One common perception, among environmentalists and others, is that
such realities reflect a change, a corruption of aboriginal culture by a culture
of poverty or too much contact with the outside world. Such a view is not to
be dismissed out of hand. There certainly have been generational changes
over time as consociate groups have passed on (see Kan 1989a). Today the

youngest people to have significant knowledge of specific places are in late middle age. It is unlikely that previous generations would have participated in the trail project in the first place; there would have been no need to educate people (especially outsiders) on Ahousaht places. Those who did not obtain knowledge through family channels would have had no right to it.

However, against this background of change, certain persistent structures of place making may be noted. There remains a healthy respect for landscape, which may be perceived by outsiders as fear. In years of hiking British Columbia backcountry, I have rarely seen aboriginal people and have never seen them alone. Solitary recreational hiking is an alien concept. Engagements with the land are much more pragmatic, and exposure to its potential dangers (both natural and supernatural, in an ethnocentric gloss) are minimized. I was teased by native people on both occasions when I hiked the Ahousaht trail, with comments about being eaten by bears or getting lost in the woods. Indeed, on the most recent trip, my thoughtful and kind boat pilot braved rough seas to look for me along stretches of the trail that crossed beaches. (Indeed, hiking alone in bad weather probably was foolhardy). This is far from the ethos of John Muir and his descendants (for whom, I suppose, being eaten by a bear would be an ecologically sound life choice). With technology and other sources of income reducing the time spent in the wild by most aboriginal people (certain exceptions exist, such as traditional herbalists), it is easy for outsiders to criticize them as having forsaken their ecological patrimony (or, in more extreme cases, to deny their legitimacy as aboriginal people). However, it is certain that their ancestors would have (and did) use technological and other measures to minimize their exposure to the dangers of place. This is, after all, simply the corollary of the notion that place can act.

Such actions are more likely to be malevolent than otherwise, although opportunities for obtaining power exist in the most dire circumstances. The emphasis of this essay is on land (reflecting current political realities as well as cultural prejudice), but certainly seascape played an equally important part in the place-making practices of Northwest Coast people (see Raban 1999). Roiling waters, whirlpools, and fantastic creatures (both with and without Linnaean designations) are truly Homeric in their active foiling of human purpose. On the land, dense forest, muskeg, caves, hollow trees, and thick underbrush were scarcely less impenetrable or resistant. The essential condition of the world is to be resistant to human intention. In Western culture we view this as a social fact (economic, political, and educational systems thwart our greater aspirations while granting certain desires). In the aboriginal view, this is a natural and cosmological fact. The land challenges us profoundly, while at the same time providing the means and very ground of our existence.

Living within such a landscape implies an interpenetration of human and nonhuman forms of intentionality. The excess of trash, from an environmentalist perspective, is a reflection of this. Traditionally, fish and animal remains were returned to the land and water; the same fate awaits the soon-to-be detritus of modern life. Objects that have lost their usefulness are simply cast aside; these include the accessories of a hunting and fishing way of life. Flashlights, coolers, batteries, bottles, and other flotsam were prominent on the beaches of the trail, while smaller amounts of trash were evident in other areas, except nearest the village, where the trail sometimes appeared to abut landfill. Along the trail the more colorful and long-lasting items, made of plastic, were playfully used to mark the trail itself: a sort of meta-commentary on the opposition between two ways of perceiving the land.

Pedestrian Discourse

The trail is both a form and referent of discourse. It is itself an argument about landscape. The most overt elements of discourse are the signs, which often cryptically suggest meanings. These meanings are arranged syntagmatically for the hiker, who goes from marker 1 through 9 (and then back again). It is a hard-fought battle for meaning, along 17 kilometers of rugged trail. At the same time, the signs can be read paradigmatically, through the mythological and historical referents of places. A trail guide (Sam 1997) hints at this, with further meanings available to those who possess deeper knowledge of Ahousaht myth-history. As with Lévi-Strauss's famous analysis of Oedipus, we may choose how to read the trail. Physically, we must proceed linearly, just as the speaker of a text, but once the trail is completed, other meanings are available to us.

To the overt signs we must add the nonverbal symbols: the trail markers made of refuse, extraordinary landscape elements, unmarked places where myth-historical events occurred. Each of these suggests other meanings, which in the end overwhelm the ability of the trail to convey propositional meaning. As Susanne Langer (1951) has said, objects that are of interest per se are less than ideal symbolic vehicles. This is part of the problem, certainly. Beyond this, the fact is that trails and trail making are so implicated in human projects and human life in general that to read a trail is no easier than to read a life. As Ricouer insists, lives can be read in retrospect, but this is a complex hermeneutic process, and one that, to my mind, is culturally and historically constructed. The problem is not that trails are inadequate symbols, but that they are too productive. The trail is an easy and obvious metaphor for lives, choices, careers, and the like. For both aboriginal and outsider, the Ahousaht trail is a hybrid sort of experiential discourse, in which the hiker participates in the explicit and implicit meanings of place.

De Certeau (1984:91–110) has compared walking to a "speech act." There is a difference, I think, between his analysis of urban walking and my notion of trail walking. Most obviously, the city is a built environment. Each square block is filled with discrete places, named or marked with numbers. Even an empty lot — whether intentional, as parks, or unintentional, as abandoned "brownfields" or undeveloped space — by virtue of its opposition to surrounding built space is a potential signifier. Signifiers attain meaning by virtue of their place in the semiotic grid, through a system of paradigmatic opposition. The act of walking is then an act of enunciation, in which readymade signifiers are appropriated by the walker, who remains a fixed point of reference through deictic interplay of locations, of "heres" and "theres" (99). Against this background of semiotic stability, the walker constructs a space of freedom in which free play with the signifiers, the choice to connect certain signifiers in new ways, the leaving out (asyndeton) of certain signifiers, and the creation of "local authority" (analogous to connotation) give him or her creative freedom within a deterministic system. In all, the walker is akin to a poet in a highly structured and officially controlled language; the walker is able to escape this particular prison house by resorting to the idiosyncratic, the random, the private, the local.

This view, while provocative, is less useful for a woodland trail, which is situated within a largely unbuilt space. Moreover, it makes certain assumptions about language and signification that go against the grain of the sort of analysis I have tried to make. Rather than imagine the overarching semiotic context as a "totalitarian" system against which the individual and the locale must constantly struggle, it seems closer to the truth to think of the creation of meaning, specifically place meaning, as an open system (de Certeau 1984:106). The walker, or speaker, is engaged in a dialogic interaction with both the natural world and the previously existing semiotic system. Nor is this prior system itself handed down from above.[7] Rather, place meanings arise from private, local, and family meanings: the ongoing praxis of place making. On the Walk the Wild Side trail, marked places arise from the historical experiences of individuals and families. In traditional Nuu-chah-nulth and Northwest Coast society, any empowered individual (i.e., not a slave) could create valid geographical meanings (see Boas 1934). Such meanings may be in conflict with prior meanings, but these prior meanings were themselves the product of individual encounters with place. Of course, chiefs were by definition more able than others to create such meanings and impose them, in certain circumstances, on others. However, their status as chiefs was itself dependent upon control of landscape meanings.

The trail markers and text represent an attempt to bring this originally private place making into the truly public realm that is a mode of discourse unrestricted by sociological boundaries. Here we could say that this is closer to de Certeau's notion of regimented spatial discourse. However, this attempt has been both incomplete and unstable. Not only are many named places left out of the marked trail, but the connections between the elements are tenuous, due to the disrepair of the trail and the sheer distance between markers. The marked places become overwhelmed by the topemic signification of rain forest, beach, and trail.

In the end the constructed trail is an argument about place. In the first instance it is a discourse about sovereignty. As in most of British Columbia, reserved land is restricted to small parcels upon which aboriginal people actually live. The rest of Flores Island, where the trail goes, is not formally part of this reserve. A claim is being made here about property rights, similar to the claim made by the nearby Tla-o-qui-aht band to land on Meares Island, on which they likewise built a public trail, although without markers. The trail is also an argument about the nature of place, and the appropriate human relation to it. It attempts to combine discrete discourses — Romantic, touristic, environmentalist, aboriginal — into a hybrid discourse, playing down the obvious contradictions between them. As I have argued, the rhetorical trail is less than fully successful. Just as the physical trail has failed to bring significant economic development to the community, the trail as argument has failed to be entirely coherent or cogent. Both physical and rhetorical trails are subject to an unstoppable entropy; just as segments of boardwalk are washed away by floods, and new detours created, elements of discourse are undermined by alternate significations. It is, indeed, in the nature of trails to resist any single meaning.

Conclusion: Steps to the World Market

The Walk the Wild Side trail may be seen as one small instance in the process of semiotic globalization, wherein local and nonlocal meanings are tossed together in a heteroglossic stew. This is especially common in the tourist context, where existing places are semiotically reframed and thereby taken out of the realm of everyday praxis and local place making. As Appadurai (1996:188) has stated the problem, it is one of producing and reproducing locality—reterritorializing—in the face of a world that is increasingly "deterritorialized" in Deleuze and Guattari's (1987) apt turn of phrase. The conflict between local and global itself destabilizes the very community that might be assumed to ground local discourse. That is, allegiances are not always what one would expect: the local person may have more subjective connections with distant places and discourses than with the local. Another way of framing the matter is that the production of locality, if unsuccessful, leads to the dissolution of the sociological entity, the "neighborhood" as Appadurai calls it.

The issue at stake is the very continuation of such neighborhoods. If localities are to continue to have access to meanings that derive from local place-making practice, some version of the local place making must survive. For this to be the case, it must hold its own against other landscape discourses and practices. It is naive to think that traditional place-making discourse such as espoused by Stanley Sam could survive in its current, preserved form. However, as an element of a larger, globalized context of discourse, it may persist.

In the end, heteroglossia and hybridity are values to be embraced, not eschewed. Mikhail Bakhtin's notion of heteroglossia was itself optimistic, seen against the Stalinist attempt to control discourse. Similarly, the forces of globalization attempt to control, in a totalitarian fashion, anything that may be seen as a "resource." The alternative to heteroglossia is not a return to some idealized culture, but rather a total absorption by global culture. However, as we know from a myriad of other cases, such disasters rarely happen, as non-Western groups have managed to reinvent themselves in the face of overwhelming pressures, including deterritorialization (see Appadurai 1996).

On a gray day in May 2000 with intermittent rainfall, the Canadian prime minister, Jean Chretien, gave a speech in Tofino proclaiming the UNESCO biosphere designation. In the audience were a mixed group of protesters and supporters, including environmentalists colorfully dressed in costumes representing local wildlife species. Some of these were protesting, others celebrating. Also present were loggers and other blue-collar workers dependent on resource extraction, members of the Ucluelet First Nation, and groups of locals and tourists who seemed to be enjoying the spectacle. Down the road were members of the Tla-o-qui-aht and Ahousaht First Nations blockading the road to protest the government's claim to land around the local airport, a former military installation.

The failure to achieve consensus on a largely symbolic measure, which moreover left room for all local interests at the expense of the province and multinational corporations, was striking but not surprising. The issue of land is inherently contentious. In areas such as Clayoquot Sound one's relation to place not merely reflects but largely defines one's identity. In this way, too, the land acts. The trail is a place where human intentionality and a subjective nature come to a mutual accommodation. The variety of spurs, turnings, secret passages, unmarked places, blockages, changes of vista, weather conditions, and the action of what de Certeau calls "local authority" allow room for a wide range of perspectives, each of which is achieved in a dialogue with place. As Stevens says "But I know, too, / That the blackbird is involved / In what I know."

Notes

1. Notions of "the sublime" were connected to both Romanticism and Christian spiritualism in the 19th century and to the developing environmentalist movement, embodied in figures such as John Muir. What Ruskin (1873:172–188) half-derides as "the pathetic fallacy" survives in the writings of both religious figures and environmentalists, such as Edward Abbey (Ellis 2001:7–11). Mountains in particular are a "motivated" sign of epiphany, abstraction, and, in a personal moral context, achievement of difficult goals.

2. The Canadian landscape movement of Carr, Barbeau, and the Group of Seven was both similar and different to contemporary developments in the United States. Regionalism, as exemplified by Thomas Hart Benton, was, as the term implied, dedicated to place making on a regional scale, in opposition to aesthetic developments on the national scene. This, too, was political but suggested a politics of regional separation rather than national unity.

3. Bourdieu's insistence on the arbitrariness of boundaries is relevant to the case of the U.S.-Canadian border and to the problem of Barbeau's reterritorialization. Borders may indeed be arbitrary, but not all meanings of place derive from them.

4. Although essentially premodern, the motif of place as actor persists into the modern era. Wagner is one obvious example. More recently, magical realist fiction and the poetry of Seamus Heaney are instances.

5. The man-eating cave motif appears widely in Northwest Coast mythology. In a Heiltsuk version a would-be shamanic initiate has his flesh stripped from his bones.

6. Superficially such formulations are similar to New Age ideas of "power points," "earth acupuncture," and the like. However, these are in fact much different. Although they appropriate elements of Native American ritual, their origins lie with the geomantic practices of alchemy. Although premodern in most senses, alchemy was a universal system, one that proposed general rules of operation. It was thus precisely not local, and the forces brought into action were impersonal.

7. The notion of a "totalitarian" semiotic system, which is already "out there," ontologically and epistemologically prior to the individual, is formally homologous to the idea of the geographic "first space." Both are, in fact, creations of discourses and institutions. In the case of language, we can think of the Port Royal grammar and the Académie française as equivalent to the forces that constructed pure universal space.

CONTEMPORARY MAKAH WHALING

Janine Bowechop

Qwi-dich-cha-at-h or Makah people inhabit the outer coast of what is now Washington State and the entrance to the Strait of Juan de Fuca. According to oral traditions and the archaeological record, Makah people have been hunting whales and other sea mammals and fishing in the Pacific Ocean waters from cedar dugout canoes for several thousand years.

Until a century ago Makahs lived in shed roof, cedar plank longhouses near the shore (Mauger 1978). The majority of food resources came from the ocean and the intertidal zone. Over the centuries Makah people developed technologically sophisticated methods and accompanying ritual for harvesting and preserving these preferred foods.

Contact with non-Indians was relatively late. Not until 1788 did the Makahs begin interacting with Europeans, as recorded by John Meares, who anchored off the coast of Tatoosh Island (Gunther 1972:56–57). Spaniards first sailed into Makah territory in 1790 and two years later made an effort to create a fort in the village of *di·ya*. After only four months the Spaniards were forced to leave, as they behaved improperly according to Makah custom (67–72).

Prior to contact with non-Indians Makahs were wealthy, in part due to the trade of whale oil. Neighboring tribes traded canoes, roots, and other goods for the whale oil and blubber that the Makah people provided. Relationships with Nuu-chah-nulth people on Vancouver Island were nurtured by gifts of whale products (Ida Jones in Kirk 1986:135).

Early explorers, traders, and settlers were also fascinated with, and even dependant upon, Makah whaling. Whale oil was used to lubricate machinery in the logging camps and was used as lamp fuel in emerging cities in the Northwest. Victoria, British Columbia, is said to have been "lit" by Makah whale oil for a period of time, and lighthouses, created to save the lives of immigrant ocean travelers, were lit by whale oil also. Native travelers did not need the lighthouses, for they knew the coastlines, islands, out-croppings, and Pacific Ocean currents and wave swell patterns. Certainly the non-Indian development of the Olympic Peninsula and parts of British Columbia was facilitated by the availability of high-quality whale oil that the Makahs provided. Nuu-chah-nulth people of Vancouver Island also supplied whale oil to non-native settlers.

Treaty of 1855: Inherent Sovereignty

With the increase of Euro-American settlers in the region, and the continued existence of trade posts and trade vessels, Makah people saw the wisdom of negotiating a treaty with the representatives of the U.S. government prior to 1855. During the treaty negotiations the Makah representatives understood that they would be giving up control of large tracts of land in order to continue living the life they chose to live on selected parts of their traditional land and to continue hunting whales and fishing in usual and accustomed grounds. "The right of taking fish and of whaling or sealing at usual and accustomed grounds and stations is further secured to said Indians in common with all citizens of the Unites States" (Article IV, Treaty of Neah Bay). The Makahs had lived in the same area from time immemorial, securing a truly indigenous position. They also governed themselves with a sophisticated system of laws and values for centuries. Their treaty-negotiating authority stemmed from this inherent sovereignty. Makah people reserved important rights within their land and ocean territories, and the U.S. government agreed, via the treaty, to reserve and protect these rights.

"In common with" was a treaty phrase that recognized the mutual but separate interest that Makahs and United States citizens had with whaling at the time of treaty signing. Makahs had engaged in whaling as a religious, subsistence, and economic activity for several thousand years or longer. Whales were abundant and were harvested by a particular portion of the population during two seasons of the year. By limiting hunting to a segment of the population, the Makah tribe had created a social and management system. And because whaling required such specialized skills, only a small number of men not born into the occupation took up whaling.

Temporary Pause in Whaling

Just after the beginning of the 20th century whales became scarce in traditional Makah territory due to unregulated whaling by non-Indian whalers.

Because of the increased difficulty of bringing whales to Makah shores and concern for whale populations, Makah whalers chose to stop pursuing whales. Between 1913 and 1921 possibly only two whales were hunted and consumed by Makah people.

Though whaling was not a regular activity after 1915, whaling and whales remained an important part of the Makah imagination. Women continued to weave whaling scenes into baskets and sold them to visitors and to the local general store, and the women brought them to Victoria and Seattle to sell to tourists directly. Thunderbirds and whales continued to figure prominently in the carvings and two-dimensional designs created by Makah people. Even through the last three decades of the 20th century when boys (and some girls) began to learn to draw and paint, they usually mastered drawing whales before moving on to other images such as thunderbirds, serpents, wolves, ravens, and eagles.

Description of the Ozette Mudslide and Excavation

During the long continuum of Makah whaling a drastic event occurred that preserved Makah material culture for three or more centuries. A large mudslide, possibly triggered by a massive earthquake, covered several houses in the Ozette village in January 1700 or perhaps earlier. The mud came down the hillside at approximately 65 miles an hour, flattening and covering everything in its path, which included several full-size cedar plank longhouses, built with a timber frame construction and shed style roofs. The mud was followed by a layer of thick gray clay, which sealed out oxygen from the buried houses. A stream of water trickled down the hillside, underground, creating a wet site, perfect for waterlogging the contents of the houses. The houses stayed buried for nearly three centuries until a violent winter storm exposed the artifacts. Some artifacts were reportedly pulled from the ocean bank by curious hikers during the winter of 1969–70. One hiker called a member of the Makah Tribal Council, alerting him to the situation at Ozette (Ed Claplanhoo, personal communication, 2001). After a brief investigation the tribal council called in Dr. Richard Daugherty of Washington State University, an archaeologist who had conducted archaeological surveys in the area and at Ozette as recently as 1966 and 1967.

At Washington State University, Daugherty, at the request of the Makah Tribal Council, prepared for site excavation starting in the spring of 1970, thinking that the excavation would continue through the fall (Dr. Richard Daugherty, personal communication, 1999). The excavation continued year-round for 11 years. Hundreds of field school students and young Makah excavators worked with the archaeologists to recover more than 55,000 artifacts. Many of the artifacts were well preserved and in near-perfect condition. Others were broken into fragments due to the pressure of the sudden mudslide.

The Makah Tribal Council determined that the artifacts would stay on the Makah reservation and would not be transported to a remote museum or university for conservation, analysis, and storage. The artifacts were stabilized at the lab at the Ozette site and then flown by helicopter to the conservation laboratory and storage center in Neah Bay, the main village of the Makah reservation. Here the artifacts were further treated, studied, organized, and shelved in a remodeled storage laboratory. In 1979 the Makah tribe opened the Makah Cultural and Research Center to provide research and education opportunities to the Makah community and others and to display the world-class collection of artifacts excavated at Ozette.

Sometimes the helicopters transporting artifacts were met by Makah elders who would identify the items for the archaeologists. Some elders were flown to the excavation site. Archaeologists and other researchers recorded elder men talking about whale hunts and seal hunts while holding the hunting tools excavated at Ozette. They were able to demonstrate how the hunting tools were made and used, as they used similar tools as young men. Ruth Kirk (1986:135) quotes a Makah elder describing a whaling harpoon shaft, excavated from the Ozette site: "This splice is here for a reason. It's so when you spear the whale [the harpoon] won't bounce back. Even if you had a long pole and made the shaft of it . . . it would bounce right back out if there's no splice." The elder is referring to a splice in the harpoon shaft, which is also called a scarf joint. It is a diagonal fitted coupling, similar in profile to two crochet hook tips joined together. Splices were also a safety feature for the whaling crew. Elder men explained that if the shaft stayed lodged in the whale with the harpoon and the whale rolled, the splice (scarf joint) provided a clean separating point. The shaft would separate into two pieces rather than damage or tip the canoe, and the two pieces could be quickly reattached. Without this added safety dimension the canoe could be in peril of capsizing if the whale rolled dramatically.

Makah youth learned a lot during the excavation. The presence of the artifacts facilitated many important cultural discussions. They also inspired thoughts and memories that were transferred to the younger generations. One young man who participated in the recent whale hunt told me he would look at the Ozette whaling gear and wonder what it would be like for the man who used that gear to bring in a whale. He wondered about the spiritual and physical training, the power and the life of the man.

Ozette revealed a complex and sophisticated whaling regime. Whaling gear was excavated and brought before the Makahs and general public. Whaling harpoons, shafts, lanyards, and float plugs were found in the houses, indicating where whalers lived. Cedar bark harpoon sheaths were found wrapped around the mussel shell and elk antler harpoons, ready for the next whale hunt. Paddles with pointed tips were stored in the houses and were perfectly preserved by the mud for centuries. These paddles were designed to silently paddle through the water while approaching whales. The water drips off the pointed ends, barely making any noise or movement.

Whalebones were plentiful at Ozette. They were even found positioned outside the houses as drainage features, similar to a storm water runoff system. All these bones were weighed and measured, and gray whale and humpback whale bones made up over 95 percent of the whalebones that were excavated (Huelsbeck 1994). Archaeologists were able to estimate that the Ozette villagers hunted two to four whales each year during the period prior to the mudslide.

The archaeological record supported what Makah elders had been saying about earlier days: that whaling was central and important to Makah people, and that whaling had been on going for centuries. The location and abundance of the whaling gear also supported elders' descriptions of whaling as a right limited to certain families but beneficial to the whole tribe. Nearly everything that Makah elders had taught to younger Makahs or told to earlier ethnographers could be supported by the artifacts excavated from Ozette. Similarly, nearly every artifact that needed interpretation could be explained by Makah elders.

Anticipation of the De-listing of the Gray Whales

As described above, the connection to whales and whaling continued even through the years while the Makahs did not go whaling. The tribe was acutely aware that the population of gray whales was rebounding and hoped that they would eventually be removed from the endangered species list. The de-listing of gray whales occurred in 1994. Now the traditional relationship between Makahs and gray whales could resume. The tribe could revitalize an important cultural tradition and create an even healthier, stronger tribal population.

Some of the younger members had continually heard old Makah men talk of the need to resume whaling. They understood that the same characteristics that made good whalers also made our community strong and vibrant. They talked again and again of the need to return to whaling. These young people listened intently and absorbed the importance from these elders. The Makah tribe inherently understood the importance of reconnecting the spiritual and cultural relationship between whales and people, thereby providing closure to the gap between the past and the present.

Announcement of the Resumption of Whaling

Within this context it was natural for the Makah tribe to announce its intention to resume hunting gray whales, just shortly after they were removed from the endangered species list. The Makah tribe understood the process involved with de-listing and knew that the population of gray whales was healthy and strong. Makahs also knew this because they could see the huge migrations of the gray whales while they were out fishing on the ocean waters. This was an exciting time for everyone. We imagined a glorious yet not uncomplicated resumption of a central cultural activity. Yet we knew that there would be those who would not understand our intentions, and that there would certainly be opposition. I do not think it was possible at that time, though, to realize the enormity and irrationality of the opposition.

The Makah Community's Preparation for Whaling

Even prior to the 1995 announcement by the Makah Tribal Council that the tribe would resume gray whale hunting, Makahs had been training and preparing for the hunt. Older members of the tribe had continually talked about the rituals to prepare for whaling. Men were taught the songs, prayers, and locations for ritual preparation. The older men also offered technical explanations concerning whale hunting, sometimes using the Ozette artifacts or old whaling gear that had been passed down from previous generations.

Younger women also were told about their roles and responsibilities for the preparations and the hunt. The wife of the harpooner is required to be still during the hunt and should not drink any liquid, for her actions are directly connected to the behavior of the whale. Grandmothers, aunts, and mothers taught the younger women how to prepare seal oil, which is similar to the preparation of whale oil.

Following the formal decision and announcement in 1995 the tribe began plans to prepare traditionally, politically, and administratively for the hunt. The Makah tribe brought the 1855 Treaty of Neah Bay to the United States Department of the Interior and explained the intention to exercise the treaty right to hunt whales, as stipulated in Article IV. This position of the Makah tribe was problematic for U.S. government officials, as they had signed an international agreement to halt whaling, not cognizant of the prior formal treaty agreement with the Makah tribe. The Department of the Interior acknowledged the tribe's legal right to hunt whales and ushered the Makah tribe to the Department of Commerce's National Marine Fisheries Service, the federal agency that oversees the management of marine mammals. The Department of Commerce sponsored the Makah tribe through the International Whaling Commission (IWC) whale quota recognition process. Makahs were eventually included as participants in the gray whale quota. This inclusion became formal at the IWC annual meeting in Monaco in the fall of 1997. The Makah tribe celebrated with a parade through the streets of Neah Bay, and the tribal council held a press conference at the Makah Cultural and Research Center.

The Makah Whaling Commission was established, which had supervisory authority over the whale hunt. In order to assure broad tribal participation the commission was set up to include representatives of all the major Makah families. It developed the whaling management plan, with input from the National Marine Fisheries Service. The Makah Whaling Commission established the training requirements for the whalers and selected men from their families to train for the first hunt in approximately 80 years. These men would be required to meet the criteria set by the Makah Whaling Commission. They began paddling in the one cedar dugout canoe that the tribe owned, first in the calmer waters near Neah Bay, then out on the open ocean. Two Makah men, working with Nuu-chah-nulth carvers on Vancouver Island, had made the canoe, named the *qwitiiqwich* (hummingbird), in

1993, prior to the journey to Bella Bella. The *qwitiiqwich* had already proved to be seaworthy.

While the rest of the world was still trying to decide whether to support what our small tribe on the tip of the Olympic Peninsula was preparing to do, the Makah community was coming together like never before. The men were paddling every day in the canoe and talked to their elder relatives seeking advice, support, and traditional knowledge. They also spent time examining the whaling gear in the Ozette collection, noticing intricate details about the gear that the curators and archaeologists had not. Some also accessed the materials in the Makah Cultural and Research Center's archives and library, which include recordings of their grandparents talking about preparations for whale hunts, among other topics.

As the training intensified, so did the protests against the pending hunt. Makahs were characterized as vicious, savage, and bloodthirsty by animal rights activists and other anti-Indian groups and individuals. Because a few Makah people believed that this was not the right time to resume whale hunting, the opposition depicted the Makah community as a divided community, one that did not listen to the reason and advice of our elders. In fact, the Makah community and our many friends and relatives were more unified than ever. Many other Indian people offered words of encouragement and prayers, sending their messages in person, over the phone, using e-mail and fax machines.

Makahs had made the decision to resume whaling for reasons that were exclusively internal, and the tribe kept its focus internal, except where involvement with governmental officials and attorneys was required. Some tribal members enjoyed the attention that the media provided, but the whalers in training kept to their regimen and ignored the repeated requests for interviews and photographs. Even the aggressive and crude insults hurled at the whalers while on the ocean were unable to break their concentration. The more vicious the attacks became against the whalers and the tribe, the firmer the resolve of the Makahs grew. Unfortunately the eldest people and the youngest people seemed the most affected by the protesters. The large, unsightly, and deliberately loud vessels that plied the waters off Neah Bay created a certain amount of discomfort for these most vulnerable members of our population, and the roadblocks were certainly an inconvenience to the community.

The whaling crew made several hunting attempts in the fall of 1998 and resumed hunting in the spring of 1999. The crew is required by the Makah tribe to secure a whaling permit prior to a hunt, and the tribe notifies the U.S. Coast Guard, who enforces the exclusionary zone. When the flag is raised on the canoe, other vessels are required by law to keep 500 yards away from the canoe. News traveled fast in the Neah Bay community when a hunt was on. People knew from dockside reports or from the media helicopters that provided up-to-the-minute coverage of an active hunt. Prayers, songs, and traditional observances were regular occurrences during these times. Meanwhile the only road in and out of Neah Bay was blocked by protesters regularly, boycotts of Neah Bay were organized (but not successful), and Makahs were often criticized by the mainstream media and more viciously by animal rights activists.

The positive outcome from the incessant media attention was that some of the more perspicacious professionals desired to learn more about what whale hunting means from a historical, legal, and cultural perspective. They moved from viewing a simple controversy to examining a social and cultural renaissance with complex, even inexplicable, meaning and importance. They learned what the Treaty of Neah Bay means to the everyday lives of Makah people. They were guests of honor at a community dinner that the tribe hosted where they learned that the Makahs could be very generous, gracious, and great cooks. Some of them grew to like our community so well that they still regularly return to visit.

The Whale Hunt

Following an evening prayer session of elders with the crew, the men paddled out to sea well before dawn on Monday morning, May 17, 1999. They left in the canoe, with no Makah chase boats. The protesters were not out early enough that morning to cause any disturbance (as some of their vessels had been recently confiscated). By the time the whale had been sighted and the canoe began its approach, the Makah chase boats were on site, ready to assist the hunters. The crew made an approach, and the harpooner lifted his harpoon, thrust it with a force that was aided by ancestral strength, and gave it a little twist to make sure it was lodged in tight. Cheers of triumph rang through our small village, and telephones began ringing, too. The conversations would have been difficult to interpret for an outsider, for they were interspersed with tears of victory and emotional outpourings of relief and accomplishment. This hunt was being watched on live television by 70 percent of the Neah Bay community (Renker 2002).

Because the tribe agreed to work within International Whaling Commission guidelines, which have requirements for humane kills, our whalers agreed to use a .577 caliber rifle as a substitute for the killing lance. The earlier hunters used these lances after the first harpoons were thrust into the whale, which were attached by lanyard to inflated sealskins. The floats kept the whales from diving and tired the whales before they could be fatally injured with the barbless lances.

A Makah man chosen by the Makah Whaling Commission (MWC) to shoot the whale after it was harpooned supplied the final shots. He is considered an expert marksman by the MWC standards, is an experienced game hunter, and is a decorated Vietnam War combat veteran. His shots killed the whale, and the whaling crew and support boats began their work of pulling the whale to the surface, tying its mouth closed, and towing it home to Neah Bay.

The whaling crew hunted the whale near the village of Ozette, approximately 17 miles south of the village of Neah Bay. The harpooner sunk the harpoon in the whale at approximately 6:55 a.m., and 12 hours later our canoe, accompanied by four canoes from neighboring tribes, brought the whale ashore on the beach at Neah Bay. The place they chose to land the whale was the same spot where other whales have been brought to shore, according to historic photos and to elders' accounts. Many tribal members were excused from work that Monday. Most of us chose to be together, in celebration of an event for which our tribe had waited three-quarters of a century. Many joyous tears were shed that day.

Like most populations of Indian tribes, just a little over half of our enrolled members live on reservation. By the time the whale was brought ashore nearly every Makah in driving distance had made the pilgrimage home. It was a rainy, drizzly day. Women who normally keep out of the rain to preserve their hairstyles were walking up and down the beach, looking happier and more full of life than ever before. Elders had arranged to have cars parked above the beach so they could be brought close when the whale came in. Even people who had doubted the timing of the hunt were hugging others, smiling and sharing in the joy.

Traditionally a whale was beached at high tide, and then after the tide receded the butchering began. Because this whale hunt was so momentous, the people could not be so patient. The whale was hauled up the beach, inch by inch, by men who heaved on the lengths of two large chains. Many men were involved in the training, had organized on behalf of the Makah Whaling Commission or Tribal Council, or offered boats to tow the whale home, and those who may not have been involved in any of those tasks offered their combined strength to pull the whale up the beach to be honored.

The whale was sung to, prayed over, and thanked for giving its life in order that our community might thrive. Media helicopters finally backed away when the arm motions of hundreds of people indicated that they were disrupting the rituals. George Bowechop, executive director of the Makah Whaling Commission, was quoted in the newspapers as saying "Today the Makah have brought the whale home." The harpooner, Theron Parker, was praised by members of the tribe and thanked by members of other tribes for exercising the most sacred treaty right the Makahs secured. His perseverance, focus, and serious study of Makah whaling traditions were, and are, truly remarkable.

Some of the whale meat and blubber was distributed to Makah tribal members the first night, and a portion of both were reserved for a feast that the Makah Tribal Council planned to host the Saturday after the hunt. During the week people were invited to the building where the whale was being cut up and stored for the meal. We found that the blubber tastes good raw, and that the meat can even be eaten raw. We cut the blubber with no blood in small pieces for everyone to taste. This clean blubber makes the best oil, and cutting any of the blubber makes the sharpest blade dull in a short time.

The feast, which was similar to a potlatch but hosted by the tribe rather than an individual family, was a spectacular event. All the Makahs who drove home for the arrival of the whale either stayed the week or returned for the feast, and so many other Indians from other tribes joined us at this celebration. The four canoes from neighboring tribes (Puyallup, Tulalip, Quileute, and Hoh) that came for support and to accompany our crew and the whale to the beach were well represented. Thousands of other friends and relatives joined our tribe in this historic celebration. Almost all the Ozette archaeologists were there, for they had learned so much about whaling during their tenure with Makah artifacts and Makah elders.

At the celebration the tribe gave special gifts and words of thanks to the United States Coast Guard, for their tireless enforcement of the exclusionary zone, which provided a safe environment for Makah whale hunting. The day before the successful hunt we understood that a high-ranking Coast Guard official had promised that no further interference would delay this hunt. The attempts to disrupt the Makah whale hunt were an affront to U.S. law. We had the backing of the U.S. government for the tribe to resume a traditional cultural activity.

The celebration lasted from noon on Saturday until nearly 8:00 the next morning. The organizers gave the floor to invited dignitaries and other special guests. Later the floor was opened up to any visitors who wished to comment. Billy Frank Jr., a Nisqually Indian who is the president of the Northwest Indian Fish Commission, gave one of the most impassioned speeches ever, and he is well known for his vigilant support of treaty rights and public speaking. A Massai warrior talked about neither being able to create nor destroy energy, only being able to transfer it. He was talking about the spirit of the whale, and he moved people to tears and a standing ovation. He also talked about the preservation of the unique characteristics of tribal rights and said that in the modern world these tribal rights are in danger of becoming extinct. The Makah whale hunt proved that you could turn back the clock to preserve these unique identities (my paraphrase of his speech from May 22, 1999). Hundreds of our Nuu-chah-nulth relatives from British Columbia came to celebrate the whale hunt with us and gave our harpooner, Theron Parker, an additional name, which translates to "getter of the fin" (the dorsal fin and the dorsal fin area, the most prized parts of the whale, receive ceremonial treatment for several days after the hunt). Our relatives from Canada and other tribes performed songs and dances to show their support and appreciation for what the Makah tribe had accomplished. Many thanked the Makah tribe for resuming this tradition, as we had set out to do. Many Indian people looked at whaling as an important affirmation of treaty rights.

Unfortunately many non-Indian people felt offended that we undertook such a tradition that did not fit into their framework of what real and good Indians are supposed to do. Even well-meaning people had created images in their minds of what Indians represent, and it usually involves worshipping all mother earth's creatures, praying to the winds, and maybe living off of vegetables and roots. Because our small tribe stood up and continued a tradition that is full of meaning and perfectly reasonable and honorable to us, we were no longer looked at as passive and needy. Since we did not ask for approval, or for sympathy, we fell out of favor with so many folks. Additionally, since we did not start out with an organized educational campaign to let others know that gray whales are abundant and that we intend to harvest very few for subsistence purposes only, we were met with an aggressive campaign of misinformation that painted us as careless and brutal.

Since 1999 the Makah tribe has not hunted another whale, though our whalers did butcher and distribute a whale that was injured and chased ashore by killer whales. By that time people had favorite recipes for whale meat and had experimented with various methods of rendering oil. The Makah Whaling Commission has recently created an educational film on Makah whaling and distributes it free to educational institutions. It is also sold to visitors on the Makah reservation.

The young man who looked at the Ozette whaling gear with wonder can now say that he knows something of what it is like to use such gear to bring a whale to the tribe, for he was the harpooner in the tribe's first hunt in approximately 80 years. The children in the tribe today have more to look forward to than ever. At a local café a child of a friend of our family looked lovingly at his mother and said, "When I get big, Mom, I'm going to get you a whale." The real possibilities for the future of the Makah tribe are brighter than ever before, and much of this is because of the existence of the opportunity for whale hunting. Whether one whale is hunted every year or every several years we will continue to apply cultural standards to our conduct in order to be prepared. We are thankful for those who offered support, or who had the patience to suspend judgment, and we are proud of the strength of our community, of the wisdom of our elders, and of the many opportunities offered to us from our ancestors.

REFERENCES

Abbott, Donald
  1981 The World Is as Sharp as a Knife: An Anthology in Honour of Wilson Duff. Victoria BC: British Columbia Provincial Museum.
Aberle, David F.
  1983 Navajo Economic Development. *In* Handbook of North American Indians, vol. 10: Southwest. Alfonso Ortiz, ed. Pp. 641–658. Washington DC: Smithsonian Institution Press.
Abram, David
  1996 The Spell of the Sensuous. New York: Vintage.
Abrams, George
  1990 Dialogue. Smithsonian Runner 90(6):2.
Abruitina, Larisa
  1997 Shamanism and Spiritual Revival in Chukotka. Paper presented at the Jesup Centenary Conference, American Museum of Natural History, New York, November 1997.
Ackerman, Charles
  1975 Tsimshian Oedipus. *In* Proceedings of the Second Congress of the Canadian Ethnology Society, vol. 1. Jim Freedman and Jerome H. Barkow, eds. Pp. 65–85. National Museum of Man, Mercury Series, Canadian Ethnology Service, 28. Ottawa: National Museums of Canada.
  1982 A Small Problem of Fish Bones. *In* The Logic of Culture: Advances in Structural Theory and Methods. Ino Rossi, ed. Pp. 113–126. South Hadley MA: J. F. Bergin.
Adams, John W.
  1973 The Gitksan Potlatch: Population Flux, Resource Ownership and Reciprocity. Toronto: Holt, Rinehart, and Winston.
  1974 Dialectics and Contingency in "The Story of Asdiwal": An Ethnographic Note. *In* The Unconscious in Culture: The Structuralism of Claude Lévi-Strauss in Perspective. Ino Rossi, ed. Pp. 170–178. New York: E. P. Dutton.

1981 Recent Anthropology on the Northwest Coast. Annual Review of Anthropology 10:361–392.

Agnew, John A., and James S. Duncan

1989 The Power of Place: Bringing Together Geographical and Sociological Imaginations. Boston: Unwin Hyman.

Alexander, Sally

1994 Women, Class and Sexual Differences in the 1830s and 1840s: Some Reflections on the Writing of a Feminist History. *In* Culture/Power/History: A Reader in Contemporary Social Theory. Nicholas B. Dirks, Geoff Eley, and Sherry B. Ortner, eds. Pp. 269–296. Princeton: Princeton University Press.

Allen, John L.

1972 An Analysis of the Exploration Process: Lewis and Clark Expedition of 1804–06. Geographical Review 62:13–39.

American Museum of Natural History

1902–60 Annual Reports. New York: American Museum of Natural History.

Ames, Michael

1981 A Note on the Contributions of Wilson Duff to Northwest Coast Ethnology and Art. *In* The World Is as Sharp as a Knife: An Anthology in Honour of Wilson Duff. Donald Abbott, ed. Pp. 17–21. Victoria BC: British Columbia Provincial Museum.

1992 Cannibal Tours and Glass Boxes. Vancouver: University of British Columbia Press.

Amoss, Pamela T.

1977 The Power of Secrecy among the Coast Salish. *In* The Anthropology of Power: Ethnographic Studies from Asia, Oceania, and the New World. Raymond D. Fogelson and Richard N. Adams, eds. Pp. 131–140. New York: Academic Press.

Anderson, Benedict

1983 Imagined Communities: Reflections on the Origin and Spread of Nationalism. London: Verso. Rev. ed., London: Verso, 1991.

Anderson, Margaret Seguin

N.d. Wilson Duff's Tsimshian File, 014–16–01. Prepared as a virtual research tool by Margaret Anderson, including introduction, detailed inventory, and full content of Tsimshian File scanned as images on ten CDs. Available at the Museum of Anthropology, University of British Columbia, Vancouver.

1998 Asdiwal on the Ground. Paper presented at the Symposium on Asdiwal, organized by John Leavitt, at the joint meetings of the American Ethnology Society/Canadian Anthropology Society, Toronto, May.

Anderson, Margaret, and Marjorie Halpin, eds.

2000 Potlatch at Gitsegukla: William Beynon's 1945 Field Notebooks. Vancouver: University of British Columbia Press.

Anonymous

1910 Ugalakhmiut. *In* Handbook of American Indians North of Mexico, vol. 2. Frederick Webb Hodge, ed. Pp. 862–863. Bureau of American Ethnology Bulletin, 30. Washington DC: Government Printing Office.

Anonymous

1993 Lack of Money Imperils Indian Cultural Center. New York Times, Sunday, June 13: 41.

Appadurai, Arjun

1996 Modernity at Large: Cultural Dimensions of Globalization. Minneapolis: University of Minnesota Press.

Archer, Christon

1980 Cannibalism in the Early History of the Northwest Coast: Enduring Myths and Neglected Realities. Canadian Historical Review 61:453–79.

Arima, Eugene, Denis St. Claire, Louis Clamhouse, Joshua Edgar, Charles Jones, and John Thomas

1991 Between Ports Renfrew and Alberni: Notes on West Coast People. Hull QC: Canadian Museum of Civilization.

Augé, Marc

1982 The Anthropological Circle: Symbol, Function, History. Martin Thom, trans. Cambridge: Cambridge University Press.

Bakhtin, Mikhail

1981 The Dialogic Imagination: Four Essays by M. M. Bakhtin. M. Holmquist, ed. Austin: University of Texas Press.

Bancroft, Hubert Howe

1887 History of British Columbia, 1792–1887. San Francisco: History Company.

Barbeau, Marius

1910 a Lettre à Marcel Mauss, juin 23, 1910. Archives Marcel Mauss. Paris: Collège de France.

1910 b The Totemic System of the Northwestern Indian Tribes of North America. B.Sc. thesis, Diploma in Anthropology, Oxford University.

1916 Henri Beuchat. American Anthropologist n.s. 18:105–110.

1930 Totem Poles: A Recent Native Art of the Northwest Coast. Geographical Review 20(2):258–272.

1950 Totem Poles. 2 vols. National Museums of Canada Bulletin, 119. Anthropological Series, 30. Ottawa: National Museums of Canada.

1957 Haida Carvers in Argillite. National Museums of Canada Bulletin, 139. Anthropological Series, 38. Ottawa: National Museums of Canada.

Barnett, Homer

N.d. Field Notebooks, Archives, University of British Columbia.

Barth, Frederik

1966 Models of Social Organization. Royal Anthropological Institute Occasional Paper, 23. Royal Anthropological Institute of Great Britain and Ireland. London: Royal Anthropological Institute.

Barthes, Roland

1987 Michelet. Richard Howard, trans. New York: Hill and Wang.

Basso, Keith H.

1984 Stalking with Stories: Names, Places, and Moral Narratives among the Western Apache. *In* Text, Play, and Story: The Construction and Reconstruction of Self and Society. Edward M. Bruner, ed. Pp. 19–55. Washington DC: American Ethnological Society, Waveland Press.

1988 Speaking with Names: Language and Landscape among the Western Apache. Cultural Anthropology 3(2):99–130.

1996 Wisdom Sits in Places: Landscape and Language among the Western Apache. Albuquerque: University of New Mexico Press.

Bataille, Georges

1967[1933] La part maudite, précédé de La notion de dépense. Introduction de Jean Piel. Paris: Les Editions de Minuit.

1998 The Accursed Share: An Essay on General Economy, vol. 1: Consumption. Robert Hurley, trans. New York: Zone.

Bataille, Gretchen M., and Kathleen Sands

1984 American Indian Women: Telling Their Lives. Lincoln: University of Nebraska Press.

Bauman, Richard

1984 Verbal Art as Performance. Rowley, MA: Newbury House.

Bauman, Richard, and Charles L. Briggs

1990 Poetics and Performance as Critical Perspectives on Language and Social Life. Annual Review of Anthropology 19:59–88.

Beals, Ralph L.

1985 The Anthropologist as Expert Witness: Illustrations from the California Indian Land Claims Case. In Irredeemable America: The Indians' Estate and Land Claims. Imre Sutton, ed. Pp. 139–155. Albuquerque: University of New Mexico Press.

Beck, Brenda

1972 Peasant Society in Konku: A Study of Right and Left Subcastes in South India. Vancouver: University of British Columbia Press.

1978 a The Logical Appropriation of Kinship as a Political Metaphor: An Indian Epic at the Civilizational and Regional Levels. Theme issue, "L'appropriation sociale de la logique: Mélanges offerts à Claude Lévi-Strauss à l'occasion de son 70e anniversaire de naissance," Pierre Maranda, ed., Anthropologica n.s. 20(1–2): 47–64.

1978 b The Metaphor as a Mediator between Semantic and Analogic Modes of Thought. Current Anthropology 19:83–97.

1982 Root Metaphor Patterns. Recherches sémiotiques/Semiotic Inquiry 2(1):86–97.

Begay, Daryl R.

1991 Navajo Preservation: The Success of the Navajo Nation Historic Preservation Department. Cultural Resource Management 14(4):3–4.

Benedict, Ruth

1934 Patterns of Culture. Boston: Houghton Mifflin.

Berlo, Janet Catherine

1990 Portraits of Dispossession in Plains Indian and Inuit Graphic Art. Art Journal 49(2):133–141.

Berman, Judith

1982 The Organization of Events in Traditional Kwakiutl Narrative.

Paper presented at the Workshop on Native American Discourse, University of Texas, Austin, April.

1991 The Seals' Sleeping Cave: The Interpretation of Boas' Kwakw'ala Texts. Ph.D. dissertation, University of Pennsylvania, Philadelphia.

1992 Oolachen-Woman's Robe: Fish, Blankets, Masks, and Meaning in Boas' Kwakw'ala Texts. *In* On the Translation of Native American Literatures. Brian Swann, ed. Pp. 125–162. Washington DC: Smithsonian Institution Press.

1994 Night Hunter and Day Hunter. *In* Coming to Light: Contemporary Translations of the Native Literatures of North America. Brian Swann, ed. Pp. 250–272. New York: Random House.

1996 The Culture as It Appears to the Indian Himself: Boas, George Hunt and the Methods of Ethnography. *In* Volksgeist as Method and Ethic: Essays on Boasian Ethnography and the German Anthropological Tradition. George Stocking, ed. Pp. 215–256. Madison: University of Wisconsin Press.

2000 Red Salmon and Red Cedar Bark: Another Look at the Nineteenth-Century Kwakwaka'wakw Winter Ceremonial. BC Studies 125/126:53–98.2001 Unpublished Materials of Franz Boas and George Hunt: A Record of 45 Years of Collaboration. *In* Gateways: Exploring the Legacy of the Jesup North Pacific Expedition, 1897–1902. Igor Krupnik and William Fitzhugh, eds. Pp. 181–213. Washington DC: National Museum of Natural History, Smithsonian Institution.

2004 Giver. *In* Voices from Four Directions: Contemporary Translations of the Native Literatures of North America. Brian Swann, ed. Lincoln: University of Nebraska Press.

Bermingham, Ann

2003 System, Order, and Abstraction: The Politics of English Landscape Drawing around 1795. *In* Landscape and Power. 2nd edition. W. J. T. Mitchell, ed. Pp. 77–102. Chicago: University of Chicago Press.

Besnard, Philippe

1985 Un conflit au sein du groupe durkheimien: La polémique autour de la Foi jurée. Revue française de sociologie 26(2):247–257.

Beynon, William

 1941 The Tsimshians of Metlakatla, Alaska. American Anthropologist
 43(1):83–88.

Bhabha, Homi

 1994 The Location of Culture. New York: Routledge.

Biddle, Lucy

 1977 Keeping Tradition Alive. Museum News, May/June: 35–42.

Bierwert, Crisca

 1999 Brushed by Cedar, Living by the River: Coast Salish Figures of
 Power. Tucson: University of Arizona Press.

Bierwert, Crisca, ed.

 1996 Lushootseed Texts: An Introduction to Puget Salish Narrative
 Aesthetics. Crisca Bierwert, Vi Hilbert, and Thomas M. Hess,
 trans., with annotations by T. C. S. Langen. Lincoln: University of
 Nebraska Press.

Biolsi, Thomas, and Larry Zimmerman

 1997 Indians and Anthropologists. Tucson: University of Arizona Press.

Birket-Smith, Kaj

 1953 The Chugach Eskimo. Nationalmuseets Skrifter, Etnografisk
 Raekke 6. Copenhagen.

Birket-Smith, Kaj, and Frederica de Laguna

 1938 The Eyak Indians of Copper River Delta, Alaska. Copenhagen:
 Levin and Munksgaard.

Black, Martha

 1999 HuupuKanum Tupaat: Out of the Mist: Treasures of the Nuu-
 chah-nulth Chiefs. Victoria: Royal British Columbia Museum.

Blackman, Margaret B.

 1981 The Changing Status of Haida Women: An Ethnohistorical and
 Life History Approach. In The World Is as Sharp as a Knife: An
 Anthology in Honour of Wilson Duff. Donald B. Abbott, ed. Pp.
 65–78. Victoria: British Columbia Provincial Museum.

 1982 During My Time: Florence Edenshaw Davidson, a Haida Woman.
 Seattle: University of Washington Press.

Blackman, Margaret B., ed.

 1977 Continuity and Change in Northwest Coast Ceremonialism.
 Theme issue, Arctic Anthropology 14(1).

Boas, Franz

1894 Chinook Texts. Bureau of American Ethnology Bulletin, 20. Washington DC: Government Printing Office.

1895 Indianische Sagen von der Nord-Pacifischen Küste Amerikas. Berlin: A. Asher.

1897 The Social Organization and the Secret Societies of the Kwakiutl Indians. In Report of the U.S. National Museum for 1895. Reprint, New York: Johnson Reprint, 1970.

1899 Twelfth and Final Report on the North-Western Tribes of Canada. Report of the British Association for the Advancement of Science for 1898. London.

1900 Ethnological Collections from the North Pacific Coast of America. Guide to Hall 105. New York: American Museum of Natural History.

1901 Kathlamet Texts. Bureau of American Ethnology Bulletin, 26. Washington DC: Government Printing Office.

1902 Tsimshian Texts, Nass River Dialect. Bureau of American Ethnology Bulletin, 27. Washington DC: Government Printing Office.

1911 a Introduction. In Handbook of American Indian Languages, vol. 1. Pp. 1–83. Bureau of American Ethnology Bulletin, 40. Washington DC: Government Printing Office.

1911 b The Mind of Primitive Man. New York: Macmillan.

1911 c Tsimshian. In Handbook of American Indian Languages, vol. 1. Pp. 283–422. Bureau of American Ethnology Bulletin, 40. Washington DC: Government Printing Office.

1912 Tsimshian Texts, New Series. Pp. 65–284. Publications of the American Ethnological Society, 3. Leyden, Netherlands: E. J. Brill.

1916 a The Origin of Totemism. American Anthropologist n.s. 18: 319–326.

1916 b Tsimshian Mythology: Based on Texts Recorded by Henry W. Tate, Smithsonian Institution. In Thirty-First Annual Report of the Bureau of American Ethnology for the Years 1909–1910. Pp. 31–1037. Washington DC.

1920 The Social Organization of the Kwakiutl Indians. American Anthropologist 22:111–126.

1921 Ethnology of the Kwakiutl: Based on Data Collected by George

Hunt. 2 vols. *In* 35th Annual Report of the Bureau of American Ethnology for the Years 1913–1914. Washington DC: Government Printing Office.

1926 Letter to Dr. M. Mauss, March 26, 1926. Paris. Archives Marcel Mauss, Collège de France.

1930 The Religion of the Kwakiutl Indians, vol. 2. Columbia University Contributions to Anthropology, 10. New York: Columbia University Press.

1934 Geographical Names of the Kwakiutl Indians. Columbia University Contributions to Anthropology, 20. New York: Columbia University Press.

1935 Kwakiutl Culture as Reflected in Mythology. Memoirs of the American Folk-lore Society 28. Reprint, New York: Kraus Reprint, 1969.1940a Race, Language and Culture. New York: Free Press.

1940b[1920] The Social Organization of the Kwakiutl. *In* Race, Language and Culture. Pp. 356–369. New York: Free Press.

1943 Kwakiutl Tales, New Series, vol. 2: Texts. Columbia University Contributions to Anthropology, 26. New York: Columbia University Press.

1955[1927] Primitive Art. Series B, vol. 8. Oslo: Instituttat for Sammenlignende Kulturforsking. Reprint, New York: Dover.

1966 Kwakiutl Ethnography. Helene Codere, ed. Chicago: University of Chicago Press.

Boas, Franz, and George Hunt

1905 Kwakiutl Texts. Publications of the Jesup North Pacific Expedition, 3. Memoirs of the American Museum of Natural History, 5. New York: G. E. Stechert.

Boelscher, Marianne

1989 The Curtain Within: Haida Social and Mythic Discourse. Vancouver: University of British Columbia Press.

Bolt, Clarence

1988 The Conversion of the Port Simpson Tsimshian: Indian Control or Missionary Manipulation. *In* Out of the Background: Readings on Canadian Native History. Robin Fisher and Kenneth Coates, eds. Pp. 219–235. Mississauga ON: Copp Clark Pittman.

Bordo, Jonathon

2003 Picture and Witness at the Site of the Wilderness. *In* Landscape and Power. 2nd edition. W. J. T. Mitchell, ed. Pp. 291–316. Chicago: University of Chicago Press.

Boss, Suzie

1993 The Museum at Warm Springs, Oregon, Preserves Art and Artifacts of a Time Long Gone. New York Times, Sunday, June 13: 23, 36.

Bourdieu, Pierre

1977 Outline of a Theory of Practice. Cambridge: Cambridge University Press.

1991 Identity and Representation: Elements for a Critical Reflection on the Idea of Region. In Language and Symbolic Power. John B. Thompson, ed. Matthew Adamson, trans. Pp. 220–228. Cambridge MA: Harvard University Press.

Boxberger, Daniel L.

1980 The Lummi Island Reef Nets. Indian Historian 13:4:48–54.

1988 a In and Out of the Labor Force: The Lummi Indians and the Development of the Commercial Salmon Fishery of North Puget Sound. Ethnohistory 35(2):161–190.

1988 b The Lummi Indians and the Canadian/American Pacific Salmon Treaty. American Indian Quarterly 12(4):299–311.

1993 Lightning Boldts and Sparrow Wings: A Comparison of Native Fishing Rights in British Columbia and Washington State. Native Studies Review 9(1):1–13.

1994 Ethnicity and Labor in the Puget Sound Fishing Industry. Ethnology 33(2):179–191.

1998 The Legal Context of Native American Land and Resource Use in Mount Rainier National Park. Seattle: National Park Service, Pacific Northwest Region.

2000 a Cultural Affiliation Study of the Kennewick Human Remains: Review of Traditional Historical and Ethnographic Information. Washington DC: United States Department of the Interior, National Park Service. Electronic document, "Cultural Affiliation Report, Chapter 3: Review of Traditional Historical and Ethnographic Information," http://www.cr.nps.gov/aad/kennewick/boxberger.htm, accessed September 15, 2003.

2000b[1989] To Fish in Common: The Ethnohistory of Lummi Indian

Salmon Fishing. Lincoln: University of Nebraska Press. Reprinted with a new introduction and epilogue. Columbia Classics in Northwest History. Seattle: University of Washington Press.

Boyd, Robert

1996 The People of the Dalles: The Indians of Wascopam Mission. Lincoln: University of Nebraska Press.

1999 The Coming of the Spirit of Pestilence: Introduced Infectious Diseases and Population Decline among Northwest Coast Indians, 1774–1874. Lincoln: University of Nebraska Press.

Boyer, Pascal

1997 Recurrence without Transmission: The Intuitive Background of Religious Tradition. *In* Present Is Past: Some Uses of Tradition in Native Societies. Marie Mauzé, ed. Pp. 23–42. Lanham MD: University Press of America.

Bridgman, Rae, Sally Cole, and Heather Howard-Bobiwash, eds.

1999 Feminist Fields: Ethnographic Insights. Peterborough ON: Broadview Press.

Bringhurst, Robert

1999 A Story as Sharp as a Knife: The Classical Haida Mythtellers and Their World. Lincoln: University of Nebraska Press.

Bringhurst, Robert, and Bill Reid

1984 The Raven Steals the Light. Vancouver: Douglas and McIntyre; Seattle: University of Washington Press.

Bringhurst, Robert, and Ulli Steltzer

1992 The Black Canoe: Bill Reid and the Spirit of the Haida Gwaii. Vancouver: Douglas and McIntyre.

Brink, Jacob H., van den

1974 The Haida Indians: Cultural Change Mainly between 1876–1970. Monographs and Theoretical Studies in Sociology in Honour of Nels Anderson, 8. Leiden: E. J. Brill.

Brown, Jennifer S. H.

1987 *I Wish to Be as I See You:* An Ojibwa-Methodist Encounter in Fur Trade Country, Rainy Lake, 1854–1865. Arctic Anthropology 24(1):19–31.

Brumble, H. David

1988 American Indian Autobiography. Berkeley: University of California Press.

Buckley, Thomas, and Thomas Gottlieb

    1988 Blood Magic: The Anthropology of Menstruation. Berkeley: University of California Press.

Bulletin du Musée d'ethnographie du Trocadéro

    1988 Decary et al., eds. Préface de Jean Jamin. Paris: Jean-Michel Place, Les cahiers de Gradhiva 9. Reprint of 8 issues: vol. 2, 1931; vol. 3, 1932.

Campbell, Brad

    1975 The Shining Youth in Tsimshian Mythology. In Proceedings of the Second Congress of the Canadian Ethnology Society, vol. 1. Jim Freedman and Jerome H. Barkow, eds. Pp. 86–109. National Museum of Man, Mercury Series, Canadian Ethnology Service, 28. Ottawa: National Museums of Canada.

Campbell, Maria

    1973 Halfbreed. Toronto: McClelland and Stewart.

Canada, Indian Claims Commission

    1999 "The Facts: What Is Oral History?" Electronic document, http://www.indianclaims.ca/download/trteng.pdf, accessed November 15, 2003.

Cannizzo, Jeanne

    1983 George Hunt and the Invention of Kwakiutl Culture. Canadian Review of Sociology and Anthropology 20:44–58.

Carpenter, Edmund

    1975 Collecting Northwest Coast Art. In Indian Art of the Northwest Coast: A Dialogue on Craftsmanship and Aesthetics. Bill Holm and Bill Reid, eds. Pp. 9–27. Houston: Institute for the Arts, Rice University; Seattle: University of Washington Press.

Casey, Edward S.

    1993 Getting Back into Place: Toward a Renewed Understanding of the Place-World. Bloomington: Indiana University Press.

    1996 How to Get from Space to Place in a Fairly Short Stretch of Time: Phenomenological Prolegomena. In Senses of Place. Steven Feld and Keith H. Basso, eds. Pp. 13–52. Santa Fe NM: School of American Research.

    1997 The Fate of Place: A Philosophical History. Berkeley: University of California Press.

Cassidy, Frank, ed.
1992 Aboriginal Title in British Columbia: Delgamuuk v. the Queen. Proceedings of a conference held September 10 and 11, 1991. Lantzville: BC: Oolichan Books; Montreal: Institute for Research on Public Policy.

Catton, Theodore
1997 Inhabited Wilderness: Indians, Eskimos, and National Parks in Alaska. Albuquerque: University of New Mexico Press.

Cefaï, Daniel, and Alain Mahé
1998 Échanges rituels de dons, obligation et contrat. Mauss, Davy, Maunier: Trois perspectives de sociologie juridique. L'Année sociologique 48(1):209–228.

Cheever, John
1969 Bullet Park. New York: Alfred A. Knopf.

Claplanhoo, Edward
1994 Oral history transcription from interview by Patricia P. Erikson, Neah Bay WA.

Claplanhoo, Ruth
1995 Oral history transcription from interview by Patricia P. Erikson, Neah Bay WA.
2001 Oral history transcription from interview by Patricia P. Erikson, Neah Bay WA.

Claret de Fleurieu, C. P.
1801 Voyage autour du monde pendant les années 1790, 1791 et 1792 par Etienne Marchand, précédé d'une introduction historique. 4 vols. Paris: Imprimerie de la République.

Clifford, James
1988 The Predicament of Culture: Twentieth-Century Ethnography, Literature, and Art. Cambridge MA: Harvard University Press.
1992 Four Northwest Coast Museums. In Exhibiting Cultures: The Poetics and Politics of Museum Display. I. Karp and S. D. Lavine, eds. Pp. 212–254. Washington DC: Smithsonian Institution Press.
1997 a Museums as Contact Zones. In Routes: Travel and Translation in the Late Twentieth Century. Pp. 188–219. Cambridge MA: Harvard University Press.
1997 b Routes: Travel and Translation in the Late Twentieth Century. Cambridge MA: Harvard University Press.

Clifford, James, and George Marcus, eds.

1986 Writing Culture: The Poetics and Politics of Ethnography. Berkeley: University of California Press.

Clifton, James, ed.

1990 The Invented Indian: Cultural Fictions and Government Policies. New Brunswick NJ: Transaction.

Codere, Helen

1950 Fighting with Property: A Study of Kwakiutl Potlatching and Warfare, 1792–1930. Monographs of the American Ethnological Society, 18. New York: J. J. Augustin.

Codere, Helen, ed.

1966 Introduction. *In* Kwakiutl Ethnography, by Franz Boas. Pp. xi–xxxii. Chicago: University of Chicago Press.

Coffee, Kevin

1991 The Restoration of the Haida Canoe Life Group. Curator 34(1):31–43.

Cohen, David William

1989 The Undefining of Oral Tradition. Ethnohistory 36(1):9–18.

Cohodas, Marvin

1986 Washoe Innovators and Their Patrons. *In* The Arts of the North American Indian. Edwin Wade, ed. Pp. 203–220. New York: Hudson Hills Press.

Cole, Douglas

1985 Captured Heritage: The Scramble for Northwest Coast Artifacts. Seattle: University of Washington Press.

1999 Franz Boas: The Early Years, 1858–1906. Seattle: University of Washington Press.

2000 The Invented Indian/The Imagined Emily. BC Studies 125/126: 147–162.

Cole, Douglas, and Ira Chaikin

1990 An Iron Hand upon the People: The Law against the Potlatch on the Northwest Coast. Vancouver: University of British Columbia Press.

Cole, Douglas, and Alex Long

1999 The Boasian Anthropological Survey Tradition: The Role of Franz Boas in North American Anthropological Surveys. *In* Surveying the Record: North American Scientific Exploration to 1930. Edward C. Carter, ed. Pp. 225–249. Philadelphia: American Philosophical Society.

Coleman, Michael C.
1980 Not Race but Grace: Presbyterian Missionaries and American Indians. Journal of American History 67(1):41–60.

Collier, Donald, and Harry Tschopik Jr.
1954 The Role of Museums in American Anthropology. American Anthropologist 56:768–779.

Collins, Henry B.
1937 Archaeology of St. Lawrence, Alaska. Smithsonian Miscellaneous Collections 96(1).

Collins, June McCormick
1950 The Growth of Class Distinctions and Political Authority among the Skagit Indians during the Contact Period. American Anthropologist 70:331–342.
1974 Valley of the Spirits: The Upper Skagit Indians of Western Washington. Seattle: University of Washington Press.

Collis, Septima M.
1890 A Woman's Trip to Alaska: Being an Account of a Voyage through the Inland Seas of the Sitkan Archipelago. New York: Cassell.

Cooper, Karen Coody
1998 About This Directory. In Tribal Museum Directory. Washington DC: Smithsonian Institution Center for Museum Studies.

Coull, Cheryl
1996 A Traveller's Guide to Aboriginal BC. Vancouver BC: Whitecap Books.

Cousineau, Phil, ed.
1990 The Hero's Journey: The World of Joseph Campbell. San Francisco: Harper and Row.

Cove, John J., and George F. MacDonald, eds.
1987 Tsimshian Narratives. Collected by Marius Barbeau and William Beynon. 2 vols. Canadian Museum of Civilization, Mercury Series, Directorate, 3. Ottawa: National Museums of Canada.

Cowling, Elizabeth
1978 The Eskimos, the American Indians and the Surrealists. Art History 1(4):484–500.

Cranmer Webster, Gloria

    1991 The Contemporary Potlatch. *In* Chiefly Feasts: The Enduring Kwakiutl Potlatch. Aldona Jonaitis, ed. Pp. 227–250. Seattle: University of Washington Press.

Cronon, William

    1995 Introduction. *In* Uncommon Ground: Toward Reinventing Nature. William Cronon, ed. Pp. 23–67. New York: Norton.

Cruikshank, Julie

    1981 Legend and Landscape: Convergence of Oral and Scientific Traditions in the Yukon Territory. Arctic Anthropology 18(2):67–93.

    1990 Getting the Words Right: Perspectives on Naming and Places in Athapaskan Oral History. Arctic Anthropology 27(1):52–65.

    1992 Images of Society in Klondike Gold Rush Narratives: Skookum Jim and the Discovery of Gold. Ethnohistory 39(1):20–41.

    1998 The Social Life of Stories: Narrative and Knowledge in the Yukon Territory. Vancouver: University of British Columbia Press; Lincoln: University of Nebraska Press.

Cruikshank, Julie, with Angela Sidney, Kitty Smith, and Annie Ned

    1990 Life Lived Like a Story: Live Stories of Three Yukon Elders. Lincoln: University of Nebraska Press.

Culhane, Dara

    1998 The Pleasure of the Crown: Anthropology, Law and First Nations. Burnaby BC: Talonbooks.

Curtis, Edward

    1915 The North American Indian, vol. 10: The Kwakiutl. Nordwood MA: Plimpton Press.

    1916 The North American Indian, vol. 11: The Nootka. Nordwood MA: Plimpton Press.

Cutler, Robin

    1994 A Gift from the Past. Indian America Series. Videocassette, 60 min., coor., 1/2 inch. Media Resource Associates, Washington DC.

Dark, Alex

    1998 Public Sphere Politics and Community Conflict over the Environment and Native Land Rights. Ph.D. dissertation, New York University.

Darnell, Regna

1990 Edward Sapir: Linguist, Anthropologist, Humanist. Berkeley: University of California Press.

1995 The Structuralism of Claude Lévi-Strauss. Historiographia Linguistica 22(1/2):217–234.

1998 And Along Came Boas: Continuity and Revolution in Americanist Anthropology. Amsterdam: John Benjamins.

2000 The Pivotal Role of the Northwest Coast in the History of Americanist Anthropology. BC Studies 125/126:33–52.

2001 Invisible Genealogies: A History of Americanist Anthropology. Lincoln: University of Nebraska Press.

Dauenhauer, Richard

2000 Syncretism, Revival, and Reinvention: Tlingit Religion, Pre- and Postcontact. In Native Religions and Cultures of North America: Anthropology of the Sacred. Lawrence E. Sullivan, ed. Pp. 160–180. New York: Continuum.

Dauenhauer, Richard, and Nora Marks Dauenhauer

1987 Haa Shuká, Our Ancestors: Tlingit Oral Narratives. Seattle: University of Washington Press.

1990 Haa Tuwunáagu Yís, for Healing Our Spirit: Tlingit Oratory. Seattle: University of Washington Press.

1994 Haa Kusteeyí, Our Culture: Tlingit Life Stories. Seattle: University of Washington Press.

1995 Oral Literature Embodied and Disembodied. In Aspects of Oral Communication. U. Quasthoff, ed. Pp. 91–111. Berlin: Walter de Gruyter.

1998 Technical, Emotional, and Ideological Issues in Reversing Language Shift: Examples from Southeast Alaska. In Endangered Languages: Language Loss and Community Response. Lenore Grenoble and Lindsay Whaley, eds. Pp. 57–98. Cambridge: Cambridge University Press.

1999 The Paradox of Talking on the Page: Some Aspects of the Tlingit and Haida Experience. In Talking on the Page: Editing Aboriginal Texts. Laura Murray and Keren Rice, eds. Pp. 3–41. Toronto: University of Toronto Press.

2002 Tlingit Clans and Shifting Patterns of Socio-political Discourse.

In Discourses in Search of Members: Festschrift in Honor of Ron Scollon. David S. C. Li, ed. Pp. 335–360. Lanham MD: University Press of America.

2003 Louis Shotridge and Indigenous Tlingit Ethnography: Then and Now. *In* Constructing Cultures Then and Now: Celebrating Franz Boas and the Jesup North Pacific Expedition. Laurel Kendall and Igor Krupnik, eds. Pp. 165–183. Contributions to Circumpolar Anthropology, 4. Washington DC: Arctic Studies Center, National Museum of Natural History, Smithsonian Institution.

Daugherty, Richard

1971 At Cape Alava: A Time Capsule Unsealed. Pacific Search 5(3):1–3.

1995 Oral history transcription from interview by Patricia P. Erikson, Lacey WA.

Daugherty, Richard, and Ruth Kirk

1976 Ancient Indian Village Where Time Stood Still. Smithsonian 7(2):68–75.

Davy, Georges

1922 La foi jurée: Etude sociologique du problème du contrat: La formation du lien contractuel. Paris: Félix Alcan.

Dawson, George M.

1888 Notes and Observations on the Kwakiool People of the Northern Part of Vancouver Island and Adjacent Coast. Proceedings and Transactions of the Royal Society of Canada for the Year 1887 5(2):63–98.

de Certeau, Michel

1984 The Practice of Everyday Life. Berkeley: University of California Press.

de Laguna, Frederica

1932–33 A Comparison of Eskimo and Paleolithic Art. American Journal of Archaeology 36:422–511, 37:77–107.

1933 Peintures rupestres eskimo. Journal de la Société des Américanistes n.s. 25:17–30.

1940 a Eskimo Lamps and Pots. Journal of the Royal Anthropological Institute 70(1):53–76.

1940 b Lévy-Bruhl's Contributions to the Study of Primitive Mentality. Philosophical Review 49(5):552–566.

1946 The Importance of the Eskimo in Northeastern Archaeology. *In* Man in Northeastern North America. Frederic Johnson, ed. Pp. 106–142. Papers of the R. S. Peabody Foundation, 3. Andover MA: Phillips Academy.

1947 The Prehistory of Northern North America as Seen from the Yukon. Memoirs of the Society for American Archaeology, 3. Menasha WI: Society for American Archaeology.

1949 *Review of* Archéologie du Pacifique-Nord: Matériaux pour l'étude des relations entre les peuples d'Asie et d'Amérique, by André Leroi-Gourhan. American Anthropologist 51(4):645–647.

1954 Tlingit Ideas about the Individual. Southwestern Journal of Anthropology 19(2):172–191.

1956 Chugach Prehistory: The Archaeology of Prince William Sound, Alaska. University of Washington Publications in Anthropology, 13. Seattle: University of Washington Press.

1960 The Story of a Tlingit Community: A Problem in Relationship between Archaeological, Ethnological, and Historical Methods. Bureau of American Ethnology Bulletin, 172. Washington DC: U.S. Government Printing Office.

1965 Childhood among the Yakutat Tlingit. *In* Context and Meaning in Cultural Anthropology. Melford Spiro, ed. Pp. 3–23. New York: Free Press.

1968 On Anthropological Inquiry. Presidential Address, American Anthropological Association. *American Anthropologist* 70: 465–476.

1972 Under Mount Saint Elias: The History and Culture of the Yakutat Tlingit. 3 vols. Smithsonian Contributions to Anthropology, 7. Washington DC: Smithsonian Institution Press.

1975a[1934] The Archaeology of Cook Inlet, Alaska. Philadelphia: University of Pennsylvania Press for the University Museum. Reprinted with a new foreword by Karen W. Workman and William B. Workman and a new preface by Frederica de Laguna. Fairbanks: Alaska Historical Society, Anchorage.

1975 b Matrilineal Kin Groups in Northwestern North America. *In* Proceedings: Northern Athapaskan Conference, 1971, vol. 1. A. McFadyen Clark, ed. Pp. 17–145. National Museum of Man,

Mercury Series, Canadian Ethnology Service Paper, 27. Ottawa: National Museums of Canada.

1977 Voyage to Greenland: A Personal Initiation into Anthropology. New York: W. W. Norton.

1994 Some Early Circumpolar Studies. *In* Circumpolar Religion and Ecology: An Anthropology of the North. Talkashi Irimoto and Takako Yamada, eds. Pp. 7–44. Tokyo: University of Tokyo Press.

1995 Tales from Dena: Indian Stories from the Tanana, Koyukuk and Yukon Rivers. Recorded in 1935 by Frederica de Laguna and Norman Reynolds. Seattle: University of Washington Press.

2000 a Field Work with My Tlingit Friends. *In* Celebration 2000: Restoring Balance through Culture. Susan W. Fair and Rosita Worl, eds. Pp. 21–40. Juneau AK: Sealaska Heritage Foundation.

2000 b Travels among the Dena: Exploring Alaska's Yukon River. Seattle: University of Washington Press.

de Laguna, Grace

1966 On Existence and the Human World. New Haven: Yale University Press.

Deleuze, Gilles, and Félix Guattari

1987 A Thousand Plateaus: Capitalism and Schizophrenia. Brian Massumi, trans. Minneapolis: University of Minnesota Press.

Deloria, Philip J.

1998 Playing Indian. New Haven: Yale University Press.

Deloria, Vine

1969 Custer Died for Your Sins. Playboy, August: 131–132, 172–175.

Descola, Philippe, and Michel Izard

1991 Amérique—Les recherches sur l'Amérique. *In* Dictionnaire de l'ethnologie et de l'anthropologie. Pierre Bonte and Michel Izard, eds. Pp. 46–53. Paris: Presses universitaires de France.

Descola, Philippe, and Anne Christine Taylor, eds.

1993 La remontée de l'Amazone. Theme issue, L'Homme 126–128.

Dickerson, Mary C.

1910 Herculean Task in Museum Exhibition: Foreword Regarding the Ceremonial Canoe Scene in the North Pacific Hall. American Museum Journal 10:227–228.

Dilworth, Leah

1996 Imagining Indians in the Southwest: Persistent Visions of a Primitive Past. Washington DC: Smithsonian Institution Press.

Dingus, Lowell

1996 Next of Kin: Extinct Fossils at the American Museum of Natural
History. New York: Rizzoli.

Dombrowski, Kirk

2001 Against Culture: Development, Politics, and Religion in Indian
Alaska. Lincoln: University of Nebraska Press.

Dominguez, Virginia

1992 Invoking Culture: The Messy Side of "Cultural Politics." South
Atlantic Quarterly 91(1):19–42.

Donald, Leland

1997 Aboriginal Slavery on the Northwest Coast of North America.
Berkeley: University of California Press.

Dosse, François

1997 History of Structuralism, vol. 2: The Sign Sets, 1967-Present.
Deborah Glassman, trans. Minneapolis: University of Minnesota
Press.

Doxtator, Deborah

1985 The Idea of the Indian and the Development of Iroquoian Museums. Museum Quarterly, Summer: 20–26.

Drucker, Philip

1940 Kwakiutl Dancing Societies. University of California Anthropological Records 2(6):201–230.

1951 The Northern and Central Nootkan Tribes. U.S. Bureau of American Ethnology Bulletin, 144. Washington DC.

Drucker, Philip, and Robert F. Heizer

1967 To Make My Name Good: A Reexamination of the Southern
Kwakiutl Potlatch. Berkeley: University of California Press.

Ducharme, Edward R.

1998[1968] J. D., D. B., Sonny, Sunny, and Holden. English Record, Decem-
ber, 54–58. Reprinted as Possible Autobiographical Elements in
Catcher. In Readings on The Catcher in the Rye. Steven Engel, ed.
Pp. 68–75. San Diego: Greenhaven Press.

Duff, Wilson

n.d. Tsimshian File. 014–16–01. Unpublished manuscript, Museum of Anthropology, University of British Columbia, Vancouver. See Margaret Seguin Anderson n.d. for an inventory of the contents and digitized ms. on CD.

1952 The Upper Stalo Indians of the Fraser Valley, British Columbia. Anthropology in British Columbia Memoir, 1. Victoria BC: British Columbia Provincial Museum.

1969 The Fort Victoria Treaties. BC Studies 3:3–57.

1975 Images, Stone, BC: Thirty Centuries of Northwest Coast Indian Sculpture. Saanichton BC: Hancock House.

1981 The World Is as Sharp as a Knife: Meaning in Northern Northwest Coast Art. *In* The World Is as Sharp as a Knife: An Anthology in Honour of Wilson Duff. Donald N. Abbott, ed. Pp. 209–224. Victoria BC: British Columbia Provincial Museum.

1996 Birds of Paradox: The Unpublished Writings of Wilson Duff. E. N. Anderson, ed. Surrey BC: Hancock House.

Duncan, Kate C.

2000 1001 Curious Things: Ye Olde Curiosity Shop and Native American Art. Seattle: University of Washington Press.

Dundes, Alan

1979 Heads or Tails: A Psychoanalytic Study of the Potlatch. Journal of Psychological Anthropology 2:395–424.

Dunn, John A.

n.d. Adáwga wila waalsga naa mmóot a dúulas nagwát. Told by Joseph Bradley to William Beynon (Columbia University Manuscript, 127) with a new transcription and poetic translation/interpretation by John Dunn. *In* Sm'algyax Level Two: First Nations Studies, 138, University of Northern British Columbia.

1984 Tsimshian Grandchildren: Redistributive Mechanisms in Personal Property Inheritance. *In* The Tsimshian and Their Neighbors of the North Pacific Coast. Jay Miller and Carol M. Eastman, eds. Pp. 36–57. Seattle: University of Washington Press.

1998 The Heat of Her Breasts: Sun's Daughter. Paper presented at the Symposium on Asdiwal, organized by John Leavitt, at the joint meetings of the American Ethnological Society/Canadian Anthropology Society, Toronto, May.

Dunn, John, and L. Dunn

1972 An Equivalence Cycle for Kitkatla Kin-Status Terms. Anthropological Linguistics 14(6):240–254.

Dunning, Mike

2000 Tourism in Ketchikan and Southeast Alaska. Alaska History 15(2):30–43.

Durkheim, Emile

1896–97 La prohibition de l'inceste et ses origines. L'Année sociologique 1:1–70.

1898–99 Review of The Social Organization and the Secret Societies of the Kwakiutl Indians, by Franz Boas. L'Année sociologique 3:336–340.

1900–1901 Sur le totémisme. L'Année sociologique 5:82–121.

1903–4 Sur l'organisation matrimoniale des sociétés australiennes. L'Année sociologique 8:119–147.

1909–12a Review of The Mind of the Primitive Man, by Franz Boas. L'Année sociologique 12:31–33.

1909–12b Review of Totemism: An Analytical Study, by A. A. Goldenweiser. L'Année sociologique 12: 100–101.

1915 The Elementary Forms of the Religious Life. London: George Allen and Unwin.

1998 Lettres à Marcel Mauss, présentées par Philippe Besnard et Marcel Fournier. Paris: Presses universitaires de France.

Durlach, T. M.

1928 The Relationship Systems of the Tlingit, Haida and Tsimshian. American Ethnological Society Publications, 11. New York: G. E. Stechert.

Dyck, Noel, and James B. Waldram, eds.

1993 Anthropology, Public Policy and Native Peoples in Canada. Montreal: McGill-Queens University Press.

Eisenstadt, Sergei N.

1973 Tradition, Change, and Modernity. New York: John Wiley and Sons.

Eliade, Mircea

1959 Cosmos and History: The Myth of the Eternal Return. Willard Trask, trans. New York: Harper.

Ellis, Reuben

2001 Vertical Margins: Mountaineering and the Landscapes of Neoimperialism. Madison: University of Wisconsin Press.

Elmendorf, William

1993 Twana Narratives: Native Historical Accounts of a Coast Salish Culture. Seattle: University of Washington Press.

Emberley, Julia V.

1993 Thresholds of Difference: Feminist Critique, Native Women's Writings, Postcolonial Theory. Toronto: University of Toronto Press.

Emmons, George T.

1910 Niska. In Handbook of American Indians North of Mexico. Pp. 75–76. Smithsonian Institution, Bureau of American Ethnology Bulletin, 30(2). Washington DC: Smithsonian Institution Press.

1911 Native Account of the Meeting between La Pérouse and the Tlingit. American Anthropologist 13(2):294–298.

1916 Whale House of the Chilkat. Pp. 1–33. American Museum of Natural History Anthropological Papers, 19(1). New York.

1991 The Tlingit Indians. Edited with additions by Frederica de Laguna. Vancouver BC: Douglas and McIntyre.

Eribon, Didier

1988 Lévi-Strauss Interviewed—Part 2. Anthropology Today 4(6):3–5.

Erikson, Patricia Pierce

1996 Encounters in the Nation's Attic: Native American Community Museums/Cultural Centers, the Smithsonian Institution, and the Politics of Knowledge Making. Ph.D. dissertation, University of California, Davis.

1999 A-Whaling We Will Go: Encounters of Knowledge and Memory at the Makah Museum. Cultural Anthropology 14(4):556–583.

Erikson, Patricia Pierce, with Helma Ward and Kirk Wachendorf

2002 Voices of a Thousand People: The Makah Cultural and Research Center. Lincoln: University of Nebraska Press.

Escobar, Arturo

2001 Culture Sits in Places: Reflections on Globalism and Subaltern Strategies of Localization. Political Geography 20:139–174.

Ewers, John C.

   1955 Problems and Procedures in Modernizing Ethnological Exhibits. American Anthropologist 57(1):1–12.

Fardon, Richard, ed.

   1990 Localizing Strategies: Regional Traditions of Ethnographic Writing. Edinburgh: Scottish Academic Press; Washington DC: Smithsonian Institution Press.

Fassett, E. C. B.

   1911 Foreword on the New Mural Paintings in the American Museum. American Museum Journal 11:129–137.

Fawcett, Melissa Jayne

   2000 Medicine Trail: The Life and Lessons of Gladys Tantaquidgeon. Tucson: University of Arizona Press.

Federal Writers' Project

   1982[1939] The WPA Guide to New York City: The Federal Writers' Project Guide to 1930s New York. Reprint, New York: Pantheon Books.

Feld, Steven, and Keith H. Basso, eds.

   1996 Senses of Place. Santa Fe NM: School of American Research.

Field, Edward

   1897 Sitka and Its Inhabitants. Alaska [Selections from The Youth's Companion]. Pp. 5–9. Boston: Perry Mason.

Finck, Henry T.

   1891 The Pacific Coast Scenic Tour. New York: Charles Scribner.

Fisher, Michael M. J.

   1986 Ethnicity and the Post-Modern Arts of Memory. In Writing Culture: The Poetics and Politics of Ethnography. James Clifford and George E. Marcus, eds. Pp. 194–233. Berkeley: University of California Press.

Fisher, Robin

   1992[1977] Contact and Conflict: Indian-European Relations in British Columbia 1884–1890. 2nd edition. Vancouver: University of British Columbia Press.

Fiske, Jo-Anne

   1996 The Womb Is to the Nation as the Heart Is to the Body: Ethnopolitical Discourses of the Canadian Indigenous Women's Movement. Studies in Political Economy 51:65–95.

Fitzhugh, William W.

1997 Ambassadors in Sealskins: Exhibiting Eskimos at the Smithsonian. *In* Exhibiting Dilemmas: Issues of Representation at the
Smithsonian. Amy Henderson and Adrienne L. Kaeppler, eds. Pp.
206–245. Washington DC: Smithsonian Institution Press.

Fitzhugh, William W., and Valérie Chaussonnet, eds.

1994 Anthropology of the North Pacific Rim. Washington DC: Smithsonian Institution Press.

Fitzhugh, William W., and Aaron Crowell, eds.

1988 Crossroads of Continents: Cultures of Siberia and Alaska. Washington DC: Smithsonian Institution Press.

Forbes, Jack

1966 Special Section. Indian Voices, April/May: 29–31.

Force, Roland W.

1999 Politics and the Museum of the American Indian: The Heye and
the Mighty. Honolulu HI: Mechas Press.

Ford, Clellan S.

1941 Smoke from Their Fires: The Life of a Kwakiutl Chief. New Haven
CT: Yale University Press.

Foster, Gwendolyn Audrey

1997 Women Filmmakers of the African and Asian Diaspora: Decolo-
nizing the Gaze, Locating Subjectivity. Carbondale: Southern
Illinois University Press.

Foucault, Michel

1979 Discipline and Punish: The Birth of the Prison. New York: Vantage
Books.

1980 Power/Knowledge: Selected Interviews and Other Writings, 1972–
1977. Colin Gordon, ed. New York: Pantheon.

1998[1964] Nietzsche, Freud, Marx. *In* Foucault: Aesthetics, Method, and
Epistemology, vol. 2. James Faubion, ed. Pp. 261–268. New York:
New Press.

Fournier, Marcel

1993 Marcel Mauss ou le don de soi. Archives européennes de sociologie 34:325–338.

1994 Marcel Mauss. Paris: Fayard.

1995 Marcel Mauss, l'ethnologie et la politique: Le don. Anthropologie
et sociétés 19(1–2):57–69.

Fox, Everett

1995 The Five Books of Moses. New York: Schocken Books.

Freed, Stanley A.

1966 The New Eastern Woodlands Indians Hall at the American Museum of Natural History. Curator 9(4):267–288.

Freed, Stanley A., and Ruth S. Freed

1983 Clark Wissler and the Development of Anthropology in the United States. American Anthropologist 85(4):800–825.

Friedrich, Paul

1970 Proto-Indo-European Trees: The Arboreal System of a Prehistoric People. Chicago: University of Chicago Press.

Fuller, Nancy

1992 The Museum as a Vehicle for Community Empowerment: The Ak-Chin Indian Community Ecomuseum Project. *In* Museums and Communities: The Politics of Public Culture. Ivan Karp, Christine Kreamer, and Steven Lavine, eds. Pp. 327–366. Washington DC: Smithsonian Institution Press.

Fuller, Nancy, and Suzanne Fabricius

1992 Native American Museums and Cultural Centers: Historical Overview and Current Issues. Zeitschrift für Ethnologie 117:223–237.

1994 Tribal Museums. *In* Native Americans in the Twentieth Century: An Encyclopedia. Pp. 655–657. New York: Garland.

Gallenkamp, Charles

2001 Dragon Hunter: Roy Chapman Andrews and the Central Asiatic Expedition. New York: Viking.

Galois, Robert

1994 Kwakwakaka'wakw Settlements, 1775–1920: A Geographical Analysis and Gazetteer. Vancouver: University of British Columbia Press, Seattle: University of Washington Press.

Gardner, George S.

1985 Old Show-Cases: Discard or Recycle? Museum, no. 146, 37(2):74–78 (Paris: UNESCO).

Garfield, Viola

1931 Change in the Marriage Customs of the Tsimshian. M.A. thesis, University of Washington.

1939 Tsimshian Clan and Society. University of Washington Publications in Anthropology, 7(3). Seattle: University of Washington.

1951 The Tsimshian and Their Neighbors. *In* The Tsimshian: Their Arts and Music. V. E. Garfield, P. S. Wingert, and M. Barbeau, eds. Pp. 1–70. Publications of the American Ethnological Society, 18. New York: J. J. Augustin.

Garfield, Viola, Paul Wingert, and Marius Barbeau
    1951 The Tsimshian: Their Arts and Music. Publications of the American Ethnological Society, 18. New York: J. J. Augustin.

Garrod, Andrew, and Colleen Larimore, eds.
    1997 First Person, First Peoples: Native American College Graduates Tell Their Life Stories. Ithaca: Cornell University Press.

Ghandl of the Qayahl Llaanas
    2000 Nine Visits to the Mythworld. Robert Bringhurst, trans. Masterworks of the Classical Haida Mythtellers, 2. Vancouver: Douglas and McIntyre; Lincoln: University of Nebraska Press.

Gibson, Ann
    1983 Painting outside the Paradigm: Indian Space. Arts Magazine 57(6):98–104.

Gibson, James R.
    1992 Otter Skins, Boston Ships and China Goods: The Maritime Fur Trade of the Northwest Coast, 1785–1841. Seattle: University of Washington Press.

Gmelch, Sharon B.
    1995 Elbridge Warren Merrill of Sitka, Alaska. History of Photography 19(2):159–172.

Goddard, Pliny Earle
    1934 Indians of the Northwest Coast. 2nd edition. American Museum of Natural History, Handbook Series, 10. New York: American Museum Press.

Godelier, Maurice
    1996 L'énigme du don. Paris: Fayard.

Goldenweiser, Alexander
    1910 Totemism: An Analytical Study. Journal of American Folklore 23:179–292.
    1918 Form and Content in Totemism. American Anthropologist n.s. 20:280–295.
    1975[1915] *Review of* Les formes élémentaires de la vie religieuse: Le sys-

tème totémique en Australie, by Emile Durkheim. *In* Durkheim on Religion. W. S. F. Pickering, ed. Pp. 209–227. London: Routledge and Kegan Paul.

Goldman, Irving

1975 The Mouth of Heaven: An Introduction to Kwakiutl Religious Thought. New York: Wiley.

Goldschmidt, Walter, and Theodore H. Haas

1946 Possessory Rights of the Natives of Southeastern Alaska. Report to the Commissioner of Indian Affairs, Bureau of Indian Affairs. WA DC.

1998[1946] Haa Aaní, Our Land: Tlingit and Haida Land Rights and Use. Thomas F. Thornton, ed. Seattle: University of Washington Press.

Golovko, Eugene

1997 Traveling Folklore: Inter-ethnic Contacts as a Cause of Folklore Exchange. Paper presented at the Oral Traditions of the North Pacific Rim Workshop, Fort Ross CA, November.

Gough, Barry

1984 Gunboat Frontier: British Maritime Authority and Northwest Coast Indians, 1846–90. Vancouver: University of British Columbia Press.

Graburn, Nelson

1999 Afterword: Ethnic and Tourist Arts Revisited. *In* Unpacking Culture: Arts and Goods in Colonial and Postcolonial Worlds. Ruth B. Phillips and Christopher B. Steiner, eds. Pp. 335–353. Berkeley: University of California Press.

Green, Rayna

1988 The Indian in Popular American Culture. *In* Handbook of North American Indians, vol. 4: History of Indian-White Relations. Wilcomb Washburn, ed. Pp. 587–606. Washington DC: Smithsonian Institution Press.

Gregory, Derek

1994 Geographical Imaginations. Cambridge MA: Blackwell.

Griffin, Kristin

1999 Early Views: Historical Vignettes of Sitka National Historical Park. Anchorage AK: U.S. Department of the Interior.

Grinev, Andrei V.

1999–2000 Frederica de Laguna and Her Contribution to the Study of the Native Population of Alaska. *In* Beyond the Wildest Dreams: Western Influences on Post-Soviet Anthropology. Anthropology and Archaeology of Eurasia 38(3):11–23.

Guédon, Marie-Françoise

1974 a People of Tetlin, Why Are You Singing? National Museum of Man, Mercury Series, Canadian Ethnology Service, 9. Ottawa: National Museums of Canada.

1974 b Chamanisme Tsimshian et Athapaskan: Un essai sur la défi-nition des méthodes chamaniques. *In* Proceedings of the First Congress of the Canadian Ethnology Society. Jerome H. Barkow, ed. Pp. 181–221. National Museum of Man, Mercury Series, Canadian Ethnology Service, 17. Ottawa: National Museums of Canada.

1984 a An Introduction to Tsimshian World View and Its Practioners. *In* The Tsimshian: Images of the Past: Views for the Present. Margaret Seguin, ed. Pp. 137–159. Vancouver: University of British Columbia Press.

1984 b Tsimshian Shamanic Images. *In* The Tsimshian: Images of the Past: Views for the Present. Margaret Seguin, ed. Pp. 174–211. Vancouver: University of British Columbia Press.

In press Le rêve et la forêt: Histoires de chamanes Nabesna. Québec: Presses de l'Université Laval.

Gunther, Erna

1972 Indian Life on the Northwest Coast of America, as Seen by Early Explorers and Fur Traders during the Last Decades of the Eighteenth Century. Chicago: University of Chicago Press.

Gupta, Akhil, and James Ferguson, eds.

1997 a Anthropological Locations: Boundaries and Grounds of a Field Science. Berkeley: University of California Press.

1997 b Culture, Power, Place: Explorations in Critical Anthropology. Durham NC: Duke University Press.

Hallock, Charles

1886 Our New Alaska: The Seward Purchase Vindicated. New York: Forest and Stream.

Hallowell, Irving A.

1926 Bear Ceremonialism in the Northern Hemisphere. American
Anthropologist 28(1):1–175.

1955 Culture and Experience. Philadelphia: University of Pennsylvania
Press.

Halpin, Marjorie

1973 The Tsimshian Crest System: A Study Based on Museum Specimens and the Marius Barbeau and the William Beynon Field
Notes. Ph.D. dissertation, University of British Columbia, Vancouver.

1984 The Structure of Tsimshian Totemism. *In* The Tsimshian and
Their Neighbors of the North Pacific Coast. Jay Miller and
Carol M. Eastman, eds. Pp. 16–35. Seattle: University of Washing-
ton Press.

Handler, R., and J. Linnekin

1984 Tradition, Genuine and Spurious. Journal of American Folklore:
97:273–290.

Hanson, F. Allan

1997 Empirical Anthropology, Post-Modernism and the Invention of
Tradition. *In* Present Is Past: Some Uses of Tradition in Native
Societies. Marie Mauzé, ed. Pp. 195–214. Lanham MD: University
Press of America.

Hanson, James

1980 The Reappearing Vanishing American. Museum News 59(2):44–
51.

Haraway, Donna

1989 Primate Visions: Gender, Race, and Nature in the World of Modern Science. New York: Routledge.

Harding, Sarah

2000 Cultural Secrecy and the Protection of Cultural Property. *In* Topics in Cultural Resource Law. Donald F. Craib, ed. Pp. 69–78.
Washington DC: Society for American Archaeology.

Harkin, Michael

1988 History, Narrative, and Temporality: Examples from the Northwest Coast. Ethnohistory 35:99–130.

1993 Power and Progress: The Evangelical Dialogue among the Heiltsuk. Ethnohistory 40:1–33.

1995 Modernist Anthropology and Tourism of the Authentic. Annals of
Tourism Research 32:650–670.

1996 Engendering Discipline: Discourse and Counterdiscourse in the
Methodist-Heiltsuk Dialogue. Ethnohistory 43:643–661.

1997 a The Heiltsuks: Dialogues of Culture and History on the Northwest Coast. Lincoln: University of Nebraska Press.

1997 b A Tradition of Invention: Modern Ceremonialism on the North-
west Coast. *In* Present Is Past: Some Uses of Tradition in Native
Societies. Marie Mauzé, ed. Pp. 97–111. Lanham MD: University
Press of America.

1998 Whales, Chiefs, and Giants: An Exploration into Nuu-chah-nulth
Political Thought. Ethnology 37:317–332.

2000 Sacred Place, Scarred Space. Wicazo Sa Review 15(1):49–70.

2001 Ethnographic Deep Play: Boas, McIlwraith, and Fictive Adoption
on the Northwest Coast. *In* Strangers to Relatives: The Adoption
and Naming of Anthropologists in Native North America. Sergei
Kan, ed. Pp. 57–79. Lincoln: University of Nebraska Press.

Harmon, Alexandra

1990–91 Writing History by Litigation: How Courts Use Historical Evidence When Making Rulings on Northwest Indian Rights Cases.
Columbia: The Magazine of Northwest History 4(4):5–15.

1998 Indians in the Making: Ethnic Relations and Indian Identities
around Puget Sound. Berkeley: University of California Press.

Harris, Kenneth B.

1974 Visitors Who Never Left: The Origin of the People of Damela-
hamid. Kenneth B. Harris, trans., with Frances M. P. Robinson.
Vancouver: University of British Columbia Press.

Hartman, Russell

1983 The Navajo Tribal Museum: Bridging the Past and Present.
American Indian Art Magazine 9(1):30–36.

Hawthorn, Audrey

1979[1967] Kwakiutl Art. Seattle: University of Washington Press.

Heath, Deborah

1994 The Politics of Appropriateness and Appropriation: Recontextualizing Women's Dance in Urban Senegal. American Ethnologist 21(1):88–103.

Heidegger, Martin

    1962 Being and Time. John Macquarrie and Edward Robinson, trans. New York: Harper and Row.

    1977 Building Dwelling Thinking. *In* Martin Heidegger, Basic Writings. Albert Hofstader, trans. Pp. 319–340. London: Harper and Row.

Heider, Karl

    1988 The Rashomon Effect: When Ethnographers Disagree. American Anthropologist 90:73–82.

Heilbrun, Carolyn G.

    1988 Writing a Woman's Life. New York: W. W. Norton.

Hellman, Geoffrey

    1969 Bankers, Bones, and Beetles: The First Century of the American Museum of Natural History. Garden City NY: Natural History Press.

Henaff, Marcel

    1998 Claude Lévi-Strauss and the Making of Structural Anthropology. Minneapolis: University of Minnesota Press.

Hendricks, Janet Wall

    1993 Creating Meaning and Evoking Emotion through Repetition: Shuar War Stories. *In* New Voices in Native American Literary Criticism. Arnold Krupat, ed. Pp. 77–119. Washington DC: Smithsonian Institution Press.

Higginson, Ella

    1910 Alaska, the Great Country. New York: Macmillan.

Hillman, James

    1999 The Force of Character, and the Lasting Life: New York: Ballantine.

Hilton, Susanne Storie, Evelyn Walkus Windsor and John C. Rath

    1982 Oowekeeno Oral Traditions as Told by the late Simon Walkus Sr. National Museum of Man, Mercury Series, Canadian Ethnology Service, 84. Ottawa: National Museums of Canada.

Hinckley, Ted C.

    1962 Sheldon Jackson, Presbyterian Lobbyist for the Great Land of Alaska. Journal of Presbyterian History 40:3–23.

1965 The Inside Passage: A Popular Gilded Age Tour. Pacific Northwest Quarterly 56:67–74.

1966 The Presbyterian Leadership in Pioneering Alaska. Mississippi Valley Historical Review 52:742–756.

1972 The Americanization of Alaska, 1867–1897. Palo Alto CA: Pacific Books.

1982 Alaskan John G. Brady: Missionary, Businessman, Judge, and Governor, 1878–1918. Columbus: Ohio State University Press.

1996 The Canoe Rocks: Alaska's Tlingit and the Euramerican Frontier. Lanham MD: University Press of America.

Hinsley, Curtis

1992 Collecting Cultures and Cultures of Collecting: The Lure of the American Southwest, 1880–1915. Museum Anthropology 16(1):12–20.

1993 Search of the New World Classical. In Collecting the Pre-Columbian Past: A Symposium at Dumbarton Oaks, 6th and 7th October 1990. E. H. Boone, ed. Pp. 105–121. Washington DC: Dumbarton Oaks Research Library.

Hirsch, Eric, and Michael O'Hanlon, eds.

1995 The Anthropology of Landscape. Oxford: Clarendon Press.

Hobsbawm, Eric, and Terence Ranger, eds.

1983 The Invention of Tradition. Cambridge: Cambridge University Press.

Holden, Madronna

1976 Making All Crooked Ways Straight. Journal of American Folklore 89:271–293.

Hollier, Denis, ed.

1988 The College of Sociology 1937–1939. Minneapolis: University of Minnesota Press.

Holm, Bill

1965 Northwest Coast Indian Art: An Analysis of Form. Thomas Burke Memorial Washington State Museum Monographs, 1. Seattle: University of Washington Press.

1977 Traditional and Contemporary Kwakiutl Winter Dance. Arctic Anthropology 14(1):5–24.

1979 Review of Objects of Bright Pride by Allen Wardwell. In American Indian Art Magazine 4(3):77–79.

Holm, Wayne
  1993 On the Use of the Navajo Language in Navajo Head Start Centers: Preliminary Considerations. Journal of Navajo Education 10:36–45.
Hooper-Greenhill, Eilean
  1989 The Museum in the Disciplinary Society. *In* Museum Studies in Material Culture. Susan M. Pearce, ed. Pp. 61–72. London: Leicester University Press.
Hoover, Alan L., ed.
  2000 Nuu-chah-nulth Voices, Histories, Objects and Journeys. Victoria BC: Royal British Columbia Museum.
Hope, Andrew, III, and Thomas F. Thornton, eds.
  2000 Will the Time Ever Come? A Tlingit Source Book. Fairbanks: University of Alaska Press.
Horse Capture, George P.
  1994 From the Reservation to the Smithsonian via Alcatraz. American Indian Culture and Research Journal 18(4):135–149.
Hovey, Edmund O., ed.
  1904 A General Guide to the American Museum of Natural History: A Guide. Leaflet, 13. New York: American Museum of Natural History.
Howard, Kathleen L., and Diana F. Pardue
  1996 Inventing the Southwest: The Fred Harvey Company and Native American Art. Flagstaff AZ: Northland.
Howard-Bobiwash, Heather
  1999 Like Her Lips to My Ear: Reading Anishnaabekweg Lives and Aboriginal Cultural Continuity in the City. *In* Feminist Fields: Ethnographic Insights. Rae Bridgman, Sally Cole, and Heather Howard-Bobiwash, eds. Pp. 117–136. New York: Broadview Press.
Huelsbeck, David R.
  1994 The Utilization of Whales at Ozette. *In* Ozette Archaeological Project Research Reports, vol. 2: Fauna. Stephan R. Samuels, ed. Washington State University, Department of Anthropology, Reports of Investigations, 66. Pullman: Washington State University.
Hunn, Eugene
  1993 What Is Traditional Ecological Knowledge. *In* Traditional Eco-

logical Knowledge: Wisdom for Sustainable Development. Nancy Williams and Graham Baines, eds. Pp. 13–15. Canberra: Centre for Resource and Environmental Studies, Australian National University.

1994 Place Names, Population Density, and the Magic Number 500. Current Anthropology 35(1):81–85.

1996 Columbia Plateau Indian Place Names: What Can They Teach Us? Journal of Linguistic Anthropology 6(1):3–26.

1999 Ethnobiology in Court: The Paradoxes of Relativism, Authenticity and Advocacy. *In* Ethnoecology: Knowledge, Resources and Rights. Ted L. Gragson and Ben G. Blount, eds. Pp. 1–11. Athens: University of Georgia Press.

Hunn, Eugene, Darryll Johnson, Pricilla Russell, and Thomas Thornton

2002 A Study of Traditional Use of Birds' Eggs by the Huna Tlingit. Technical Report NPS D-113. Seattle: National Park Service Pacific Northwest Cooperative Ecosystem Studies Unit.

Hyde, Anne F.

1990 An American Vision: Far Western Landscape and National Culture, 1830–1920. New York: New York University Press.

Hymes, Dell H.

1965 Some North Pacific Coast Poems: A Problem in Anthropological Philology. American Anthropologist, 67(1):316–341.

1981 In Vain I Tried to Tell You: Essays in Native American Ethnopoetics. Philadelphia: University of Pennsylvania Press.

1982 The Wife Who Goes Out Like a Man: Reinterpretation of a Clackamas Chinook Myth. *In* Structural Analysis of Oral Tradition. Pierre Maranda and Elli Kongas Maranda, eds. Pp. 49–80. Philadelphia: University of Pennsylvania Press.

1990 Mythology. *In* Handbook of North American Indians, vol. 7: Northwest Coast. Wayne Suttles, ed. Pp. 593–601. Washington DC: Smithsonian Institution Press.

1996 Coyote, the Thinking (Wo)man's Trickster. *In* Monsters, Tricksters, and Sacred Cows: Animal Tales and American Identities. A. James Arnold, ed. Pp. 108–137. Charlottesville: University Press of Virginia.

1999 Boas on the Threshold of Ethnopoetics. *In* Theorizing the Americanist Tradition. Lisa Philips Valentine and Regna Darnell, eds. Pp. 84–108. Toronto: University of Toronto Press.

2002 Loon Woman. *In* Surviving through the Ways. Translations of Native California Stories and Songs. Herbert W. Luthin, ed. pp. 192–218. Berkeley: University of California Press.

Inglis, Joy

 1989 Assu of Cape Mudge: Recollections of a Coastal Indian Chief. Vancouver: University of British Columbia Press.

Irvin, Terry

 1977 The Northwest Coast Potlatch since Boas, 1897–1972. Anthropology 1(1):65–77.

Irving, Margaret

 1995 Field notes from an interview with Patricia P. Erikson. Neah Bay WA.

Jacknis, Ira

 1984 Franz Boas and Photography. Studies in Visual Communication 10(1):2–60.

 1985 Franz Boas and Exhibits: On the Limitations of the Museum Method of Anthropology. *In* Objects and Others: Essays on Museums and Material Culture. George W. Stocking Jr., ed. Pp. 75–111. Madison: University of Wisconsin Press.

 1991 George Hunt, Collector of Indian Specimens. *In* Chiefly Feasts: The Enduring Kwakiutl Potlatch. Aldona Jonaitis, ed. Pp. 177–225. New York: American Museum of Natural History. Seattle: University of Washington Press.

 2002 The Storage Box of Tradition: Kwakiutl Art, Anthropologists, and Museums, 1881–1981. Washington DC: Smithsonian Institution Press.

Jackson, Sheldon

 1880 Alaska and the Missions of the North Pacific Coast. New York: Dodd, Mead.

James, Wendy, and Nick J. Allen, eds.

 1998 Marcel Mauss: A Centenary Tribute. New York: Berghahn Books.

Jamin, Jean

 1991 L'anthropologie française. *In* Dictionnaire de l'ethnologie et de l'anthropologie. Pierre Bonte and Michel Izard, eds. Pp. 289–295. Paris: Presses universitaires de France.

Jasen, Patricia

1995 Wild Things: Nature, Culture, and Tourism in Ontario, 1790–1914. Toronto: University of Toronto Press.

Jeffcott, P. R.

1949 Nooksack Tales and Trails. Ferndale WA: Sedro-Wooley Courier-Times.

Jenness, Diamond

1955 The Faith of a Coast Salish Indian. Anthropology in British Columbia Memoir, 3. Victoria BC: British Columbia Provincial Museum.

1991 Artic Odyssey: The Diary of Diamond Jenness, Ethnologist with the Canadian Artic Expedition in Northern Alaska and Canada, 1913–1916. Stuart E. Jenness, ed. and annotator. Foreword by William E. Taylor Jr. Hull QC: Canadian Museum of Civilization.

Jensen, Allan

1980 A Structural Approach to the Tsimshian Raven Myths: Lévi-Strauss on the Beach. Anthropologica 22:159–186.

Jilek, Wolgang, and Louise Jilek-Aal

1974 Meletinsky in the Okanagan: An Attempt to Apply Meletinsky's Analytic Criteria to Canadian Indian Folklore. In Soviet Structural Folkloristics. Pierre Maranda, ed. Pp. 143–151. The Hague: Mouton.

Jocks, Christopher Ronwaniente

1996 Spirituality for Sale: Sacred Knowledge in the Consumer Age. American Indian Quarterly 20(3):415–431.

Jonaitis, Aldona

1981 Creations of Mystics and Philosophers: The White Man's Perceptions of Northwest Coast Art from the 1930s to the Present. American Indian Culture and Research Journal 5(1):1–45.

1986 Art of the Northern Tlingit. Seattle: University of Washington Press.

1988 From the Land of the Totem Poles: The Northwest Coast Indian Art Collection at the American Museum of Natural History. New York: American Museum of Natural History; Seattle: University of Washington Press.

1999 The Yuquot Whalers' Shrine. With research contributions by Richard Inglis. Seattle: University of Washington Press.

Jonaitis, Aldona, ed.

1991 Chiefly Feasts: The Enduring Kwakiutl Potlatch. New York: American Museum of Natural History; Seattle: University of Washington Press.

1995 A Wealth of Thought: Franz Boas on Native American Art. Seattle: University of Washington Press.

Jonaitis, Aldona, and Richard Inglis

1992 Power, History, and Authenticity: The Mowachaht Whalers' Washing Shrine. South Atlantic Quarterly 91(1):193–213.

Jones, Livingstone

1914 A Study of the Thlingets of Alaska. New York: Fleming H. Revell.

Jorgensen, Joseph G.

1972 The Sun Dance Religion: Power for the Powerless. Chicago: University of Chicago Press.

1978 A Century of Political-Economic Effects on American Indian Society. Journal of Ethnic Studies 6(3):1–82.

1990 Oil Age Eskimos. Berkeley: University of California Press.

Junod, Henri A.

1912–13 Life of a South African Tribe. 2 vols. Neuchâtel, Switzerland: Attinger Frères.

Kahn, Miriam

2000 Tahiti Intertwined: Ancestral Land, Tourist Postcard, and Nuclear Test Site. American Anthropologist 102:7–26.

Kan, Sergei

1983 Words That Heal the Soul: An Analysis of the Tlingit Potlatch Oratory. Arctic Anthropology 20(2):47–59.

1985 Russian Orthodox Brotherhoods among the Tlingit: Missionary Goals and Native Response. Ethnohistory 32:196–222.

1987 Memory Eternal: Russian Orthodox Christianity and the Tlingit Mortuary Complex. Arctic Anthropology 24:32–55.

1989 a Cohorts, Generations, and Their Culture: The Tlingit Potlatch in the 1980s. Anthropos 84:405–422.

1989 b Symbolic Immortality: Tlingit Potlatch of the Nineteenth Century. Washington DC: Smithsonian Institution Press.

1989 c Why the Aristocrats Were Heavy, or How Ethnopsychology Legitimized Inequality among the Tlingit. Dialectical Anthropology 14:81–94.

1990 The Sacred and the Secular: Tlingit Potlatch Songs outside the Potlatch. American Indian Quarterly 14:355–366.

1996 Clan Mothers and Godmothers: Tlingit Women and Russian Orthodox Church Christianity, 1840–1940. Ethnohistory 43(4): 613–641.

1998 Whose Heritage Is It Anyway? Representing, Contesting, and Marketing Sitka's History and Culture. Paper presented at the Annual Meeting of the American Society for Ethnohistory, Minneapolis, Minnesota, November 12–14.

1999 Memory Eternal: Tlingit Culture and Russian Orthodox Christianity through Two Centuries. Seattle: University of Washington Press.

2001 Friendship, Family, and Fieldwork: One Anthropologist's Adoption by Two Tlingit Families. *In* Strangers to Relatives: The Adoption and Naming of Anthropologists in Native North America. Sergei Kan, ed. Pp. 185–217. Lincoln: University of Nebraska Press.

Karp, Ivan, and Steven D. Lavine, eds.

1991 Exhibiting Cultures: The Poetics and Politics of Museum Display. Washington DC: Smithsonian Institution.

Kasakoff, Alice

1974 Lévi-Strauss's Idea of the Social Unconscious: The Problem of Elementary and Complex Structures in Gitksan Marriage Choice. *In* The Unconscious in Culture: The Structuralism of Claude Lévi-Strauss in Perspective. Ino Rossi, ed. Pp. 143–169. New York: E. P. Dutton.

Katz, Adria H.

1986 The Raven Cape, a Tahitian Breastplate Collected by Louis Shotridge. *In* Raven's Journey: The World of Alaska's Native People. Susan A. Kaplan and Kristin J. Barsness, eds. Pp. 78–90. Philadelphia: University Museum, University of Pennsylvania.

Kawaky, Joseph

1981 Haa Shagóon (Video). Berkeley: University of California Extension, Center for Media and Independent Learning.

Kennedy, John Michael

1968 Philanthropy and Science in New York City: The American Museum of Natural History, 1868–1968. Ph.D. dissertation, Yale University.

Kennedy, Robert F., Jr.

 1997 Foreword. *In* Ahousaht Wild Side Heritage Trail Guidebook, by Stanley Sam. P. 15. Vancouver: Western Canada Wilderness Committee.

Kew, J. E. Michael

 1976 Salmon Abundance, Technology, and Human Populations on the Fraser River Watershed. Unpublished manuscript, Department of Anthropology and Sociology, University of British Columbia.

 1990 Central and Southern Coast Salish Ceremonies since 1900. *In* Handbook of North American Indians, vol. 7, Northwest Coast. Wayne Suttles, ed. Pp. 476–480. Washington DC: Smithsonian Institution Press.

King, Jonathan C. H.

 1997 Marketing Magic: Process, Identity and the Creation and Selling of Native Art. *In* Present Is Past: Some Uses of Tradition in Native Societies. Marie Mauzé, ed. Pp. 81–96. Lanham MD: University Press of America.

Kinkade, M. Dale

 1990 History of Research in Linguistics. *In* Handbook of North American Indians, vol. 7: The Northwest Coast. Wayne Suttles, ed. Pp. 98–106. Washington DC: Smithsonian Institution.

Kirk, Ruth

 1980 The Pompeii of the Northwest. Historic Preservation 32(2):2 9.

 1986 Tradition and Change on the Northwest Coast: The Makah, Nuu-chah-nulth, Southern Kwakiutl, and Nuxalk. Seattle: University of Washington Press. *Reprinted in* Wisdom of the Elders: Native Traditions on the Northwest Coast, by Ruth Kirk. Vancouver: Douglas and McIntyre, with the Royal British Columbia Museum, 1987.

Kirshenblatt-Gimblett, Barbara

 1998 Destination Culture: Tourism, Museums, and Heritage. Berkeley: University of California Press.

Kitka, Herman, Sr.

 1998 Deep Ties to Deep Bay: A Tlingit Elder's Training. Cultural Survival Quarterly 22(3): 47–48.

Kluckhohn, Clyde

1945 The Personal Document in Anthropological Science. *In* The Use of Personal Documents in History, Anthropology, and Sociology. Louis Gottschalk, Clyde Kluckhohn, and Robert Angell, eds. Pp. 78–173. New York: Social Sciences Research Council.

Knapp, Frances, and Rheta L. Childe

1896 The Thlinkets of Southeastern Alaska. Chicago: Stone and Kimball.

Knecht, Rick

1994 Working Together: Archaeology and Alutiiq Cultural Identity on Kodiak Island. Society for American Archaeology 12(5):8–10.

Knight, Rolf

1978 Indians at Work: An Informal History of Native Indian Labor in British Columbia, 1858–1930. Vancouver: New Star Books.

Kobrinsky, Vernon

1975 Dynamics of the Fort Rupert Class Struggle: Fighting with Property Vertically Revisited. *In* Papers in Honour of Harry Hawthorn. Vernon C. Serl and Herbert Taylor, eds. Pp. 32–59. Bellingham: Western Washington State College.

Kosek, Jon

1993 Ethics, Economics, and Ecosystems: Can British Columbia's Indigenous People Blend the Economic Potential of Forest Resources with Traditional Philosophies? Cultural Survival Quarterly 17(1):19.

Krause, Aurel

1956 The Tlingit Indians. Erna Gunther, trans. Seattle: University of Washington Press.

Krauss, Michael E.

1970 a Eyak Dictionary. Fairbanks: University of Alaska.

1970 b Eyak Texts. University of Alaska and Massachusetts Institute of Technology. Mimeo.

Krech, Shepard, III

1991 The State of Ethnohistory. Annual Review of Anthropology 20:345–375.

1999 The Ecological Indian. New York: Norton.

Krech, Shepard, III, and Barbara A. Hail, eds.

1999 Collecting Native America, 1870–1960. Washington: Smithsonian Institution Press.

Kroeber, Alfred L.

1923 American Culture and the Northwest Coast. American Anthropologist 25:1–20.

1939 Cultural and Natural Areas of Native North America. University of California Publications in American Archaeology and Ethnology, 38. Berkeley: University of California Press.

1944 Configurations of Culture Growth. Berkeley: University of California Press.

1948 Anthropology: Race, Language, Culture, Psychology, Pre-history. New York: Harcourt Brace.

Kronenfeld, David, and Henry W. Decker

1979 Structuralism. Annual Review of Anthropology 8:503–541.

Krupat, Arnold

1985 For Those Who Came After: A Study of Native American Autobiography. Berkeley: University of California Press.

1990 Irony in Anthropology: The Work of Franz Boas. In Modernist Anthropology: From Fieldwork to Text. Marc Magnaro, ed. Pp. 133–145. Princeton: Princeton University Press.

Kuhn, Thomas

1970 The Structure of Scientific Revolutions. 2nd edition. Chicago: University of Chicago Press.

Lakoff, George

1987 Women, Fire, and Dangerous Things: What Categories Reveal about the Mind. Chicago: University of Chicago Press.

Langer, Susanne

1951 Philosophy in a New Key. New York: New American Library.

Langness, L. L.

1965 The Life History in Anthropological Science. New York: Holt, Rinehart and Winston.

Lapérouse, Jean-Galaup, de

1985 Le voyage de Lapérouse, 1785–1788. Récits et documents originaux présentés par John Dunmore et Maurice de Brossard. Paris: Imprimerie nationale.

Laponce, Jean

    1981 Left and Right: The Topography of Political Perception. Toronto: University of Toronto Press.

Layton, Monique J.

    1974 Semantic Classification of Dramatis Personae in Some Breton Lays. *In* Soviet Structural Folkloristics. Pierre Maranda, ed. Pp. 173–194. The Hague: Mouton.

Layton, Robert

    1995 Relating to the Country in the Western Desert. *In* The Anthropology of Landscape. Erich Hirsch and Michael O'Hanlon, eds. Pp. 210–231. Oxford: Clarendon.

Leach, William

    1993 Land of Desire: Merchants, Power, and the Rise of a New American Culture. New York: Random House.

Lee, Molly

    1991 Appropriating the Primitive: Turn-of-the-Century Collection and Display of Native Alaskan Art. Arctic Anthropology 28(1):6–15.

Lefebvre, Henri

    1991 The Production of Space. Oxford: Blackwell.

Legros, Dominique

    1978 Instrumentalismes contradictoires de la logique des idéologies dans une formation sociale inuit aborigène. Theme issue, "L'appropriation sociale de la logique: Mélanges offerts à Claude Lévi-Strauss à l'occasion de son 70e anniversaire de naissance," Pierre Maranda, ed., Anthropologica n.s. 20(1–2):145–180.

Lejeune, Philippe

    1975 Le pacte autobiographique. Paris: Editions du Seuil.

Lenoir, Raymond

    1924 L'institution du potlatch. Revue philosophique de France et de l'étranger 49(2):234–257.

Leroi-Gourhan, André

    1946 Archéologie du Pacifique-Nord: Matériaux pour l'étude des relations entre les peuples d'Asie et d'Amérique. Paris: Institut d'ethnologie.

Levin, Gail

    1984 American Art. *In* Primitivism in 20th Century Art. William Rubin, ed. Pp. 453–473. New York: Museum of Modern Art.

Lévi-Strauss, Claude

1943 The Art of the Northwest Coast at the American Museum of Natural History. Gazette des Beaux-Arts, series 6, 24:175–182.

1949 Les structures élémentaires de la parenté. Paris: Presses universitaires de France.

1955 a The Structural Study of Myth. Journal of the American Folklore 68:428–444.

1955 b Tristes Tropiques. Paris: Plon.

1958 a Anthropologie structurale. Paris: Plon.

1958b[1945] Le dédoublement de la représentation dans les arts de l'Asie et de l'Amérique. *In* Anthropologie structurale. Pp. 269–299. Paris: Plon.

1958 c La geste d'Asdiwal: Annuaire de l'Ecole pratique des hautes études, VIe section (Sciences religieuses). Pp. 3–43. Paris.

1961 a La geste d'Asdiwal. Les Temps modernes 16:1080–1123.

1961b[1955] A World on the Wane. John Russel, trans. London: Hutchinson.

1962 a La pensée sauvage. Paris: Plon.

1962 b Le totémisme aujourd'hui. Paris: Presses universitaires de France.

1963 a Structural Anthropology. Claire Jacobson and Brooke Grundfest Schoepf, trans. 2 vols. New York: Basic Books.

1963 b Totemism. Rodney Needham, trans. Boston: Beacon Press.

1964 Mythologiques, vol. 1: Le cru et le cuit. Paris: Plon.

1966 a Mythologiques, vol. 2: Du miel aux cendres. Paris: Plon.

1966 b The Savage Mind. Chicago: University of Chicago Press.

1967 The Story of Asdiwal. *In* The Structural Study of Myth and Totemism. Edmund Leach, ed. Nicholas Mann, trans. Pp. 1–17. Association of Social Anthropologists Monographs, 5. London: Tavistock Press.

1968 Mythologiques, vol. 3: L'origine des manières de table. Paris: Plon.

1969 a The Elementary Structures of Kinship. James Harle Ball and John Richard von Sturmer, trans. Rodney Needham, ed. Boston: Beacon Press.

1969 b The Raw and the Cooked. Vol. 1 of Introduction to a Science of Mythology. John and Doreen Weightman, trans. New York: Harper and Row.

1971 Mythologiques, vol. 4: L'homme nu. Paris: Plon.

1973 a From Honey to Ashes. Vol. 2 of Introduction to a Science of Mythology. John and Doreen Weightman, trans. New York: Harper and Row.

1973 b La geste d'Asdiwal. *In* Anthropologie structurale, vol. 2. Pp. 175–233. Paris: Plon.

1975 La voie des masques. Genève: Skira.

1976 Structural Anthropology, vol. 2. New York: Basic Books.

1978 Origin of Table Manners. Vol. 3 of Introduction to a Science of Mythology. John and Doreen Weightman, trans. New York: Harper and Row.

1979 La voie des masques. Edition revue et augmentée de trois excursions. Paris: Plon.

1981 a The Naked Man. Vol. 4 of Introduction to a Science of Mythology. John and Doreen Weightman, trans. New York: Harper and Row.

1981 b Three Memories of Wilson Duff. *In* The World Is as Sharp as a Knife: An Anthology in Honour of Wilson Duff. Donald M. Abbott, ed. Pp. 259–260. Victoria, BC: British Columbia Provincial Museum.

1982 The Way of the Masks. Sylvia Modelski, trans. Vancouver: Douglas and McIntyre.

1984 Claude Lévi-Strauss's Testimony on Franz Boas. Inuit Studies 8(1):7–10.

1985 a New York in 1941. *In* The View from Afar. Joachim Neugroschel and Phoebe Hoss, trans. Pp. 258–267. New York: Basic Books.

1985 b The View from Afar. Joachim Neugroschel and Phoebe Hoss, trans. New York: Basic Books.

1986 Comment by Claude Lévi-Strauss. American Ethnologist 13:804.

1987 a *Review of* Art of the Northern Tlingit, by A. Jonaitis. L'Homme 104:104–105.

1987 b Introduction to the Work of Marcel Mauss. London: Routledge and Kegan Paul.

1988 The Jealous Potter. Bénédicte Chorier, trans. Chicago: University of Chicago Press.

1991 a Boas, Franz. *In* Dictionnaire de l'ethnologie et de l'anthropologie. Pierre Bonte and Michel Izard, eds. Pp. 116–118. Paris: Presses universitaires de France.

1991 b Bohemian Life in New York. *In* Conversations with Claude Lévi-Strauss, by Claude Lévi-Strauss and Didier Eribon. Pp. 25–46. Chicago: University of Chicago Press.

1991 c Maison. *In* Dictionnaire de l'ethnologie et de l'anthropologie. Pierre Bonte and Michel Izard, eds. Pp. 434–436. Paris: Presses universitaires de France.

1995a[1978] Myth and Meaning. Foreword by Wendy Doniger. New York: Schocken Books.

1995 b The Story of Lynx. Catherine Tihanyi, trans. Chicago: University of Chicago Press.

2000 *Review of* Lushootseed Culture and the Shamanic Odyssey: An Anchored Radiance, by J. Miller. L'Homme 156:287–288.

Lévi-Strauss, Claude, and Didier Eribon

1991 Conversations with Claude Lévi-Strauss. Paula Wissing, trans. Chicago: University of Chicago Press.

Lévy-Bruhl, Lucien

1922 La mentalité primitive. Paris: Presses universitaires de France.

Lilley, Rozanna

1989 Gungarakayn Women Speak: Reproduction and the Transformation of Tradition. Oceania 60(2):81–98.

Lincoln, Neville, and John Rath

1980 North Wakashan Comparative Root List. National Museums of Man, Mercury Series, Canadian Ethnology Service, 68. Ottawa: National Museums of Man.

Linnekin, Jocelyn

1991 Cultural Invention and the Dilemma of Authenticity. American Anthropologist 93:446–449.

1992 On the Theory and Politics of Cultural Construction in the Pacific. Oceania 62:249–263.

Lukens, Matilda B.

1889 The Inland Passage: A Journal of a Trip to Alaska. N.p.

Lukes, Steven

1973 Emile Durkheim, His Life and Work: A Historical and Critical Study. London: Penguin Books.

Lurie, Nancy

    1961 Mountain Wolf Woman, Sister of Crashing Thunder: Autobiography of a Winnebago Indian. Ann Arbor: University of Michigan Press.

MacClancy, Jeremy, ed.

    1997 Contesting Art: Art, Politics and Identity in the Modern World. London: Berg.

MacDonald, George F.

    1981 Cosmic Equations in Northwest Coast Indian Art. *In* The World Is as Sharp as a Knife: An Anthology in Honour of Wilson Duff. Donald M. Abbott, ed. Pp. 225–238. Victoria: British Columbia Provincial Museum.

    1984 The Epic of Nekt: The Archaeology of Metaphor. *In* The Tsimshian: Images of the Past, Views for the Present. Margaret Seguin, ed. Pp. 65–82. Vancouver: University of British Columbia Press.

    1989 Kitwanga Fort Report. Canadian Museum of Civilization, Mercury Series, Directorate, 4.

Macdonald, Sharon, and Gordon Fyfe, eds.

    1996 Theorizing Museums: Representing Identity and Diversity in a Changing World. Cambridge MA: Blackwell.

MacIsaac, Ron, and Anne Champagne

    1994 Mass Trials: Defending the Rainforest. Philadelphia: New Society.

Macnair, Peter L., Robert Joseph, and Bruce Grenville

    1998 Down from the Shimmering Sky: Masks of the Northwest Coast. Vancouver: Vancouver Art Gallery and Douglas and McIntyre; Seattle: University of Washington Press.

Makah Cultural and Research Center (MCRC)

    1989 Riding in His Canoe: The Continuing Legacy of Young Doctor. An Exhibit in Celebration of Our 10th Year. Neah Bay WA: Makah Tribal Council.

Malinowski, Bronislaw

    1922 Argonauts of the Western Pacific: An Account of Native Enterprise and Adventure in the Archipelagos of Melanesian New Guinea. New York: E. P. Dutton.

    1924 Magic, Science and Religion. *In* Science, Religion, and Reality. J. Needham, ed. Pp. 19–84. New York: Macmillan.

Manners, Robert A.
  1956 The Land Claims Cases: Anthropologists in Conflict. Ethno-
    history 3(1):72–81.
Maranda, Pierre
  1971 L'analyse des mythes. Theme issue, "Informatique et sciences so-
    ciales," Marc Barbut, ed., UNESCO, International Social Science
    Journal: 244–254.
  1972 a Cendrillon: Théorie des ensembles et théorie des graphes. *In* Sé-
    miotique narrative et textuelle. Claude Chabrol, ed. pp. 122–136.
    Paris: Larousse.
  1972 b Structural Analysis in Cultural Anthropology. Annual Review of
    Anthropology 1:329–348.
Maranda, Pierre, ed.
  1972 Mythology. Penguin Books.
  1974 Soviet Structural Folkloristics. The Hague: Mouton.
  1978 L'appropriation sociale de la logique. Theme issue, "Mélanges
    offerts à Claude Lévi-Strauss à l'occasion de son 70 anniversaire
    de naissance," Pierre Maranda, ed., Anthropologica n.s. 20(1–2).
  2001 The Double Twist: From Ethnography to Morphodynamics.
    Toronto: University of Toronto Press.
Maranda, Pierre, and Elli K. Maranda
  1970 Le crâne et l'utérus: Deux théorèmes nord-malaïtains. *In* Echanges
    et communications: Mélanges offerts à C. Lévi-Strauss à l'occasion
    de son 60e anniversaire, vol. 2. Jean Pouillon and Pierre Maranda,
    eds. Pp. 829–861. The Hague: Mouton.
  1971 Structural Models in Folklore and Transformational Essays. The
    Hague: Mouton.
  1974 a French Kinship: Structure and History. The Hague: Mouton.
  1974 b Myth as a Cognitive Map: A Sketch of the Okanagan Myth
    Automaton. *In* Proceedings of the International Social Science
    Council Conference on Content Analysis. P. Stone, ed. Pisa:
    UNESCO. Reprinted in TextProcessing/Textverabeitung. W. Burg-
    hart and H. Holker, eds. Pp. 253–272. Hamburg: Walter de
    Gruyter.
Maranda, Pierre, and Elli K. Maranda, eds.
  1971 Structural Analysis of Oral Tradition. Philadelphia: University of
    Pennsylvania Press.

Maranda, Pierre, Brock Taylor, and Frank Flynn, eds.

1984 Automatic Text Reading: An Attempt at Artificially Intelligent Interpretation. Québec City: Laboratoire de recherches anthropologiques de l'Université Laval.

Marr, Carolyn, et al.

1987 Portrait in Time: Photographs of the Makah by Samuel G. Morse, 1869–1903. Seattle: Makah Cultural Center and Washington State Historical Society.

Marriott, Alice

1948 Maria: The Potter of San Ildefonso. Norman: University of Oklahoma Press.

Marsden, Susan

2001 Defending the Mouth of the Skeena: Perspectives on Tsimshian-Tlingit Relations. *In* Perspectives on Northern Northwest Coast Prehistory. Jerome S. Cybulski, ed. Pp. 61–106. Archaelogy Survey of Canada, 60. Hull QC: Canadian Museum of Civilization.

Masco, Joseph

1995 It Is a Strict Law That Bids Us Dance: Cosmologies, Colonialism, Death and Ritual Authority in the Kwakwaka'wakw Potlatch, 1849–1922. Comparative Studies in Society and History 37:41–75.

Mathé, Barbara, and Thomas R. Miller

2001 Kwazi'nik's Eyes: Vision and Symbol in Boasian Representation. *In* Gateways: Exploring the Legacy of the Jesup North Pacific Expedition, 1897–1902. Igor Krupnik and William Fitzhugh, eds. Pp. 107–138. Washington DC: Smithsonian Institution Arctic Studies Center.

Maud, Ralph

2000 Transmission Difficulties: Franz Boas and Tsimshian Mythology. Burnaby BC: Talonbooks.

Mauger, Jeffrey E.

1978 Shed Roof Houses at the Ozette Archaeological Site: A Protohistoric Architectural System. Washington Archaeological Research Center Project Report, 73. Pullman: Washington State University.

1991 Part 2: Shed Roof Houses at Ozette and in a Regional Perspective. *In* House Structure and Floor Midden, Ozette Archaeological Project Research Reports, vol. 1. Stephan R. Samuels, ed. Pp.

29–173. Pullman: Washington State University Department of Anthropology.

Mauger, Jeffrey, and Janine Bowechop

1995 Tribal Collections Management at the Makah Cultural and Researach Center. Perspectives: A Resource for Tribal Museums 2:1–7. American Indian Museum Studies Program, Smithsonian Institution.

Maurer, Evan

1984 Dada and Surrealism. *In* Primitivism in 20th Century Art. William Rubin, ed. Pp. 535–593. New York: Museum of Modern Art.

Mauss, Marcel

1898–99 *Review of* Traditions of the Thompson River Indians of British Columbia, by James Teit, with an introduction by Franz Boas. L'Année sociologique 3:278–280.

1901–2 *Review of* Memoirs of the American Museum of Natural History—Anthropology. Vol. 2: The Mythology of the Bella Coola Indians, by Franz Boas. Vol. 5, pt. 1: Kwakiutl Texts, by Franz Boas and George Hunt. Vol. 3, pt. 1: The Symbolism of the Huichol Indians, by Carl Lumholtz. L'Année sociologique 6:247–253.

1904–5 Essai sur les variations saisonnières des sociétés eskimos. Essai de morphologie sociale. L'Année sociologique 9:39–132.

1905–6 *Review of* Report on the Ethnology of the Statlumh of British Columbia, by C. Hill Tout. L'Année sociologique 10:235–238.

1906–9 *Review of* Contributions to the Ethnology of the Haida, by J. R. Swanton. Social Condition, Beliefs and Linguistic Relationship of the Tlingit Indians, by J. R. Swanton. Haida Texts and Myths: Skidegate Dialect, by J. R. Swanton. L'Année sociologique 11:110–119.

1909–12 *Review of* The Kwakiutl of Vancouver Island, by Franz Boas. L'Année sociologique 12:857–858.

1925 a In Memoriam: Henri Beuchat. Année sociologique n.s. 1: 20.

1925 b Essai sur le don: Forme et raison de l'échange dans les sociétés archaïques. L'Année sociologique n.s. 1:30–186. *Reprinted in* Sociologie et anthropologie avec une introduction de Claude Lévi-Strauss. Paris: Presses universitaires de France, 1950.

1947 Manuel d'ethnographie. Denise Paulme, ed. Paris: Payot.

1950[1925] Essai sur le don: Forme et raison de l'échange dans les sociétés archaïques. L'Année sociologique n.s. 1. *Reprinted in* Sociologie et anthropologie avec une introduction de Claude Lévi-Strauss. Paris: Presses universitaires de France.

1967 The Gift: Forms and Functions of Exchange in Archaic Societies. Introduction by E. E. Evans Pritchard. New York: W. W. Norton.

1969 Oeuvres, vol. 3: Cohésion sociale et divisions de la sociologie. Présentation de Victor Karady. Paris: Les Editions de Minuit.

1979 Seasonal Variations of the Eskimo: A Study in Social Morphology. James Fox, trans. London: Routledge and Kegan Paul.

1998 An Intellectual Self-Portrait. *In* Marcel Mauss: A Centenary Tribute. Wendy James and Nick Allen, eds. Pp. 29–42. New York: Berghahn Books.

Mauss, Marcel, with Henri Beuchat

1906 Essai sur les variations saisonnières: Etude de morphologie sociale. L'Année sociologique 9:39–132.

Mauzé, Marie

1986 Boas, les Kwagul et le potlatch: Éléments pour une réévaluation, suivi des commentaires de C. Meillassoux, A. Testart, D. Legros, S. Gruzinski et d'une réponse de M. Mauzé. L'Homme 100:21–63.

1987 Georges Bataille et le potlatch: À propos de La part maudite. *In* Ecrits d'ailleurs: Georges Bataille et les ethnologues. Dominique Lecocq and Jean-Luc Lory, eds. Pp. 31–38. Paris: Editions de la Maison des sciences de l'Homme.

1989 Le canoë dans le potlatch lekwiltoq. L'Homme 109:117–128.

1990 In Honor of Lévi-Strauss. European Review of Native American Studies 4(1):51–53.

1991 Le destin d'un sanctuaire. Gradhiva 10:11–25.

1992 a Exhibiting One's Culture: Two Case Studies. European Review of Native American Studies 6(1):27–30.

1992 b Les fils de Wakai: Une histoire des Indiens Lekwiltoq. Paris: Éditions Recherche sur les civilisations.

1992 c Premiers contacts entre les surréalistes et l'art de la côte Nord-Ouest: Le tambour d'eau des castors. *In* Destins Croisés: Cinq siècles de rencontres avec les Amérindiens. Pp. 283–296. Paris: Albin Michel, UNESCO.

1994 Le tambour d'eau des castors: L'art de la Cote Nord-Ouest et le surréalisme. Arts d'Afrique Noire, 89:35–45.

1997 On Concepts of Tradition: An Introduction. *In* Present Is Past: Some Uses of Tradition in Native Societies. Marie Mauzé, ed. Pp. 1–16. Lanham MD: University Press of America.

1998 a Northwest Coast Trees: From Metaphors in Culture to Symbols for Culture. *In* The Social Life of Trees: Anthropological Perspectives on Tree Symbolism. Laura Rival, ed. Pp. 233–251. London: Berg.

1998 b Rivages totémiques. Theme issue, "Totémismes," Systèmes de pensée en Afrique noire 15:127–168.

1999 Un patrimoine, deux musées: La restitution de la Potlatch Collection. Ethnologie française 1999(3):419–430.

2000 a Les objets américains dans les collections françaises. *In* Sculptures Afrique, Asie, Océanie, Amériques. Jacques Kerchache, ed. Pp. 28–33. Paris: Réunion des musées nationaux.

2000 b Sculpture kwakwaka'wakw: Masque à transformation. *In* Sculptures: Afrique, Océanie, Asie, Amériques. Jacques Kerchache, ed. Pp. 362–365. Paris. Réunion des musées nationaux.

2000 c Sculpture nisga'a: Masque frontal. *In* Sculptures: Afrique, Océanie, Asie, Amériques. Jacques Kerchache, ed. Pp. 360–361. Paris: Réunion des musées nationaux.

2000 d Sculpture tlingit: Heaume. *In* Sculptures: Afrique, Océanie, Asie, Amériques. Jacques Kerchache, ed. Pp. 366–369. Paris. Réunion des musées nationaux.

McBeth, Sally
1983 Indian Boarding Schools and Ethnic Identity: An Example from the Southern Plains Tribes of Oklahoma. Plains Anthropologist 28:119–128.

McBride, Bunny
1990 Our Lives in Our Hands: Micmac Indian Basketmakers. Halifax NS: Nimbus.

McClellan, Catharine
1988 Frederica de Laguna. *In* Women Anthropologists: A Biographical Dictionary. U. Gacs et al., eds. Pp. 37–44. New York: Greenwood Press.

1989 Frederica de Laguna and the Pleasures of Anthropology. American Ethnologist 16:766–785.

McClusky, Sally
1972 Black Elk Speaks, and So Does John Neihardt. Western American Literature 6:231–242.

McDonald, James
1989 Poles, Potlatching, and Public Affairs: The Use of Aboriginal Culture in Development. Culture 10(2):103–120.

McDowell, Jim
1997 Hamatsa: The Enigma of Cannibalism on the Pacific Northwest Coast. Vancouver: Ronsdale Press.

McFeat, Tom, ed.
1966 Indians of the North Pacific Coast. Seattle: University of Washington Press.

McHalsie, Albert (Sonny)
1999 That the Business Was Done: Stories of Conflict and Leadership in Stó:lo Oral History. Paper given to Stó:lo: People of the River ll Conference at the session titled A Community Forged in Violence, Chilliwack, BC, October 22.

McLaren, Carol
1978 Moment of Death: Gift of Life; A Reinterpretation of the Northwest Coast Image "Hawk." Theme issue, "L'appropriation sociale de la logique: Mélanges offerts à Claude Lévi-Strauss à l'occasion de son 70e anniversaire de naissance," Pierre Maranda, ed., Anthropologica n.s. 20(1–2):65–90.

McMullen, Ann, and Russell G. Handsman, eds.
1987 A Key into the Language of Woodsplit Baskets. Washington CT: American Indian Archaeological Institute.

McNeary, Stephen
1976 When Fire Came Down: Social and Economic Life of the Niska. Ph.D. dissertation, Bryn Mawr College.

Means, Russell
1995 Where White Men Fear to Tread: The Autobiography of Russell Means. New York: St. Martin's Press.

Medicine, Beatrice
1971 The Anthropologist and American Indian Studies Programs. Indian Historian 4(1):15–18, 63.

Mertz, Douglas Kemp

1994 The Role of the Anthropologist as an Expert Witness in Litigation. Paper delivered at the Annual Conference of the Alaska Anthropological Association, Anchorage, April 6–9. http://www.alaska.net/~dkmertz/expert.htm, accessed September 15, 2003.

Métraux, Alfred

1963 Rencontre avec les ethnologues. Critique 195/196:677–678.

Milburn, Maureen

1997 Politics of Possession: Louis Shotridge and the Tlingit Collections of the University Museum. Ph.D. dissertation, University of British Columbia, Vancouver.

Miller, Bruce

2001 The Problem of Justice: Tradition and Law in the Coast Salish World. Lincoln: University of Nebraska Press.

Miller, Bruce, ed.

1992 Anthropology and History in the Courts. Theme issue, BC Studies 95.

Miller, Jay

1997 Tsimshian Culture: A Light through the Ages. Lincoln: University of Nebraska Press.

1999 a Lushootseed Culture and the Shamanic Odyssey: An Anchored Radiance. Lincoln: University of Nebraska Press.

1999 b The Shell(Fish) Game: Rhetoric, Images, and (Dis)Illusions in Federal Court. American Indian Culture and Research Journal 23(4):159–173.

Miller, Jay, and Carol Eastman, eds.

1984 The Tsimshian and Their Neighbors of the Northwest Coast. Seattle: University of Washington Press.

Mills, Antonia

1994 Eagle Down Is Our Law: Witsuwit'en Law, Feasts, and Land Claims. Vancouver: University of British Columbia Press.

Misch, Georg

1951 A History of Autobiography in Antiquity. 2 vols. Cambridge MA: Harvard University Press.

Mitchell, W. J. T.

2003 Imperial Landscape. *In* Landscape and Power. 2nd edition. W. J. T. Mitchell, ed. Pp. 5–34. Chicago: University of Chicago Press.

Momaday, N. Scott

1976 The Names: A Memoir. Tucson: University of Arizona Press.

Monet, Don, and Skanu'u (Ardythe Wilson)

1993 Colonialism on Trial: Indigenous Land Rights and the Gitksan and Wet'suwet'en Sovereignty Case. Philadelphia: New Society.

Morgan, Lewis Henry

1877 Ancient Society. New York: Henry Holt.

Morphy, Howard

1995 Landscape and the Reproduction of the Ancestral Past. *In* The Anthropology of Landscape. Erich Hirsch and Michael O'Hanlon, eds. Pp. 184–209. Oxford: Clarendon.

Moyer, David

1978 The Ideology of Social Reform in a Nineteenth Century South Sumatra Legal Code. *In* L'appropriation sociale de la logique: Mélanges offerts à Claude Lévi-Strauss à l'occasion de son 70e anniversaire de naissance. Theme issue, Anthropologica n.s. 20(1–2): 223–248.

Muir, John

1988[1915] Travels in Alaska. San Francisco: Sierra Club Books.

1993[1879–80] Letters from Alaska. Madison: University of Wisconsin Press.

Munn, Nancy

1973 Walbiri Iconography: Graphic Representation and Cultural Symbolism in a Central Australian Society. Ithaca NY: Cornell University Press.

Myers, Fred

1986 Pintupi Country, Pintupi Self. Canberra: Australian Institute of Aboriginal Studies.

Nandan, Nash

1980 Emile Durkheim: Contributions to L'Année sociologique. New York: Free Press.

Neandross, Sigurd

1910 Work on the Ceremonial Canoe. American Museum Journal 10:238–243.

Neel, David
    1992 Chiefs and Elders: Words and Photographs of Native Leaders. Vancouver: University of British Columbia Press.

Neihardt, John, G., ed.
    1972[1932] Black Elk Speaks. New York: Washington Square Press.

Newell, Dianne
    1993 Tangled Webs of History: Indians and the Law in Canada's Pacific Coast Fisheries. Toronto: University of Toronto Press.

Newman, Barnett
    1946 Northwest Coast Indian Painting. New York: Betty Parsons Gallery.

Niaussat, P.-M
    1983 Journal de voyage autour du monde du chirurgien G.-TH: Vimont, 1816–1819. Vincennes: Archives et bibliothèque centrale de la Marine Nationale.

Nicks, Trudy
    1996 Dr. Oronhyatekha's History Lessons: Reading Museum Collections as Texts. In Reading beyond Words: Contexts for Native History. Jennifer S. H. Brown and Elizabeth Vibert, eds. Pp. 483–508. Orchard Park NY: Broadview.

Northwest Intertribal Court System (NICS)
    1991 a Summary: Traditional and Informal Dispute Resolution Processes in Tribes of the Puget Sound and Olympic Peninsula Region. Edmonds WA: NICS.
    1991 b Traditional and Informal Dispute Resolution Processes in Tribes of the Puget Sound and Olympic Peninsula Region. Edmonds WA: NICS.

Nowry, Laurence
    1995 Man of Mana, Marius Barbeau: A Biography. Toronto: NC Press.

Olson, Ronald L.
    1956 Channeling Character in Tlingit Society. In Personal Character and Cultural Milieu. Douglas G. Haring, ed. Pp. 675–687. Syracuse: Syracuse University Press.
    1967 Social Structure and Social Life of the Tlingit in Alaska. Anthropological Records, 26. Berkeley: University of California Press.

Orosz, Joel J.

1990 Curators and Culture: The Museum Movement in America, 1740–1870. Tuscaloosa: University of Alabama Press.

Ortner, Sherry

1996 Making Gender: The Politics and Erotics of Culture. Boston: Beacon Press.

Osgood, Cornelius

1936 a Contributions to the Ethnography of the Kutchin. Yale University Publications in Anthropology, 14. New Haven CT: Yale University Press.

1936 b The Distribution of the Northern Athapaskan Indians. Yale University Publications in Anthropology, 7. New Haven CT: Yale University Press.

1937 The Ethnography of the Tanaina. Yale University Publications in Anthropology, 16. New Haven CT: Yale University Press.

Ostrowitz, Judith M.

1999 Privileging the Past: Reconstructing History in Northwest Coast Art. Seattle: University of Washington Press.

Pacific Coast Steamship Company

1887–94 About Alaska. Brochures. San Francisco: Goodall, Perkins.

Papanikolas, Zeese

1995 Trickster in the Land of Dreams. Lincoln: University of Nebraska Press.

Parker, Patricia L.

1991 America's Tribal Cultures—A Renaissance in the 1990s. Cultural Resource Management 14(5):1, 3.

Parmenter, Ross

1966 Explorer, Linguist and Ethnologist: A Descriptive Bibliography of the Published Works of Alphonse Louis Pinart. Los Angeles: Southwest Museum.

Parsons, Elsie W. C.

1991 Pueblo Mothers and Children: Essays. Barbara A. Babcock, ed. Santa Fe NM: Ancient City Press.

Paul, William L.

1971 The Real Story of the Lincoln Pole. Alaska Journal 1(3):2–16.

Pelikan, Jaroslav
   1985 Jesus through the Centuries: His Place in the History of Culture. New Haven: Yale University Press.

Penney, David W.
   1981 The Nootka Wild Man Masquerade and the Forest Spirit Tradition of the Southern Northwest Coast. Northwest Coast Research Notes 1: 95–109.

Persky, Stan
   2000 Delgamuukw: The Supreme Court of Canada Decision on Aboriginal Title. Vancouver: Greystone, Seattle: University of Washington Press.

Petitot, Émile Fortune Stanislaus
   1886 Traditions indiennes du Canada nord-ouest. Paris: Maisonneuve and LeClerc.
   1888 Traditions indiennes du Canada nord-ouest: Textes originaux et traduction littérale. Actes de la société philologique, 16–17. Alençon, France: Renaut de Broise.

Phillips, Ruth B.
   1998 Trading Identities: The Souvenir in Native North American Art from the Northeast, 1700–1900. Seattle: University of Washington Press.

Pickering, W. S. F.
   1975 Durkheim on Religion: A Selection of Readings with Bibliographies. London: Routledge and Kegan Paul.

Piddocke, Stuart
   1965 The Potlatch System of the Southern Kwakiutl: A New Perspective. Southwestern Journal of Anthropology 21(3):244–264.

Pierrepont, Edward
   1884 Fifth Avenue to Alaska. New York: G. P. Putnam's Sons.

Pomeroy, Earl
   1957 In Search of the Golden West: The Tourist in Western America. New York: Alfred A. Knopf.

Pouillon, Jean
   1980 Anthropological Traditions: Their Uses and Misuses. *In* Anthropology: Ancestors and Heirs. Stanley Diamond, ed. Pp. 36–51. The Hague: Mouton.

1997 The Ambiguity of Tradition: Begetting the Father. *In* Present Is Past: Some Uses of Tradition in Native Societies. Marie Mauzé, ed. Pp. 17–21. Lanham MD: University Press of America.

Pouillon, Jean, and Pierre Maranda, eds.

1970 Echanges et communications: Mélanges offerts à Claude Lévi-Strauss à l'occasion de son soixantième anniversaire. 2 vols. Studies in General Anthropology, 5. The Hague: Mouton.

Pratt, Mary Louise

1992 Imperial Eyes: Travel Writing and Transculturation. New York: Routledge.

Quimby, George I.

1948 Culture Contact on the Northwest Coast between 1785 and 1795. American Anthropologist 50(2):247–255.

Raban, Jonathan

1999 Passage to Juneau: A Sea and Its Meanings. New York: Pantheon.

2001 Battleground of the Eye. Atlantic Monthly 287(3):40–52.

Radin, Paul

1983[1926] Crashing Thunder: The Autobiography of an American Indian. Foreword and appendix by Arnold Krupat. Lincoln: University of Nebraska Press.

Rainger, Ronald

1991 An Agenda for Antiquity: Henry Fairfield Osborn and Vertebrate Paleontology at the American Museum of Natural History, 1890–1935. Tuscaloosa: University of Alabama Press.

Rasmus, Stacy

2001 Repatriating Words: Local Knowledge in a Global Context. M.A. thesis, Western Washington University, Bellingham.

Reid, Bill

1981 The Box Painting by the Master of the Black Field. *In* The World Is as Sharp as a Knife: An Anthology in Honour of Wilson Duff. Donald N. Abbott, ed. Pp. 300–301. Victoria: British Columbia Provincial Museum.

Reid, Bill, and Robert Bringhurst

2000 Solitary Raven: The Selected Writings of Bill Reid, with an Afterword by Martine Reid. Vancouver: Douglas and McIntyre; Seattle: University of Washington Press.

Reid, Martine J.

    1981 La cérémonie hamatsa des Kwagul: Approche structuraliste des rapports mythe-rituel. Ph.D. dissertation, University of British Columbia, Vancouver.

    1984 Le mythe de Baxbakwalanuxsiwae: Une affaire de famille. Recherches amérindiennes au Québec 14(2):25–34.

Reid, Martine, ed., and Daisy Sewid-Smith, trans.

In press Paddling to Where I Stand: Agnes Alfred, Qwiqwasut'inuxw Noblewoman. Vancouver: University of British Columbia Press.

Reid, Susan

    1974 Myth as Metastructure of the Fairytale. In Soviet Structural Folkloristics. Pierre Maranda, ed. Pp. 151–172. The Hague: Mouton.

    1976 The Origins of the Tsetseqa in the Baxus: A Study of Kwakiutl Prayers, Myths, and Rituals. Ph.D. dissertation, University of British Columbia, Vancouver.

    1979 The Kwakiutl Man-Eater. Anthropologica 21: 247–275.

Relph, Edward

    1976 Place and Placelessness. London: Pion.

Renker, An M.

    2002 Whale Hunting and the Makah Tribe: A Needs Statement. International Whaling Commission Document no. 50-AS5. Shimononosiki, Japan.

Rice, David G.

    1997 The Seeds of Common Ground: Experimentations in Indian Consultation. In Native Americans and Archaeologists: Stepping Stones to Common Ground. Nina Swidler, Kurt E. Dongoske, Roger Anyon, and Alan S. Downer, eds. Pp. 217–226. Walnut Creek CA: Altamira.

Richard, Gladys

1975[1923] Dogmatic Atheism in the Sociology of Religion. In Durkheim on Religion. W. S. F. Pickering, ed. Pp. 228–276. London: Routledge and Kegan Paul.

Richman, Michele H.

    1982 Reading Georges Bataille: Beyond the Gift. Baltimore: John Hopkins University Press.

Rodman, Margaret C.

1992 Empowering Place: Mutilocality and Multivocality. American Anthropologist 94(3):640–656.

Rohner, Ronald P.

1966 Franz Boas, Ethnographer on the Northwest Coast. *In* Pioneers of American Anthropology: The Uses of Biography. June Helm, ed. Pp. 151–222. Seattle: University of Washington Press.

Rohner, Ronald P., ed.

1969 The Ethnography of Franz Boas: Letters and Diaries of Franz Boas Written on the Northwest Coast from 1886 to 1931. Chicago: University of Chicago Press.

Roquefeuil, Camille de

1823 Journal d'un voyage autour du monde fait pendant les années 1816, 1817, 1818, 1819. Paris: Ponthieu.

Roseberry, William

1996 Hegemony, Power, and Languages of Contention. *In* The Politics of Difference: Ethnic Premises in a World of Power. Edwin N. Wilmsen and Patrick McAllister, eds. Pp. 61–84. Chicago: University of Chicago Press.

Rosen, Lawrence

1977 The Anthropologist as Expert Witness. American Anthropologist 79(3):555–578.

Rosenthal, H. D.

1990 Their Day in Court: A History of the Indian Claims Commission. New York: Garland.

Rosman, Abraham, and Paula G. Rubel

1971 Feasting with Mine Enemy: Rank and Exchange among Northwest Coast Societies. New York: Columbia University Press.

1990 Structural Patterning in Kwakiutl Art and Ritual. Man n.s. 25(4):620–639.

Rossi, Ino

1982 On the Assumptions of Structural Analysis: Revisiting Its Linguistic and Epistemological Premises. *In* The Logic of Culture: Advances in Structural Theory and Methods. Ino Rossi et al., eds. Pp. 3–22. South Hadley, MA: J. F. Bergin.

Rousselot, Jean-Loup

    2001 La collection d'Alphonse Pinart: Alaska, 1871–1872. Gradhiva 29:87–99.

Rubel, Paula G., and Abraham Rosman, eds.

    2003 Translating Cultures: Perspectives on Translation and Anthropology. New York: Berg.

Rubin, William, ed.

    1984 Primitivism in 20th Century Art. New York: Museum of Modern Art.

Rushing, W. Jackson, III

    1992 Marketing the Affinity of the Primitive and the Modern: René d'Harnoncourt and Indian Art of the United States. *In* The Early Years of Native American Art History: Essays on the Politics of Scholarship and Collecting. Janet C. Berlo, ed. Pp. 191–236. Seattle: University of Washington Press.

    1995 Native American Art and the New York Avant-Garde: A History of Cultural Primitivism. Austin: University of Texas Press.

Ruskin, John

    1873 Modern Painters. *In* Ruskin's Works. New York: Lovell, Coryyell.

Sadongei, Alyce

    1991 New Training Opportunities for American Indians at the Smithsonian Institution: The American Indian Studies Program. Cultural Resource Management 14(5):11–12.

Sahlins, Marshall

    1993 Goodbye to Tristes Tropes: Ethnography in the Context of Modern World History. Journal of Modern History 65:1–25.

Sahlins, Peter

    1989 Boundaries: The Making of France and Spain in the Pyrenees. Berkeley: University of California Press.

Salabelle, Marie-Amélie

    2001 La caverne aux masques: La collection Pinart du musée de Boulogne-sur-Mer. Gradhiva 29:101–107.

Salinger, J. D.

    1951 The Catcher in the Rye. Boston: Little, Brown.

Salomon, Albert

    1960 The Legacy of Durkheim. *In* Emile Durkheim, 1858–1917. Kurt H. Wolff, ed. Pp. 247–266. Columbus: Ohio State University Press.

Sam, Stanley

1997 Ahousaht Wild Side Heritage Trail Guidebook. Vancouver: Western Canada Wilderness Committee.

Sapir, Edward

1915 A Sketch of the Social Organization of the Nass River Indians. Canada Department of Mines, Geological Survey Museum Bulletin 19:1–30.

1921 The Life of a Nootka Indian. Queen's Quarterly 28:232–243, 351–367.

Sarris, Greg

1993 Keeping Slug Woman Alive: A Holistic Approach to American Indian Texts. Berkeley: University of California Press.

1994 Mabel McKay: Weaving the Dream. Berkeley: University of California Press.

Saunders, Barbara

1997 Contested Ethnie in Two Kwakak'awakw Museums. *In* Contesting Art. Jeremy MacClancy, ed. Pp. 85–130. London: Berg.

Saunders, Deidre, Kathleen Mooney, Naneen Stuckey, and Leland Donald

1999 What the People Said: Kwakwaka'wakw, Nuu-Chah-Nulth, and Tsimsian Testimonies before the Royal Commission on Indian Affairs for the Province of British Columbia (1913–1916). Canadian Journal of Native Studies 19(2):213–248.

Schama, Simon

1995 Landscape and Memory. New York: Alfred A. Knopf.

Schulte-Tenckhoff, Isabelle

1986 Potlatch: Conquête et invention: Réflexion sur un concept anthropologique. Lausanne, Switzerland: Editions d'en bas.

Schwimmer, Eric

1967 Modern Orokaiva Leadership. Journal of the Papua New Guinea Society 1(2):52–60.

1969 a Cultural Consequences of a Volcanic Eruption Experienced by the Mount Lamongton Orokaiva. Eugene: University of Oregon.

1969 b Virgin Birth. Man 4:132–133.

1970 Alternance de l'échange restreint et de l'échange généralisé dans le système matrimonial orokaiva. L'Homme 10(4):5–34.

1973 Exchange in the Social Structure of the Orokaiva: Traditional and

Emergent Ideologies in the Northern District of Papua. London: Hurst.

1978 Lévi-Strauss and Maori Social Structure. Theme issue, "L'appropriation sociale de la logique: Mélanges offerts à Claude Lévi-Strauss à l'occasion de son 70e anniversaire de naissance." Anthropologica n.s. 20(1–2):201–222.

Scidmore, Eliza R.

1885 Alaska: Its Southern Coast and Sitka Archipelago. Boston: D. Lothrop.

Scientific Panel for Sustainable Forest Practices in Clayoquot Sound

1995 First Nations' Perspectives Relating to Forest Practice Standards in Clayoquot Sound. Report 3. Victoria: Queen's Printer for British Columbia.

Scott, James C.

1998 Seeing Like a State: How Certain Schemes to Improve the Human Condition Have Failed. New Haven CT: Yale University Press.

Seguin, Margaret, ed.

1984 The Tsimshian: Images of the Past, Views for the Present. Vancouver: University of British Columbia Press.

Seligman Charles G.

1976[1910] The Melanesians of British New Guinea. New York: AMS Press.

Sessions, Francis C.

1890 From Yellowstone Park to Alaska. New York: Welch, Fracker.

Sewid-Smith, Daisy

1979 Prosecution or Persecution. Cape Mudge BC: Nu-yum-baleess Society.

1997 The Continuing Reshaping of Our Ritual World by Academic Adjuncts. Anthropology and Education Quarterly 28:594–602.

1998 Liqwala/Kwakwala, Book 1. Campbell River BC: School District no. 72.

Shadbolt, Doris

1979 The Art of Emily Carr. Vancouver: Douglas and McIntyre.

Shapiro, Warren

1991 Claude Lévi-Strauss Meets Alexander Goldenweiser: Boasian Anthropology and the Study of Totemism. American Anthropologist 93:599–610.

Shelikhov, Grigorii I.

    1991 A Voyage to America, 1783–1785. Kingston ON: Limestone Press.

Sherzer, Joel

    1976 An Areal-Typological Study of American Indian Languages. Amsterdam: North Holland.

Shils, Edward

    1981 Tradition. Chicago: University of Chicago Press.

Shotridge, Louis

    1919 War Helmets and Clan Hats of the Tlingit Indians. Museum Journal 10(2):43–48.

    1920 Ghost of Courageous Adventurer. Museum Journal 11(1):11–26.

    1922 Land Otter-Man. Museum Journal 13(1):55–59.

    1928 The Emblems of the Tlingit Culture. Museum Journal 19(3):350–377.

    1929 The Bride of Tongass: A Study of the Tlingit Marriage Ceremony. Museum Journal 20(2):131–156.

Skaay of the Qquuna Qiighawaay

    2001 Being in Being: The Collected Works of Skaay of the Qquuna Qiighawaay. Robert Bringhurst, ed. and trans. Masterworks of the Classical Haida Mythtellers, 3. Vancouver: Douglas and McIntyre; Lincoln: University of Nebraska Press.

Slaney, Frances

    2000 Working for a Canadian Sense of Place(s): The Role of Landscape Painters in Marius Barbeau's Ethnology. *In* Excluded Ancestors, Inventible Traditions: Essays toward a More Inclusive History of Anthropology. Richard Handler, ed. Pp. 31–122. History of Anthropology, 9. Madison: University of Wisconsin Press.

Smith, Marion W.

    1940 The Puyallup-Nisqually. Columbia University Contributions to Anthropology 32. New York: Columbia University Press.

Snyder, Joel

    2003 Territorial Photography. *In* Landscape and Power. 2nd edition. Pp. 175–202. Chicago: University of Chicago Press.

Snyder, Sally

    N.d. Fieldnotes, Melville Jacobs Collection, University of Washington Manuscript Collection, Seattle.

1964 Skagit Society and Its Existential Basis: An Ethnofolkloristic Reconstruction. Ph.D. dissertation, University of Washington.

Sollors, Werner
1986 Beyond Ethnicity: Consent and Descent in American Culture. New York: Oxford University Press.

Southeast Native Subsistence Commission (SENSC)
1995–2002 Native Place Names Project. Maps and data on file at Central Council of Tlingit and Haida Tribes of Alaska, Juneau.

Spector, Janet
1993 What This Awl Means: Feminist Archaeology at a Wahpeton Dakota Village. St. Paul: Minnesota Historical Society.

Spradley, James P., ed.
1969 Guests Never Leave Hungry: The Autobiography of James Sewid, A Kwakiutl Indian. New Haven CT: Yale University Press.

Sproat, Gilbert Malcolm
1987[1868] The Nootka: Scenes and Studies of Savage Life. Charles Lillard, ed. Victoria BC: Sono Nis Press.

Staniszewski, Mary Ann
1998 The Power of Display: A History of Exhibition Installations at the Museum of Modern Art. Cambridge MA: MIT Press.

Stearns, Mary Lee
1981 Haida Culture in Custody: The Masset Band. Seattle: University of Washington Press.

Steinhart, Edward I.
1989 Introduction. Theme issue, "Ethnohistory and Africa," Ethnohistory 36(1):1–8.

Stern, Bernhard J.
1969[1934] The Lummi Indians of Northwest Washington. Columbia University Contributions to Anthropology, 17. New York: Columbia University Press. Reprint, New York: AMS Press.

Stern, Pamela R.
1999 Learning to Be Smart: An Exploration of the Culture of Intelligence in a Canadian Inuit Community. American Anthropologist 101(3):502–514.

Sterritt, Neil J., Susan Marsden, Robert Galois, Peter R. Grant, and Richard Overstall

    1998 Tribal Boundaries in the Nass Watershed. Vancouver: University of British Columbia Press.

Steward, Julian

    1955 Theory and Application in Social Science. Ethnohistory 2:292–302.

Stewart, Omer C.

    1979 An Expert Witness Answers Rosen. American Anthropologist 81(1):108–111.

Stocking, George W.

    1968 Race, Culture, and Evolution: Essays in the History of Anthropology. Chicago: University of Chicago Press.

Stocking, George W., ed.

    1974 The Shaping of American Anthropology, 1883–1911. New York: Basic Books.

    1985 Objects and Others: Essays on Museums and Material Culture. Madison: University of Wisconsin Press.

Strathern, Marilyn

    1972 Women in Between: Females Roles in a Male World. London: Seminar Press.

    1988 The Gender of the Gift: Problems with Women and Problems with Society in Melanesia. Berkeley: University of California Press.

Strehlow, T. G. H.

    1947 Aranda Traditions. Melbourne: Melbourne University Press.

Suttles, Wayne

    1987 Private Knowledge, Morality, and Social Class among the Coast Salish. *In* Coast Salish Essays. Wayne Suttles, ed. Pp. 3–14. Vancouver: Talonbooks; Seattle: University of Washington Press.

Suttles, Wayne, ed.

    1990 Handbook of North American Indians, vol. 7: Northwest Coast. Washington DC: Smithsonian Institution Press.

Suttles, Wayne, and Aldona Jonaitis

    1990 History of Research in Ethnology. *In* Handbook of North American Indians, vol. 7: Northwest Coast. Wayne Suttles, ed. Pp. 73–87. Washington DC: Smithsonian Institution Press.

Swanton, John R.

1905 a Contributions to the Ethnology of the Haida. Jesup North Pacific Expedition, 5(1). New York: American Museum of Natural History.

1905 b Haida Texts and Myths: Skidegate Dialect. Bureau of American Ethnology Bulletin, 29. Washington DC: Government Printing Office.

1908 Social Condition, Beliefs and Linguistic Relationships of the Tlingit Indians. *In* 26th Annual Report of the Bureau of American Ethnology for the Years 1904–1905. Washington.

1909 a Contributions to the Ethnology of the Haida. Jesup North Pacific Expedition, 5(1). Memoirs of American Museum of Natural History, 8. New York: G. E. Stechert.

1909 b Tlingit Myths and Texts. Bureau of American Ethnology Bulletin, 39. Washington DC: Government Printing Office.

1952 The Indian Tribes of North America. Bureau of American Ethnology Bulletin, 145. Washington DC: Government Printing Office.

Swineford, Alfred P.

1898 Alaska: Its History, Climate, and Natural Resources. Chicago: Rand, McNally.

Swinomish Tribal Mental Health Project

1991 A Gathering of Wisdoms. LaConner WA: Swinomish Tribal Community.

Tarot, Camille

1999 De Durkheim à Mauss: L'invention du symbolique. Sociologie et sciences des religions. Paris: Éditions La Découverte/M.A.U.S.S.

Taylor, Charles M., Jr.

1901 Touring Alaska and the Yellowstone. Philadelphia: George W. Jacobs.

Taylor, Will S.

1910 Results of an Art Trip to the Northwest Coast. American Museum Journal 10:42–47.

Tennant, Paul

1990 Aboriginal Peoples and Politics: The Indian Land Question in British Columbia, 1849–1989. Vancouver: University of British Columbia Press.

Testart, Alain

1998 Uncertainties of the Obligation to Reciprocate: A Critique of Mauss. *In* Marcel Mauss. A Centenary Tribute. Wendy James and N. J. Allen, eds. Pp. 97–110. New York: Berghahn Books.

Thom, Brian David

1995 The Dead and the Living: Burial Mounds and Cairns and the Development of Social Classes in the Gulf of Georgia Region. M.A. thesis, University of British Columbia.

2001 Harlan I. Smith's Jesup Fieldwork on the Northwest Coast. *In* Gateways: Exploring the Legacy of the Jesup North Pacific Expedition, 1897–1902. Igor Krupnik and William Fitzhugh, eds. Pp. 139–180. Washington DC: Smithsonian Institution Arctic Studies Center.

Thomas, Lynn L., Judy Z. Kronenfeld, and David B. Kronenfeld

1976 Asdiwal Crumbles: A Critique of Lévi-Straussian Myth Analysis. American Ethnologist 3:147–173.

Thomas, Nicholas

1992 The Inversion of Tradition. American Ethnologist 19:213–232.

Thompson, Laurence C., and Dale Kinkade

1990 Languages. *In* Handbook of North American Indians, vol. 7: Northwest Coast. Wayne Suttles, ed. Pp. 30–51. Washington DC: Smithsonian Institution Press.

Thornton, Thomas F.

1995 Tlingit and Euro-American Toponymies in Glacier Bay. *In* Proceedings of the Third Glacier Bay Science Symposium. Daniel Engstrom, ed. Pp. 294–301. Anchorage: National Park Service.

1997 a Anthropological Studies of North American Indian Place Naming. American Indian Quarterly 21(2):208–228.

1997 b Know Your Place: The Organization of Tlingit Geographic Knowledge. Ethnology 36(4):295–307.

1999 What's in a Name? Indigenous Place Names in Southeast Alaska. Artic Research of the United States 13 (Spring/Summer):40–48.

2000 Person and Place: Lessons from Tlingit Teachers. *In* Celebration 2000: Restoring Balance through Culture. Susan W. Fair and Rosita Worl, eds. Pp. 79–86. Juneau AK: Sealaska Heritage Foundation.

Thornton, Thomas F., ed.

1998 Crisis in the Last Frontier: The Alaskan Subsistence Debate. Theme issue, Cultural Survival Quarterly 22(3).

Tikhmenev, P. A.

1978[1861–63] A History of the Russian-American Company. Richard A. Pierce and Alton S. Donnelly, trans. and eds. Seattle: University of Washington Press.

Tla-o-qui-aht First Nation

2000 Press Release. May 5, 2000.

Tollefson, Kenneth

1977 A Structural Change in Tlingit Potlatching. Western Canadian Journal of Anthropology 7:16–27.

1978 From Localized Clans to Regional Corporation: The Acculturation of the Tlingit. Western Canadian Journal of Anthropology. 8:1–20.

1984 Tlingit Acculturation: An Institutional Perspective. Ethnology 23:229–247.

Tuan, Yi Fu

1974 Topophilia: A Study of Environmental Perception, Attitudes, and Values. Englewood Cliffs NJ: Prentice-Hall.

1977 Space and Place: The Perspective of Experience. Minneapolis: University of Minnesota Press.

Tuleja, Tad, ed.

1997 Usable Pasts: Traditions and Group Expressions in North America. Logan: Utah State University Press.

Turner, David

1978 Ideology and Elementary Structures. Theme issue, "L'appropriation sociale de la logique: Mélanges offerts à Claude Lévi-Strauss à l'occasion de son 70e anniversaire de naissance." Anthropologica n.s. 20(1–2):223–248.

Tylor, Sir Edward B.

1946[1881] Anthropology: An Introduction to the Study of Man and Civilization, vol. 1. London: Watts.

U.S. Department of the Interior, Bureau of Indian Affairs, Branch of Acknowledgment and Research

N.d. "Acknowledgment Guidelines." Electronic document. http://

www.doi.gov/bureau-indian-affairs.html, accessed May 18, 2000. (This particular document is currently unavailable due to the Cobell Litigation.)

Usher, Jean

    1974 William Duncan of Metlakatla: A Victorian Missionary in British Columbia. National Museum of Man, Publications in History 5. Ottawa: National Museums of Canada.

Vakhtin, Nikolai

    1997 Environmental Change and Indigenous Knowledge in Chukotka. Paper presented at the Oral Traditions of the North Pacific Rim Workshop, Fort Ross CA, November.

Valentine, Lisa, and Regna Darnell, eds.

    1999 Theorizing the Americanist Tradition. Toronto: University of Toronto Press.

Vansina, Jan

    1985 Oral Tradition as History. Madison: University of Wisconsin Press.

Varnedoe, Kirk

    1984 Abstract Expressionism. *In* Primitivism in 20th Century Art. William Rubin, ed. Pp. 615–659. New York: Museum of Modern Art.

Wade, Edwin L.

    1985 The Ethnic Art Market in the American Southwest, 1880–1980. *In* Objects and Others: Essays on Museums and Material Culture. George W. Stocking Jr., ed. Pp. 167–191. Madison: University of Wisconsin Press.

Wagner, Roy

    1981 The Invention of Culture. Chicago: University of Chicago Press.

Waldberg, Patrick, and Isabelle Waldberg

    1992 Un amour acéphale: Correspondance, 1940–1949. Edition établie et présentée par Michel Waldberg. Paris: Editions de la Différence.

Wallas, James

    1981 Kwakiutl Legends as Told to Pamela Whitaker. North Vancouver: Hancock House.

Walter, E. V.

    1998 Placeways: A Theory of the Human Environment. Chapel Hill: University of North Carolina Press.

Wardman, George

1884 A Trip to Alaska. Boston: Lee and Shepard.

Wardwell, Allen

1978 Objects of Bright Pride: Northwest Coast Indian Art from the American Museum of Natural History. New York: Center for Inter-American Relations and the American Federation of Arts.

1996 Tangible Visions: Northwest Coast Indian Shamanism and Its Art. New York: Monacelli Press.

Warren, Winonah

1991 A Model Cultural Center at Pojoaque Pueblo. Cultural Resource Management 14(4):4-6.

Washburne, H. C., and Anauta

1940 Land of the Good Shadows: The Life Story of Anauta, an Eskimo Woman. New York: AMS Press.

Waterman, Thomas T.

1922 The Geographic Names Used by the Indians of the Pacific Coast. Geographical Review 12(2):175–194.

Wei Tchen, John Kuo

1992 Creating a Dialogic Museum. In Museums and Communities: The Politics of Public Culture. Ivan Karp, Christine Mullen Kreamer, and Steven D. Lavine, eds. Pp. 285–326. Washington DC: Smithsonian Institution Press.

Weigle, Martha

1990 Southwest Lures: Innocents Detoured, Incensed Determined. Journal of the Southwest 32:499–540.

Weiner, Annette

1992 Inalienable Possessions: The Paradox of Keeping-While-Giving. Berkeley: University of California Press.

Weintraub, Karl J.

1978 The Value of the Individual: Self and Circumstance in Autobiography. Chicago: University of Chicago Press.

Weiss, Jeffrey

1983 Science and Primitivism: A Fearful Symmetry in the Early New York School. Arts Magazine 57(7):81–87.

White, Hayden

1978 Tropics of Discourse. Baltimore: Johns Hopkins University Press.

White, Leslie

    1963 The Ethnography and Ethnology of Franz Boas. Bulletin of the Texas Memorial Museum 6:1–76.

White, Richard

    1983 The Roots of Dependency: Subsistence, Environment and Social Change among the Choctaws, Pawnees, and Navajos. Lincoln: University of Nebraska Press.

Wickwire, Wendy, ed.

    2000 Ethnographic Eyes: Essays in Memory of Douglas Cole. Special double issue, BC Studies 125/126 (Spring/Summer).

Widerspach-Thor, Martine de (a.k.a. Martine Reid)

    1978 Kwakiutl Marine Mythology. Unpublished manuscript. National Museum of Man Archives. Urgent Ethnology Division, Ottawa.

    1981 The Equation of Copper. In The World Is as Sharp as a Knife. Donald N. Abbott, ed. Pp. 157–174. Victoria: British Columbia Provincial Museum.

Wike, Joyce

    1951 The Effect of the Maritime Fur Trade on Northwest Coast Indian Society. Ph.D. dissertation, Columbia University, New York.

    1984 A Reevaluation of Northwest Coast Cannibalism. In The Tsimshian and Their Neighbors on the North Pacific Coast. Jay Miller and Carol Eastman, eds. Pp. 239–254. Seattle: University of Washington Press.

Wiley, William H., and Sara King Wiley

    1893 The Yosemite, Alaska, and the Yellowstone. New York: J. Wiley.

Wilkins, David E.

    1993 Modernization, Colonialism, Dependency: How Appropriate Are These Models for Providing an Explanation of North American Indian 'Underdevelopment'? Ethnic and Racial Studies 16:3:390–419.

Willard, Mrs. Eugene

1995[1883] Carrie M. Willard among the Tlingits: The Letters of 1881–1882. Sitka AK: Mountain Meadow Press.

Willis, Jane

    1973 Geneish: An Indian Girlhood. Toronto: New Press.

Wilson, Chris

1997 The Myth of Santa Fe: Creating a Modern Regional Tradition. Albuquerque: University of New Mexico Press.

Wissler, Clark

1943 Survey of the American Museum of Natural History, Made at the Request of the Management Board in 1942–43. Typescript, Central Archives, American Museum of Natural History, New York.

Wolf, Eric

1999 Envisioning Power: Ideologies of Dominance and Crisis. Berkeley: University of California Press.

Wollheim, Richard

1984 The Thread of Life. Cambridge: Harvard University Press.

Wonders, Karen

1993 Habitat Dioramas: Illusions of Wilderness in Museums of Natural History. Acta Universitatis Upsaliensis, figura nova series, 25. Uppsala, Sweden: Uppsala University.

Woodman, Abby J.

1889 Picturesque Alaska. Boston: Houghton, Mifflin.

Wright, Chief Walter

1962 Men of Medeek. Kitimat BC: Sentinel Press.

Wyatt, Victoria

1989 Images of the Inside Passage: An Alaskan Portrait by Winter and Pond. Seattle: University of Washington Press.

Archival Works Cited

AHL Louis Shotridge Manuscripts. Alaska Historical Library, Juneau AK.

BBN Marius Barbeau and William Beynon Field Notes (1914–56). Canadian Centre for Folk Culture Studies, Canadian Museum of Civilization, Ottawa.

BCU William Beynon, Tsimshean Manuscripts. Rare Book and Manuscript Library, Columbia University Libraries, New York City.

BPC Franz Boas Professional Correspondence. American Philosophical Society, Philadelphia.

HCU George Hunt, Manuscript in the Language of the Kwakiutl Indians of Vancouver Island. Preface by Franz Boas, reviser. 14 vols. Rare Book and Manuscript Library, Columbia University Libraries, New York City.

KM Franz Boas [and George Hunt], Kwakiutl Materials (1896–1933). 6 vols. American Philosophical Society, Philadelphia.

LSC Louis Shotridge Correspondence. University of Pennsylvania Museum Archives, Philadelphia.

ROP Ronald Olson Papers. Bancroft Library, University of California, Berkeley CA.

UEN Unpublished Ethnographic Notes of Louis Shotridge. University of Pennsylvania Museum Archives, Philadelphia.

Margaret Seguin Anderson is Professor of First Nations Studies at the University of Northern British Columbia. Dr. Anderson works with the Tsimshian, Nisga'a, and Gitksan peoples of the university's northwest region, establishing collaborative programs to make First Nations languages available for university credit. Dr. Anderson is currently researching the question of a Tsimshian aboriginal right to a commercial fishery and working on several First Nations language documentation projects, including a multimedia "talking dictionary" developed under the auspices of the Ts'msyen Sm'algyax Authority: http://web.unbc.ca/~smalgyax/. She is also the principal researcher on a three-year grant from the Social Sciences and Humanities Research Council of Canada to edit scholarly versions of *adawx* collected by William Beynon and to have fluent speakers record these on CD.

Judith Berman is a research associate at the University of Pennsylvania Museum of Archaeology and Anthropology in Philadelphia. In addition to two decades of research and publications on the voluminous Kwakwaka'wakw materials of Franz Boas and George Hunt, she has also worked extensively with the manuscripts and collections of Louis Shotridge. Her research interests include oral literature and the ethnohistory of contact on the North Pacific Coast.

Janine Ledford Bowechop, enrolled member of the Makah Indian tribe, lives in Neah Bay, Washington, on the Makah reservation. She is currently the executive director of the Makah Cultural and Research Center (MCRC), a position she has held since 1995. She has worked extensively with the Ozette archaeological collection and currently focuses on language revitalization, the Tribal Historic Preservation Office, library and archives acquisitions, and education programming. In 1990, after finishing her undergraduate studies in cultural anthropology at Dartmouth College, she returned to her childhood home of Neah Bay and began work at the MCRC, first as a researcher and then within the (archaeological) collections department. Ms. Bowechop regularly participates in community cultural activities and spends the spring and summer training and racing with the Makah women's racing canoe team, the Spirit Paddlers.

Daniel L. Boxberger is Professor of Anthropology at Western Washington University. His research has focused on the political economy of indigenous peoples, in particular on the issues of natural resource use and control. Much of his recent work has been with the National Park Service on issues of Native American access and use of public lands. His current focus is on comparative analyses of resource issues in the United States, Canada, and Mexico.

Robert Bringhurst is the author of a major study of Haida oral literature (*A Story as Sharp as a Knife: The Classical Haida Mythtellers and Their World*) and the translator of two volumes of Haida narrative poetry (*Nine Visits to the Mythworld* by Ghandl of the Qayahl Llaanas and *Being in Being: The Collected Works of Skaay of the Qquuna Qiighawaay*). With Haida sculptor Bill Reid he is coauthor of *The Raven Steals the Light*. His other books include *The Black Canoe,* a study of Reid's largest and most complex work of sculpture.

Regna Darnell is Professor of Anthropology and Director of First Nations Studies and the Centre for Research and Teaching of Canadian Native Languages at the University of Western Ontario. Recent works include *Invisible Genealogies: A History of Americanist Anthropology* (2001), *Theorizing the Americanist Tradition* (edited with Lisa Valentine, 1999), and *Along Came Boas: Continuity and Revolution in Americanist Anthropology* (1998). Her interests include history of anthropology, linguistic anthropology, Canadian First Nations, Canadian national identity, and social theory. She is a fellow of the Royal Society of Canada.

Richard and Nora Marks Dauenhauer, partners in marriage and scholarship, worked nearly 14 years at Sealaska Heritage Foundation in Juneau, where they developed the Language and Cultural Studies Program. This was downsized in 1997, and they are now freelance writers and consultants. In addition to pedagogical materials for Tlingit, their most important collaborative work is the bilingual series Classics of Tlingit Oral Literature. Volumes include *Haa Shuká, Our Ancestors: Tlingit Oral Narratives* (1987); *Haa Tuwunáagu Yís, For Healing Our Spirit: Tlingit Oratory* (1990); and *Haa Kusteeyí, Our Culture: Tlingit Life Stories* (1994). They are now completing a volume of Tlingit Raven stories and a volume about the Battles of Sitka of 1802 and 1804. They have received numerous honors and awards individually and as a team. Nora Marks Dauenhauer was raised on a family fishing boat in a traditional Tlingit-speaking family. After raising a family, she completed her GED and a B.A. in anthropology. In 2002 she received an honorary doctorate from the University of Alaska Southeast. She has been working with Tlingit oral tradition for over 30 years. Her work in creative writing and Tlingit folklore has been widely published and anthologized. Her most recent book of creative writing is *Life Woven with Song* (2000). Richard Dauenhauer received his academic training in European languages and comparative literature. He has lived in Alaska since 1969 and is a former poet laureate of Alaska. His publications include three volumes of poetry, many poems and translations in various books, journals, and anthologies, and many scholarly articles. Major works in progress include completed drafts of *Erotic Epigrams: Love Poems,* translated from the Greek anthology, the first English translation of the Buriat-Mongol oral epic *Young Alamzhi Mergen,* and an adventure-mystery novel written for and about his grandchildren.

Frederica de Laguna is an American ethnologist and archaeologist especially known for her pioneering work in northwestern North America. Born in 1906, she received her Ph.D. from Columbia University in 1933. Over the years de Laguna has conducted archaeological and ethnological research in Prince William Sound and Cook Inlet, among several Dena (Athapaskan) peoples of Alaska, and the Tlingits. Her numerous publications include such seminal works as *The Prehistory of Northern North America a Seen from the Yukon* (1947), *Chugach Prehistory* (1956), *The Story of a Tlingit Community: A Problem in the Relationship between Archaeological, Ethnological and Historical Methods* (1960), and especially her monumental *Under Mount Saint Elias: The History and Culture of the Yakutat Tlingit* (1972). Most of her teaching career has been associated with Bryn Mawr College, from which she retired in 1975. She served as the president of the American Anthropological Association in 1966–67. Still an active researcher, she published *Tales from the Dena: Indian Stories from the Tanana, Koyukuk and Yukon Rivers* in 1995 and *Travels among the Dena: Exploring Alaska's Yukon River* in 2000b.

Patricia Pierce Erikson is a museum anthropologist and Native American Studies scholar who has taught at Smith College and the University of Southern Maine. Her recent publications include the book *Voices of a Thousand People: The Makah Cultural and Research Center* (2002) and the article "A-Whaling We Will Go: Encounters of Knowledge and Memory at the Makah Museum" (1999) in *Cultural Anthropology.* Her exhibitions include *Excavating the Museum: Journeys of Native American Art* at the Smith College Art Museum, Northampton, Massachusetts, in 1999. Her interests include the anthropology of museums, oral history, and indigenous social movements in the Western Hemisphere.

Aaron Glass works primarily with Kwakwaka'wakw communities, exploring issues surrounding the local and global politics of contemporary art and cultural performance. In addition, he has conducted research on the circulation of totem poles (for a planned publication with Aldona Jonaitis), the social history of the Northwest Coast art world, repatriation in a comparative perspective, and the role of indigenous artists and anthropologists as culture brokers. He has an M.A. in anthropology from the University of British Columbia and is currently a Ph.D candidate at New York University, working on the representational history of the Hamat'sa Dance.

Marie-Françoise Guédon is Professor of Anthropology at the Department of Religious Studies at the University of Ottawa. She has conducted fieldwork among the Inuit, the Tsimshian, the Ahtna of the Copper River Valley, and Upper Tanana people. She is the author of many articles published in American and Canadian journals. Her most recent book, *Le rêve et la forêt: Histoires de chamanes Nabesna,* on Northern Athapaskan shamanism, has been accepted for publication by the Presses de l'Université Laval in Québec.

Marjorie Myers Halpin (1937–2001) was Northwest Coast Curator at the Museum of Anthropology MOA at the University of British Columbia and had also taught in the Department of Anthropology and Sociology at UBC since 1973. Dr. Halpin's research deepened scholarly understanding of the meanings of the art of Northwest Coast societies, notably the crest art of the Tsimshianic groups that was an enduring interest from the time of her doctoral studies. Dr. Halpin published several academic books and numerous articles and curated exhibitions at MOA. Her public communication also included a highly regarded book on totem poles of the Northwest Coast and a Web site exploring the various meanings of a specific totem pole. Dr. Halpin died in August 2001 after a brief illness, just two months after she presented her paper at the conference in Paris.

Michael E. Harkin is a cultural anthropologist and ethnohistorian. He received an M.A. and Ph.D. in anthropology from the University of Chicago. He is author of *The Heiltsuks: Dialogues of Culture and History on the Northwest Coast* (1997) and editor of a forthcoming volume, *Reconsidering Revitalization: Case Studies from Native North America and Oceania*. He is associate editor of the journal *Ethnohistory*. He is Professor of Anthropology and American Indian Studies at the University of Wyoming and has taught previously at Emory University and Montana State University.

Ira Jacknis is research anthropologist at the Phoebe A. Hearst Museum of Anthropology, University of California at Berkeley. Among his research specialties are the art and cultures of Native North America (especially the Northwest Coast and California), the history of anthropology, museums, and photography, film, and sound recording as modes of ethnographic representation. He is the author of *Carving Traditions of Northwest California* (1995) and *The Storage Box of Tradition: Kwakiutl Art, Anthropologists, and Museums, 1881–1981* (2002).

Sergei Kan, born in Russia, began his undergraduate education there but completed it in the United States and went on to receive his Ph.D. in anthropology from the University of Chicago in 1982. He is currently Professor of Anthropology and Native American Studies at Dartmouth College. He has been conducting ethnographic and archival research in southeastern Alaska since 1979 and is the author of numerous articles and book chapters on the culture and history of the Tlingit Indians, the history of the Russian Orthodox mission in Siberia and Alaska, and the history of anthropology. His 1989 monograph, *Symbolic Immortality: The Tlingit Potlatch of the Nineteenth Century,* received the 1990 American Book Award from the Before Columbus Foundation. In 1999 he published another book, *Memory Eternal: Tlingit Culture and Russian Orthodox Christianity through Two Centuries.* His most recent publication is an edited volume, *Strangers to Relatives: The Adoption and Naming of Anthropologists in Native North America* (2001). Currently he is coediting a collection of essays, "Native Peoples of North America: Cultures, Histories, and Representations," and is writing a biography of Lev Shternberg, a prominent Russian anthropologist of the late 19th and early 20th centuries.

Claude Lévi-Strauss is the author of many distinguished works such as *Structural Anthropology* (2 vols.; 1963a), *The Elementary Structures of Kinship* (1969a), *Tristes Tropiques* (1955b), and the seminal series on mythology, which includes *The Raw and the Cooked* (1969b), *From Honey to Ashes* (1973a), *The Origin of Table Manners* (1978), and *The Naked Man* (1981a). He is also the author of *The Way of the Masks* (1982), *The View from Afar* (1985b), *The Story of Lynx* (1995b), and *The Jealous Potter* (1988). He is honorary professor at the College de France, where he taught social anthropology from 1960 to 1982, and the founder of the Laboratoire d'anthropologie sociale. He is also a member of the Académie française.

Pierre Maranda, Professor Emeritus of Anthropology, Université Laval, Québec, Canada. Ph.D. in anthropology, Harvard University (1966). Fieldwork in Malaita, Solomon Islands (1966–68, 1974, 1975, 1980, 1987, 1989). Visiting professor, École des hautes études en sciences sociales (Paris), Collège de France, Universidade federal do Rio de Janeiro, Université Omar Bongo, University of Toronto. Author/editor of 12 books and over 90 papers in anthropological journals or collective works.

Marie Mauzé is Directeur de recherche at the Centre national de la recherche scientifique (CNRS), Paris, and a member of the Laboratoire d'anthropologie sociale. She has conducted fieldwork in British Columbia with the Kwakwak'awakw since 1980. She has published several articles in *L'Homme, Gradhiva, Journal des Américanistes,* and the *European Review of Native American Studies.* She is the author of *Les fils de Wakai: Une histoire des Lekwiltoq* (1992) and the editor of *Present Is Past: Some Uses of Tradition in Native Societies* (1997). She is coauthor with Marine Degli of *Arts premiers: Le temps de la reconnaissance* (2000). Her current interests include the anthropology of art, the history of anthropology, the history of museum collections, and the relationship between museums and native peoples.

Bruce G. Miller is a professor in the Department of Anthropology and Sociology at the University of British Columbia. His work concerns ethnography and ethnohistory of the Northwest Coast, particularly issues of governance and justice. Recent publications include *The Problem of Justice: Tradition and Law on the Northwest Coast* and *Invisible Indigenes: The Politics of Nonrecognition.* He was editor of *Culture,* the journal of the Canadian Anthropological Association, from 1996 to 1998 and guest editor of a *BC Studies* issue on anthropology and history in the courts. He won the UBC Killam Teaching Prize in 1999.

Martine J. Reid is an independent researcher. She was born and educated in France, where she received the Diplôme de l'ecole des hautes etudes en sciences sociales in the field of Northwest Coast cultural and symbolic anthropology in 1975 under the name Martine de Widerspach-Thor. She has conducted field research among the Kʷaguł since 1976 and in 1981 received her doctorate from the University of British Columbia's Department of Anthropology, where she lectured from 1978 to 1982. Her doctoral dissertation was a structural analysis of the Kʷaguł Hamatsa ritual. She has published on Kʷaguł art and culture and has regularly spent research time among the Kʷaguł. She has curated and co-curated several international Northwest Coast art exhibits, among them *The Spirit Sings* in 1988, Bill Reid in Paris in 1989 (contributing a chapter in *Des symboles et leurs doubles* by Claude Lévi-Strauss in 1989), Budapest in 1992, and Tokyo in 1997. In 2000 she lectured on Haida artist Bill Reid at the British Museum. She is currently collaborating on the American Museum of Natural History's 2004 exhibit

From Totems to Turquoise: Native North American Jewelry Arts of the Northwest and Southwest and its companion book.

Daisy Sewid-Smith [Mayanilh], LLD, is a teacher and consultant. Born in Alert Bay BC and daughter of the late Chief James Sewid, Daisy is a member of the Mamaliliqəlla- Qʷiqʷasutinux̌ʷ tribe of Village Island. Daisy has written several articles on Kʷagul̓ culture and is the author of *Prosecution or Persecution,* published by the Cape Mudge Museum (1979). As a teacher, Daisy has been employed by School District no. 72 (Campbell River) for 20 years and was the head of the First Nations Education department. In recognition of her contribution to the advancement of knowledge about Kʷagul̓ language and culture, Daisy Sewid-Smith was conferred with the title and degree of Honorary Doctor of Laws by the University of Victoria in 1998.

Thomas F. Thornton, Ph.D., is Associate Professor of Global Studies at St. Lawrence University, having taught anthropology at the University of Alaska from 1994 to 2000. He has conducted extensive research on Tlingit and Alaska Native ethnogeography and subsistence issues since 1989. In addition to numerous published articles, he edited the fall 1998 issue of *Cultural Survival Quarterly* on Alaska Native subsistence and is the editor of *Haa Aaní, Our Land: Tlingit and Haida Land Rights and Use* (1998) and coeditor of *Will the Time Ever Come? A Tlingit Sourcebook* (2000). His book *Being and Place among the Tlingit* is forthcoming.

INDEX

CPSIA information can be obtained
at www.ICGtesting.com
Printed in the USA
LVHW080514301019
635801LV00009B/71/P

9 780803 282964